THE COMPLETE FOUR SPORT STADIUM GUIDE

By the Sports Staff of USA TODAY

Edited by Balliett & Fitzgerald, Inc.

Updated by Larry Peterson and Liz Barrett

A Balliett & Fitzgerald Book

for Fodor's Travel Publications, Inc.

NEW YORK · LONDON · SYDNEY · AUCKLAND

While every care has been taken to ensure the accuracy of the information in this guide, time brings change, and consequently, the publisher cannot accept responsibility for errors that may occur. Prudent travelers will therefore want to call ahead to verify prices and other "perishable" information.

Second Edition
ISBN: 0-679-03296-7

Book design: Sue Canavan
Cover design: Allison Saltzman
Cover illustrations: Mike Powell/AllSport (baseball player); Stephen Parker/Syracuse University S.I.D. (basketball player); Brian Drake/Sportschrome (hockey player); Robert Tringali, Jr./Sportschrome (football player)

Project editor: Tom Dyja
Production editors: Susan Canavan, Duncan Bock
Art editor: Maria Fernandez
Graphic artists: Maria Fernandez, Ronan Coyle, Tracy Liu
Assistant editor: Howard Slatkin
Editorial assistants: Catie O'Brien, Ruth Ro, Donna Spillane, Bindu Poulose, John Ciba, Chuck Ciba

Special thanks to Susan Bokern and Betty Boyd-George at Gannett along with Keith Cutler and Susan Mayoralgo.

MANUFACTURED IN THE UNITED STATES OF AMERICA

10 9 8 7 6 5 4 3 2 1

Since the first edition of THE USA TODAY FOUR
SPORT STADIUM GUIDE came out in 1994, there's
been an unprecedented amount of movement in the world
of sports. Nowadays it seems if a team hasn't moved cities
in the last two years, it either has a new stadium or is in the
process of getting one. This revised edition of THE USA
TODAY FOUR SPORT STADIUM GUIDE is the only
book that will give fans at home and on the road a detailed,
insider's look at who's playing where in each of the four
major sports, and what it's like to
watch a game there. This unique volume delivers team trivia and strate-
gic tips for those following a game at home and up-to-date,
direct and savvy practical information for those visiting the
park. Each stadium includes a color illustration and seating
diagram. Along with giving you a look at all the new stadiums for established teams, we'll even show you the as-
yet unopened ballparks for the Arizona Diamondbacks and
Tampa Bay Devil Rays. Only the Atlanta Braves' new
home hadn't been reconfigured from the Olympics in time
for us to include a seating diagram.

The Guide is divided into four sections: baseball, football, basketball, and hockey. Each entry covers the venue
for the current or upcoming season, even if it's just a temporary home. If a venue is used by teams in two sports, it
is covered in each sport's section. Venue chapters are 1 to
3 pages long, depending on the sport and the length and
eventfulness of a team's stay in its current home, with as
much information about each team as space will allow.
Topics covered differ only slightly from sport to sport.

Ticket scalping, although a common practice, is illegal
in some cities. While we have included information about
it, that is in no way an endorsement of the practice. Check
local ordinances if you plan to obtain tickets from sources
other than the team or its ticket agency.

The stadium and arena illustrations, while as realistic as
possible, are by necessity not to scale because they must also
function as seating diagrams. Prices provided are primarily
for the single-game, rather than season, ticket buyer.

Note: *All prices, contacts, and programs listed in
the book, as well as our stadium illustrations and
seating diagrams, are current as of our closing
editorial date in the summer of 1996. Minor
league baseball affiliations change frequently.
Call before you make your plans.*

How to use the Four Sport Stadium Guide

contents

baseball

football

TEAM	STADIUM	CITY	PAGE
Arizona Cardinals	Sun Devil Stadium	Tempe, AZ	94
Atlanta Falcons	Georgia Dome	Atlanta	96
Baltimore Ravens	Memorial Stadium	Baltimore	98
Buffalo Bills	Rich Stadium	Orchard Park, NY	100
Carolina Panthers	Ericsson Stadium	Charlotte, NC	102
Chicago Bears	Soldier Field	Chicago	104
Cincinnati Bengals	Cinergy Field	Cincinnati	106
Dallas Cowboys	Texas Stadium	Irving, TX	108
Denver Broncos	Mile High Stadium	Denver	110
Detroit Lions	Pontiac Silverdome	Pontiac, MI	112
Green Bay Packers	Lambeau Field	Green Bay, WI	114
Houston Oilers	Astrodome	Houston	116
Indianapolis Colts	RCA Dome	Indianapolis	118
Jacksonville Jaguars	Jacksonville Stadium	Jacksonville, FL	120
Kansas City Chiefs	Arrowhead Stadium	Kansas City	122
Miami Dolphins	Pro Player Stadium	Miami	124
Minnesota Vikings	HHH Metrodome	Minneapolis	126
New England Patriots	Foxboro Stadium	Foxboro, MA	128
New Orleans Saints	Louisiana Superdome	New Orleans	130
New York Giants	Giants Stadium	E. Rutherford, NJ	132
New York Jets	Giants Stadium	E. Rutherford, NJ	134
Oakland Raiders	Oakland Coliseum	Oakland	135
Philadelphia Eagles	Veterans Stadium	Philadelphia	137
Pittsburgh Steelers	Three Rivers Stadium	Pittsburgh	139
St. Louis Rams	Trans World Dome	St. Louis	141
San Diego Chargers	San Diego Jack Murphy Stadium	San Diego	143
San Francisco 49ers	3Com Park	San Francisco	145
Seattle Seahawks	Kingdome	Seattle	147
Tampa Bay Buccaneers	Tampa Stadium	Tampa	149
Washington Redskins	RFK Memorial Stadium	Washington, D.C.	151

basketball

TEAM	STADIUM	CITY	PAGE
Atlanta Hawks	The Omni	Atlanta	154
Boston Celtics	FleetCenter	Boston	156
Charlotte Hornets	Charlotte Coliseum	Charlotte, NC	158
Chicago Bulls	United Center	Chicago	159
Cleveland Cavaliers	Gund Arena	Cleveland	161
Dallas Mavericks	Reunion Arena	Dallas	162
Denver Nuggets	McNichols Arena	Denver	163
Detroit Pistons	The Palace of Auburn Hills	Auburn Hills, MI	165
Golden State Warriors	San Jose Arena	San Jose, CA	167
Houston Rockets	The Summit	Houston	169
Indiana Pacers	Market Square Arena	Indianapolis	171
Los Angeles Clippers	Memorial Sports Arena	Los Angeles	172
Los Angeles Lakers	Great Western Forum	Los Angeles	173
Miami Heat	Miami Arena	Miami	175
Milwaukee Bucks	Bradley Center	Milwaukee	176
Minnesota Timberwolves	Target Center	Minneapolis	177
New Jersey Nets	Continental Airlines Arena	E. Rutherford, NJ	178
New York Knicks	Madison Square Garden	New York City	179
Orlando Magic	Orlando Arena	Orlando	181
Philadelphia 76ers	CoreStates Center	Philadelphia	183
Phoenix Suns	America West Arena	Phoenix	185
Portland Trail Blazers	The Rose Garden	Portland, OR	187
Sacramento Kings	ARCO Arena	Sacramento	189
San Antonio Spurs	Alamodome	San Antonio	191
Seattle SuperSonics	Key Arena	Seattle	193
Toronto Raptors	SkyDome	Toronto	195
Utah Jazz	Delta Center	Salt Lake City	196
Vancouver Grizzlies	General Motors Place	Vancouver	198
Washington Bullets	USAir Arena	Landover, MD	199

hockey

TEAM	STADIUM	CITY	PAGE
Boston Bruins	FleetCenter	Boston	202
Buffalo Sabres	Marine Midland Arena	Buffalo	204
Calgary Flames	Canadian Airlines Saddledome	Calgary	206
Chicago Blackhawks	United Center	Chicago	207
Colorado Avalanche	McNichols Arena	Denver	209
Dallas Stars	Reunion Arena	Dallas	210
Detroit Red Wings	Joe Louis Arena	Detroit	211
Edmonton Oilers	Edmonton Coliseum	Edmonton	213
Florida Panthers	Miami Arena	Miami	215
Hartford Whalers	Hartford Civic Center	Hartford, CT	217
Los Angeles Kings	Great Western Forum	Los Angeles	218
Mighty Ducks of Anaheim	Arrowhead Pond of Anaheim	Anaheim, CA	219
Montreal Canadiens	Molson Centre	Montreal	220
New Jersey Devils	Continental Airlines Arena	E. Rutherford, NJ	222
New York Islanders	Nassau Veterans Mem. Coliseum	Uniondale, NY	223
New York Rangers	Madison Square Garden	New York City	225
Ottawa Senators	Corel Centre	Kanata, ON	227
Philadelphia Flyers	CoreStates Center	Philadelphia	228
Phoenix Coyotes	America West Arena	Phoenix	230
Pittsburgh Penguins	Pittsburgh Civic Arena	Pittsburgh	231
St. Louis Blues	Kiel Center	St. Louis	233
San Jose Sharks	San Jose Arena	San Jose, CA	234
Tampa Bay Lightning	Ice Palace	Tampa	236
Toronto Maple Leafs	Maple Leaf Gardens	Toronto	237
Vancouver Canucks	General Motors Place	Vancouver	239
Washington Capitals	USAir Arena	Landover, MD	240

baseball

AMERICAN LEAGUE

ANAHEIM ANGELS

Anaheim Stadium

When the Angels take to the field for the first time at home in 1997, it will be under new ownership (Disney), with a new name (the "Anaheim," not "California" Angels), and in a mostly renovated baseball-only stadium. After the Rams moved to St. Louis, Southern California baseball fans' fondest hope was that the "Big A" (so named for its 230-foot-tall, haloed A-frame scoreboard) would again become a baseball-only stadium. In walks Disney—well known for making dreams come true. Disney bought the team in early 1996, and, after some wrangling with the city of Anaheim over who would foot how much of the very big bill for the municipally-owned stadium's renovations, bought the stadium, too. Disney's plans include plenty of things that should warm the hearts of baseball purists, starting with the fact that the architects doing the renovations are HOK, who brought us Coors Field, Camden Yards, and Jacobs Field.

The overall plan is to create a more intimate setting and to generate a more festive (uh-oh) atmosphere. Seats added in 1979 to accommodate the Rams will be removed, bringing the park's capacity down to about 45,000; the Big A scoreboard will be reinstalled in the outfield (earthquake damage had forced its move to the parking lot); a stadium club at the end of the third-base line will be added, along with several luxury boxes and suites; all seats will be replaced, and outfield seats will be angled to face home plate; more food courts will be added, and concourses that are currently closed in will be exposed for more light and more space. Disney's intentions for the playing field and the comfort of the players (upgraded team facilities and locker rooms) and fans seem of the highest order, but their plans for the exterior and landscaping lean toward the whimsical; an "extravaganza" (probably an elaborate water fountain) behind the outfield, and such "architectural icons" as huge sculptures of baseball caps and bats outside. Renovations will commence when the 1996 season ends, and only work that won't interfere with games will continue during '97, with major work picking up again in the next off-season for completion by the start of the 1998 schedule.

PARKING
On-site parking for 15,000 automobiles provided adequate space for the stadium when it held 64,000, and should be more than enough for the baseball-only crowds of 45,000 max. Parking has cost $6 in recent seasons. A number of nearby private lots charge about $4–$5, and many fans park on area side streets. Traffic flow is smooth in and out of the stadium; the three main entrances are off major freeways.

WEATHER
The temperature is normally mild year-round in Southern Califor-nia. The average weather conditions are sunny and 75 degrees.

MEDIA
Radio: KMPC (710 AM). Bob Starr and Mario Impemba are the announcers.
TV: KCAL (Channel 9) and Prime Sports Cable. Ken Wilson and former major-league pitcher Ken Brett are the announcers. Once media giant Disney is fully in charge, you can bet that there will be wider broadcast coverage of Angels' games.

CUISINE
The traditional stadium fare—with a few popular local twists—have done well here, and although they haven't chosen the specific concessionaires, Disney plans to expand the menus to include more diverse and international cuisine. What's offered at the Mighty Ducks' Pond of Anaheim might be a good indication of things to come at Anaheim Stadium. Given that Disney's stock in trade is in striking just the right balance of nostalgia and innovation, it's a safe bet that hot dogs and peanuts will still be available, and the stadium has long offered Mexican, Japanese, and Italian foods. The renowned cinnamon rolls will probably also make the cut. Along with whichever slate of domestic and imported beers that will be sold, a microbrewery—seemingly a must in any baseball stadium these days—will be added. Popular postgame hangouts along State College Boulevard include T.G.I. Friday's (714-978-3308), El Torito's (714-956-4880), The Catch (714-634-1829), and Charlie Brown's (714-634-2211), all located across the street from the stadium.

LODGING NEAR THE STADIUM
Doubletree Hotel
100 The City Dr.
Anaheim, CA 92668
(714) 634-4511/(800) 222-8733
1½ miles from the stadium.

In the Hot Seats at Anaheim Stadium

The Angels have sold an average of about 13,000 season tickets for the past several years, so tickets have been readily available for every game at every price level. The smaller capacity of the renovated ballpark may make a difference in this regard, but only if the Angels start burning up the baselines as well. Big games generally sell out level by level. Season ticketholders generally fill the seats along the baselines.

GOOD SEATS
Along with adding several new revenue-generating luxury boxes and suites in prime spots, Disney is replacing every seat in the house with newer, comfier seats, and angling outfield seats to face home plate. The removal of the football seating will provide a view beyond the fence, and/or of whatever "extravaganza" (possibly an elaborate spouting water fountain) that gets installed behind center field. No matter what is done to improve the so-so seats, the best will still be along the baselines, and sun worshipers should try for the first-base side or right and center fields.

BAD SEATS
The stadium's sight lines were already very good, and proposed renovations will make them even better; if the upper-level section in dead center is still around, avoid it—it's too far from the field. While it isn't known if any obstructed-view seats will remain, they have traditionally been sold last and only at the customer's request.

SCALPING
It's illegal to scalp tickets in California, and it isn't like Disney to let anyone cut into their profits. Besides, even with the smaller capacity, tickets should be pretty easy to come by.

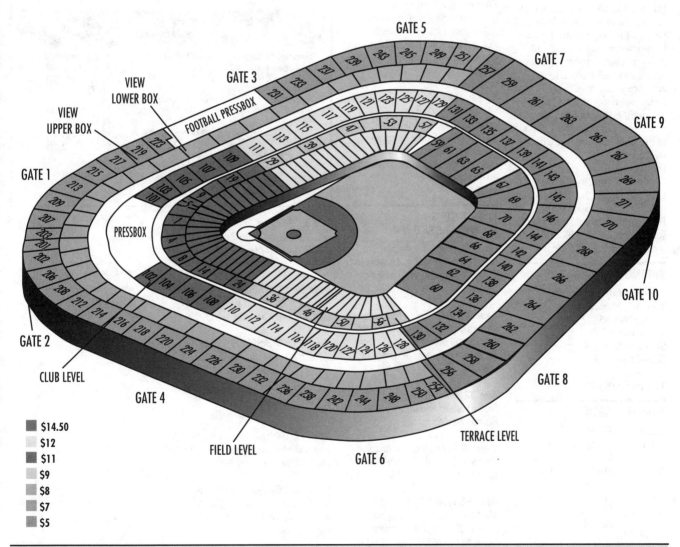

Price legend:
- ■ $14.50
- ▨ $12
- ■ $11
- ▨ $9
- ▨ $8
- ■ $7
- ■ $5

TICKET INFORMATION
Address: 2000 Gene Autry Way, Anaheim, CA 92806
Phone: (714) 634-2000, (714) 663-9000, or TicketMaster at (714) 740-2000, (213) 480-3232, (805) 583-8700, or (619) 278-TIXS

By mail: Orders must be received at least seven days before the game. Include $4 an order for postage and handling. Gift certificates are also available by mail. Mail orders to: Angels Tickets, P.O. Box 2000, Anaheim, CA 92803.

Hours: Mon.–Sat. 9–5:30, beginning Mar. 11 at Gate No. 1 advance-ticket window.
Prices: $14.50: MVP; $12: field box; $11: terrace MVP; $9: terrace box; $8: view level lower box; $7: view level upper box; $5: pavilion reserved.

The Anaheim Ramada Inn
1331 E. Katella Ave.
Anaheim, CA 92805
(714) 978-8088/(800) 228-0586
1½ blocks from the stadium.

GETTING TO ANAHEIM STADIUM

Public transportation: The No. 49 and No. 50 buses run to Anaheim Stadium. For more information, call Orange County Transit Authority at (714) 636-7433.

By car: From the northwest, drive south on I-5 toward Anaheim, and exit at Katella Avenue. Turn left and continue on Katella about 1½ miles to State College Boulevard. Turn right and continue about ¼ mile to the stadium.
From the south, drive north on I-5, and exit to Highway 57 (called Orange Freeway) north. Exit at Orangewood. Continue about 2 miles and turn left onto Orangewood. Proceed 1 block to the entrance to the stadium.
From points north, take Highway 57 south, get off at Orangewood, turn right, and continue 1 block to the stadium entrance, which is on the right.
From Long Beach, go east on Highway 22 to City Centre Drive and turn left. After about a mile it becomes State College Boulevard. Continue north to the stadium entrance, 6 blocks up on the right side.

SPRING TRAINING

Tempe Diablo Stadium
2200 W. Alameda
Tempe, AZ 85282
Capacity: 9,785
Surface: Bermuda grass
Game time: 1:05 p.m. or 7:05 p.m.
Tickets: (602) 350-5200

MINOR LEAGUES

Class	Team
AAA	Vancouver (BC) Canadians
AA	Midland (TX) Angels
A	Lake Elsinore (CA) Storm
A	Cedar Rapids (IA) Kernels
Short Season A	Boise (ID) Hawks
Rookie	Mesa (AZ) Angels

The Angels' nearest minor-league affiliate is the Class A Lake Elsinore Storm of the California League. The Storm's nickname was selected by team owner Ken Stickney who, as owner of the Storm's league rival, the Rancho Cucamonga Quakes, as well as the Las Vegas Thunder of the International Hockey League, has expressed a decided preference for monikers inspired by natural phenomena. A farm club of the Angels since 1986, the Storm moved from Palm Springs to Lake Elsinore in 1994, giving this growing community its first pro team.
The park's Diamond Club restaurant recently added a terrace from which diners can watch the action on the field.
To reach the Storm's stadium from Anaheim, which is only 50 miles away, take I-15 south and exit at Diamond Drive/Railroad Canyon Road. Turn right on Diamond and follow it straight to the stadium.
Ticket prices: $5.50: box seats; $4.50: reserved seats; $3.50: general admission. $7 gets you a table on the terrace overlooking the field from outside the Diamond Club restaurant. For more information, call (909) 245-4487.

THE ANGELS AT ANAHEIM STADIUM

April 20, 1966: *The Angels top the White Sox 4–3 in 11 innings for their first win at Anaheim Stadium.*

Sept. 27, 1973: *Nolan Ryan strikes out 16 Minnesota Twins, setting the major-league record for most strikeouts in a season with 383.*

Aug. 12, 1974: *Ryan sets a team record when he strikes out 19 Boston Red Sox.*

Sept. 28, 1974: *Ryan no-hits the Twins 4–0, his third no-hitter as an Angel.*

Sept. 12, 1976: *53-year-old Minnie Minoso of the Chicago White Sox singles off Sid Monge to become the oldest player to get a hit in a major-league game.*

HOME-FIELD ADVANTAGE

The two low fences in the right- and left-field corners that have made it possible for outfielders to pull homers out of the stands, but that have also made it possible for fans to pull long fly outs into the stands for home runs, may or may not be around much longer. Disney's plans call for a more intimate ballpark, on the order of Jacobs Field, Camden Yards, and Coors Field, so it seems likely that, if anything, the field dimensions will get smaller, favoring the hitters rather than the pitchers or the fielders. Anaheim Stadium is already known to be favorable to long-ball hitters, even if the Angels have not always stocked their teams with them, although Reggie Jackson, Wally Joyner, and Brian Downing all took advantage of the situation. The Big A's days as a strong pitchers' park, with a lower batting average than most, as well as fewer walks, doubles, and triples, may be over.

ANGELS TEAM NOTEBOOK

Franchise history
Los Angeles Angels, 1961–1965; California Angels, 1966–1996; Anaheim Angels, 1997–present

Division titles
1979, 1982, 1986

Most Valuable Player
Don Baylor, 1979

Rookie of the Year
Tim Salmon, 1993

Cy Young Award
Dean Chance, 1964

Hall of Fame
Frank Robinson, 1982

Hoyt Wilhelm, 1985
Rod Carew, 1991
Reggie Jackson, 1993

Retired numbers
26 Gene Autry
29 Rod Carew
30 Nolan Ryan

Oct. 5, 1979: *The Angels beat the Orioles 4–3 in Game 3 of the ALCS, the first playoff game ever at Anaheim Stadium.*

Sept. 17, 1984: *Reggie Jackson hits his 500th home run, off Bud Black of the Kansas City Royals.*

Aug. 4, 1985: *Rod Carew gets his 3,000th hit, against the Twins.*

June 18, 1986: *Don Sutton wins his 300th as the Angels beat the Rangers 5–1.*

April 11, 1990: *Mark Langston and Mike Witt combine to no-hit the Seattle Mariners 1–0.*

Sept. 30, 1992: *George Brett of the Kansas City Royals gets his 3,000th hit, off Tim Fortugno of the Angels.*

ARIZONA DIAMONDBACKS

Bank One Ballpark

STADIUM STATS

Location: Jefferson St. between 4th and 7th Sts., Phoenix, AZ 85001
Opens: April 1998
Surface: Grass
Capacity: 48,500
Outfield dimensions: LF 328, LC 376, CF 402, RC 376, RF 335
Services for fans with disabilities: Seating available throughout the stadium.

TEAM NOTEBOOK

Franchise history:
Arizona Diamondbacks, 1998.

Yes, but it's a dry heat. If you're lucky, you'll hear this phrase only a dozen or so times while you're in Phoenix. If you're even luckier, the daytime temperatures won't go too far into the triple digits while you're in town, either. It does get hot here; Phoenix fans have sat through games in 120-degree heat. Baseball fans needn't worry; once they're inside the Arizona Diamondbacks' Bank One Ballpark, the only heat should be coming off the pitcher's mound. Strategically placed fans will send cool air to various points of the stadium to keep it comfy.

Set across a parking lot from the NHL Phoenix Coyotes' home, America West Arena, the Arizona Diamondbacks' Bank One Ballpark—at press time still more than a year from completion—has already been affectionately nicknamed "Bob." This $238 million (so far) ballpark is a creation of the same firm that designed Boston's FleetCenter and Atlanta's Olympic Stadium. The stadium's exterior is sort of southwestern-style postmodern; the facade somewhat resembles the Texas Rangers' park in Arlington, with its columns and aged-brick colors, and fits well into Phoenix's landmark warehouse district. Bank One's most unique feature is its retractable roof, which is made up of separate bowed panels that telescope out along rails, using a winch-and-cable drive mechanism common in mining and manufacturing; it looks more like an airplane hangar than a dome. The adjustable exposure will allow in enough sun to play ball in true daylight without heating up the building's concrete-and-metal support structure.

Shaded plazas and walkways, two huge beer gardens overlooking the field of real grass, and a design that keeps everything to a human scale should make this park a favorite of new and visiting fans.

HOT TIPS FOR VISITING FANS

PARKING
Bank One will have a lot that will hold about 1,500 cars, and another 18,000 spots are available in private lots nearby. Street parking is extremely limited.

WEATHER
Although the summer daytime temperature can routinely go over 100 degrees, the stadium's roof and cooling system will keep the sun out during day games. What may surprise out-of-state visitors is how cool it can get here at night, even in summer. Bring a light jacket for night games.

MEDIA
Radio: KTAR (620 AM) is scheduled to carry all games; no Spanish-language radio station has yet been designated.
TV: KTVK (Channel 3) is on deck to broadcast the games.

CUISINE
Concessionaires haven't been chosen yet, but if the food is like that of its neighboring America West Arena, it won't be half bad; and they might even try to top all of the other teams in town. The premier sports bar in Phoenix is Majerle's Sports Grill (602-253-0118), which is owned by former Suns' star and local hero Dan Majerle. It's just up the street at 24 North Second Street. The Arizona Center, a mall on North Third Street, has several bars and restaurants, many of them already favorites of Phoenix sports fans. The local brew pub is Coyote Springs (no relation to the ice hockey team), downtown at First and Washington streets.

LODGING NEAR THE STADIUM

Hilton Suites at Phoenix Plaza
10 E. Thomas Rd.
Phoenix, AZ 85012
(602) 222-1111/(800) HILTONS
2 miles from the stadium.

Hyatt Regency
122 N. Second St.
Phoenix, AZ 85004
(602) 252-1234/(800) 233-1234
1 block from the stadium.

SPRING TRAINING

The Diamondbacks and Chicago White Sox will share a new facility in Tucson that will be ready for the 1998 spring training season.

MINOR LEAGUES

Class	Team
Rookie	Lethbridge (AB) Black Diamonds
Rookie	Phoenix (AZ) Diamondbacks

Until they start playing big-league ball in 1998, the Diamondbacks will have a chance to break in some of their players and coaching staff at the very lowest minor-league levels. In the Pioneer League, the Black Diamonds play at Henderson Stadium in the city of Lethbridge, Alberta, Canada. Closer to home, the Phoenix Diamondbacks began playing in the Arizona League's schedule in the summer of 1996. The Arizona League is, like the Gulf Coast League, the minors' minors, where games are like spring training in extra innings. You might get a sneak peek at some future Diamondbacks' star in the rough. For information, call (602) 327-7975.

In the Hot Seats at Bank One Ballpark

With 48,500 seats, there ought to be enough to go around. Season tickets for the Diamondbacks' first year of major-league play haven't gone on sale yet (summer 1996), so there's no way to know how eager local fans are to see baseball played at the big-league level for the entire season. They've seen plenty of rookie baseball through the Arizona League and various pro teams' spring training, but the Arizona League's viewing stands are populated mostly by major-league scouts who haven't come for the peanuts and Cracker Jack. It's also too soon to know whether Phoenix residents have enough enthusiasm (and money) to support four professional sports teams. Baseball has the inherent advantage of the longest stretch of play unrivaled by other sports.

GOOD SEATS

There are no obstructed seats in Bank One Ballpark, and until some games get played, drawbacks to any of the seats are unknown. Seats even in upper decks should be excellent; the steepness of the rise of the stands increases as they get higher, keeping the higher seats closer to the action.

SCALPING

Rules for Bank One Ballpark haven't been set, but will likely follow those of America West Arena; scalping is legal in Phoenix but isn't allowed on arena grounds. If this turns out to also be the case at Bank One, and there's a market for Diamondback tickets, sellers will probably just cross the street to conduct business, the way they do for Coyotes games now.

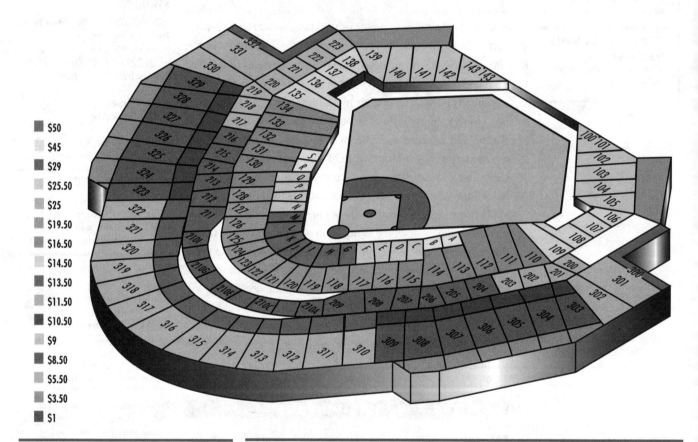

- $50
- $45
- $29
- $25.50
- $25
- $19.50
- $16.50
- $14.50
- $13.50
- $11.50
- $10.50
- $9
- $8.50
- $5.50
- $3.50
- $1

HOME-FIELD ADVANTAGE

Nothing about the stadium or the field offers the Diamondbacks any obvious edge over visitors. The retractable roof and efficient cool air circulation will keep the daytime heat down. The fans, however, might be harder to keep cool. Phoenix is in the midst of a sports Big Bang, and when the Diamondbacks take to the field in 1998, the only sport missing will be soccer. With less overlap into other sports seasons, baseball will rule this town all summer.

GETTING TO BANK ONE BALLPARK

Public transportation: Phoenix transit buses stop one block from the stadium. The main bus station is across the street, and any bus through downtown passes near the stadium. Call (602) 253-5000 for more information.
By car: From the north, take the I-17 Black Canyon Freeway to Jefferson/Washington exit. Go left onto Washington Street, then left on First Street. The stadium will be on the left.

From the south, take the I-10 Maricopa north to Jefferson Street. Go left onto Jefferson. The ballpark will be on the right.
From the east, take the SR-360 Superstition Freeway to the I-10 Maricopa, heading north.
From the west, take the I-10 Papago to First Street. Go right onto First Street. The stadium will be on the right.

TICKET INFORMATION
Address: Box 2095, Phoenix, AZ 85001
Phone: (602) 514-8400
By mail: 455 N. Third St., Suite 224,

Phoenix, AZ 85004
Hours: Mon.–Fri. 10–5, Wed. 10–8
Prices: $50: clubhouse lower level; $45: dugout lower level; $25.50, $19.50,

$16.50, $14.50, and $9: lower level; $29 and $25: diamond level; $13.50, $11.50, $10.50, $8.50, $5.50, $3.50, and $1: upper level.

Olympic Stadium

STADIUM STATS

Location: *Capitol Ave. S.W. & Ralph David Abernathy Blvd., Atlanta, GA 30312*
Opened: *July 1996*
Surface: *Prescription Athletic Turf (PAT grass)*
Capacity: *49,831*
Outfield dimensions: *LF 335, LC 380, CF 400, RC 385, RF 330.*
Services for fans with disabilities: *Seating available throughout the stadium.*

TICKET INFORMATION

Address: *521 Capitol Ave. S.W., Atlanta, GA 30312*
Phone: *(800) 326-4000*
By mail: *List the date, the kind of ticket and the number of tickets you want, and mail to: Atlanta Braves, P.O. Box 4064, Atlanta, GA 30302. Add a $5 handling charge and make your check payable to the Atlanta Braves.*
Hours: *Mon.–Sat. 8:30–5, Sun. 1–5.*
Prices: *To be determined.*

Gold, silver, and bronze medals are all very nice, but as well as the American athletes and teams did at the 1996 Olympics in Atlanta, the Braves and their fans got the better keepsake: a new ballpark. Baseball-only, state-of-the-art, built to last, and a real looker. Set right next door to Atlanta–Fulton County Stadium (which will be torn down and the site converted to a parking facility), the new home of the Braves follows the recent trend toward attractive, tradition-conscious stadium design and uses a red, white, blue, and green color scheme. The field is 20 feet below street level, so that even the upper-level seats aren't a killer climb.

The field is nearly the same size as Fulton County's, although it is asymmetrical, and infielders will have to adjust to the narrower foul territory. Braves power hitters will like the similar dimensions and the eight-foot fences. A quarter of the Olympic Stadium will be carved out to create an open plaza and the arched red-brick entrance that will lead fans into the park from the outfield end. Fans will like just about everything in this park. They'll be closer to the action, and home plate faces downtown Atlanta, offering spectacular views of the city skyline, especially during night games.

Atlanta–Fulton County Stadium will be remembered as "the Launching Pad," partly for some of the great home runs hit there, including Henry Aaron's 715th, which broke Babe Ruth's record, as well as for being the place where the Braves went from worst to first in a single season and rose to perpetual league-leader status. But no one will shed many tears for the stadium itself, a rather indistinctive mid-'60s creation without much character. Aside from the home runs, the stadium once was known primarily for having the worst field in the majors.

The various mascots in American Indian regalia had ceased even before the move, but the tomahawk chop, politically incorrect as it is, lives on and probably will continue in the new digs. No one knows yet what the stadium will be called once the Braves move in. Will it be Coca-Cola Park? Margaret Mitchell Stadium? With Ted Turner at the helm, maybe the FondaDome is possible.

HOT TIPS FOR VISITING FANS

PARKING

Once Atlanta–Fulton County Stadium is demolished and paved over, there will be 8,700 parking spots available. Prices had not been set at press time (summer '96), but the existing lots charge $7. Gypsy lots farther out run from $5 to $10, but beware: They sometimes park cars so tightly that you have to wait until well after the game for stragglers blocking you in. Plus, the area around the stadium is not very well lighted or considered particularly safe. Three freeways converge nearby, so traffic isn't a problem.

WEATHER

Often steamy, and be prepared for rain, too. The Braves might lead the majors in rain delays from all the early-evening thunderstorms that race through.

MEDIA

Radio: WSB (750 AM).
TV: Superstation WTBS (Channel 17) and SportSouth (cable). The Braves' broadcasters on WTBS are Skip Caray, Pete Van Wieren, Joe Simpson, and Don Sutton. Ernie Johnson, Tim Brando, and Ernie Johnson Jr. work strictly on SportsSouth.

CUISINE

Concession stands will be located throughout the ballpark, ensuring that you don't have to go too far to refuel. Regular fans are looking forward to the upgraded selections in the Braves' new home; offerings will include higher-quality traditional ballpark fare as well as gourmet ice creams, Italian specialties (remarkably popular at Atlanta–Fulton County), and a host of domestic and imported beers along with some microbrewery selections. Manuel's (404-525-3447) is the best and closest spot for a drink and a bite after the game, but plenty of young fans prefer the Hard Rock Cafe (404-688-7625). Jocks 'n' Jills (404-873-5405) on Peachtree and Champions (404-521-0000) in the Marriott are two sports-oriented places that also draw big crowds. If you want even more to choose from, head for Underground Atlanta, a huge complex that features many bars and restaurants.

LODGING NEAR THE STADIUM

Ritz Carlton
181 Peachtree St. N.E.
Atlanta, GA 30303
(404) 659-0400/(800) 241-3333
2 miles from the stadium.

Hyatt Regency
265 Peachtree St. N.E.

Atlanta, GA 30303
(404) 577-1234/(800) 233-1234
2½ miles from the stadium.

GETTING TO OLYMPIC STADIUM

Public transportation:
MARTA (Metropolitan Atlanta Rapid Transit Authority) bus service is available to the stadium. For more information, call (404) 848-3456 or (404) 848-4711.
By car: From the south, take I-75/85 north to exit 90, Ralph David Abernathy Avenue/ Stadium. Go left at stop sign on Washington Street and then right onto Abernathy Avenue. The stadium will be on the left.
From the north, take I-75/85 south to exit 91, Fulton Street/Stadium. Go left onto Fulton Street; the stadium will be on the right.
From the east, take I-20 west to exit 24, Capitol Avenue. Go left about ¼ of a mile; the stadium will be on the right.
From the west, take I-20 east to exit 22, Windsor Street/ Stadium. Go right about ¼ of a mile. Left onto Fulton. The Stadium will be about ¾ mile on the right.

IN THE HOT SEATS AT OLYMPIC STADIUM

Tickets were already hard to come by before the Braves won a World Series and moved into a new—and smaller—stadium. Not only that, but the team is still one of the few that doesn't hold back tickets for game-day sales. This can make it a scalper's market.

SCALPING

Scalpers are not hard to find. They line Capitol Avenue along the east side of the Stadium, and Fulton Street along the north side, ready to bargain.

SPRING TRAINING

Municipal Stadium
715 Hank Aaron Dr.
West Palm Beach, FL 33401
Capacity: 7,200
Surface: Grass
Game time: 1:05 p.m. or 7:05 p.m.
Tickets: (407) 471-6100

MINOR LEAGUES

Class	Team
AAA	Richmond (VA) Braves
AA	Greenville (SC) Braves
A	Durham (NC) Bulls
A	Macon (GA) Braves
Short Season A	Danville (VA) Braves
Rookie	Gulf Coast (FL) Braves

The minor-league affiliate closest to Atlanta is the Class A Macon Braves of the South Atlantic League. Macon's ballpark, Luther Williams Field, which opened in 1929, is one of baseball's oldest. Not surprisingly, baseball has a long history in Macon; in 1904, the league's first season, the team captured the Class C South Atlantic League pennant with a record of 67–45. Among Macon's famous alumni are Tony Perez and Pete Rose. The field was also used in the movie *Bingo Long and the Traveling All-Stars and Motor Kings* (another Braves minor league club, the Durham Bulls, was depicted in the almost-eponymous film *Bull Durham*). The stadium's newest concession, The Spud Shack, serves up all manner of tasty fried potatoes.
To reach Williams Field, which is approximately 80 miles from Atlanta, take the Coliseum exit from I-16. Turn right at the foot of the exit ramp. Go 1 block and turn left on Riverside Drive. The ballpark is ½ block in front of you.
Ticket prices: $6: box seats; $5: general admission. For information, call (912) 745-8943.

HOME-FIELD ADVANTAGE

The new home of the Braves will probably pick up right where Atlanta–Fulton County Stadium left off as a launching pad. The dimensions are nearly identical, and the squad still features some of the long-ball hitters from the '95 World Series. The eight-foot fence heights won't hurt, either.

The new park's smaller foul territory will leave infielders less room to chase, much less catch, pop-up fouls, as well as bringing the crowd closer to the action, which will only accentuate the highly charged atmosphere that can build to such a fevered pitch with Braves fans. The home crowd turned zealous in 1991, when the Braves won their first NL pennant since moving to Atlanta in 1966, and with each subsequent World Series appearance the tomahawk chops have become more emphatic. The World Series win in 1995 only confirmed the Braves as the team of the '90s; chances are that with Series momentum and a new, Olympic-caliber stadium, they'll finish out the century at or near the top—in the hearts of their fans if not in the league.

Braves fans, in fact, may benefit more from the new park than the team does. Since it was built for larger, Olympic-sized crowds, getting into, around, and back out of the new stadium should be a snap; field level seats are much closer to the action; the food available is more varied and of a much higher quality; and when Atlanta–Fulton County Stadium is razed there'll be lots more parking.

BRAVES TEAM NOTEBOOK

Franchise history
Boston Red Stockings, Reds or Red Caps, 1876–82; Boston Beaneaters, 1883–1906; Boston Doves, 1907–10; Boston Rustlers, 1911; Boston Braves, 1912–1935; Boston Bees, 1936–40; Boston Braves, 1941–52; Milwaukee Braves, 1953–65; Atlanta Braves, 1966–present

World Series titles
1914, 1957, 1995

National League pennants
1877, 1878, 1883, 1891, 1892, 1893, 1897, 1898, 1914, 1948, 1957, 1958, 1991, 1992, 1995

Division titles
1969, 1982, 1991, 1992, 1993, 1995

Most Valuable Players
John Evers, 1914
Bob Elliott, 1947

Henry Aaron, 1957
Dale Murphy, 1982, 1983
Terry Pendleton, 1991

Rookies of the Year
Alvin Dark, 1948
Sam Jethroe, 1950
Earl Williams, 1971
Bob Horner, 1978
David Justice, 1990

Cy Young Awards
Warren Spahn, 1957
Tom Glavine, 1991
Greg Maddux, 1993

Hall of Fame
Babe Ruth, 1936
George Wright, 1937
Cy Young, 1937
Hoss Radbourne, 1939
George Sisler, 1939
Rogers Hornsby, 1942
Dan Brouthers, 1945
James Collins, 1945
Hugh Duffy, 1945
King Kelly, 1945
Jim O'Rourke, 1945
Johnny Evers, 1946
Tommy McCarthy, 1946
Ed Walsh, 1946
Kid Nichols, 1949

Paul Waner, 1952
Al Simmons, 1953
Harry Wright, 1953
Rabbit Maranville, 1954
Billy Hamilton, 1961
Bill McKechnie, 1962
John Clarkson, 1963
Burleigh Grimes, 1964
Casey Stengel, 1966
Lloyd Waner, 1967
Joe "Ducky" Medwick, 1968
Dave Bancroft, 1971
Rube Marquard, 1971
Joe Kelley, 1971
Warren Spahn, 1973
Earl Averill, 1975
Billy Herman, 1975
Al Lopez, 1977
Eddie Mathews, 1978
Henry Aaron, 1982
Enos Slaughter, 1985
Hoyt Wilhelm, 1985
Ernie Lombardi, 1986
Red Schoendienst, 1989
Gaylord Perry, 1991

Retired numbers
3 Dale Murphy
21 Warren Spahn
35 Phil Niekro
41 Eddie Mathews
44 Hank Aaron

Oriole Park at Camden Yards

STADIUM STATS

Location: 333 W. Camden St., Baltimore, MD 21201
Opened: April 6, 1992
Surface: Grass
Capacity: 48,262
Outfield dimensions: LF 333, LC 410, CF 400, RC 386, RF 318
Services for fans with disabilities: Seating available throughout the stadium. Call (410) 685-9800 ext. 6600 for more information.

STADIUM FIRSTS

Regular-season game: April 6, 1992, 2–0 loss to the Cleveland Indians.
Pitcher: Rick Sutcliffe of the Orioles.
Batter: Kenny Lofton of the Indians.
Hit: Paul Sorrento of the Indians.
Home run: April 8, 1992, by Paul Sorrento.

GROUND RULES

• Foul poles with screens attached are judged outside of playing field.
• Thrown or fairly batted ball that remains behind or under the canvas or canvas holder is two bases. Ball rebounding in playing field is in play.
• Ball striking surfaces, pillars or facings surrounding the dugout is ruled in dugout.
• Ball striking railing around photographers' booths is in play.
• Fair bounding ball striking railings above cement wall down right field line is out of play
• Fly ball hitting the grounds crew shed roof in right field and bouncing back onto field is a home run.

Opened in 1992 with the idea that tradition would take precedence over the flashy technology that's usually associated with new sports facilities, Oriole Park at Camden Yards, 2 blocks from where the legendary Babe Ruth was born, is a ballpark that honors its elder counterparts—Chicago's Wrigley Field, Boston's Fenway Park, and New York's Polo Grounds. While it was intended to be reminiscent of old-time parks, Camden Yards' architecture has a distinctly local flavor and its facilities are thoroughly modern. The stadium has become a favorite of players and fans alike, and the model against which all other new or proposed ballparks are measured.

The park has also given new life to the B&O Warehouse, a turn-of-the-century building 1,016 feet long and 51 feet wide now housing restaurants, sports bars, and the Orioles' offices and situated past right field. Although it has never been hit during a game, Ken Griffey, Jr., bounced one off the building in a home run contest before the 1993 All-Star Game.

Camden Yards revived the out-of-town scoreboard, another feature of the old-fashioned parks, that spews out up-to-the-minute scores, pitching changes, and assorted details from other games.

The stadium is double-decked. There are outfield bleacher seats that soak up the sun. Fans enter the stadium through wrought-iron gates and arched portals.

Walkways are spacious, and concessions stands provide excellent service. The new stadium has become the place to be, which often results in diehard fans being shut out. The suit-and-tie crowd also tends to be quieter.

HOT TIPS FOR VISITING FANS

PARKING

If you want to get one of the 5,000 spaces in the parking lots, make sure to arrive at least 45 minutes before the first pitch. If you miss out, don't fret: Another 30,000 spaces are available in lots and garages throughout downtown, all within a mile's walk of Oriole Park. Actually, it's not all bad to park outside the stadium site. A bracingly short 10- to 15-minute walk will get fans quickly out of the most congested areas, allowing them to hit the road ahead of traffic. If you're arriving by boat, you can dock at the Inner Harbor marina, 3 blocks from the stadium.

WEATHER

April and September are unpredictable: Temperatures can swing to either extreme, but those months may also offer gorgeous weather. The one sure bet is the heavy humidity during the summer months, particularly in July and August. For those games, wear loose clothing and prepare for oven-like temperatures, even in the late innings of a night game. Rain delays are shorter than at most parks, once precipitation stops. The park has a drainage system that can remove 75,000 gallons of water from the field in one hour. Club suites are a good deal in hot weather because they are air conditioned.

MEDIA

Radio: WBAL (1090 AM) with Jon Miller, Fred Manfra, Chuck Thompson, and Josh Lewin.
TV: WMAR (Channel 2) with Scott Garceau and Keith Mills; and Home Team Sports (cable) with Mel Proctor, Mike Flanagan, Jim Palmer, and Tom Davis. Orioles' broadcaster Jon Miller is nationally known from his work on ESPN. His voice is soothing, his descriptions are crisp, and the best part is that he can do imitations of legendary broadcasters from other teams. However, if you're listening to a broadcasted game on radio or TV, you'll miss the highly entertaining public-address announcing of Rex Barney, a flame-throwing pitcher for the Brooklyn Dodgers in 1943–50. When a fan catches a foul ball, Barney says, "Give that fan a contract." At the end of announcements, his "thank youuuuuu" has become a Baltimore staple.

CUISINE

The fabulous taste of Maryland's Chesapeake Bay crab cakes are as much a part of Baltimore baseball as bats and balls. They are served with tartar or cocktail sauce, and lemon wedges. Stands at Oriole Park sell a dozen different imported beers to wash down the crab cakes. Most popular: Corona with a slice of lime. Out in center field there's a stand serving kosher food; if there's a game during afternoon or evening prayers, observant Jews are welcome to join the proprietors.
After the game, try Eutaw Street, where former first baseman Boog Powell cooks up beef sandwiches and talks baseball at his barbecue pit just outside the stadium. How to find the pit? Follow the aromatic clouds of smoke that billow up from behind center field. Nearby is another stand run by the folks who own the Bambino's Pub sports bar and restaurant.

LODGING NEAR THE STADIUM

Renaissance Harborplace Hotel
202 E. Pratt St.
Baltimore, MD 21201

In the Hot Seats at Oriole Park at Camden Yards

Tickets for Orioles games at Camden Yards are hard to get for fans who just show up hoping to buy a ticket for that day's game. Attendance averages 44,000 a game, and by mid-May of the 1996 season total attendance had already hit the 1 million mark; most games are near sellouts. There's competition and long lines for any individual tickets that go on sale. It is best to plan ahead—as early as December, when the Orioles put 1 million tickets on sale at First Pitch, a festive event that, in addition to ticket sales, allows fans to tour the park, get players' autographs, visit Santa Claus, and buy memorabilia. The Orioles cut off season-ticket sales at 27,500 to ensure an ample supply of single-game tickets, but with a season-ticket waiting list of more than 8,000, it's easy to imagine how fast tickets

get gobbled up. Section 90, another bleacher section in center field, was recently added.

EXTRA VIEW
Seats down the third-base line in the first deck are the best for getting a view of Baltimore's skyline.

BAD SEATS
Word is, there isn't a bad seat in the house, but it ain't so. Still, some improvements have been made. Seats that wrap around the corner in left field and in a couple of sections down the right-field line and that used to face the center-field wall have been "redirected" to face the infield. However, several rows of seats at the back of the lower deck have an obstructed view: Fans can't see outfielders because of the second deck's overhang.

SPECIAL PROGRAM
For a $4 membership fee, fans 16 and under can join the Dugout Club, a program that gets them a T-shirt and discount ticket prices. There are eight dates in which upper-reserve tickets are available at half price. Call (410) 685-9800 for dates.

SCALPING
The ballpark has become quite the trendy place to be, a social event at which a good number of those who show up have only a fleeting interest in baseball. That leaves some of the hard-core fans on the outside, dealing with scalpers. The market can be competitive, and for big regular-season games, prices can double.

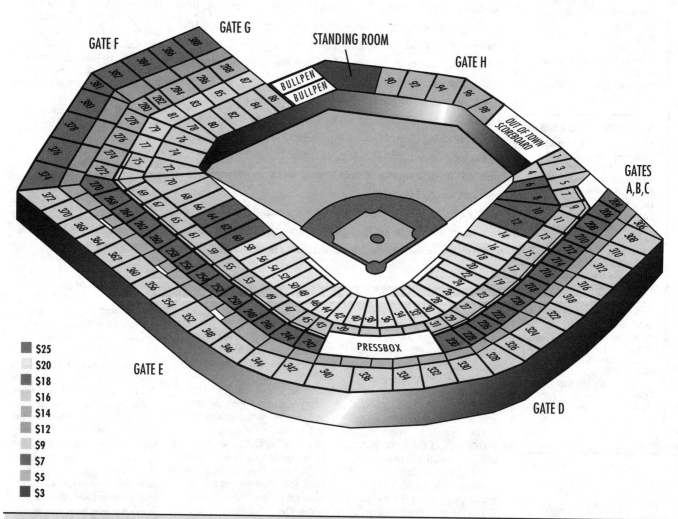

- $25
- $20
- $18
- $16
- $14
- $12
- $9
- $7
- $5
- $3

TICKET INFORMATION
Address: 333 W. Camden St., Baltimore, MD 21201
Phone: (410) 685-9800 or TicketMaster at (410) 481-SEAT (greater Baltimore), (202) 432-SEAT (greater Washington, D.C., and Maryland, or (703) 573-SEAT (greater northern Virginia) .
Hours: Mon.–Sat. 9–6, Sun. 12–5
Prices: $25: club box; $20: field box; $18: lower box; $16: LF club and terrace box; $14: upper box and LF box; $12: LF upper box; $9: upper and lower reserve; $7 LF upper reserve; $5: bleachers; $3: standing room.

(410) 547-1200/(800) 535-1201
A few blocks from the stadium.

**Baltimore Marriott
Inner Harbor**
110 S. Eutaw St.
Baltimore, MD 21201
(410) 962-0202/(800) 228-9290
Across the street from the stadium.

GETTING TO CAMDEN YARDS

Public transportation: More than 20 bus lines go within 4 blocks of the stadium. The Baltimore Metro is speedy, and it provides more than 8,000 free parking spots. Take the Metro to Lexington Market or Charles Center stations, and pick up a shuttle to the park. MTA information: (410) 539-5000.
By car: Take MD 295, I-83, or U.S. 40 to downtown Baltimore, or I-95 to exit 53, 52, or 51.

SPRING TRAINING

Ft. Lauderdale Stadium
5301 N.W. 12 Ave.
Ft. Lauderdale, FL 33309
Capacity: 8,340
Surface: Grass
Game time: 1:05 p.m. or 7:05 p.m.
Tickets: (954) 776-1921

MINOR LEAGUES

Class	Team
AAA	Rochester (NY) Redwings
AA	Bowie (MD) Baysox
A	Frederick (MD) Keys
A	High Desert (CA) Mavericks
Rookie	Bluefield (WV) Orioles
Rookie	Sarasota (FL) Orioles

The Frederick Keys compete in the Carolina League. To get to Frederick from Baltimore, take I-70 west and go 40 miles. Harry Grove Stadium (seating 5,500) is at exit 54.
Ticket prices: $9 and $7: box seats; $5: general admission; $3: general admission for children 6–12. Call (301) 662-0013 for information.
The Class AA Bowie Baysox play at the Prince George Stadium, located 40 miles south of

Oriole Park and 25 minutes east of Washington, D.C. The stadium, which seats 10,000, is surrounded by woods.
Ticket prices: $9, $7: box seats; $5: general admission; $3: children 6–12, senior citizens and active military. Free for kids in Little League uniforms and children under 5. Call (301) 805-6000 for more information.

THE ORIOLES AT CAMDEN YARDS

June 28, 1989: Razing of the 85-acre parcel on which Baltimore's new stadium will be constructed begins.

Oct. 6, 1991: The Orioles play their last game in Memorial Stadium, which has been home to the Orioles for 38 years (and 3,036 games). On this final day, more than 100 past and present Orioles return to the field in an emotional postgame tribute. Bringing tears to the eyes of players and fans alike, Orioles management brings back scores of ex-Orioles, puts them in their old uniforms, and has them return to their positions on the field. No introductions are necessary.

April 6, 1992: Oriole Park at Camden Yards becomes the official home of the Orioles.

1992: The Orioles bring their magic with them to their new stadium in their first season at Oriole Park at Camden Yards. The Orioles' 22-game improvement is second only to the record-breaking 32½-game improvement in 1989.

June 22, 1992: The game at Camden Yards draws 45,156 spectators, giving the Orioles their 12th consecutive sellout and their 20th full house of 1992.

Jan. 4, 1993: Time magazine names Oriole Park at Camden Yards among the Top 10 Best Designs of '92.

July 15, 1993: Cal Ripken hits his 278th homer, passing Ernie Banks for most home runs by a shortstop.

HOME-FIELD ADVANTAGE

With a close right field—the corner is 318 feet from home plate—you'd think there would be baseballs banging off the 25-foot wall every night. That's not the case. In 1993, for example, only 21 hits bounced off the right-field scoreboard, and it's still a rare occurrence. The theory is that a wind blows over the scoreboard toward center field. It's not strong enough to hold in a well-hit ball that goes for a home run, but it can take an average line drive destined for the wall and turn it into a fly-ball out.

The left- and center-field fences are 7 feet high, so the home-run-robbing catch is back. There's usually about a dozen heists a year, and more than half belong to Orioles outfielders who've got the move down cold.

Players love playing in Oriole Park because for the most part they enjoy small stadiums that are full of fans. They say it adds to the electricity of the game.

They also like the real conditions: fresh air, green grass, and the views out from the stadium. And they appreciate Oriole Park for the state-of-the-art facilities: roomy clubhouses, comfortable lounges, well-lighted indoor batting cages and plenty of exercise equipment.

And the Orioles are the lucky ones who call this stadium home.

ORIOLES TEAM NOTEBOOK

Franchise history
Milwaukee Brewers, 1901; St. Louis Browns, 1902-53; Baltimore Orioles, 1954–present

World Series titles
1966, 1970, 1983

American League pennants
1944, 1966, 1969, 1970, 1971, 1979, 1983

Division titles
1969, 1970, 1971, 1973, 1974, 1979, 1983

Most Valuable Players
Brooks Robinson, 1964
Frank Robinson, 1966
Boog Powell, 1970

Cal Ripken Jr., 1983, 1991

Rookies of the Year
Roy Sievers, 1949
Ron Hansen, 1960
Curt Blefary, 1965
Al Bumbry, 1973
Eddie Murray, 1977
Cal Ripken Jr., 1982
Gregg Olson, 1989

Cy Young Awards
Mike Cuellar, 1969 (tie)
Jim Palmer, 1973, 1975, 1976
Mike Flanagan, 1979
Steve Stone, 1980

Hall of Fame
George Sisler, 1939
Rogers Hornsby, 1942
Hugh Duffy, 1945
Jessie Burkett, 1946
Eddie Plank, 1946
Rube Waddell, 1946

Dizzy Dean, 1953
Bobby Wallace, 1953
Heinie Manush, 1964
Branch Rickey, 1967
Goose Goslin, 1968
Satchel Paige, 1971
Jim Bottomley, 1974
Robin Roberts, 1976
Frank Robinson, 1982
Brooks Robinson, 1983
George Kell, 1983
Luis Aparicio, 1984
Rick Ferrell, 1984
Hoyt Wilhelm, 1985
Jim Palmer, 1990
Bill Veeck, 1991
Reggie Jackson, 1993
Earl Weaver, 1996

Retired numbers
4 Earl Weaver
5 Brooks Robinson
20 Frank Robinson
22 Jim Palmer

Aug. 7, 1993: Cal Ripken hits two homers for the first time at Camden Yards and drives in four runs as the Orioles beat Cleveland 8–6. It is the 12th two-homer game of Ripken's career.
Sept. 6, 1995: The Record is broken. Ripken plays in his 2,131st consecutive game, overtaking the Iron Horse, Lou Gehrig.

BOSTON RED SOX

Fenway Park

A warm, sunny afternoon at Fenway Park is baseball's version of a religious experience.

Except for the electronic scoreboard in center field, the park has changed little since it was built in 1912. The 2-story red-brick facade still goes well with Boston's worn-down urban setting. Inside, you'll find baseball's only single-deck park and certainly its coziest, given that some of the seats are closer to home plate than the dugouts are. However, the most distinctive feature of Fenway is the Green Monster, the intimidating 37-foot wall in left field. It was created to keep cheap home runs from flying out of the stadium. At its base is a hand-operated scoreboard that shows scores and pitching changes from games around the American League. Completing the scene are the famous Citgo sign looming over the Green Monster and the Prudential Building over the right-field fence.

Even through a long championship drought—the last time the Red Sox won the World Series was 1918, before they sold Babe Ruth to the New York Yankees—and the painful teases of 1975 and 1986, New England fans love their team. The traditions of the Red Sox and the beauty of the park outweigh any of the inconveniences of a small, old-fashioned stadium. Just go with a mitt and be ready to talk baseball—that's how Red Sox fans pass the time while waiting in long lines at the hot-dog stands, ticket windows, and bathrooms.

Do not wear a Yankees shirt. Or a Mets shirt, for that matter. Legend has it that the sale of the Babe to the Yankees put a curse on Boston baseball, a curse that felt all too real when the ball rolled between Bill Buckner's legs in 1986 at the other New York ballpark. Curse or not, an eerie reminder is posted on the green facade above the right-field grandstand. The Red Sox have retired only four numbers—Ted Williams' No. 9, Joe Cronin's No. 4, Bobby Doerr's No. 1, and Carl Yastrzemski's No. 8. As Boston author Dan Shaughnessy points out, the numbers are arranged 9-4-1-8, or 9/4/18—the eve of the 1918 World Series.

Castiglione and Jerry Trupiano are the announcers.
TV: WABU (Channel 68) and NESN (cable). Sean McDonough and Jerry Remy do the games on WABU, and Bob Kurtz joins Jerry Remy to handle the NESN games.

CUISINE
In a city of tradition, what else would be the most popular concessions item but the Fenway frank? The Fenway frank is a legend—you can even buy them in supermarkets, where they're marked with a Red Sox logo. But the supermarket frank has a different taste from the ballpark's frank, which is all beef and has more spice. Locals add mustard, ketchup, onions, and relish. Starting at $2.25, the Fenway Frank is a steal; even its largest and toppings-heavy version is only $3.25. They are eaten for the nostalgia, not necessarily the taste. Specialty foods at Fenway are for show only.

After the game, try the Cask 'N Flagon (617-536-4840) on the corner of Landsdowne and Brookline. Loaded with Red Sox memorabilia going back to the days of Babe Ruth, even Yankee fans say it's a must-stop when they come to town. Two wide-screen and six 20-inch TVs mean you won't miss a play while enjoying your Green Monster burger, piled with green peppers and onions. In fact, it's close enough to the park that the original Green Monster can be seen from the bar's front door. Two or three home runs a year land on the roof, and employees see them on TV and then climb up to get the baseballs.

LODGING NEAR THE PARK

Sheraton Boston Hotel and Towers
39 Dalton St.
Boston, MA 02199
(617) 236-2000/(800) 325-3535
About 5 blocks from the stadium.

Boston Marriott Copley Place
110 Huntington Ave.
Boston, MA 02116
(617) 236-5800/(800) 228-9290
About ½ mile from the stadium.

HOT TIPS FOR VISITING FANS

PARKING
Some limited parking is available at the Prudential Center Garage a few blocks away and at the Riverside MBTA Station. A number of private lots are around the park at Kenmore Square and at Boston University. All these lots can be pretty inconvenient, though. If you know you have to leave early, park where you can get out, because getting blocked in is common. Parking in and around Fenway costs $5–$15.

WEATHER
Don't be surprised if it snows during April. September can be cool. Summer months can be hot.

MEDIA
Radio: WEEI (850 AM). Joe

In the Hot Seats at Fenway Park

Tickets go on sale Dec. 1 at Fenway Park. Tickets can be difficult to get on game day, depending on who's playing, but you may have better luck later in the season if the Sox aren't in a pennant race.

GOOD SEATS

Outside of the pole seats, virtually any seat in the grandstand is good, but some are better than others. For example, several sections of seats down the right-field line point toward center field, not the infield. The advantage of sitting in right field is that both bullpens are in front of the bleachers. Opposing relievers sometimes have to warm up with soda cups bouncing off their heads. Fans can get rowdy, but Fenway's crowd-control personnel keep things under control.

All bleacher seats have excellent views. They're great for getting sun, and they're the same price as the seats down the right-field line. Bleacher fans usually start the wave. The best seat in the bleachers is the red one in row 33. It's easy to find because all the other seats are green. It marks the longest home run hit to right field, by Ted Williams. The ball went 502 feet and broke the straw hat of a sun-blinded fan.

BAD SEATS

Pole seats are a fact of life at every old-fashioned ballpark, and while they can be a pain, they're better than nothing at Fenway. Ticket sellers will warn fans before they sell a seat with an obstructed view. Locals say pole seats aren't ideal, but if fans can bend their heads to the left and right, the game can be seen.

FAMILY SECTIONS

Sections 32 and 33, located down the left-field line, are good for families because they're non-drinking, non-smoking sections. Also, the overhang protects children in case of rain.

SCALPING

You'd think that with fewer than 34,000 seats, scalpers would have a field day, but tickets usually go on the scalp market with minimal inflation.

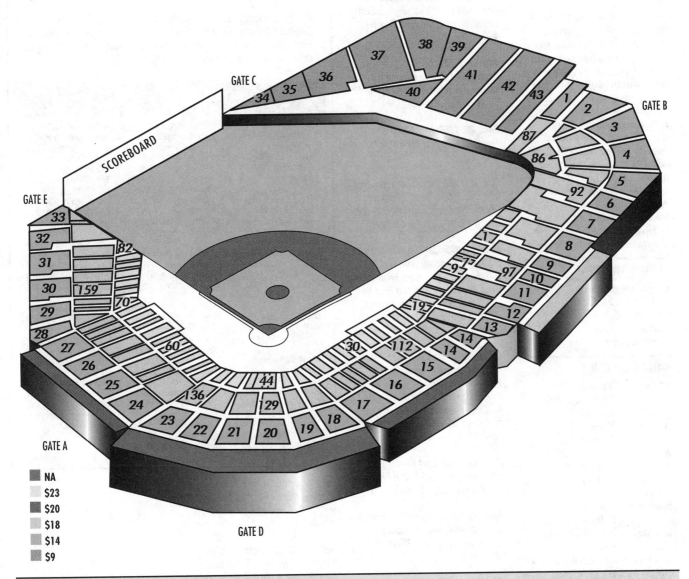

TICKET INFORMATION
Address: 4 Yawkey Way, Boston, MA 02215
Phone: (617) 267-8661
Hours: Mon.–Sat. 9–5.
Prices: $23: field box; $20: infield roof; $18: right-field roof and upper box; $14: reserved grandstand; $9: bleachers.

GETTING TO FENWAY PARK

Public transportation: The Nos. 8, 8A, 47, 55, 57, 60, and 65 buses go to Kenmore Square, which is about 3 blocks north of the park, as does the Green Line on the T. Commuter trains from the western suburbs stop at Yawkey Station, 2 blocks west of Fenway. For more information, call (617) 722-3200 or (800) 392-6100.

By car: From the west, take the Massachusetts Turnpike to the Prudential exit. Make a right onto Dalton Street, then a left at the light onto Boylston Street. At the second set of lights, turn right onto Ipswich Street. Continue for ¼ mile (Ipswich becomes Van Ness Street) and make a right onto Yawkey Way. The stadium is on the left.
From the north, take Route 93 south and follow signs to Storrow Drive. Take Storrow to the Kenway/Kenmore Square exit. At the top of the exit ramp, bear right onto Boylston Street, then proceed as above.
From the south, take I-95 north. Follow the Dedham–Maine/New Hampshire split. Take exit 20A/Route 9 east off I-95. Continue on Route 9 east about 10 or 12 miles, past the Chestnut Hill Reservoir. Turn left onto Brookline Avenue, continue on to Boylston Street, and take a right. Go ¼ mile and make a left onto Yawkey Way. The stadium will be on your right.

SPRING TRAINING

City of Palms Park
Fort Myers, FL 33901
Capacity: 6,990
Surface: Grass
Game time: 1:05 p.m.

MINOR LEAGUES

Class	Team
AAA	Pawtucket (RI) Red Sox
AA	Trenton (NJ) Thunder Red Sox
A	Michigan Battle Cats
A	Sarasota (FL) Red Sox
Short Season A	Lowell (MA) Spinners
Rookie	Fort Myers (FL) Red Sox

The Pawtucket Red Sox are the closest minor-league team. McCoy Stadium has been the Pawsox' home since 1942. This is where, on April 18, 1981, Pawtucket and the Rochester Red Wings played the longest game in organized baseball history. After 8 hours, 7 minutes, and 32 innings, the game was called at 4:09 a.m. with the score 2–2. When play resumed on June 23, Pawtucket won 3–2 in the 33rd inning.
To get to McCoy Stadium from I-95 south, take exit 2A, then go on Newport Avenue for 2 miles. Turn right on Columbus and follow for about 1 mile. McCoy Stadium will be on the right.

THE RED SOX AT FENWAY PARK

June 23, 1917: After the starting pitcher, Babe Ruth, walks the first batter and is ejected for arguing, Ernie Shore comes on and retires 27 Washington Senators in a row. The Red Sox win 4–0.

June 8, 1950: The Red Sox tie an American League record for most runs when they beat the St. Louis Browns 29–4.

Sept. 28, 1960: In his last at-bat, Ted Williams hits his 521st home run.

Oct. 11, 1967: Rico Petrocelli hits two home runs as the Red Sox top the St. Louis Cardinals 8–4 in Game 6 of the World Series.

Oct. 21, 1975: Carlton Fisk leads off the 12th inning with a home run that barely curves around the foul pole, giving the Red Sox a 7–6 win over the Cincinnati Reds in Game 6 of the World Series.

Oct. 2, 1978: Tied in the standings after the regular-season, the Yankees and Red Sox play a one-game playoff to decide the AL East. Homers by Bucky Dent and Reggie Jackson give the Yankees a 5–4 win.

Sept. 12, 1979: Carl Yastrzemski gets his 3,000th hit, off the Yankees' Jim Beattie.

April 29, 1986: Roger Clemens sets a major-league record when he strikes out 20 Seattle Mariners.

Oct. 15, 1986: Clemens pitches seven shutout innings and Jim

HOME-FIELD ADVANTAGE

Fenway Park's outfield is a maze of difficulties for opposing outfielders, which gives the Red Sox the biggest home-field advantage in the American League.

The outfield wall's height starts with the 37-foot Green Monster in left and then, as the fence zigzags its way to right field, it drops to 17, 5, and then 3 feet. Opposing outfielders reserve an extra 20 minutes a day to practice catching line drives off the wall.

The right-field fence is waist-high. The trick here is to shut out the verbal abuse from the bleachers fans and concentrate on trying to make a catch while falling over the fence and into the bullpen. Nobody did that better than Dwight Evans.

The proximity of the fans to the field can be distracting. Hitters, not pitchers, have the advantage because infielders have little room—and outfielders have none—to catch foul pop-ups. Unfortunately for pitchers, cheap outs are rare.

But pitchers, at least some, take advantage of how the Green Monster looms in left field. Many a batter has left Fenway with an inflated strikeout total, a few meager pop-ups and an out-of-sync swing.

RED SOX TEAM NOTEBOOK

Franchise history Boston Americans or Pilgrims, 1901–1907; Boston Red Sox, 1907–present	Fred Lynn, 1975 Jim Rice, 1978 Roger Clemens, 1986 Mo Vaughn, 1995	Al Simmons, 1953 Joe Cronin, 1956 Joe McCarthy, 1957 Heinie Manush, 1964 Ted Williams, 1966
World Series titles 1903, 1912, 1915, 1916, 1918	**Rookies of the Year** Walt Dropo, 1950 Don Schwall, 1961 Carlton Fisk, 1972 Fred Lynn, 1975	Red Ruffing, 1967 Waite Hoyt, 1969 Lou Boudreau, 1970 Harry Hooper, 1971
American League pennants 1903, 1904, 1912, 1915, 1916, 1918, 1946, 1967, 1975, 1986	**Cy Young Awards** Jim Lonborg, 1967 Roger Clemens, 1986, 1987, 1991	Bucky Harris, 1975 Billy Herman, 1975 Tom Yawkey, 1980 George Kell, 1983 Juan Marichal, 1983 Luis Aparicio, 1984 Rick Ferrell, 1984
Division titles 1975, 1986, 1988, 1990, 1995	**Hall of Fame** Babe Ruth, 1936 Tris Speaker, 1937 Cy Young, 1937 Eddie Collins, 1939 Jimmy Collins, 1945	Bobby Doerr, 1986 Carl Yastrzemski, 1989 Ferguson Jenkins, 1991 Tom Seaver, 1992
Most Valuable Players Tris Speaker, 1912 Jimmie Foxx, 1938 Ted Williams, 1946, 1949 Jackie Jensen, 1958 Carl Yastrzemski, 1967	Hugh Duffy, 1945 Jesse Burkett, 1946 Frank Chance, 1946 Jack Chesbro, 1946 Lefty Grove, 1947 Herb Pennock, 1948 Jimmie Foxx, 1951 Ed Barrow, 1953	**Retired numbers** 1 Bobby Doerr 4 Joe Cronin 8 Carl Yastrzemski 9 Ted Williams

Rice hits a three-run home run, leading the Sox to the pennant with a 8–1 win over the California Angels.

July 8, 1994: Shortstop John Valentin makes only the tenth unassisted triple play in major-league history. The Sox beat Seattle 4–3.

STADIUM STATS

Location: *1060 W. Addison St., Chicago, IL 60613*
Opened: *1914*
Surface: *Grass*
Capacity: *38,765*
Outfield dimensions: *LF 355, LC 368, CF 400, RC 368, RF 353*
Services for fans with disabilities: *Call (312) 404-2827 for information.*

STADIUM FIRSTS

Regular-season game: *April 20, 1916, 7–6 over the Cincinnati Reds in 11 innings.*
Pitcher: *Claude Hendrix, Cubs.*
Batter: *Red Killefer, Reds.*
Home run: *Johnny Beall, Reds.*

GROUND RULES

• *If the ball hits the railing or screen above the bleacher wall and bounces back onto the playing field, it is in play.*
• *If the ball hits the top of the screen and drops between the screen and wall, or hits the screen and bounces into the bleachers, it is a home run.*
• *If the ball sticks in the screen or in the vines, it is a double.*
• *If the ball hits foul markers above the painted mark, it is a home run.*
• *If the ball goes under the grates in left field or right field and remains there, it is a double.*
• *If the ball hits the foul markers below the painted mark and bounces back onto the playing field, it is in play.*
• *If the ball goes in or under the grates on either side of home plate and remains there, it's one base on a pitched ball and two bases on a thrown ball.*

Known as "the Friendly Confines" and tucked into a neighborhood of vintage brownstones on Chicago's North Side, Wrigley Field is the ballpark down the street and feels like home the minute you walk in. Wrigley has kept up with modern times at its own pace, not adding lights until 1988 or sky boxes until 1989.

But even those changes do little to alter the nostalgic feel one has here. Wrigley is one of the few ballparks that can sell out even if the home team is in last place. This is the park with the best bleachers in baseball, the only place where Harry Caray sings "Take Me Out to the Ball Game," and the stadium where there are more day games than anywhere else.

The ivy vines clinging to the outfield walls were planted in 1937 by Bill Veeck, but you have to wait until May for them to turn green against the 11-foot-high brick wall. The scoreboard, constructed in 1937, also by Veeck (you can look it up!), presides over the park from center field and is still operated manually. It was built before expansion and lacks room for all the games played. The only ball hit off the scoreboard was a golf ball, teed up by pro Sam Snead in 1951; Roberto Clemente homered just left, Bill Nicholson missed just to the right.

Originally known as Weeghman Park and built for the Whales of the extinct Federal League, the park was renamed for team owner William Wrigley, Jr., in 1926. The current owners, the Tribune Company, bought the team in 1981. Everyone who comes to Wrigley knows there's something special about the park, so the normal rules don't apply. Players actually have fun interacting with fans here. Visiting pitchers especially will play catch with the bleacher fans during batting practice and usually right up until game time. Those who don't will hear about it until they can escape to the clubhouse after the game.

HOT TIPS FOR VISITING FANS

PARKING

Parking is almost nonexistent, with no single main lot and only several small vendors along Clark Street. The Cubs offer prepaid parking through their ticket office and through TicketMaster. Wrigleyville and Lake View residents have special stickers that allow them to park in the neighborhood, and regulations are strictly enforced. Tow trucks do good business at Cubs night games, so pay to park somewhere legitimate. The vendors know that.

They raise parking prices for night games.

WEATHER

Former Cubs manager Don Zimmer used to call the ballpark "Wrigley Field I" and "Wrigley Field II," depending on which way the breeze was blowing off Lake Michigan. If it's from the west or southwest, you want a seat in the bleachers because balls will usually be flying out of the ballpark. If the wind is from the east or northeast, bring a jacket. April, May, and September can be significantly colder because of gusts off the water.

MEDIA

Radio: WGN (720 AM); Cubs great Ron Santo is color commentator and Pat Hughes does the play by play.
TV: WGN (Channel 9); 140 games are broadcast on superstation WGN with Steve Stone and Wayne Larrivee announcing. Harry Caray does all home games and only selected road games due to health concerns. Ten away games are carried by CLTV (cable), and another eight games appear on Fox Sports Saturday.

CUISINE

Wrigley Field has three restaurants—the Stadium Club, the Friendly Confines Café, and the Sheffield Grill. Inside the ballpark, concessions offer everything from Italian beef sandwiches to traditional fare such as hot dogs, hamburgers, popcorn, pretzels, and peanuts. Across the street, The Cubby Bear (312-327-1662) is usually jammed for both pre- and postgame refreshments, along with nearby Sluggers (312-248-0055) and Murphy's Bleachers, on Waveland and Sheffield. Some flock to Hi-Tops (312-348-0009), another sports bar, located on Sheffield and Addison. For a taste of Chicago-style pizza, go to Gino's East (312-321-1000). Visit Harry Caray's in River North (312-465-9269) for Italian food and maybe another glimpse of Harry if you weren't satisfied with your seventh-inning sing-along, or Billy Goat's Tavern (312-222-1525), a newspaper dive full of Chicago atmosphere, for a "chee' burger."

LODGING NEAR THE STADIUM

Hyatt Regency
151 E. Wacker Dr.
Chicago, IL 60601
(312) 565-1234/(800) 233-1234
About 5 miles from the stadium.

Westin Hotel
909 N. Michigan Ave.

In the Hot Seats at Wrigley Field

The Cubs have a season-ticket base of about 11,000 for weekday games, 19,000 for weekends, but you usually can get a ticket unless it's Opening Day. Tickets are also tough to get for night games, which always feel like a Saturday night no matter what day of the week it is. Because of an agreement with the city of Chicago, only 18 night games are played out of the 81 home dates. Day games on Friday usually start one hour later than the regular 1:20 p.m. first pitch.

The most difficult tickets are for dates against the St. Louis Cardinals. Busloads of folks from Peoria have bought seats well in advance, and the ballpark is always loud and red. Plan far ahead for the Cards as well as for summer weekends. A three-game series against Cincinnati in July 1994 drew a record 120,000 people—and the Cubs were in last place at the time.

GOOD SEATS

The sun-drenched bleachers are the prime location and are still general admission. Although they can be bought in advance, some are held back each day for that game. The bleachers have their regulars, and the left-field and the right-field sections have a friendly rivalry. One rule is observed by both: Any home run hit by the opposing team is thrown back onto the field.

If you want sunshine and can't get in the bleachers, the terrace, or lower section, along the first-base line is the warm side of the ballpark. The third-base side is usually in the shade midway through the game. A rule of thumb: Bleachers are for grown-ups; boxes and reserved are for kids.

BAD SEATS

The back rows of the terrace reserved area are the few bad seats because of the claustro-phobic upper-deck overhang. When sky boxes were added, they reduced the visibility for those seats. You will be able to see the field, and television screens provide instant replays. But you can't see the scoreboard, there are a few obstructing posts, and the seats are always in the shade.

SPECIAL PROGRAMS

Wrigley offers a non-alcoholic family section in the left-field corner of the bleachers, and a group section in the right-field corner. If you're looking for a bargain, all sections are discounted weekdays in April, May, and September.

SCALPING

Scalpers are plentiful, especially across from the main entrance at Clark and Addison, and near the el tracks on Addison and Sheffield. Police and stadium security do monitor them.

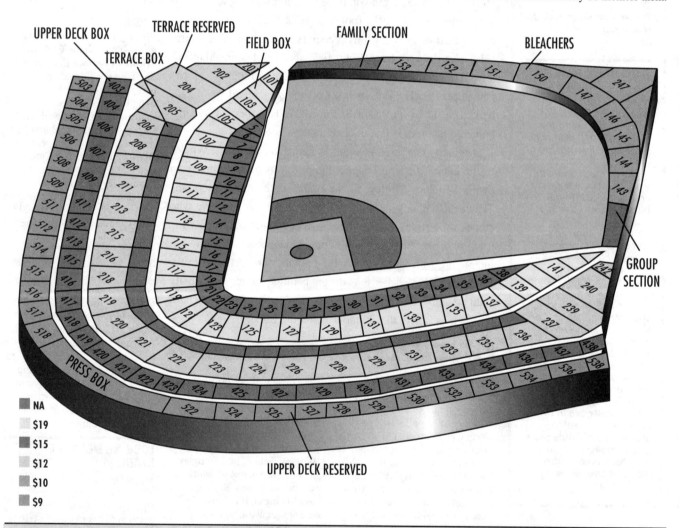

- NA
- $19
- $15
- $12
- $10
- $9

TICKET INFORMATION
Address: 1060 W. Addison St., Chicago, IL 60613
Phone: TicketMaster at (312) 831-CUBS; out of state, call (800) 347-CUBS
Hours: Mon.–Fri. 9–6, Sat.–Sun. 9–4.
Prices: $19: club box, field box; $15: terrace box, upper-deck box, family section; $12: terrace reserved; $10: bleachers; $9: upper-deck reserved. All sections are discounted weekdays in April, May, and September.

Chicago, IL 60611
(312) 943-7200/(800) 228-3000
About 4 miles from the stadium.

GETTING TO WRIGLEY FIELD

Public transportation: The Howard–Dan Ryan (Red Line) el line stops at the Addison Street station next to the stadium. The No. 152 Addison Street bus and the No. 22 Clark Street bus stop at the park. For more information, call (312) 836-7000.

By car: From the south, head north on Lake Shore Drive; exit at Belmont (3200 North) to Clark Street. Turn right and continue to Addison Street. The stadium is on the corner of Clark and Addison streets.

From the north, head south on Lake Shore Drive. Exit at Irving Park (4000 North), take a left on Clark, and continue to Addison.

SPRING TRAINING

HoHoKam Park
1235 N. Center St.
Mesa, AZ 85201
Capacity: 8,963
Surface: Grass
Game time: 1:05 p.m.
Tickets: (602) 678-2222
Training facility: Fitch Park
655 N. Center St.
Mesa, AZ 85201

MINOR LEAGUES

Class	Team
AAA	Iowa Cubs
AA	Orlando Cubs
A	Daytona (FL) Cubs
A	Rockford (IL) Cubbies
Short	
Season A	Williamsport (PA) Cubs
Rookie	Ft. Myers (FL) Cubs

The Cubs' closest minor-league team is the Rockford Cubbies of the Class A Midwest League. The team has been a Cubs farm team since 1995, but Rockford has a long baseball history going back to a team fielded within months of the end of the Civil War. More recently, it was the home of the Rockford Peaches of the All-American Girls' Professional Baseball League, immortalized in the film *A League of Their Own.*

To get to the Cubbies' Marinelli Stadium from Chicago, take I-90 west to the mile-post 61 exit (U.S. 20), go west on U.S. 20 to Main Street, turn right on 15th Street. **Ticket prices:** $6: box seats; $4: reserved; $3: general admission. For more information, call (815) 962-2827.

THE CUBS AT WRIGLEY FIELD

May 2, 1917: Jim "Hippo" Vaughn of the Cubs and Fred Toney of the Reds both throw no-hitters through nine innings until Jim Thorpe, then playing with the Reds, singles in the winning run in the 10th.

Oct. 1, 1932: After an exchange between Babe Ruth and Cubs pitcher Charlie Root during Game 3 of the World Series, Ruth allegedly points to the bleachers and hits a home run to that spot.

Oct. 8, 1945: The Cubs edge the Tigers 8–7 in Game 6 of the World Series, the last home Series win for the Cubs. Hank Borowy gets the win in relief, despite having started two days earlier.

May 13, 1958: Stan Musial doubles off Moe Drabowsky for his 3,000th hit.

May 4, 1960: Announcer Lou Boudreau trades jobs with Cubs manager Charlie Grimm. The Cubs win 5–1 over the Pirates.

May 12, 1970: Ernie Banks hits his 500th career home run, off Pat Jarvis of the Atlanta Braves.

Sept. 2, 1972: Milt Pappas no-hits the Padres 8–0.

Sept. 16, 1975: Rennie Stennett goes 7-for-7 as the Pirates beat the Cubs 22–0.

May 17, 1979: The Phillies give up a 21–9 lead but win 23–22 in 10 innings. Dave Kingman has three home runs and six RBIs.

Oct. 2, 1984: Gary Matthews homers twice, leading the Cubs to a 13–0 Game 1 romp over the Padres in the NLCS.

Sept. 8, 1985: Pete Rose singles for his 4,191st hit, tying him with Ty Cobb for most hits in baseball history.

Aug. 9, 1988: The Cubs beat the New York Mets 6–4 in the first official night game at Wrigley.

HOME-FIELD ADVANTAGE

Check the flags on top of the scoreboard when you enter. That will tell you what kind of day it'll be at Wrigley Field. Many a pitcher is left shaking his head after a game because of the unexpected wind currents that turn routine fly-ball outs into home runs. The small foul territory benefits fans and hitters. Foul balls end up as souvenirs, giving batters another pitch. The groundskeepers tend to keep the grass long, which slows any bunt attempts.

Day baseball might be great for out-of-town fans but is a tough adjustment for visiting ballplayers, who are used to starts at 7 p.m., not 1:20 p.m.

The home dugout is along the third-base line, and Cubs managers say it gives them the worst view of the game. The infield is slightly sloped, and from their ground-level perch they can barely see a close play at first base. Forget about trying to track a fly ball into the left-field corner.

Bullpens are next to the seats down the left- and right-field lines, and relievers, being who they are, will talk to the crowd before the game or between innings. The pens also provide a little obstacle course for outfielders trying to chase balls into foul territory. The ivy-covered outfield walls are lovely but not very friendly. Nothing but brick sits behind the lush green leaves, and many a rookie outfielder finds that out quickly and painfully. Balls lost in the ivy are ground-rule doubles.

All of this doesn't necessarily work in the home team's favor—the Cubs had better records on the road than at home in both '94 and '95.

CUBS TEAM NOTEBOOK

Franchise history
Various names, 1876–1904; Chicago Cubs, 1905–present

World Series titles
1907, 1908

National League pennants
1876, 1880, 1881, 1882, 1885, 1886, 1906, 1907, 1908, 1910, 1918, 1929, 1932, 1935, 1938, 1945

Division titles
1984, 1989

Most Valuable Players
Frank Schulte, 1911
Rogers Hornsby, 1929
Gabby Hartnett, 1935
Phil Cavarretta, 1945
Hank Sauer, 1952
Ernie Banks, 1958, 1959
Ryne Sandberg, 1984
Andre Dawson, 1987

Rookies of the Year
Billy Williams, 1961
Ken Hubbs, 1962
Jerome Walton, 1989

Cy Young Awards
Ferguson Jenkins, 1971
Bruce Sutter, 1979
Rick Sutcliffe, 1984
Greg Maddux, 1992

Hall of Fame
Grover Cleveland Alexander, 1938
Cap Anson, 1939
A. G. Spalding, 1939
Rogers Hornsby, 1942
Roger Bresnahan, 1945
Hugh Duffy, 1945
King Kelly, 1945
Frank Chance, 1946
Johnny Evers, 1946
Clark C. Griffith, 1946
Joe Tinker, 1946
Rube Waddell, 1946
Frankie Frisch, 1947
Mordecai Brown, 1949
Jimmie Foxx, 1951

Dizzy Dean, 1953
Rabbit Maranville, 1954
Gabby Hartnett, 1955
Joe McCarthy, 1957
John Clarkson, 1963
Burleigh Grimes, 1964
Kiki Cuyler, 1968
Lou Boudreau, 1970
Monte Irvin, 1973
George Kelly, 1973
Billy Herman, 1975
Ralph Kiner, 1975
Fred Lindstrom, 1976
Robin Roberts, 1976
Ernie Banks, 1977
Hack Wilson, 1979
Chuck Klein, 1980
Lou Brock, 1985
Hoyt Wilhelm, 1985
Billy Williams, 1987
Ferguson Jenkins, 1991
Tony Lazzeri, 1991
Leo Durocher, 1994
William Hulbert, 1995

Retired numbers
14 Ernie Banks
26 Billy Williams

CHICAGO WHITE SOX

Comiskey Park

On April 18, 1991, Comiskey Park became the first new sports facility to open in the Windy City since Chicago Stadium in 1929. It was also the first baseball-only stadium since Royals Stadium opened in Kansas City in 1972. The White Sox didn't go far when they moved into the second Comiskey. The $137 million ballpark is just across the street from the old park, which was razed and replaced by a parking lot.

The architecture firm HOK—which also designed Camden Yards, Jacobs Field, and Coors Field—took pains to capture old Comiskey's charm. The rose-colored, precast-concrete exterior reflects the original look. The brick arches are emulated with arched windows. But unlike old Comiskey, which had beams that obstructed views, the new Comiskey is column-free.

Among other notable features of the ballpark are a Sony JumboTron videoscreen, a 140-by-30-foot center-field scoreboard, and an exploding scoreboard with huge pinwheels that can been seen from outside the stadium after White Sox home runs. Eight kinds of grass make up the lush playing field, and the infield uses dirt from the original park. The team clubhouses are spacious and plush, and there are 90 sky boxes for corporate spectators. The Bullpen Sports Bar under the right-field stands affords a view of the visiting team's bullpen as well as the game. Fan amenities include a picnic patio area for pregame parties and six kennels for pets.

Comiskey Park fans are family-oriented, and their loyalty runs deep. Few White Sox fans share the same sentiment for the Cubs, considered the North Side's team. Crowds are generally into the game, knowledgeable, and well behaved.

Along with all of the food and off-field entertainment to be found at Comiskey, the White Sox have kept the spirit of late, legendary owner Bill Veeck alive in a way that he would truly appreciate.

HOT TIPS FOR VISITING FANS

PARKING
The stadium has a little more than 7,000 parking spaces at $10 a space, including a big lot where old Comiskey Park was. The old park's home plate and batters' box are marked in the parking lot. A few private lots are around; a lot at the school across the railroad tracks charges $6–$8. The park is in a residential neighborhood, and side-street parking is limited-to-nonexistent.

WEATHER
They don't call Chicago the Windy City for nothing. The wind shifts wreak havoc with the ball, benefiting hitters. Summer average temperatures can range from the mid-60s at night to 85 in the daytime, so bring a jacket. Rain has no lasting effect on the quick-draining field.

MEDIA
Radio: WMVP (1000 AM— English); WIND (560AM— Spanish). John Rooney and Ed Farmer announce on WMVP; Hector Molina and former White Sox shortstop Chico Carrasquel are on WIND.
TV: WGN-TV (Channel 9) and SportsChannel (cable). Ken Harrelson and Tom Paciorek are the announcers. Every game is televised by one of the two stations or ESPN; WFLD (Channel 32) is the local Fox affiliate.

CUISINE
Concession stands, decorated with ceramic-tile fronts and neon signs, are dispersed throughout the main and upper concourses. The stands feature ethnic dishes that reflect the city's diversity, including Tex-Mex, pizza, dipped Italian beef, perogis, and various desserts. Most of the stands have adjacent seating areas. Comiskey favorites are the grilled chicken-breast sandwich, chicken fajitas, Maxwell Street–style pork chops, fried onions, and—perhaps best of all—grilled kosher hot dogs that everyone who's had one insists is the best they've ever tasted. A unique offering is Corn Off the Cob; cooked kernels are the main ingredient of a do-it-yourself saladlike creation. Another new addition is Lemon Chill, a frozen lemonade concoction that's the perfect treat during a sundrenched day game. Several Shortstop ministands offer a limited menu of hot dogs, bratwurst, beer, and soda, as well as "value meals" comprised of a hot dog or burger, fries or chips, and a soda for a lower price than each would cost individually. The new Bullpen Sports Bar under the right-field stands offers fans a view of either the action on the field or a close-up look at the visiting team's pitchers warming up; the place is chock-full of Sox memorabilia. The Kids Corner is a pint-sized concessions stand with pint-sized meals (hot dogs and soda, peanut butter and jelly sandwiches) for pint-sized prices. Adults must be accompanied by children.

The South Side has several pop-

In the Hot Seats at Comiskey Park

White Sox attendance has dropped off a bit since the initial rush of fans to the new Comiskey made them one of the American League's top draws, averaging more than 30,000 fans a game. The crowds are closer to 20,000 these days, and season-ticket sales are hovering between 17,000 and 20,000; walk-up sales are brisk, and tickets are available.

GOOD SEATS

With a capacity of more than 44,000,

Comiskey Park has an abundance of good seats. In addition to the traditionally good lower boxes between the bases, the club level also has good views. The upper-deck boxes are worth a look if you can't get anything lower down. The bleachers get the most sun.

BAD SEATS

A couple dozen seats are just behind the foul poles. These obstructed-view seats are sold last and marked as such on the ticket.

SPECIAL PROGRAMS

On Mondays all seats in the park are half price.

SCALPING

Scalpers are hard to miss along 35th Street, toward the Dan Ryan Expressway, but you won't need them, what with good seats available at the box office.

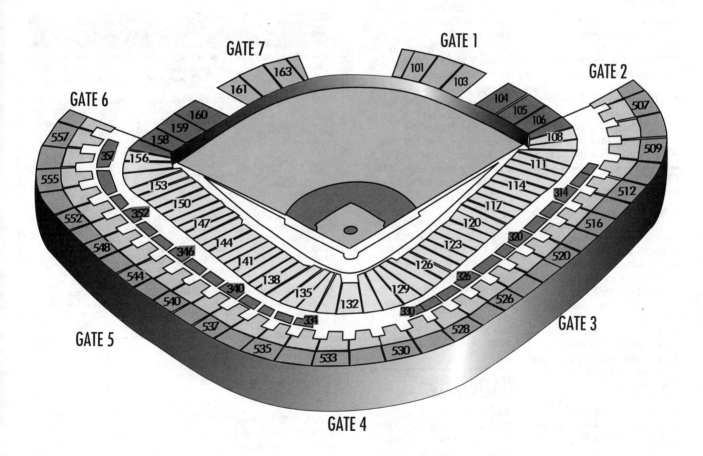

- ■ NA
- ☐ $20
- ■ $15
- ▨ $13
- ☐ $12
- ▨ $8 Fri -Sun/ $4 Mon-Thur

TICKET INFORMATION
Address: 333 W. 35th St., Chicago, IL 60616
Phone: (312) 924-1000 or TicketMaster at

(312) 831-1769
Hours: Mon.–Fri. 10–6, Sat.–Sun. 10–4; during home stands, hours are extended to Mon.–Sat. 9–9, Sun. 9–4.

Prices: $20: club level and lower-deck boxes; $15: lower-deck reserved; $13: upper-deck boxes; $12: bleacher reserved; $8: upper-deck reserved.

ular postgame spots, including Jimbo's, a couple of blocks from the stadium, and Connie's Pizzeria (312-326-3443), at 26th Street and Archer. If you're interested in heading back toward the Loop and the North Side, Pizzeria Uno (312-321-1000) is the home of the deep-dish pizza, and Ed Debevic's (312-664-1707) offers a retro-diner experience. In a town that loves its meat, Carson's, The Place for Ribs (312-280-9200), has some of the very best. Not to be missed by baseball or basketball aficionados is Michael Jordan's restaurant at 500 North LaSalle in the River North neighborhood (312-644-3865).

LODGING NEAR THE STADIUM

Ramada
520 S. Michigan Ave.
Chicago, IL 60605
(312) 786-0000/(800) 727-6232
1 mile from the stadium.

Hyatt Regency
151 E. Wacker Dr.
Chicago, IL 60601
(312) 565-1234/(800) 233-1234
About 5 miles from the stadium.

GETTING TO COMISKEY PARK

Public transportation: Take the Dan Ryan el to 35th Street or the No. 24 Wentworth, No. 44 Wallace/Racine, or No. 35 35th Street bus to the park. Call (312) 836-7000 for more information.
By car: From the south, drive north on I-94 and exit at 35th Street.
From the north, head south on Lake Shore Drive to the Dan Ryan Expressway and get off at 31st Street or 35th Street.
From the west, head east on I-290 to I-94. Proceed south and exit at 31st or 35th streets.

SPRING TRAINING

Ed Smith Stadium
12th St. and Tuttle Ave.
Sarasota, FL 34237.
Ticket office: (813) 953-3388
Capacity: 7,500
Surface: Grass
Game time: 1:05 p.m. or 7:05 p.m.

In 1998 the Sox will move to a new spring training camp in Tucson that they'll share with the Arizona Diamondbacks.

MINOR LEAGUES

Class	Team
AAA	Nashville (TN) Sounds
AA	Birmingham (AL) Barons
A	Prince William (VA) Cannons
A	South Bend (IN) Silver Hawks
A	Hickory (NC) Crawdads
Rookie	Sarasota (FL) White Sox

The minor-league team nearest to Chicago is the Class A Kane County Cougars of the Midwest League. The Cougars' opponents include the Peoria Chiefs and the South Bend Silver Hawks, Midwest League affiliates of the Cubs and the White Sox, respectively. Since Kane County made its debut in 1991, the franchise has set league records for highest total attendance in 1992 (323,769) and 1993 (354,327). In '93 the Cougars drew more fans to the ballpark than any other Class A team. They've continued to break their own records each year since, reaching 477,550 in 1995. To reach Kane County's Elfstorm Stadium in suburban Geneva, approximately 35 miles from Chicago, take I-290 west to I-88 west. Exit at (north) Farnsworth Road, then at Cherry Lane, go west until you reach the ballpark. **Ticket prices:** $7: box seats; $6: reserved seats; $5: bleachers; $4: lawn general admission; For more information, call (708) 232-8811.

THE WHITE SOX AT COMISKEY PARK

April 22, 1991: Frank Thomas hits the Sox' first homer at the new Comiskey Park during the stadium's first night game. The Sox beat the Baltimore Orioles 8–7.

April 9, 1993: Bo Jackson, playing with an artificial hip, hits a home run with his first swing on Opening Day.

HOME-FIELD ADVANTAGE

Fans have responded enthusiastically to the new Comiskey Park since it opened in 1991. Starting with a franchise-record attendance of 2,934,154 in 1991, the team has experienced similar success in subsequent seasons, although the total yearly attendance has not matched that of 1991. In 1993 Chicago area fans, still excited about their new ballpark, plus a team that ranked among the league's best, flocked to the park to see Frank "the Big Hurt" Thomas, one of baseball's top players, as well as a White Sox team that was involved in postseason play for the first time since 1983.

Fan support is about the only clear advantage that Comiskey Park gives the White Sox. Whereas the center-field wall at the old Comiskey was moved in and out in various seasons, depending on the power of the team, the new Comiskey is not quite as adaptable.

WHITE SOX TEAM NOTEBOOK

Franchise history Chicago White Sox, 1901–present	Tommie Agee, 1966 Ron Kittle, 1983 Ozzie Guillen, 1985	Red Faber, 1964 Luke Appling, 1964 Charles "Red" Ruffing, 1967
World Series titles 1906, 1917	**Cy Young Awards** Early Wynn, 1959 LaMarr Hoyt, 1983 Jack McDowell, 1993	Harry Hooper, 1971 Early Wynn, 1972 John "Jocko" Conlan, 1974
American League pennants 1900, 1901, 1906, 1917, 1919, 1959	**Hall of Fame** Eddie Collins, 1939 Charles Comiskey, 1939	Bob Lemon, 1976 Al Lopez, 1977 George Kell, 1983 Luis Aparicio, 1984
Division titles 1983, 1993	Hugh Duffy, 1945 Frank Chance, 1946 Johnny Evers, 1946	Hoyt Wilhelm, 1985 Bill Veeck, 1991 Tom Seaver, 1992
Most Valuable Players Nellie Fox, 1959 Dick Allen, 1972 Frank Thomas, 1993, 1994	Clark Griffith, 1946 Ed Walsh, 1946 Chief Bender, 1953 Al Simmons, 1953 Ted Lyons, 1955 Ray Schalk, 1955	Steve Carlton, 1994 **Retired numbers** 2 Nellie Fox 3 Harold Baines 4 Luke Appling
Rookies of the Year Luis Aparicio, 1956 Gary Peters, 1963	Hank Greenberg, 1956 Edd Roush, 1962	9 Minnie Minoso 11 Luis Aparicio 16 Ted Lyons 19 Billy Pierce

June 22, 1993: Carlton Fisk catches his 2,226th game, putting him past Bob Boone for most games caught.

Sept. 27, 1993: The White Sox win the West with a 4–2 victory over the Seattle Mariners on a three-run homer by Bo Jackson.

Oct. 5, 1993: The Toronto Blue Jays beat the White Sox in Game 1 of the ALCS 7–3, but rumors of Michael Jordan's retirement steal the show.

Cinergy Field

STADIUM STATS

Location: *100 Cinergy Field, Cincinnati, OH 45202*
Opened: *June 30, 1970*
Surface: *AstroTurf 8*
Capacity: *52,952*
Outfield dimensions: *LF 330, LC 375, CF 404, RC 375, RF 330*
Services for fans with disabilities: *Seating available on the green and blue levels. Call (513) 421-4510 for more information.*

STADIUM FIRSTS

Regular-season game: *June 30, 1970, 8–2 loss to the Atlanta Braves.*
Pitcher: *Jim McGlothlin of the Reds.*
Batter: *Sonny Jackson of the Braves.*
Hit: *Felix Millan of the Braves.*
Home run: *Hank Aaron of the Braves.*

GROUND RULES

• *Any ball hitting foul screen in left or right field is a home run.*
• *Any ball bouncing over the fence is a two-base hit.*
• *Any ball hit down right-field or left-field line and bouncing into box seats in stands is a two-base hit.*
• *Ball remaining behind or underneath canvas is one base on pitch and two bases on throw by fielder and two bases on a batted ball. Fielder may make catch standing on canvas.*
• *Everything else in play unless the ball goes into the dugout.*

Enough about Marge Schott. The real baseball news in Cincinnati is that a voter referendum has finally cleared the way for a new—and exclusively baseball—stadium. It won't open till after the turn of the century, but whenever it is, it'll be about time. It's a shame that a team with such a rich baseball history has had to share such a sterile environment as Cinergy Field, a facility with all the charm and tradition of a six-lane highway. Opened in 1970, Cinergy is pleasant enough, and clean; it just doesn't feel like a ballpark. Like its cousins in Pittsburgh and Philadelphia, the circular stadium has artificial turf, sliding pits, no view of downtown, and no sense of the city, which is too bad, because just outside the park, it's quite nice. The stadium is set on the banks of the Ohio River next to the historic John A. Roebling Suspension Bridge; Roebling, the architect, used it as a prototype for his next project, the Brooklyn Bridge. The plaza outside the stadium overlooks the Ohio River on one side and offers a marvelous view of the downtown skyline on the other. Pedestrian bridges cross an interstate highway and connect the site to downtown, which is clean and safe.

The atmosphere in the ballpark will never be described as circus-like, but descriptions of it as a morgue are a bit harsh. Unlike some of the newer parks in which corporate America has bought up the box seats, Cincy's regulars are serious baseball fans. They're just not rowdy. Maybe the Reds' usually conservative policies will loosen during Schott's years away from the helm, and Cinergy will get just a little livelier.

HOT TIPS FOR VISITING FANS

PARKING
It's rarely a problem, and traffic clears out quickly after the games. A three-level city garage surrounds the stadium, but that's sold out on a season-subscription basis. Open-air city lots adjacent to the stadium can handle about 1,800 cars and charge $3.50. Within a 12-block radius, facilities can handle about 20,000 cars. Garages and open lots are easy to find—if you look hard enough, you often can find a free spot on the street after business hours. Or you can park across the river in Covington, Kentucky, and walk across the Roebling Bridge to the stadium.

WEATHER
From snow delays on Opening Day to blistering heat in August, you can expect almost anything in Cincinnati. Night games in April can be chilly, but spring and fall in the Queen City are usually very pleasant. Heat and humidity can be oppressive in the middle of summer, especially in the blue seats near the artificial turf.

MEDIA
Radio: WLW (700 AM) is the radio flagship. Marty Brenneman, who joined the team in 1974, is a solid pro and one of the best announcers in baseball. His distinctive voice and tell-it-like-it-is approach make him one of the city's most treasured assets. He does both radio and television. Radio sidekick Joe Nuxhall, a former Reds pitcher who has been in the booth since 1967, is an acquired taste. Cincinnati natives love his folksy style and his unabashed partisanship. Don't knock Joe to a native. Marty and Joe are a Cincinnati institution, having worked as a team for more than 20 years. **TV:** WSTR-TV (Channel 64) and SportsChannel Cincinnati (cable). George Grande and ex-Red Chris Welsh handle the announcing.

CUISINE
Marge Schott was the champion of the $1 hot dog. She consistently lobbied the concessions service to keep the price of the basic frank at a buck. Time will tell if her absence will change that. The dog is nothing special, but Cincinnati's culinary traditions are in evidence in other menu items. Metts and brats (German sausages) by Kahn's are at several stands, and that local delicacy Cincinnati chili is represented. You can buy a cheese coney (a hot dog with Cincinnati chili and shredded cheese) at eight Gold Star Chili stands. Cincinnati, with its German roots, has a glorious tradition in beer brewing. Unfortunately, only one local beermaker, Hudepohl-Schoenling, remains, but it makes several fine brews. Try Hudepohl's Christian Moerlein or Little King's Bruin Pale Ale. Also recommended are any of the brews from the local microbrewery, Oldenburg. Other premium and imported beers are available at the bar on the blue level behind home plate and four auxiliary locations, and a host of brews at the two J. M. Malthaus microbrew stands.

Several popular pregame and postgame spots can be found on Pete Rose Way (formerly Second Street), a five-minute walk from the stadium. Caddy's (513-721-3636) and Flanagan's Landing (513-421-4055) are the standbys. The waterfront features several popular places, including Covington Landing (606-291-9992) on the Kentucky side and the

In the Hot Seats at Cinergy Field

The Reds don't often sell out, but the bulk of the 10,400 field boxes are sold on a season-ticket basis. Ditto the green (second-level) seats on the infield. Many of the attractive weekend dates have brisk advance sales, as fans from Kentucky, Indiana, and central Ohio make their annual weekend trips to catch the Reds.

GOOD SEATS

If you're not afraid of heights and haven't planned ahead, try the "top six" seats—one of the best bargains in baseball. The top six rows of the entire stadium are sold only on game days (unless all other tickets are sold in advance). You can walk up to the box office the day of the game and, for $3.50, buy a

ticket behind home plate—albeit at the top of the upper deck. The seats are high, but for real fans who like to be in the infield, they're a bonus.

BAD SEATS

The green seats in the outfield are very popular, but if you sit in them, you might wonder why. You get a fine view of outfielders' backs, but you're a long way from the plate without any of the atmosphere of a bleacher section. The same goes for the limited number of blue seats in the outfield.

SCALPING

Ticket brokers, a.k.a. scalpers, are legal in Cincinnati as long as they have vendor

licenses issued by the city. However, they aren't permitted to sell Reds tickets for more than face value on the stadium grounds or Pete Rose Way. Legally, they should be north of Fourth Street (about 3 blocks from the stadium), but they are frequently found by the entrance to the pedestrian walkway, a block closer. The city's policy also has spawned brokerages, some with offices downtown, that sell tickets to all games. For an average game, buyers can pay about $20 for blues (face value: $11.50). For weekend series against a team battling the Reds in a pennant race, though, that can go up to $50–$75. Fans selling extra tickets at face value or below are permitted on the plaza, so buyers sometimes try there first.

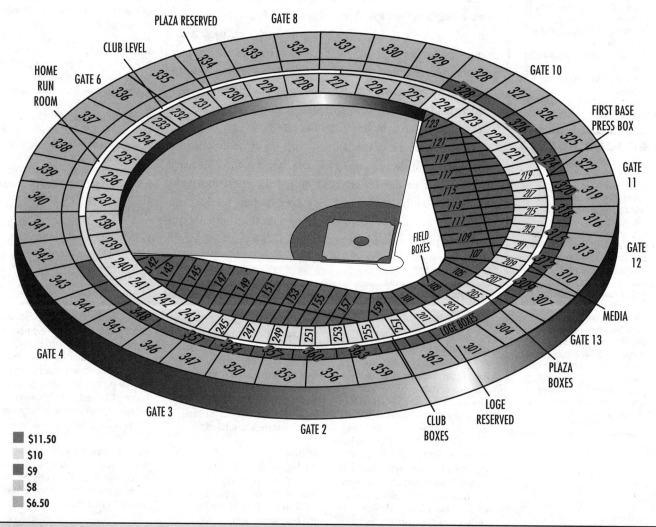

- ■ $11.50
- ▢ $10
- ■ $9
- ▨ $8
- ▨ $6.50

TICKET INFORMATION
Ticket Office: 100 Cinergy Field, Cincinnati, OH 45202
Phone: (513) 421-4510 (513) 749-4949 or (513) 421-GOREDS in Cincinnati, or (800)

829-5353 from outside Cincinnati
Hours: Mon.–Fri. 9–5:30.
Prices: $11.50: blue level box seats; $10: green level box seats and yellow level box seats; $9: red level; $8: green level

reserved; $6.50: red level reserved; $3.50; top six reserved (top six only sold day of game unless all other tickets are sold in advance).

Montgomery Inn Boathouse (renowned for its ribs) on the Cincinnati side (513-721-7427). Chili parlors serving the traditional Cincinnati fare are all over downtown; the two top chains are Skyline and Gold Star. Izzy's has great corned-beef sandwiches and two downtown locations. Ice cream lovers must sample Graeter's creamy ice cream, with chips the size of a Hershey bar.

LODGING NEAR THE STADIUM

Westin Hotel
21 E. Fifth St. (corner of Vine St. and Fountain Sq.)
Cincinnati, OH 45202
(513) 621-7700/(800) 228-3000
About 5 blocks from the stadium.

Hyatt Regency
151 W. Fifth St.
Cincinnati, OH 45202
(513) 579-1234/(800) 233-1234
About 5 blocks from the stadium.

GETTING TO CINERGY FIELD

Public transportation: Metro Center's Nos. 28 and 49 buses go to Fourth Street and Broadway, 1½ blocks from the stadium. For more information, call (513) 621-4455.
By car: From points north in Ohio, go south on I-75, get onto the I-71 northbound lane for exit 1 downtown; from there get onto Pete Rose Way. Take Pete Rose Way fewer than 1½ miles to the stadium, which will be on the left. From the south, head north on I-75, stay right, and exit at 3rd Street and Elm Street; from ramp go right on 3rd Street which leads to Pete Rose Way, which leads to the stadium.
From the west, head east on I-74 to I-75 south, then follow instructions above from the north.

SPRING TRAINING

Plant City Stadium
1900 S. Park Rd.
Plant City, FL 33564
(813) 752-1878
Capacity: 6,700
Surface: Grass
Game time: 1:05 p.m. or 7:05 p.m.

MINOR LEAGUES

Class	Team
AAA	Indianapolis Indians
AA	Chattanooga (TN) Lookouts
A	Winston-Salem (NC) Warthogs
A	Charleston (WV) Alley Cats
Rookie	Billings (MT) Mustangs
Rookie	Princeton (WV) Reds

The Reds' closest minor-league affiliate is the Class AAA Indianapolis Indians of the American Association. Baseball first came to this city in 1903, when Indianapolis was one of the American Association's charter franchises. The Indians play in Bush Stadium, the oldest ballpark in the Association, having opened in 1931.
To reach Indianapolis' Bush Stadium, approximately 110 miles from Cincinnati, take the Meridian Street exit from I-65. Turn right and head to 16th Street, then turn left onto 16th Street. The stadium is 1½ miles ahead on the left.

THE REDS AT CINERGY FIELD

July 1, 1970: Reds get their first win at Cinergy, 9–2 over the Atlanta Braves. Tommy Helms becomes the first Red to hit a home run at the new park.

Oct. 5, 1970: Reds sink the Pittsburgh Pirates 3–2 to complete a three-game sweep of the National League Championship Series and win their first league pennant since 1961.

Oct. 11, 1972: Reds score two in the bottom of the ninth inning to beat the Pirates 4–3 in the fifth and deciding game of the NLCS.

Oct. 15, 1972: Oakland's Joe Rudi makes a leaping, backhanded catch against the wall to stop a two-run homer in the ninth inning of Game 2 in the World Series. The A's win the game 2–1, and the Series.

April 4, 1974: Hank Aaron ties Babe Ruth's all-time home-run record on Opening Day.

May 5, 1978: Pete Rose gets his 3,000th hit, a single off the Montreal Expos' Steve Rogers.

June 16, 1978: Tom Seaver throws the Reds' first no-hitter at Cinergy, beating the St. Louis Cardinals 4–0.

July 15, 1980: Johnny Bench breaks Yogi Berra's major-

HOME-FIELD ADVANTAGE

In keeping with the city's reputation as a polite town, Cinergy Field is perfectly fair: symmetrical, average dimensions (330 feet down the lines, 404 to center), favoring neither hitter nor pitcher. The stadium is not the kind you can build a team for, but as on all artificial surfaces, the home team needs speed. The Reds have a slightly better record at home than on the road.

REDS TEAM NOTEBOOK

Franchise history
Cincinnati Reds (AA), 1882–1889; merged with Washington Senators in 1889; Cincinnati Reds, 1890–1943 (NL); Cincinnati Redlegs, 1944–1945; Cincinnati Reds, 1946–present

World Series titles
1919, 1940, 1975, 1976, 1990

National League pennants
1919, 1939, 1940, 1961, 1970, 1972, 1975, 1976, 1990

Division titles
1970, 1972, 1973, 1975, 1976, 1979, 1990, 1994, 1995

Most Valuable Players
Ernie Lombardi, 1938
Bucky Walters, 1939
Frank McCormick, 1940
Frank Robinson, 1961

Johnny Bench, 1970, 1972
Pete Rose, 1973
Joe Morgan, 1975, 1976
George Foster, 1977
Barry Larkin, 1995

Rookies of the Year
Frank Robinson, 1956
Pete Rose, 1963
Tommy Helms, 1966
Johnny Bench, 1968
Pat Zachry, 1976 (tie)
Chris Sabo, 1988

Hall of Fame
Christy Mathewson, 1936
George Wright, 1937
Candy Cummings, 1939
Buck Ewing, 1939
Charles "Hoss" Radbourne, 1939
Rogers Hornsby, 1942
King Kelly, 1945
Clark Griffith, 1946
Joe Tinker, 1946
Mordecai Brown, 1949
Harry Heilmann, 1952

Al Simmons, 1953
Rod "Bobby" Wallace, 1953
Harry Wright, 1953
Arthur "Dazzy" Vance, 1955
Sam Crawford, 1957
Bill McKechnie, 1962
Edd Roush, 1962
Eppa Rixey, 1963
Miller Huggins, 1964
Lloyd Waner, 1967
Kiki Cuyler, 1968
Jesse Haynes, 1970
Jake Beckley, 1971
Chick Hafey, 1971
Joe Kelley, 1971
Rube Marquard, 1971
George Kelly, 1973
Jim Bottomley, 1974
Amos Rusie, 1977
Larry MacPhail, 1978
Warren Giles, 1979
Frank Robinson, 1982
Ernie Lombardi, 1986
Johnny Bench, 1989
Joe Morgan, 1990
Tom Seaver, 1992

Retired numbers
1 Fred Hutchinson
5 Johnny Bench

league record for catchers with a homer off the Expos' David Palmer.

April 18, 1981: Tom Seaver records strikeout No. 3,000, getting St. Louis' Keith Hernandez.

Sept. 11, 1985: Pete Rose becomes baseball's all-time hit leader at 4,192, with a single to left-center field off San Diego Padre Eric Show.

Sept. 16, 1988: Tom Browning becomes the first pitcher in Reds history to throw a perfect game, beating the Los Angeles Dodgers 1–0.

Oct. 12, 1990: Reds sink the Pirates 2–1 in the sixth and final game of the 1990 NLCS for their

first pennant since 1976.

Oct. 16, 1990: Billy Hatcher goes 3-for-3 in Game 1 and 4-for-4 in Game 2 of the World Series, setting a World Series record with seven consecutive hits.

Sept. 7, 1993: Cardinal Mark Whiten hits four homers and drives in 12 runs (both of which tie major-league records) in the second game of a doubleheader.

CLEVELAND INDIANS

Jacobs Field

Downtown Cleveland got a big boost from the opening of Jacobs Field in 1994 and so did the Indians, who reacted to their new park like a new team. They finished the shortened '94 season in second place, and in '95 grabbed the division title, league pennant, and made their first World Series appearance since 1954.

Part of the Gateway Sports Complex, which includes a multi-purpose arena for the NBA's Cleveland Cavaliers, Jacobs Field was designed as the antithesis of Oriole Park at Camden Yards in Baltimore. Cleveland didn't want its ballpark to be a throwback to yesteryear, so the city opted instead for a contemporary marvel. The urban setting and brick give the stadium some traditional feel, but Jacobs Field is modern in every sense, from its white color to its steel beams, which were purposely left exposed to blend with the architecture of Cleveland's bridges and to foster the city's steel-town image. The ballpark's vertical light towers, unlike any in North America, echo the smokestacks and skyscrapers visible from the stands.

In the excitement over the Indians' present and future, the Tribe's past has not been forgotten: Bob Feller's statue sits just outside the stadium, where 3-foot-high granite blocks spell out "Who's on first?" People sit on the blocks and have lunch. Inside, huge full-color and backlighted murals of current players line the walls. There are 25 (so far) "great moment" signs throughout the park, one of which depicts Lem Barker's perfect game.

The Indians want to create a family-style atmosphere, although the huge number of sellout crowds sometimes makes this hard to maintain. All in all, the park combines the modern features of baseball with the best of its traditions.

HOT TIPS FOR VISITING FANS

PARKING
With 34,000 spaces within a 15-minute walk, including 17,000 within a 10-minute walk, parking is not a concern. Parking is $10 at the stadium, $8–$10 in surrounding lots. The parking was intentionally dispersed to create business in different parts of the downtown area.

WEATHER
The former stadium was on Lake Erie, so the move to the heart of downtown has provided the Indians with a somewhat warmer climate. Still, on any given night, temperatures can dip, and fans are recommended to bring a jacket or sweater.
Strangely enough, despite the move away from the lake, Jacobs Field is more prone to winds than old Municipal Stadium. The open spaces in the outfield help the breezes come through, creating a swirling effect on the playing field, 18 feet below street level. During the first few weeks after Jacobs Field opened, officials thought they had another Wrigley Field because the wind changed directions every other inning. Preliminary wind studies had suggested the ball would travel straight to right field, but that hasn't been the case; left field has seen even more homers fly into its seats.

MEDIA
Radio: WKNR (1220 AM) is the flagship station.
TV: WUAB (Channel 43) and SportsChannel Ohio (cable).

CUISINE
The Indians have 80 kinds of foods on the menu at Jacobs Field, ranging from standard fare such as hot dogs and beer, to Caesar salad and Evian water. Jacobs Field also has a bakery where goods are baked on the premises and a delicatessen that offers a choice of breads. Fans can eat in Picnic Plaza areas throughout the ballpark; the largest is in center field.
Although the park is in one of the poorer sections of the city, development of Cleveland Flats and Jacobs Field had enhanced the economic status of the area. Businesses and restaurants are investing more heavily because of the volume of people now visiting the area. Popular after-game spots include Mel's Grill (216-781-1771) and Alvie's (216-273-7351), both within walking distance.

LODGING NEAR THE STADIUM

Cleveland Marriott Society Center
127 Public Sq.
Cleveland, OH 44114
(216) 696-9200/(800) 228-9290
10 blocks from the stadium.

The Renaissance Tower City Plaza
24 Public Sq.
Cleveland, OH 44113
(216) 696-5600/(800) 468-3571
Less than a mile to the stadium via an indoor walkway in the mall at Tower City Plaza.

GETTING TO JACOBS FIELD

Public transportation: All RTA (Regional Transit Authority) trains go to Tower City. Then either take the RTA bus from

STADIUM STATS
Location: 2401 Ontario St., Cleveland, OH 44115
Opened: April 4, 1994
Surface: Grass
Capacity: 42,865
Outfield dimensions: LF 325, LC 370, CF 405, RC 375, RF 325
Services for fans with disabilities: Seating available throughout the stadium. For information, call (216) 241-8888.

STADIUM FIRSTS
Regular-season game: April 4, 1994, a 4–3 win over the Seattle Mariners in 11 innings.
Pitcher: Dennis Martinez of the Indians.
Batter: Rich Amaral of the Mariners.
Hit: Rich Amaral.
Home run: Eric Anthony of the Mariners.

GROUND RULES
• A batted ball hitting the foul pole or attached screen is a fair ball.
• A thrown or fair batted ball that goes behind or under the field tarp or drum covers and remains there is two bases. A ball that rebounds into the playing field is in play.
• A ball striking the roof or the colored facing of the dugout, camera pits, or diamond suites is considered in the dugout and equals two bases.
• A thrown ball that enters the camera pits, dugouts, or diamond suites and remains is two bases.
• A pitched ball that strikes the roof or facing, or enters the camera pits, dugouts, or diamond suites is one base.

In the Hot Seats at Jacobs Field

Good luck if you're looking for tickets at the box office. The park's capacity is 42,865, and after the Indians' World Series appearance in 1995, every one of those seats was sold for 1996 before Christmas. That includes the standing-room-only section in left field, which you used to be able to get into up to an hour before the game. Now when a home run is hit into the area, some people scramble for the ball, but others don't want to risk losing their spots.

GOOD SEATS
The best seats are between home plate and the bases in the lower deck, but bargains exist. A $6 bleacher seat is the toughest ticket in town—understandable when you consider that the bleachers are patterned after Wrigley Field's, and the 19-foot left-field wall, just 370 feet from home plate, is a mini version of Fenway Park's Green Monster. Another good buy, at $12, are the middle-level mezzanine seats in right field.

BAD SEATS
A few obstructed-view seats are in the upper corners of left and right field. Those seats are traditionally sold last, and fans buying them are told they might have problems seeing certain parts of the field. Nobody will be all that picky, though, with the team poised to get back into post season play, so these will probably be just as hard to get as box seats along the first-base line.

SPECIAL PROGRAM
Jacobs Field has no "official" family section, arguing that the whole ballpark caters to families. However, a designated area for youngsters, Kidsland, is in the lower deck in right field.

SCALPING
This is a seller's market, with a markup of 10 times or more of face value. Since the Indians' resurgence, baseball fever has swept through the city. Officials had begun to crack down on scalpers, but the market is there, and so are the scalpers.

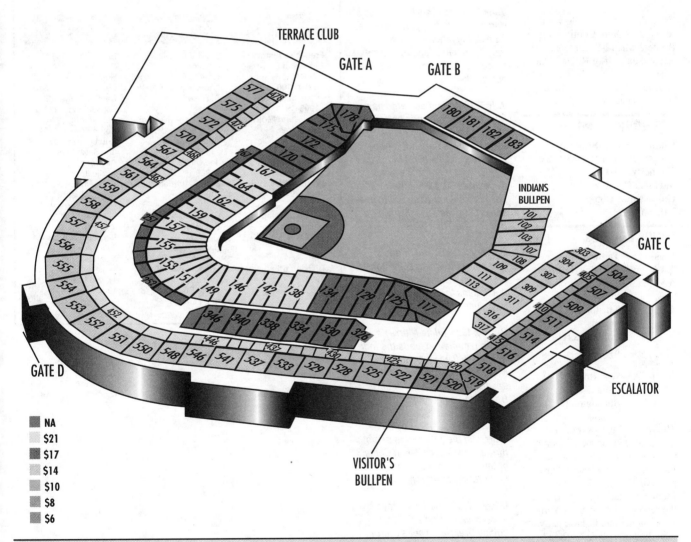

Legend:
- NA
- $21
- $17
- $14
- $10
- $8
- $6

TICKET INFORMATION
Address: 2401 Ontario St., Cleveland, OH 44115
Phone: (216) 241-8888 or TicketMaster at (216) 241-5555 or (216) 861-1200

Hours: Mon.–Fri. 9–5, Sat. 10–4, and from 9 until the game ends during home games.
By mail: Call to request a mail-order form, or send a letter with your requested game, number of tickets and a check (including $3 for shipping and handling) to: Cleveland Stadium, Gate A, 1805 W. Third St., Cleveland, OH 44114.
Prices: $21, $17, $14, $10, $8, $6.

Public Square and Tower City Center/Prospect Avenue to the stadium or walk (approximately 10 minutes) via the the walkway at Tower Center. For more bus and rail routes, contact the Regional Transit Authority at (216) 621-9500.

By car: From the south, take I-77 north to the East Ninth Street exit. Continue south on East Ninth a little less then a mile to Gateway area parking. From the southwest, take I-90 or I-71 north to the Inner Belt merge. Continue on I-90 to the Ontario Street exit. Take Ontario to Gateway parking.

From the west, take West Shoreway from Lakewood and continue across the Main Avenue Bridge. Continue ½ mile and exit right onto West Sixth Street. Continue on West Sixth to area parking.

From the east, take I-90 west/Route 2 to Ohio. Continue on Route 2 when I-90 curves to the left and exit off of Route 2 onto East Ninth Street. Make a left onto East Ninth and continue south to Gateway parking.

SPRING TRAINING

Chain of Lakes Stadium
Winter Haven, FL 33880
Capacity: 7,042
Surface: Grass
Game time: 1:05 p.m. or 7:05 p.m.

MINOR LEAGUES

Class	Team
AAA	Buffalo (NY) Bisons
AA	Canton/Akron (OH) Indians
A	Kinston (NC) Indians
A	Columbus (GA) Redstixx
Short Season A	Watertown (NY) Indians
Rookie	Burlington (NC) Indians

The Indians' closest minor-league affiliate is the Class AA Canton/Akron Indians of the Eastern League. Canton/Akron plays in Thurman Munson Memorial Stadium, named after the renowned New York Yankees catcher and Canton native who died in a plane crash in 1979. Before heading to the ball-park, fans can relive their favorite gridiron memories by stopping at the nearby Pro Football Hall of Fame in Canton. To reach the stadium, which is approximately 60 miles from Cleveland, take the Cleveland Avenue exit from I-77. From Cleveland Avenue, turn left on Mill Road and then left on Allen Avenue.

Ticket prices: $6: reserved seats; $5: general admission; $4.50 for seniors and children under 14.

For information call (216) 456-5100.

THE INDIANS AT JACOBS FIELD

June 13, 1994: The Indians beat the Toronto Blue Jays 7–3 and go into a tie for first place in the AL Central Division.

June 25, 1994: Cleveland opens a home stand in first place by four games, the latest in the season they have had a lead that large since their pennant-winning season in 1954.

July 3, 1994: Paul Sorrento has four hits and four runs batted in, including a game-winning single, as the Indians defeat the Minnesota Twins 10–9 in 11 innings.

September 30, 1995: Albert Belle hits his 50th home run of the season off Kansas City's Melvin Bunch. The Tribe wins 3–2.

October 3, 1995: Tony Peña's two-out, 13th-inning solor homer off Boston's Zane Smith gives the Indians their first playoff victory since 1954.

Oct. 14, 1995: Eddie Murray's two-run home run leads the Indians to a 7–0 win over the Mariners in Game 4 of the ALCS, despite the absence of Albert Belle and Sandy Alomar.

Oct. 24, 1995: A single by Eddie Murray in the 11th inning beats the Atlanta Braves 7–6 in Game 3 of the World Series, Cleveland's first World Series win since 1948.

Oct. 26, 1995: The Tribe stays alive, winning Game 5, 5–4, behind Orel Hershiser's fourth victory in the postseason.

HOME-FIELD ADVANTAGE

The biggest advantage comes in playing before sellout crowds in a cozy, first-class ballpark after years of playing before small audiences in an old, dank, sprawling stadium. Players are in love with the park's plush grass field. Five different strands of Kentucky bluegrass make the turf durable enough to deal with Cleveland's harsh winters. A top-of-the-line drainage system allows the field to dry quickly. Other than a couple of symphonic concerts, few other events are deemed suitable for Jacobs Field. Tractor pulls? Not. Jacobs Field is intended to be a shrine to baseball and so far the Tribe has honored it; they've had one of the best home records in baseball since the park opened.

Though Jacobs Field is friendly to power hitters, this isn't an easy park in which to hit doubles. Balls hit down the lines, especially in left field, where the ball bounces back quickly, have made easy outs of base runners trying to stretch a single.

INDIANS TEAM NOTEBOOK

Franchise history
Cleveland Broncos, 1901; Cleveland Blues, 1902–1904; Cleveland Naps, 1905–1911; Cleveland Molly McGuires, 1912–1914; Cleveland Indians, 1915–present

World Series titles
1920, 1948

American League pennants
1920, 1948, 1954, 1995

Division titles
1995

Most Valuable Players
George Burns, 1926
Lou Boudreau, 1948
Al Rosen, 1953

Rookies of the Year
Herb Score, 1955
Chris Chambliss, 1971
Joe Charboneau, 1980
Sandy Alomar, Jr., 1990

Cy Young Award
Gaylord Perry, 1972

Hall of Fame
Nap Lajoie, 1937
Tris Speaker, 1937
Cy Young, 1937
Jesse Burkett, 1946
Bob Feller, 1962

Elmer Flick, 1963
Sam Rice, 1963
Stan Coveleski, 1969
Lou Boudreau, 1970
Satchel Paige, 1971
Early Wynn, 1972
Earl Averill, 1975
Ralph Kiner, 1975
Bob Lemon, 1976
Joe Sewell, 1977
Al Lopez, 1977
Addie Joss, 1978
Frank Robinson, 1982
Hoyt Wilhelm, 1985
Gaylord Perry, 1991
Bill Veeck, 1991

Retired numbers
3 Earl Averill
5 Lou Boudreau
14 Larry Doby
18 Mel Harder
19 Bob Feller

Coors Field

STADIUM STATS

Location: 20th and Blake Sts., Denver, CO 80204
Opened: April 1995
Surface: Grass
Capacity: 50,249
Outfield dimensions: RF 350, CF 415, LF 347
Services for fans with disabilities: Seating for 500 wheelchair users is available in the front row behind the screen, and in the first rows along the leftfield and rightfield lines.

STADIUM FIRSTS

Regular-season game: April 26, 1995, 11–9 over the New York Mets.
Pitcher: Bill Swift of the Rockies.
Batter: Brett Butler of the Mets.
Hit: Brett Butler.
Home Run: Rico Brogna of the Mets.

GROUND RULES

• Everything is in play unless ball goes in the dugout. Photographers' areas are considered part of the dugout.
• A ball hitting any part of the screen area supported by poles down left or right field lines is a home run.
• A ball hitting the net in the left field and bouncing back onto the playing field is in play.
• A ball remaining behind or underneath tarp is one base on a pitch and two bases on a throw by a fielder or battered ball, other wise in play. A fielder may make a catch standing on the tarp.
• A ball going through the scoreboard, either on the bound or fly is two bases.

Coors Field, the Rockies' new ballpark, is a perfect fit—both with Denver's long baseball tradition and with the trend of building new stadiums that recall the game's early days. Coors Field, located in a 25-square-block historic district known as lower downtown, or LoDo to locals, was built on the site of an 1876 railroad depot, and designed to look as if it has always belonged there. And, with its brick and steel design and intimate dimensions, it does. And, as if fulfilling the ballpark's aspirations for historic continuity, a 66-million-year-old dinosaur bone was unearthed as the field was being built.

The folks at HOK who designed Coors Field are the same bunch who built Camden Yards and Jacobs Field, and they know baseball stadiums. Coors Field features the majors' smallest foul territory between the seats and the infield corners, and other than the right-field wall, which is necessarily taller to accommodate the out-of-town scoreboard, the outfield fence is 8 feet high. This is, perhaps, one of the reasons that Coors Field is a launching pad for homers. Fans are also treated to one of the most spectacular views in baseball: the Rocky Mountains, which loom beyond the left-field fence.

Long hungry for a baseball franchise, Denver fans have been rooting for this team since Day One; Attendance at Mile High Stadium, with its total capacity of 76,000, averaged nearly 57,000 fans per game over the two seasons the Rockies played there. Denver fans loved this park even before it was built; a plaza outside the stadium is paved with bricks that 5,000 locals paid $75 to have inscribed and set down. Baseball at Coors Field is a quality experience; between the team's quick rise to major-league credibility, the field's home-run-spawning conditions, the first-class stadium's attention to details both big and small, the picture-perfect setting, and the enthusiastic support of the home crowd, this is a place meant for memorable baseball games, and so far it hasn't failed.

HOT TIPS FOR VISITING FANS

PARKING
There are approximately 6,000 parking spaces at Coors Field, and prices run from $5–$8. Within a 20-minute walk of the stadium there are another 40,000 spots in private lots, with prices ranging from $5–$25 depending on their walking distance from the field. If you are here in April or October, it might be worth it to pay the extra dollars.

WEATHER
Anyone who has watched the Rockies or Denver Broncos on television knows early spring and fall can be downright chilly into out-and-out cold. Snow can fall as late as April (remember the snow-outs that began the 1996 season?), so be sure to dress warmly if you decide to visit Coors Field any time other than in the summer.

MEDIA
Radio: KOA (850 AM). Wayne Hagin and Jeff Kingery provide the English-language play-by-play. KCUV (1150 AM). Francisco Gamez and Carlos Bido are announcers for the Spanish-language broadcast.
TV: KWGN (Channel 2). Dave Armstrong and Dave Campbell call the games for television. Campbell occasionally calls national games for ESPN.

CUISINE
There are some 35 concession stands throughout Coors Field, and they offer everything from traditional ballpark fare to Buffalo Burgers (yes, bison) and deep fried Rocky Mountain Oysters (no, not the seagoing bivalve kind). For the less adventuresome, Domino's Pizza, Taco Bell, and Quiznos Sandwiches are plentiful. A kids-oriented stand on the left-field main level offers peanut butter and jelly sandwiches, corn dogs, and other children's favorites.

You'll never guess what brand of beer they serve here. Just about everything Coors makes can be had in the park, and the Sandlot Brewery on the concourse level in the right-field corner offers a host of microbrews and imports.

After the game, head across the street to Jackson's Hole sports bar (303-388-2883), or the Sports Column (303-296-1930). The Wynkoop Brewing Co. (303-297-2700) was Colorado's first brew pub. They make seven beers on the premises, which you can try along with some local specialties such as buffalo steak, pheasant quesadilla, and elk medallions. Brooklyn's (303-572-3999) is near Mile High Stadium, in an area that was once called "Little Brooklyn." With 30 televisions in the bar and four satellite systems, sports fans will find a home in this comfortable place housed in a Victorian-style building. Zang Brewing Company (303-455-2500) is also popular with Denver fans and sports personalities. Along with the requisite televisions and satellite systems, it's loaded with memorabilia.

In the Hot Seats at Coors Field

Coors Field, which holds just over 50,000 and has sold out every game, makes Rockies seats much harder to come by. Game-day tickets from the box office are available only for the Rockpile.

GOOD SEATS

They're all pretty good. The right-field stands afford a view of the not-so-distant peaks of the Rocky Mountains and provide afternoon sunshine. Mile-High row is the ring of seats in the 21st row of the upper level, and are painted purple to mark them as being exactly a mile above sea level.

The Club-level seats throughout the park have more leg room, are 22 inches wide, and are padded, allowing comfort for a range of fan girth; the wait service offered can help fans create their own padding. A climate-controlled private lounge with gourmet concessions and even comfier chairs is just behind the seating area.

BAD SEATS

There are a dozen or so semi-obstructed seats in the right-field mezzanine, so if you're getting tickets for that section, be sure to ask. The Rockpile, a holdover concept from Mile High Stadium, offers low-cost seats in an isolated upper-level section in straightaway center field. Calling these seats "bad" is a little harsh, since you can see the game just fine, and you get a view of the downtown Denver skyline to boot. And you can't beat the price ($4 for adults, $1 for kids), and they will probably be the only seats available. Bring binoculars and a glove; given the number of homers routinely being belted out of this park, odds are one of them's bound to head your way.

SCALPING

Scalping is illegal in Denver, but with the smaller capacity of Coors Field and constant sellouts, scalping Rockies tickets is a growth industry. Because of Coors Field's downtown location, side streets leading to the park will be prime locations for those with tickets to sell. The team's strong start and the excitement of the new park make this a seller's market. Expect dramatic markups over face value.

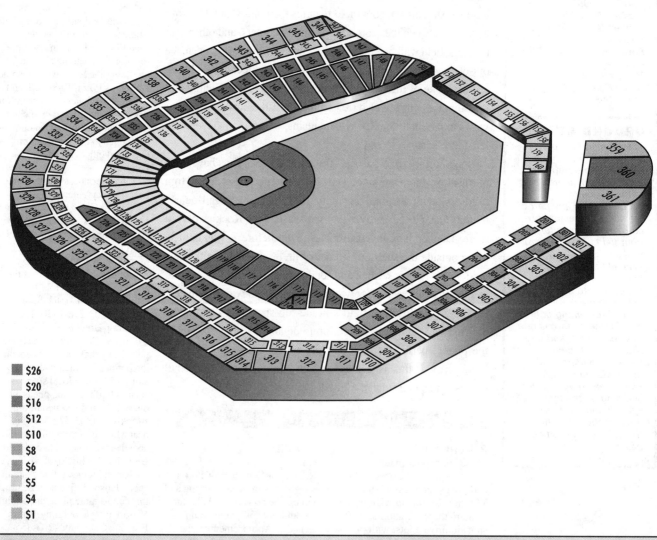

- $26
- $20
- $16
- $12
- $10
- $8
- $6
- $5
- $4
- $1

TICKET INFORMATION
Address: 1700 Broadway, Suite 2100, Denver, CO 80290
Phone: (303) ROCKIES or (800) 388-ROCK

Hours: Mon.–Sat. 9–6.
Prices: $26: club level; $20: infield box; $16: outfield box; $12: lower box; $10: upper reserved and right-field box; $8: right-field mezzanine; $6: Lower right-field reserve; $5: Upper right-field reserve, pavilion; $4: Rockpile; $1: Rockpile, 12 and under and 55 and older.

LODGING NEAR THE STADIUM

Westin Hotel
1672 Lawrence St.
Denver, CO 80202
(303) 572-9100/(800) 228-3000
About 1 mile from the stadium.

Hyatt Regency
1750 Welton St.
Denver, CO 80202
(303) 295-1234/(800) 233-1234
About 1½ miles from the stadium.

GETTING TO COORS FIELD

Public transportation: The RTD provides 16 buses to the downtown area. Call (303) 299-6000 for more information.
By car: Coors Field is at 20th and Blake streets. From I-25, take the 22nd Street Viaduct, which leads into the parking lot.

SPRING TRAINING

Hi Corbett Field
3400 E. Camino Campestre
Tucson, AZ 85716
Capacity: 7,726
Surface: Grass
Game time: 1:05 p.m. or 7:05 p.m.

MINOR LEAGUES

Class	Team
AAA	Colorado Springs (CO) Sky Sox
AA	New Haven (CT) Ravens
A	Salem (VA) Avalanche
A	Asheville (NC) Tourists
Short Season A	Portland (OR) Rockies
Rookie	Chandler (AZ) Rockies

The Rockies' closest minor-league affiliate is the Class AAA Colorado Springs Sky Sox of the Pacific Coast League. Sky Sox Stadium, 6,400-plus feet above sea level, some 1,200 feet higher than Coors Field, touts itself as the highest ballpark in North America.

To reach Colorado Springs' Sky Sox Stadium, approximately 70 miles from Denver, take the Woodman Road exit from I-25 south. Turn left and go through several traffic lights until you reach Powers Boulevard. Turn right. To reach the ballpark, visible on your left, turn left on Barns Road.

Ticket prices: $6: box seats; $5: children under 13 and senior citizens 60 and over; $4: general admission.

THE ROCKIES AT COORS FIELD

April 26, 1995: Dante Bichette's 3-run homer in the bottom of the 14th inning gives the Rockies an 11–9 win on Opening Day against the New York Mets.

July 3, 1995: Andres "Big Cat" Galarraga gets six hits against the Astros in a 15–0 win.

October 1, 1995: The Rockies defeat the San Francisco Giants 10–9 to earn a National League wild-card spot and become the first expansion team to reach postseason play before its eighth season.

October 3, 1995: The Atlanta Braves score in the top of the ninth to edge the Rockies 5–4 in Game 1 of the 1995 Divisional Series.

HOME-FIELD ADVANTAGE

There's no better home-field advantage than an enthusiastic and supportive crowd, and Coors Field has that in spades. The thin-air theory explaining the high number of home runs and long hits at Coors Field is at best overstated and at worst completely groundless; the aerodynamics of the altitude were figured into the dimensions of the park, and Mile High Stadium has the same air but didn't produce these numbers. A combination of good hitting, so-so pitching, and the roar of the crowd is a likelier, if less romantic, explanation. Coors Field's asymmetrical shape can sometimes produce funny hops when balls bounce off a fence, and the small foul territory allows less room to chase pop-ups. Air density aside, the Rockies do have an edge, being used to Denver's high altitude and cool temperatures (even the occasional snow squall). Still, the park led the league in homers hit in 1995 by a huge margin.

ROCKIES TEAM NOTEBOOK

Franchise history:
Colorado Rockies,
1993–present.

Wild Card: 1995

Tiger Stadium

If you've ever thought about seeing a game at Tiger Stadium, come soon. A Motor City fixture since its concrete-and-steel grandstand was built in 1912, the grand playground at the corner of Michigan and Trumbull in Detroit is one of the most fabled sites in professional sports. Although Tiger Stadium underwent an $8 million face-lift in 1993, now its days are numbered and a new stadium is planned that will include the inevitable revenue-enhancing frills such as skyboxes. The start of construction is hung up in court battles over financing, but the current goal is for the Tigers to begin the 1999 season in a new home.

Despite all the wrangling for a new park, Tiger Stadium is a great place to see a game, not in spite of its age, but because of it. Baseball at the Tiger Stadium site dates to 1896 and the Western League. Although there have been several name changes—Bennett Park, Navin Field, Briggs Stadium, and, finally, Tiger Stadium—little else has changed about one of the last remaining classic ballparks. It has remained remarkably free of splashy gimmicks. Detroit fans know their baseball and don't have to be egged on by applause signs to cheer for their team.

Given the fans' love of the Tigers, it's unlikely that any dismay over the move will be taken out on the team, but a few years ago, fans did form a human chain around the stadium in hopes that it would stay. The new park will have to be amazing to top Tiger Stadium, at least for memories and atmosphere.

HOT TIPS FOR VISITING FANS

PARKING
Tiger Stadium has no on-site parking, but the number of private lots in the vicinity is more than adequate. The freedom of choice benefits consumers, with the closer lots charging $5 or $6 and the lots 2 or 3 blocks farther away charging $2 or $3. The surface streets and extensive freeway system have been developed to accommodate easy movement of traffic before and after games.

WEATHER
Temperatures rise and fall in the course of a summer day in Detroit, generally ranging from the mid-60s to the high 70s. But it can get colder or hotter.

MEDIA
Radio: WJR (760 AM).
TV: WKBD (Channel 50) and the PASS (Pro-Am Sports System) cable network. Al Kaline handles analysis on WKBD and the legendary Ernie Harwell works play-by-play on PASS.

CUISINE
Part of the stadium's recent renovation included Tiger Plaza, a food court outside the stadium. It offers 208 menu items, including standard ballpark fare and, of course, pizza, which has become the local favorite. The brand has changed, though, from previous owner Tom Monaghan's Domino's to current owner Mike Illitch's Little Caesar's.
The Lindell A.C. (313-964-1122) remains one of the stadium area's most popular watering holes. Nemo's (313-965-3180) and Reedy's Saloon (313-961-1722) are also good haunts for fans.

The Greektown area, about a mile away, is a good stopping-off point for dining before and after the game.

LODGING NEAR THE STADIUM

Ritz-Carlton Dearborn
Fairlane Plaza
300 Town Center Dr.
Dearborn, MI 48126
(313) 441-2000
About 15 miles from the stadium.

Hyatt Regency Dearborn
Fairlane Town Center
Dearborn, MI 48126
(313) 593-1234/(800) 233-1234
About 15 miles from the stadium.

GETTING TO TIGER STADIUM

Public transportation: The Linwood bus line runs to Tiger Stadium. For more information, call (313) 935-4910.
By car: From the north, take the Lodge Freeway (Highway 10) south to the I-75/Flint-Toledo exit. Stay in the right lane while exiting. Then, almost immediately, exit I-75 at Trumbull Avenue. The stadium is on your right. From the south, take I-75 north to exit 49A, Rosa Parks Boulevard. Continue on Rosa Parks to the stadium, which is on the left. From the west, take I-96, the Jeffries Freeway. Stay in the left lane and exit at Lodge Freeway. Continue 1 mile on the Lodge Freeway to the Rosa Parks Boulevard and Civic Center exit. The stadium will be straight ahead. From the east, take I-94 west. Stay to the left, and take exit 215A, the Lodge Freeway (Highway 10 south). Continue about 1½ miles to I-75, the Fisher Freeway to Flint-Toledo. Continue on I-75, and exit at Trumbull Avenue. The stadium will be directly ahead.

SPRING TRAINING

Marchant Stadium
P.O. Box 90187
Lakeland, FL 33804
Capacity: 7,027
Surface: Grass
Game time: 7 p.m.
Tickets: (813) 688-7911

STADIUM STATS
Location: 2121 Trumbull Ave., Detroit, MI 48216
Opened: April 20, 1912
Surface: Grass
Capacity: 52,416
Outfield dimensions: LF 340, LC 365, CF 440, RC 370, RF 325
Services for fans with disabilities: Seating available in the Tiger Den behind home plate, the reserved section along the third-base line, and in the left-field grandstand.

STADIUM FIRSTS
Regular-season game: April 20, 1912, 6–5 over the Cleveland Indians.
Pitcher: George Mullin of the Tigers.
Batter: Jack Graney of the Indians.

GROUND RULES
• Foul poles are outside the playing field.
• A batted ball striking the facing or any part of the upper stands in fair territory and bouncing back onto field is a home run.
• Fly balls that strike lights underneath the upper stands from right field to center field in fair territory and bounce back onto the field are home runs.
• Balls striking the yellow line of the flagpole or below it and caroming into stands count for two bases.
• Balls striking the yellow line of the flagpole or below it and bouncing back onto the field are in play.
• Balls striking above the yellow line on the flagpole are home runs.
• A fair bounding ball going onto the roof of either bullpen dugout counts for two bases.
• A ball going through or sticking in the screen on fair ground is two bases.
• A pitched ball sticking or remaining on the backstop screen is one base, while a thrown ball doing the same is two bases.

In the Hot Seats at Tiger Stadium

The Tigers' attendance is directly related to their success on the field, although the team has sold 1 million tickets per season for 31 years, and passed the 100 million mark in 1994. Give the fans a winner, and they will come. Give them a loser, and, well, the last couple of seasons have not been box-office smashes. Given the team's mediocre state, tickets are easy to get for almost any game. The exception is the season opener, which is virtually always sold out way ahead of time. The Tigers do most of their business with single-game advance and walk-up sales.

GOOD SEATS
Tiger Stadium's seating is closer to the field than any other ballpark. The upper deck sits right on top of the lower deck, so even the higher seats have an excellent viewpoint. Despite its capacity of 52,416, Tiger Stadium is fan-friendly. It also boasts a center-field bleacher section of 10,000 seats priced at $5, one of the best buys in baseball. Except for a few seats along the lines and the bleachers, the roof provides refuge from the rain.

BAD SEATS
The one drawback of Tiger Stadium is the number of obstructed-view seats, about 5,000. The beams that obstruct the view of the field are reminiscent of those of the Polo Grounds and Ebbets Field.

SCALPING
Though scalping is illegal in Michigan, there are plenty of scalpers around the ballpark. Fans rarely need them, however.
A few years back, a scandal erupted when club officials held back good tickets for scalping purposes, rather than selling them at the box office.

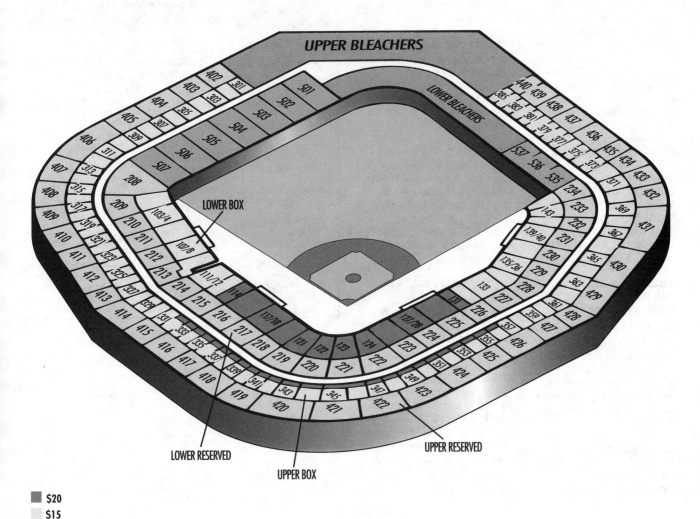

- $20
- $15
- $12
- $8
- $2.50

TICKET INFORMATION
Address: 2121 Trumbull Ave., Detroit, MI 48216

Phone: (313) 962-4000
Hours: Mon.–Sun. 9–6 (until 8 on game nights).

Prices: $20: Tiger's Den; $15: box seats; $12: reserved seats; $8: grandstand reserved seats; $2.50: bleachers.

MINOR LEAGUES

Class	Team
AAA	Toledo (OH) Mudhens
AA	Jacksonville (FL) Suns
A	Visalia (CA) Oaks
A	Fayetteville (NC) Generals
Short	
Season A	Jamestown (NY) Jammers
Rookie	Lakeland (FL) Tigers

The Tigers' closest minor-league affiliate is the Class AAA Toledo Mudhens of the International League. Pro baseball came to Toledo in 1883. The next season, Moses "Fleet" Walker and his brother, Welday, became the first African-American ballplayers in major-league history; 43 years later, Casey Stengel, who later became the New York Yankees' manager, led Toledo to a Junior World Series title as that team's skipper.

To reach Toledo's Ned Skeldon Stadium, approximately 60 miles from Detroit, take exit 4 from the I-475 bypass and follow U.S. 24 for 2 miles. Turn left onto Key Street; the park will be on your right.

Ticket prices: $6: box seats; $5: reserved seats; $3: general admission; children 14 and under and senior citizens over 60 receive a $2 discount on all seats.

THE TIGERS AT TIGER STADIUM

Oct. 9, 1934: Commissioner Kenesaw Mountain Landis removes St. Louis Cardinal Ducky Medwick from Game 7 of the World Series as Tigers fans shower Medwick with fruit and vegetables in left field. St. Louis wins 11–0.

Oct. 7, 1935: The Tigers beat the Chicago Cubs 4–3 in the sixth game of the World Series to win the title.

May 15, 1937: Tigers great Mickey Cochrane is hit in the head with a pitch by New York Yankee Bump Hadley, ending Cochrane's career.

Sept. 30, 1945: Hank Greenberg returns from World War II to hit a pennant-clinching home run in the last game of the season.

June 15, 1948: The Tigers play their first night game at Tiger Stadium. The gates open at 6, but management doesn't start the game until 9:30, thinking that the lights won't take effect until it is dark.

May 15, 1952: Virgil Trucks wins his no-hitter 1–0 when Vic Wertz homers off the Washington Senators with two outs in the bottom of the ninth.

Sept. 14, 1968: Denny McLain wins his 30th of the season, against the Oakland A's.

Sept. 17, 1968: The Tigers clinch the pennant with a 2–1 win over the Yankees.

June 18, 1975: Fred Lynn of the Boston Red Sox enjoys one of the best days in big-league history, hitting three home runs and driving in 10 runs in a 15–1 victory.

June 1, 1976: Mark "the Bird" Fidrych makes his debut at Tiger Stadium.

Oct. 4, 1984: Kirk Gibson's two home runs lead the Tigers to an 8–4 win over the San Diego Padres in Game 5, clinching the World Series title.

May 28, 1995: The Tigers and White Sox combine for a major-league record of 12 home runs in a single game. Kirk Gibson celebrates his 38th birthday with a solo homer, one of 10 in this contest; four players hit multiple homers.

HOME-FIELD ADVANTAGE

Although the wasteland in center field—440 feet to dead center, the deepest outfield in baseball—can help a smart pitcher, this is a hitter's park, so the Tigers have traditionally emphasized power hitting over speed. The short right-field line, with an overhanging upper deck, is a left-handed power hitter's dream. The limited foul territory also gives hitters an advantage. The proof is in the numbers: Tiger Stadium led the American League in homers in both '94 and '95. Lowering the fences has only helped the balls leave the yard that much faster. Unfortunately, most of those homers were hit by opposing teams.

The Tigers' grounds crew has been accused of doing all kinds of things, from watering down the basepaths to growing really thick infield grass, to accentuate the home-field advantage.

TIGERS TEAM NOTEBOOK

Franchise history
Detroit Tigers, 1901–present

World Series titles
1935, 1945, 1968, 1984

American League pennants
1907, 1908, 1909, 1934, 1935, 1940, 1945, 1968, 1984

Division titles
1972, 1984, 1987

Most Valuable Players
Mickey Cochrane, 1934
Hank Greenberg, 1935, 1940
Charlie Gehringer, 1937

Hal Newhouser, 1944, 1945
Denny McLain, 1968
Willie Hernandez, 1984

Rookies of the Year
Harvey Kuenn, 1953
Mark Fidrych, 1976
Lou Whitaker, 1978

Cy Young Awards
Denny McLain, 1968, 1969 (tie)
Willie Hernandez, 1984

Hall of Fame
Ty Cobb, 1936
Dan Brouthers, 1945
Hughie Jennings, 1945
Mickey Cochrane, 1947
Al Simmons, 1953

Charlie Gehringer, 1956
Edward G. Barrow, 1956
Hank Greenberg, 1956
Sam Crawford, 1957
Heinie Manush, 1964
Goose Goslin, 1968
Waite Hoyt, 1969
Billy Evans, 1973
Sam Thompson, 1974
Earl Averill, 1975
Bucky Harris, 1975
Eddie Mathews, 1978
Al Kaline, 1980
George Kell, 1983
Rick Ferrell, 1984

Retired numbers
2 Charlie Gehringer
5 Hank Greenberg
6 Al Kaline

STADIUM STATS

Location: *2269 N.W. 199th St., Miami, FL 33056*
Opened: *Aug. 16, 1987*
Surface: *Grass*
Capacity: *40,585*
Outfield dimensions: *LF 330, LC 385, CF 434, RC 385, RF 345*
Services for fans with disabilities: *Seating available in sections 103, 125, 128, 131, 153, and 156.*

STADIUM FIRSTS

Regular-season game: *April 5, 1993, 6–3 over the Los Angeles Dodgers.*
Pitcher: *Charlie Hough of the Marlins.*
Batter: *José Offerman of the Dodgers.*
Hit: *Bret Barberie of the Marlins.*
Home run: *Tim Wallach of the Dodgers.*

GROUND RULES

• *If a ball bounds off any portion of the railing around the photographers' booths, it is in play.*
• *If a ball strikes any portion of the left-field scoreboard below the uppermost edge, it is in play.*
• *If a ball strikes any portion of the foul poles in left field above any edge of the scoreboard, or in right field above the top of the wall, it is a home run.*

When H. Wayne Huizenga first mentioned adapting Pro Player Stadium to house an expansion baseball team, purists howled. Visions of Toronto's old Exhibition Stadium haunted fans. The only way Huizenga could convince the fans (and baseball owners) that it could be done was to build it. And convince them he did.

Constructed as a football-only stadium for the NFL Dolphins in 1987, Huizenga and company spent about $20 million to convert Pro Player Stadium to dual-purpose in 1990. While the home of the Florida Marlins is no Camden Yards, it's better than purists expected. The capacity for baseball is about 40,500—reduced from the 73,000 for football by both a desire for a more intimate atmosphere and the reality that some of the upper-deck outfield seats would've been awful. Because of the conversion, the outfield configuration is a little unusual in center field, making for some interesting caroms off the nooks and crannies—all the better for baseball flavor.

The 202-foot-long out-of-town scoreboard in left and left-center field also contributes to the nice baseball feel. Nicknamed the Blue Blocker or the Teal Tower, it's a manually operated board that, like Wrigley Field's, provides an inning-by-inning score of every other major-league game. It comes into play quite a bit, sometimes in unlikely ways. Atlanta's Ryan Klesko crashed into the left-field wall beneath it in 1993 and knocked a few of the numbers off the scoreboard.

Since acquiring full ownership of the stadium in 1994, Huizenga has instituted $15 million worth of improvements inside and out, such as adding 7,500 parking spaces, a food and entertainment complex, a second JumboTron, and a state-of-the-art turf drainage system.

The crowd has outgrown its status as rookie big-league fans. There is a much more family atmosphere at Marlins games, with less of the sort of heckling and vulgarity that you get from a Dolphins crowd.

HOT TIPS FOR VISITING FANS

PARKING

The parking lot was built to accommodate crowds of 70,000-plus for football, so it handles the baseball crowds easily. It's probably the best in the National League. Spaces are available for 23,000 cars, 254 buses, and a helicopter (yes, there's a helipad). Cost for cars is $5. On Opening Day and occasional other dates when huge crowds are expected, alternate lots open. The only drawback: With crowds of 35,000-plus, getting out of the lot can take a long time.

WEATHER

Hot and humid, and then summer comes. In South Florida, early spring is perfect and fall is very nice. But June, July, and August get very steamy. The Marlins play very few day games in the summer. From June 1 to mid-September, most Sunday games start at 6:05 p.m. and Saturday games at 7:05 p.m. Nights are rarely uncomfortable. Florida also gets lots of rain in the summer, but the Marlins have had fewer rainouts than expected. In their first three seasons they've only been rained out four times; although there was also that game canceled in '95 because of a hurricane warning.

Fans who show up for batting practice are more affected by the weather; late-afternoon thundershowers frequently force players to hit in indoor cages. But the recently upgraded drainage system and the stadium's excellent grounds crew almost always get the field ready in time for the first pitch.

MEDIA

Radio: WQAM (560 AM) has English-language broadcasts with Joe Angel and Dave O'Brien; WCMQ (1210 AM), with Felo Ramirez and Manolo Alvarez, broadcasts in Spanish. **TV:** WBFS (Channel 33) and Sunshine Network (cable), with Jay Randolph and Gary Carter, broadcast in English.

CUISINE

Excellent variety, including several tasty dishes that reflect the Latin influence in South Florida. The arepa, a South American dish made of two grilled cornbread "pancakes" stuffed with mozzarella cheese, is particularly popular. Try the medinoche sandwich (sliced pork, ham, cheese, mustard, and pickle served hot on oval-shaped egg bread) and a Cuban sandwich that's similar, but on Cuban bread. Also tasty is the empanada, a turnover-like pastry filled with chicken or beef. Cuban coffee is available. Reflecting New York's influence in Miami, a fully kosher concessions stand sits behind home plate; it's closed on Friday and Saturday. Carts around the concourses serve Hebrew National hot dogs and Italian sausage with

In the Hot Seats at Pro Player Stadium

The Marlins have about 20,000 season-ticket holders, so all box seats on or near the infield are sold out on a season basis. Individual-game tickets are available for boxes down the lines. You can buy a ticket for a future game without leaving your seat at Pro Player. In a service called Ticket Express, ticket sellers roam the stadium like vendors, take your order at your seat, and return with the ticket.

GOOD SEATS

If you don't mind a premium price, buy a seat on the club (200) level, still on the lower deck. It gives you access to luxury-box concessions and waiter service at your seat.

Tickets are $30 behind the plate, $20 around the bases, and $13 out by the foul poles.

BAD SEATS

Sight lines from the lower-level seats between the infield edge and the foul poles present a problem. Since they were built for football, seats are pointed toward what would be the 50-yard line, which is center field. You have to twist to watch the action at home plate. Some terrace boxes (at the corners in the football configuration) are pointed more toward the infield, but from those you have to look over the bullpen.

FAMILY SECTIONS

The park has two no-smoking, no-alcohol sections, one on each level. On the lower level, it's section 134 (down the right-field line near the foul pole); upstairs it's section 403 (down the left-field line).

SCALPING

Scalpers who work the Dolphins, Heat, and Panthers games seem to take the summer off. Scalping is illegal, the club is working to police it, and the market isn't very profitable because good seats are usually available at the gate.

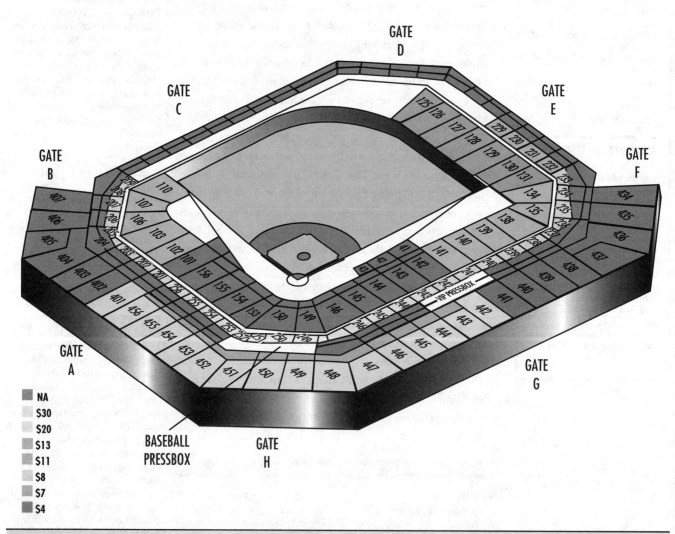

Legend:
- NA
- $30
- $20
- $13
- $11
- $8
- $7
- $4

GATE D
GATE C
GATE E
GATE B
GATE F
GATE A
GATE G
GATE H
BASEBALL PRESSBOX

TICKET INFORMATION
Address: 2269 N.W. 199th St., Miami, FL 33056
Phone: (305) 626-7200 or TicketMaster at (305) 350-5050 in Dade, (813) 287-8844 in west Florida, (407) 966-3309 in West Palm, (904) 353-3309 in north Florida, (407) 839-3900 in central Florida, or (954) 523-3309 in Broward.
Hours: Mon.–Fri. 8–6.
By mail: Florida Marlins Ticket Office, 100 N.E. Third Ave., Third Floor, Fort Lauderdale, FL 33301.
Prices: $30: zone A club seats; $20: zone B club seats; $13: terrace box and zone C club seats; $11: mezzanine box; $7: mezzanine reserved seats; $8: outfield reserved (adults); $3.50: outfield reserved (children); $4: general admission (adults); $1.50: general admission (children).

pepper and onion. Domino's vendors sell small pizzas in the stands, and such regional and national chains as Carvel and TCBY have outposts in the concourses. The Ports O'Call concession in sections 138–139 offers some 40 imported and specialty beers, including Heineken and Molson Ice, but the stadium's most popular drink is 16 ounces of ice-cold bottled water.

When Marlins' owner Wayne Huizenga purchased the remaining 50% of the stadium in 1994 (he'd bought the other 50% in 1990), he promised better concessions and/or reduced prices. The result is SportsTown, a complex of two 7,500-square-foot, tent-covered expanses of food stands, bars, interactive games, ticket and souvenir stands, as well as two entertainment stages, eight 32-inch color TV monitors, and a state-of-the-art sound system. SportsTown is between Gates F and H, at the south side of the stadium.

There aren't any popular postgame spots within walking distance of the stadium. The neighborhood is sandwiched by interstates and populated with small plazas, supermarkets, fast-food restaurants, and a variety of businesses aimed at interstate traffic. The area isn't particularly dangerous, but pedestrian traffic isn't recommended. Fans in search of postgame fun drive a couple of miles to an area around Pines Boulevard and University Drive, where a number of bar-restaurants (Friday's, Hooter's, etc.) cater to a stadium crowd. North Miami Beach, with a number of nightspots, is also a relatively short drive.

LODGING NEAR THE STADIUM

Don Shula Hotel and Golf Club
15255 Bull Run Rd.
Miami Lakes, FL 33014
(305) 821-1150/(800) 247-4852
About 12 miles from the stadium.

Turnberry Isle Resort
19999 W. Country Club Dr.
Aventura, FL 33180
(305) 932-6200/(800) 327-7028
About 7 miles from the stadium.

GETTING TO PRO PLAYER STADIUM

Public transportation: Metro-Dade Transit Agency provides transportation to the stadium via bus service. Call (305) 638-6700 for more information.
By car: From South Miami and the Keys, take U.S. 1 to I-95 north. Take I-95 north to the Ives Dairy Road exit. Proceed west on Ives Dairy for 5 miles; the stadium will be on your right. From West Palm Beach and Fort Lauderdale, either take I-95 south to the Ives Dairy exit, or take the Florida Turnpike south to the Honey Hill Road stadium exit. The stadium will be on your right.
From Naples and Fort Myers, take I-75 to I-595 east. Get off at the Florida Turnpike south and continue to the Honey Hill Road stadium exit.

SPRING TRAINING

Space Coast Stadium and Carl Barger Baseball Complex
5600 Stadium Pkwy.
Melbourne, FL 32940
Capacity: 7,200
Surface: Grass
Game time: 1:05 p.m. or 7:35 p.m.

MINOR LEAGUES

Class	Team
AAA	Charlotte (NC) Knights
AA	Portland (ME) Sea Dogs
A	Brevard County (FL) Manatees
A	Kane County (IL) Cougars
Short Season A	Oneida (NY) Blue Marlins
Rookie	Gulf Coast (FL) Marlins

The minor-league team closest to Miami is the Class A West Palm Beach Expos of the Florida State League. One of the Expos' opponents is the Brevard County Manatees, the Marlins' affiliate in the Florida State League. Montreal Expos manager Felipe Alou rates West Palm Beach as his favorite among the five cities he managed in during his minor-league career. His first season

was 1990, when his team captured the FSL regular-season title with 92 wins, best among all minor-league teams.
To reach West Palm Beach's Municipal Stadium, which is about 70 miles from Miami, take exit 53, Palm Beach Lakes Boulevard, from I-95 and head east. The ballpark will be on the right, about ¾ mile from the highway.
Ticket prices: $5: general admission; $4: children under 13; $3: senior citizens 65 and over; For more information, call (407) 684-6801.

THE MARLINS AT PRO PLAYER STADIUM

May 1, 1993: Jeff Conine hits the first grand slam at Pro Player, off Colorado Rockies' David Nied.

Oct. 2, 1993: A crowd of 43,210 shows up to see the Marlins, putting the team over the 3 million mark in attendance.

April 17, 1994: Catcher Benito Santiago charges San Francisco Giants pitcher Kevin Rogers, starting the Marlins' first regular-season on-field brawl.

May 1, 1994: Gary Sheffield homers, leading the Marlins to a 9–4 win over the Cincinnati Reds. Florida's 13–12 record marks the second time they are over .500 in their history.

June 6, 1994: Jesus Tavarez hits a game-winning pinch-hit single in the bottom of the ninth to give the Marlins an 11–10 comeback win over the Los Angeles Dodgers.

HOME-FIELD ADVANTAGE

The layout of the ballpark makes it tough to hit home runs. It's 434 feet to center field, the 22- to 33-foot scoreboard makes the left-field fence tough to clear, and the ball doesn't carry well to right. The heavy, humid air doesn't help much either. The outfield gaps are spacious, so the Marlins have placed a priority on stockpiling speedy outfielders. The stadium's dimensions probably help the young Marlins by cutting their expansion-caliber pitching some slack. The Marlins posted their first winning record at home in 1995.

MARLINS TEAM NOTEBOOK

Franchise history	Retired number
Florida Marlins, 1993–present	5 Carl F. Barger

Astrodome

Few people would call it the Eighth Wonder of the World now, but the Astrodome was, after all, the first major-league ballpark to be enclosed.

Houston's first ballclub, the Colt 45s, played in Colt Stadium in 1962–64, and all the near-tropical pleasures of the city became part of the fan experience: the periodic torrential rains, usually just before game time, the Amazonian rain-forest humidity, and especially the mosquitos, almost as big as the ball in play. The Astrodome was eagerly anticipated—if not for its new inhabitants, then for the air conditioning it promised.

The stadium was built for $31.6 million, and the roof went up with 4,796 panes of glass. But the architects forgot that players must peer up to follow the flight of a batted ball. The panes made that nearly impossible, so they were painted, and everyone thought the problem was solved.

Then the grass died. To remedy the situation, the Monsanto Corporation developed a short, plush carpet called AstroTurf. The game was never the same again.

Visiting players soon had another surprise: The still air had a chilling effect on home runs. Power hitters were punished by the ball's not carrying. The Astrodome quickly gained a reputation as one of the long-ball hitters' least favorite parks.

As well as changing the height of the outfield walls, the Astros have tried to liven things up over the years with such embellishments as a Wild West scoreboard extravaganza that went off whenever an Astros player homered. That was dropped after the 1987 season. For a short time, ushers wore space outfits. Thankfully, that, too, was dropped.

With a long line of imitators and a history as rich as the oilmen and tycoons who put it in Texas, the Astrodome is a unique—and pleasantly cool—repository of great baseball moments.

HOT TIPS FOR VISITING FANS

PARKING
The Astrodome is ringed with acres of parking lots. There's room for 24,600 cars, so private lots are unnecessary. Parking is $4. The Astros have an early-bird lot for $1 in the northwest corner of the property, a decent walk from the ballpark. It opens three hours before game time and remains open for two hours afterward.

WEATHER
You can get rained out at the Astrodome. It happened once. On June 15, 1976, 10 inches of rain fell on Houston, and the flooding was too bad to hold a game. The weather inside is man-made, though. You can count on real relief from Houston's humidity when you take your seat at the Astrodome. The AC has 6,600 tons of cooling capacity, and the temperature always hovers around 72.

MEDIA
Radio: KILT (610 AM) is the flagship station, with Milo Hamilton and Larry Dierker as the primary announcers. Bill Brown, Vince Cotroneo, and Bill Worrell also broadcast for the Astros. KXYZ (1320 AM) does the Spanish-language broadcasts, with Francisco Ernesto Ruiz and Danny Gonzalez announcing. Former Astro Enos Cabell has a weekly call-in show on KCOH (1430 AM).
TV: KTXH (Channel 20) and the Home Sports Entertainment channel do telecasts. Brown does play-by-play for TV, with Dierker and Worrell helping.

CUISINE
The Astrodome features several items with a distinctive Texas flair. Luther's Barbecue Stand, run by a popular local chain, sells beef barbecue and a gigantic barbecued potato, with a variety of toppings. You can get nachos with chili, cheese, and plenty of jalapeño peppers. Other foods include oversized Dome Dogs, grilled burgers, and grilled Italian sausages. A variety of beers, including Heineken and Mexican brews, are sold.
Pappasito's (713-784-5253) is about 10 minutes from the Astrodome and is a good choice for a postgame Tex-Mex meal; check out the athlete-autographed menus on the ceiling over the bar. Astros and visiting players are occasional customers. Willie G's (713-840-7190) is also nearby. This New Orleans–style restaurant serves Cajun dishes and specializes in fresh seafood; it also features Shiner's, a popular Texas brew. Dave & Busters is one of several spots along Richmond Avenue that are convenient postgame hangouts, but they're geared more to the local singles scene than to sports fans.

LODGING NEAR THE STADIUM

Sheraton Astrodome
8686 Kirby Dr.
Houston, TX 77054
(713) 748-3221/(800) 325-3635
1 block from the stadium.

STADIUM STATS
Location: 8400 Kirby Dr., Houston, TX 77054
Opened: April 9, 1965
Surface: Artificial turf (Magic Carpet)
Capacity: 54,370
Outfield dimensions: LF 325, LC 375, CF 400, RC 375, RF 325
Services for fans with disabilities: Seating available on the field box level behind home plate, and on the mezzanine level in right and left fields.

STADIUM FIRSTS
Regular-season game: April 12, 1965, 2–0 loss to the Philadelphia Phillies.
Pitcher: Bob Bruce of the Astros.
Batter: Tony Taylor of the Phillies.
Hit: Tony Taylor.
Home run: Dick Allen of the Phillies.

GROUND RULES
• Dugouts: The ball remains in play unless it enters the dugout or crosses the yellow line therein. If it enters the dugout, it counts for one base on a throw by a pitcher or two bases on a throw by a fielder.
• Behind home plate: Any thrown ball hitting above, on, or below the padding or screen behind the home-plate area remains in play if it rebounds onto field; if the ball lodges in the padding or behind the Plexiglas camera shield, it counts for one base on a pitch or two bases on a throw by a fielder.
• Hitting roof or speakers: A ball hitting the roof or speakers in fair territory is playable if caught by a fielder. The batter is then out.

In the Hot Seats at the Astrodome

The capacity for baseball is 54,370. The Astros, even in their best seasons and when they had Nolan Ryan, were rarely a threat to sell out and though they've contended the past few years, walk-up tickets are still no problem. Those who buy them in the early afternoon at the stadium can take the Astrodome tour to kill time. It is fascinating, and fans are allowed to stand on the field.

GOOD SEATS
All seats face the diamond, which isn't always the case in multi-use domes, and they're almost all upholstered, so in those ways they're all good seats. The Diamond Level boxes around the plate are where President Bush sits. This is as good as it gets here. There are 150 of them, they cost $8,300 for the season and none are available, so be satisfied with your upholstered loge seat.

BAD SEATS
Outfield seats are far from the action. Avoid the general-admission seats in left and right field on either side of the pavilion; some of these are obstructed by supports. Once you get in, don't plan to move down to better seats, especially the Diamond Level boxes. The ushers vigorously enforce the sit-in-your-seat edict.

SCALPING
Though it's legal, it's unknown around the Astrodome. Longtime fans don't even recall seeing them in 1986, when the Astros were in the playoffs.

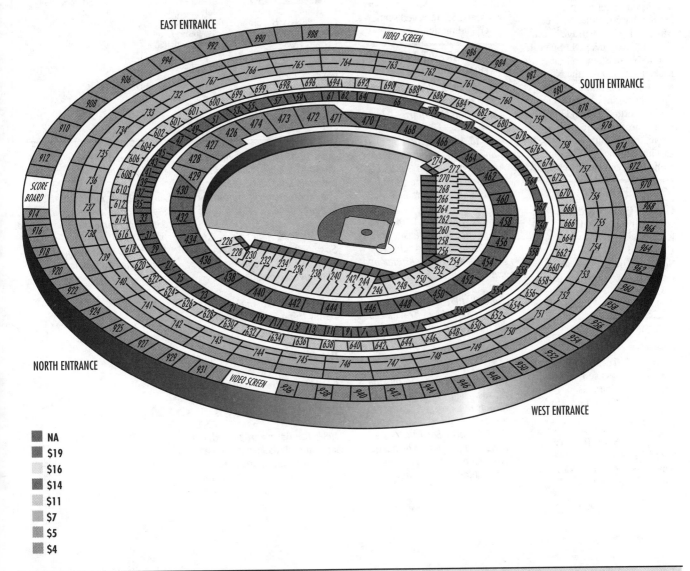

- ■ NA
- ■ $19
- ■ $16
- ■ $14
- ■ $11
- ■ $7
- ■ $5
- ■ $4

TICKET INFORMATION
Address: 8400 Kirby Dr., Houston, TX 77054
Phone: (713) 799-9555 or TicketMaster at

(713) 629-3700
By mail: Houston Astros, Ticket Dept., P.O. Box 1691, Houston, TX 77001
Hours: Daily 9–5.

Prices: $19: stardeck; $16: field; $14: mezzanine; $11: loge; $7: upper box; $5: upper reserved; $4: pavilion ($1 for children 14 and under).

Holiday Inn Astrodome
8111 Kirby Dr.
Houston, TX 77054
(713) 790-1900/(800) 552-0942
¾ mile from the stadium.

GETTING TO THE ASTRODOME

Public transportation: You can catch a Metro bus from downtown: the No. 18 Kirby or the No. 15 Hiram-Clark. For more information, call (713) 635-4000.

By car: From the South Loop 610, exit at Kirby Street or continue about ½ mile and exit at Fannin Street. From Kirby, the parking-lot entrances are at Westridge, Murworth, and McNee streets. From Fannin, the entrances are at Naomi, Holly Hall, and Northwest Drive. Or take Main Street north and approach from either McNee, Murworth, or Westridge streets. From the east, take Old Spanish trail to North Stadium Drive. Make a left and use the North Stadium Drive entrance. From the north, go south on I-45 to North Sheridan Drive, which turns into GreenBriar Drive, then Fannin Street. Use the parking entrances off Naomi, Holly Hall, and Northwest Drive.

SPRING TRAINING

Osceola County Stadium
1000 Bill Beck Blvd.
Kissimmee, FL 34744
Capacity: 5,100
Surface: Grass
Game time: 12:05 p.m. or 6:35 p.m.
Tickets: (407) 933-2520

MINOR LEAGUES

Class	Team
AAA	Tucson (AZ) Toros
AA	Jackson (MS) Generals
A	Kissimmee (FL) Cobras
A	Quad City (IA) River Bandits
Short Season A	Auburn (NY) Astros
Rookie	Gulf Coast (FL) Astros

The closest minor-league team to Houston is the Class AA San Antonio Missions of the Texas League. One of the Missions' opponents is the Jackson Generals, Houston's Texas League affiliate; 1994 marked the Missions' first season in their new ballpark, Municipal Stadium, designed by the architects of Cleveland's Jacobs Field. Except for five years (1943–45, 1965–66), pro baseball has been played in this city since 1903. To reach San Antonio's Municipal Stadium, approximately 200 miles from Houston, take Route 35 south from downtown to Highway 90 west. The park is at the intersection of 90 and Callaghan Road.

Ticket prices: $8: executive box seats; $7: box seats; $6: upper box seats; $5: reserved seats; $4: general admission.

THE ASTROS AT THE ASTRODOME

Sept. 13, 1965: Willie Mays hits his 500th home run, off the Astros' Don Nottebart.

April 18, 1966: The first official game played on AstroTurf. Los Angeles rookie Don Sutton beats the Astros and future Hall of Famer Robin Roberts 6–3.

June 22, 1966: The Astrodome attendance record is set as 50,908 see the Los Angeles Dodgers and Sandy Koufax beat the Astros 5–2.

June 18, 1967: Don Wilson no-hits the Atlanta Braves 2–0 for the first no-hitter in the Astrodome.

April 30, 1969: Jim Maloney of the Cincinnati Reds no-hits the Astros. The next night, Wilson no-hits the Reds.

April 29, 1974: Lee May ties a major-league record by hitting two home runs in one inning against the Chicago Cubs.

June 10, 1974: Mike Schmidt of the Philadelphia Phillies hits a towering shot that deflects off a speaker hanging in fair territory in center field.

July 30, 1975: Relief pitcher Jose Sosa homers in his first major league at-bat, becoming the first Astro ever to do so.

July 11, 1985: Nolan Ryan fans Danny Heep for his 4,000th strikeout.

Oct. 15, 1986: In one of the most exciting games ever played, the New York Mets beat the Astros 7–6 in 16 innings to earn a trip to the World Series.

1992: The Astros are forced to go on a 26-day road trip because the Astrodome is hosting the Republican National Convention.

September 8, 1993: Darryl Kile no-hits the Mets for a 7–1 victory.

Aug. 5, 1994: Jeff Bagwell sets team records when he hits his 38th home run of the season and has five RBI, to bring his total to 112, in a 12–4 win against the San Francisco Giants.

Kauffman Stadium

STADIUM STATS

Location: *1 Royal Way, Kansas City, MO 64129*
Opened: *April 10, 1973*
Surface: *Grass*
Capacity: *40,625*
Outfield dimensions: *LF 330, LC 375, CF 400, RC 375, RF 330*
Services for fans with disabilities: *Sections 100–102 and 140–141.*

STADIUM FIRSTS

Regular-season game: *April 10, 1973, 12–1 over the Texas Rangers.*
Pitcher: *Paul Splittorff of the Royals.*
Batter: *Dave Nelson of the Rangers.*
Home run: *John Mayberry of the Royals.*

GROUND RULES

• *Foul poles: on or above yellow, home run; below yellow, in play.*
• *Ball going into dugout or hitting padded protective railings is out of play.*
• *Ball hitting guy wires supporting backstop screen is out of play.*
• *Batted or thrown ball that hits tarpaulin area cover is in play.*
• *Thrown ball lodging in or under backstop protective canvas and remaining is two bases; pitched ball, one base.*

Known as one of baseball's most beautiful ballparks, Kauffman Stadium was one of the first baseball-only stadiums built in the past two decades. Its football cousin, the Kansas City Chiefs' Arrowhead Stadium, sits next door, and together the two stadiums make up the Harry S. Truman Sports Complex. The stadium is named after Ewing M. Kauffman, who bought the Royals as an expansion team in 1968.

Kauffman Stadium's most prominent feature is a 322-foot-wide water spectacular behind the outfield wall; it's the largest privately funded fountain in the world. The stadium also features a 12-story-high scoreboard built in the shape of the Royals' crest and a state-of-the-art Sony JumboTron color video-display board. These snazzy extras are all very nice, but they pale in comparison to the stadium's switch from artificial turf to grass in 1995. Instead of plastic, now five strains of bluegrass and one kind of rye cover the field, and more people than the groundskeeper have had to get used to the change. While Kauffman Stadium formerly provided a happy home to the sort of fast, average-over-power teams that artificial turf engenders, the Royals are still trying to adjust to the natural surface.

This isn't the kind of salty, colorful venue you get in some big cities. The Royals' organization is focused on fostering a family-type crowd, which has proved to be very successful for the organization and popular with the fans. Kauffman Stadium encourages this atmosphere with features such as a picnic-and-music area, known as the Royal Courtyard, and an amusement area with a pitching booth.

HOT TIPS FOR VISITING FANS

PARKING
The stadium has 22,000 parking spaces available for $5 a vehicle, more than enough to handle a sell-out crowd. Traffic moves swiftly on and off the nearby freeway.

WEATHER
Kansas City is traditionally hot in August and September. Rain is not much of a threat, thanks to the excellent drainage system installed for use with the late, unlamented AstroTurf. It's so effective that it leaves the grass field dry in no time, resulting in fewer postponed games.

MEDIA
Radio: WIBW (580 AM).

Denny Matthews and Fred White call the play-by-play and John Waltham and Paul Splittorff provide the color.
TV: KSMO (Channel 62). Splittorff also adds some color to fellow former Royal Steve Busby's play-by-play for televised games.

CUISINE
Barbecued pork and beef are favorites. Ice-cream sundaes and deli foods also are very popular. Budweiser, Miller, and Coors are among the national brands of beer sold. A local brew, Boulevard Beer, also is popular. Quincy's, in the Adams Mark Hotel, is a popular postgame watering hole for Royals and

Chiefs fans (it used to host the Chiefs official team postgame party), and within easy walking distance of Kauffman Stadium. Although not a sports bar, Alison's House is also nearby and pulls in a lot of business from both Chiefs and Royals fans hungry after a game. In Westport, a neighborhood about 20 minutes' drive south of Kansas City, is the area's most famous watering hole: Kelly's (816-753-9193). Any trip to Kansas City to see the Royals—or even if you're not going to a game at all—should include a stop here. Kansas City is also famous for barbecue, and the most famous place for barbecue here is Arthur Bryant's (816-231-1123), a mecca for all barbecue lovers.

LODGING NEAR THE STADIUM

Westin Crown Center
1 Pershing Rd.
Kansas City, MO 64108
(816) 474-4400/(800) 228-3000
About 10 miles from the stadium.

Holiday Inn Sports Complex
4011 Blue Ridge Cutoff
Kansas City, MO 64133
(816) 353-5300/(800) HOLIDAY
Across the street from the stadium.

GETTING TO KAUFFMAN STADIUM

Public transportation: Stadium Express Bus service runs from downtown, the Crown Center, and Country Club Plaza to Kauffman Stadium. Service begins 1 hour and 50 minutes before game time. Call (816) 221-0660 for more information.
By car: From the south, take I-435 to the stadium exit at Stadium Drive. The stadium will be ahead.
From the north, take I-435 to I-70. Take I-70 to the Harry S. Truman Sports Complex exit, then take Blue Ridge Cutoff to the stadium.
From both east and west, take I-70 to the Harry S. Truman Sports Complex exit, then take Blue Ridge Cutoff to the stadium.

In the Hot Seats at Kauffman Stadium

Walk-up sales are very common because games rarely sell out. In addition, 5,000 general-admission seats go on sale an hour and a half before the start of each game. These seats are split equally between right and left fields.

Fireworks nights, typically on holidays, always attract big crowds and are generally sellouts. The Royals have big rivalries with the Oakland A's, who formerly played in Kansas City, and the Chicago White Sox. A rivalry is also developing with the Cleveland

Indians, but their biggest rivalry for a number of years has been with the New York Yankees; tickets for home games against any of these teams will be harder to get.

GOOD SEATS

Being a baseball-only stadium, Kauffman Stadium has no bad seats. For sunbathers, the left-field stands are generally the best place to be. Some fans prefer plaza reserved seats or box seats, but any ticket will do.

SPECIAL PROGRAMS

The Royals offer half-price reserved seats on Mondays and Thursdays. A limited number of standing-room-only tickets are available for most otherwise sold-out games.

SCALPING

Ticket availability limits scalping activity, but some can be found off the stadium premises.

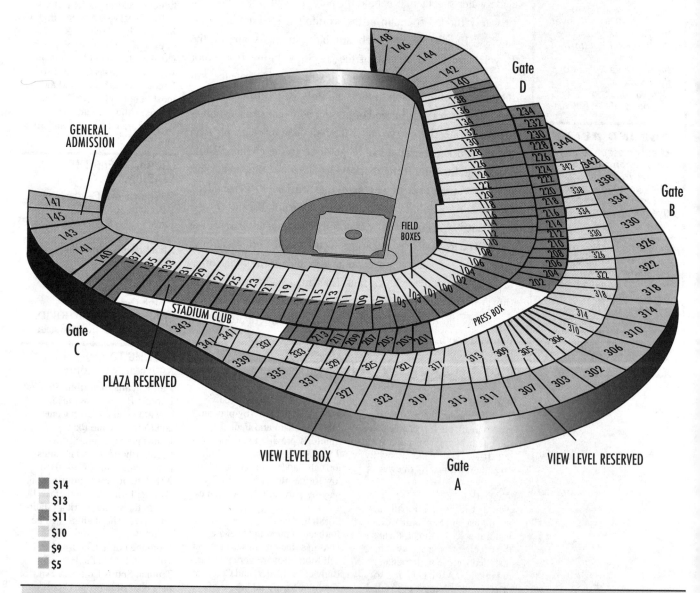

- $14
- $13
- $11
- $10
- $9
- $5

TICKET INFORMATION

Address: 1 Royal Way, Kansas City, MO 64129
Phone: (800) 6-ROYALS or (816) 921-8000
By mail: P.O. Box 419969, Kansas City, MO 64141. Specify dates, number of tickets, and preferred location. Include $2 postage and handling.
Hours: Daily 9–6.
Prices: $14: club-level box; $13: field-level box; $11: plaza-level reserved; $10: view-level (upper) box; $9: reserved; $5: general admission.

SPRING TRAINING

Baseball City Stadium
300 Stadium Way
Davenport, FL 33837
Capacity: 7,000
Surface: Grass
Game time: 1:05 p.m.
Tickets: (813) 424-7211

MINOR LEAGUES

Class	Team
AAA	Omaha Royals
AA	Wichita (KS) Wranglers
A	Wilmington (DE) Blue Rocks
A	Rockford (IL) Royals
A	Lansing (MI) Lugnuts
Short Season A	Spokane (WA) Indians
Rookie	Fort Myers (FL) Royals

The Royals' closest minor-league affiliate is the Class AAA Omaha Royals of the American Association.
Omaha's Rosenblatt Stadium is the site of the NCAA college World Series since the mid-1950s. Omaha has had a professional ballclub since 1879, part of the first league established that included cities not on the Eastern Seaboard. Affliated with the Kansas City Royals since 1969, Omaha has been the launch pad for such Royalty as George Brett, who played here in 1973 and 1974, Frank White, also class of '73, and Dennis Leonard, who holds Omaha's record for most innings pitched (223) in a single season (1974). David Cone, Paul Splittorff, Steve Farr, Danny Jackson, and Bob Hamelin also spent time here before moving up to the majors.
Pizza is made fresh at the ballpark daily, and the concessions offer six different grilled sausages. There is a picnic area at the park, and a three-level stadium club (sorry, members only) down the right-field line. It's fronted with glass and allows those watching an unbeatable view of the proceedings.
To reach Omaha's Rosenblatt Stadium, approximately 190 miles from Kansas City, take the 13th Street exit from I-80. The stadium will be visible.
Ticket prices: $6.50: field seats; $5.50: view box; $3.50: general admission. For more information, call (402) 734-2550.

THE ROYALS AT KAUFFMAN STADIUM

May 15, 1973: Nolan Ryan throws his first no-hitter and the first at the Stadium, striking out 12 as the California Angels win 3–0.

Oct. 10, 1976: The Royals get their first playoff win at the Stadium, beating the New York Yankees 7–3.

May 14, 1977: Jim Colborn no-hits the Rangers 6–0.

Oct. 4, 1978: Larry Gura and Fred Patek lead the Royals to a 10–4 win over the Yankees in Game 3 of the ALCS.

Oct. 17, 1980: The Royals get their first World Series victory, edging the Philadelphia Phillies 4–3 in 10 innings behind homers by George Brett and Amos Otis.

Oct. 27, 1985: A five-hitter by Bret Saberhagen and a two-run homer by Daryl Motley key an 11–0 win over the St. Louis Cardinals in Game 7 of the World Series. The Royals also had trailed this series 3–1.

Aug. 2, 1987: Kevin Seitzer ties a team record with 6 hits, against the Boston Red Sox.

HOME-FIELD ADVANTAGE

The 1995 season saw the arrival of real grass at Kauffman Stadium. Despite the great sentimental value of going to grass, playing baseball on artificial turf had been very, very good to the Royals. Their winning percentage on the fake stuff was .569 for 1995, .582 overall; on grass it was .467. Perhaps they just need a little more time to adjust to the difference in the speed of play.

In 1994 the Royals moved the outfield fences in by about 10 feet and lowered them from 12 feet to 9 feet as well. At first, the closer and lower fences didn't seem to have a dramatic effect; there were 38 homers at Kauffman in '95, even fewer than in '94 (46). Then in 1996 everything seemed to click. In the first 27 games, 41 homers got belted over the fence. Was it the grass? Was it the fences? Was it the current state of major league pitching? Go figure. The lower fences also, of course, allow fielders to make leaping saves and get themselves onto the occasional sports highlight footage.

ROYALS TEAM NOTEBOOK

Franchise history	Rookies of the Year	Hall of Fame
Kansas City Royals, 1969–present	Lou Pinella, 1969 Bob Hamelin, 1994	Bob Lemon, 1976 Harmon Killebrew, 1984 Gaylord Perry, 1991
World Series title 1985	**Cy Young** Bret Saberhagen, 1985, 1989 David Cone, 1994	**Retired numbers** 10 Dick Howser 5 George Brett 20 Frank White
American League pennants 1980, 1985	**Most Valuable Player** George Brett, 1980	
Division titles 1976, 1977, 1978, 1980, 1984, 1985		

Aug. 26, 1991: Bret Saberhagen no-hits the White Sox 7–0.

Sept. 29, 1993: Future Hall of Famer George Brett singles in his final at-bat, off the Cleveland Indians' Jeremy Hernandez.

June 17, 1996: Cal Ripken breaks Japanese baseball player Sachio Kinugasa's record for most consecutive games anywhere.

LOS ANGELES DODGERS

Dodger Stadium

The story goes like this: Walter O'Malley was riding in a helicopter over Los Angeles, scouting for the Dodgers' new home, when he noticed a spot where several freeways converged, and asked the government official with him, "Can I have that?"

The rest is Dodgers history. O'Malley got what he wanted: As the Dodgers began their West Coast life in 1958 at Los Angeles Coliseum, construction was under way on Dodger Stadium at Chavez Ravine. Some squatters and goatherds were evicted first, including one family that had to be carted away kicking and screaming and even biting the marshals who took them. The result was a jewel—a gorgeous, clean, friendly, and efficient ballpark on a hilltop overlooking downtown Los Angeles. Among the ushers in their straw boaters, the tasty Dodger dogs, and the great views of the San Gabriel Mountains on one side and the city skyline on the other, this park has as much personality as any of its older cousins off to the east.

The presence of figures like recently retired manager Tommy Lasorda (who, contrary to rumors, never lived here) and Mike Brito (a Dodgers employee who sports a Panama hat, cigar, and radar gun in his role as goodwill ambassador, occasional scout, and recorder of pitch velocities) has lent a sense of tradition to the place that offsets the "come late, leave early" attitude of many fans. Still, Dodger Stadium was the first ballpark to draw 3 million fans in one season, so even if the fans don't always show it, Dodger blue definitely runs through the veins of Angelenos.

HOT TIPS FOR VISITING FANS

PARKING
The stadium has parking for 16,000 cars; the cost is $5. Lots funnel into nearby freeways much more easily than the common perception has it, helped by fans leaving early. No lot empties much faster than the others. If you arrive early by the Elysian Park Road entrance, you can see "Dodger Mom," a rabid fan who's always first in line waiting for the parking gates to open.

WEATHER
The climate is almost never a factor. The Dodgers have not had a rainout since April 21, 1988. You can count on warm weather generally, but ocean breezes and high elevation usually preclude stifling heat. It can get cool in the evenings, especially in April and September, so long sleeves help at those times of the year. Another, more ominous, natural phenomenon is always in the back of the minds of those attending Dodgers games. Dodger Stadium is built on a fault line, so the earthquake that shook up Candlestick Park could look minor league compared to what could happen if the Big One ever hits Southern California.

MEDIA
Radio: The Dodgers' flagship radio station is KABC (790 AM), with legendary Vin Scully behind the microphone. Color is handled by Ross Porter and Rick Monday, a former Cub and Dodger famed for the game in which, as a visiting Cub, he tore a U.S. flag away from people who had trotted onto the outfield with intentions of burning the Stars and Stripes. The Spanish broadcasts are on KWKW (1330 AM), with Jaime Jarrin and Rene Cardenas.
TV: KTLA (Channel 5) carries the games on television.

CUISINE
Dodger Dogs are required eating. Long, thin, and grilled to perfection, it's the best hot dog in baseball. Insiders recommend the "Red Hot" spicy dog. Order it grilled, not steamed. Take the time to find the Gulden's mustard dispensers. Pizza Hut, and Carl's Jr. are on hand to serve less traditional fare, and TCBY draws long lines for its frozen yogurt served in plastic, mini Dodger batting helmets.
The Outfield Bar, near the food court on the club level along the first-base line, serves a variety of wines and beers until the seventh inning.
Don't miss the loge-level peanut vendor who is renowned for throwing peanuts across sections to customers with accuracy that would shame many NBA guards. Drop the bag and you risk his wrath.
There are many choices for after the game. The stadium bumps against Chinatown, which has any number of quality spots. On Broadway, an Italian place called Little Joe's (213-489-4900) is highly recommended. Felipe's (213-628-3781), on Alameda just below Chinatown, is where the French-dip sandwich was invented; it has great food, and sawdust on the floor. Downtown, near the Coliseum, is Mr. Jim's barbecue spot, whose slogan is "You Don't Need Teeth to Eat Mr. Jim's Beef." Those with the bucks can head for Morton's or Spago's, where the Hollywood big shots schmooze, dine, and do business.

LODGING NEAR THE STADIUM

Sheraton Grande
333 S. Figueroa St.
Los Angeles, CA 90017
(213) 617-1133/(800) 325-3535
About 8 miles from the stadium.

STADIUM STATS
Location: 1000 Elysian Park Ave., Los Angeles, CA 90012
Opened: April 10, 1962
Surface: Prescription Athletic Turf (PAT)
Capacity: 56,000
Outfield dimensions: LF 330, LC 385, CF 395, RC 385, RF 330
Services for fans with disabilities: Seating available throughout the stadium. Call (213) 224-1HIT for more information.

STADIUM FIRSTS
Game: April 10, 1962, 6–3 loss to the Cincinnati Reds.
Pitcher: Johnny Podres of the Dodgers.
Batter: Eddie Kasko of the Reds.
Hit: A double by Eddie Kasko.
Home run: Wally Post of the Reds.

GROUND RULES
• Ball is in play when it hits below railing (white section) of left- and right-field foul poles.
• Home run on ball hitting foul pole above railing (yellow section).
• Dugouts—all television and photography booths, as well as dugouts, considered bench.
• Ball striking any forward facing of dugouts is in play.
• Backstop screen—screen roof of fans' dugout boxes considered same as sloping area of a backstop.
• Ball striking guy wire supporting backstop is out of play.

In the Hot Seats at Dodger Stadium

Dodger Stadium is the only ballpark in the majors (excluding new yards for the Baltimore Orioles, the Chicago White Sox, and the Texas Rangers) that has never changed capacity. It has always held 56,000. Though architect Emil Praeger designed the ballpark so the outfield could be enclosed and capacity raised to 85,000, that has never been done. Prime seats can be had for most games on a walk-up basis.

GOOD SEATS
The seats nearly everyone wants are the dugout-level seats right behind the plate. You get serious airtime when you sit there.

BAD SEATS
Counting the club level, five decks rise from behind the plate. If you are in the top deck, you might as well be trying to spot the waves in Malibu for all the distance you are from the field. Top-deck seats in foul ground down the lines are even more daunting. No wonder people leave early—if they get home before the game ends, they might actually see a player. The pavilion seats (a.k.a. the bleachers) are superior to top-deck spots; they're closer to the action, and no alcohol is sold there.

SCALPING
Scalpers line the streets encircling the stadium. Those willing to pay can get premium seats from them, but should have a seating chart for verification and be prepared to pay plenty. After all, this is Los Angeles, and the stadium is just off the Hollywood Freeway. Plenty of high rollers are willing to pay top dollar for a good ticket, so the scalpers have a strong bargaining position.

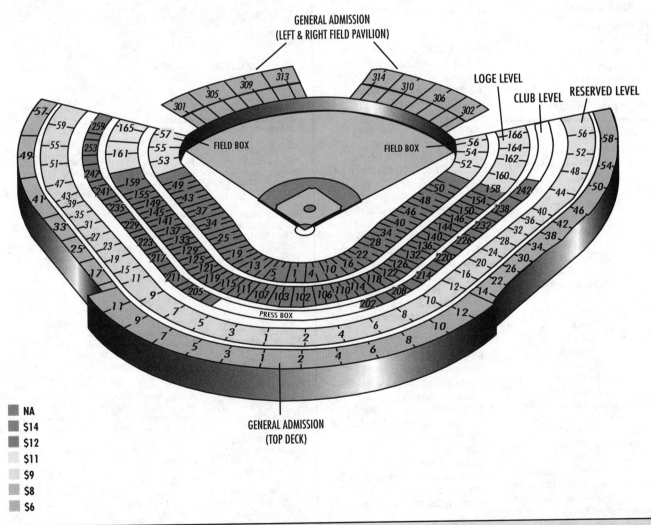

Legend:
- NA
- $14
- $12
- $11
- $9
- $8
- $6

TICKET INFORMATION
Address: 1000 Elysian Park Ave., Los Angeles, CA 90012
Phone: (213) 224-1HIT or TicketMaster at (213) 480-3232
By mail: Send checks or money orders payable to: Ticket Manager, Los Angeles Dodgers, File No. 51100, Los Angeles, CA 90074-1100. Add $3 for handling and mailing.
Hours: Mon.–Sat. 8:30–5:30.
Prices: $14: field box; $12: loge box; $11: loge level; $9: front reserved; $8: back reserved; $6: top deck and pavilion (reserved); $3: top deck and pavilion for children 12 years of age or under (when purchased at the stadium one hour before game time).

Inter-Continental
251 S. Olive St.
Los Angeles, CA 90017
(800) 327 0200/(213) 617-3300
About 2 miles from the stadium.

GETTING TO DODGER STADIUM

Public transportation: There is no public transportation to Dodger Stadium.

By car: From the north, take Freeway 101 south to the Alvarado exit. Turn left and then make a right onto Sunset Boulevard. Continue on Sunset for about 2 miles and make a left onto Elysian Park Avenue. Go 1 mile on Elysian to the stadium. From the south, take Freeway 101 north to the Alvarado exit. Turn right onto Sunset Boulevard and proceed as above.

SPRING TRAINING

Holman Stadium
P.O. Box 2887
4001 26th St.
Vero Beach, FL 32961
Capacity: 6,500
Surface: Grass
Game time: 1:05 p.m.

MINOR LEAGUES

Class	Team
AAA	Albuquerque (NM) Dukes
AA	San Antonio (TX) Missions
A	San Bernadino (CA) Stampede
A	Vero Beach (FL) Dodgers
A	Savannah (GA) Sand Gnats
Short Season A	Yakima (WA) Bears
Rookie	Great Falls (MT) Dodgers

The Dodgers' closest minor-league team is the San Bernardino Stampede of the Class A California League. After winning the California League championship in 1996, the Stampede got a new name (they used to be the Spirit) and a new stadium, a state-of-the-art, 2-tiered, 5,000-seat California Mission style ballpark, The Ranch, in downtown San Bernardino, about 60 miles southeast of Los Angeles. To reach The Ranch from Los

Angeles, take I-10 east to I-215 north, exit, and go right at Mill Street. Turn left on G Street; the stadium will be on the right. **Ticket prices:** $7: executive box; $6: field box; $5 upper box; $4: general admission; $3: children under 12 and senior citizens.
For more information, call (909) 888-9922.

THE DODGERS AT DODGER STADIUM

April 11, 1962: The Dodgers get their first win at Dodger Stadium, beating the Reds 6–2.

Oct. 6, 1963: Sandy Koufax six-hits the Yankees as the Dodgers sweep the World Series.

Sept. 9, 1965: Koufax fires a 1–0 perfect game against the Chicago Cubs, his fourth no-hitter in as many years.

Oct. 14, 1965: Koufax shuts out the Minnesota Twins for the second time, as the Dodgers win Game 7, 2–0, for their fourth World Championship.

June 13, 1973: Steve Garvey, Davey Lopes, Bill Russell, and Ron Cey start together in the Dodgers' infield for the first time, beginning a record 8½-year run.

Sept. 2, 1979: Manny Mota cracks his 145th career pinch-hit in a 6–2 come-from-behind win over the Pittsburgh Pirates, the major-league record.

Sept. 6, 1981: Fernando Valenzuela blanks St. Louis 5–0 for his seventh shutout, tying the record for rookies.

Oct. 15, 1988: Kirk Gibson makes his only appearance in the 1988 World Series, pinch-hitting with two out in the bottom of the ninth, and hits a game-winning two-run homer off Oakland A's closer Dennis Eckersley.

June 4, 1990: Rookie Ramon Martinez fans 18 batters in a victory over the Atlanta Braves, matching Koufax's club high.

July 14, 1995: Ramon Martinez no-hits the Florida Marlins 7–0.

HOME-FIELD ADVANTAGE

Dodger players are used to the rock-hard crushed-brick infield that leads to bad hops. The mound is often alleged to be a little higher than anywhere else, an advantage for pitching, which historically has been a Dodger strength. The outfield corners are sometimes a challenge because of the waist-level fence right at the line, leading to some strange caroms.

The "come late, leave early" ritual is not something the team boasts about, either. Large segments of fans tend to wander in a few innings into the game, possibly because of the traffic or the fashionably late lifestyle of Lotusland. These same people like to leave two or three innings early. They're trying to beat traffic, but traffic is a 24-hour problem in Los Angeles, so what's the point? A team can't get charged up for a late-inning rally when it sees droves of fans walking out.

DODGERS TEAM NOTEBOOK

Franchise history
Brooklyns, 1884–88 (AA); Brooklyn Bridegrooms, 1889 (AA); Brooklyn Bridegrooms 1890–98; Brooklyn Superbas, 1899–1910; Brooklyn Infants, 1911–13; Brooklyn Robins, 1914–31; Brooklyn Dodgers, 1932–57; Los Angeles Dodgers, 1958–present

World Series titles
1955, 1959, 1963, 1965, 1981, 1988

National League pennants
1880, 1899, 1900, 1916, 1920, 1941, 1947, 1949, 1952, 1953, 1955, 1956, 1959, 1963, 1965, 1966, 1974, 1977, 1978, 1981, 1988

Division titles
1974, 1977, 1978, 1981, 1983, 1985, 1988, 1995

Most Valuable Players
Jake Daubert, 1913
Dazzy Vance, 1924
Dolph Camilli, 1941
Jackie Robinson, 1949
Roy Campanella, 1951, 1953, 1955
Don Newcombe, 1956
Maury Wills, 1962
Sandy Koufax, 1963

Steve Garvey, 1974
Kirk Gibson, 1988
Rookies of the Year
Jackie Robinson, 1947
Don Newcombe, 1949
Joe Black, 1952
Jim Gilliam, 1953
Frank Howard, 1960
Jim Lefebvre, 1965
Ted Sizemore, 1969
Rick Sutcliffe, 1979
Steve Howe, 1980
Fernando Valenzuela, 1981
Steve Sax, 1982
Eric Karros, 1992
Mike Piazza, 1993
Raul Mondesi, 1994
Hideo Nomo, 1995

Cy Young Awards
Don Newcombe, 1956
Don Drysdale, 1962
Sandy Koufax, 1963, 1965, 1966
Mike Marshall, 1974
Fernando Valenzuela, 1981
Orel Hershiser, 1988

Hall of Fame
Willie Keeler, 1939
George Sisler, 1939
Dan Brouthers, 1945
Hugh Jennings, 1945
Wilbert Robinson, 1945
Thomas McCarthy, 1946
Joe McGinnity, 1946
Paul Waner, 1952
Rabbit Maranville, 1954
Ted Lyons, 1955
Dazzy Vance, 1955
Zack Wheat, 1959

Max Carey, 1961
Jackie Robinson, 1962
Burleigh Grimes, 1964
Heinie Manush, 1964
Monte Ward, 1964
Casey Stengel, 1966
Branch Rickey, 1967
Lloyd Waner, 1967
Kiki Cuyler, 1968
Joe "Ducky" Medwick, 1968
Roy Campanella, 1969
Waite Hoyt, 1969
Dave Bancroft, 1971
Joe Kelley, 1971
Rube Marquard, 1971
Sandy Koufax, 1972
George Kelly, 1973
Billy Herman, 1975
Fred Lindstrom, 1976
Al Lopez, 1977
Larry MacPhail, 1978
Hack Wilson, 1979
Duke Snider, 1980
Frank Robinson, 1982
Walter Alston, 1983
Juan Marichal, 1983
Don Drysdale, 1984
Pee Wee Reese, 1984
Arky Vaughan, 1985
Hoyt Wilhelm, 1985
Ernie Lombardi, 1986
Tony Lazzeri, 1991
Leo Durocher, 1994

Retired numbers
1 Pee Wee Reese
4 Duke Snider
19 Jim Gilliam
24 Walter Alston
32 Sandy Koufax
39 Roy Campanella
42 Jackie Robinson
53 Don Drysdale

MILWAUKEE BREWERS

Milwaukee County Stadium

STADIUM STATS

Location: 201 S. 46th St., Milwaukee, WI 53201
Opened: April 6, 1953
Surface: Grass
Capacity: 53,192
Outfield dimensions: LF 362, LC 392, CF 402, RC 392, RF 362
Services for fans with disabilities: Seating available in the 35th row of the lower grandstand and in the first row of the bleacher section.

STADIUM FIRSTS

Brewers regular season game: April 7, 1970, 12–0 loss to the California Angels.
Pitcher: Lew Krauss of the Brewers.
Batter: Sandy Alomar of the Angels.

GROUND RULES

• Foul poles and the screens attached are outside the playing field.
• A ball hitting the bats or bat rack is considered in the dugout.
• A ball hitting the facing of the dugout roof is considered in the dugout.
• A ball hitting the cable or above the break on the screen behind home plate is out of play.
• A ball staying under or behind the tarp is out of play; if it rebounds onto the field, it is in play.
• A ball hitting the top of the outfield padding in fair territory and bouncing into stands is two bases.
• A ball hitting the railings of the photographer's well and rebounding is in play; if it bounces into the well or dugout area of stands, the ball is out of play.

Another on the ever-growing list of ballparks slated for oblivion, Milwaukee County Stadium won't be around for baseball in the 21st century. Miller Park, to be erected just southeast of the current stadium, should be completed and ready for play for the 1999 season, thanks to the machinations of Acting Commissioner Bud Selig. If Fenway represents baseball's early days and SkyDome its future, then Milwaukee County Stadium is a snapshot of baseball in the 1950s. It sits next to I-94, several miles from downtown Milwaukee, with towering light poles, real bleachers, and real grass. The city's skyline—church steeples, smokestacks, and all—is visible from the two decks of seats, and on clear nights the Allen Brady Tower's clock hovers like a full moon. There may not be too many tears shed over Milwaukee County Stadium, but the place is crowd-friendly, and does its job without drawing undo attention to itself, two qualities rarely found anywhere in major-league baseball today.

The Brewers have followed tough acts since they moved from Seattle in 1970. Milwaukee fans loved their National League Braves, who moved there from Boston in 1953. With players such as Hall of Famers Henry Aaron, Eddie Mathews, and Warren Spahn, who could blame them? The Braves left for Atlanta in 1966, and Milwaukee fans still miss them.

For the most part, Beer City fans are loyal blue-collar workers with little sympathy for whining millionaire players. They tend to relate more to players with Robin Yount's no-nonsense work ethic or the decidedly nonglamor-boy persona of stubbly-faced Gorman Thomas. What would you expect in a stadium where a home team home run sends a guy in lederhosen sliding into a gigantic mug of beer in center field?

HOT TIPS FOR VISITING FANS

PARKING

County Stadium has 11,000 spaces, and at $5 a space, the price is a bargain. For those interested in a little exercise before sitting down with an Italian sausage, plenty of spaces beyond the stadium are cheaper but require a good hike.

WEATHER

Temperatures can take nasty dips in April and May, so be prepared to dress as if you are attending a Green Bay Packers' football game (though they don't have those here anymore). September afternoons are beautiful. The most relaxing time to attend is in the sunshine of a weekday afternoon.

MEDIA

Radio: WTMJ (620 AM). Jim Powell has joined Bob Uecker—a local hero who has made a second career out of his lack of playing ability—in the broadcast booth.
TV: WVTV (Channel 18). Jim Paschke and ex-Brewer Bill Schroeder announce the games for television.

CUISINE

Brats and brewskis. Before a game, clouds of smoke and the aroma of fired-up grills linger in the stadium's parking lots as tailgate parties swirl around RVs, pickup trucks, and the trunks of cars. The bratwursts are out of this world. First they're browned on a grill for 10 minutes, then put into a mixture of beer, green peppers, and onions to cook for a half hour or so. Pop open a beer and experience a true Wisconsin tradition. Inside, the Brewers feature baseball's best bratwurst—with a secret sauce so popular that it's sold in supermarkets throughout Wisconsin—and Italian and Polish sausages. Other popular items include corned beef, steak, roast-beef sandwiches, fresh-dough pizza, garlic bread, and meatball subs.

Not surprisingly, County Stadium features Milwaukee's hometown beer, Miller. Milwaukee has always meant beer, though (why do you think they're called the Brewers?), so instead of singing "Take Me Out to the Ball Game" during the seventh-inning stretch, Brewers fans sing "Roll Out the Barrel." It doesn't stop there. "Bernie Brewer" lives in a chalet just above a giant-sized stein of beer beyond the center-field bleachers. Every time the Brewers hit a home run or win a game, Bernie slides down a chute into the beer stein.

Former Brewer Gorman Thomas now runs Gorman's Grill, which is accessible from the park during games. Those who want to find Brewers fans to talk baseball with before and after the game should check out Kelly's Bleachers, just outside gate 6, or Saz's (414-453-2410), a rib restaurant 1 mile north of the stadium. The specialty is a rack of ribs with Saz's own barbecue sauce. Saz's has parking and runs buses to Brewers games. Luke's Sports Bar (414-223-3210) is popular with the Brewers and opposing players; check out the 50 television sets and three bars with different sports themes.

In the Hot Seats at Milwaukee County Stadium

Good seats are almost always available for a walk-up fan. Normally, the Brewers have two and three times as many seats as fans. That fact, of course, kills the scalping market. The toughest ticket is Opening Day, no matter how wet, cold, and snowy Wisconsin's weather may be.

GOOD SEATS

Outfield seats are all bleachers, but the best of the bleachers are in right field. They overlook the action in the bullpen—from reliev-ers loosening up to sunflower-seed-spitting contests. The left-field bleachers are good, too, but they don't have the bullpen view. In the afternoon, both sets of bleachers are great for working on a tan.

The upper deck has no bad seats. You can see the field and the whole city of Milwaukee. Sections J and K are non-smoking and non-drinking, making them favorites for families.

BAD SEATS

The worst seats in the house are the four or five rows in the back of the first deck. Because of the second deck's overhang, long fly balls get cut from view. But hey, because the stadium is virtually empty, just move. Some seats are directly behind a pole, but they're seldom sold.

SCALPING

Because of ticket availability, not much of a market exists.

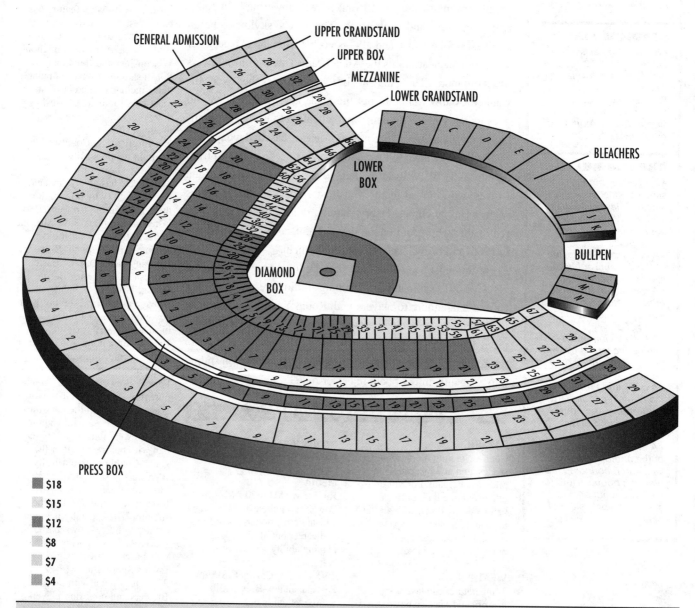

$18
$15
$12
$8
$7
$4

TICKET INFORMATION
Address: 201 S. 46th St., Milwaukee, WI 53201
Phone: (414) 933-1818

Hours: Mon.–Fri. 9–7, Sat. 9–5, Sun. 11–3.
Prices: $18: deluxe mezzanine, mezzanine diamond, lower-box diamond; $15: mezzanine, lower box; $12: upper box, lower grandstand; $8: upper grandstand; $7: general admission; $4: bleachers.

LODGING NEAR THE STADIUM

Pfister Hotel
424 E. Wisconsin Ave.
Milwaukee, WI 53201
(414) 273-8222/(800) 558-8222
About 2 miles from the stadium.

Hyatt Regency
333 W. Kilbourn Ave.
Milwaukee, WI 53201
(414) 276-1234/(800) 233-1234
About 4 miles from the stadium.

GETTING TO MILWAUKEE COUNTY STADIUM

Public transportation: On game days, a special bus line, No. 99, runs along Wisconsin Avenue directly to County Stadium. For more information, call (414) 344-6711.
By car: From the north, go south on U.S. 41 to the County Stadium exit.
From the south, take U.S. 41 north, and enter the stadium at gate 6.
From the west, take I-94 east to the County Stadium exit. Enter the stadium at gate 1.
From the east, take I-94 west to U.S. 41. Continue south on U.S. 41 and enter the stadium at gate 6.

SPRING TRAINING

Campadre Stadium
4001 S. Alma School Rd.
Chandler, AZ 85248
(602) 895-6000
Capacity: More than 10,000
Surface: Grass
Game time: 1 p.m.

MINOR LEAGUES

Class	Team
AAA	New Orleans Zephyrs
AA	El Paso (TX) Diablos
A	Stockton (CA) Ports
A	Beloit (WI) Snappers
Rookie	Helena (MT) Brewers
Rookie	Chandler (AZ) Brewers

The Brewers' closest minor-league affiliate is the Class A

Beloit Snappers of the Midwest League. After the 1905 season, in which Beloit's entry in the Class D Wisconsin Association won 50 of 109 games and finished 18 games behind first-place La Crosse, the community's team left town. Beloit was without baseball for 75 years, until 1982, when the minor leagues returned.
To reach Beloit's Pohlman Field, approximately 45 miles from Milwaukee, exit at Route 81 west from I-90. Take 81 to Cranston Road. Turn right and head to Pohlman Field.
Ticket prices: $4: reserved seats; $3: general admission. For more information, call (608) 362-2272.

THE BRAVES AND BREWERS AT MILWAUKEE COUNTY STADIUM

May 26, 1959: Harvey Haddix of the Pittsburgh Pirates pitches 12 perfect innings against the Milwaukee Braves, but he loses 1–0 in the 13th.

May 6, 1970: The Brewers notch their first home win, behind pitcher Bob Bolin.

June 19, 1974: Steve Busby of the Kansas City Royals no-hits the Brewers.

July 15, 1975: Bill Madlock drives in two runs in the ninth to win the 46th All-Star Game for the National League.

July 20, 1976: Hank Aaron hits his 755th and last home run, off Dick Drago of the California Angels.

Aug. 27, 1982: The Oakland A's Rickey Henderson breaks Lou Brock's single-season record when he steals his 119th base. He finishes the season with 130.

Oct. 10, 1982: Cecil Cooper singles in two runs in the seventh that put the Brewers ahead for good in Game 5 of the ALCS. The

HOME-FIELD ADVANTAGE

Except for the temperature, which can turn a baseball crowd into a football crowd as late as June, no stadium is more neutral than County Stadium, despite frequent remodelings and a complete reseeding of the field in 1995. The outfield fences are nondescript and the infield grass is level, but ever try to hit a baseball with a wooden bat when it's freezing? Opposing teams dread coming into Milwaukee when it's cold. Brewers players don't care for it either, but they have become used to hot-water bottles in the on-deck circle.

At the ripe old age of 43, County Stadium finds itself on the endangered-species list. The Brewers' new home, Miller Park, has long been planned but was hampered by a variety of obstacles that delayed groundbreaking. These have now been overcome, and the Brewers should be in their new digs on time for the next millennium.

BREWERS TEAM NOTEBOOK

Franchise history	Division title	Cy Young Awards
Seattle Pilots, 1969; Milwaukee Brewers, 1970–present	1982	Rollie Fingers, 1981 Peter Vuckovich, 1982
	Most Valuable Players	
American League pennant 1982	Rollie Fingers, 1981 Robin Yount, 1982, 1989	**Retired numbers** 34 Rollie Fingers 44 Hank Aaron 19 Robin Yount

Brewers beat the California Angels 4–3.

Oct. 16, 1982: The Brewers get their first home win in the World Series, 10–2 over the St. Louis Cardinals in Game 4.

July 31, 1990: Nolan Ryan gets his 300th win, beating the Brewers 11–3.

September 14, 1991: Cecil Fielder hits the longest home run in County Stadium history—502 feet, over the left-field bleachers.

Sept. 9, 1992: Robin Yount gets his 3,000th hit, off the Cleveland Indians' Jose Mesa, becoming the third-youngest player to reach that milestone.

MINNESOTA TWINS

HHH Metrodome

The billowy roof looks like one of Grandma's lemon-meringue pies against the Minneapolis skyline. Inside, thousands of blue seats rise above the green turf in a cramped stadium that has nothing but basic necessities. No flash, no extra conveniences. Except for a muddy replay board, high technology is nonexistent.

Minnesota's Hubert H. Humphrey Metrodome—named for the state's favorite son, a former U.S. vice president—is everything Minnesota isn't. The·state's favorite activities are outdoors. It leads the nation in fishing and snowmobile licenses, and the boundary waters in northern Minnesota offer the most breathtaking recreation scenery in the world. Given their love of fresh air and weather, local baseball fans had trouble parting with Metropolitan Stadium, a classic ballpark from the 1960s.

The Twins, though, belong to more than Minnesota. Twins fever runs high along the country roads of the Dakotas and battles with Cubs fever in Iowa's small towns and Wisconsin's dairy farms. The Dome was built for these out-of-state fans who appreciate the roof because they can make four- and five-hour one-way trips without having to worry about rainouts.

Players don't appreciate the stadium, though. They detest the turf, poor lighting, and size. Home runs crash into the 7,600 retractable football seats that hang like vultures in right field. A 16-foot tarp, known as the "trash bag," extends the height of the right-field fence to 23 feet. The seats are better situated for football, and the stadium is remarkably loud.

All this adds up to a less-than-premier baseball viewing experience. But then again, you won't get wet if you drove all the way from Watertown, South Dakota.

HOT TIPS FOR VISITING FANS

PARKING
Arrive early and park a block or two from the Metrodome on the street, using eight-hour meters. The cost is $3, about half of what it costs for a parking lot or garage. If the metered spaces aren't available, park far away from the stadium and enjoy a nice walk in a clean, safe city. In most cases, the closer fans park to the Metrodome, the better chance they have of getting clogged in postgame traffic. Some parking lots are situated so fans can use walkways over the Mississippi River.

WEATHER
Not a problem, unless you park several blocks away and have a long walk in early April or late September. Even with football weather outdoors, inside the dome is always 68–70 degrees. Even dome games, though, can be postponed because of weather: On April 14, 1983, heavy snowfall caved in the air-inflated roof, causing the Metrodome's only postponement.

MEDIA
Radio: WCCO (830 AM). Play-by-play man Herb Carneal is as much a part of Twins history as Oliva, Killebrew, and Carew. He shares the microphone with John Gordon.

TV: WCCO (Channel 4). Al Newman, Tommy John, Dick Bremer, and Bob Carpenter are the announcers, and former Twins pitcher Bert Blyleven stops by frequently to act as guest commentator and color man.

CUISINE
The Metrodome offers basic baseball food: hot dogs, beer, pop, pizza, popcorn, and snow cones. The place hasn't—yet—been overrun with fast-food franchises. The burger stands behind home plate offer delicious hamburgers and crisp onion rings. Other stands offer a kids specialty—a hot dog, chips, soft drink with licorice straw, and a surprise snack, all in a pail with Twins logo for $3.75. Though nothing is special about his beer, local fans actually get a charge out of buying their cold ones from Wally the Beerman. He has a deep "beer here" voice, but other than that, he pours his beers like any other beer vendor in the country. Still, Wally has become a local hero and a virtual institution, with his own baseball card and T-shirt, and he plugs local liquor stores on TV. He's available for birthdays and weddings parties, too.

For a meal or a drink before or after a game, head over a few blocks to the cluster of 19 restaurants at the City Center mall at 7th Street and Hennepin Avenue. The Mall of America, the nation's largest retail and amusement park, is in Bloomington at the site of the Twins' old park. The mall has 430 stores, roller-coaster rides, and Knott's Camp Snoopy. The location of Metropolitan Stadium's home plate is marked, as is the location of the seat that marks the longest home run hit in Met Stadium, by Hall of Famer Harmon Killebrew.

LODGING NEAR THE STADIUM

Hyatt Regency
1300 Nicollet Mall
Minneapolis, MN 55403
(612) 370-1234/(800) 233-1234
15 blocks from the stadium.

STADIUM STATS
Location: 501 Chicago Ave. S., Minneapolis, MN 55415
Opened: April 3, 1982
Surface: AstroTurf
Capacity: 56,144
Outfield dimensions: LF 343, LC 385, CF 408, RC 367, RF 327
Services for fans with disabilities: Seating available in the upper and lower decks.

STADIUM FIRSTS
Regular-season game: April 6, 1982, 11–7 loss to the Seattle Mariners.
Pitcher: Peter Redfern of the Twins.
Batter: Julio Cruz of the Mariners.
Hit: Dave Engle of the Twins.
Home run: Dave Engle.

GROUND RULES
• Foul poles are in fair territory.
• Balls that hit the roof or speakers in fair territory. If the ball is caught by a fielder, the batter is out and base runners advance at their own risk.
• A ball hitting the roof or speakers in fair territory shall be judged fair or foul in relation to where it hits the ground or is touched by a fielder.
• Any ball that hits the speaker or roof in foul territory is a foul ball; however, if the ball is caught by a fielder, the batter is out and base runners advance at their own risk.
• A ball that hits a speaker in foul territory and ricochets back into fair territory is still a foul ball; if the ball is caught by a fielder, the batter is out and the base runners advance at their own risk.

In the Hot Seats at the HHH Metrodome

Twins tickets sell well, but walk up to the ticket office on virtually any game day and tickets will be available.

GOOD SEATS

The best seats for baseball are between sections 119 and 132 in the first deck and 220–229 in the second deck. These seats offer the best possible view of the diamond. If you can't get a ticket for "the baseball section," the next-best location is left field, particularly sections 141, 100, and 101. Get seats at least 10 rows up in the middle of the row. They'll give a straight view of the field, and you won't have to stand up every time another fan wants to leave. Also, if you're 10 rows up, you'll be over the Plexiglas atop the left-field seats. For a cheap ticket with a cheap view, try the right-field seats. Arrive early and chase home-run balls from batting practice. But plan on watching the replay of any plays in right on TV—the right fielder can't be seen from these seats.

BAD SEATS

This is primarily a football stadium, so bad baseball seats abound. The outfield seats, aside from those mentioned above, are way out there, and try to stay out of anything in the upper decks that's not in the first couple rows. In sections 133–135 or 229–232 down the left-field line or sections 116–118 or 217–220 down the right-field line, make sure not to get an aisle seat. Vendors and fans constantly block the view by walking in front of the seats.

SPECIAL PLANS

The Metrodome doesn't have rowdy fans, but section 231, in the second deck just beyond third base, is a no-alcohol family section. Thirteen knothole days (all Sundays) are sponsored by SuperAmerica. An adult who buys a $4 general admission ticket gets two free tickets to be used by kids 14 or under.

SCALPING

Scalpers are plentiful but, because of competition, are usually not much of a factor. Perhaps because of the low-key, hardworking honesty of the Midwest, season ticketholders sell their extra tickets at cost outside the door.

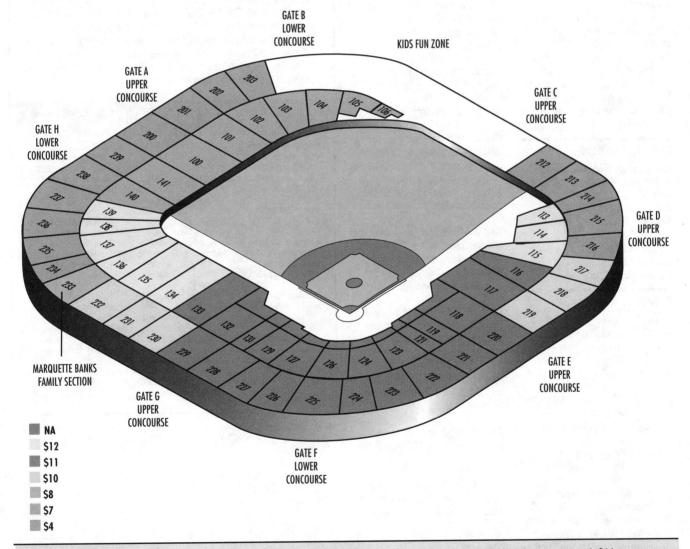

Legend:
- NA
- $12
- $11
- $10
- $8
- $7
- $4

TICKET INFORMATION
Address: 500 11th Ave. S., Minneapolis, MN 55415
Phone: (612) 375-7444 or (612) 375-1116; for charges, call (612) 33-TWINS or (800) 33-TWINS
Hours: Mon.–Fri. 9–5, Sat. 9–4, 9–9 when night games are scheduled.
Prices: $12: lower reserved; $11: upper club; $10: upper reserved; $8: lower-deck general admission; $4: upper-deck general admission.

The Minneapolis City Center
30 S. Seventh St.
Minneapolis, MN 55402
(612) 349-4000/(800) 228-9290
2 miles from the stadium.

GETTING TO THE HHH METRODOME

Public transportation: A shuttle bus operates from downtown Minneapolis one hour before and one hour after well-attended games. Stops are marked with shuttle bus signs. To check the schedule, call (612) 349-7000.
By car: From the south, drive north on I-35 west to the Third Street exit. Continue on Third to stadium lots.
From the north, head south on I-35 west to the Washington Avenue exit. Turn left onto Washington, then left onto Chicago Avenue. Continue to the stadium.
From the east, go west on I-94. Exit onto Fifth Street. The stadium is visible.
From the west, take I-394 East to the Fourth Street exit. Head east and turn on any street west of the Metrodome for parking. Or go east on I-94 and follow Fourth Street north signs.

SPRING TRAINING

Lee County Sports Complex
14100 Six Mile Cypress Pkwy.
Fort Myers, FL 33912
(941) 768-4280
South of Fort Myers, Florida, near I-75
Capacity: 7,500
Surface: Grass
Game time: 1:05 p.m.

MINOR LEAGUES

Class	Team
AAA	Salt Lake City Buzz
AA	Hardware City (CT) Rock Cats
A	Fort Myers (FL) Miracle
A	Fort Wayne (IN) Wizards
Rookie	Elizabethton (TN) Twins
Rookie	Fort Myers (FL) Twins

The nearest minor-league team to Minneapolis is the Class A Wisconsin Timber Rattlers (formerly the Appleton Foxes), of Appleton, Wisconsin, an affiliate of the Seattle Mariners. Rattlers Stadium is built with both the players and fans in mind; grassy knolls just beyond first and third allow fans to watch from blankets or folding chairs, and the stadium's open concourse makes it possible to keep track of the game while you're at the concession stands. Home-run hitters will have to give it their all to hit one out of this park: The 16-foot-high right-center wall is a daunting 405 feet from home. To reach Rattlers Stadium, 250 miles from Minneapolis, take the Wisconsin Avenue exit west off U.S. 41, and turn right onto Casaloma Drive, the ballpark is on the right.
Ticket prices: $5: box seats; $4: reserved; $3: general admission.

THE TWINS AT THE METRODOME

July 27, 1983: Ben Oglivie of the Milwaukee Brewers hits the longest homer at the Metrodome, a 481-foot shot to the second deck.

Oct. 25, 1987: Frank Viola gets the win as the Twins take Game 7 and the World Series against the St. Louis Cardinals.

Oct. 27, 1991: In what has been called the greatest of all World Series games, the Twins break a scoreless tie in the bottom of the 10th to win Game 7 against the Atlanta Braves.

Aug. 31, 1993: The Twins play the longest game at the Metrodome, beating the Indians 5–4 on a Pedro Muñoz homer in the bottom of the 22nd inning.

Sept. 16, 1993: Dave Winfield gets his 3,000th hit off Dennis Eckersley, in an 8–3 loss to the Oakland A's.

April 8, 1994: Kirby Puckett gets his 2,000th hit, off Bobby Witt of Oakland.

April 27, 1994: Scott Erickson no-hits the Brewers. The Twins win 6–0.

June 30, 1995: Eddie Murray gets his 3,000th hit, off Twins pitcher Mike Trombley.

HOME-FIELD ADVANTAGE

Four factors give the Twins a definite edge when they have a team that can take advantage of them:

The noise: The Metrodome can be deafening. During the 1987 and 1991 World Series, some St. Louis and Atlanta players wore earplugs to try to block thundering sounds that rivaled an airplane's decibel level. The Twins, by the way, took both World Series, winning all eight games at home.

The ceiling: This is the only stadium where an outfielder can't take his eye off a fly ball. General rule: At least one Twins fly ball each series is lost in the roof by opposing outfielders. The roof is white, but the lights cast eerie shadows that demand major adjustments by outfielders.

The center-field fence: The outfield fence in center field is 7 feet high, and that makes for the acrobatic, home-run-robbing catches that Kirby Puckett made famous.

Weird ground rules: The speakers are in play. So is the roof, 195 feet at its highest point above the playing field. Dave Kingman once hit a ball into the roof while he was with the A's. The ball never came down, so it was ruled a ground-rule double. On the other hand, Twins DH Chili Davis hit a ball that would have been a home run to right until it hit a speaker and was caught by Baltimore second baseman Mark McLemore, proving that the Metrodome doesn't always play favorites.

TWINS TEAM NOTEBOOK

Franchise history
Washington Senators, 1901–60;
Minnesota Twins, 1961–present

World Series titles
1924, 1987, 1991

American League pennants
1924, 1925, 1933, 1965, 1987, 1991

Division titles
1969, 1970, 1987, 1991

Most Valuable Players
Walter Johnson 1913, 1924
Roger Peckinpaugh, 1925

Zoilo Versalles, 1965
Harmon Killebrew, 1969
Rod Carew, 1977

Rookies of the Year
Albie Pearson, 1958
Bob Allison, 1959
Tony Oliva, 1964
Rod Carew, 1967
John Castino, 1979 (tie)
Chuck Knoblauch, 1991
Marty Cordova, 1995

Cy Young Awards
Jim Perry, 1970
Frank Viola, 1988

Hall of Fame
Walter Johnson, 1936
Tris Speaker, 1937
George Sisler, 1939

Ed Delahanty, 1945
Clark Griffith, 1946
Al Simmons, 1953
Joe Cronin, 1956
Sam Rice, 1963
Heinie Manush, 1964
Goose Goslin, 1968
Stan Coveleski, 1969
Lefty Gomez, 1972
Early Wynn, 1972
Bucky Harris, 1975
Harmon Killebrew, 1984
Rick Ferrell, 1984
Rod Carew, 1991
Steve Carlton, 1994

Retired numbers
3 Harmon Killebrew
6 Tony Oliva
14 Kent Hrbek
29 Rod Carew

MONTREAL EXPOS

Olympic Stadium

ance 80.

STADIUM FIRSTS

Regular-season game:
April 15, 1977, 7–2 loss to
the Philadelphia Phillies.
Pitcher: Don Stanhouse
of the Expos.
Batter: Jay Johnstone of
the Phillies.
Home run: Ellis Valentine
of the Expos.

GROUND RULES

• A ball hitting the con-
crete rim below the roof
on the outfield side of the
yellow line is a home
run.
• A ball hitting the overhanging speakers in fair
territory is a home run.
• A ball hitting the orange
roof is in play.
• A ball hitting the con-
crete rim below the roof
on the home-plate side of
the yellow line is out of
play (foul ball).
• Everything in play
except:
  • a ball entering the
  dugout;
  • pop up or fly ball hit
  into any one of the four
  designated camera
  areas;
  • a ball crossing the line
  at the entrance to the
  corridor leading from
  the dugout to the club-
  house. If the ball hits
  the overhanging speak-
  ers in foul territory it is
  a dead ball.

A Montreal Expos game is the closest thing you'll find in the major leagues to European baseball. The French-speaking city's European flavor is apparent even in the sterile confines of Olympic Stadium. Pitchers are *lanceurs,* the shortstop is the *arrêt-court,* and a balk is a *feinte irregulière.*

The fans here are polite and even a bit restrained. It could be their Canadian nature, or it could be the recent yo-yo fortunes of their team. Whatever the reason, the atmosphere here can be less electric than most fans in the States are accustomed to, although attendance is up again, due in part to baseball's growing popularity among Canadian teenagers. The blandness of the stadium doesn't help much, though the club and the stadium authorities have tried to make improvements to the ambience. Home plate was moved 40 feet closer to the backstop to improve sight lines and bring fans closer to the action. The outfield bleachers also were moved and brought behind the fences in left and right fields. A faraway section in center field was closed, and a new, larger scoreboard with a video board was installed. It's not homey, but it's an improvement.

Other improvements are awaited. The stadium was designed for the 1976 Olympics, and the plan included a retractable fabric roof, but the tower and roof weren't completed until 1987. Since then, retracting the roof has proved troublesome—the canvas-like surface has torn in the process. The dome is now on most of the time. A permanent roof is a distant promise.

Such problems aren't new here. In September 1991, a 55-ton block of concrete dropped from the side of the stadium, forcing its closure. The Expos had to play the final 13 games of their home schedule on the road.

The stadium is a marvel from a distance. With its lights on at night, it looks like a huge flying saucer. Public tours are available, and a cable car whisks you to the top of the world's largest inclined tower for an excellent view of the city.

HOT TIPS FOR VISITING FANS

PARKING
Olympic Stadium brags that it has Canada's largest indoor parking garage under the stadium—space for 4,000 vehicles, at C$8 for games. You can also park in street lots for C$7, and there's plenty of outdoor parking on steets and lots within ½ mile of the park.

WEATHER
Summers are generally cool and

pleasant in Montreal, but early or late in the season, pack a sweater at least. The park itself is domed and climate-controlled.

MEDIA
Radio: CIQC (600 AM), with Dave Van Horne, Ken Singleton, Elliott Price, Richard Griffin, and Mike Stenhouse, is the English-language flagship station. CKAC (730 AM) is the

French-language flagship, with Jacques Doucet, Rodger Brulotte, and Alain Chantelois.
TV: The Sports Network (TSN, national cable) with Van Horne and Singleton, is in English. CBFT (Channel 2) and RDS (cable) broadcast in French.

CUISINE
C'est magnifique! OK, that might be a slight exaggeration, but it's very good. You won't find authentic French cooking at the Big O, but an excellent variety of ballpark food is available. The main food court is on the 100 level behind home plate. Smoked meat, a Montreal specialty that (according to one New Yorker) is a cross between corned beef and pastrami, is available at Briskets. Another tasty dish is Kojax Sou-flaki; it's souvlaki, but that's not the French spelling—they say that's the way it's pronounced. It's served as a sandwich or plate, in chicken or beef, and is a favorite of the ballpark employ-ees, which says something. Also popular are the Expos Burger and Poulet Frix Kentucky (Kentucky Fried Chicken). Ice cream, pas-tries, hot dogs, and Cordero wine from Chile are also available at individual stands.
Rusty's, a sit-down restaurant/ sports bar, is located on the 100 level between home and third base. The bar area is decorated with dozens of old photos of the team. The place is named after Rusty Staub, one of the most pop-ular players in team history, who also happens to be a gourmet chef. For the kids, Expo Fest, a base-ball amusement area, is on the 100 level down the left-field line. *Le cage des frappeurs* (batting cage), a radar gun pitching cage, and video games are featured. Olympic Stadium is just outside downtown Montreal, and the size of the complex doesn't lend itself to sports bars nearby. Most fans ready for entertainment head downtown, a 15- to 20-minute Metro ride or a $10–$15 cab ride. Crescent Street has several excel-lent spots, from the distinguished Les Halles (514-844-2328) restaurant for a late dinner, to the

In the Hot Seats at Olympic Stadium

Expos tickets are never in great demand, even when the team is winning. You usually can walk up and obtain a good seat.

GOOD SEATS

Field-level box seats on the infield between home and third base or between home and first are called the VIP section and feature waiter service at your seat. The new seats (complete with cupholders) are bigger and much more comfortable than the rest and provide an excellent view of the game. They cost C$25 a pop. Most, but not all, are bought by season ticketholders. Sit in one of the "regular" seats and you half expect to see Captain Kirk next to you. Made in the futuristic mode of the 1970s, they're small and made of mold-

ed plastic in pastel colors. Still, they're much more comfortable than they look.

BAD SEATS

Even with the restructuring of the playing field, many seats are a long way from the action. Avoid the higher rows in the C$19 seats on the 100 level. Technically they're boxes, but think of them as lower reserve. The upper deck is also quite high, so when you get to the top rows there you might feel closer to the roof than to the batter's box. Montreal is a hockey town, something you're reminded of on the 100 level. A walkway separates lower boxes from mid-level boxes. In front of the first row of the mid-level seats, a pane of Plexiglas protects fans (pre-

sumably from foul balls). If you don't like sitting behind the glass at hockey games, avoid these seats. Also, some of the lower rows in the upper reserve have a view obstructed by safety crossbars.

SCALPING

Though technically a no-no, scalping is out in the open, and the bigger the game, the more visible the hawkers. They greet fans on the walk from the subway to the stadium and in the lobby area by the souvenir shop. Big regular-season games have commanded C$40 and up for a box seat (about double the face value), depending on the location, but how well things are going on the field will ultimately dictate the price.

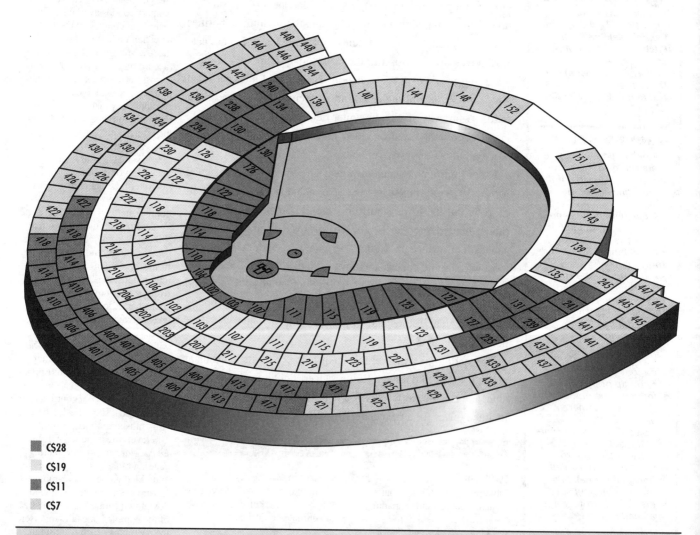

- ■ C$28
- ■ C$19
- ■ C$11
- ■ C$7

TICKET INFORMATION

Address: 4549 av. Pierre de Coubertin, Montreal, PQ, Canada H1V 3N7

By phone: (514) 8GO-EXPOS or Admission at (514) 790-1245 (in Montreal), (800) 361-4595 (elsewhere in Canada), or (800) 678-5440 (in the U.S.A.).

By mail: P.O. Box 500, Station M, Montreal, PQ, H1V 3P2, Canada. Send check or money order payable to Montreal Baseball Club, Inc. There is a C$4 service charge for mail orders.

Hours: Mon.–Sat. 9–5, and until an hour before home games.

Prices: C$28: president's club, loges, VIP box seats; C$19: box seats; C$11: terrace; C$7: general admission. A C$2 discount applies to wheelchair-accessible seating, to children 15 or under, and to senior citizens 65 or over.

Hard Rock Cafe (514-987-1420). And of course, sightseers will want to visit Old Montreal and the port. For deli fare, Dunn's (514-866-4377) downtown is popular. A reminder: Many of the nicer spots require gentlemen to wear a jacket.

LODGING NEAR THE STADIUM

Le Centre Sheraton
1201 blvd. René-Lévesque
Montreal, PQ P3H 2L7
Canada
(514) 878-2000/(800) 325-3535
About 3 miles from the stadium.

Days Inn
1005 rue Guy
Montreal, PQ H3A 2K4
Canada
(514) 938-4611/(800) 329-7466
About 8 miles from the stadium.

GETTING TO OLYMPIC STADIUM

Public transportation: Metro trains run daily from downtown Montreal to the Olympic Stadium's Pie IX station.
By car: From the United States, take I-87 north from New York to Quebec Highway 15. Take Highway 15 through Montreal to the Jacques Cartier Bridge. Stay left as you exit. Continue to the first stop light and turn right onto Sherbrooke Street. Continue on Sherbrooke to the stadium.
From farther west, take I-81 north to the Canadian Highway 401. Take 401 east to Quebec Highway 20. Go north to Highway 40. Take Highway 40 to the boulevard Pie IX exit south. Proceed to the stadium.
From Ontario, take Highway 417 east to Quebec Highway 40 north. Take 40 north to the boulevard Pie IX exit south. Proceed to the stadium.

SPRING TRAINING

Municipal Stadium
715 Hank Aaron Dr.
West Palm Beach, FL 33401
(407) 684-6801
Capacity: 7,500
Surface: Grass
Game time: 1:05 p.m.

MINOR LEAGUES

Class	Team
AAA	Ottawa Lynx
AA	Harrisburg (PA) Senators
A	West Palm Beach (FL) Expos
A	Burlington (IA) Bees
Short Season A	Vermont Expos
Rookie	West Palm Beach (FL) Expos

The Expos' closest minor-league affiliate is the Class AAA Ottawa Lynx of the International League. After a 38-year absence, pro baseball received a big reception upon its return to Ottawa in 1993. That season, the Lynx were second among all minor league teams in attendance, attracting 663,926 fans. The team's nickname was selected for a uniquely Canadian reason: lynx, the name for a type of cat found in northern Canada, is spelled the same in English and French.
To reach Ottawa's stadium, approximately 130 miles from Montreal, take route 417 to the Vanier Parkway. Go over the overpass and turn right on Coventry Road. The ballpark will be on your right.
Ticket prices: C$8.45 and C$6.35: field box seats; C$4.25: reserved seats. For more information, call (613) 747-5969.

THE EXPOS AT OLYMPIC STADIUM

May 20, 1978: Willie Stargell of the Pittsburgh Pirates hits a 535-foot home run into the second deck of right field.

May 10, 1981: Charlie Lea no-hits the San Francisco Giants 4–0.

Oct. 19, 1981: Rick Monday of the Los Angeles Dodgers hits a two-out home run in the ninth to give the Dodgers a 2–1 win over the Expos in the deciding Game 5 of the NLCS.

July 13, 1982: Olympic Stadium hosts the first All-Star Game to be played outside the U.S.A.

HOME-FIELD ADVANTAGE

While the ball carries well in the dome in the summer months, Olympic Stadium is not a home-run hitters' park. As such, the Expos generally build a ballclub around speed and moderate power. The Expos' base-stealing tradition was etablished by Ron LeFlore and Tim Raines and carried on recently by Marquis Grissom and Delino De Shields; the team often has several players with 15 home runs and 15 stolen bases a year. Generally, the crowds are small. The dome, of course, is a major factor. During big games with good attendance, the place can actually rock with the best of them. The Expos usually are about five games a year better at Olympic Stadium, but five times since 1982 they've had a better record on the road than at home.

EXPOS TEAM NOTEBOOK

Franchise history	Rookies of the Year	Retired numbers
Montreal Expos, 1969–present	Carl Morton, 1970	8 Gary Carter
	Andre Dawson, 1977	10 Rusty Staub
Division title		
1981		

April 4, 1988: The New York Mets' Darryl Strawberry hits a 525-foot home run off the lip of the roof in right field.

Aug. 23, 1989: The Expos lose the longest game in their history to the Dodgers 1–0. The game lasts 22 innings and includes the ejection of Expos mascot Youppi! in the 11th.

May 23, 1991: Tommy Greene of the Philadelphia Phillies no-hits the Expos 2–0.

Sept. 28, 1995: Greg Harris becomes the first pitcher in this century to throw both left- and right-handed in a game.

Shea Stadium

OK, this isn't The House That Stengel Built. The only monument in the outfield is a giant top hat with an apple inside. Shea Stadium will never have the history and tradition of its crosstown neighbor in the Bronx, and at 30-plus years old it's showing some age, but overall it's a fine ballpark. Built as a dual-purpose facility (and home to the NFL Jets until 1984), Shea is now a baseball-only stadium and is better for it.

Named after New York lawyer William A. Shea, who helped bring the National League back to the city after the Dodgers and the Giants left, it was one of the first dual-purpose stadiums with movable box seats to rotate between football and baseball configurations. The Mets moved to the new park in the third year of their existence; the 1969 World Series upset of Baltimore and the dramatic come-from-behind victory over Boston in Game 6 of the 1986 Series have helped create a lore for the park, if not a strong sense of history.

Shea's main landmark is the huge scoreboard in right-center field. The 86-foot-high, 175-foot-long structure was originally called the Stadiarama Scoreboard (it was the '60s, folks). On the top was a rear-projection screen that was used to display full-color slides of players at night games—a breakthrough at the time. But the screen was used only sporadically and was eventually replaced by a display depicting the New York skyline. The large part of the old matrix board is now a beer ad. A Diamond Vision video replay board is in left-center field, and the top hat (from which the "Big Apple" pops up when a Met homers) is in center.

Watching baseball in New York is an interactive experience—the fans are part of the show. The local faithful are extremely knowledgeable and are not shy about sharing their insights. For the most part, the play-by-play from the stands is funny and relatively good-natured. The vocabulary is not always PG, however. Overall, the atmosphere is pure baseball—the smell of hot dogs permeates the park, and the chatter centers on the game, not that day's Dow Jones Industrial Average.

HOT TIPS FOR VISITING FANS

PARKING
About 8,000 spaces are available in stadium parking, at $6. For heavy crowds, secondary lots are opened across Roosevelt Avenue. Very limited on-street parking is within walking distance, but vandalism makes it inadvisable.

Check the dates of the U.S. Tennis Open next door at Flushing Meadows, and proceed on those days with fair warning: It's a logjam. Some New Yorkers avoid going to Shea during tennis time. If you have to be there, consider taking public transportation, because you might end up being routed to alternate parking several blocks from the park.

If you're visiting New York and driving to Shea, get a map and plan the route. New York's expressways can be a maze to the uninitiated, but they're well marked if you know where you're going. (It also helps to know which bridge or tunnel is located in the direction you want to head, because signs are frequently marked that way). Crime on New York subways is publicized worldwide, but most New Yorkers feel that if you come and go with the ballpark crowd, you shouldn't have any problem.

WEATHER
Like the rest of the Northeast, New York can have wet, chilly springs, and day games in the summer can be scorchers. Shea usually doesn't get as hot as midtown, however, so this is often the perfect place to be on a stifling summer afternoon.

MEDIA
Radio: WFAN (660 AM) is the radio flagship with Hall of Fame announcer Bob Murphy, along with Gary Cohen and Ed Coleman. **TV:** WWOR (Channel 9) or SportsChannel (cable). Former slugger Ralph Kiner does play-by-play, and Tim McCarver is nationally known for his insightful color commentary. Gary Thorne and Fran Healy also contribute.

CUISINE
Specialty stands offer deli sandwiches and the like. But if you want a real taste of New York, try one of the knishes and the Kahn's hot dogs. Pizza Hut supplies the slices, and Carvel ice cream, a popular soft-serve brand, is sold in the stands. Premium beers such as Beck's and Molson are available at the 16 Beers of the World stands, and a microbrew, New Amsterdam, has its own four locations. There's a lot to do before the game if scouting out food isn't a priority. The gates at Shea open two hours before game time, so autograph hunting is possible by the field.

STADIUM STATS
Location: 126th St. and Roosevelt Ave., Flushing, Queens, NY 11368
Opened: April 17, 1964
Surface: Grass
Capacity: 55,777
Outfield dimensions: LF 338, LC 378, CF 410, RC 378, RF 338
Services for fans with disabilities: Seating available behind home plate and near third base at the field level.

STADIUM FIRSTS
Regular-season game: April 17, 1964, 4–3 loss to the Pittsburgh Pirates.
Pitcher: Jack Fisher of the Mets.
Batter: Dick Schofield of the Pirates.
Hit: A home run by Willie Stargell of the Pirates.

GROUND RULES
• A ball rolling under any part of the field boxes and staying out of sight is one base on a throw by a pitcher from the rubber, or two bases on throw by a fielder.
• A ball hitting the side of the facing of the dugout is considered in the dugout.
• A ball going into the dugout is one base on a throw by a pitcher from the rubber and two bases from the field.
• A fair ball bouncing over the fence is two bases.
• A fair ball bouncing over the temporary fence in foul territory in left or right field is two bases.
• A ball caught in the padding of the outfield fence is two bases.

In the Hot Seats at Shea Stadium

Shea was originally designed with the option to enclose it into a circular stadium (like Anaheim Stadium), but because that was never done, outfield seating is nearly nonexistent. About 95% of the seats are in foul territory. The design has one drawback. When you put 50,000 seats between the left-field and right-field lines, something has to give, so the upper deck is up. Seats there still have good sight lines, but they are high and set back.

GOOD SEATS

The loge and mezzanine provide excellent seats in the infield. A small bleacher area is set up in left-center field, but it's strictly for picnic groups. With the team rebuilding, ticket availability is not a problem.

BAD SEATS

Avoid the last two or three rows of the loge (blue) and mezzanine (green) levels (rows K and L in loge and N, O, and P in the mezzanine). The deck above creates an overhang that blocks all or part of the scoreboards and leaves you guessing on high fly balls. The last row is awful, third-from-the-top passable but still a distraction for serious fans. The club discounts these tickets sharply (from $12 to $6.50), but most fans would be happier taking a seat in the upper deck for the same price.

No-alcohol sections are set aside in the upper deck, but at least they're not in sections that are a long-distance call to home plate. They're sections 10–16, between home and third base. Smoking anywhere in the stadium was banned in 1995, in keeping with city ordinances. The sun sets behind home plate, but fans on the third-base side get a few more rays than first-base fans.

SCALPING

You could almost gauge the Mets' standings from the presence and volume of scalpers. When the team is down and out, good seats can be got at the gate. When the team is playing well, the scalpers appear like ants at a picnic and are a lot easier to spot.

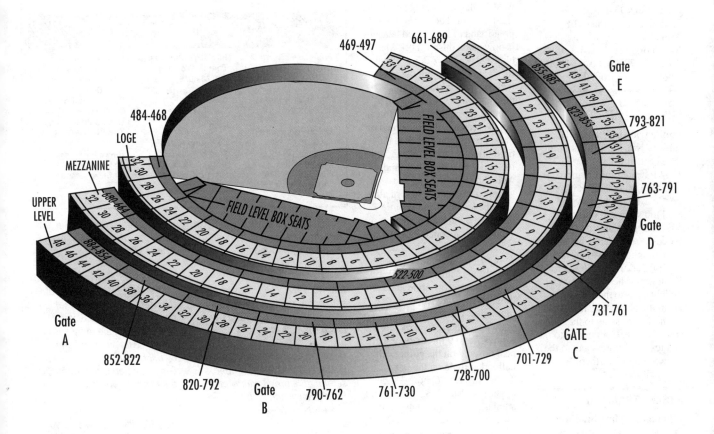

- ■ $17
- □ $13
- ▨ $12
- ▨ $6.50

TICKET INFORMATION
Address: 126th St. and Roosevelt Ave., Flushing, NY 11368

Phone: (718) 507-TIXX
Hours: Mon.–Fri. 9:30–5:30.
Prices: $17: MVP, lower box; $13: loge and mezzanine reserved; $12: upper box, lower reserved; $6.50: upper reserved, pavilion; senior citizen discounts.

After the game, go to Manhattan. A city as diverse as New York doesn't have any one or two spots that qualify as the postgame hangouts, but you will find sports fans in Mickey Mantle's (212-688-7777) on Central Park South, and sportswriters like Runyon's (212-223-9592) and P. J. Clarke's (212-759-1650) on the East Side. Times Square has the All-Star Cafe (212-840-8326), which is owned by Ken Griffey, Jr., Wayne Gretzky, Andre Agassi, Shaq, and Joe Montana, and Carmine's (212-221-3800), high-quality Italian meant for crowds.

LODGING NEAR THE STADIUM

Grand Hyatt
Park Ave. at Grand Central
New York, NY 10017
(212) 883-1234/(800) 233-1234
About 7 miles from the stadium.

Doral Park Hotel
70 Park Ave. (corner of E. 38th St.)
New York, NY 10016
(212) 687-7050/(800) 22-DORAL
About 7 miles from the stadium.

GETTING TO SHEA STADIUM

Public transportation: Take subway No. 7 to Willets Point (Shea Stadium); call (718) 330-1234 for more information. Or take the Long Island Railroad Port Washington line to the Shea Stadium stop; call (718) 217-5477 for more information.
By car: From Manhattan, take the Triborough Bridge to the Grand Central Parkway to Northern Boulevard (Shea Stadium) exit. Follow signs to the stadium. From the north, take the Cross-Bronx Expressway to the Whitestone Bridge. Continue onto the Whitestone Expressway to the Shea Stadium/Northern Boulevard exit.

SPRING TRAINING

Thomas J. White Stadium
St. Lucie County Sports Complex
525 N.W. Peacock Blvd.
Port St. Lucie, FL 34986
Capacity: 7,400
Surface: Grass
Game time: 1:10 p.m.
Tickets: (407) 871-2115

MINOR LEAGUES

Class	Team
AAA	Norfolk (VA) Tides
AA	Binghamton (NY) Mets
A	St. Lucie (FL) Mets
A	Capital City (SC) Bombers
Short Season A	Pittsfield (MA) Mets
Rookie	Kingsport (TN) Mets
Rookie	St. Lucie (FL) Mets

The Mets' closest minor-league affiliate is the Pittsfield Mets, a short-season Class A club of the New York–Penn League, in the Berkshire hills of western Massachusetts. Pittsfield's Wahconah Park, built in 1919, is one of the oldest operating stadiums in the minors. Any tears in batters' eyes aren't from sentimental feelings for this traditional ballfield; they're because the park faces west, so that the setting sun blasts right at them. The original wood grandstand of long wood benches is now painted New York Met blue and orange. Adding to the rustic atmosphere are the plastic owls on the roof to ward off pigeons. Carlton Fisk played 97 games here in 1969 before finishing the season at the other end of the state with the Red Sox. Pittsfield offers a variety of standard ballpark fare along with sundaes with chocolate topping and whipped cream, but, best of all, it sells the locally made Wohrle's hot dogs, a Berkshires treat. To reach Wahconah Park, take exit 2 off the Massachusetts Turnpike to State Route 7 north. Take Route 7 into Pittsfield. Go around the traffic circle and continue north along Route 7 for a mile or so. Go left at the fork onto Wahconah Street, where Routes 7 and 9 meet (there will be a hospital on the corner); the ballpark will be on the left.
Ticket prices: $6: box; $3.75: upper grandstand; $2.75: general admission. Call (413) 499-6387 for more information.

THE METS AT SHEA STADIUM

Sept. 24, 1969: The Mets beat the St. Louis Cardinals 6–0, clinching their first division title.

Oct. 16, 1969: Future Mets manager Davey Johnson makes the final out of Game 5 of the World

HOME-FIELD ADVANTAGE

When the Mets win and fans pack Shea, the crowd is a big plus. In the championship (mostly near-championship) days of the 1980s, the atmosphere was electric and pumped up the team. The crowd would cheer for players to make a curtain call from the dugout after a big home run, which led to the team's reputation for being arrogant showboaters. In the lean days of the '90s, the crowd is more subdued. Those wearing a jersey or the colors of the opposing team should still expect some comment on their wardrobe, though. It's usually good-natured but can be persistent. If you don't want to take any lip, restrict your logo emblems to alligators, penguins, and polo ponies.

Some players are bothered by the low-flying planes landing or taking off at nearby LaGuardia Airport. The jets generally buzz the stadium beyond left field, and some players opt to step out of the batter's box when they hear 'em coming. Former Mets slugger Bobby Bonilla wore earplugs at Shea to block out the plane noise in his first year in New York, but skeptics thought it was to muffle the boos he was getting from disgruntled fans.

METS TEAM NOTEBOOK

Franchise history	Rookies of the Year	Hall of Fame
New York Mets, 1962–present	Tom Seaver, 1967	Casey Stengel, 1966
	Jon Matlack, 1972	George Weiss, 1971
World Series titles	Darryl Strawberry, 1983	Yogi Berra, 1972
1969, 1986	Dwight Gooden, 1984	Warren Spahn, 1973
		Willie Mays, 1979
League pennants		Duke Snider, 1980
1969, 1973, 1986	**Cy Young Awards**	Tom Seaver, 1992
	Tom Seaver, 1969, 1973, 1975	
Division titles	Dwight Gooden, 1985	**Retired numbers**
1969, 1973, 1986, 1988		14 Gil Hodges
		37 Casey Stengel
		41 Tom Seaver

Series, giving the Mets a 5–3 win over the Baltimore Orioles and the team's first world championship.

May 14, 1972: Willie Mays hits a solo home run in his first game as a Met to beat the San Francisco Giants 5–4.

Oct. 8, 1973: Cincinnati Red Pete Rose slides hard into second, setting off a brawl with Met Buddy Harrelson in the NLCS. The Mets win 9–2.

April 5, 1983: Tom Seaver begins his second tour as a Met, starting before the largest opening-day crowd at Shea since 1968. The Mets beat the Philadelphia Phillies 2–0.

July 24, 1984: Keith Hernandez hits a two-out single to beat the Cardinals 9–8. The Mets go 20

games over .500 and are in first place the latest in the season since 1973.

Oct. 25, 1986: Down 5–3 with two outs in the bottom of the ninth, the Mets stage a remarkable comeback in Game 6 of the World Series, aided by a Bob Stanley wild pitch and an error by Bill Buckner. The Mets win 6–5 and go on to win Game 7 and their second world championship.

July 18, 1991: Darryl Strawberry and Gary Carter return to Shea as Los Angeles Dodgers, and both hit home runs as the Mets fall 10–5.

July 28, 1993: Anthony Young breaks a major-league-record 27-game losing streak with a relief appearance in a 5–4 win over the Florida Marlins.

STADIUM STATS

Location: *The Bronx, NY 10451*
Opened: *April 18, 1923*
Surface: *Merion blue-grass*
Capacity: *57,545*
Outfield dimensions: *LF 318, LC 399, CF 408, RC 385, RF 314*
Services for fans with disabilities: *Seating available in main reserve sections 2, 7, 8 and 10.*

STADIUM FIRSTS

Regular-season game: *April 22, 1923, 4–1 over the Boston Red Sox.*
Pitcher: *Bob Shawkey of the Yankees.*
Batter: *Chick Fewster of the Red Sox.*
Hit: *George Burns of the Red Sox.*
Home run: *Babe Ruth of the Yankees.*

GROUND RULES

• *The four poles are outside the playing field.*
• *Any batted ball hitting a foul pole above the fence line is a home run.*
• *Bat racks are within the dugout.*
• *Any thrown ball hitting the dugout railing or foundation and rebounding on field is in play.*
• *Any ball going into the dugout or hitting other parts of dugout is out of play.*

Few stadiums have thicker history books than Yankee Stadium: 33 American League pennants, 22 World Series championships, Monument Park, pinstripes, and the Yankee Clipper. But talk that "The House That Ruth Built" might start the 21st century with a For Sale sign out front haunted the early weeks of the '96 season, overshadowing the team's strong '95 finish and the loss of Mattingly and Showalter. The specter of the Yankees moving out of the Bronx—out of New York, even!—when their lease expires in 2002 has been the buzz of Broadway. Is Steinbrenner bluffing? Will the Bronx Bombers need a new nickname? Stay tuned...

As soon as fans step off the subway platform outside Yankee Stadium's right-field corner, the Big Apple sights and sounds hit them. The area is crowded and well lighted, with softball and basketball games going on across the street, and the air is thick with the smell of fresh pretzels on an open grill. Inside, Yankee Stadium is a sea of blue seats and the blue outfield fence rising around the green. It's a handsome, relaxing baseball site that merges the best of past and present.

Inside, familiar black-and-white images come to life; home plate is where Ruth and Lou Gehrig delivered their famous farewells. Fans can stand 15 feet from where the Iron Horse set his consecutive-game record of 2,130. A look down the third-base line brings back memories of Yogi Berra hugging Don Larsen after the perfect game in the '56 World Series, and the ornate facade lacing the top of the outfield calls to mind Reggie Jackson's three-homer Game 6 in 1977.

Given all that has happened within these walls, Yankee Stadium is not just an important site in sports history—it's a landmark in American history.

HOT TIPS FOR VISITING FANS

PARKING
Driving is not recommended, because parking is extremely tight (only 6,900 spaces). But if you must, arrive by 5 p.m. to be assured of a parking place. Or park at Grand Concourse, 3 blocks east of the Stadium on 161st Street. The cost is $8, and you get a jump on postgame traffic congestion.

WEATHER
Hot in June, July, August and probably even September. Snow is possible in April and bring a jacket in May.

MEDIA
Radio: WABC (770 AM). John Sterling and Michael Kay are the announcers.
TV: WPIX (Channel 11) and MSG Network (cable). Al Trautwig, David Cohen, Jim Kaat for MSG; former Yankees Bobby Murcer and Rick Cerone, along with Suzyn Waldman, are in the WPIX booth, joined for home games (and a few road trips) by Hall of Famer Phil "Scooter" Rizzuto.

CUISINE
The Café Olé Stand serves eight types of international coffee. The Yankees bakery has cookies, pie, cake, and rolls. Vanilla cookies are the specialty. The goods are baked fresh every day. The food court on the lower level and the "Fries in the Sky" on the tier level feature beers and a wide range of foods. Beers of the World offers exactly that.
For those fans who drive and arrive early, try the Sidewalk Cafe, between the stadium and Garage No. 8. For ticketholders only, it serves barbecued ribs, sandwiches, hot dogs, chicken, French fries, imported beers, and soft drinks. It opens at 5 p.m. for night games and 11 a.m. for day games.
Though the area has an image of blight, an image built up by no one less than George Steinbrenner himself, a 3-block area on 161st Street near Yankee Stadium is flush with convenience stores and ethnic restaurants, including Indian, Chinese, Irish, Spanish, and fried-chicken spots. Another option is to go into Manhattan. Mickey Mantle's Restaurant and Sports Bar (212-688-7777) is a fine choice, considering it's loaded with sports memorabilia, including jerseys worn by Mantle, DiMaggio, and Stan Musial.

LODGING NEAR THE STADIUM

Grand Hyatt
Park Ave. at Grand Central
New York, NY 10017
(212) 883-1234/(800) 233-1234
About 6 miles from the stadium.

Doral Inn
541 Lexington Ave. (49th St.)
New York, NY 10022
(212) 755-1200/(800) 22-DORAL
About 6 miles from the stadium.

GETTING TO YANKEE STADIUM

Public transportation: Take the No. 4, the C or the D subway train to the 161 Street Station, or take the BX6, BX13, or BX 35 (free transfer) bus to 161st Street. For more information, call (718) 330-1234.
By car: From Manhattan, take

In the Hot Seats at Yankee Stadium

There was little talk of low attendance at Yankee Stadium in 1995, but the murmurs began again in 1996 that there were a surprising number of empty seats in The House That Ruth Built. When the team is hot, the tickets get, well, warm. Even during a winning streak good seats are available on game day. They probably won't be behind home plate, but they'll certainly be good baseball seats. Single-game tickets go on sale in December.

GOOD SEATS

If first-deck box seats are not an option, the tier-level reserved in the second deck are good. The seats are high, but the entire playing field can be seen, and it's good territory for foul balls. And, if you're not afraid of heights, go to the top row and check out the view. The sights include parts of New Jersey,

the Hudson River, the Empire State Building, and the World Trade Center.

The outfield bleachers are filled mostly with diehard, blue-collar fans who make at least a dozen trips a season to Yankee Stadium. The regulars in the bleachers feel like family—some only see each other at games, but still send Christmas cards. Bleacher fans are generally rowdy, but the party people sit near the top and they respect those who don't come to party. Newcomers and families sit in the front rows and are not bothered.

The loge seats are good if you don't want to feel the elements. Shielded from the sun and rain, the seats are squeezed in under the second deck, but the view of the field is excellent. For a few dollars more, the new "MVP" seating—5,000 seats in sections 21–22 on the field level, and 8, 10, and 12 on the loge

level—offers fans a cushioned seat with a cupholder, a menu of goodies beyond the concessions, and waiter service to bring it to you.

BAD SEATS

The lower-tier box seats down the left-field line (main boxes 202–350 and field boxes 2–136) are no place for young kids or fans with slow reflexes. The seats are close to the field, and line drives come ripping in at 110 m.p.h. More than a few fans have been hit.

SCALPING

Not many fans use scalpers, because the Yankees usually sell only 20,000 to 30,000 tickets a game. Those who buy from scalpers often pay 20% more than the face value.

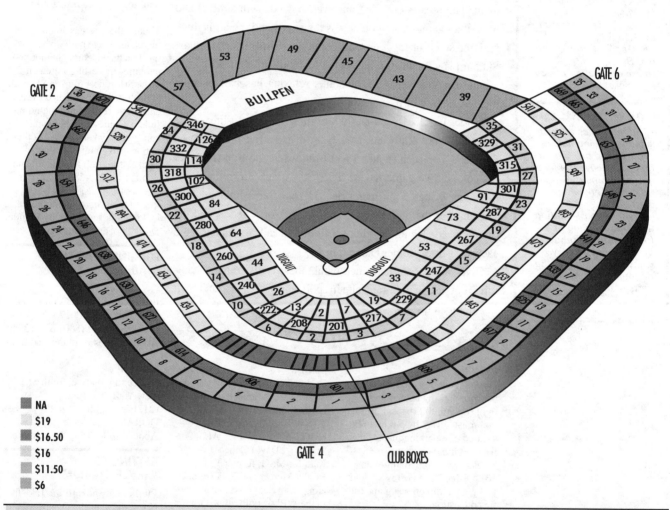

Legend:
- NA
- $19
- $16.50
- $16
- $11.50
- $6

TICKET INFORMATION
Address: The Bronx, New York, NY 10451
Phone: (718) 293-6000 or TicketMaster at (212) 307-7171
Hours: Mon-Sun. 9–5, and through the conclusion of all night games.

By mail: Make check or money orders payable to the New York Yankees; add $2 to cover postage and handling. Address to Mail Order Department, New York Yankees, Yankee Stadium, The Bronx, NY 10451.

Prices: $19: lower/loge box seats; $16.50: tier box; $16: lower reserved; $11.50: tier reserved; $6: bleachers (sold only at the stadium on game day); $2: senior citizen; $3: youth groups of 25 or more (if purchased in advance).

the FDR Drive north to Harlem River Drive north. Continue to West 155 Street. Continue east via the Macombs Dam Bridge to Jerome Avenue.

From the north, take I-87 south across the Tappan Zee Bridge. Exit I-87 at exit 6; the stadium is straight ahead.

SPRING TRAINING

Legends Field
3802 Martin Luther King Blvd.
Tampa, FL 33614
Capacity: 10,382
Surface: Grass
Game time: 1:05 p.m. or 7:05 p.m.
Tickets: (813) 879-2244

MINOR LEAGUES

Class	Team
AAA	Columbus (OH) Clippers
AA	Norwich (CT) Navigators
A	Tampa Yankees
A	Greensboro (NC) Bats
Short Season A	Oneonta (NY) Yankees
Rookie	Tampa Yankees

The closest minor-league team to New York City is the Short Season Class A Hudson Valley Renegades of the NY-Penn League (one of the Texas Rangers' minor-league teams). 1994 was Hudson Valley's first season. That was also the first year an organized baseball team was based in Fishkill, a suburban community in Dutchess County, north of N.Y.C.

To reach Fishkill's Dutchess Stadium, approximately 55 miles from N.Y.C., take I-684 to I-84 west. Exit at No. 11, Route 9D, and turn right on 9D. The ballpark is about a mile up on the right.

THE YANKEES AT YANKEE STADIUM

June 1, 1925: *Lou Gehrig replaces Wally Pipp at first base.*

Sept. 30, 1927: *Babe Ruth hits his 60th home run of the season, off Washington Senator Tom Zachary.*

April 18, 1929: *The Yankees become the first major-league team to wear numbers on their uniforms.*

Oct. 8, 1956: *Don Larsen pitches a perfect game against the Brooklyn Dodgers in Game 5 of the World Series.*

Oct. 1, 1961: *Roger Maris breaks Ruth's record with his 61st home run of the season.*

May 14, 1967: *Mickey Mantle hits his 500th home run, off Baltimore Oriole Stu Miller.*

Oct. 14, 1976: *Chris Chambliss homers in the ninth inning of Game 5 of the ALCS to clinch the Yankees' 30th pennant.*

Oct. 18, 1977: *Reggie Jackson hits three home runs in Game 6 as the Yankees take their 21st World Championship by beating the Los Angeles Dodgers.*

July 4, 1983: *Dave Righetti no-hits the Boston Red Sox.*

July 24, 1983: *George Brett of the Kansas City Royals hits a two-run home run in the ninth inning to put the Royals ahead 5–4, but a check of his bat reveals pine tar past the 18-inch limit. Brett is called out to end the game. The Royals protest successfully and the rest of the game is played August 18, ending in a 5–4 Kansas City win.*

Sept. 29, 1987: *Don Mattingly breaks Ernie Banks' major-league record when he hits his sixth grand slam of the season, off Bruce Hurst of the Red Sox.*

Sept. 4, 1993: *Jim Abbott no-hits the Cleveland Indians 4–0.*

May 14, 1996: *Dwight Gooden, returning to New York baseball after years of arm and substance-abuse problems, pitches a no-hitter against the Seattle Mariners.*

HOME-FIELD ADVANTAGE

Yankee Stadium's spacious, sloping outfield is a challenge to visiting outfielders. The fence from right center to the right-field corner takes a drastic curve. Batted balls can bounce like a pinball in the corner, and an outfielder has to work in confined space. A strong arm, though, can nail runners advancing to second or third base.

Death Valley, the left-center-field area, is 399 feet from home plate, and center field is 408 feet away. That means outfielders need speed and a strong arm to patrol the area adequately. Any batted ball that gets away from an outfielder can turn into an inside-the-park home run.

Pitchers despise the short right-field fence as much as they love the space in the other direction. The right-field fence is 314 feet from home plate. The best way to defend against a cheap home run here is to pitch lefties to the outside part of the plate and make batters go the other way.

Foul territory behind home plate is roomy. Foul territory wide of third and first bases is shallow, giving batters a big advantage.

YANKEES TEAM NOTEBOOK

Franchise history
Baltimore Orioles, 1901–02; New York Highlanders, 1903–12; New York Yankees, 1913–present

World Series titles
1923, 1927, 1928, 1932, 1936, 1937, 1938, 1939, 1941, 1943, 1947, 1949, 1950, 1951, 1952, 1953, 1956, 1958, 1961, 1962, 1977, 1978

American League pennants
1921, 1922, 1923, 1926, 1927, 1928, 1932, 1936, 1937, 1938, 1939, 1941, 1942, 1943, 1947, 1949, 1950, 1951, 1952, 1953, 1955, 1956, 1957, 1958, 1960, 1961, 1962, 1963, 1964, 1976, 1977, 1978, 1981

Division titles
1976, 1977, 1978, 1980, 1981

Wild Card
1995

Most Valuable Players
Babe Ruth, 1923
Lou Gehrig, 1927, 1936
Joe DiMaggio, 1939, 1941, 1947

Joe Gordon, 1942
Spud Chandler, 1943
Phil Rizzuto, 1950
Yogi Berra, 1951, 1954, 1955
Mickey Mantle, 1956, 1957, 1962
Roger Maris, 1960, 1961
Elston Howard, 1963
Thurman Munson, 1976
Don Mattingly, 1985

Rookies of the Year
Gil McDougald, 1951
Bob Grim, 1954
Tony Kubek, 1957
Tom Tresh, 1962
Stan Bahnsen, 1968
Thurman Munson, 1970
Dave Righetti, 1981

Cy Young Awards
Bob Turley, 1958
Whitey Ford, 1961
Sparky Lyle, 1977
Ron Guidry, 1978

Hall of Fame
Babe Ruth, 1936
Lou Gehrig, 1939
Willie Keeler, 1939
Clark Griffith, 1945
Frank Chance, 1946
Jack Chesbro, 1946
Herb Pennock, 1948
Paul Waner, 1952
Edw. G. Barrow, 1953
Bill Dickey, 1954
Frank "Home Run" Baker, 1955
Joe DiMaggio, 1955
Dazzy Vance, 1955
Joe McCarthy, 1957

Bill McKechnie, 1962
Burleigh Grimes, 1964
Miller Huggins, 1964
Casey Stengel, 1966
Branch Rickey, 1967
Red Ruffing, 1967
Stan Coveleski, 1967
Waite Hoyt, 1969
Earl Combs, 1970
Geo. M. Weiss, 1970
Yogi Berra, 1971
Lefty Gomez, 1972
Mickey Mantle, 1974
Whitey Ford, 1974
Bucky Harris, 1975
Joe Sewell, 1977
Larry MacPhail, 1978
Johnny Mize, 1981
Enos Slaughter, 1985
Catfish Hunter, 1987
Gaylord Perry, 1991
Tony Lazzeri, 1991
Reggie Jackson, 1993
Phil Rizzuto, 1994

Retired numbers
1 Billy Martin
3 Babe Ruth
4 Lou Gehrig
5 Joe DiMaggio
7 Mickey Mantle
8 Bill Dickey and Yogi Berra
9 Roger Maris
10 Phil Rizzuto
15 Thurman Munson
16 Whitey Ford
32 Elston Howard
37 Casey Stengel
44 Reggie Jackson

OAKLAND ATHLETICS

Oakland Coliseum

Bucking the trend for neo-traditional, baseball-only stadiums, Oakland–Alameda County Coliseum is welcoming its prodigal football team, the Raiders, back from L.A. with open arms and a refitted stadium with 22,000 new seats. Let's just hope that history doesn't play out in reverse here. The bowl-shaped Coliseum was originally built for the then-Oakland Raiders in 1965. A couple of years later the Athletics moved in and the place got a makeover to suit its dual purpose. Then the Raiders moved to L.A., and the stadium was (somewhat) retro-fitted to be exclusively for baseball. Now it's back to both. Yipes! What would Charlie Finley say?

The flamboyant Finley, who moved the team to the Bay Area from Kansas City, would probably suggest ways to capitalize on playing ball while construction goes on in the outfield.

It took the Bash Brothers—Jose Canseco and Mark McGwire—to put the energy back into the stadium after Finley's departure and several lackluster seasons that had earned it the nickname "the Mausoleum." The A's have fallen from those World Series days of the late '80s, but fan loyalty, and sometimes even excitement, remain.

New locally based ownership in 1996 seems determined to improve the team and the stadium's fortunes, and the brisk pace of preparations for the new co-tenants indicates an activist approach by those in charge. The A's weren't all that amused early in the 1996 season, though, when the construction forced them to open their season at a minor-league stadium in Las Vegas. The grumbling got louder throughout the campaign, with some even casting their eyes toward other, calmer homes.

Despite its circular configuration, the Coliseum has always had generally good sight lines for baseball, and football seating shouldn't change that. Some of the new seats will be available for A's games and—so it is hoped—will be necessary for the throngs pouring into the Coliseum for the playoffs and Series to come.

Spanish). Ken Korach, Bill King, and Ray Fosse do the English broadcasts, and Carlos Caesar Rivera and Raul Collindres announce the games in Spanish. **TV:** KRON (Channel 4) and SportsChannel (cable). Ken Wilson and Ray Fosse are the broadcasters on Channel 4.

CUISINE
The Coliseum offers a wide variety of food, from basic hot dogs, all sorts of barbecued meats, pastas, soft-serve ice cream, Chinese food, Roundtable pizza and Subway sandwiches, to health-conscious foods such as veggie burgers and salads. The popular microbrewery stand offers brands from Seattle and California. Name brands such as Miller and Budweiser also are sold. Pre-game tailgating is very popular, but most people go home after the games. Near the stadium, the Hyatt Hotel is a popular haunt for visiting and hometown players, as is the Hilton Sports Bar across the street. Francesco's (510-569-0653) is also nearby. Downtown, try the Pacific Coast Brewing Co. (510-836-2739), and the Old Spaghetti Factory (510-893-0222) in Jack London Square.

LODGING NEAR THE STADIUM

Oakland Airport Hilton
1 Hegenberger Rd.
Oakland, CA 94621
(510) 635-5000/(800) 445-8667
7 blocks from the stadium.

Waterfront Plaza
10 Washington St.
Oakland, CA 94607
(510) 836-3800/(800) 729-3638
About 5 miles from the stadium.

GETTING TO OAKLAND COLISEUM

Public transportation: Bay Area Rapid Transit (BART) trains go from San Francisco and other adjacent areas to the Coliseum BART station. From there you walk over a bridge to the stadium. For more information, call (510) 465-2278 or (510) 464-6000.

HOT TIPS FOR VISITING FANS

PARKING
The stadium has 11,500 spaces at $7 each. If the game is sold out, free overflow parking is across the freeway, a 10-minute walk away. Try to arrive at least half an hour to an hour before the game.

WEATHER
The Bay Area rarely gets too cold or too hot or too windy, and Oakland is a few degrees warmer than San Francisco, but you should dress for the summer like the locals do—in layers. The fog sometimes moves in at night, making the air heavy and home runs harder to hit. But rainouts are rare, and conditions are most often ideal.

MEDIA
Radio: KFRC (610 AM—English), KNTA (1430 AM—

In the Hot Seats at Oakland Coliseum

Because the stadium holds nearly 40,000 and season-ticket sales usually number closer to 15,000, and the fact that the A's have spent a couple of seasons in the cellar, tickets are available on a walk-up basis for almost every game. Generally some good seats are available on all levels.

GOOD SEATS

The $17.50 MVP seats, in the lower level along the baselines, are considered the best. The lowest-priced ticket is a $4.50 bleacher seat behind the outfield fence. If you enjoy sun and a more involved atmosphere, these seats are a great deal.

In the event of inexplicable sellout crowds or postseason play, newly built Raiders' seating can be pressed into service. Some of the new Raiders' seats will be made available for the A's on a regular basis—more outfield bleachers behind the current outfield bleachers. The prices for these gems weren't available at press time (All-Star break, '96), but they will probably be on the inexpensive side.

BAD SEATS

There are no obstructed views or peculiarities that make any seats very bad, nor is the stadium so large that distance is a serious factor. Foul poles are in sections 103 and 131 at the field level, so avoid these if possible. Also, the foul ground is one of the largest in the major leagues, so anyone who sits in the boxes hoping to get a close look at their favorite players might be disappointed. This is especially true of the seats directly behind the plate; a notch in the backstop wall places them farther back than at other parks.

SCALPING

Scalpers aren't allowed on stadium property, and, frankly, these days none of them has any reason to be. With good seats readily available even when the team is doing fairly well, fans don't need to use them.

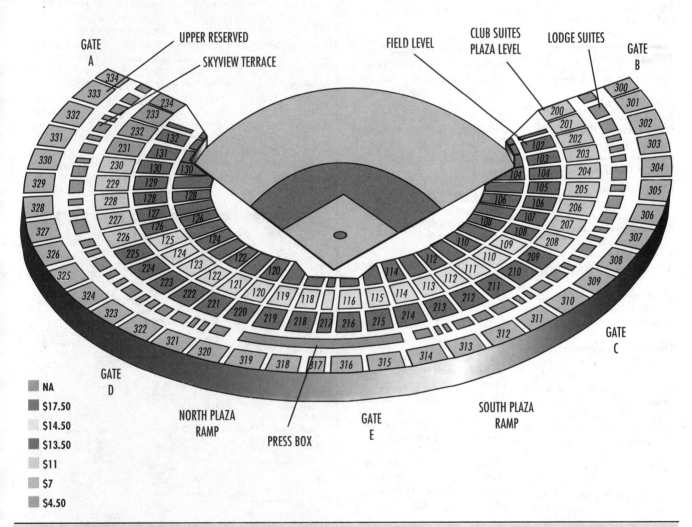

Legend:
- NA
- $17.50
- $14.50
- $13.50
- $11
- $7
- $4.50

TICKET INFORMATION

Address: 7000 Coliseum Way, Oakland, CA 94621

Phone: (510) 638-0500 or Bass outlets at (510) 762-BASS, (408) 998-BASS, (707) 546-BASS, (916) 923-BASS

By mail: Oakland A's Tickets, P.O. Box 2220, Oakland, CA 94621. Send a check or money order payable to the Oakland Athletics Baseball Company or a Visa or Master-Card number and expiration date. Specify the date of game, and price and location of tickets. Include a $4 handling fee.

Hours: Mon.–Fri. 9–6, Sat. 10–4. On game days, the office is open until half an hour after the game.

Prices: $17.50: MVP; $14.50: field level infield; $13.50: field level, plaza level infield; $11: plaza level; $7: upper reserved; $4.50: bleachers.

By car: The Coliseum is adjacent to I-880 on Coliseum Way, about 6 miles south of downtown Oakland. Take the 66th Avenue or Hegenberger Road exit off I-880.

From San Francisco, drive east over the Bay Bridge to I-580 toward Hayward. Take I-980 to Oakland and get on I-880 south. Get off at 66th Avenue and follow signs to the Coliseum.

From Marin County, take I-580 over the San Rafael Bridge to I-80. Take I-80 to I-580 toward Hayward and follow above directions.

From Sacramento, take I-80 west toward Oakland. Get on I-580 toward Hayward and follow low directions provided above.

From Contra Costa County, take Highway 24 through Caldecott Tunnel into downtown Oakland and get onto I-980. Follow directions provided above.

SPRING TRAINING

Phoenix Municipal Stadium
5999 E. Van Buren
Phoenix, AZ 85008
Surface: Grass
Game time: 1:05 p.m.
Tickets: (602) 392-0074

MINOR LEAGUE

Class	Team
AAA	Edmonton (AB) Trappers
AA	Huntsville (AL) Stars
A	Modesto (CA) A's
A	West Michigan Whitecaps
Short	
Season A	Southern Oregon A's
Rookie	Scottsdale (AZ) A's

The closest minor-league team to Oakland is the Class A San Jose Giants of the California League. San Jose (one of San Francisco's minor-league teams) frequently plays the Modesto A's, Oakland's California League affiliate. With the exception of five years—1959–61 and 1977–78—pro baseball has been played in San Jose since 1947. But this city's baseball history goes back even farther, to 1896, when San Jose was a charter franchise in the California State League, which folded after the '96 season ended.

To reach San Jose from the Bay Area, fewer than 45 miles away, take I-880 south to I-280 south. Exit at 10th Street. Turn right on 10th and then left on Alma; Municipal Stadium will be on the right.

Ticket prices: $7: box seats; $5: adults; $3: children under 10 (children under 4 are free); $3: senior citizens 65 or over. For more information, call (408) 297-1435.

THE A'S AT OAKLAND COLISEUM

May 8, 1968: Catfish Hunter throws a perfect game against the Minnesota Twins.

Oct. 21, 1973: A 5–2 win over the New York Mets in Game 7 of the World Series gives the A's their second world championship in Oakland.

Oct. 17, 1974: The A's take their third consecutive World Series by beating the Los Angeles Dodgers 3–2 in Game 5.

Sept. 28, 1975: Vida Blue, Glenn Abbott, Paul Lindblad, and Rollie Fingers combine to no-hit the California Angels in the final game of the season.

Oct. 15, 1981: Fan "Crazy" George Henderson creates "the wave," at least for the first time in a baseball stadium.

Oct. 14, 1989: The A's win Game 2 of the World Series 5–1 over the San Francisco Giants. Game 3 in San Francisco is postponed after a 7.1 earthquake hits the Bay Area.

May 1, 1991: Rickey Henderson of the A's steals his 939th base, passing Lou Brock to become the all-time leader.

June 8, 1994: Ruben Sierra hits homers against Milwaukee from both sides of the plate in the same game, becoming the first Oakland Athletic ever to do so, and the first player on any A's team to do this since 1916.

HOME-FIELD ADVANTAGE

The Coliseum's natural-grass field is arguably the best in baseball. A noteworthy trait of the field is the large foul territory, making the park pitcher-friendly. The stadium has always had tall outfield grass, making triples in the alleys few and far between. Fears that the addition of the Raiders' cleats will change this are at least premature, if not unwarranted. The only certain long-term effects of the stadium's renovations for the returning Raiders are the new outfield fence and the loss of an expansive view of the East Bay Hills.

The outfield fence, which used to be eight feet tall all the way across, now rises from that height to 15 feet in two dromedary-style humps at the end of each of the power alleys, dipping again to eight feet in the middle. This might compensate for the football luxury boxes now behind the fence, which will keep the wind from blowing in, making this a potential launching pad. The loss of the view is a shame for fans, but shouldn't much bother players, who shouldn't have been gazing at it anyway.

At least during the construction of the new sections, the home team had a slight edge over visitors, although the construction workers had it over both of them—mostly. In the rush to finish renovations in time for the Raiders 1996 season, construction work adding the 22,000 new seats went on during A's day games. Even though work was restricted to "quieter" tasks at game time (no pile driving, for instance), the remaining noise still often made it impossible for outfielders on either team to hear how hard a ball had been hit, and therefore difficult to know how to react. For their part, the construction workers were supposed to ignore the game, those caught watching were reassigned to work out of sight of the field.

ATHLETICS TEAM NOTEBOOK

Franchise history
Philadelphia Athletics, 1901–54; Kansas City Athletics, 1955–67; Oakland Athletics, 1968–present

World Series titles
1910, 1911, 1913, 1929, 1930, 1972, 1973, 1974, 1989

American League pennants
1902, 1905, 1910, 1911, 1913, 1914, 1929, 1930, 1931, 1972, 1973, 1974, 1988, 1989, 1990

Division titles
1971, 1972, 1973, 1974, 1975, 1981, 1988, 1989, 1990, 1992

Most Valuable Players
Eddie Collins, 1914
Mickey Cochrane, 1928
Lefty Grove, 1931
Jimmie Foxx, 1932, 1933
Bobby Shantz, 1952
Vida Blue, 1971
Reggie Jackson, 1973
Jose Canesco, 1988
Rickey Henderson, 1990
Dennis Eckersley, 1992

Rookies of the Year
Harry Byrd, 1952
Jose Canesco, 1986
Mark McGwire, 1987
Walt Weiss, 1988

Cy Young Awards
Vida Blue, 1971
Jim "Catfish" Hunter, 1974
Bob Welch, 1990
Dennis Eckersley, 1992

Hall of Fame
Ty Cobb, 1936
Nap Lajoie, 1937
Connie Mack, 1937
Tris Speaker, 1937
Eddie Collins, 1939
Jimmy Collins, 1945
Eddie Plank, 1946
Rube Waddell, 1946
Mickey Cochrane, 1947
Lefty Grove, 1947
Herb Pennock, 1948
Jimmie Foxx, 1951
Chief Bender, 1951
Al Simmons, 1953
Frank "Home Run" Baker, 1955
Zack Wheat, 1959
Elmer Flick, 1963
Luke Appling, 1964
Stan Coveleski, 1969
Waite Hoyt, 1969
Lou Boudreau, 1970
Satchel Paige, 1971
George Kell, 1983
Enos Slaughter, 1985
Willie McCovey, 1986
Jim "Catfish" Hunter, 1987
Billy Williams, 1987
Joe Morgan, 1990
Rollie Fingers, 1992
Reggie Jackson, 1993

Retired numbers
27 Jim "Catfish" Hunter
34 Rollie Fingers

Veterans Stadium

STADIUM STATS

Location: *3501 S. Broad St., Philadelphia, PA 19148*
Opened: *April 10, 1971*
Surface: *AstroTurf*
Capacity: *62,263*
Outfield Dimensions: *LF 330, CF 408, RF 330*
Services for fans with disabilities: *Seating available behind sections 205, 251, and throughout the 300 level.*

STADIUM FIRSTS

Regular-season game: *April 10, 1971, 4–1 over the Montreal Expos.*
Pitcher: *Jim Bunning of the Phillies.*
Batter: *Boots Day of the Expos.*
Hit: *Larry Bowa of the Phillies.*
Home run: *Don Money of the Phillies.*

GROUND RULES

• *Dugout: A ball has to enter the dugout or hit the yellow bars or yellow line to be considered out of play. A ball entering the open area above the end of the dugout inside the yellow line is considered out of play.*
• *Fences: Glass area has openings at top. If a ball sticks in the opening, it is a ground-rule double. A ball sticking under the padding in the outfield fence is in play. In left and right field the stands protrude to a point near the foul lines. If a ball lands in fair territory and bounces over the points and lands in the playing area, it is considered to be in the stands and is a ground-rule double.*
• *A ball off the screen behind home plate is in play. A ball hitting the pipe to the right of the right-field foul pole is in play.*

Veteran Stadium often is used as an example of all that is wrong with the ballparks of the 1970s. Carpeted with an artificial surface, fully enclosed but with no roof, heavy on the concrete and impersonal, the ballpark is part of the sprawling sports complex in South Philadelphia that includes the Spectrum. The Vet is a concrete structure, roundish, marked by huge vertical pillars. The highest seats are as elevated as those in any ballpark in North America.

Pittsburgh has first dibs on state money marked for building a new ballpark. When the Phillies do build a new stadium, owner Bill Giles is looking for a baseball-only stadium modeled after Camden Yards or Jacobs Field. His motivation is obvious. For one thing, the upkeep at Veterans Stadium is handled mostly by Giles, and the Vet needs plenty of it. No matter how the Phillies fare, no matter how much the Phillie Phanatic distracts fans' attention, those who visit the Vet can't help but notice that it's not a good ballpark. All of the seats in the stadium were replaced in 1995 with blue and, allegedly, more comfortable chairs.

The artificial surface is reviled by players as the worst in the National League. It's been repaced several times, but there always seem to be worn and bare spots, and it is hard almost everywhere. There's even a myth that the stadium is actually crumbling. The rumor is false, but the yard does feel as if it's decaying; Mike Schmidt even complained of a "cat stink" smell in the dugouts and runways in the late '80s.

At least some good things have happened here. The Phillies won their first World Series championship in 1980. They got back to the World Series and lost in 1983 and '93 and reached the NL playoffs in 1976–78. Given the sorry history of the Phillies, this was a real turnaround. The Phillies reached the Series in 1915 (and won one game) and in 1950 (and won none). They previously had played in Baker Bowl, the ultimate hitter's park, where the stands once collapsed, killing 12. They played in Shibe Park, later renamed Connie Mack Stadium, through the 1970 season.

HOT TIPS FOR VISITING FANS

PARKING
The lots surrounding the stadium charge $5 and have spaces for about 14,000 cars. Don't be afraid to pull into the Spectrum lot next door. In fact, it might be a smart move because you can walk briskly to your car after the game and get out faster. This tactic is especially effective if you are driving onto southbound I-95.

Another main artery is the Schuylkill Expressway. It is nicknamed "Sure-kill" for a reason. Also avoid Broad Street—too many lights.

WEATHER
It's plenty cold in Philadelphia in April and September, not to mention October, and it gets fairly steamy in the summer. A waste-treatment center sits a few miles from the stadium, and every now and then breezes waft that aroma to the ballpark.

MEDIA
Radio: WGMP (1210 AM).
TV: WB17 (Channel 17) and PRISM (cable). Richie Ashburn, Harry Kalas, Andy Musser, Kent Tekulve, Chris Wheeler, and Todd Kalas are the broadcasters.

CUISINE
The Phillies may have upgraded their concessions, but the cheese steaks are still not as good as those at stands outside the ballpark, and are more expensive to boot. The Italian water ices in the stadium have the same problems. Pennsylvania funnel cake, a local pastry specialty, is available, and there's the usual stuff—Pizza Hut, grilled chicken, etc. Stands offering a wide variety of imported beers were added in 1995, one each on the upper and lower levels.
South Street is nice for pregame dining or postgame revelry. Café Nola (215-627-2590) serves excellent Cajun fare that visiting ballplayers love. Susanna Foo (215-545-2666) has first-rate Chinese food. Better yet, go to the Italian Market in South Philadelphia and find your way to Pat's King of Steaks (215-339-9872) for that Philadelphia specialty, the cheese steak. Yummy, but tell your arteries to expect heavy traffic. Get an Italian water ice if you can find room after the cheese steak. There's a stand near Pat's. Lemon water ice is the best.
For those interested in more action, the happening place is Legends at the Stadium Holiday Inn (215-755-9500). One of the owners is Ron Jaworski, a former Philadelphia Eagles quarterback.

LODGING NEAR THE STADIUM

Sheraton Society Hill
1 Dock St. (corner of Second and Walnut)
Philadelphia, PA 19103
(215) 238-6000/(800) 325-3535
3 miles from the stadium.

In the Hot Seats at Veterans Stadium

You can walk up and get seats—the ballpark has plenty of room—but getting great ones is another matter. Forget about the field boxes; they go as season tickets.

GOOD SEATS

The best bargain is a general admission ($5) seat at the 700 (top) level. Arrive early and you can claim a seat right behind home plate. You'll be in nosebleed territory (no, conces-

sionaires do not stroll aisles selling oxygen), but behind the plate is a great spot, regardless. The seats in left and center field get the most sun during day games; the deluxe seats (200 level) get it almost all through the game.

BAD SEATS

Try to avoid seats in the 700 level down the foul lines. The angles make it difficult to follow the ball off the bat. You're better off at

the 600 level in the outfield or in the newly expanded 500 level in which aisles were filled in with additional seats, making the section 18 seats deep.

SCALPING

Tickets for good seats are peddled outside the stadium. The demand is not great for marked-up seats, so you can take a tough negotiating stance.

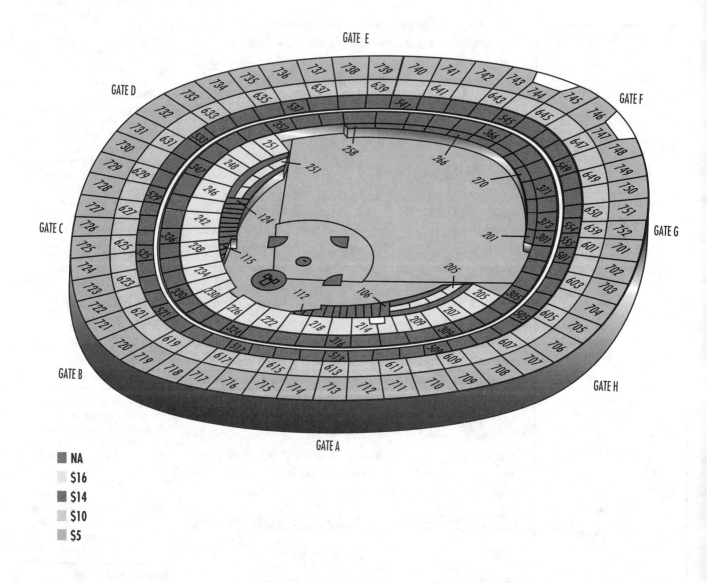

- ■ NA
- ■ $16
- ■ $14
- ■ $10
- ■ $5

TICKET INFORMATION
Address: 3501 S. Broad St., Philadelphia, PA 19148
Phone: (215) 463-1000
By mail: Note the date you want, the num-

ber and price of tickets, and send a check or money order (including a $4 service charge) to: Philadelphia Phillies, P.O. Box 7575, Philadelphia, PA 19101.
Hours: Mon.–Fri. 9–8, Sat.–Sun. 10–4.

Prices: $16: field box, 200 level. $14: field box, sections 258–274; terrace box, 300 level; loge box, 500 level. $10: reserved, 600 level. $5: reserved, 700 level.

The Ritz Carlton
17th and Chestnut Sts.
at Liberty Place
Philadelphia, PA 19106
(215) 563-1600/(800) 241-3333
7 miles from the stadium.

GETTING TO VETERANS STADIUM

Public transportation: By subway, take the Broad Street line from 15th and Market southbound to the last stop, Broad and Pattison. The stadium is ½-block away. Call (215) 580-7800 for more information.

By car: From the north, take I-95 south to the Broad Street exit. Go to the first light (Zinkoff Boulevard) and turn right. The stadium is on your left.
From the south, take I-95 north to the Broad Street exit and proceed as above.
From the west, take I-76 east. At Century City, stay to the right and follow signs for New Jersey and the Sports Complex, heading toward the Walt Whitman Bridge. Take the Broad Street exit, No. 45 (Sports Complex), and go right at the bottom of the ramp onto Broad Street. Stay to the far left, to Pattison Avenue. The stadium is on the left.
From the east, cross Walt Whitman Bridge to I-76 west through the tolls, to exit 46B, South Seventh Street. Go through one traffic light to Pattison Avenue. Right to the first traffic light. Go left onto 11th Street. The stadium is on your right.

SPRING TRAINING

Jack Russell Memorial Stadium
800 Phillies Dr.
Clearwater, FL 34615
Capacity: 6,025
Surface: Grass
Game time: 1:05 p.m. or 7:05 p.m.
Tickets: (215) 463-6000

MINOR LEAGUES

Class	Team
AAA	Scranton/Wilkes-Barre (PA) Red Barons
AA	Reading (PA) Phillies
A	Clearwater (FL) Phillies
A	Piedmont (NC) Boll Weevils
Short	
Season A	Batavia (NY) Clippers
Rookie	Martinsville (VA) Phillies

The Phillies' closest minor-league affiliate is the Class AA Reading Phillies of the Eastern League. Since Reading became one of Philadelphia's farm teams in 1967, this team has sent more than 130 players to the big leagues. Among the alumni: Phillies Mike Schmidt, Greg Luzinski, Bob Boone, and Larry Bowa, plus such other stars as Ryne Sandberg and Julio Franco. To reach Reading Municipal Memorial Stadium, which is approximately 60 miles from Philadelphia, take U.S. 422 west to Route 222 north. Exit at Route 61 south. The ballpark is 1 block past the exit on your right.
Ticket prices: $7: box seats; $6: reserved seats; $5: left-field reserved; $4 general admission; $2.50: children under 14 and senior citizens. For more information, call (610) 375-8469.

THE PHILLIES AT VETERANS STADIUM

Aug. 17, 1972: Steve Carlton gets his 20th win of the season and his 15th in a row as the Phillies beat the Cincinnati Reds 9–4.

Oct. 7, 1980: Greg Luzinski hits a two-run homer, bringing the Phillies a 3–1 win over the Houston Astros in the opening game of the League Championship Series.

Oct. 14, 1980: The Phillies win Game 1 of the World Series against the Kansas City Royals 7–6, with the help of Bake McBride's three-run homer.

Oct. 21, 1980: The Phillies win their only world championship when Tug McGraw strikes out the Royals' Willie Wilson at 11:29 p.m.

April 29, 1981: Steve Carlton strikes out the Montreal Expos' Tim Wallach to reach 3,000 strikeouts.

Aug. 10, 1981: Pete Rose singles to break Stan Musial's NL record for hits.

June 7, 1983: Steve Carlton passes Nolan Ryan on the all-time strikeout list by striking out the St. Louis Cardinals' Lonnie Smith, victim number 3,552.

Oct. 8, 1983: The Phillies take the pennant, with Gary Matthews' three-run homer leading a 7–2

HOME-FIELD ADVANTAGE

Veterans Stadium, like its nearly identical twins in Pittsburgh and Cincinnati, has a large, cavernous feel. Fans in the upper-deck sections really do have "Bob Uecker" seats, far from the field. But this distance does not prevent the Phillies or opposing players from hearing the boos that rain down from the stands with a regularity and ferocity that might surprise those unaccustomed to watching pro sports in Philadelphia. Even Hall of Fame third baseman Mike Schmidt was not spared from receiving the occasional wrath of the hometown fans during his 15-year career.

As tough as the fans can be with the Phillies, opposing players, especially those from such arch rivals as the Mets and the Braves, can get even harsher treatment. The Vet, as this ballpark is known to Philadelphians, can be a surprise to unsuspecting rookies and other uninitiated souls.

Veterans Stadium is a good hitter's park with a hard, fast, artificial surface that the Phillies fielders cope with better than visitors do.

PHILLIES TEAM NOTEBOOK

Franchise history
Worcester Brown Stockings, 1880–82; Philadelphia Phillies, 1883–present

World Series title
1980

National League pennants
1915, 1950, 1980, 1983, 1993

Division titles
1976, 1977, 1978, 1980, 1983, 1993

Most Valuable Players
Chuck Klein, 1932
Jim Konstanty, 1950
Mike Schmidt, 1980, 1981, 1986

Rookies of the Year
Jack Sanford, 1957

Dick Allen, 1964

Cy Young Awards
Steve Carlton, 1972, 1977, 1980, 1982
John Denny, 1983
Steve Bedrosian, 1987

Hall of Fame
Nap Lajoie, 1937
Grover Cleveland Alexander, 1938
Dan Brouthers, 1945
Ed Delahanty, 1945
Hugh Duffy, 1945
Hughie Jennings, 1945
Johnny Evers, 1946
Tommy McCarthy, 1946
Kid Nichols, 1949
Jimmie Foxx, 1951
Chief Bender, 1953
Harry Wright, 1953
Billy Hamilton, 1961
John Clarkson, 1963
Elmer Flick, 1963

Eppa Rixey, 1963
Tim Keefe, 1964
Casey Stengel, 1966
Lloyd Waner, 1967
Dave Bancroft, 1971
Sam Thompson, 1974
Bucky Harris, 1975
Roger Connor, 1976
Robin Roberts, 1976
Hack Wilson, 1979
Chuck Klein, 1980
Joe Morgan, 1990
Ferguson Jenkins, 1991
Steve Carlton, 1994
Richie Ashburn, 1995
Mike Schmidt, 1995

Retired numbers
1 Richie Ashburn
20 Mike Schmidt
32 Steve Carlton
36 Robin Roberts

win over the Los Angeles Dodgers.

June 11, 1985: Von Hayes homers twice in the first inning as the Phillies bomb the New York Mets 26–7.

June 29, 1989: The Phillies retire Steve Carlton's No. 32, then go on to defeat the Pittsburgh Pirates 6–2.

May 26, 1990: The Phillies retire Mike Schmidt's No. 20.

Aug. 15, 1990: Terry Mullholland pitches the first no-hitter in Veterans Stadium history and the Phillies' first no-hitter this century, beating the San Francisco Giants, 6–0.

October 13, 1993: The Phillies beat the Braves 6–3 in the sixth game of the the NLCS to win the National League title.

PITTSBURGH PIRATES

Three Rivers Stadium

When Three Rivers Stadium opened in 1970, the master plan called for a sprawling complex of office buildings and businesses to sprout around it on the north side of the Allegheny River by the year 2000. Today, new team owners and city planners are aiming to have the Pirates out of the Stadium and into a new "baseball only" ballpark downtown shortly after the turn of the century. It's still very early in the process, but there's a lot of wishful talk of a Forbes Field reincarnation or a Camden Yards clone. The problems? Some of the team's potential buyers had not been fully committed to keeping the Pirates in Pittsburgh, making any new stadium plan a bit premature, and Three Rivers—although difficult to love—is still in good shape and perfectly functional.

In the meantime the Pirates, the city, and the Stadium Authority are trying hard to recraft the atmosphere. They covered the upper-deck outfield seats with decorative tarps in 1993 to add baseball flavor and a sense of intimacy to the park. As a gesture to the club's 110-year history, they installed a statue honoring Hall of Famer Roberto Clemente in the plaza, and at each base on the field, planted a patch of "hallowed ground" from fields where he played. They added a baseball boardwalk of distinctive concessions and banners on the lower-level concourse. They put in a new $4.3 million Sony JumboTron video board in 1994 and added two out-of-town scoreboards just over the outfield walls. All these measures help, but you can't make Fenway Park out of a cereal bowl.

For all the efforts to get rid of it, the Pirates have been one of baseball's most successful teams since they moved into Three Rivers. In their first 26 years in the park (through 1995), they won nine NL East Division titles and two World Series and had 16 winning seasons. Clemente played there for 2½ seasons before his death in a plane crash, and Willie Stargell thrilled fans with his titanic home runs. He reached the upper deck four times—no one else has done it more than once.

PARKING
Stadium lots can handle 4,000 cars, which is OK for your average game but a problem with a big crowd. Cost is $4. Signs around the stadium will direct you to alternate lots east and north of the park. You'll also find a few lots on or near Allegheny Avenue (northwest), an easy walk through an underpass to the park. Count on paying $4–$5.

WEATHER
Bundle up in April, as the nights can be downright cold. (Stadium veterans report having seen a fire or two in the bullpens over the years.) Pittsburgh summers are usually quite pleasant. Temperatures hit 90 degrees on occasion in July and August, but that's not the norm, and evenings are cooler. September days and evenings are mild, making for fine baseball weather.

MEDIA
Radio: KDKA (1020 AM).
TV: WPXI (Channel 11) and KBL Sports Network (cable). The announcers on both are Lanny Frattare, Steve Blass, Greg Brown, and Bob Walk.

CUISINE
In the past few years, the stadium has put some Pittsburgh flavor into its concessions, a move that has proved to be a hit. Dagwood would love Primanti Bros. on the lower level; their specialty sandwiches ($4.75) come piled with meat, cheese, coleslaw, tomatoes, and French fries—all stuffed between fresh slices of bread. The standby is cheese steak, but you can also get pastrami, corned beef, sausage, and more. Fish lovers head around the corner to Benkovitz's stand for lightly breaded fresh fish fillets; the sandwich comes with two fillets on a kaiser roll with fixings. Imported beers—Beck's, Molson Golden, and Amstel Light—and local brews, such as Iron City, and a host of microbrews, are available at the Penn Brewery. Parents might want to check out the Kidcession on the lower level, where $1.75 buys a hot dog, soda, chips, and a coloring book for younger fans.
Tailgate parties are a Pittsburgh tradition that started at Steelers football games but carried over to Pirates outings. Throw a small grill and some dogs in the trunk, and you'll fit right in. If concrete with yellow stripes isn't your idea of ambience, the Clark Bar & Grill Restaurant (412-231-5720) is the best option. Located in the Clark Building on Martindale Street across the parking lot from Gate B, it's popular with players and fans alike. Retired Pirate Mike LaValliere and John Smiley (now a Cincinnati Red) are part owners. The north side by the river is mostly residential

In the Hot Seats at Three Rivers Stadium

With the upper-deck outfield seats now covered (the tarps would be removed for World Series games), capacity is reduced from 58,729 to 48,044. But tickets still are no problem. The team averages about 25,000 in its best seasons. You can almost always walk up the day of the game and buy a good seat. Opening Day and playoffs, of course, are exceptions.

GOOD SEATS

Getting a very good box seat with little notice is possible, particularly if you're seeking a single seat. The stands are close to the action, so anything in the club boxes on the infield is a treat. If that's still not close enough you could shell out $75 for a seat in the recently installed "Batter's Box," 100 seats in four rows just behind home plate. The terrace boxes in the upper deck are excellent and not too high. Upper reserves are about the same as with any of the cookie-cutter stadiums—excellent sight lines but too high. The sunny side of the stadium is down the third-base line out to left field. It gets plenty of sun and can get hot on July afternoons.

BAD SEATS

During day games it can be difficult to pick up the ball off the bat from the club boxes down the lines. The angle and the light-green color of the artificial surface contribute to the problem. If you're down the left-field line, the problem is with balls hit to the right side of the infield (away from you) and vice versa. This problem can take a couple of innings to get used to and seems to be more of a problem on bright days. Sections 177–183, the lower-deck left field, are no smoking, and one section is no-smoking/no-drinking.

SCALPING

Because ticket demand is rarely overwhelming, scalping isn't big business. It's illegal, and the club says the stadium grounds are policed. Still, scalpers can be found near the gate ramps, but on most nights it is a buyer's market.

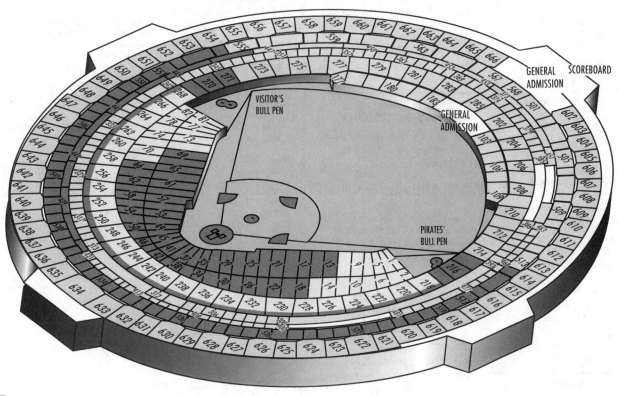

- ▩ NA
- ▢ $15
- ▉ $10
- ▨ $8
- ▧ $5

TICKET INFORMATION

Address: Advance Ticket Office, under Gate A, 600 Stadium Circle, Pittsburgh, PA 15212
Phone: (412) 321-BUCS, (800) BUY-BUCS or TicketMaster at (412) 323-1919
Hours: Mon.–Sat. 9–6.

By mail: Specify the date, number, and price of tickets you want and send a check or money order (including $3 for processing charges) to: Pittsburgh Pirates, Three Rivers Stadium, P.O. Box 7000, Pittsburgh, PA 15212.

Prices: $15: club boxes; $10: terrace boxes; $8: terrace and outfield reserved, and family sections; $5: general admission (adults); $1: general admission (children under 14).

or warehouses, so there aren't many other businesses or restaurants nearby. Many fans jump in their cars and cross the Fort Duquesne Bridge to downtown.

LODGING NEAR THE STADIUM

Doubletree Hotel at Libery Center
1000 Penn Ave.
Pittsburgh, PA 15222
(412) 281-3700/(800) 222-8733
1 mile from the stadium.

Westin in William Penn
530 William Penn Pl.
Pittsburgh, PA 15219
(412) 281-7100/(800) 228-3000
About 3 miles from the stadium.

GETTING TO THREE RIVERS STADIUM

Public transportation: Call Port Authority Transit at (412) 231-5707 for information.
By car: From the south, take I-79 north to I-279 north. Go over the Fort Pitt Bridge and the Fort Duquesne Bridge to exit 11B. The stadium lots are directly off I-279. From the north, take I-79 south to I-279 south to the stadium exit. From the east, take the Pennsylvania Turnpike to I-376 west to downtown and the stadium exit. From the west, take the Ohio Turnpike to the Pennsylvania Turnpike, then head south on I-79 to I-279 south to the stadium exit.

SPRING TRAINING

Pirate City
1701 27th St. E.
Bradenton, FL 34208

McKechnie Field
17th Ave. W. and Ninth St. W.
Bradenton, FL 34208
Capacity: 6,562
Surface: Grass
Game time: 1:05 p.m.

MINOR LEAGUES

Class	Team
AAA	Calgary (AB) Cannons
AA	Carolina (NC) Mudcats
A	Lynchburg (VA) Hillcats
A	Augusta (GA) Green Jackets
Short Season A	Erie (PA) Seawolves
Rookie	Bradenton (FL) Pirates

The Pirates' closest minor-league affiliate is the Short Season Class A Erie Seawolves of the New York–Penn League. That the Seawolves' new home, Jerry Uht Park, is reminiscent of such classic stadiums as Wrigley Field is only fitting for a town that's had a pro baseball club since the 1870s. The 6,000-seat park, however, is not just about nostalgia; its very own "green monster"—an 18-foot-high left-field wall—will provide a memorable challenge for would-be power hitters.
Along with traditional stadium fare, grilled chicken, pizza, and a spicy delicacy called "Pepperoni Balls" are on the menu. For do-it-yourselfers there is a grill and picnic area.
To reach Erie's Jerry Uht Park, which is about 130 miles from Pittsburgh, take the 12th Street exit from I-79 to State Street, then turn right onto 10th Street; the ballpark will be to your left. Ticket prices: $6: box seats; $5: reserved; $3: general admission. For more information, call (814) 456-1300.

THE PIRATES AT THREE RIVERS STADIUM

Aug. 14, 1971: Bob Gibson no-hits the Pirates in an 11–0 St. Louis Cardinals win.

Oct. 6, 1971: Homers by Al Oliver and Richie Hebner lead the Bucs to a 9–5 win in Game 4 of the NLCS over the San Francisco Giants, earning a trip to the World Series.

Oct. 13, 1971: The Pirates and Baltimore Orioles play the first night game in the history of the World Series. Pittsburgh wins Game 4, 4–3.

Aug. 9, 1976: John Candelaria no-hits the Los Angeles Dodgers 2–0.

May 11, 1977: Ted Turner enjoys the shortest managerial career ever as he takes over his Atlanta Braves for one game. The Pirates win 2–1, and Turner is suspended by Commissioner Bowie Kuhn.

April 18, 1979: The Philadelphia Phillies' Greg Luzinski hits the longest home run in Three Rivers history, a 483-foot shot off Don Robinson.

HOME-FIELD ADVANTAGE

Like its dual-purpose, artificial-surface, symmetrical cousins of the late '60s and early '70s, Three Rivers offers little edge to the home team. In the early 1970s the team won with big, power-hitting players and was nicknamed "the Lumber Company." In the late '70s they lost some of that power but added speed and won with the moniker "Lumber 'n' Lightning." In the early 1990s they used a blend of pitching, power, and defense to win three consecutive NL East crowns. All three eras produced solid teams that could have won in any park. Over the years the Pirates have posted a better record at Three Rivers than on the road, but not unusually so.

PIRATES TEAM NOTEBOOK

Franchise history
Pittsburgh Pirates, 1887–present

World Series titles
1909, 1925, 1960, 1971, 1979

National League pennants
1901, 1902, 1903, 1909, 1925, 1927, 1960, 1971, 1979

Division titles
1970, 1971, 1972, 1974, 1975, 1979, 1990, 1991, 1992

Most Valuable Players
Paul Waner, 1927
Dick Groat, 1960
Roberto Clemente, 1966
Dave Parker, 1978
Willie Stargell, 1979 (tie)
Barry Bonds, 1990, 1992

Cy Young Awards
Vernon Law, 1960
Doug Drabek, 1990

Hall of Fame
Honus Wagner, 1936
Connie Mack, 1937
Fred Clarke, 1945
Jack Chesbro, 1946
Rube Waddell, 1946
Frankie Frisch, 1947
Pie Traynor, 1948
Paul Waner, 1952
Rabbit Maranville, 1954
Arthur "Dazzy" Vance, 1955
Joe Cronin, 1956
Hank Greenberg, 1956
Max Carey, 1961
Bill McKechnie, 1962
Burleigh Grimes, 1964
Heinie Manush, 1964
James "Pud" Galvin, 1965
Casey Stengel, 1966
Branch Rickey, 1967
Lloyd Waner, 1967

Kiki Cuyler, 1968
Waite Hoyt, 1969
Jake Beckley, 1971
Joe Kelley, 1971
Roberto Clemente, 1973
George Kelly, 1973
Billy Herman, 1975
Ralph Kiner, 1975
Fred Lindstrom, 1976
Al Lopez, 1977
Chuck Klein, 1980
Arky Vaughan, 1985
Willie Stargell, 1988

Retired numbers
1 Billy Meyer
4 Ralph Kiner
8 Willie Stargell
9 Bill Mazeroski
20 Pie Traynor
21 Roberto Clemente
33 Honus Wagner
40 Danny Murtaugh

Oct. 5, 1979: Willie Stargell and Bill Madlock homer, and the Pirates beat the Cincinnati Reds 7–1 to take the National League Pennant in Game 3 of the NLCS.

Oct. 14, 1979: Bert Blyleven gets the win as the Pirates take Game 5 of the World Series, 7–1 over the Orioles.

April 18, 1987: Philadelphia's Mike Schmidt hits his 500th home run, off Don Robinson.

Sept. 20, 1992: Mickey Morandini of the Phillies turns an unassisted triple play.

July 8, 1994: The Pirates unveil a

statue honoring Roberto Clemente as part of the All-Star Game festivities at Three Rivers.

Busch Stadium

STADIUM STATS

Location: *250 Stadium Plaza, St. Louis, MO 63102*
Opened: *May 12, 1966*
Surface: *Grass*
Capacity: *57,673*
Outfield dimensions: *LF 330, LC 372, CF 402, RC 375, RF 330*
Services for fans with disabilities: *Seating available behind home plate in the field-box and loge-reserve sections.*

STADIUM FIRSTS

Regular season game: *May 12, 1966, 4–3 over the Atlanta Braves in 12 innings.*
Pitcher: *Ray Washburn of the Cardinals.*
Batter: *Felipe Alou of the Braves.*
Hit: *Gary Geiger of the Braves.*
Home Run: *May 13, 1966, by Julian Javier of the Cardinals.*

GROUND RULES

• *A fly ball hitting above yellow line on the outfield wall is a home run.*
• *A fair ball bounding into field boxes, bleachers, over the fence in the outfield or an enclosed area in left- or right-field corners, or going through or under fences is a double.*
• *A ball rolling onto the top step of a dugout is in play. The photographers' area is part of the dugout.*
• *A pitched, thrown, or batted ball that hits anyone on the field, except as otherwise provided for in the Official Rules, is in play.*
• *Any batted ball hitting a tarpaulin is a foul ball.*
• *A ball going through the wire behind the plate or lodging in it is one base on a throw by a pitcher and two bases if thrown by a fielder.*

Busch Stadium was the second of the oval, dual-purpose cookie-cutter stadiums, and among its genre, Busch is considered a cut above the average (which isn't saying much). But the reasons for this advantage rest more with the fans and surrounding area than with the ballpark.

St. Louis is a baseball town, and the game's traditions run deep here. The park is splashed with red as fans wear apparel in the team colors. The crowd isn't rowdy, but it's always into the game. The franchise has a rich history of colorful teams and winning—from the Gashouse Gang of the 1930s and early '40s to Whitey Herzog's base-stealing ballclubs of the 1980s. A statue of Hall of Famer Stan "The Man" Musial, and a monument honoring the Cards' World Championship teams greet visitors by the prime entrance.

The park was part of a huge urban-renewal project that included construction of the Gateway Arch on the banks of the Mississippi River. It worked. Small arches are built into the rim of the stadium in the upper deck, and the Gateway Arch (about 8 blocks away) is visible from the stands beyond the left-field foul pole.

In 1996 two heartfelt baseball traditions returned to the park. First and foremost was grass. Real grass. A distant second was the reinstatement of singing of "Take Me Out to the Ball Game" at the seventh-inning stretch, instead of the famous Budweiser jingle "When You Say Bud…." The famous beermaker sold the team prior to the '96 season, and the new ownership removed many of the logos and did away with a lot of the company tie-ins to the stadium and the game. Anheuser-Busch beers will still dominate the market here, and the stadium name won't change, but it might be a while before any Clydesdales are seen trotting around the infield.

HOT TIPS FOR VISITING FANS

PARKING

Unless you are in a great rush to leave after the game, use the two stadium garages ($5) across the street on the east and west sides. They're convenient—connected to the park by a pedestrian bridge. Together they offer room for 5,000 cars, and while they fill close to capacity most every game, you usually can get in. Several other lots and garages are within a few blocks of the park, charging from $2 to $10-plus.

WEATHER

If you've never been to St. Louis in summer, brace yourself. The summer months are hot and very humid. And nights aren't necessarily cooler in July and August—90 degrees at 6 p.m. isn't news. You have to take your chances—you could find a perfect day for baseball, or an afternoon in a 50,000-seat sauna. April nights can be chilly, but September is usually very pleasant.

MEDIA

Radio: KMOX (1120 AM). Hall of Famer Jack Buck, his son Joe, and ex-Cardinal Mike Shannon handle the announcing chores on radio and on Channel 11.
TV: KPLR-TV (Channel 11) and Prime Network (cable), which has commentary by Joe Buck, Bob Carpenter, and ex-Cards reliever Al "The Mad Hungarian" Hrabosky.

CUISINE

OK, but nothing special. St. Louis is basically a hot-dog-and-beer town at the park. The dogs are pretty tasty, and the bratwurst is definitely a cut above normal. The beer is Anheuser-Busch in all its glory. A food court on the lower concourse offers a nice selection of burgers, brats, etc. A kids' area on the lower concourse features a play area and kids' menu at concessions.

Because the park is downtown, fans have an excellent choice of pre- and postgame spots. Mike Shannon's (314-421-1540) on North Seventh Street, which has steaks and seafood and lots of sports memorabilia, is a very popular spot just a couple of blocks from the stadium. Umpires and writers frequent Randy's (314-231-2234) on North Tucker Boulevard, across from the *St. Louis Post Dispatch*. Before Sunday afternoon games, head for Chestnuts restaurant in the Adams Mark Hotel (314-241-7400) for its wonderful brunch. It's just a 3-block walk from the stadium. One of the best steakhouses in the Midwest is Dierdorf & Hart's Restaurant (ex-football Cardinals Dan Dierdorf and Jim Hart are part owners) in Union Station (314-421-1772)—a five-minute cab ride out to Market Street.

LODGING NEAR THE STADIUM

Adams Mark Hotel
Fourth and Chestnut
St. Louis, MO 63102
(314) 241-7400/(800) 444-2326
3 blocks from the stadium.

The St. Louis Marriott Pavilion
1 S. Broadway
St. Louis, MO 63102
(314)421-1776/(800) 228-9290
Across the street from the stadium.

In the Hot Seats at Busch Stadium

The Cardinals attract 2 million fans a year—they have a season-ticket base of more than 17,000 and draw from all over Missouri and four neighboring states, so advance sales are brisk and start in the offseason. The Cards begin to receive mail orders for the coming season in September, four months before they begin processing them. All the field boxes are sold on a season-ticket basis (except for disabled-accessible seating), as are loge boxes and reserves on the infield. You can still get behind home plate in the upper deck—terrace boxes, reserve, and general admission. On the lower levels you have to go down the lines, but the sight lines in the park are pretty good.

GOOD SEATS

Upper decks in the circular stadiums of the 1970s are high, no getting around it. But the Busch top level is not as steep as some of its cousins, so it's not a bad seat. The terrace boxes (at $12, not exactly a bargain) are fine seats if you can get on the infield. The bleachers in left-center and right-center fields are also popular. They're sold on the day of game only, for just $5. But one word of warning: You're in the sun during day games, and the heat can be oppressive. Seats at the end of the foul lines have been redirected to face home plate. A new picnic area called Homers Landing has been established along the left-center line and overlooking the bullpen.

BAD SEATS

Be careful of the back rows in the loge reserve. Like most of the parks in Busch's mold, an overhang problem exists under the second deck. And they tuck you back a fair piece at Busch. You won't get wet during rain delays, but you'll miss high flies and the gorgeous view of the Arch.

SCALPING

Scalpers will work the bridge connecting the stadium to the parking garage, and sometimes you'll find them in front of the main gates. Demand is high for Cubs games. Fans sometimes buy from season ticketholders selling an extra or two at face value in front of the park.

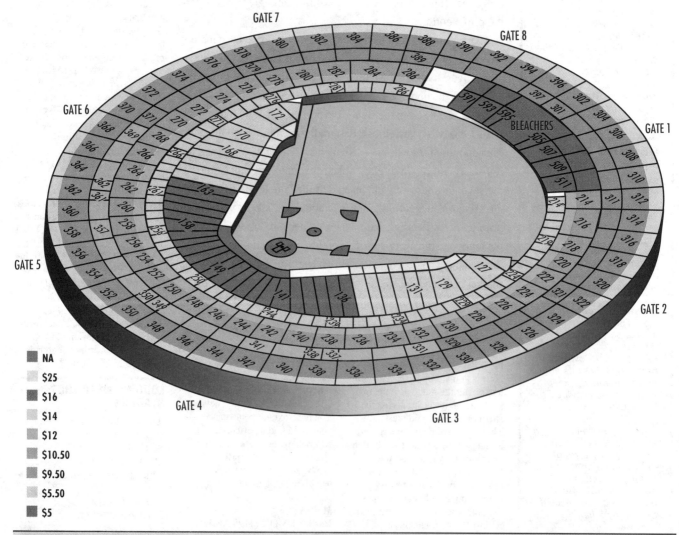

Legend:
- NA
- $25
- $16
- $14
- $12
- $10.50
- $9.50
- $5.50
- $5

TICKET INFORMATION

Address: 250 Stadium Plaza, St. Louis, MO 63102
Phone: (314) 421-2400

Hours: Mon.–Sat. 9–5:30, and 9 until game time on game days.
Prices: $25: dugout level boxes; $16: baseline boxes; $14: field boxes, loge boxes (rows 1–4); $12: terrace boxes, loge boxes (rows 5–7); $10.50: loge reserved; $9.50: terrace reserved; $5.50: general admission reserved; $5: bleachers.

GETTING TO BUSCH STADIUM

Public transportation: Bi-State Development buses go to the stadium. For more information, call (314) 231-2345.

By car: From the north, take I-55 south, I-64 west. Then I-70 West or U.S. 40 west to the Poplar Street Bridge. Continue to the Busch Stadium exit and follow signs to the stadium.
From the west or the south, use I-55 north, I-70 east, I-44 east or U.S. 40 east to St. Louis, then go to the Busch Stadium exit. Follow signs to the stadium.

SPRING TRAINING

Al Lang Stadium
180 Second Ave. S.E.
St. Petersburg, FL 33701
Capacity: 7,600
Surface: Grass
Game time: 1:05 p.m.

MINOR LEAGUES

Class	Team
AAA	Louisville (KY) Redbirds
AA	Arkansas Travelers
A	St. Petersburg (FL) Cardinals
A	Peoria (IL) Chiefs
Short Season A	New Jersey Cardinals
Rookie	Johnson City (TN) Cardinals
Rookie	Chandler (AZ) Cardinals

The closest minor-league team is the Class A Peoria Chiefs of the Midwest League. Pro baseball returned to Peoria in 1983 after a 26-year absence. One of the Chiefs' opponents is the Madison Hatters, the Cardinals' Midwest League affiliate. The Chiefs, a Chicago Cubs farm team since 1985, have sent such prominent players as Greg Maddux, Mark Grace, and Derrick May on to Wrigley Field.
To reach Peoria's Pete Vonachen Stadium, approximately 150 miles from St. Louis, take the North University exit from I-74. Turn left on North University and then left on Nebraska. The ballpark will be on your left. Ticket prices: $5: box seats; $4: reserved seats; $3: general admission. For more information, call (309) 688-1622.

THE CARDINALS AT BUSCH STADIUM

Oct. 8, 1967: Bob Gibson wins his second game of the World Series, beating the Boston Red Sox 6–0.

Oct. 2, 1968: In Game 1 of the 1968 fall classic, Gibson strikes out a World Series-record 17 batters in the Cardinals' 4–0 victory over the Detroit Tigers.

Set. 15, 1969: Steve Carlton strikes out 19 New York Mets in a 4–3 loss.

Sept. 10, 1974: Lou Brock breaks Maury Wills' record for steals in a season, getting his 105th against the Philadelphia Phillies.

April 16, 1978: Bob Forsch throws a no-hitter against the Phillies, winning 5–0.

Aug. 13, 1979: Lou Brock singles off Dennis Lamp of the Chicago Cubs for his 3,000th hit.

Sept. 23, 1979: Brock steals his 938th base, establishing an all-time record not broken until Rickey Henderson.

Oct. 20, 1982: Joaquin Andujar and Bruce Sutter team up to win Game 7 of the World Series, 6–3 over the Milwaukee Brewers.

Oct. 14, 1985: With the game tied in the bottom of the ninth, Ozzie Smith hits his first-ever left-handed homer to give the Cards a 3–2 win and a 3–2 edge in the NLCS vs. Los Angeles.

Oct. 14, 1987: Danny Cox shuts out the Giants 6–0 in the seventh game of the NLCS.

July 3, 1995: Newly acquired relief pitcher Mike Morgan holds Montreal batters hitless for 8½ innings in a 6–0 shutout.

September 15, 1995: 40-year-old Ozzie Smith inspires aging baby boomers nationwide when he gets his 1,554th double play, a league record for shortstops.

HOME-FIELD ADVANTAGE

Busch Stadium is not a home-run hitters' park. It traditionally has been considered a big park geared to line-drive hitters who could sting the ball into the gaps of a spacious AstroTurf outfield. Over the years, outfield speed was a tradmark of the club. Lou Brock, Lonnie Smith, Willie McGee, and Vince Coleman patrolled the plastic grass in the '70s and '80s, and the Cards finished with the best record in the NL East Division four times and appeared in three World Series in the '80s. The Cardinals haven't ranked higher than eighth in the National League in home runs since 1967. Between 1982 and '91 they finished last every year but one.

The reputation of the park is on the verge of a complete revision. Grass, real grass, was planted before the 1996 season, and although the returns aren't in yet on how this affects the need for speed in the outfield, or the number of bases a long-ball hitter can take if he doesn't get it over the fence, stadium stats will likely start to look different from now on. The walls had already been lowered from 10 feet to eight feet, and the center-field fence is 402 feet—12 feet shorter than previously. The walls are now also painted green (the color was chosen by fans' votes). The power alleys are about 20 feet closer than they once were. Still, the Cards tend to be a club built around line-drive hitters (center fielder Ray Lankford represents the speed and power combination they seek), and they're traditionally much tougher at home than on the road. In 1993 they were 17 games over .500 at Busch, five games under .500 elsewhere; in 1995 they went 39–33 at home.

CARDINALS TEAM NOTEBOOK

Franchise history
St. Louis Cardinals, 1892–present

World Series titles
1926, 1931, 1934, 1942, 1944, 1946, 1964, 1967, 1982

National League pennants
1926, 1928, 1930, 1931, 1934, 1942, 1943, 1944, 1946, 1964, 1967, 1968, 1982, 1985, 1987

Division titles
1982, 1985, 1987

Most Valuable Players
Rogers Hornsby 1925
Bob O'Farrell, 1926
Jim Bottomley, 1928
Frankie Frisch, 1931
Dizzy Dean, 1934
Joe "Ducky" Medwick, 1937
Mort Cooper, 1942
Stan Musial, 1943, 1946, 1948
Marty Marion, 1944
Ken Boyer, 1964
Orlando Cepeda, 1967

Bob Gibson, 1968
Joe Torre, 1971
Keith Hernandez, 1979 (tie)
Willie McGee, 1985

Rookie of the Year
Wally Moon, 1954
Bill Virdon, 1955
Bake McBride, 1974
Vince Coleman, 1985
Todd Worrell, 1986

Cy Young Awards
Bob Gibson, 1968, 1970

Hall of Fame
John McGraw, 1937
Cy Young, 1937
Grover Cleveland Alexander, 1938
Rogers Hornsby, 1942
Roger Bresnahan, 1945
Wilbert Robinson, 1945
Frankie Frisch, 1947
Jesse Burkett, 1948
Mordecai Brown, 1949
Kid Nichols, 1949
Dizzy Dean, 1953
Bobby Wallace, 1953
Rabbit Maranville, 1954

Dazzy Vance, 1955
Bill McKechnie, 1962
Burleigh Grimes, 1964
Miller Huggins, 1964
Pud Galvin, 1965
Branch Rickey, 1967
Joe "Ducky" Medwick, 1968
Stan Musial, 1969
Jesse Haines, 1970
Jake Beckley, 1971
Chick Hafey, 1971
Jim Bottomley, 1974
Roger Connor, 1976
Bob Gibson, 1981
John Mize, 1981
Walter Alson, 1983
Lou Brock, 1985
Enos Slaughter, 1985
Hoyt Wilhelm, 1985
Red Schoendienst, 1989
Steve Carlton, 1994

Retired numbers
6 Stan Musial
14 Ken Boyer
17 Dizzy Dean
20 Lou Brock
45 Bob Gibson
85 August A. Busch, Jr.

SAN DIEGO PADRES

San Diego Jack Murphy Stadium

Think San Diego has no baseball tradition? Think again. Ted Williams, one of the greatest hitters of all time, was born in San Diego and started his career there. Tony Gwynn, a four-time National League batting champion, is from San Diego, too, and he has become almost as much of a cultural icon here as the surfboard. There were even Padres before these Padres. They played in Lane Field.

This time around the Padres play in Jack Murphy Stadium, named after the sportswriter who helped San Diego land major-league franchises in football and baseball. Some longtime baseball observers recall the crowds from the summer of 1984—the year the team reached the World Series—as the loudest they'd ever heard at an open-air stadium.

The cheering isn't quite as loud now. After nearly giving away every player of value short of Tony Gwynn, the team came close to losing all its fans, too. Coupled with Roseanne's controversial rendition of the national anthem before a 1990 game, the team's trading habits made things pretty dark for a while. Then, in 1995, the Padres and Astros worked out the largest trade in baseball history, which gave the Padres a jump start. The team's swinging friar mascot, dating back to its days as a minor-league club, was reactivated in 1996 to commemorate 60 years of Padre baseball in San Diego, and perhaps to appeal to wayward fans' sense of tradition. The Murph is slowly coming back to life.

The ballpark is still attractive, even if the team isn't. Set in Mission Valley, between two steep ridges, it's about 8 miles from the Pacific Ocean, near the junction of Interstates 15 and 8. The Murph has an open end in the outfield and five levels (including a club level) stacked in three decks. A larger JumboTron screen (24 feet by 33 feet) was installed in 1996, and a new 9½-foot-tall, 86-foot-long out-of-town scoreboard in right field will prove hazardous to left-handed sluggers; Tony Gwynn bounced one off the board in the first game played with it in the park.

PARKING
Stadium lots have space for 18,000 cars, the second-largest in the major leagues. Street parking is extremely limited. Traffic congestion can be a problem, but when the club isn't drawing, you can easily get out to the two interstates.

WEATHER
Don't look for rain delays. The weather is divine—that's why San Diego is such a popular vacation destination. The Padres, who have not been rained out since April 20, 1983, don't have a full-time rain-delay squad. Instead, designated concession-aires and cleanup crew members will spring to the field and unroll the tarp if necessary. All of which accounts for the skunk who lives inside the tarp rolled up under the stands along the first-base line. So far, no one has been sprayed, and his annual visits make highlight reels every year (something that few Padres can boast of recently), along with a family of foxes that dwell under the stands and have been known to interrupt play.

MEDIA
Radio: KFMB (760 AM); XEXX (1420 AM) in Tijuana does the Spanish-language broadcasts, with Mario T. Zapiain, Eduardo Ortega, and Matias Santosas announcing.
TV: KUSI-TV (Channel 51) shows road games. The broadcasters are Jerry ("Oh, Doctor") Coleman, Bob Chandler, and Ted Leitner, who also do KFMB's radio shows.

CUISINE
Sushi is no longer sold. It was eliminated this season to a few howls of indignation (none from local fish). You can get fish tacos from Rubio's, a local fast-food taco outlet. Consisting of crisp fried fish with lettuce and salsa, they're well worth trying. Other notable options include java from gourmet coffee carts, Rally-burgers for those with more traditional tastes, and deluxe sausages. Randy Jones' barbecue stand has ribs, chicken, hot dogs, and corn on the cob, served up and supervised by the former Padres pitcher who won 42 games over the 1975–76 seasons. The Stadium Club is on the press level on the third-base side; it's open to season ticketholders and offers dinner before and during the game. The Sports Club is on the plaza level on the third-base side. It is open to the public and offers table seating, food, a bar, and a dozen imported beers. After the game, one possible destination is the Gaslamp Quarter, a restored turn-of-the century section of downtown about 6 miles from the stadium. It's known for its nightlife, with numerous restaurants and clubs that range from upscale to funky. The area is adjacent to several new waterfront hotels, the convention center, and the Horton Plaza

Location: 9449 Friars Rd., San Diego, CA 92108
Opened: Aug. 30, 1967
Surface: Santa Ana Bermuda Grass
Capacity: 48,639
Outfield dimensions: LF 327, LC 370, CF 405, RC 370, RF 330
Services for fans with disabilities: Seating in plaza level, sections 17, 25, 44–46, and 57–59; in loge level, section 31.

Regular-season game: April 8, 1969, 2–1 over the Houston Astros.
Pitcher: Dick Selma of the Padres.
Batter: Jesus Alou of the Astros.
Hit: Jesus Alou.
Home run: Ed Spiezio of the Padres.

• Photographers' areas adjacent to first-base and third-base dugouts are considered part of dugouts. Ball in these areas is out of play, same as both dugouts.
• Bullpens are in play.
• Everything else is standard ground rules.

In the Hot Seats at San Diego Jack Murphy Stadium

Capacity is 48,639, with maybe one-quarter of the seats used in a typical game. The Padres sell only about 8,000 season tickets, so you can get good seats on a walk-up basis. The top deck is closed from left-center field to the right-field corner. In an attempt to put the best face on things, each closed section is covered by a tarp, but unoccupied seats still abound. Nonetheless, don't try to move down to a better location—ushers are vigilant about letting customers sit only in their assigned seats. In an effort to lure back fans, some novelty seating has been created; 69 seats behind home plate—closer to the batter than the pitcher is—are available as season tickets, and a dozen or so seats at the field level next to the dugouts and photographers' bays are sold for each game.

All seats in the stadium are reserved, including the $5 pavilion seats beyond right field, which aren't as bad as you might think, even with the scoreboard; they get lots of sun during day games, so you can strip down and catch some rays.

GOOD SEATS

Some outfield seats are actually prized. The right-field stands, in particular, allow fans to commune with Tony Gwynn, whose popularity exceeds that of any San Diego athlete, even Chargers linebacker Junior Seau.

BAD SEATS

All seats have unobstructed views of the field, but fans in the pavilion seats can't see the main scoreboard, or the JumboTron videoboard that towers above the section. Beyond center field, many seats are more than 500 feet from home plate. Seats on the field level beyond the dugouts extend close to the playing field down both foul lines, so fans there must be prepared to dodge foul line drives.

SPECIAL PROGRAMS

The junior Padres' program for youngsters 14 or under offers tickets to eight games for $6. The seniors' program offers tickets to eight games for $6. Also, every Friday night is family night. For $32, families receive four loge-level seats, four hot dogs, four Cokes, a game program, and parking. Special nights for Little League and the military are scheduled.

SCALPING

Fans needn't bother. Although 1996 showed signs of improved attendance over the previous couple of seasons, the state of ticket sales still makes scalping fairly pointless for both seller and buyer. These days, whatever market there is favors the buyers.

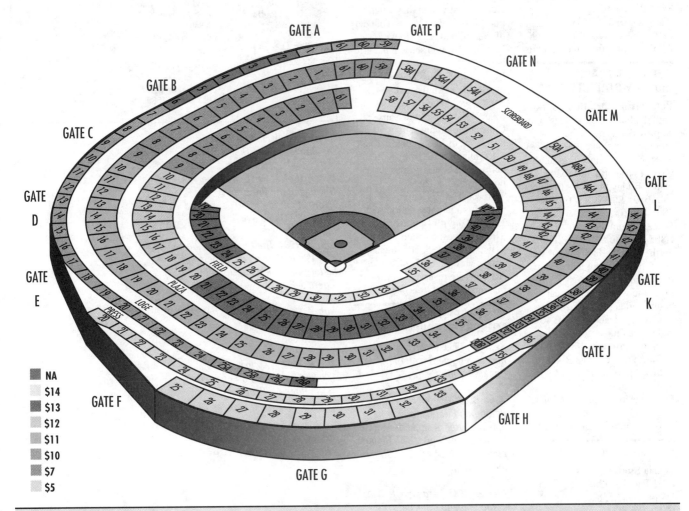

Legend:
- NA
- $14
- $13
- $12
- $11
- $10
- $7
- $5

TICKET INFORMATION
Address: Gate C, 9449 Friars Rd., San Diego, CA 92108
Phone: (619) 283-4494.
Hours: Daily 9–5.

By Mail: San Diego Padres Ticket Department, P.O. Box 12900, San Diego, CA, 92112. Send a check or money order. Please specify the date of game and the number and location of seats.

Prices: $14: field level (infield); $13: field level (outfield), plaza level (infield); $12: plaza level (outfield); $11: loge; $10: press level; $7: left-field grandstand; $5 view level bleachers.

downtown shopping center. Try Kansas City Barbecue (619-231-9680), downtown near the Marriott. Some of the bar scenes from the Tom Cruise movie *Top Gun* were filmed in this popular stop. Order the tasty Hot Links. Closer to the stadium, 2 or so miles away, is Mission Valley's Hotel Circle and Restaurant Row. Padres Pub in the Hilton Mission Valley is a good choice. Also try Trophy's Bar & Grill (619-296-9600) on Friars Road near the ballpark, and Bully's East on Texas Street.

LODGING NEAR THE STADIUM

Hyatt Regency
1 Market Pl.
San Diego, CA 92101
(619) 232-1234/(800) 233-1234
10 miles from the stadium.

The Mission Valley Marriott
8757 Rio San Diego Dr.
San Diego, CA 92108
(619) 692-3800/(800) 228-9290
About 2 miles from the stadium.

GETTING TO JACK MURPHY STADIUM

Public transportation: Working with the Padres, San Diego transit provides a shuttle bus. For more information call (619) 233-3004. North County Transit also provides a shuttle bus to the games Friday through Sunday; call (619) 722-NCTD or (619) 685-4800 for details.
By car: From the north, take I-805 south to I-8 east to I-15 north. Take the Friars Road west and follow it about half a mile to the stadium.
From the west, take I-8 east bound and get off at Stadium Way, which leads to Friars Road and the stadium.
From the east, take I-8 West to I-15 North to the Friars Road exit. Follow Friars Road west ½ mile to the stadium.
From the south, take I-805 north to I-8 and follow the directions provided above from the west.

SPRING TRAINING

Peoria Stadium
8131 Paradise Lane
Peoria, AZ, 85382
(602) 486-7000
Capacity: 7,000 permanent seating, 3,000 in grass seating in the outfield.

Surface: Grass
Game time: 1:05 p.m. or 7:05 p.m.

MINOR LEAGUES

Class	Team
AAA	Las Vegas (NV) Stars
AA	Memphis (TN) Chicks
A	Rancho Cucamonga (CA) Quakes
A	Clinton (IA) Lumber Kings
Short Season A	Idaho Falls (ID) Braves
Rookie	Peoria (AZ) Padres

The closest minor-league affiliate team to San Diego is the 1994 California League champion Class A Rancho Cucamonga Quakes. Quakes owner Hank Stickney also owns the Lake Elsinore Storm (an Angels farm club against whom they often play) and the Las Vegas Thunder of the International Hockey League. (Do you sense a pattern here?)
Built in 1993, the Quakes' state-of-the-art stadium is called—what else—"The Epicenter," and is set at the foot of the San Gabriel Mountains, about 50 miles east of Los Angeles, about a 40-minute drive from Anaheim, and about a 2-hour drive north from San Diego.
To reach The Epicenter, take I-15 north from its intersection with I-10 to Foothill Boulevard.
Ticket prices: $7: field box seats; $6: box; $5: club level; $4.50: view box; $3: bleachers. All seats are reserved. For more information call (909) 481-5000.

THE PADRES AT JACK MURPHY STADIUM

Sept. 22, 1969: *Willie Mays hits his 600th home run off of Mike Cockins of the Padres.*

June 12, 1970: *Dock Ellis of the Pittsburgh Pirates throws the only no-hitter in stadium history, blanking the Padres 2–0. He later claims to have been on LSD during the game.*

May 25, 1982: *Ferguson Jenkins of the Chicago Cubs gets his 3,000th strikeout.*

Sept. 20, 1984: *The Padres clinch*

HOME-FIELD ADVANTAGE

The stadium's reputation as a launching pad may change, at least for lefties, since the addition of an out-of-town scoreboard that rises 9½ feet above the right field fence. Sluggers batting from the left side of the plate now have to clear a 17-foot, 9-inch barrier to get the ball into the stands beyond right. The board is in play, which means fewer highlight appearances by Tony Gwynn leaping up to steal a homer at the fence. Right-handed hitters still have only the 8' foot fence in left field, and left-fielders can still make their leaping catches at the wall.
Balls hit down the lines and into foul territory in the left- and right-field corners can cause problems. Fair balls that hit the stands that extend close to the field midway down the line can kick back into right field. Gwynn often plays the carom instead of heading for the corner, fields the ball in medium right, and throws the runner out at second.

PADRES TEAM NOTEBOOK

Franchise history	Rookies of the Year	Hall of Fame
San Diego Padres, 1969–present	Butch Metzger, 1976 (tied)	Willie McCovey, 1986
	Benito Santiago, 1987	Gaylord Perry, 1991
National League pennant		Rollie Fingers, 1992
1984	**Cy Young Awards**	
	Randy Jones, 1976	**Retired number**
Division title	Gaylord Perry, 1978	6 Steve Garvey
1984	Mark Davis, 1989	

their first division title, beating the San Francisco Giants 5–4.

Oct. 7, 1984: *An error by Leon Durham of the Cubs allows the Padres to erase a 3–0 deficit and win 8–3 in Game 5 of the NLCS.*

Oct. 10, 1984: *The Padres get the only World Series win in their history, defeating the Detroit Tigers 5–3.*

Aug. 4, 1993: *Tony Gwynn has six hits against the Giants, his career best.*

Aug. 6, 1993: *Gwynn gets his 2,000th hit, a single off of the Colorado Rockies' Bruce Ruffin.*

3Com Park

It is loved, it is loathed, and pretty soon it'll be history. In its 30-plus years of service, Candlestick has been home to Willie Mays and Barry Bonds, but it remains best known for its weather conditions. It's been shaken by an earthquake and rattled by wind. Some fans riff on Mark Twain's line and claim that the coldest winter they've ever spent was a summer evening at Candlestick. The Giants' new park in China Basin is scheduled to open on time for the 2000 season. It will be the first in 30 years to be built with private funds, which is a reason to like it already.

Developer Charles Harney was the man—the villain, really—who in 1958 offered Candlestick Point, a rocky outcropping into San Francisco Bay, for the Giants' home here. Mayor George Christopher loved the site, as did Giants' owner Horace Stoneham. After two years at downtown Seals Stadium, the Giants moved into Candlestick in 1960; by the time the ballpark was expanded and enclosed in 1971–72 to make room for the NFL 49ers, the Stick had become a meteorological legend. Unfortunately, the mayor and the owner had toured the area during the day. Days at Candlestick are gorgeous—the chill, fog, and wind arrive at dusk.

To get around the elements, the Giants play more day games than any team in baseball other than the Chicago Cubs: 57 in 1994, up from 53 in '93 and 44 in '92. Go at night only if you're interested in the bizarre. During night games, hot-dog wrappers and other paper products are routinely pushed into the outfield corners and trapped there by gusty winds, occasionally forcing outfielders to sift wildly through several inches of trash to recover a ball still in play. Flocks of birds have dive-bombed players, and caps have been blown off the heads of infielders and pinned against the outfield wall at Candlestick.

Oh, but it's 3Com Park now, you say? Well, even the Giants' media guide still calls it Candlestick. Enough said.

HOT TIPS FOR VISITING FANS

PARKING

There are 8,300 spots for cars and 200 for buses in 77 acres around the stadium. Lots generally charge $10. It helps to arrive early—about an hour ahead—if you want to avoid bottlenecks. Traffic backs up in a particularly frustrating manner at the two exits off U.S. 101, the nearby north-south highway (and one very harrowing drive). Don't park in the surrounding area. The neighborhood can be rough, and your car might be damaged.

WEATHER

The wind and cold aren't the only odd conditions. Dense fog tends to stream over the top of the stands like smoke from a major forest fire, then it settles on the field like an apparition. Bundle up for night games, and though the weather is usually pleasant and warm during the day, a sweater or light jacket is never a bad idea.

MEDIA

Radio: KNBR (680 AM) has Hank Greenwald on play-by-play with Ted Robinson and Mike Krukow. There is also a Spanish-language broadcast on KIQI (1010 AM) of all home games and selected road games. Amaury Pi-Gonzalez, Rene De La Rosa, and Edgar Martinez handle the duties.
TV: KTVU-Fox (Channel 2) and SportsChannel (cable). Sports-Channel has Mike Krukow and Duane Kuiper, both of whom are joined by legendary Giants announcer Lon Simmons and Ted Robinson on KTVU.

CUISINE

Yum! Polish sausage is regarded by aficionados as one of the better concessions foods anywhere. Other fans say the top concessions item is a 12-clove garlic-chicken sandwich provided by The Stinking Rose, a hot spot in North Beach. The Mexican stand offers sensational garlic-chili French fries; if you're partial to hot foods, don't miss them. Gordon Biersch microbrewery serves cold drafts of its exquisite beer, plus good pub food. As far as anyone knows, this was the first major-league ballpark to serve wine. Concessions stands were recently widened, which means lines are shorter, but there are more of them.

After the game, head into town. San Francisco is as wonderful as you've heard; the city supports more restaurants per capita than any other in the country. If you're a mystery fan, order chops just like Sam Spade at John's Grill on Ellis Street (415-986-0069). Try Chinese at the nationally renowned (but inexpensive) House of Nanking (415-421-1429) on Kearney Street off Columbus Avenue. Also off Columbus, the Washington Square Bar & Grill (415-982-8123), affectionately known as "The Washbag," is a baseball insiders' hangout.

LODGING NEAR THE STADIUM

Parc 55 Hotel
55 Cyril Magnin St.

In the Hot Seats at 3Com Park

The Giants have a small season-ticket base. You can get good walk-up seats for almost every game. The Mets and the Dodgers are the leading draws.

GOOD SEATS

There are some nights when it gets so cold, there are no good seats, save the super boxes on the mezzanine level. They have heat. The rows in the lower stands rise gradually, so your view is limited if you sit behind anyone tall.

BAD SEATS

The left-field bleachers once stopped 20 to 30 feet from the fence, prompting fans to scramble from their seats and fight wildly over home-run balls that fell into the demilitarized zone. One reason the Giants moved their bleachers right to the wall before the 1993 season was to eliminate that kind of scramble. They are still not great seats, but at least you won't get stepped on anymore. The JumboTron scoreboard in right-center pro-vides a clear picture, but those sitting in the center or right-field upper deck can't see it.

SCALPING

There's not much of a market, because buyers can always walk up to the window and get a seat.

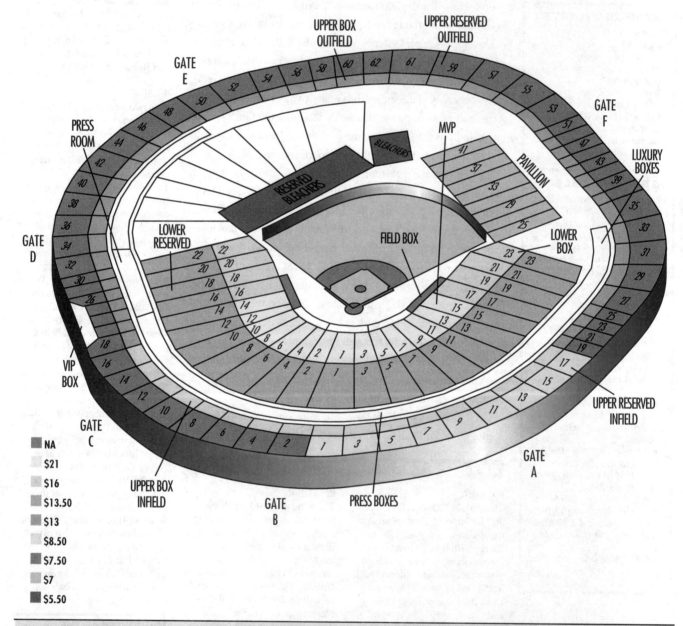

Legend:
- NA
- $21
- $16
- $13.50
- $13
- $8.50
- $7.50
- $7
- $5.50

TICKET INFORMATION
Address: 3Com Park, San Francisco, CA 94124
Phone: (415) 467-8000

Hours: Mon.–Fri. 9–5.
Prices: $21: MVP; $16: upper box sections 1–17 infield, lower box; $13.50: lower reserved; $13: upper box outfield; $8.50: upper reserved sections 1–17 infield; $7.50: upper reserved outfield; $7: pavilion; $5.50: reserved bleachers.

San Francisco, CA 94102
(415) 392-8000/(800) 338-1338
About 3 miles from the stadium.

Westin St. Francis
335 Powell St.
San Francisco, CA 94102
(415) 397-7000/(800) 228-3000
About 7 miles from the stadium.

GETTING TO 3COM PARK

Public transportation: The Municipal Railway (MUNI) and the San Mateo County Transit District (SamTrans) provide bus service to the stadium. For schedule information, call (415) 673-MUNI or SamTrans at (800) 660-4287.

By car: From San Francisco and points north, take U.S. 101 to the Cow Palace–Brisbane exit, not the 3Com Park exit. Continue to Third and turn left over the freeway, continuing on Third Street, about ¼ mile, then make a right onto Jamestown Avenue. Go about 1¼ miles to the main lot. From the south, exit from 101 onto Third. Then follow the directions above.

SPRING TRAINING

Scottsdale Stadium
7408 E. Osborn Rd.
Scottsdale, AR 85251
Capacity: 10,500 (8,500 fixed seats and 2,000 lawn seating)
Surface: Grass
Game time: 1:05 p.m. or 7:05 p.m.

MINOR LEAGUES

Class	Team
AAA	Phoenix (AZ) Firebirds
AA	Shreveport (LA) Captains
A	San Jose (CA) Giants
A	Burlington (IA) Bees
Short Season A	Bellingham (WA) Giants
Rookie	San Pedro (DR) Giants

The closest minor-league team to San Francisco is the Class A San Jose Giants of the California League. San Jose (one of the Giants' minor-league teams) frequently plays the Modesto A's, Oakland's California League affiliate. With the exception of only five years, 1959–61 and 1977–78, pro baseball has been played continuously in San Jose since 1942. But this city's baseball history goes back even farther, to 1896, when San Jose was a charter franchise in the California State League, which folded after its first season ended. To reach San Jose from the Bay Area, which is fewer than 45 miles away, take I-880 South to I-280 south. Exit at 10th Street. Turn right on 10th and then left on Alma; Municipal Stadium will be on the right.
Ticket prices: $7: box seats; $6: adults; $3: children under 10 (children under 4 are free); $2: senior citizens 65 or over. For more information call (408) 297-1435.

THE GIANTS AT 3COM PARK

Oct. 5, 1962: The Giants win their first World Series game at Candlestick, 2–0 over the Yankees.

Oct. 15, 1962: Billy Pierce holds the Yankees in a 5–2 win in Game 6 of the World Series.

Sept. 22, 1963: Willie McCovey hits three consecutive home runs against the New York Mets.

Aug. 22, 1965: Juan Marichal attacks Los Angeles Dodgers catcher John Roseboro with his bat.

July 3, 1966: Atlanta's Tony Cloninger, a pitcher, becomes the only player in National League history to hit two grand slams in one game. The Braves win 17–3.

July 14, 1967: Marichal is the victim of Eddie Mathews' 500th home run.

Sept. 17, 1968: Gaylord Perry of the Giants no-hits the St. Louis Cardinals 1–0. The next afternoon, Ray Washburn of the Cardinals returns the favor, no-hitting the Giants 2–0.

August 24, 1975: Ed Halicki no-hits the Mets 6-0.

July 10, 1984: Fernando Valenzuela strikes out Dave Winfield, Reggie Jackson, and George Brett in order. The next inning, Doc Gooden strikes out three more American Leaguers, and the National League wins the All-Star Game 3–1.

HOME-FIELD ADVANTAGE

When Roger Craig managed the Giants, he ordered players not to complain about conditions. He knew the opposition would be unhappy and eager to leave, and figured the Giants would hold a home-field advantage.

Visiting clubs have a good deal to complain about. Only the home dugout has runway access to the clubhouse, so a visiting player has to walk from the left-field dugout, across the field, and up the right-field line to reach the visitors' clubhouse. Until 1994 only the Giants' dugout had a heater, and the home team is still in sole possession of a little heated hut for a bullpen.

Since the Giants are moving out, don't expect any improvements to be made at 3Com Park in regard to baseball. The 49ers, on the other hand, are licking their chops at the prospect of having the place to themselves.

GIANTS TEAM NOTEBOOK

Franchise history
Troy Trojans, 1879–82; New York Gothams, 1883–84; New York Giants, 1885–1957; San Francisco Giants, 1958–present.

World Series titles
1905, 1921, 1922, 1933, 1954

National League pennants
1905, 1911, 1912, 1913, 1917, 1921, 1922, 1923, 1924, 1933, 1936, 1937, 1951, 1954, 1962, 1989

Division titles
1971, 1987, 1989

Most Valuable Players
Larry Doyle, 1912
Bill Terry, 1930
Carl Hubbell, 1933, 1936
Willie Mays, 1954, 1965
Willie McCovey, 1969
Kevin Mitchell, 1989
Barry Bonds, 1993

Rookies of the Year
Willie Mays, 1951
Orlando Cepeda, 1958

Willie McCovey, 1959
Gary Matthews, 1973
John Montefusco, 1975

Cy Young Award
Mike McCormick, 1967

Hall of Fame
Christy Mathewson, 1936
John McGraw, 1937
William "Buck" Ewing, 1939
Willie Keeler 1939
Rogers Hornsby, 1942
Roger Bresnahan, 1945
Dan Brouthers, 1945
King Kelly, 1945
James O'Rourke, 1945
Jesse Burkett, 1946
Joe McGinnity, 1946
Frankie Frisch, 1947
Carl Hubbell, 1947
Mel Ott, 1951
Bill Terry, 1954
Gabby Hartnett, 1955
Ray Schalk, 1955
Bill McKechnie, 1962
Edd Roush, 1962
Burleigh Grimes, 1964
Tim Keefe, 1964
Monte Ward, 1964
Casey Stengel, 1966
Joe "Ducky" Medwick, 1968
Waite Hoyt, 1969

Dave Bancroft, 1971
Jake Beckley, 1971
Rube Marquard, 1971
Ross Youngs, 1972
Monte Irvin, 1973
George Kelly, 1973
Warren Spahn, 1973
Mickey Welch, 1973
Roger Conner, 1976
Fred Lindstrom, 1976
Amos Rusie, 1977
Willie Mays, 1979
Hack Wilson, 1979
Duke Snider, 1980
Johnny Mize, 1981
Travis Jackson, 1982
Juan Marichal, 1983
Hoyt Wilhelm, 1985
Ernie Lombardi, 1986
Willie McCovey, 1986
Joe Morgan, 1990
Gaylord Perry, 1991
Steve Carlton, 1994

Retired numbers
Christy Mathewson (Did not wear a number during career)
John McGraw (Did not wear a number during career)
3 Bill Terry
11 Carl Hubbell
14 Mel Ott
24 Willie Mays
27 Juan Marichal
44 Willie McCovey

Oct. 10, 1987: The Giants hit three homers to edge past the Cardinals in Game 4 of the NLCS 4–2.

Oct. 17, 1989: An earthquake rocks the Bay Area, damaging Candlestick Park and causing the postponement of Game 3 of the World Series. Ten days later, the Series resumes.

SEATTLE MARINERS

Kingdome

The Kingdome's roof and ceiling have been fixed, and the Mariners are serious contenders not only for another division series berth, but also for the attention and enthusiasm of the more football-oriented Seattle sports fans. But the Mariners will be moving on soon. Legislation slating $320 million of funding for a new stadium was passed in 1996, clearing the way for a long-hoped-for, new, baseball-only home for the Mariners. The new ballpark will be by the Seattle-based architecture firm of NJJB, which is also creating a new ballpark for the Milwaukee Brewers. The Mariners' new stadium will have a retractable roof and real grass, and is scheduled for completion in time for Opening Day of the 1999 season.

For the Mariners, it won't be a moment too soon. Despite the recent upturn of the team's fortunes, it's had a troubled tenancy at the Kingdome. Falling ceiling tiles forced the Mariners into an extended road trip in 1994 before the players' strike ended the season early. About the only regal thing about baseball in the Kingdome has been Ken Griffey, Jr., heir apparent to the crown of baseball's best all-around player, and the team's thrilling home-stand victory in its first appearance in postseason play, against the New York Yankees in 1995.

Opened in 1976, the $67 million, multi-purpose facility also houses the NFL's Seahawks, and is used for all manner of other events, from concerts and exhibitions to tractor pulls.

The Kingdome's new acoustical ceiling is supposed to cut down on the sort of echo that used to reverberate in the place during Mariners games when the place wasn't close to being full, but the bigger crowds have also helped muffle the roar. Baseball is finally an "in" thing to do in Seattle, and the combination of a winning team and the anticipation of a new stadium has created momentum that could make this tradionally football town a first-class baseball town as well.

HOT TIPS FOR VISITING FANS

PARKING
The Kingdome has three lots— one to the north and two to the south—with a combined 4,000 spaces that are adequate for the crowds the Mariners draw. Parking is $5, but car pools of three or more persons receive a $1 discount. Another 30,000 spaces are in private lots close to the stadium. Plan on spending $5–$10 for a spot depending upon how close they are to the dome.

WEATHER
Rain is not uncommon, so a light jacket and an umbrella are always good to have as you make your way to the Kingdome. But, as long as the new roof holds up, you won't need any raingear once you get inside.

MEDIA
Radio: KIRO (710 AM).
TV: KIRO-TV (Channel 7) and Prime Sports (cable). Dave

Niehaus, Ron Fairly, and Rick Rizzo call the action for KIRO.

CUISINE
The Mariners offer a variety of brand-name foods and traditional ballpark fare at concessions stands and portable carts throughout the Kingdome. Offerings include Coca-Cola products, Dreyer's ice cream, Ezell's fried chicken, Cow Chip cookies, TCBY frozen yogurt, Fletcher's ballpark franks, and a wide variety of Starbucks coffee beverages. There's more than just coffee here, though. Seattle was at the forefront of the microbrewery trend, and they've got something for just about any particular taste in beer at the concessions stands, which offer microbrews from the numerous local breweries. If you just want to quench your thirst or clear your palate with nothing more than some tasty bottled water, they've got Crystal Geyser.

For pre- or post-game, nearby Pioneer Square, the area where Seattle grew into a city in the 1890s, has several fine restaurants. Among the most popular are F. X. McRory's (206-623-4800), which features an oyster bar and a great liquor list, Duke's (206-622-1092), which has steaks and seafood, and, farther uptown, McCormick's Fish House & Bar (206-682-3900), which has more fish on the menu than you'll see at the aquarium. No visit to Seattle would be complete without a stop at the justly famous Ray's Boathouse (206-789-3770), about a half hour drive north of town on the beach of Elliot Bay.

Visitors also can take advantage of the waterfront, which is a short walk northwest of the Kingdome and features several seafood eateries as well as an expansive view of Puget Sound and the Olympic Mountains.

LODGING NEAR THE STADIUM

Westin Hotel Seattle
1900 Fifth Ave.

STADIUM STATS
Location: 201 S. King St., Seattle WA 98104
Opened: 1976
Surface: AstroTurf
Capacity: 59,856
Outfield dimensions: LF 331, LCF 389, CF 405, RCF 380, RF 312
Services for fans with disabilities: Seating available in several sections on the 100 and 200 levels. For more information, call the ticket office.

STADIUM FIRSTS
Regular-season game: April 6, 1977, 7–0 loss to the California Angels.
Pitcher: Diego Segui of the Mariners.
Batter: Jerry Remy of the Angels.
Hit: Don Baylor of the Angels.
Home run: Joe Rudi of the Angels.

GROUND RULES
Photographers' area:
• The ball is in play if it hits the retaining fence and bounces back into the playing field.
Hitting suspended objects:
• A batted ball hitting any suspended object, such as speakers, wires, streamers, etc., in fair territory shall be judged fair or foul in relation to where it lands or is touched by a fielder. If caught by a fielder, the batter is out and base runners advance at their own risk.
• A batted ball hitting any suspended object in foul territory is a foul ball, regardless of where it lands or is touched by a fielder. If the ball is caught by a fielder, the batter is out and the base runners advance at their own risk.
• A batted ball sticking in any supended object in foul territory will be called a strike. A batted ball sticking in any suspended object in fair territory will be a ground-rule double.
Outfield area:
• A ball batted fair clearing the wall is a home
continued on p. 84

In the Hot Seats at the Kingdome

The Mariners' season ticket base is about 13,300. It is usually possible to walk up and get tickets, although for games against the Yankees expect good seats to be harder to get.

BAD SEATS

The worst seats are in the upper deck. They're quite a distance from the field. You still can see the game, but it looks like a scale-model version from up there.

SPECIAL PROGRAMS

Every Sunday home game is seniors day, which offers half-price tickets for fans 62 or older. Also offered are a $23 birthday package and a $33 anniversary package, with ticket costs extra. Paid "will call" tickets can be picked up at the courtesy window outside gate D.

SCALPING

Games rarely sell out, so even with the team being a bigger draw in town than ever, there's still not much of a market for scalpers.

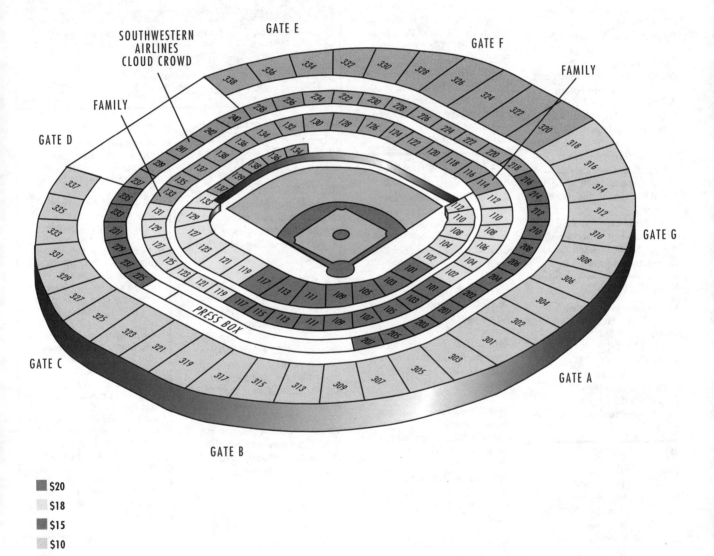

- $20
- $18
- $15
- $10
- $7
- $5

TICKET INFORMATION
Address: 201 S. King St., Seattle, WA 98104
Phone: TicketMaster, (206) 622-HITS or

(206) 627-TIXS
Hours: Mon.–Sat. 8:30–5:30, Sun. 12–5.
By mail: P.O. Box 4100, 411 First Ave. S., Seattle, WA 98104

Prices: $20: box; $18: field level; $15: club level; $10: view ($8 for children under 14); $7: general admission; $5: Southwest Airlines section.

Seattle, WA 98101
(800) 228-3000/(206) 728-1000
2 miles from the stadium.

Holiday Inn Crown Plaza
1113 Sixth Ave.
Seattle, WA 98101
(206) 464-1980/(800) HOLIDAY
About 1 mile from the stadium.

GETTING TO THE KINGDOME

Public transportation: Most downtown buses stop within walking distance of the King-dome. The most direct may be the southbound bus on Third Avenue. Get off at Third and South Jackson, about 2 blocks from the stadium. For more information, call Metro Transit at (206) 553-3000.

By car: From the north, I-5 to the Airport Way exit, no. 164. Right onto Dearborn Street to Airport Way South. Go left and then left again onto Fourth Avenue South. Go ¼ mile to South Royal Brougham Way. Right to Kingdome lot B or C. From the south, Spokane Street exit (no. 163) on I-5 North. Fol-low Spokane (lower level) to Fourth Avenue South, to South Royal Brougham, and proceed to lot B or C.
From the east, I-90 to the Dear-born Street exit. Left on Fourth Avenue South to South Royal Brougham. Right to lot B or C.

SPRING TRAINING

Peoria Sports Complex
15707 N. 83 Ave.
Peoria, AZ 85382
(602) 412-9000
Capacity: 10,000 (7,000 seats and 3,000 on lawn)
Surface: Grass
Game time: 1:05 p.m.
Ticket information: (602) 784-4444

MINOR LEAGUES

Class	Team
AAA	Tacoma (WA) Rainiers
AA	Port City (NC) Roosters
A	Lancaster (CA) JetHawks
A	Wisconsin Timber Rattlers
Short Season A	Everett (WA) Aquasox
Rookie	Peoria (AZ) Mariners

The closest minor-league team to Seattle is the short-season Class A Everett Aquasox of the North-west League. The Sox frequently play the Bellingham Giants, an affiliate of the San Francisco Giants. Everett's first pro team, the Smokestackers, disbanded after only one season in 1905. Baseball did not return until 1984, when the Giants estab-lished a team here. The Mariners organization took over in 1995. The Sox play in Everett Memori-al Stadium, where Ken Griffey, Jr., hit his first professional home run, in 1987. The team has proved popular enough to prompt plans for a new, larger stadium.
To reach Everett Stadium from Seattle, which is 28 miles away, take I-5 north to the Broadway exit, no. 192. The ballpark is ¼ mile down Broadway.
Ticket prices: $7: adult reserved seats; $5: reserved seats; $5: adult general admission; $4: gen-eral admission for children 14 and under. For more information, call (206) 258-3673.

THE MARINERS AT THE KINGDOME

June 9, 1979: "Willie Horton Night" sees Horton (no relation to the rapist infamous for spoil-ing Michael Dukakis's 1988 pres-idential campaign) hit his 300th home run.

May 6, 1982: Gaylord Perry gets his 300th win, beating the New York Yankees 7–3.

April 2, 1990: Brian Holman sets down the first 26 Oakland A's before Ken Phelps homers. The Mariners win 6–1.

June 2, 1990: Randy Johnson throws the first no-hitter in Mariners history, beating the Detroit Tigers 2–0.

Aug. 31, 1990: Ken Griffey and Ken Griffey, Jr., became the first father and son to play in the same game.

April 22, 1993: Chris Bosio no-hits the Boston Red Sox 7–0.

July 28, 1993: Ken Griffey, Jr., homers in his eighth consecutive game, but the Mariners lose 5–1 to the Minnesota Twins.

Sept. 22, 1993: Nolan Ryan's last appearance: He pitches to six batters and is unable to retire any.

May 23, 1994: Ken Griffey, Jr., breaks Mickey Mantle's record for most home runs in the first two months of the season, hitting his 21st in a 7–5 loss to the Oak-land A's.

Oct. 7, 1995: Edgar Martinez dri-ves in 7 runs, setting a postsea-son record, en route to a 11–8 win over the Yankees.

October 8, 1995: Edgar Martinez hits a two-RBI double in the 11th inning that clinches a come-from-behind victory in the fifth game of the division series against New York, capping the Mariners' first appearance in postseason play, and only the fifth postseason series to be decided in extra innings.

HOME-FIELD ADVANTAGE

The Kingdome's troublesome roof has been repaired, and the Mariners have finally got perennially lukewarm fans' attention—if not affection—with a division series victory over the New York Yankees. The late-inning rallies that buoyed the team into the ACLS were aided by the deafening roar of a crowd that spent much of the game on its feet. But it's still too little, too late for the Kingdome. The Mariners' new ballpark, slated for completion in time for the 1999 season, will have a retractable roof and real grass. In the meantime, the team will continue to play the high hops off the artificial turf of the Kingdome, reasonably secure that the new roof won't fall in on them.

MARINERS TEAM NOTEBOOK

Franchise history	Cy Young Award	Hall of Fame
Seattle Mariners, 1977–present	Randy Johnson 1995	Gaylord Perry, 1991
Division title 1995	**Rookie of the Year** Alvin Davis, 1984	

continued from p. 82
run. A ball batted fair bouncing over the wall is a ground-rule double. Dugouts:
• *A ball will be consid-ered thrown into the dugout only if it hits an object or person within the dugout. A thrown ball hitting the lip at the base of the dugout or the frame around the dugout and bouncing back into the playing field is in play.*
• *A thrown ball hitting any player's equipment that is left on or in front of the lip at the base of the dugout will be con-sidered in the dugout. Bullpen areas:*
• *A ball will be consid-ered in play going into the bullpen area and coming back out onto the playing field. A ball going into the bullpen area and obstructed by a player, equipment or bench will be called dead.*

ThunderDome

ARENA STATS

Location: 1 Stadium Dr., St. Petersburg, FL 33705
Opened: March 3, 1990
Capacity: 45,000
Surface: AstroTurf
Services for fans with disabilities: Seating will be available in various sections of the stadium.

TEAM NOTEBOOK

Franchise history: Tampa Bay Devil Rays, 1998.

Long before multiple microbreweries and Starbuck's coffee bars became the mark of metropolitan sophistication, domed stadiums were all the rage. St. Petersburg's Suncoast Dome was one of the last domes to go up, and it was almost too late; they built it but no one came. Intended to lure a baseball team to Tampa Bay by 1990, when the doughnut-shaped Suncoast opened, the trend in stadiums was for traditional, open-air, baseball-only parks with a more intimate feel. Luckily, the NHL Tampa Bay Lightning were looking for a bigger temporary home after a year at Tampa's tiny Expo Hall. In a marvel of resourcefulness and speed, the base-ball-ready Suncoast Dome was quickly transformed into an ice hockey arena. What began as a marriage of convenience became a success story, in terms of attendance and technology. But all good things come to an end, and it was never meant to last. The Lightning got their own Ice Palace, and Tampa Bay finally got an expansion franchise.

Ebbets Field is a model for various touches in and around the dome; the outfield walls will be asymmetrical, and outside, a rotunda at the entrance will recall the one that long greeted Dodgers fans; it will also face the main parking lot; the dome's old main entrance was around back. The stadium's exterior will be expanded to accommodate an enclosed promenade that will essentially be a baseball-themed shopping mall. There will be a three-tiered sports bar behind center field with batting cages, pitching machines, and miniature golf; and a "Scouts Section" 50 feet behind home plate will offer seats on a per-game basis in which fans will get a radar gun and a private TV monitor from which they can punch up the view from any camera in the park.

By the time it opens in 1998, don't look for it in the phone book under ThunderDome, it will be rechristened with whatever name the highest corporate bidder wants it to have.

HOT TIPS FOR VISITING FANS

PARKING
The neighborhood around the dome isn't the greatest, so you might want to pay the extra buck or three that the stadium lot will charge. Spots filled up quickly when this arena held only 28,000, so you can imagine how much-harder it's going to be for 45,000. Many lots around the dome are not well lighted. For Lightning games, a shuttle bus used to swing by the free lots in downtown St. Petersburg starting about an hour before face-off; a similar arrangement will probably be made for the Rays.

MEDIA
Radio: A flagship radio station hasn't been chosen.
TV: So far, SportsChannel Florida (cable) is the only TV broadcaster of Devil Rays games to have been announced.

CUISINE
Vendors haven't been designated, but Volume Services, which provides concessions for the Bucs and several other NFL and major-league baseball stadiums, is taste-testing even as you read this. One thing is for sure: You should get here hungry; the plan calls for 260 places selling food and/or drink—more than double the number when the Lightning played here. An enclosed promenade with bars, shops, restaurants, and a kids' zone will wrap around the outside of the stadium. Plans also call for a food court called Taste of Tampa Bay that will feature local specialties.

After a game, amble across the street to Ferg's Sports Bar (813-822-4562). They've got big pitchers of beer and decent food. But get there early—it fills up fast. If you want a beachier experience, head out to the Hurricane (813-822-4562). It offers grouper sandwiches, late-night music, and a breathtaking view of the Sunshine Skyway Bridge from the rooftop.

LODGING NEAR THE STADIUM

Hilton
333 First St. S.
St. Petersburg, FL 33701
(813) 894-5000/(800) HILTON
16 blocks from the stadium

Renaissance Vinoy Resort
501 Fifth Ave. N.E.
St. Petersburg, FL 33701
(813) 894-1000/(800) HOTELS1
2 miles from the stadium.

MINOR LEAGUES

Class	Team
Short Season A	Hudson Valley (NY) Renegades
Rookie	Gulf Coast (FL) Devil Rays

In 1999 the Devil Rays will acquire the Class AA Southern League franchise in Orlando from the Chicago Cubs; until then the Rays will operate the team as a Cubs' affiliate, under a player development contract with the Cubs for 1997 and 1998. The Short Season A and rookie affiliates will also serve as training for future and would-be Rays who will be available to round out the roster once the ready-for-prime-time-players are enlisted.

In the Hot Seats at the ThunderDome

Season-ticket sales began in the summer of 1996, with an emphasis on the suites and luxury boxes. Single-game prices hadn't been set, and how many tickets might be held for single-game sales wasn't known.

There weren't any obstructed seats for hockey, and no new obstructions are planned for baseball, so the sight lines should be as good as ever.

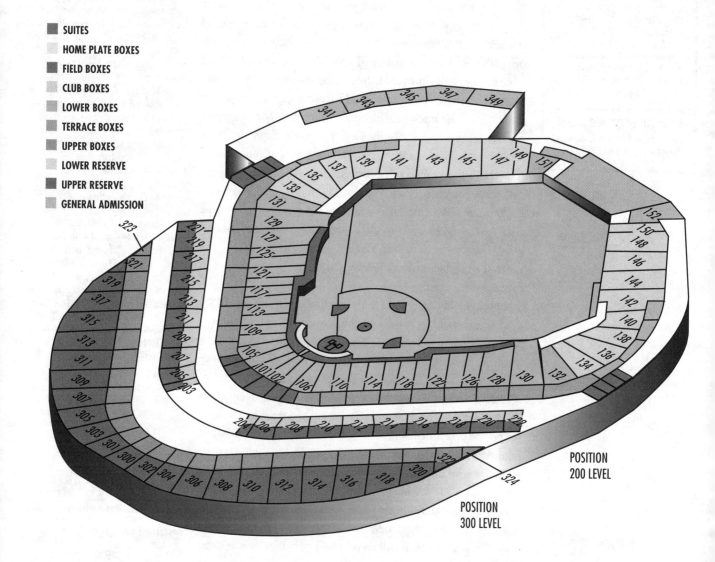

- ■ SUITES
- ▫ HOME PLATE BOXES
- ■ FIELD BOXES
- ▨ CLUB BOXES
- ■ LOWER BOXES
- ■ TERRACE BOXES
- ■ UPPER BOXES
- ▫ LOWER RESERVE
- ■ UPPER RESERVE
- ▨ GENERAL ADMISSION

POSITION 200 LEVEL

POSITION 300 LEVEL

HOME-FIELD ADVANTAGE

The dome's irregular outfield shape and its fake turf/real dirt combo may hold some surprises, but, since the Rays won't play here until the start of the '98 season, it'll take them a while to figure out their new home's idiosyncrasies. Plans are for a turf that will cut down on AstroTurf-created ground-rule doubles. At least for a while both teams will be equally unfamiliar. Certainly the home crowds will be happy to see baseball played at the major-league level (at least that's the plan) all season long. Fans hereabouts have had to make do watching the pros shake off the dust of the off-season in spring training, and then watch them head north for the real thing once they were starting to play halfway decently.

GETTING TO THE THUNDERDOME

Public transportation: Numerous buses pass near the stadium; the No. 18 stops right at it. Call (813) 530-9911 for more information.
By car: From the north, take I-275 going south. The dome is clearly visible from the highway. Take the dome exit off I-275 and follow signs to the stadium.
From the south, take I-275 north to the dome exit. Follow signs to the stadium.

TICKET INFORMATION
Address: 501 E. Kennedy Blvd., Suite 175, Tampa, FL 33602 or 1 Stadium Dr., St. Petersburg, FL 33705
Phone: (813) 825-3250
Hours: Mon.–Fri. 9–5.

Ticket prices: Individual ticket prices to be determined in late 1997.

The Ballpark in Arlington

STADIUM STATS

Location: *1000 Ballpark Way, Arlington, TX 76011*
Opened: *April 1, 1994*
Surface: *Grass*
Capacity: *49,178*
Outfield dimensions: *LF 332, LC 390, CF 400, RC 377–381, RF 325*
Services for fans with disabilities: *Call (817) 273-5222 for information.*

STADIUM FIRSTS

Regular-season game: *April 11, 1994, 4–3 loss to the Milwaukee Brewers.*
Pitcher: *Kenny Rogers of the Rangers.*
Batter: *Pat Listach of the Brewers.*
Hit: *Pat Listach of the Brewers.*
Home run: *Dave Nilsson of the Brewers.*

GROUND RULES

• *Ball striking railing separating photographers' bench or facing of dugout roof and rebounding to field is considered in the dugout.*
• *A fly ball hitting the foul poles or screens above the fence line is a home run.*
• *A ball lodging in the outfield-fence padding or in the manually operated scoreboard in the left-field fence is a ground-rule double.*

Is anything done on a small scale in Texas? Of course not. That's why The Ballpark in Arlington—even the name is gigantic—is definitely Texas. It's the tallest building in an area where one- and two-story buildings spread across the Texas plains and flatlands. It takes up 1.4 million square feet. Even the grass reflects the grand scale of the Lone Star State—it was grown on a farm in "nearby" Combine, three hours away.

While the exterior facade is all Texas—granite from Texas quarries, Texas-style cast-stone carvings, 35 Longhorn steer heads, and 21 Lone Star emblems—its arches bring memories of the original Comiskey Park in Chicago. Inside, the ballpark continues its salute to baseball's most-treasured scenes. In left field, a 14-foot wall and a hand-operated scoreboard bring a touch of Fenway Park. The foul poles made the trip across the street from old Arlington Stadium. In right field, the two-deck porch recalls Detroit's Tiger Stadium; atop sits a sign that reads "Hit It Here and Win a Free Suit," à la Brooklyn's Ebbets Field. If you begin to forget where you are, the Lone Star emblems on the aisle seats (which have cup holders) should bring you back to Texas.

The Ballpark is in the suburbs, so there's no downtown view. No matter: The Rangers built one, and what they built looks like a block of buildings out of New Orleans. The main structure is a four-story office building with floor-to-ceiling glass walls and steel trusses. Those who work in it can watch the game from their balconies. One complaint fans have is that the replay board is on top of the right-field porch, but designers planned it that way. They didn't want the board to detract from the game.

The Ballpark in Arlington is enclosed, with one small tunnel that runs between the right-field porch and the foul pole. It lets in a tad of light, an idiosyncrasy that makes it unique. On the right day, a left-handed batter might get just the right pitch and crash a baseball completely out of the stadium. It's a once-in-a-century shot. But that's Texas for you.

HOT TIPS FOR VISITING FANS

PARKING
Nine lots are available, each costing $5. Each lot is color-coded and is named for a Texas historical figure from the era of the Republic of Texas, in the 1830s and 1840s.
Check out the Walk of Fame on your way in. It's a brick walk, ranging from 18 to 70 feet wide, which rings the perimeter of the park. It's divided into panels featuring each year the Rangers have been in the American League (their first season was 1972), with the entire roster from each season included on the bricks. Fans can buy bricks and make their own inscriptions.

WEATHER
With the exception of the occasional gullywasher, Texas weather in baseball season is always hot.

MEDIA
Radio: KRLD (1080 AM—English), KXEB (910 AM—Spanish).
TV: KXAS (Channel 5) and KXTX (Channel 39), sister stations, cover the games with Mark Holtz and former Ranger Tom Grieve in the broadcast booth.

CUISINE
Aside from the traditional stadium food of hot dogs and pizza, The Ballpark in Arlington serves smoked meats made in the team's own smokehouse. Also, a sports grill run by T.G.I. Friday's behind the upper home-run porch in right field draws a crowd because of its full view of the playing field. The Ballpark also houses its own bakery, which supplies fresh-baked cookies and other desserts. The concessions stands sell Miller, Coors, and Budweiser beers. For more formal dining, the private Diamond Club is open to members before and after games. The club seats about 500 on four tiers and provides a full view of the field. After the game some fans head to Bobby Valentine's Sports Gallery Cafe (817-467-9922), a five-minute drive from the ballpark. The walls are filled with sports memorabilia, including mementos from Valentine's career; the Nolan Ryan Room features baseball cards from each of Ryan's 5,217 strikeout victims. If you don't want to watch one of the 25 televisions, there is free shuttle service to and from every home game.

LODGING NEAR THE STADIUM

Arlington Marriott
1500 Convention Center Dr.
Arlington, TX 76011
(817) 261-8200/(800) 228-9290
Across the street from the park.

Hyatt Regency Dallas (at Reunion Tower)
300 Reunion Blvd.
Dallas, TX 75207
(214) 651-1234/(800) 233-1234
Approximately 20 miles from the park.

In the Hot Seats at The Ballpark in Arlington

Though the Ballpark has been drawing large crowds, it hasn't been selling out as consistently as some other new parks. Tickets are available for all games on a walk-up basis.

GOOD SEATS

There are 1,500 bleacher seats. Always a ballpark delight, the benches were moved from old Arlington Stadium, and they are sun-drenched. For a real old-time, knothole-gang feel, ask for tickets in the right-field porch that allow you to view the game through an opening in the fence.

BAD SEATS

The terrace club boxes in the last few rows of the lower deck can be blocked by railings and the overhang, and the grandstand reserved seats on the upper deck give you as good a view of the traffic pattern at the Dallas–Fort Worth airport as of the ball game.

SCALPING

The new stadium is drawing big crowds, but plenty of ticketholders are willing to sell for face value.

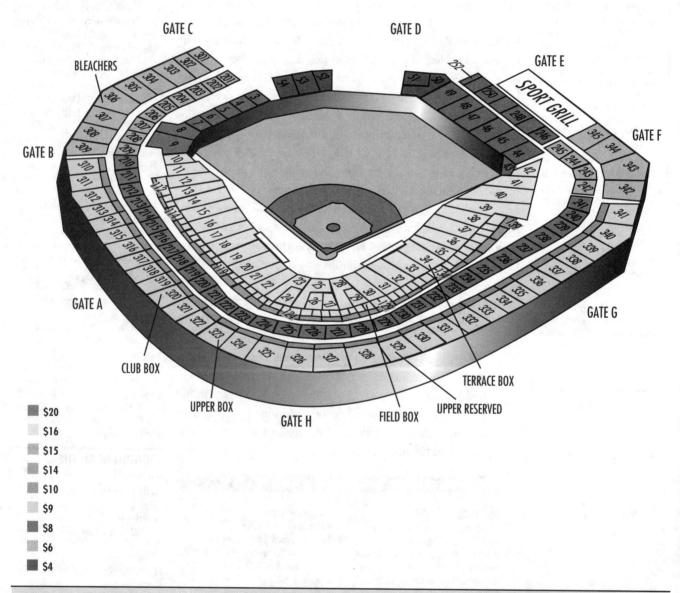

Legend:
- $20
- $16
- $15
- $14
- $10
- $9
- $8
- $6
- $4

TICKET INFORMATION

Address: 1000 Ballpark Way, Arlington, TX 76011
Phone: (817) 273-5100
By mail: Texas Rangers Ticket Office, P.O. Box 90111, Arlington, TX 76004.
Hours: Mon.–Fri. 9–6, Sat. 10–4; on days of home games, Sat. 9–9; for day games, Sun. 9–3:30 and for all night games, noon–9.
Prices: $20: club box; $16: field box; $15: terrace club box; $14: terrace box; $10: upper box; $9: upper reserved; $8: home-run porch, left-field reserved; $6: grandstand reserved (children $3); $4: bleachers (children $2); bleachers sold day of game only.

GETTING TO THE BALLPARK IN ARLINGTON

Public transportation: There is no public transportation to the Ballpark in Arlington.

By car: From Dallas, take I-30 west to The Ballpark Way exit. Go left on Stadium Drive east to parking lots.

From Fort Worth, take I-30 east to the Cooper Street exit. Go south to Randol Mill Road, then left to parking lots.

From South Arlington, take Highway 360 north to Division Street. Go left to Stadium Drive, then right to parking lots.

SPRING TRAINING

Charlotte County Stadium
Rangers Complex
2300 El Jobean Rd.
Port Charlotte, FL 33948
Capacity: 6,026
Surface: Bermuda grass
Game time: 1:30 p.m.
Tickets: (813) 625-9500

MINOR LEAGUES

Class	Team
AAA	Oklahoma City (OK) 89ers
AA	Tulsa (OK) Drillers
A	Port Charlotte (FL) Rangers
A	Charleston (SC) Riverdogs
Short Season A	Hudson Valley (NY) Renegades
Rookie	Port Charlotte (FL) Rangers

The Rangers' closest minor-league affiliate is the AAA Oklahoma City 89ers of the American Association. The team's nickname was selected by a local schoolteacher in honor of the land rush of 1889 and the western pioneers from that era. Since the team played its first game in 1961, such prominent players as Rusty Staub, Ryne Sandberg, Ruben Sierra, and Juan Gonzalez have been 89ers.

To reach Oklahoma City's All-Sports Stadium, approximately 210 miles from Arlington, take the State Fairgrounds/10th Street exit from I-44 at the intersection of I-44 and I-40. Go east on N.W. 10th Street which heads you to the ballpark.

Ticket prices: $6: lower box seats; $5: upper box seats; $3: upper reserved; $2: general admission. For more information, call (405) 946-8989.

THE RANGERS AT THE BALLPARK IN ARLINGTON

April 26, 1994: Starting pitcher Rick Kelly is blown off the mound by a gust of wind, as 50 m.p.h. winds cause a 45-minute wind delay during a 6–1 win over Detroit.

April 27, 1994: Joe Carter of the Toronto Blue Jays drives in his 30th run of the month, setting a major-league record for RBIs in April.

May 14, 1994: Texas moves into first place with a 5–2 win over the Chicago White Sox.

June 13, 1994: Jose Canseco hits three home runs and knocks in a career-high eight runs as Texas beats Seattle, 17–9.

July 5, 1994: First-place Texas beats the first-place Cleveland Indians and goes on to take the series, two games to one.

July 28, 1994: Kenny Rogers of the Rangers pitches the 12th perfect game in major-league history, beating the California Angels 4–0.

HOME-FIELD ADVANTAGE

It pays to be a left-handed batter at The Ballpark in Arlington. The right-field foul pole is 325 feet from home plate, and the fence is only 8 feet high. In the two years after The Ballpark opened, eleven home-run balls reached the upper porch in right field.

Other than that, home runs aren't easy to get. The fence moves out to 407 feet in right-center field, its deepest point. The power alley goes from 381 to 377 feet at one corner of the bullpen. That quirk can make life difficult for opponents' outfielders. Playing the indentation is one more thing they have to be aware of when they come to town.

While the hitters don't get a break with the outfield fence, they do get a break with the limited foul territory. The distance between home plate and the screen is 60 feet, meaning the fans are closer to the batter than the pitcher is. Down the lines, the first row of seats is only 9½ feet from the foul poles.

RANGERS TEAM NOTEBOOK

Franchise history
Washington Senators, 1961–71; Texas Rangers, 1972–present

Most Valuable Player
Jeff Burroughs, 1974

Rookie of the Year
Mike Hargrove, 1974

Hall of Fame
Ted Williams, 1966
Ferguson Jenkins, 1991
Gaylord Perry, 1991

Retired Number
34 Nolan Ryan

TORONTO BLUE JAYS

SkyDome

SkyDome brings a set of numbers to baseball that is even more impressive than the numbers the Blue Jays posted inside it during their championship years. The retractable roof covers 8 acres and weighs 11,000 tons, the equivalent of 3,372 automobiles. It takes 20 minutes to open or close. When closed, a 31-story building could fit inside. The field is large enough to store eight Boeing 747s, or 516 African and 743 Indian elephants. SkyDome—Canadians don't use "the" in its name—is made of enough concrete to build a sidewalk from St. Louis to Toronto. It looks like a giant turtle on the Toronto skyline and sits under the CN Tower, the tallest freestanding structure in the world. A 348-room hotel is integrated into the facility, as well as seven restaurants and bars.

And they even play baseball in it! If you've never seen a baseball game in Canada, you're in for some surprises. Clean aisles, orderly lines, polite fans; it's all very, well, Canadian. Fans here tend to be more sedate than their counterparts in the States, too. They may applaud an opponent's noteworthy play, but don't be fooled: Though the Blue Jays have slid down from their World Series-winning form, SkyDome fans are still doggedly loyal to their team. Only one thing can divert attention from the Blue Jays in Toronto, and that's hockey. The Jays may have won two World Series—back to back, no less—but what Toronto really wants is the Stanley Cup back at Maple Leaf Gardens.

HOT TIPS FOR VISITING FANS

PARKING
If you drive, be prepared to pay. There are 14,000 spaces within a 20-minute walk, but parking-lot owners usually jack up the parking rates to more than double the usual cost. Prices depend on how much time is left before the ballgame starts. The closer it is to game time, the higher the price. Prices usually start at C$8 and can run as high as C$20 by the first pitch. Also, be aware that Toronto has strict laws about illegal on-street parking during morning (7–9 a.m.) and afternoon (3:30–6:30 p.m.) rush hours, so cars parked illegally have a great chance of being towed.

WEATHER
SkyDome combines the best of both worlds: when the weather's nice, games are played under blue skies and sun, but in the cold of April and September and on rainy days, the roof closes.

MEDIA
Radio: THE FAN (590 AM). Tom Cheek and Jerry Howarth handle play-by-play. **TV:** CFTO and the Total Sports Network (cable). Don Chevrier and Tommy Hutton announce for CFTO, and TSN features Dan Shulman and Buck Martinez. Hutton and Martinez played in the big leagues for a combined total of nearly 30 seasons, including the six seasons that Martinez caught for the Blue Jays.

CUISINE
In addition to offering McDonald's (which runs the concessions here), SkyDome features such popular items as Italian sausages, corned beef, and Chicago Gyros. Molson and Labatt's beers are available on tap and in bottles. There's also Sightlines, a bar with seats facing the field, a 520-seat restaurant called Windows on SkyDome, and a Hard Rock Cafe, if you must.

The closest postgame restaurant is in the CN Tower next door. The tower has a mind-warp theater, laser-beam games, a revolving restaurant, and Horizon's Bar. Call (416) 868-6937 for more information. Alice Fazooli's (416-979-1910) is 2 blocks south of SkyDome and is well known for its large collection of baseball art and memorabilia. Blue Jays players are frequent customers. Al Frisco's, about 5 blocks away, has home-brewed beers on tap and a dozen bottled, mostly Canadian, varieties. Downtown is Eaton Centre, a large mall with 340 shops and services, and many restaurants.

LODGING NEAR THE STADIUM

Westin Harbour Castle
1 Harbour Sq.
Toronto, ON M5J 1A6
Canada
(416) 869-1600/(800) 228-3000
About 1¼ miles from the stadium.

Toronto Hilton
145 Richmond St. W.
Toronto, ON M5H 2L2
Canada
(416) 869-3456/(800) 445-8667
5 blocks south of the stadium.

GETTING TO SKYDOME

Public transportation: Take the Yonge–University–Spadina subway line to Union Station at Front and Bay streets. For more information call the Toronto Transit Commission at (416) 393-4636.
By car: From the south, take the Queen Elizabeth Expressway east toward Toronto. Exit at the Gardener Expressway exit. Take the Gardener Expressway to the Spadina Avenue exit. Take Spadina north and make a right on Blue Jay Way; the stadium will be on your left.

STADIUM STATS
Location: 1 Blue Jays Way, Toronto, ON, M5V J3 Canada
Opened: June 5, 1989
Surface: AstroTurf 8
Capacity: 50,516
Outfield dimensions: LF 328, LC 375, CF 400, RC 375, RF 328
Services for fans with disabilities: Seating available in the first and second level between home plate and the bases in sections 115–128. Additional seating is in sections 109–112 and 131–134 in the outfield first level, and in sections 207–208 and 240–241 in the outfield second level.

STADIUM FIRSTS
Regular-season game: June 5, 1989, 5–3 loss to the Milwaukee Brewers.
Pitcher: Jimmy Key of the Blue Jays.
Batter: Paul Molitor of the Brewers.
Hit: Paul Molitor.
Home run: Fred McGriff of the Blue Jays.

GROUND RULES
• A ball hitting the fence or screen in back of home plate is in play.
• Ball going into camera booth behind home plate is one base if thrown by pitcher from rubber; other thrown balls, two bases.
• A ball hitting the padding and bouncing over the fence is two bases.
• A ball batted or thrown fair lodged in the padding is worth two bases.
• A ball batted or thrown fair that is on the steps of the dugout is considered in the dugout.
• A ball hitting padding on an outfield fence in foul territory is dead.

In the Hot Seats at SkyDome

Tickets are no longer as hard to get as they were in the early '90s when the Jays were pulling in more than 4 million fans a year; the team's charge line, once difficult to get through to, doesn't involve such a long wait anymore. Still, it's better to plan ahead and write away for tickets weeks ahead; fans have been remarkably loyal, even as their team went from first to last in just one season. Also check the ticket windows at gate 9 on game day, since there are often unused season tickets and players' tickets.

GOOD SEATS
Like all newer parks, SkyDome was planned so virtually all seats are good for baseball,

but the 200-level seats are probably the best of all. The sections are smaller, the seats are padded, and most fans believe sitting a level up makes for better angles on the game. First-deck seats are nice, too, but those behind home plate have to contend with the safety net. If all that's left is the outfield, don't fret. Any of the lower-deck outfield seats are good. Fans can see the pitches and the flight of the ball, and unlike in other parks across both leagues, the fans aren't known to be rowdy.

BAD SEATS
The seats in the 500 level put the "Sky" in SkyDome. The view and the angles are

excellent, but the seats are candidates for the steepest in the league. Try not to get dizzy, and watch your step. Use the rail between the aisles on your way up.

SCALPING
The Blue Jays do not own the property surrounding the ballpark and can't prevent scalpers from congregating as close as possible to the ticket windows, but with plenty of seats available, scalping, like the team, is in a slump.

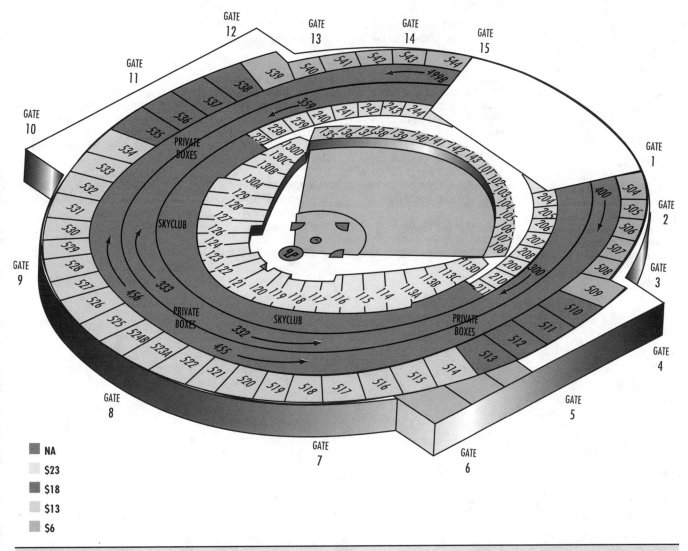

Legend:
- ■ NA
- □ $23
- ■ $18
- ▨ $13
- ▨ $6

TICKET INFORMATION
Address: 1 Blue Jays Way, Suite 3200, Skydome, Toronto, ON, M5V 1J3 Canada

Phone: (416) 341-1234
Hours: Daily 9–6 on non-game days, 9–9 on game days.

Prices: C$23: sky club level 200; C$18: lower sky box level 300; C$13: upper sky box level 400; C$6: sky box level 500.

From the east, take the Gardener Expressway and follow the directions given above.

From the west, take the Dun Valley Parkway to the Gardener Expressway and continue as directed above.

SPRING TRAINING

Dunedin Stadium at Grant Field
311 Douglas Ave.
Dunedin, FL 34698
Capacity: 6,218
Game time: 1:05 p.m., 1:35 p.m., or 7:35 p.m.
Tickets: (813) 733-0429

MINOR LEAGUES

Class	Team
AAA	Syracuse (NY) Chiefs
AA	Knoxville (TN) Smokies
A	Dunedin (FL) Blue Jays
A	Hagerstown (MD) Suns
Short Season A	St. Catharines (ON) Stompers
Rookie	Medicine Hat (AB) Blue Jays
Rookie	Dunedin (FL) Blue Jays

The Blue Jays' closest minor-league affiliate is the Short Season A St. Catharines Stompers of the NY–Penn League. In 1986, when St. Catharines fielded its first pro team since 1930, this small Ontario community just west of Niagara Falls made base-ball history. At that time, St. Catharines became the first pro baseball franchise run by women.

To reach St. Catharines' Community Park, approximately 70 miles from Toronto, take the QEW to Route 406 south. Exit at Glendale and turn left. Stay on Glendale to the end and turn left on Merritt. Stay in the left lane, cross a railroad bridge, and turn right on Weymour. The ballpark will be on your right, across the street from Merritton High School.

Ticket prices: C$5: reserved seats; C$4: general admission. Children 13 and under and senior citizens 60 and over can deduct C$1 from the above prices. For more information call (905) 641-5297.

THE BLUE JAYS AT SKYDOME

June 29, 1990: *The Oakland A's Dave Stewart pitches the first no-hitter at SkyDome.*

Oct. 2, 1991: *Toronto clinches the American League East with a 6–5 win over the California Angels in the last game of the season.*

October 3, 1991: *The Blue Jays draw 4,001,526 fans to SkyDome for the season, the first team to break 4,000,000 attendance.*

September 4, 1992: *The Blue Jays tie an American League record with ten consecutive hits* during an 8-run inning against the Twins.

Sept. 24, 1992: *Dave Winfield sets a team single-season record for homers by a DH with his 23rd. He also becomes the oldest player in major-league history to get more than 100 RBIs.*

Oct. 8, 1992: *The Jays win their first postseason game at Sky-Dome, beating the A's 3–1 behind David Cone.*

Oct. 20, 1992: *In the first World* Series game played outside the U.S.A., the Jays beat the Atlanta Braves 1–0.

Sept. 26, 1993: *The Jays draw 50,518 fans, raising their season attendance to 4,057,947.*

Oct. 23, 1993: *Joe Carter's three-run home run in the bottom of the ninth gives Toronto an 8–6 Game 6 win against the Philadel-phia Phillies, clinching their sec-ond consecutive World Series title.*

football

ARIZONA CARDINALS

Sun Devil Stadium

The sun always seems to shine on Sun Devil Stadium, the only NFL arena on a college campus. It's a dry heat, but the fans roasting in the stands for August pre-season games are not usually cheered up by the lack of humidity. Temperatures have climbed as high as 122 degrees, and it's worse on the field. Most regular-season games are played in the hottest part of the day—1 p.m. in September and early October, and 2 p.m. the rest of the season.

The sun and the gorgeous setting between two mountain buttes provide most of the heat and color at Sun Devil Stadium. Visiting fans sometimes outnumber Cardinals supporters, especially when the Cowboys come to town; on those weekends, I-10 in New Mexico and Arizona is filled with Texas license plates. Cowboys fans from West Texas drive to Phoenix and pack the stadium, creating a sea of blue that irritates Cardinals players. Transplanted Phoenix residents—especially retirees—have been slow to switch loyalties from their previous home-town teams, and the high number of snow birds doesn't help matters. Neither does the Cardinals' record, and until the team starts heating things up in the stadium, the sun will have to suffice.

The team is slowly building a following among the younger fans, visible proof being "The Wild Cards," or "Zonies," a rowdy group in the north end zone who paint their faces and wear red wigs and Cardinals garb. Perhaps having hosted Super Bowl XXX and having adopted hockey and baseball teams in quick succession has begun to raise Phoenix's overall sports awareness and, therefore, fan enthusiasm.

HOT TIPS FOR VISITING FANS

PARKING
Even though only 3,500 spaces are around the stadium, parking is ample. Another 10,000 spots are less than a mile from the stadium, and the school's band practice fields are also used. Many regular fans consider the $5 lot across Rio Salado from the stadium the premium spot at the best price. In addition, many fans park in the downtown Tempe area only a few blocks away and walk to the game. A nearby ramp on and off the Red Mountain Freeway (202) that was added recently has greatly eased the traffic congestion that used to clog up the area on game days.

WEATHER
Fans at Miami's Joe Robbie Stadium might argue, but Sun Devil Stadium is the NFL's best tanning salon. You can catch the best rays in the east stands. Just make sure you bring plenty of sunblock. Stadium officials are well-prepared to handle those who bake too long. The medical staff is the largest in the league: Seven paramedic teams are inside the stadium, a force that includes six physicians and six nurses. The team also provides chilled water throughout the stadium. Stadium officials experimented with misting systems but are not convinced of their effectiveness.

MEDIA
Radio: KIDR (740 AM) and KHPC (99.9 FM) broadcast in English; KVVA (850 AM) in Spanish.
TV: KPHO (Channel 5, CBS), shows pre- and some regular-season Cardinals games; KNXV (Channel 15) is the Fox affiliate.

CUISINE
Hot dogs, hamburgers, nachos, pretzels, soft drinks, and beer. Fans can purchase only two beers at a time, and no alcohol is sold after halftime.
Outside, there's Macayo's Depot Cantina (602-966-6677) for Mexican. Stan's Metro Deli (602-921-3505) is a favorite of the students. McDuffy's is a sports bar that has off-track betting. Fans also often dine at the Mill Landing (602-966-1700) for seafood, or at the Paradise Bar and Grill (602-829-0606). Fans who don't want to walk the several blocks to Mill Avenue go to nearby Mission Palms Hotel (602-894-1400), site of pre-game and post-game parties. The Arizona Center mall on North Third St. has several bars and restaurants.

LODGING NEAR THE STADIUM

Mesa Pavilion Hilton
1011 West Holmes Ave.
Phoenix, AZ 85210
(602) 833-5555/(800) HILTONS
8 miles from the stadium.

Hyatt Regency
122 N. Second St.
Phoenix, AZ 85004
(602) 252-1234/(800) 233-1234
15 miles from the stadium.

THE CARDINALS AT SUN DEVIL STADIUM

Nov. 13, 1988: Roy Green has nine receptions for 176 yards as the Cards beat the New York Giants 24–17.

Dec. 10, 1988: Neil Lomax throws for 384 yards in a 23–17 loss to the Philadelphia Eagles.

Dec. 12, 1992: Johnny Johnson rushes for 156 yards in a 19–0 win over the Giants.

In the Hot Seats at Sun Devil Stadium

Ticket prices were the highest in the league in 1988, the team's first year in Arizona. They averaged $38 a ticket, but the club quickly realized its mistake. Now the average cost is about $32—middle of the pack in the NFL—and 40,000 seats are available at $30 a ticket or less. Individual tickets go on sale in mid-July.

For the time that Buddy Ryan was coaching here, tickets were pretty much gone by game day. He's gone and game day tickets are back; unless the game's against the Dolphins, Cowboys, or Bears. The large number of midwestern expatriates explains why the Bears are the second-biggest draw at Sun Devil. The Cardinals were originally a Chicago team, so the rivalry and fan base remain.

BAD SEATS
The field was lowered in 1992, so no seats are obstructed: From the front row you can see the entire field. Those in the upper deck get a nice breeze and a good view of the breathtaking sunsets. Only about 27,000 seats have chair backs; the rest are benches. Chair backs can be rented, though, for $2. Nearly 5,000 no-alcohol seats are available, in sections 9, 12, 13, 41, and 201.

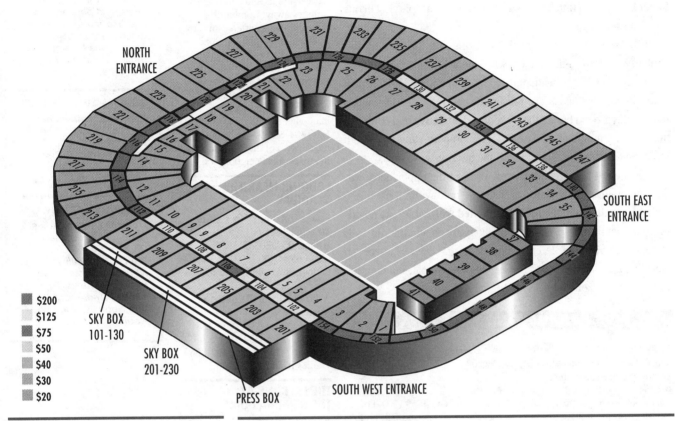

NORTH ENTRANCE

SOUTH EAST ENTRANCE

$200
$125
$75
$50
$40
$30
$20

SKY BOX 101-130

SKY BOX 201-230

PRESS BOX

SOUTH WEST ENTRANCE

HOME-FIELD ADVANTAGE

The heat can wreak havoc on opposing teams. Just ask the New England Patriots, who melted under the 120 degree heat during a 1991 game. The Cards don't put thermometers on the visiting sideline but make sure the opposition thinks about the heat. A sign outside one locker room reads: "Make sure you get plenty of fluids." A sign since removed read: "Warning: The Surgeon General reports that exertion coupled with high temperatures can lead to dehydration." The Cardinals also get to wear white at home so opponents have to suffer in the darker colors.

GETTING TO SUN DEVIL STADIUM

Public transportation: The system does not run on Sundays. Call (602) 253-5000 for information concerning non-Sunday games. **By car:** From Sky Harbor International Airport, take 143 north to the 44th Street/Hohokam Expressway exit northbound. Continue to Washington Street and turn right. Washington Street merges with Van Buren Street, which runs across the Salt River bridge before becoming Mill Avenue. Go left off Mill at Fifth Street. The stadium is 3 blocks on the north side of Fifth Street. From 202 (Red Mountain Fwy.), take the Scottsdale Rd. exit; turn right onto Scottsdale Rd., over Salt River bridge to Rio Salado Rd.; the stadium will be on the right.

TICKET INFORMATION
Address: Box 888, Phoenix, AZ 85001-0888
Phone: (602) 379-0102/(800) 999-1402
Hours: Mon.–Fri. 8:30–5.
Prices: $200: sections 106 and 134; $125: sections 101–105, 107–111, 129–133 and 135–139; $75: sections 112–128 and 140–154; $50: sections 5/6–8/9, 29–31, 205–207 and 241–243; $40: sections 4–5, 9–10, 28, 32, 201–204, 208–211, 239–240 and 244–245; $30: sections 1–3, 11–27, 33–36, 212–238, and 246–247; $20: sections 37–41.
Training camp: Northern Arizona University, Flagstaff, AZ

ATLANTA FALCONS

Georgia Dome

The Georgia Dome, not the worst-to-first Braves or the '96 Olympics, began the transformation of Atlanta's professional-sports image from Losersville U.S.A. to big league—and when you see the Dome, it's easy to understand why. The Falcons have one of the best venues in the NFL, suitable to host the Super Bowl, even if the chances of the host team's playing in one any time soon appear dim.

Built especially for football, the Dome sparkles and draws applause even from the pundits who said they'd never root for a team in, or even go inside, an enclosed stadium. Unlike most other domes, this one doesn't resemble an Erector Set. Atlanta's indoor playground has a billowy roof and attractive teal colors on the outside; more than 150 trees dot the property, and mammoth windows allow natural light to fill the interior walkways.

It gets even better inside. Seats, even in the upper-deck corners, are angled so spectators can see the field without having to turn their bodies, and the roof is supported with cables, so no pillars obstruct the view. When the Falcons are on and the run-and-shoot is carving up defenses, the Georgia Dome can be an electric place. Music blares and a 300-pound break-dancing fan in the east end zone revs up his engine and gyrates.

HOT TIPS FOR VISITING FANS

PARKING
Traffic is not a huge hassle, even an hour before game time, because city officials discourage fans from driving to the Dome. But if you want to drive, the Georgia Dome advertises 17,000 spaces available in the vicinity of the Dome. However, unless you're a luxury-suite owner with a parking pass to the Gold or Green lots, or you want to arrive three hours early and pay $10 or $15 at a private lot, don't try parking at the Dome.
If you want to pay $3 and don't mind a 15-minute walk, you can leave your car in the parking decks at Underground Atlanta (see Cuisine).

WEATHER
Because of the domed stadium, football fans can't enjoy the splendid fall Sunday afternoons, but they also don't have to brave the chill that comes from 9 p.m. starts for Monday night games or the blustery weather that can overtake Atlanta in December.

MEDIA
Radio: WZGC (92.9 FM). Former Falcons Neal and Bill Fralic call the games.
TV: Preseason games are televised on WSB-TV (Channel 2), the ABC affiliate. WAGA (Channel 5) is the Fox affiliate.

CUISINE
You are not allowed to bring food and beverages into the Dome, but the Food Court is well stocked. Whatever you want, you can probably find: Mexican and deli food, pizza, ice cream, salads, and so on; the Varsity Burger is a local favorite.
A variety of imported beers is available on the Executive Club level, and club-level ticketholders can have a cold one brought to their seat. The Kickers Bar on the lower-level concourse offers the same selection and is open to all ticketholders.

A five-minute walk from the Dome is the CNN Center, which features five restaurants, including a sports bar, and a variety of fast-food eateries.
Underground Atlanta, with 150 stores and pushcarts, as well as 12 restaurants and clubs, is 15 minutes away. Lombardi's (404-522-6568) is an after-game stop that opens at 5 p.m. on Sundays. Jocks 'n' Jills (404-873-5405), at the corner of 10th Street and Peachtree Road, and Bones (404-237-2663), on Piedmont in Buckhead, are popular local sports hangouts, as is Frankie's Sports Bar (404-843-9444), about 10 miles north of the stadium in the Sandy Springs neighorhood.

LODGING NEAR THE STADIUM
Omni Hotel at CNN Center
100 CNN Center
Atlanta, GA 30335
(404) 659-0000/(800) 843-6664
2 blocks from the stadium.

Atlanta Airport Hilton and Towers
1031 Virginia Ave.
Atlanta, GA 30354
(404) 767-9000/(800) 445-8667
7 miles from the stadium.

THE FALCONS AT THE GEORGIA DOME

Aug. 23, 1992: A sellout crowd watches the Falcons win the first football game in the Georgia Dome, 20–10 over the Philadelphia Eagles.

Sept. 6, 1992: The Falcons win their first regular-season game, against the New York Jets 20–17.

Nov. 1, 1992: Billy Joe Tolliver comes off the bench to throw a 13-yard touchdown to Michael Haynes, leading the Falcons to a 30–28 victory over the Los Angeles Rams.

Nov. 29, 1992: The Falcons beat the New England Patriots 34–0 in their first shutout since 1988. Atlanta gives up just 15 passing yards, and Deion Sanders has two interceptions.

STADIUM STATS
Location: 1 Georgia Dome Dr. N.W., Atlanta, GA 30313
Opened: Aug. 12, 1992
Surface: AstroTurf
Capacity: 71,228
Services for fans with disabilities: Besides 700 wheelchair-accessible seats, text phones (TTY) and hearing-amplification devices are available. Guide dogs for sight-impaired guests are welcome.

STADIUM FIRSTS
Regular-season game: Sept. 6, 1992, 20–17 over the New York Jets.
Points scored: A 25-yard field goal by Norm Johnson of the Falcons.

TEAM NOTEBOOK
Franchise history: Atlanta Falcons, 1966–present.
Division title: 1980.
Pro Football Hall of Fame: Norm Van Brocklin, 1971.
Retired numbers: 31, William Andrews; 57, Jeff Van Note; 60, Tommy Nobis.

In the Hot Seats at the Georgia Dome

Until recently every seat in this stadium went for the same price, no matter how close to the action it was. Not anymore. The price range is extremely reasonable, however, and the upper-level end-zone seats cost even less than the old one-size-fits-all price. Although the Falcons sold out only one game in 1995, it might be hard to get tickets for games against the Saints and 49ers.

GOOD SEATS

The Falcons have about 36,000 season ticket-holders, leaving nearly 35,000 seats for walk-up and sale by phone. Single-game tickets go on sale in mid-July. You can usually find a good seat close to the field with little or no difficulty.

BAD SEATS

Decent seats are available in the thinner air of the upper deck between the 20-yard lines. But like any major football stadium, when you get upper-deck seats outside the 20s (behind the end zone, for instance) the view can be remote, to say the least.

SCALPING

With tickets readily available there's no need to resort to scalpers. If the team should suddenly heat up and tickets become hard to get, fans can easily find tickets from brokers on the street. CNN Center, which is five minutes away, usually is a gathering spot for people unloading tickets.

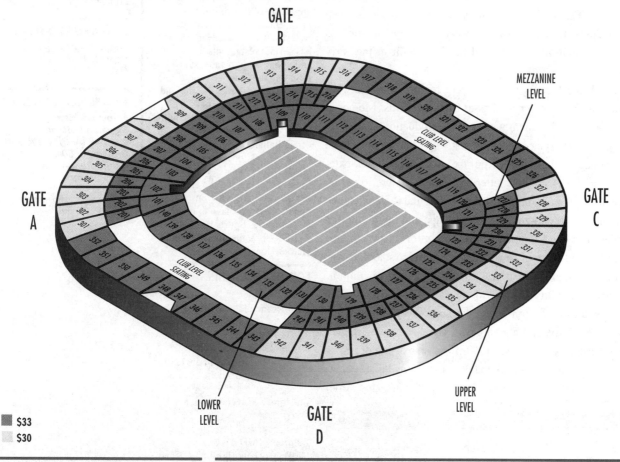

$33
$30

HOME-FIELD ADVANTAGE

Though the Falcons have had below-average teams (combined record 35-45) in their first five years in the Dome, they've gone 26–14 at home, including 7–1 at home in '95. The team has been built for the Dome's racetrack rug: Small, speedy receivers who are extra fast inside on artificial surface and helpful in the pass-first offense that the Falcons tend to use are always high on the draft-pick list.

GETTING TO THE GEORGIA DOME

Public transportation: The Omni/Dome/GWCC and Vine City MARTA stations are within close proximity. Use the former if your ticket tells you to enter at Gate C or D; the latter for Gate A, B, or E. Bus service is available from the airport. Call (404) 848-4711 for more information.
By car: From Hartsfield Atlanta International Airport take I-75/85 north about 11 miles to Exit 96 (Georgia World Congress Center/International Boulevard). At the end of the exit ramp make a left onto International, and continue 10 blocks to the Georgia World Congress Center. Turn left at the fork to Magnum Street, where you can make a right into the stadium parking lot.

TICKET INFORMATION
Address: 1 Georgia Dome Dr. N.W., Atlanta, GA 30313

Phone: (404) 223-8000 or TicketMaster at (404) 429-6400 or (800) 326-4000
Hours: Mon.–Fri. 9–5.

Prices: $33, $30.
Training camp: One Falcon Pl., Suwanee, GA

BALTIMORE RAVENS

Memorial Stadium

The Baltimore Ravens' (a.k.a. the NFL team formerly known as the Cleveland Browns) arrival in Memorial Stadium is only the latest chapter in the long, proud, and storied history of this stadium and this site. The stadium was the home turf of the Baltimore Colts from 1950 right up until they left in 1983, and served as the Orioles' stadium from 1954 until they moved into their fine new home at Camden Yards in 1991. Memorial also hosted the CFL Baltimore Stallions in 1994 and 1995. Even before the present stadium was constructed in 1949, this site was occupied by Baltimore Municipal Stadium, built in the early 1920s.

Although the Ravens will play here for only two seasons, until they more over to new digs at Camden Yards, Memorial Stadium will provide them with a fine introduction to the city of Baltimore. The place looks almost like a movie-set for an old-fashioned football game, from the oval-shaped brick exterior and the Art Deco-style lettering to the two-tiered seating. The stadium got a major refurbishing before the Ravens moved in, adding 12,000 end-zone and field seats, and upgrading fan amenities. The one truly new innovation in this historic venue is the turf: The field will be covered in SportGrass, a high-tech hybrid of artificial and real grass that is supposed to combine AstroTurf's durability with the look and feel of real grass. If it delivers, you can count on seeing this stuff everywhere.

The Ravens arrive in Baltimore with several advantages: their own long history as the Cleveland Browns, an existing organization and coaching staff, a town that loves sports and that is eager to cheer its own team again, and a brand-new stadium in the works.

HOT TIPS FOR VISITING FANS

PARKING
The Venable lot and the parking lot at Eastern High School, both directly accross 33rd Street from the stadium, are open to the general public. Other nearby lots are at Johns Hopkins University, Mergenthaler High School, and Lake Montebello. Street parking is extremely limited.
For information about parking, call (410) 347-9330.

WEATHER
September can be unpredictable: Temperatures can swing to either extreme, but it may provide gorgeous weather. There might be a humid day or three left over from Baltimore's steamy summers. Winter here is fairly mild, but it can get cold, and snow is not unheard of.

MEDIA
Radio: WLIF (101.9 FM) and WJFK (1300 AM) are the Ravens' flagship stations.
TV: WBFF (Channel 45) is the local Fox affiliate. WNUV (UPN, Channel 54) broadcasts the Ravens' Insider highlight show.

CUISINE
Memorial Stadium's 30-plus concession stands will offer a variety of food and drink, ranging from traditional stadium fare to local specialties. Maryland crab cakes, the signature foodstuff of Baltimore, is always a crowd pleaser, and has proven to be a popular item over at Camden Yards.

Pre-game tailgating isn't allowed, so fans will have to brunch elsewhere. Luckily, there are plenty of possibilities in town. Baltimore's refurbished waterfront complex, Harborside, has several restaurants inside, and, along with the area surrounding the Inner Harbor, offers diners a fine view of the city and the harbor. Strapacca (410-547-1160), two blocks from the Baltimore Marriot Inner Harbor, offers Italian cuisine, and Ruth Chris's Steakhouse (410-783-0033) is sure to satisfy any beef-lover's appetite. Until a sports bar devoted to the Ravens debuts, fans will have to make do at the Orioles Sports Bar (410-962-8300), in the Sheraton Inner Harbor Hotel.

LODING NEAR THE STADIUM

Renaissance Harborplace Hotel
202 E. Pratt St.
Baltimore, MD 21201
(410) 547-1200/(800) 535-1201
About 2 miles from the stadium.

Baltimore Marriott Inner Harbor
110 S. Eutaw St.
Baltimore, MD 21201
(410) 962-0202/(800) 228-9290
About 2 miles from the stadium.

STADIUM STATS
Location: 1000 E. 33rd St., Baltimore, MD 21218
Opened: 1954
Surface: SportGrass
Capacity: 65,248
Services for fans with disabilites: Seating is available on the lower concourse in sections 11, 29, 32, and 40, and in the upper concourse in sections 12 and 31.

STADIUM FIRSTS
Regular season game: Sept. 1, 1996, vs. the Oakland Raiders.

TEAM NOTEBOOK
Franchise history: Cleveland Browns, 1946–49 (AFC); Cleveland Browns, 1950–95; Baltimore Ravens, 1996–present.

In the Hot Seats at Memorial Stadium

Memorial Stadium is an oldie-but-goodie. Bowl-shaped and open at one end, the upper decks go only to the 20-yard-line at one end of the field. But there isn't any obstructed seating. The Ravens are counting on a hefty season-ticket base, and have been selling private seat licenses for the two seasons that the Ravens will play here. Still, the team is making some 6,000 single-game tickets available for each game.

SCALPING

If the Ravens prove to be a hot ticket, those 6,000 single-game tickets will go fast, and many of them will be resold by scalpers. If Orioles ticket scalping is any indicator, competition will be fierce, and the markup may be stratospheric.

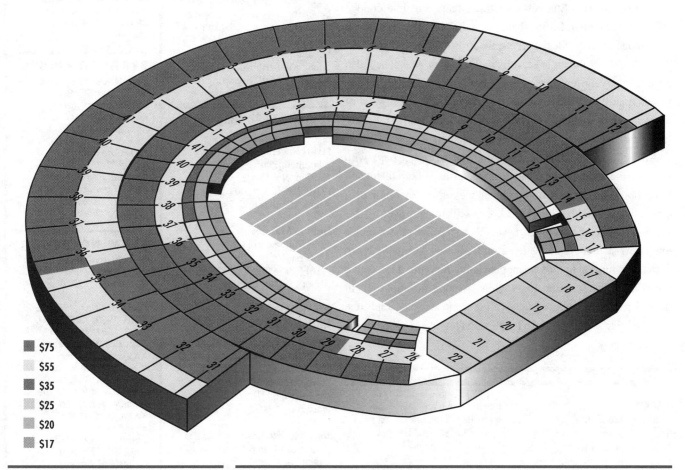

- $75
- $55
- $35
- $25
- $20
- $17

HOME-FIELD ADVANTAGE

Fan enthusiasm will be the best thing that the Ravens have going for them in their two seasons at Memorial. Baltimore has been without an NFL franchise since the Colts bolted in 1983. Memorial was originally built for football, and even with subsequent renovations, it fairly oozes gridiron tradition—it looks like a place meant for great football. The highly touted SportGrass field surface is an unknown quantity and will be new to eveybody, but the Ravens will play it more often.

GETTING TO MEMORIAL STADIUM

Public transportation: The #3 and #22 buses stop at Memorial Stadium on their regular runs. Additional buses have been added for game days. The MTA has also instituted several park-and-ride spots in and around the city. Call (410) 539-5000 or (800) 543-9809 for more information.

By car: From the south, take I-95 to exit at I-395 downtown, follow signs to Martin Luther King Blvd.; take Martin Luther King Blvd., then go left onto Howard Street and follow it to Wyman Park Drive (right) for one block. Turn left onto Charles, then right onto 33rd Street.

From the north: Take I-83 to I-695. Go west on I-695 to exit 23 (Jones Falls Expressway) to 28th Street. Head east to and make a right onto Calvert and follow it to 33rd Street and turn right. The stadium is nine blocks farther. From the west: Take US 40 or I-70 to I-695. Head to Towson to exit 30 south, at Perring Parkway. Follow Perring Parkway to 33rd Street. Turn right.

TICKET INFORMATION
Address: Memorial Stadium, 1000 E. 33rd St., Baltimore, MD 21218

Phone: (888) 972-8367 or TicketMaster (410) 481-SEAT, (202) 432-SEAT
Hours: 10–1 on game Sundays; opens 3 hours before kickoff for Saturday evening games.
Prices: $75, $55, $35, $25, $20, $17.

BUFFALO BILLS

Rich Stadium

The Buffalo Bills of recent vintage have had one of the most distinct home-field advantages in the NFL. The reasons are Rich Stadium and those who fill its seats. Bills fans are so rabid that games at Rich Stadium sometimes feel more like college games. Even though Buffalo has one of the NFL's biggest stadiums in one of its smallest markets, the Bills led the NFL in attendance for six of the eight seasons in the early 1990s. They also have a relatively low season-ticket base (about 50,000), which means not all the tickets are held by corporate fat cats. Most of those at Rich Stadium are real fans—the kind who paint their faces and show up no matter what the weather.

After the glory years of O. J. Simpson's playing days with Buffalo, the team hit some lean years in terms of both talent and fan support; but their frustrating run at the Super Bowl built up a devoted fan base that everyone hopes will remain even if this squad's best years have passed. There's been some talk of building a new stadium once the lease on Rich runs out in 1997, but with a $20 million improvement plan going forward, it looks like the Bills will be around for a while. Among the most recent upgrades are new enclosed club seating sections in each end zone and the NFL's largest JumboTron (31½ feet by 41½ feet) in the north end zone.

HOT TIPS FOR VISITING FANS

PARKING
In theory, the stadium lots hold 15,000 cars, but in reality they hold only about 11,000—unless it snows, in which case plowed piles of snow take up another 1,000 spaces. That means about 8,000 or more cars must be absorbed by the lot at the college across the street, at nearby restaurants and bars, and in the yards of local residents ready to make a quick buck. If you really want to park in a stadium lot, arrive at least two hours before the game. Many fans arrive early for elaborate tailgate parties.

WEATHER
An old joke has it that there are two seasons in Buffalo: winter and the Fourth of July. That may not seem so funny in the fourth quarter of a January playoff game. The truth is, the NFL loads up the Bills' home schedule early so that most years they play only one regular-season game late in the season. At its worst, Buffalo weather can be brutally cold, snowy, and windy.

MEDIA
Radio: WBEN (930 AM). Van Miller does play-by-play, which he's been doing off and on since 1960.
TV: WGRZ (Channel 2) is the NBC affiliate; WUTV (Channel 29) is the local Fox station.

CUISINE
Only the usual stadium fare—no Buffalo specialties such as chicken wings or roast beef on kümmelweck rolls. Your best bet is the Italian sausage with peppers and onions. The hot dogs are made by Sahlen's (which is good), but they're steamed instead of grilled (which isn't). You can get Polish sausage, but for real kielbasa try the Broadway Market

near downtown. There are two kinds of beer for sale: reduced alcohol (3.2%) and no alcohol; no alcohol at all is served at night games. For real beer and better food, try restaurants near the stadium such as Salfranco's (716-649-7644) or Ilio DiPaulo's (716-825-3675). Along Milestrip Road, near the McKinley Mall, is a string of national restaurant chains.

LODGING NEAR THE STADIUM

Hyatt Regency Buffalo
2 Fountain Plaza
Buffalo, NY 14202
(716) 856-1234/(800) 233-1234
About 15 miles to the stadium.

Buffalo Marriot
1340 Millersport Hwy.
Amherst, NY 14221
(716) 689-6900/(800) 228-9290
About 15 miles from the stadium.

THE BILLS AT RICH STADIUM

Dec. 16, 1973: O. J. Simpson runs for 200 yards, bringing his total to 2,003 and becoming the first player to rush for 2,000 yards in a single season. The Bills beat the New York Jets 34–14.

Dec. 23, 1990: A crowd of 80,235 at Rich Stadium watches the Bills clinch their fourth AFC Eastern Division title by defeating the Dolphins 24–14.

Jan. 20, 1991: The Bills rack up 502 yards in total offense and destroy the Raiders 51–3 for their first AFC championship.

Sept. 6, 1992: James Lofton breaks Steve Largent's career record for receiving yards (13,089) in a 40–7 win over the Rams.

Jan. 3, 1993: Down by 32 points in the third quarter of an AFC wild-card game, the Bills, led by quarterback Frank Reich, beat the Houston Oilers 41–38.

Jan. 23, 1994: The Bills become the only team to reach the Super

Bowl four straight years when they beat the Chiefs 30–13 for the AFC title.

In the Hot Seats at Rich Stadium

Single-game tickets go on sale in early July. Tickets for the hottest games—against the Dolphins and Cowboys, especially—sell out early. For other games tickets are sometimes available at the stadium on game day.

BAD SEATS

The beauty of this football-only stadium is that it affords arguably the best sight lines in the NFL. The closest thing to bad seats are the first several rows of the lower-level end zone, which are sometimes obstructed by personnel on the field, and the last several rows on the home-side upper level, which take the brunt of the northwest wind in bad weather.

SPECIAL PROGRAMS

There is a family section with no alcohol in the upper level at the end-zone corner near Gate 1.

SCALPING

Because the stadium is so big, scalpers don't often get big prices, but for the best games—the playoffs, the Dolphins, glamor NFC visitors—scalpers may get as much as double a ticket's face value. Just in case you care, scalping is not legal in Buffalo.

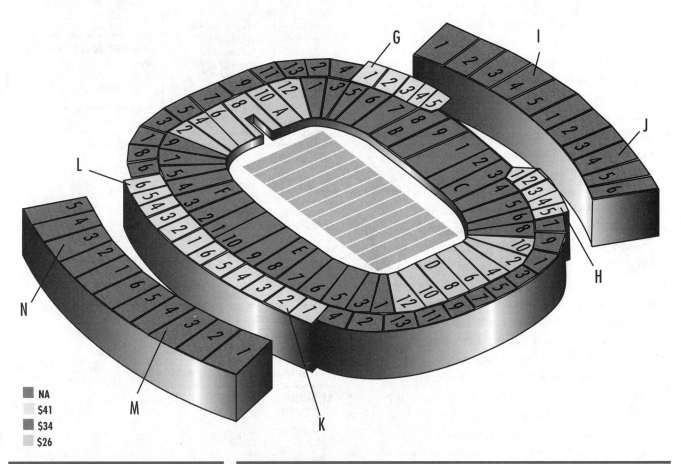

- ■ NA
- ■ $41
- ■ $34
- ■ $26

HOME-FIELD ADVANTAGE

It comes from two things. One is 80,000 screaming fans. And the second? The answer is blowing in the wind—usually out of the northwest. If you want to know which end zone will see more action, just determine which way the wind is blowing at game time. How pronounced is Buffalo's home-field advantage? The Bills have played 10 playoff games at Rich Stadium and won all of them. Too bad for the Bills that they can't play Super Bowls here.

GETTING TO RICH STADIUM

Public transportation: Metro buses Nos. 14B and 14C stop at the stadium. Call (716) 855-7300 for more information.
By car: From either downtown or Greater Buffalo International Airport, take Kensington Expressway to the southbound New York State Thruway (Route 90). Go approximately 8 miles, then exit at Orchard Park (exit 55). From exit 55, follow Route 219 south toward Orchard Park. Exit on Milestrip Road west and continue to the first traffic light, at Abbott Road. Take a left onto Abbott and continue straight through the traffic light. The stadium is on the left.

TICKET INFORMATION

Address: 1 Bills Dr., Orchard Park, NY 14217
Phone number: (716) 649-0015

Hours: Mon.-Thurs. 8–6, Fri. 8–7, Sat. 8–4 (Mon.–Fri. 9–5 during the off-season).
Prices: $41: club level; $34: sidelines, corners, and club-level end zone; $26: lower-level end zone.
Training camp: Fredonia State University, Fredonia, NY

CAROLINA PANTHERS

Ericsson Stadium

Built on 31 parcels of land in a barren end of downtown Charlotte, the Panthers' Ericsson Stadium features three 75-foot-tall, black-granite entry portals, each flanked by two 18-foot statues of fierce-looking panthers, and the stadium colors—royal blue and silver inside, black outside—reflect the team colors. Bold, colorful, and unique, the stadium is exactly what owner Jerry Richardson had in mind when Charlotte was awarded an NFL expansion franchise.

Instead of the usual parking lots, the stadium is ringed by a promenade of spacious grass lawns, and 150 oak trees and other regional plants sure to delight picnickers. The "Cat Walk" area outside the north entrance at Graham Street is the site for pre-game fan pep rallies. There are picnic tables in two areas at the 100-level concourse, in the west end zone. The grounds' overall look resembles the old southern college campus tradition; those who have seen both liken Ericsson Stadium to Sanford Stadium at the University of Georgia in Athens.

Inside, Ericsson's huge scoreboard displays tower above each end zone. Each scoreboard is 40 feet by 210 feet and includes a 24-foot by 32-foot videoboard and a similarly sized matrix board.

The man who put it all together is Richardson, who used to catch passes from Baltimore Colts legend Johnny Unitas. Richardson is president of Flagstar, the United States' fourth-largest food company (Denny's, Hardee's). Richardson follows George (Papa Bear) Halas as only the second NFL player to become a majority owner. Richardson hopes the "powerful look" of the stadium will be memorable and intimidating to rival teams. The proximity of the seats to the field—50 feet to the first sideline row and just 20 feet to the end zone—means a favorable noise factor for the home team, and will make games in Charlotte exciting experiences.

HOT TIPS FOR VISITING FANS

PARKING
The tiny stadium lot is reserved for season club seat ticket holders. City-owned lots around the stadium, however, have room for more than 20,000 cars, and there are also several corporate and private lots in the area. Prices range from $5–$15 depending upon how close you can get to Ericsson.

WEATHER
Charlotte enjoys a moderate climate, with short, mild winters and cool summer nights. The average temperature in July is 79 degrees; in December, 42 degrees. Carolinians wear lightweight summer clothes into late October. After that, bring a sweater or light jacket. The first frost usually doesn't arrive until Thanksgiving.

MEDIA
Radio: WBT (1110 AM) and WRAL (101.5 FM) with Jim Sozoke, Bill Roszinski, and ex-Rams quarterback Roman Gabriel announcing.
TV: WCCB (Channel 18, Fox) broadcasts Panthers games with Tom Hammond, James Lofton, and Tim Brando announcing.

CUISINE
Ericsson's 426 concession stands may be a league record. Given Richardson's corporation, stadium service will no doubt reflect the fast-food end of his business. More than 200 concession stands will offer eight kinds of hot dogs, hamburgers, bratwursts, salads, and other Denny's or Hardee's products. Plans are to sell beer inside the stadium. Sales are permitted starting at 11:45 a.m. on Sundays.
More than 50 restaurants are within walking distance of the stadium. Several of these are in hotels (Marriott, Radisson, Holiday Inn, Omni). The Starlight Café at the Holiday Inn features '50s-style decor. There are several bars along Cedar Street. A virtual institution in Charlotte that survived the inner-city decay of the '60s and '70s is the Open Kitchen (704-375-7449), an old-fashioned Italian bistro on Morehead Street.

LODGING NEAR THE STADIUM

Marriott City Center
100 West Trade Street
Charlotte, NC 28202
(704) 333–9000/(800) 228-9290
½ mile from the stadium.

Holiday Inn Center City
230 N. College St.
Charlotte, NC 28202
(704) 335–5400/(800) 465–4329
4 blocks from the stadium.

STADIUM STATS
Location: 800 South Mint St., Charlotte, NC 28202
Opened: August, 1996
Surface: Grass
Capacity: 72,685
Services for fans with disabilites: Seating available in sections 105, 108–109, 112, 118–125, 138, 322, 512, 522–525, and 534.

TEAM NOTEBOOK
Franchise history:
Carolina Panthers, 1995–present.

In the Hot Seats at Ericsson Stadium

There isn't a bad seat in the house. The problem will be getting one. Panthers tickets were a hot item long before the team ever set foot inside Ericsson Stadium. The Panthers' ticket plan—a permanent seat license scheme—offers the better of the seats to folks who buy the exclusive rights to purchase season tickets for those seats. The plan helped build up a healthy season ticketholder base, although not all of them had been sold before the start of the inaugural season. The 8,000 or so single-game tickets went on sale in May, and by the season's start only a few scattered individual seats for select games were still available; you can just forget about getting two seats together.

SCALPING

Where there are buyers, there will be sellers. Given the local excitement surrounding this team and the scarcity of single-game tickets, you can expect scalping. The new team's fortunes, too, will determine how much demand there is for tickets.

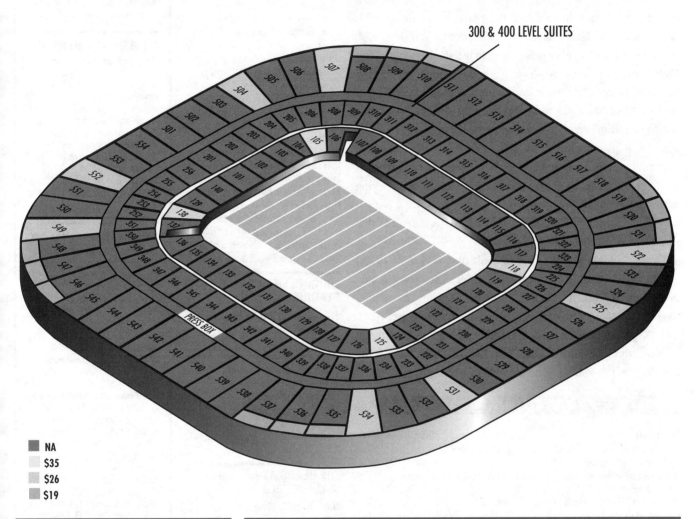

300 & 400 LEVEL SUITES

- ■ NA
- ■ $35
- ■ $26
- ■ $19

HOME-FIELD ADVANTAGE

Ericsson Stadium is supposed to reflect strength and power. The euphoria that's sure to sweep the stadium could help the home team. But remember, Tampa Bay fans were euphoric, too, and the Buccaneers lost their first 26 games. The Panthers went 7–9 at their temporary home in Clemson Stadium in 1995, but perhaps knowing that, they'll be able to settle in at Ericsson and it will boost their play at home.

GETTING TO ERICSSON STADIUM

Public Transportation: Special buses stop at the park and ride lots throughout the city and suburbs and drop riders off three blocks from the stadium. For more information, call (704) 336-2261.

By Car: From the north or south; take I-77 to the John Belk Freeway exit, to Carson Street; follow Carson and make a left onto Mint Street to the stadium.

TICKET INFORMATION
Address: Ericsson Stadium, 800 South Mint St., Charlotte, NC 28202

Phone: (704) 358-7800 or TicketMaster (704) 522-6500
Hours: Mon.–Fri. 9–5.

Prices: $60; $50; $42; $35; $32; $26; $19.

CHICAGO BEARS

Soldier Field

Even after 70 years, people still get it wrong: It's Soldier Field, not Soldier's Field. Opened in 1926 as a memorial to veterans of World War I, Soldier Field has hosted everything from boxing matches to religious conventions. Its best-known tenants, the Bears, have called the place home since 1971. Before then, the Bears shared the Cubs' den at Wrigley Field, but the Mike Ditka years—all played in the shadows of Soldier Field's majestic columns—have made this stadium as much a hallowed place as the "friendly confines" of Wrigley Field.

With Lake Michigan to the east and the downtown skyline serving as an impressive backdrop to the north, Soldier Field's location is awe-inspiring. As befits the Windy City, breezes that range from comfortably cool in September to downright arctic in December often blow across the stadium. Still, during a Monday-night game with the skyline aglow, the view is magical enough to make fans forget they're frozen stiff (and that the Bears are probably losing).

Despite a multimillion-dollar face-lift (the third in 15 years) for the 1994 World Cup, there's been much talk about a new city-financed home for the Bears. The only hitch is that neither the city nor some 90% of Chicagoans polled want to pay for it. Unless the ownership is willing to follow through on their threat to move to Gary, Indiana (the Gary Bears!), expect to see the Monsters of the Midway here at Soldier Field.

The best dog in the house is the Chicago-style, which comes with tomato, onion, relish, mustard, celery salt, pickle, and hot pepper. Also worthy of mention: Chicago-style thick-crust pizza, chicken-breast sandwiches, and bratwurst and Polish and Italian sausages.

To wash all that down, there's a wide selection of beers, with 14 imported brews, as well as local favorite brand Leinenkugel and the usual stadium standbys such as Miller and Budweiser. For later, there are several watering holes within a 5-mile drive or taxi ride of the stadium. Try Blackie's, Kitty O'Shea's (in the Hilton Towers hotel), America's Bar, Planet Hollywood (312-266-7827), the Hard Rock Cafe (312-943-2252), and just about any bar in the famed Rush Street and Division Street corridor.

LODGING NEAR THE STADIUM

The Westin Hotel Chicago
909 N. Michigan Ave.
Chicago, IL 60611
(312) 943-7200/(800) 228-3000
3 miles from the stadium.

The Hyatt Regency
151 E. Wacker Dr.
Chicago, IL 60601
(312) 565-1234/(800) 233-1234
3 miles from the stadium.

THE BEARS AT SOLDIER FIELD

Nov. 20, 1977: Walter Payton rushes for an NFL-record 275 yards in a 10–7 win over the Minnesota Vikings.

Dec. 7, 1980: The Bears beat the Packers 61–7, matching their regular-season team record for points.

Dec. 20, 1987: Future Hall of Famer Walter Payton scores two touchdowns in his final regular-season game at Soldier Field.

Dec. 29, 1994: Kevin Butler's field goal vs. New England makes him the first Bear to score 1,000 points.

HOT TIPS FOR VISITING FANS

PARKING
Nearly a third of the 6,000 spaces in the three lots surrounding Soldier Field have—temporarily—been taken over for the reconstruction of Lakeshore Drive, scheduled to last through 1996. Fans lucky enough to get into what's left pay $10. Get there early, at least two or three hours before kickoff. The better option is to park in the downtown Grant Park underground garage and catch a free shuttle. Fans who risked vandalism and break-ins by parking free on nearby streets will find even these spots harder to come by.

WEATHER
Because temperatures along the lakefront sometimes can be 10–15 degrees lower than inland, always wear a warmer jacket or coat than usual. If you're going to a game in late fall or early winter, be prepared to bring boots, blankets, and gloves or mittens, because the windchill index is often below zero.

MEDIA
Radio: WGN (720 AM). Wayne Larrivee does play-by-play, and former Bears Dan Hampton and Hub Arkush provide analysis.
TV: WBBM (Channel 2) broadcasts preseason games. For regular-season games, WFLD (Channel 32) is the Fox affiliate.

CUISINE
If there's something Chicago fans like just as much as their Bears, it's their food, and Soldier Field has plenty of options. For those who don't do their cooking at pre- and postgame tailgate parties, Ballpark Franks and Kosher Hot Dogs make good starters.

In the Hot Seats at Soldier Field

Soldier Field has 100,000 seats, but fewer than 67,000 are used for Bears games. With 60,000 season ticketholders and a waiting list of more than 9,000 (the turnover rate is about 1%), your best bet is to buy remaining single-game tickets, which almost always are for end-zone seats. The Bears have a mail-order sale every year, but the request must be postmarked by June 1. Once mail requests are filled, the team usually holds a one-day ticket sale at Soldier Field in July. Any leftovers are often on sale through TicketMaster.

GOOD SEATS
If you have a choice, get a seat on the east side of the stadium, preferably not too high and not too close to the field. That way, you have a clear view of the field and will be less likely to feel the bitter breezes that can blow in from Lake Michigan. Also, the east side of the stadium gets more sun. The seats throughout are relatively comfortable.

BAD SEATS
Avoid the far corners of the stadium because trying to see the opposite end of the field is next to impossible.

SPECIAL PROGRAMS
The team has 820 tickets in sections 29 and 31 for sale at the ticket office in Lake Forest or, during the season, at the box office at Soldier Field. Alcohol is not allowed. If you're caught nipping in these sections, you'll be ejected.

SCALPING
It's generally possible to buy scattered game-day tickets in front of Gate 0, at the south end of the stadium. Tickets usually can be bought at face value unless they're for a divisional or other high-profile game, when prices can double or even triple. Word of warning: Chicago police launch occasional stings. Those caught scalping are arrested, their tickets are confiscated, and they face a fine.

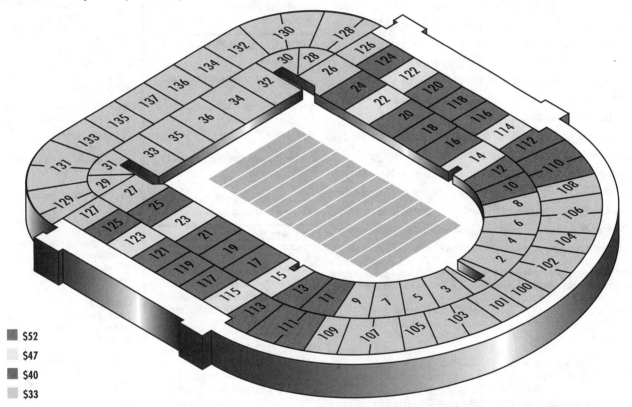

- ■ $52
- ▫ $47
- ■ $40
- ▪ $33

HOME-FIELD ADVANTAGE

During the mid- to late '80s, "Bear weather" was the ultimate home advantage. If under 40 degrees and the wind blustery—snow was an added plus— smart money would be on a win for the Bears. In the five seasons from 1984 to 1988 they went 36–8 at Soldier Field, but in recent years Chicago's advantage has eroded. Since 1989 the Bears are just 34–21 at home.

One factor that affects play is the wind off Lake Michigan. It swirls from the north one minute and gusts in from the south the next, usually, it seems, just before a field goal or extra-point kick goes up.

GETTING TO SOLDIER FIELD
Public transportation: Two Chicago Transportation Authority bus lines, No. 146 (Marine Drive/Michigan Ave.) and No. 128 (Soldier Field Express), stop at the stadium. Call (312) 836-7000 for more information.
By car: From O'Hare Airport, Kennedy Expressway east to Ohio Street exit. Go east to Columbus Drive. Turn right and follow the signs.

TICKET INFORMATION
Address: 950 N. Western Ave., Lake Forest, IL 60045
Phone: (847) 615-BEAR (2327)
Hours: Mon.–Fri. 9-4 (8-4 in the off-season).

Prices: $52: sections 16–21, 116–121; $47: sections 14, 15, 22, 23, 114, 115, 122–123; $40: sections 10–13, 110–113, 24, 25, 124 and 125; $33: sections 1–9, 100–109, 26–36 and 126–137. Sections 29 and 31 are no-alcohol sections.
Training camp: Bears Training Complex, Conway Park, Lake Forest IL (starting late 1996)

CINCINNATI BENGALS

Cinergy Field

The no-frills atmosphere in Cinergy Field may be easing up a bit. First they brought back the Ben-Gals cheerleading squad, and now there's talk of reintroducing the team mascot, Benzoo, a (real) white tiger cub that the Cincinnati Zoo would bring over for games (safety concerns benched the old Benzoo when he grew to full size). Still, Cinergy is fairly buttoned-down, overall, which is in keeping the image of Cincinnati. The franchise founded by Paul Brown believes that fans come to see football and not a circus, so you won't see much to distract you from the action. The field has no logos or marks on it other than the hashmarks and sidelines; there's not even a Bengals logo in the end zone. (When the Reds marked the spot of Pete Rose's hit that broke Ty Cobb's record, the Bengals erased it for their next game, even though it wasn't on the field of play.)

The city-owned stadium is the typical multi-purpose facility built in the early 1970s, and while it's functional, it has far less character than the historic John A. Roebling Suspension Bridge, which crosses the Ohio River next to the stadium. Bengal fans do get cranked up when the team is winning. Though New Orleans gets credit for it, the "Who Dey" chant started in Cincinnati in 1981 as the Bengals marched to the Super Bowl. It goes, "Who dey think gonna beat dem Bengals? Noooo-body." And it's still used (under appropriate game conditions).

HOT TIPS FOR VISITING FANS

PARKING
A three-level garage surrounds the stadium, but that's sold out on a season-subscription basis. Open-air city lots adjacent to the stadium can handle about 1,800 cars and charge $3.50, but a good 50% of those spaces are season subscriptions, so show up a couple of hours early to get in. There are also facilities for about 20,000 cars within 12 blocks of the stadium. Or you can park across the river in Covington and walk across the Roebling Bridge to the stadium. Postgame traffic is rarely a problem.

WEATHER
Fall weather in Cincinnati is generally quite pleasant—it's comfortable past election day. Average temperature in December is 42 degrees, perfect football weather for some. But it also can get very cold—people still talk about the 9-below-zero AFC championship game in January 1982.

MEDIA
Radio: Paul Keels and former Bengal Dave Lapham handle the broadcasts. The flagship station is WCKY (550 AM).
TV: Preseason games are telecast on WKRC (Channel 12). For regular-season games, WLWT (Channel 5) is the NBC affiliate.

CUISINE
The standard ballpark fare is available, along with some upscale sandwich selctions, but Cincinnati's culinary traditions are much in evidence. Metts and brats (German sausages) by Kahn's are sold, as is the cheese coney (a hot dog with Cincinnati chili and shredded cheese). The local brewery, Hudepohl-Schoenling, makes several fine beers, as does the Oldenburg microbrewery. A host of beers are available on the blue level at the two JM Malthaus stands. Postgame crowds head for Pete Rose Way and the hot spots on the waterfront. Caddy's (513-721-3636) and Flanagan's Landing (513-421-4055) are the standbys. Montgomery Inn Boathouse (513-721-7427), famous for their ribs, and Covington Landing (606-291-9992) are just across the river in Covington, KY.

LODGING NEAR THE STADIUM

Hyatt Regency of Cincinnati
151 W. 5th St.
Cincinnati, OH 45202
(513) 579-1234/(800) 233-1234
4 to 5 blocks from the stadium.

Omni Netherland Plaza Hotel
35 W. 5th St.
Cincinnati, OH 45202
(513) 421-9100/(800) 843-6664
2 blocks from the stadium.

THE BENGALS AT CINERGY FIELD

Nov. 17, 1975: Ken Anderson completes 30 of 46 passing attempts for 447 yards. The Bengals win 33–24 over the Buffalo Bills.

Jan. 10, 1982: The Bengals brave 9-below-zero temperatures and a minus-59 windchill to play in their first AFC championship game, against the San Diego Chargers, which the Bengals win 27–7.

Jan. 8, 1989: The Bengals make it to their second Super Bowl by defeating the Buffalo Bills 21–10 for the AFC championship.

Dec. 17, 1989: Led by Boomer Esiason's four touchdown passes, the Bengals trounce the Houston Oilers 61–7 at Cinergy Field.

Dec. 23, 1990: James Brooks sets a team record by rushing for 201 yards in a 40–20 victory over the Houston Oilers.

STADIUM STATS
Location: 1 Bengal Dr., Cincinnati, OH 45204
Opened: June 30, 1970
Surface: AstroTurf 8
Capacity: 60,389
Services for fans with disabilities: Seating available in the plaza level.

STADIUM FIRSTS
Regular-season game: Sept. 20, 1970, 31–21 over the Oakland Raiders.
Points scored: Five-yard touchdown run by Sam Wyche of the Bengals.
Overtime game: Oct. 30, 1977, 13–10 over the Houston Oilers.
Playoff game: Jan. 3, 1982, 28–21 over the Buffalo Bills.

TEAM NOTEBOOK
Franchise history: Cincinnati Bengals, 1968–69 (AFL); Cincinnati Bengals, 1970–present (NFL).
Division titles: 1970, 1973, 1981, 1988, 1990.
Super Bowl appearances: XVI, January 24, 1982, 26–21 loss to the 49ers; XXIII, January 22, 1989, 20–16 loss to the 49ers.
Pro Football Hall of Fame: Paul Brown, 1967; Forrest Gregg, 1977; Bill Walsh, 1993; Charlie Joiner, 1996.
Retired number: 54, Bob Johnson.

In the Hot Seats at Cinergy Field

Cinergy is one of the smaller-capacity NFL stadiums, so tickets are usually in demand. A game against a rival such as Pittsburgh will sell out quickly. The season-ticket base is about 46,000, so there are only 5,000 to 10,000 seats on sale for each individual game.

GOOD SEATS

When the Reds' baseball season is finished, 3,600 seats are added in the lower end zones; most are available for individual games. The Bengals can't sell those tickets until the Reds are officially eliminated, so last-minute buyers can sometimes get lucky.

Also, a limited number of $37 seats under cover on the club level are available, with a

catch or two. They're portable folding chairs that are on the spot that's eventually supposed to be made into a stadium restaurant. The city's been saying it would build one for years. Maybe the county will actually get around to it when they take over the place.

BAD SEATS

The bulk of the tickets not sold on a season basis are in the upper-deck reserved sections, and they're just fine. Some of the most overrated seats are the blue-level field boxes along the sidelines, which are almost all season tickets, anyway. Cincinnati is essentially a baseball town—fans like to sit close to the action and feel that way about football as

well. But many of those "prime" boxes are actually poor football seats. The angles are bad, and you have to look over the heads of players walking the bench.

SCALPING

Ticket scalpers and brokers are legal in Cincinnati. Figure on paying about double the face value for upper-deck seats and about triple the face value for ones closer to the field. You have to go north of 4th Street to find them—scalping is not permitted on the stadium plaza, Pete Rose Way, 3rd Street, or 4th Street. However, you may want to try the plaza first—fans selling extra tickets at face value or below are permitted to sell there.

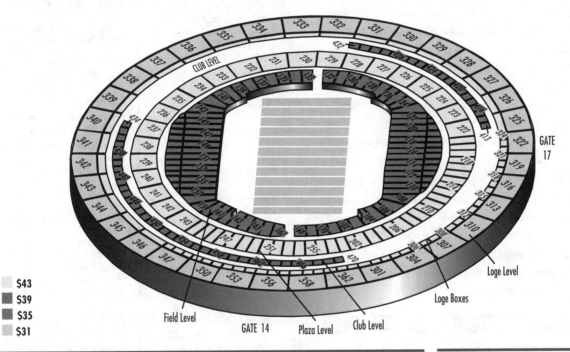

$43
$39
$35
$31

Field Level   GATE 14   Plaza Level   Club Level

GATE 17

Loge Level

Loge Boxes

HOME-FIELD ADVANTAGE

Like most stadiums of similar style, Cinergy holds little home-field advantage for the Bengals besides the crowd. But that can be a formidable edge when the team is a contender—Cincinnati was undefeated in 10 games at home (regular season and playoff) in their last Super Bowl season, 1988. The Bengals don't hold many practices here, so the players don't have the feel for the turf that comes with daily workouts. Certain sections of the turf (especially the southwest corner of the field) don't get much sun in the later part of the season and stay wetter and slicker than the rest of the field. Vet-

eran Bengal receivers know the areas and their characteristics and try to play them during games, though this isn't nearly the factor it was in the early to mid-1980s, when the turf was getting worn. It has since been replaced, and the field has a much better drainage system. Also, the sliding pits for the baseball bases and the mound are covered with artificial-turf inserts for football. A sixth sense for where the inserts are and the difference in the turf (it's much less worn than the rest, so traction is greater) are also small edges for the home team.

GETTING TO CINERGY FIELD

Public transportation: Shuttle buses run on game day from various shopping areas in the city. Call (513) 621-4455 for information.
By car: From the south, take I-75 north. Stay in the right lane as you cross Brent Spence Bridge over the Ohio River. Take the first exit after the bridge onto Pete Rose Way. The stadium is on the right.
From the north, take I-75 south. Follow signs for downtown. Exit onto Pete Rose Way. The stadium is on the right.

TICKET INFORMATION
Address: 1 Bengal Dr., Cincinnati, OH 45204
Phone number: (513) 621-3550
Hours: Mon.–Fri. 9–5.
Prices: $43: club; $39: plaza; $35: lower field; $31: upper level.
Training camp: Wilmington College, Wilmington, OH

DALLAS COWBOYS

Texas Stadium

Even if you've never been to Texas Stadium, if you follow pro football, this sparkling palace home will feel familiar. The Dallas Cowboys have been one of the NFL's most popular and most televised teams, frequently beaming their stadium into many of the nation's living rooms.

The hole in the roof is the most striking difference from other NFL facilities. The truth of the old joke that the hole is there "so God can watch his favorite football team play" has not been confirmed, but the partial roof combines an outdoor atmosphere with an indoor environment and does a decent job of protecting fans from inclement conditions. The stadium is clean, well maintained, and plush, with few if any bad seats; the proximity of the stands to the field generates intimacy on game days. Meanwhile, the Dallas Cowboys cheerleaders, the Ring of Honor around the facade, and the enormous support generated by Cowboys fans all create a bigger-than-life, Lone Star State atmosphere. Not to mention all the seemingly endless controversies that now attach to this team.

Texas Stadium crowds once were criticized because upscale fans in fur coats and three-piece suits seemed to be "too cool" to cheer, but in recent years Cowboys fans have become younger and more boisterous. Since Jerry Jones's purchase of the team in 1989, the Cowboys have gone to great lengths to accommodate this new generation, which explains why the old Cowboys Band has been replaced with blaring, up-tempo music and why Texas Stadium, long distinguished as a "dry" stadium, began selling beer and wine coolers in 1993.

HOT TIPS FOR VISITING FANS

PARKING
About 130 acres of parking provide more than 16,500 spaces on three lots distinguishable by color, as well as another 500 spots for buses. The Blue Lot ($15) is directly outside the stadium, but season ticketholders gobble these up. The Red Lot ($10) also is reserved parking, and the waiting list exceeds 500. The Green Lot ($7) is beyond the Red Lot and operates on a cash-only, unreserved basis.
Virtually no options exist beyond the stadium lots. However, the Days Inn across Highway 183 from the stadium is one option that fills up fast. Fans who park in the hotel lot (about $10) still have to hike across a bridge.

WEATHER
The start of the season generally produces excruciating heat. And when it's hot outside, the humidity inside is even worse because of the half dome/half outdoor configuration. For the rest of the season, though, weather is not a major factor.

MEDIA
Radio: KVIL-FM (103.7) is the flagship station.
TV: WFAA (Channel 8, ABC). KDFW (Channel 4) is the local Fox affiliate.

CUISINE
Texas Stadium features 52 full concession stands, 16 specialty stands, and 20 vendor stands divided almost evenly between the lower and upper levels. In recent years, Tex-Mex items have become extremely popular, particularly the chicken fajitas and jalapeño hot dogs.
Options abound for after the game. Cowboys Sports Café (214-401-3939), owned by ex-Cowboys Tony Dorsett and Everson Walls, is frequented by current players. The center of Dallas nightlife is along Greenville Avenue, north of downtown, where there's just about every sort of food, drink, and entertainment possibility.

LODGING NEAR THE STADIUM

Holiday North Dallas
2645 LBJ Freeway
Dallas, TX 75234
(214) 243-3363
6 miles from the stadium.

Love Field Courtyard
2383 Stemmons Trail
Dallas, TX 75234
(214) 352-7676
1 mile from the stadium.

THE COWBOYS AT TEXAS STADIUM

Dec. 9, 1972: Calvin Hill rushes for 111 yards in a 34–24 win over the Washington Redskins, becoming the first Cowboy to gain 1,000 yards in a season.

Jan. 1, 1978: The Cowboys slam the Vikings 23–6, taking their fourth NFC championship on the way to a Super Bowl victory over the Denver Broncos.

Dec. 28, 1980: Tom Landry wins his 200th when the Cowboys beat the Los Angeles Rams 34–13.

Dec. 27, 1992: The Cowboys set a team record for victories in a season (13) by beating the Chicago Bears 27–14.

Jan. 23, 1994: The Cowboys beat the 49ers 38–21 in the NFC championship game.

Jan. 14, 1996: The Cowboys go to their eighth Super Bowl after trouncing the Packers 38–27.

In the Hot Seats at Texas Stadium

If you're not a season ticketholder, the best bet is to get in line the day single-game tickets go on sale, from late June to mid-July. After the 56,000 or so season tickets are accounted for, the entire slate of games goes on sale, starting with fewer than 6,000 tickets per game. The most attractive games—such as those against the Redskins or the 49ers—usually sell out within hours, and playoff games are known to sell out within 20 minutes. To cut down on scalping and to offer opportunities for more fans to buy tickets, the Cowboys limit the number of tickets an individual can purchase for a single game—generally 10 for regular-season games and four to six for playoff contests.

On game days, scattered single seats sometimes are available at the Texas Stadium box office. It is extremely rare for two seats to be sold together in these cases, but the quality of seats might surprise you.

SCALPING

Although not illegal in Texas, a city ordinance makes the selling of tickets on Texas Stadium grounds illegal. At one time this was hardly enforced and scalpers would turn deals outside the gate entrances, but uniformed police officers have cracked down in recent years, and scalpers now work the freeway shoulders and parking lots. Of course, the bigger the game, the higher the price. Bargains usually can be found during the panic period right after kickoff.

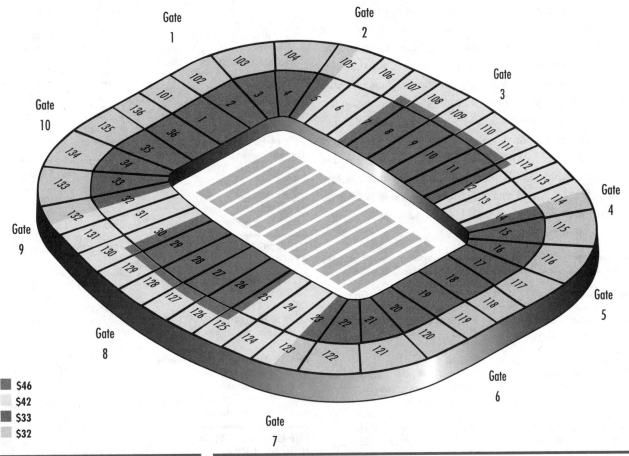

- ■ $46
- ▨ $42
- ■ $33
- ▨ $32

HOME-FIELD ADVANTAGE

In addition to noise, other nuances at Texas Stadium might favor the Cowboys. The field isn't completely level—it slopes toward the sidelines. Also, during day games, distinct sunny and shaded areas can hamper visibility. And some visiting teams have complained that Texas Stadium has a slower field because crews dampen the artificial turf before games.

GETTING TO TEXAS STADIUM

Public transportation: Special stadium buses provided by Dallas Area Rapid Transit (DART)—"The Cowboy Flyer"—are available on game days from various locations, including downtown. Call (214) 979-1111 for information.

By car: Texas Stadium is at the intersection of Loop 12, Highway 114, and Highway 183.

From Dallas–Fort Worth International Airport, take 114 east to the stadium.

From the east and west, follow I-30 to Loop 12 northbound.

TICKET INFORMATION
Address: 2401 E. Airport Freeway, Irving TX 75062
Phone: (214) 579-5000 or TicketMaster at (214) 373-8000

Hours: Mon.–Fri. 9–4.
Prices: $46: prime sidelines; $42: upper sidelines and corners; $33: lower level end zones; $32: upper level end zones.
Special packages: Dallas Cowboys Travel (214-556-9986) books trips for home and away games; packages include tickets.
Training camp: St. Edward's University, Austin, TX

DENVER BRONCOS

Mile High Stadium

Constructed by the Howsam family on a rat-infested city dump west of downtown Denver, Bears Stadium was originally meant for baseball when it opened in August 1948. Not until December 1968 did it become Mile High Stadium, but since the Broncos' first game in 1960, Denver hasn't been the same.

Broncos fans are so devoted that Mile High has been called the loudest outdoor arena in North America, which says something about how deafening a home game can be. For Denver fans, rooting for the Broncos is a religious experience, not a social occasion. If it's snowing, the visiting team might have as much to fear from snowballs thrown from the south stands as from John Elway's passes. Watching over the mayhem is Bucky the Bronco, the signature horse that has stood atop the south-stands scoreboard since 1976; 30 feet tall and made of white fiberglass, Bucky was modeled after Trigger, the Roy Rogers horse of cinema fame. While Bucky might be the only one that doesn't mind Mile High's plumbing problems and too few restrooms, the fans put up with the aging stadium simply because of the electric atmosphere. In their eyes, Sundays at Mile High have no equal in the NFL.

HOT TIPS FOR VISITING FANS

PARKING
Space for 9,010 vehicles in city-owned lots at the Denver Sports Complex; cost: $8 per space. However, most of the city-owned lots north of 17th Avenue (closest to Mile High) are by permit only. Private lots charge $5–$20, depending on the distance from the stadium. Shuttle service is available from far-flung parking areas. Additional parking is available across I-25 at various Auraria Campus sites.
To beat the traffic, arrive two hours before kickoff and enjoy a tailgate party. Immediately before and after the game, the sellout crowds create massive traffic jams. City police do a consistently remarkable job of getting traffic flowing 30-45 minutes after the game.

WEATHER
The Broncos have played several ice-cold games at home, but Denver's fall and winter weather usually is mild, more so than NFL cities in the Midwest and the Northeast. Only at three Broncos home games has the temperature at kickoff been below 20 degrees, and at none since 1978.

MEDIA
Radio: KOA (850 AM) is the flagship station for the Broncos radio network. Larry Zimmer does play-by-play for home games, and Browns and Broncos veteran Dave Logan handles color commentary all season.
TV: KUSA (Channel 9) is the NBC affiliate; WDVR (Channel 31) is the Fox station.

CUISINE
New concessions were added in 1996. Along with traditional stadium fare, fans can now sample from grilled specialties, deli foods, Buffalo burgers, hand-made pretzels, and fresh popcorn. Dominos provides the pizza, Taco Bell handles the south-of-the-border fare, Mona Lisa offers Cajun foods, the Main Street Deli serves up tasty sandwiches, and former Bronco

Simon Fletcher's Doghouse stand has hot dogs of all types. You can quench your thirst with a frozen lemonade concoction from Squishy's, or sample one of the many domestic beers—Coors, Bud, etc.—as well as local microbrews.
Several sports bars, including Zang Brewing Company (303-455-2500) and Brooklyn's (303-572-3999), are nearby. Zang's, as locals call it, is 3 blocks from Mile High in a brick building that dates from 1871. It has 16 televisions, two satellite systems, and sports memorabilia. Broncos safety Steve Atwater often comes by, as do several Nuggets and Rockies players. Brooklyn's is 200 yards south of the stadium, in an area that was known many years ago as "Little Brooklyn." The bar has 30 televisions and four satellite systems. Both spots are wall-to-wall with people before and after Broncos home games.

LODGING NEAR THE STADIUM
Westin Hotel Tabor Center
1672 Lawrence St.
Denver, CO 80202
(303) 572-9100/(800) 228-3000
1 mile from the stadium.

Denver Marriott City Center
1701 California St.
Denver, CO 80202
(303) 297-1300/(800) 228-9290
5 miles from the stadium.

THE BRONCOS AT MILE HIGH STADIUM

Oct. 22, 1973: Before a stirred-up Monday-night crowd, the Broncos come back to tie the Oakland Raiders 23–23 with a Jim Turner field goal.

Jan. 1, 1978: The Broncos earn a place in the Super Bowl by defeating the Raiders 20–17.

Jan. 10, 1988: A 34–10 victory over the Houston Oilers puts the Broncos in the AFC championship game. They make it all the way to the Super Bowl, where they lose to the Washington Redskins.

Jan. 14, 1990: The Broncos take their fourth AFC championship by beating the Cleveland Browns 37–21.

Jan. 4, 1992: Down 21–6, the Broncos come back to beat the Houston Oilers 26–24 in an AFC divisional playoff game.

STADIUM STATS
Location: 1900 Eliot St., Denver, CO 80204
Opened: 1948
Surface: Grass
Capacity: 76,273
Services for fans with disabilities: Seating available in sections 101, 111, 113, 123, and 136.

STADIUM FIRSTS
Regular-season game: Oct. 2, 1960, 31–14 over the Oakland Raiders.
Points scored: 17–yard field goal by Eugene Mingo of the Broncos.
Overtime game: Nov. 30, 1975, 13–10 over the San Diego Chargers.
Playoff game: Dec. 24, 1977, 34–21 over the Pittsburgh Steelers.

TEAM NOTEBOOK
Franchise history: Denver Broncos, 1960–69 (AFL), Denver Broncos 1970–present (NFL).
Division titles: 1977, 1978, 1984, 1986, 1987, 1989, 1991.
Super Bowl appearances: XII, Jan. 15, 1978, 27–10 loss to the Dallas Cowboys; XXI, Jan. 25, 1987, 39–20 loss to the New York Giants; XXII, Jan. 31, 1988, 42–10 loss to the Washington Redskins; XXIV, Jan. 28, 1990, 55–10 loss to the San Francisco 49ers.
Pro Football Hall of Fame: Fred Gehrke, 1972; Willie Brown, 1984; Doak Walker, 1986; Stan Jones, 1991.
Retired numbers: 18, Frank Tripucka; 44, Floyd Little.

In the Hot Seats at Mile High Stadium

Every non-strike regular-season and post-season game hosted by the Broncos has been sold out since 1970. That streak of 188 sellouts dates to Denver's first NFL season. The Broncos have sold more than 70,000 season tickets every year since 1977. The waiting list for season tickets reached a high of 18,000 in 1987 and is now at 3,500. Most ticket prices jumped by $8 in 1994, but the team felt no major backlash from fans, perhaps because the last price hike had been before the 1989 season.

The very few available single-game tickets go on sale in July, and they go fast. The week of a home game, you might be able to purchase scattered singles from the team, but those occasions are rare. Generally, the only tickets available are those returned by the visiting team.

GOOD SEATS
Though the stadium was built for baseball, it doesn't have a bad seat for football. No seats have obstructed views at Mile High (unless you count the railings over which some first-row fans can't see), which has five levels. Among the best seats are those in the third level, sections 301 through 346.

SCALPING
There aren't any bargains.

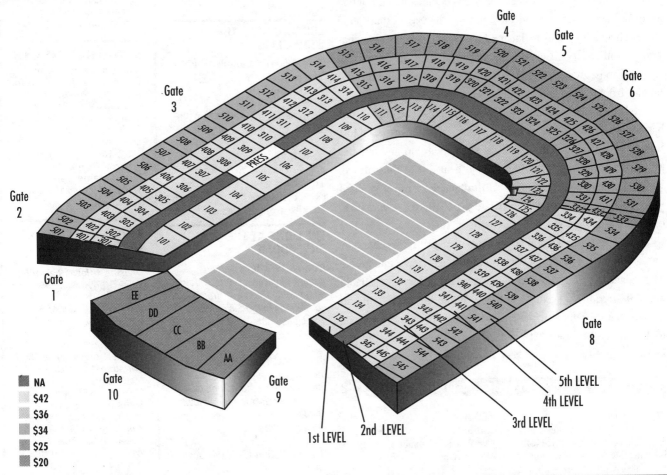

Legend:
- ■ NA
- ■ $42
- ■ $36
- ■ $34
- ■ $25
- ■ $20

HOME-FIELD ADVANTAGE

It's no exaggeration to say the Broncos enjoy the biggest advantage in the NFL. Between 1977, their first playoff season, and 1995, the Broncos were the league's winningest home team, with a 105–35 record in regular-season games. Part of the advantage surely comes from being the only team that plays at 5,280 feet. Visiting teams, particularly those outside the AFC West, often place oxygen tanks and masks behind their benches.

GETTING TO MILE HIGH STADIUM

Public transportation: Buses stop on Federal Boulevard, at the southeast corner of the stadium. Call RTD at (303) 299-6000 for more information.
By car: From the north or south: I-25 to the Mile High Stadium exit. The stadium is off 19th Avenue and Federal.

TICKET INFORMATION
Address: 1900 Eliot St., Denver, CO 80204
Phone: (303) 433-7466
Hours: Mon.–Fri. 8–5 (also open game day during the season).
Prices: $42: first-level sections 101–110 and 125–136, third-level sections 301–314 and 334–346, and fourth-level sections 401–414 and 434–446; $36: first-level sections 111–124; $34: third-level sections 315–333, fourth-level sections 415–433, and fifth-level sections 501–514 and 534–546; $25: fifth-level sections 515–533; $20: south end-zone sections AA, BB, CC, DD, and EE.
Training camp: Lawrenson Hall, University of Northern Colorado, Greeley, CO

DETROIT LIONS

Pontiac Silverdome

The idea for a domed stadium in the Detroit area had been kicked around for years, but it took firm hold in Tiger Stadium on Thanksgiving Day 1968. The Lions lost to the Philadelphia Eagles in a nationally televised game in which the mud was so deep that 11 pairs of football shoes were lost and not recovered until the spring.

Fewer than seven years later, the Lions debuted in the Pontiac Metropolitan Stadium, and they haven't lost a football shoe since. The stadium was nicknamed "PonMet," much to the chagrin of Pontiac city officials. It got its current name in 1976 when retired Lions vice president Edwin J. Anderson, viewing the facility from the air, called it "a silver dome."

The Silverdome has had its share of problems. The Teflon roof has collapsed twice, and in 1978 a plan to clean the artificial turf backfired: The AstroTurf was shipped to an airport and laid out on a runway in hopes that rain would beat dirt to the surface, where it could be vacuumed off. Unfortunately, it never stopped raining, so the Stadium Authority had to pay to have several tons of excess rainwater shipped back with the turf.

The stadium has several advantages over Detroit's other arenas. Unlike Tiger Stadium, it has no obstructed views, and unlike The Palace and Joe Louis Arena, tickets are generally available and don't require a second mortgage. While the basketball and hockey venues cater to white-collar fans, the Silverdome appeals to the shot-and-beer crowd—and as long as the Lions continue to show signs of life, fans will keep coming.

HOT TIPS FOR VISITING FANS

PARKING
There are 15,000 parking spaces available on-site. The price ($8) is controlled by the Silverdome. Several private lots are within ½ mile of the arena, most of which cost about $6–$7. Some prefer to save a couple of bucks by using the shuttle from Phoenix Center in downtown Pontiac, about 2 miles from the Silverdome. The fee is $5 per car, and the shuttle bus is free. Traffic generally isn't a problem.

WEATHER
Always 70 degrees inside the stadium, which is great for those chilly December games. However, with 60,000 warm bodies inside, preseason games in August can get toasty.

MEDIA
Radio: WXYT (1270 AM).
TV: WJBK (Channel 2, Fox); WXYZ (Channel 7, ABC).

CUISINE
The best-selling items are hot dogs, foot-long chili dogs, fresh kielbasa and Italian sausage with all the trimmings. The beer, all premium and all draft, comes in 14- and 22-ounce cups. Before the game, try the Main Event Sports Bar and Grille, at the north end of the Silverdome at club level. The restaurant can handle about 1,000 people at a time, and most come for the 15-entrée, pregame buffet at about $25 per person. Because only 150 people can get tables with any kind of view, most fans head for their seats by the end of the first quarter.

There are few bars or restaurants around the Silverdome, and Lellie's (810-373-4440) is the only one within walking distance. In downtown Pontiac just a short drive away, Griff's Grill (810-334-9292) offers burgers and rock 'n' roll.

LODGING NEAR THE STADIUM

Troy Warren Auburn Hills Marriott
200 W. Big Beaver
Troy, MI 48084
(810) 680-9797/(800) 228-9290
10 miles from the stadium.

Troy Doubletree Guest Suites
850 Tower Dr.
Troy, MI 48098
(810) 879-7500/(800) 424-2900
10 miles from the stadium.

THE LIONS AT THE SILVERDOME

Nov. 12, 1978: Horace King sprints 75 yards for a touchdown in the longest run ever from scrimmage in the Silverdome. The Lions beat the Tampa Bay Buccaneers 34–23.

Oct. 19, 1981: Eric Hipple throws the longest pass completed in the dome to Leonard Thompson—94 yards, for a touchdown. The Lions win 48–17 over the Chicago Bears.

Dec. 18, 1983: A 23–20 win over the Buccaneers clinches the Lions' first division title since 1957.

Nov. 23, 1989: Barry Sanders breaks the 1,000-yard mark when he runs for 145 yards in a 13–10 win over the Cleveland Browns.

Jan. 5, 1992: The Lions beat the Dallas Cowboys 38–6 in their first home playoff game in 35 years, and the first in the Silverdome.

Nov. 13, 1994: Barry Sanders sets a team record when he runs for 237 yards in a 14–9 win over the Buccaneers.

STADIUM STATS

Location: 1200 Featherstone Rd., Pontiac, MI 48342
Opened: Aug. 23, 1975
Surface: AstroTurf
Capacity: 80,368
Services for fans with disabilities: Seating available in the bleachers and in a dozen or more sections of the 100 level. Tickets go on sale two Mondays before game day.

STADIUM FIRSTS

Regular-season game: Oct. 6, 1975, 36–10 loss to the Dallas Cowboys.
Points scored: 21-yard field goal by Toni Fritsch of the Cowboys.
Overtime game: Nov. 27, 1980, 23–17 loss to the Chicago Bears.
Playoff game: Jan. 5, 1992, 38–6 over the Dallas Cowboys.

TEAM NOTEBOOK

Franchise history: Detroit Lions, 1934–present.
Division titles: 1935, 1952-1954, 1957, 1983, 1991, 1993.
Pro Football Hall of Fame: Earl (Dutch) Clark, 1963; Bill Dudley, 1966; Bobby Layne, 1967; Alex Wojciechowicz, 1968; Jack Christiansen, 1970; Hugh McElhenny, 1970; Ollie Matson, 1972; Joe Schmidt, 1973; Dick (Night Train) Lane, 1974; Yale Lary, 1979; Frank Gatski, 1985; Doak Walker, 1986; John Henry Johnson, 1987; Lem Barney, 1992; Lou Creekmur, 1996.
Retired Numbers: 7, Dutch Clark; 22, Bobby Layne; 37, Doak Walker; 56, Joe Schmidt; 85, Chuck Hughes; 88, Charlie Sanders.

In the Hot Seats at the Pontiac Silverdome

The size of the Silverdome is a double-edged sword. While the large capacity makes it easier for more fans to watch the Lions, it also makes it more difficult to sell out, so many home games are blacked out locally. Even the Lions' playoff game against the Packers in 1993—just the second playoff game at the Silverdome— wasn't sold out in time to lift the blackout.

GOOD SEATS

The bleachers on the lower level in the corner of the south end zone are a tremendous bargain. The seats are better situated than

many in the house and are cheaper than all the seats in the upper level. They go on sale two weeks before game day.

BAD SEATS

Although no seats have an obstructed view of the field, the only DiamondVision scoreboard is in the south end zone, so people sitting in the south side of the stadium miss out.

SPECIAL PROGRAMS

Season ticketholders—there are 35,000, 25,000 of whom date from the Silverdome's

first year—get a discount by purchasing early. During the preseason, a variety of two-for-one specials are sponsored by various corporations.

SCALPING

The size of the stadium limits scalping, since good seats usually are available at bargain rates. When demand is high, though, the Pontiac police aggressively monitor ticket scalpers on stadium grounds. The best place to find tickets is near the privately owned parking lots that surround the stadium.

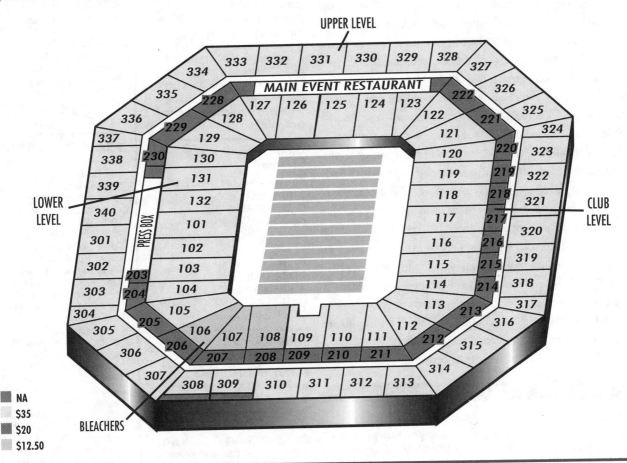

- NA
- $35
- $20
- $12.50

BLEACHERS

HOME-FIELD ADVANTAGE

It doesn't happen often, but when the Silverdome is packed with 80,000 fans, the noise resembles screaming with a metal bucket over your head. The bench area is only 12 feet from the front row of seats, so opposing players have no place to hide from biting comments from Detroit fans.

Since they moved to Pontiac in 1975, the Lions have gone 98–72–1 under the dome.

GETTING TO THE PONTIAC SILVERDOME

Public transportation: There is no way to reach the Silverdome by public transportation.
By car: From Chicago, I-90 east to I-94 east to I-275 north to I-696 east to M-24 north (Telegraph Road) to Square Lake Road. Follow Square Lake Road east to the first exit, Opdyke Road. At the stop sign at the end of the ramp, turn right to the first stoplight, then

right onto Opdyke Road. The Silverdome is fewer than 3 miles ahead, on the left.
From Detroit, I-75 north to M-59 west. Take the first exit and turn left onto Opdyke Road. The Silverdome is on the corner of M-59 and Opdyke Road.
From Port Huron, I-94 west to M-59 west, left on Opdyke Road. The Silverdome is on the corner.

TICKET INFORMATION
Address: Pontiac Silverdome, 1200 Featherstone Rd., Pontiac, MI 48342
Phone: (810) 335-4151 or TicketMaster at

(810) 645-6666
Hours: Mon.–Sat. 10–6 (Sat. 10–2 when game is away; Mon.–Fri. 9–5 in off-season).
Prices: $45: club level; $35: upper and lower

deck; $12.50: bleachers.
Training camp: Pontiac Silverdome, Pontiac, MI

GREEN BAY PACKERS

Lambeau Field

This immaculate, oval-shaped structure (named after Earl L. "Curly" Lambeau, founder and first coach of the Green Bay Packers) in tiny Green Bay, Wisconsin, gives football fans exactly what they want—seats close to the action, no upper decks, terrific sight lines, and a huge parking lot for tailgating. All these things make Lambeau Field perhaps the best pro football stadium in the country. Never mind that the steel benches do little for the gluteus maximus—the action is so close to the stands that you can almost hear the quarterback call signals and the pads collide. The backs of the end zones aren't more than a few yards from the first row of the stadium, and the sideline benches are close enough that players can hear insults hurled at them from the front row. Fans arrive early and are rabid in their enthusiasm. And the feeling seems to be mutual—the Packers were undefeated at home in 1994 and went 8–1 there in 1995.

The long tradition of the Packers playing a few games in Milwaukee County Stadium is now over. Started in the team's early years to boost attendance, it was never a comfortable arrangement. The stadium was built for baseball and made only the bare minimal required adjustments to accommodate football. Both teams shared the sideline, separated only by a piece of tape at the 50-yard line. Another problem was that County Stadium held just 56,051, and several thousand seats had obstructed views.

Even with a new JumboTron replay board in the north end zone, and new private boxes, Lambeau Field is a place to see football played the old-fashioned way: outdoors, in the cold, often in the mud, and all to the roar of a cheering crowd.

HOT TIPS FOR VISITING FANS

PARKING
Approximately 5,800 spots are around Lambeau Field, with an additional 1,000 behind the nearby Brown County Arena. About half of Lambeau spots ($7) are reserved, and fans start filing into the lots three hours before the game to get prime tailgating spots. If the main lots are full, park in the makeshift lots in the neighborhood; these range from $7–$10. Most of the major streets around the stadium don't allow parking on game day. Getting to the stadium can be a time-consuming affair. Generally all nearby highway exits are backed up on game day. One alternative is to overshoot the Lombardi Avenue exit on Highway 41 and peel back to the stadium through the side streets.

WEATHER
Headgear, thick socks, and heavy shoes or boots are musts once October rolls around. Typically, the Packers play one late-season game at Lambeau, which is almost always bitterly cold. The most common outfit for these occasions is bright-orange hunting overalls and snow boots.

MEDIA
Radio: WTMJ (620 AM) is the flagship station of the Packer Radio Network. Jim Irwin and Packers greats Max McGee and Larry McCarren are the announcers.
TV: WLUK (Channel 11) is the Fox station.

CUISINE
Lambeau Field offers standard fare: bratwurst, hot dogs, popcorn, candy, beer, and soda. Most people bring their own eats. Tailgaters grill anything from hot dogs and bratwurst to steaks. The most popular eatery is Kroll's (414-468-4422), which specializes in hamburgers and chili. The restaurant is full for hours after the game. Two local bars, the 50-Yard Line and the Stadium View, are pregame and postgame hangouts.

LODGING NEAR THE STADIUM

The Radisson in Green Bay
2040 Airport Dr.
Green Bay, WI 54313
(414) 494-7300/(800) 333-3333
About 4 miles from the stadium.

Paper Valley Hotel
333 W. College Ave.
Appleton, WI 54911
(414) 733-8000/(800) 242-3499
40 miles from the stadium.

THE PACKERS AT LAMBEAU FIELD

Dec. 31, 1961: The Packers take their seventh NFL championship with a 37–0 win over the New York Giants.

Dec. 26, 1965: Don Chandler hits a 25-yard field goal in the second overtime of a playoff game to beat the Baltimore Colts 13–10.

Dec. 31, 1967: In 16-below-zero temperature, Bart Starr sneaks over from the 1-yard line in the last minute, leading the Pack to a 21–17 win over the Dallas Cowboys and their third consecutive NFL title.

Dec. 21, 1969: Don Horn passes for five touchdowns and 410 yards in a 45–28 rout of the St. Louis Cardinals.

Jan. 8, 1983: Playing their first playoff game at Lambeau Field since 1967, the Packers top the Cardinals 41–16 behind four Lynn Dickey touchdown passes.

Dec. 31, 1994: Packers holds Barry Sanders to -1 yard, beating the Lions 16–12 in the NFC title game.

Dec. 31, 1995: The Pack puts away the Falcons 37–20 in the wild-card game.

STADIUM STATS
Location: 1265 Lombardi Ave., Green Bay, WI 54307
Opened: Sept. 29, 1957
Surface: Grass
Capacity: 60,790
Services for fans with disabilities: Seating in club sections 90 and 91.

STADIUM FIRSTS
Regular-season game: Sept. 29, 1957, 21–17 over the Chicago Bears.
Points scored: 95-yard touchdown run by Ed Brown of Chicago.
Playoff game: Dec. 1931, 1961, 37–0 over the New York Giants.

TEAM NOTEBOOK
Franchise history: Green Bay Packers, 1921–present.
Division titles: 1929, 1930, 1931, 1936, 1938, 1939, 1944, 1960, 1961, 1962, 1965, 1966, 1967, 1972, 1978, 1982, 1989.
Super Bowl appearances: I, Jan. 15, 1967, 35–10 over the Kansas City Chiefs; II, Jan. 14, 1968, 33–14 over the Oakland Raiders.
Pro Football Hall of Fame: R. Hubbard, D. Hutson, E. Lambeau, J. McNally, 1963; C. Hinkle, 1964; M. Michalske, A. Herber, W. Kiesling, 1966; E. Tunnell, 1967; V. Lombardi, 1971; T. Canadeo, 1974; L. Ford, J. Taylor, 1976; F. Gregg, B. Starr, 1977; R. Nitschke, 1978; H. Adderley, 1980; W. Davis, J. Ringo, 1981; P. Hornung, 1986; W. Wood, 1989; T. Hendricks, 1990; J. Stenerud, 1991; H. Jordan, 1995.
Retired numbers: 3, T. Canadeo; 14, D. Hutson; 15, B. Starr; 66, R. Nitschke.

In the Hot Seats at Lambeau Field

About 23,000 people are on the waiting list for season tickets, and in the past two years, only a dozen or so names moved up. Because the Packers sell out on a season-ticket basis in Green Bay, they don't offer single-game tickets until the week of the game—and even then only a couple of hundred seats turned in by the opposing team are available; still, it may be worth a try, and may be your only hope for getting a ticket anywhere near face value. The season ticket waiting list and overall ticket demand jumped way up after the Packers stopped playing their traditional four yearly games at Milwaukee County Stadium. In addition, several new private boxes were installed in the end zones for the 1995 season.

GOOD SEATS
Lambeau has no poles, and sight lines are excellent. A long-awaited second JumboTron replay board has been installed in the south end zone, so you don't have to be a contortionist to twist around to see those exciting plays again if you're sitting in the north end of the stadium.

SCALPING
A Green Bay city ordinance prohibits the sale of tickets for more than face value, and undercover agents patrol outside the stadium. Three of the streets around the stadium, however, border the village of Ashwaubenon, where scalping isn't illegal. Only Lombardi Avenue connects the stadium to the rest of the city of Green Bay. Tickets are hard to get, especially with the former Milwaukee County season ticketholders now coming to Lambeau. The best way to buy a ticket for a single game is to check the local newspapers. But for the most part, the "tickets wanted" ads far outnumber the "tickets for sale" ads.

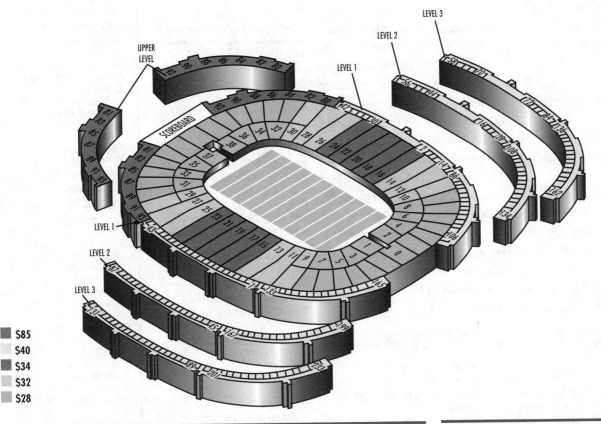

- $85
- $40
- $34
- $32
- $28

HOME-FIELD ADVANTAGE

The cold: The Packers live in the bitter cold day-to-day, and their bodies are used to it. Whether they do it just to intimidate the visiting team or they really don't mind it, some Packers come onto the field without sleeves in subzero weather.

The field: A heating system used for defrosting the field is kept operating until shortly before game time, creating a mushy field surface made up of chunks of moist earth; often, by the fourth quarter of a game on a very cold day, those chunks have started to freeze again. The Packers can better gauge which cleats will work best during their warm-ups, but opponents usually have to make do with what they brought.

Familiarity: The team practices here in the preseason (the St. Norbert training camp is just the dorm where they eat and sleep), and now plays all of its home games here as well.

GETTING TO LAMBEAU FIELD

Public transportation: Lambeau Field can't be reached by public transportation on weekends.

By car: From Highway 41 take the Lombardi Avenue exit. Go right and follow Lombardi for 1 mile to Lambeau Field. From Highway 172 take the Oneida Street exit to the right for 3 miles to the stadium.

TICKET INFORMATION
Address: 1265 Lombardi Ave., Green Bay, WI 54307
Phone: (414) 496-5719

Hours: Mon.–Fri. 9–5.
Prices: $85: club seats; $40: private boxes; $34: mid and upper level sidelines; $32, $28: end zones.

Training camp: St. Norbert College, West De Pere, WI

HOUSTON OILERS

Astrodome

If you want to catch a football game at the Astrodome, a.k.a. the Eighth Wonder of the World, the Mother of All Domes, you'd better move fast. The Oilers will be relocating in 1998 to the Nashville vicinity in a stadium to be named later. In the meantime they'll continue to play in Harris County Domed Stadium, better known as the Astrodome, with its surprisingly intimate atmosphere, good visibility, and hair-raising crowd noise. Among its many nicknames is "Astrodome. The Original," because it was built in 1961, long before its closed-top offspring in New Orleans, Pontiac, Seattle, Indianapolis, and Minneapolis.

Like many elderly NFL venues, the Astrodome has been spruced up to provide better amenities and expanded seating. Most recently, in 1988, 10,000 seats were added to satisfy Texas's football-hungry fans, and a new football-only Astro-Turf system was also installed, making the Astrodome the only artificial-turf stadium in the U.S.A. with entirely separate fields for football and baseball. This was the fourth new rug for the Astrodome.

All Texas football fans are sophisticated when it come to the Science of the Pigskin, and Oilers fans are certainly no different. While the fans go wild when the Oilers "do the right thing" on the field, they can become boobirds at the drop of a pass. Games at the Astrodome remain a pulsating experience for everyone—players, coaches, and fans. Sometimes the place can get so loud that the dome feels about ready to blow off.

HOT TIPS FOR VISITING FANS

PARKING
It's excellent, with terrific access. There are more than 24,500 spaces, all at a reasonable $4. Houston traffic is notoriously bad during rush hour on weekdays, so plan to come at least an hour early for Monday night games to avoid any tieups. Don't bother coming early for tailgating—the prohibition of cooking with an open flame extinguished that idea years ago.

WEATHER
Houston's late-summer and early-fall parking-lot weather can still be sticky with humidity. Generally, falls are gorgeous, and winters are typically moderate.

MEDIA
Radio: KTRH (740 AM). Russ Small annoues and Gifford Nielson does the color commentary. **TV:** KPRC (Channel 2, NBC) and KRIV (Fox, Channel 26) broadcast most of the Oilers games; KHTV (Channel 39) shows preseason games.

CUISINE
Stadium fare at the 120 food and drink outlets was recently upgraded from the standard hot dogs and burgers to also include pizza, deli foods, and offerings from local favorite Luther's Barbecue. There are multiple brands of Dome Foam (a.k.a. beer). Nearby restaurants include the Hard Rock Cafe (713-520-1134), the Palm (713-977-2544) for steak, and Pappasito's (713-668-5756) for Mexican.

LODGING NEAR THE STADIUM

Sheraton Astrodome
8686 Kirby Dr.
Houston, TX 77054
(713) 748-3221/(800) 325-3535
1 block from the stadium.

Holiday Inn Astrodome
8111 Kirby Dr.
Houston, TX 77054
(713) 790-1900/(800) 465-4329
About 6 blocks from the stadium.

THE OILERS AT THE ASTRODOME

Dec. 14, 1969: The Oilers come from behind to beat the Boston Patriots 27–23 and assure themselves a playoff spot.

Oct. 1, 1972: The Oilers stun Joe Namath and the New York Jets 26–20 in the Astrodome for their only 1972 victory.

Oct. 19, 1975: The Oilers come from behind to defeat Washington 13–10 in the Astrodome for their first win over an NFC team.

Dec. 21, 1980: A 20–16 victory over the Minnesota Vikings in the Astrodome clinches the Oilers' third playoff spot in three years. Earl Campbell sets an NFL record by rushing over 200 yards in a single game for the fourth time that season.

Dec. 27, 1987: The Oilers clinch their first playoff berth since 1980 as they defeat the Bengals 21–17.

Dec. 16, 1990: Quarterback Warren Moon has the second-best passing performance in NFL history, completing 27 of 45 for 527 yards in a 27–10 win over the Kansas City Chiefs.

Dec. 29, 1991: Safety Bubba McDowell intercepts two passes near the Oilers' goal line to nail down a 17–10 wild-card victory over the New York Jets.

STADIUM STATS

Location: Loop 610, Kirby and Fannin Sts., Houston, TX 77054
Opened: April 12, 1965
Surface: "Magic Carpet" AstroTurf
Capacity: 59,969
Services for fans with disabilities: Tickets for accessible seating may be purchased at West Gate B, Mon.–Fri. 9–5, or by calling (713) 799-9555.

STADIUM FIRSTS

Regular-season game: Sept. 9, 1968, 26–21 loss to the Kansas City Chiefs.
Points scored: 5-yard touchdown run by Hoyle Granger of the Oilers.
Overtime game: Oct.28, 1979, 27–24 over the New York Jets.
Playoff game: Dec.24, 1979, 13–7 over the Denver Broncos.

TEAM NOTEBOOK

Franchise history: Houston Oilers, 1960–69 (AFL); Houston Oilers, 1970–present (NFL).
Division titles: 1960, 1961, 1962, 1967, 1991, 1993.
Pro Football Hall of Fame: George Blanda, 1981; Sid Gillman, 1983; Ken Houston, 1986; John Henry Johnson, 1987; Earl Campbell, 1991; Charlie Joiner, 1996.
Retired numbers: 34, Earl Campbell; 43, Jim Norton; 65, Elvin Bethea; 63, Mike Munchak.

In the Hot Seats at the Astrodome

Season tickets go on sale in March, and individual-game tickets are available in mid-summer. There is no ticket lottery, though mail orders with requests for specific seats can be sent in July. For large groups, mail order is suggested, but only price range can be selected; the Oilers pick the seats. Tickets are often available right up until game day; complete sellouts are rare. Sometimes local merchants buy up blocks of tickets in advance to prevent local TV blackouts. No such arrangement for 1996–97 has been announced, but it would be worth looking into.

BAD SEATS
The Oilers stopped selling tickets for some 2,500 obstructed-view seats in 1993 (there are now only about 20 seats with obstructions), but there are still some bad ones in the very back rows of the upper deck (bring your binoculars!).

SCALPING
Although scalping is legal in Texas, a municipal ordinance requiring a vendor's license to sell in public includes Oilers and other event tickets. Reselling Oilers tickets is not permitted on stadium grounds. Scalpers may stand along the roadsides adjoining stadium property. Another option is to look in the Yellow Pages under "Tickets," in search of legitimate vendors.

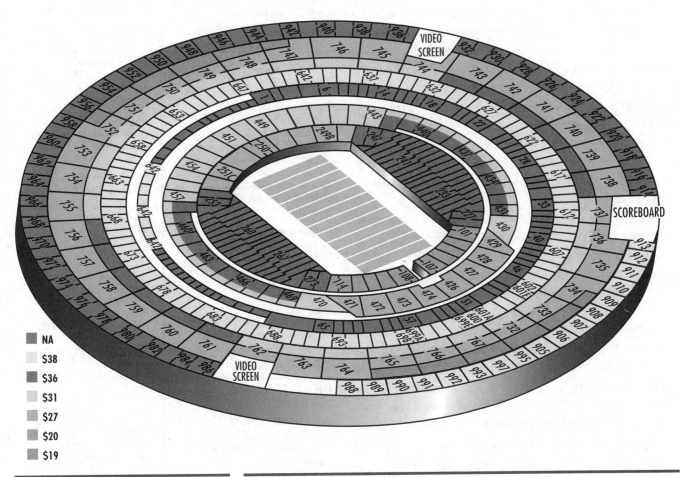

- ■ NA
- ■ $38
- ■ $36
- ■ $31
- ■ $27
- ■ $20
- ■ $19

HOME-FIELD ADVANTAGE

During the rough-and-tumble Jerry Glanville era, the dome was fondly referred to as "The House of Pain" by rabid Oilers fans. Glanville is gone, but visiting teams still find the acoustics deafening and the surface rock-hard. It's a nasty place to play when on the road.

GETTING TO THE ASTRODOME

Public transportation: The No. 15 Hiram–Clark and No. 18 Kirby buses stop at the Astrodome. Call (713) 635-4000 for more information.
By car: From Intercontinental Airport, take Highway 59 south to Highway 288 south. Take exit 288 at Holly Hall Street and make a right onto Holly Hall, which dead-ends at the Astrodome parking lot.

From Hobby Airport, take Broadway heading north to I-45 north. On I-45, get into the left lane and exit onto Loop 610. Take Loop 610 to the Kirby Drive exit and make a right onto Kirby. The Astrodome will be on your right.

TICKET INFORMATION
Address: Houston Oilers Ticket Office, P.O. Box 1516, Houston, TX 77251; the Astrodome; or the Houston Oilers new offices at 8030 El Rio, Houston, TX 77054.
Phone: (713) 797-1000 or TicketMaster at (713) 629-3700
Hours: Mon.–Fri. 8:30–5 plus Sat. 9–5 before a home game.
Prices: $38: loge, sky club; $36: field level, mezzanine, upper boxes (rows 20–38); $31: all other mezzanine and upper boxes; $27: lower west reserved, upper reserved (rows 6–19), pavilion; $20: lower east reserved; $19: upper reserved.
Training camp: Trinity University, San Antonio, TX

INDIANAPOLIS COLTS

RCA Dome

For a dozen years, NFL games hadn't changed one fact about the RCA Dome: It was pleasant place to spend a Sunday. Not provocative. Not exciting. Not loud. Just pleasant.

Since their move, the Colts had never really done much of anything before 1995 that approached the kind of success they had in Baltimore, and Indianapolis sports fans had yet to build a bandwagon for the team, let alone jump on it. The Dickerson years felt more like a blip on the screen than a storied past. In fact, many fans seemed to view home games as a way to avoid raking the leaves on Sunday afternoons. Typical midwestern politeness permeates the dome, which made for a relaxed and, well, pleasant atmosphere rather than the kind of heart-stopping, ear-ringing drama and noise at many other stadiums. If the Bears, Bengals, or Browns were in town, the excitement did ratchet up and some folks went so far as to paint their faces. Still, the atmosphere on game days rarely—if ever—matched the electricity of the Indiana high-school basketball tournament, the state's true sporting passion.

But then there was 1995 and Marshall Faulk. The Colts' surprise underdog run at the AFC title created a stir here in Hoosierland. How much of a stir is yet to be seen, since all of their 1995 playoff games were on the road, but if the NBA Pacers are any indication, the fans here will rise to the occasion and turn the formerly sleepy RCA Dome into one of the louder venues in the league.

People still stumble a bit over the stadium's new name, but they're getting more used to it. Renamed from the Hoosier Dome in 1994, the RCA Dome sits near the heart of Indianapolis. It has a Teflon-coated fiberglass roof 19 stories high and weighing 257 tons. The dome is part of a huge convention center complex and hosts a wide variety of trade shows and concerts, A day and a half are needed to set up the dome for a Colts game, because workers have to roll out 28 15-foot rolls of AstroTurf, each weighing two tons.

HOT TIPS FOR VISITING FANS

PARKING
Considering the dome is downtown, parking isn't a problem: 44,300 spaces are within a square mile of the dome; spots go for about $8–$15.

WEATHER
In September it's 70 degrees outside. But in November and December the dome's Teflon roof offers welcome relief from snow and temperatures in the teens and lower.

MEDIA
Radio: The Colts' flagship radio station is WIBC (1070 AM). Former Colts and San Diego Chargers quarterback Mark Hermann does the color commentary for the Colts' radio broadcasts.
TV: WTHR-TV (Channel 13) is the local NBC affiliate.

CUISINE
As in any other stadium, the usual hot dogs, popcorn, and pretzels are available. They're also worth avoiding. Smart fans frequent the small stands in the dome's concourse. Pizza Hut is a favorite, as is one stand that serves shrimp and crab legs, and another that features Bavarian roasted almonds. The choicest eats, however, are at Ma & Pa's Barbecue. The menu includes barbecue sandwiches, ribs, red-hots, and sweet-potato pie. After the game, Union Station, which harbors dozens of shops and restaurants, is within easy punting distance. Rick's Cafe Americain (317-634-6666) and Norman's (317-269-2545) are popular with sports crowds. The Circle Center Mall, adjacent to the RCA Dome complex, opened in late 1995 and offers a host of restaurants and entertainment.

LODGING NEAR THE STADIUM

Indianapolis Westin Hotel
50 S. Capital Ave.
Indianapolis, IN 46204
(317) 262-8100/(800) 228-3000
Adjacent to the stadium.

Omni Severin
40 W. Jackson Pl.
Indianapolis, IN 46225
(317) 634-6664/(800) 843-6664
1 block from the stadium.

THE COLTS AT THE RCA DOME

Dec. 27, 1987: A 24–6 win over the Tampa Bay Buccaneers gives the Colts the AFC Eastern Conference title.

Oct. 31, 1988: Monday Night Football comes to Indianapolis for the first time. The Colts beat Denver 55–23 behind 4 touchdowns by Eric Dickerson.

October, 30, 1994: In a 28–25 victory over the New York Jets, Marshall Faulk posts his third 100-yard rushing outing of the season, tying Alan Ameche's 1955 rookie club record; the Colts also have their first penalty-free game since 1969.

In the Hot Seats at the RCA Dome

The Colts' season-ticket base dipped to approximately 40,000 a couple of years back and has hung steady. That's in stark contrast to the first year, when well over 100,000 people sent in season-ticket requests. Single-game tickets go on sale in mid-July. Although attendance is down, generally 50,000-plus show up. It isn't difficult to get tickets, even on the day of the game, except perhaps when Miami, Chicago, Dallas, or San Francisco comes to town.

GOOD SEATS
The best seats in the house, on the lower levels all around, and even up a few rows up from the sidelines, are sold as season tickets only.

BAD SEATS
The $15 tickets include the topmost rows and "obstructed seating," and buyers are duly warned that that's what they're getting for their money. Team officials insist that fewer than 1,000 are sold, all in the top row.

SCALPING
Scalping is legal in Indianapolis but not allowed on stadium grounds. What few scalpers you'll see will be as close as the sidewalk outside the dome, which is city, not stadium, property. But with tickets so easy to come by, there's little or no reason to buy from anywhere besides the box office.

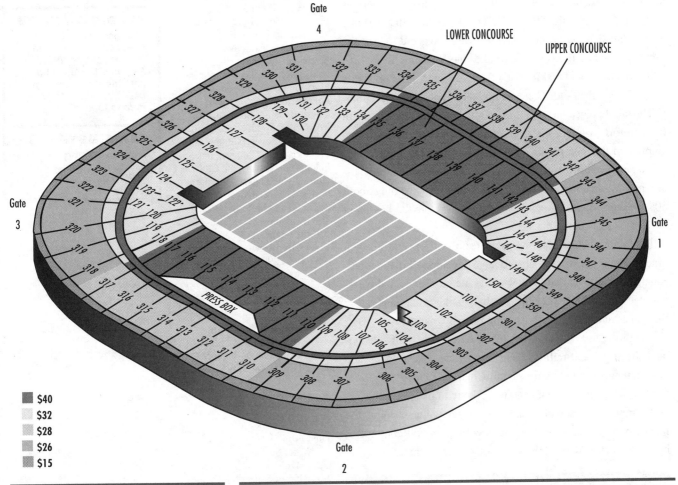

- $40
- $32
- $28
- $26
- $15

HOME-FIELD ADVANTAGE

Since their relocation to the Hoosier/RCA Dome in 1984, the Colts are 42–56 at home. They have posted a winning record at home in only four seasons, going 6–2 in 1988 and 1989, and 5–3 in 1994 and 1995. Subtract those 22 wins and you've got a lot of Colts fans driving home unhappy.

GETTING TO THE RCA DOME

Public transportation: Nearly every city bus in Indianapolis runs along Capital Street out front of the RCA Dome. Call (317) 635-3344 for Metro bus information.
By car: From Chicago, take 65S to West Street (or Martin Luther King Drive—exit 114) to Maryland Street.
From Indianapolis International Airport, follow 465S to 70E to West Street. Exit left, then north to Maryland.
From Louisville, take 65N to 70W to West Street. Exit and go north.

TICKET INFORMATION
Address: 7001 W. 56th St., Indianapolis, IN 46254
Phone: (317) 297-7000
Hours: Mon.–Fri. 9–5.
Order by mail: P.O. Box 53200, Indianapolis, IN 46253
Prices: $40: 200 section along sidelines; $32: upper and lower corners and end zones; $28: upper level sight lines, from sections 10 onward; $26: upper-level corners and end zones, sections 10 and above; $15: top rows and obstructed seats.
Training camp: Anderson University, Anderson, IN

JACKSONVILLE JAGUARS

Jacksonville Municipal Stadium

The Jacksonville Jaguars' sparkling new home is not just a renovated Gator Bowl: It bears only a passing resemblance to the previous structure that had been on the site, and all that remains of the old bowl is an upper deck and a ramping system. Jacksonville Municipal Stadium is more a cousin to the Buffalo Bills' Rich Stadium or the San Diego Chargers' Jack Murphy Stadium. Jacksonville Municipal is a large bowl with rows extending from the field level to the upper deck, with a partially open south side that in Jacksonville's case looks out toward the Jaguars' practice fields and beyond to the St. Johns River, just 200 yards away and making for a fine view regardless of what's happening on the field. There are no poles to obstruct sight lines.

The whole place has a plush feel and has been designed with fan comfort in mind, although clearly aimed primarily to the comfort of the club patron. The open-air club seats are concentrated between the 30-yard lines, rather than encircling the stadium, as is more common; while many stadiums have only about 50% of their seating along the sidelines, Jacksonville has about 70% of its seats along the sides.

The facility, which also houses the team's offices and adjacent practice fields, is still too new to have developed a distinct personality, but it is already renowned as a comfortable and pleasant place in which to take in a football game. Some fans sail to the games and dock their boats at the nearby marina.

The thrill of having pro football in Jacksonville is already evident, from the $50 million spent to upgrade infrastructure and landscaping surrounding the stadium, to the 80-foot glass atrium built at the stadium's main entrance, the twin giant scoreboards with JumboTron screens, and the instant enthusiasm of the locals. As did its predecessor, the new stadium will continue to host the Gator Bowl and the Florida-Georgia clash.

HOT TIPS FOR VISITING FANS

PARKING
Adjacent to the stadium are 3,500 spaces, all of which are only available to season ticketholders. Only cars with a valid pass are allowed inside the complex area. Another estimated 3,500 spaces are available on city-owned lots in outlying areas. Numerous side streets near the stadium may provide parking options for those who don't mind a short walk. The city is trying to acquire additional land in nearby areas for expanded parking facilities.

WEATHER
Average temperatures range from the hot and humid low 80s in August to the mid-50s in January. Florida is noted for its rainy climate, but Jacksonville's yearly average of 54 inches doesn't keep it as wet as Miami.

MEDIA
Radio: The Jaguars' flagship radio station is WOKV (690 AM). Brian Sexton does play-by-play, while Deron Cherry and Matt Robinson provide color analysis.
TV: WTLV (Channel 12, NBC).

CUISINE
Food at the stadium runs the range of traditional arena fare—pizza, hot dogs, burgers, pretzels, and nachos—along with some better-than-average bratwurst and onion rings. The concessions are broken into six kinds of areas scattered throughout the stadium: American Food Court, Boselli's Pizzeria, Gridiron Grille, South of the Cantina, Extra Point Sweet Shoppe, and Pressbox Deli. Club seat ticket holders can get into the Club House, which has an upscale buffet. The usual array of domestic and imported beers is also available.
After the game, you can try River City Brewing Company (904-398-2299), a microbrewery on the banks of the St. John's River, along the Southbank Riverwalk. Their light ale—Jag Light—is named after the team. If you're in a Hooter's sort of mood, there are three in Jacksonville; the one on Independence Drive (904-356-5400) is closest.

LODGING NEAR THE STADIUM
The Omni
245 Water St.
Jacksonville, FL 32202
(904) 355-6664/(800) 843-6664
About 3 miles from the stadium.

The Jacksonville Marriott
4670 Salisbury Rd.
Jacksonville, FL 32256
(904) 296-2222/(800) 228-9290
12 miles from the stadium.

THE JAGUARS AT JACKSONVILLE MUNICIPAL STADIUM
October 8, 1995: The Jaguars beat the Pittsburgh Steelers 20–16 for their first home win.

STADIUM STATS
Location: One Stadium Place, Jacksonville, FL 32202
Opening: Aug. 18, 1995
Surface: PAT/Grass
Capacity: 73,000
Services for fans with disabilities: Seating available throughout the stadium.

STADIUM FIRSTS
First game: Sept. 3, 1995, the Jaguars lose to the Houston Oilers 10–3.
First points: Heywood Jefferies takes a 4-yard pass from Chris Chandler in for a touchdown.

TEAM NOTEBOOK
Franchise history: Jacksonville Jaguars, 1995–present.

In the Hot Seats at Jacksonville Municipal Stadium

Jaguars club seats sold out in fewer than 10 days when Jacksonville was still in the final stages of its quest for an expansion team. Between the 30-yard lines are 12,000 club seats valued at $150 a pop.

State-of-the-art luxury suites feature large seating areas, wet bars, catered food, and television monitors with satellite feeds for other NFL games. And designers didn't forget the rich finishes and fax machines. There's also a club for suite patrons. Virtually all of the suites were leased within months of the franchise's birth.

Sellouts have been the rule so far, and the only seats available close to game time may be the opposing team's returned tickets—as few as 500 seats a game. Because so many Floridians are northern transplants, teams from the Northeast pull in bigger crowds.

GOOD SEATS

There's hardly a bad seat in the place. Sight lines are good, and there are no obstructed seats. The open south end of the stadium offers a view of the boats docked at the marina on the St. Johns River.

BAD SEATS

The higher seats really are up there, so bring binoculars.

SCALPING

Selling tickets for more than face value is illegal in Jacksonville, but considering the demand for Jaguars tickets and the roster of big events that are held at this site, such as the annual Florida-Georgia clash and the Gator Bowl, seats can probably be found, albeit, no doubt, at tremendously inflated prices. With parking and the area surrounding the stadium still somewhat unfinished, scalpers haven't yet staked out any particular turf nearby.

Legend:
- $75
- $60
- $50
- $40
- $30
- $20
- $15

HOME-FIELD ADVANTAGE

Expansion teams don't have many advantages in the NFL, and historically haven't made it to the Super Bowl for their first couple of decades. The Jaguars did start out with tremendous fan support and that is an incalculable boost for any team. Like their fellow Floridians the Miami Dolphins, the Jaguars may also benefit from the weather; the great, hulking icemen on teams from the frozen North tend to wilt fairly quickly under Jacksonville's heat and humidity.

GETTING TO JACKSONVILLE MUNICIPAL STADIUM

Public transportation: A number of buses pass by Jacksonville Municipal Stadium. Call (904) 630-3100 for more information.
By car: From Jacksonville International Airport, pick up I-95 south and proceed to the 20th Street Expressway exit. Follow the 20th Street Expressway and make a right onto the stadium grounds.

From the south, take I-95 north to Emerson Street East over the Hart Bridge to the stadium.

TICKET INFORMATION
Address: One Stadium Place, Jacksonville, FL 32202

Phone: Call (904) 633-2000 or TicketMaster at (904) 353-3309.
Hours: Mon.–Fri. 8–8 and Sat. 10–6.

Prices: $75, $60, $50, $40, $30, $20, $15.
Training camp: Jacksonville Municipal Stadium, Jacksonville, FL

KANSAS CITY CHIEFS

Arrowhead Stadium

Since it was dedicated on August 12, 1972, Kansas City's Arrowhead Stadium has been one of the jewels in the crown of NFL stadiums. It looks even better today than it did when it opened, and the sleek design means there isn't a bad seat in the house. It's hard to remember the days before the glittering era of Joe Montana and Marcus Allen that the Chiefs ever had a down time.

In those days, as former All-Pro nose tackle Bill Maas remembers, "I went into a gas station and left my car unlocked. I had four tickets on the dash, and I came back out and you'll never believe what happened—there were eight tickets on the dash." Perhaps the lowest day in Chiefs' history came on Jan. 2, 1983, when they drew a meager 11,902 fans to a season-ending 37–13 win over the New York Jets; the same day a now-defunct pro soccer team pulled in 15,000 across town.

Times have changed. In 1995 attendance averaged 78,000 during a 13–3 season. As a waiting list for season tickets grows, fans pack Arrowhead Stadium to cheer a team that has reached the playoffs every year since 1990. They wear red and gold, wave their banners, and pound their tom-toms. While they can be rowdy, it's a good-natured rowdiness preserved by Arrowhead's strict policing of drunkenness and obscenity. Arrowhead is one of the league's loudest stadiums and one of the most exciting places to watch a football game.

HOT TIPS FOR VISITING FANS

PARKING
Arrive early if you don't want to park in Outer Mongolia. Although the Chiefs offer on-site parking for 26,000 vehicles, the situation has drawn heat from fans who were used to the days when the Chiefs attracted 40,000, not 77,000. Still, it's better than most NFL cities—in fact, only the Meadowlands offers more. The red reserved stadium lots cost $11; gold reserved lots are $13 but are for season ticketholders only. Other lots are $9. The other reason to come early is that Chiefs fans love tailgating parties. Gates open three hours before the game, and that's when the tailgaters arrive.

WEATHER
The Chiefs have played very few snowy games at Arrowhead, but be prepared for cold, as the wind often swirls around inside the stadium.

MEDIA
Radio: KCFX (101 FM).
TV: Channel 4, the NBC affiliate, carries most games, though former Chiefs quarterback Len Dawson is sports director of the competing Channel 9.

CUISINE
The best food is outside before the game. Arrive early and sample some of the tailgating fare. Most of those tending pits are happy to share their food with appreciative lovers of barbecue. Inside, it's typical ballpark fare. The Chiefs offer barbecue, hot dogs, hamburgers, and such, but the stadium has no signature food item. Most common U.S. brands of beer are available. The once-famous postgame barbecues in Lot E, hosted by All-Pros Derrick Thomas and Neil Smith, are no more, and the official postgame party and radio show are at the VIP tent on the gate D apron.

Luckily for non-VIPs, Quincy's, in the Adams Mark Hotel, which used to host the team's postgame parties now has more room for fans and is within easy walking distance of Arrowhead. Although not a sports bar, Alison's House (816-923-6666) pulls in a lot of business from both Chiefs and Royals fans hungry after a game. In Westport, just south of Kansas City, is the area's most famous watering hole. A trip to see the Chiefs should include a stop at Kelly's (816-753-9193), where you can find any number of athletes and sports fans at the bar.

LODGING NEAR THE STADIUM

The Westin Crown Center
1 Pershing Rd.
Kansas City, MO 64108
(816) 474-4400/(800) 228-3000
8 miles from the stadium.

Ritz Carlton
401 Ward Pkwy.
Kansas City, MO 64112
(816) 756-1500/(800) 241-3333
About 12 miles from the stadium.

THE CHIEFS AT ARROWHEAD STADIUM

Sept. 14, 1980: Kicker Nick Lowery sets an NFL record by hitting two 50-plus-yard field goals in one game. The Chiefs still lose to the Seattle Seahawks 17–16.

Sept. 29, 1985: Deron Cherry ties an NFL record with four interceptions in a 28–7 win over Seattle.

Oct. 14, 1990: Barry Word sets a team record by rushing for 200 yards in a 43–24 win against the Detroit Lions.

Dec. 27, 1992: On the last Sunday of the season, the Chiefs lock up a playoff spot by crushing the Denver Broncos 42–20.

STADIUM STATS
Location: 1 Arrowhead Dr., Kansas City, MO 64129
Opened: Aug. 12, 1972
Surface: AstroTurf 8
Capacity: 79,101
Services for fans with disabilities: Seating available in sections 109, 110, 127, and 128.

STADIUM FIRSTS
Regular-season game: Sept. 17, 1972, 20–10 loss to the Miami Dolphins.
Points scored: 14-yard touchdown reception by Marlin Briscoe of the Dolphins.
Overtime game: Nov. 23, 1975, 24–21 over the Detroit Lions.
Playoff game: Dec. 28, 1991, 10–6 over the Los Angeles Raiders.

TEAM NOTEBOOK
Franchise history: Dallas Texans, 1960–62 (AFL); Kansas City Chiefs, 1963–69 (AFL); 1970–present (NFL).
Division titles: 1962, 1966, 1968 (tie), 1971, 1993, 1995.
Super Bowl appearances: I, Jan. 15, 1967, 35–10 loss to the Green Bay Packers; IV, Jan. 11, 1970, 23–7 over the Minnesota Vikings.
Pro Football Hall of Fame: Lamar Hunt, 1972; Bobby Bell, 1983; Willie Lanier, 1986; Len Dawson, 1987; Buck Buchanan, 1990; Jan Stenerud, 1991.
Retired numbers: 3, Jan Stenerud; 16, Len Dawson; 28, Abner Haynes; 33, Stone Johnson; 36, Mack Lee Hill; 63, Willie Lanier; 78, Bobby Bell; 86, Buck Buchanan.

Jan. 8, 1994: With Joe Montana orchestrating a fourth-quarter comeback, the Chiefs win 27–24 in overtime over the Steelers in the first round of the playoffs.

In the Hot Seats at Arrowhead Stadium

The Chiefs are the hottest ticket in town and one of the hottest in the league. The team cut off season ticket sales at 70,000 in 1995, and the resulting waiting list does not bode well for the casual fan. The few remaining single-game seats go on sale in mid-July. Ticket prices went up in 1994 and 1996, but the Chiefs' tickets still are among the lower-priced in the NFL. Occasionally tickets are turned back in before games, so sometimes seats are available the week, or even the day, of the game—but don't hold your breath.

GOOD SEATS

Arrowhead has no obstructed-view seats, with JumboTron scoreboards at each end of the field. Many fans ask for tickets in the north stands because they're in the sun for most of the noon games and some of the 3 p.m. starts. The visitors' bench is on the north side as well, so it's also a favorite spot for hecklers.

There's no plan to revive the no-alcohol section, but the Chiefs strictly enforce stadium rules against drunkenness.

SCALPING

Those who arrive at Arrowhead and need a ticket should beware. Scalping is illegal in K.C., and anyone attempting to sell a ticket—even for face value—can be arrested. Still, plenty of tickets seem to be available outside: Most scalpers can be found tying up traffic. It's a seller's market, and markups run between $25 and $50 for regular-season games, with playoff tickets going in the $150–$300 range.

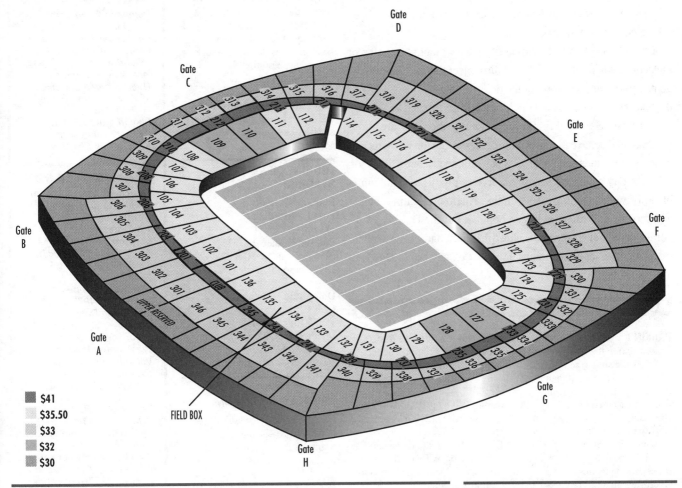

- ■ $41
- ▫ $35.50
- ▨ $33
- ▨ $32
- ▨ $30

FIELD BOX

HOME-FIELD ADVANTAGE

Talk to visiting quarterbacks about Kansas City fans. John Elway has called Arrowhead the toughest stadium in the NFL. The Chiefs make no bones about the importance of playing at home. They lost just one game there in 1993, and some of the noisiest fans in the NFL were a big reason. Linebacker Derrick Thomas says, "They are so noisy and crazy, I can't believe it. When an opponent gets in the red zone, the fans make it awfully tough. There's no way to audible down there, and that makes our job easier."

The numbers bear this out—the Chiefs have lost only four games at home since 1993.

GETTING TO ARROWHEAD STADIUM

Public transportation: Special shuttles run on game day. Call Metro Bus at (816) 221-0660 for information.

By car: From Heart Airport, take I-435 south. Follow I-435 to I-70 east. Exit to the left. Take I-70 ¼ mile to Blue Ridge Cutoff. The stadium is on the right.

TICKET INFORMATION
Address: 1 Arrowhead Dr., Kansas City, MO 64129
Phone: (816) 924-9400

Hours: Mon.–Fri. 8:30–5 (also Sat. 9–12 in season).
Prices: $41: club level; $35.50: field box; $33: upper box; $32 field reserve; $30: upper reserved.
Training camp: University of Wisconsin–River Falls, River Falls, WI

MIAMI DOLPHINS

Pro Player Stadium

Built in 1987 with the comfort of the spectator in mind, Pro Player Stadium has everything you'd expect from a state-of-the-art facility: grass field, unobstructed views, 19-inch-wide seats with chair backs and armrests, TV monitors at the 40 concessions stands, restrooms aplenty, and giant TV screens at either end of the field. It certainly beats the old Orange Bowl in amenities, parking, cleanliness, and sight lines, but the old excitement the fans had for their team seems not to have been rekindled in this new, more sterile abode.

In the Orange Bowl, the closed end put a wall of fans on top of the action, where they could (and did) inject themselves into the game by roaring in support of the defense on goal-line stands. At the open end, palm trees and a dolphin tank contributed to the tropical atmosphere. At Pro Player Stadium, the fans are more removed and behave that way. Some suggest that the well-stocked concessions stands and plush seats have softened a once-hardy lot.

Game day continues to bring a diverse mix to the stadium, a blend of wealthy and not-so-wealthy, Anglo and Latino, native and snowbird. Tailgating is also popular, but the Dolphins supporters have yet to recapture the spirit they had at the Orange Bowl. Of course, the Dolphins haven't won any Super Bowls in a while, either.

plus a Stadium Cafe for more varied selections. Seats on the club level have automated menu service, so patrons never have to leave their seats. As beers go, teetotalers can enjoy O'Doul's; the regular and light beers of the major brewers are on sale. Tailgaters show up at Sports Town Jr., a tent city at the east side of the stadium with interactive games, kickoff contests, and a variety of food and drink. After the game, many fans tuck into the huge portions served at Coach Shula's Steakhouse (305-820-8102) in nearby Miami Lakes. Joe's Stone Crab (305-673-0365) is probably the busiest and best-known restaurant in Miami.

HOT TIPS FOR VISITING FANS

PARKING
Spaces next to the stadium are reserved and sold to season ticketholders at $100 for 10 games. Persons holding single-game tickets are steered by parking attendants to lots on the east and west sides of the stadium, where parking is $10. Shuttle buses ferry patrons to the stadium. On-street parking is limited. Overflow situations rarely occur; when they do arise, it's usually on Monday nights, when car-pooling breaks down because of the late start. Smart shoppers arrive about two hours before kickoff. Traffic tends to back up on N.W. 199th Street (Ives Dairy Road), which leads to Pro Player from I-95.

WEATHER
Sultry and steamy. Fans are encouraged to drink plenty of fluids (not just soft drinks and beer) and wear hats, sunglasses, and light-colored clothing. It's

also smart to bring a fold-up raincoat since brief downpours are not uncommon.

MEDIA
Radio: WIOD (610 AM—English), WCMQ (1210 AM—Spanish).
TV: Sold-out regular-season games are on WTVJ (Channel 6, NBC); WSVN (Channel 7) is the local Fox affiliate.

CUISINE
A person could forget he or she is in a stadium. Mrs. Field's Cookies, Carvel, Domino's, Arby's, and Burger King await, as do ethnic specialties such as Cuban sandwiches and kosher cuisine. Choices among the expanded selection of standard fare: hot dogs, sausages, chicken breast sandwiches, and stuffed potatoes.
Grill and deli stands are sprinkled throughout the concourses,

LODGING NEAR THE STADIUM

Marina Marriott Fort Lauderdale
1881 S.E. 17th St.
Fort Lauderdale, FL 33316
(954) 463-4000/(800) 228-9290
19 miles south of the stadium.

Don Shula Hotel and Golf Club
15255 Bullrun Rd.
Miami Lakes, FL 33014
(305) 821-1150
10 miles from the stadium.

THE DOLPHINS AT PRO PLAYER STADIUM

Nov. 1, 1987: The Dolphins beat Pittsburgh 35–24, giving Don Shula his 250th regular-season victory.

Oct. 23, 1988: Dan Marino throws for 521 yards—the second most in NFL history—but the Dolphins lose to the New York Jets 44–30.

Dec. 12, 1988: Marino tosses his 193rd touchdown pass and becomes the first NFL quarterback to pass for more than 4,000 yards in four seasons as the Dolphins top the Browns 37–31.

Jan. 10, 1993: Miami wins 31–0 over the Chargers in an AFC playoff game, their largest postseason margin of victory.

STADIUM STATS
Location: 2269 N.W. 199th St., Miami, FL 33056
Opened: Aug. 16, 1987
Surface: Grass
Capacity: 74,916
Services for fans with disabilities: Seating available in sections 103, 125, 128, 131, 153, and 156.

STADIUM FIRSTS
Regular-season game: Oct. 11, 1987, 42–0 over the Kansas City Chiefs.
Points scored: 6-yard touchdown run by Ricky Isam of the Dolphins.
Overtime game: Oct. 25, 1987: 34–31 loss to the Buffalo Bills.
Playoff game: Jan. 5, 1991, 17–16 over the Kansas City Chiefs.

TEAM NOTEBOOK
Franchise history: Miami Dolphins, 1966–69 (AFL); Miami Dolphins, 1970–present (NFL).
Division titles: 1971, 1972, 1973, 1974, 1979, 1981, 1983, 1984, 1985, 1992, 1994.
Super Bowl appearances: VI, Jan. 16, 1972, 24–3 loss to the Dallas Cowboys; VII, Jan. 14, 1973, 14–7 over the Washington Redskins; VIII, Jan. 13, 1974, 24–7 over the Minnesota Vikings; XVII, Jan. 30, 1983, 27–17 loss to the Washington Redskins; XIX, Jan. 20, 1985, 38–16 loss to the San Francisco 49ers.
Pro Football Hall of Fame: Paul Warfield, 1983; Larry Csonka, 1987; Jim Langer, 1987; Bob Griese, 1990; Larry Little, 1993.
Retired number: 12, Bob Griese.

Sept. 4, 1994: Marino throws for 5 touchdowns and 473 yards, including his 300th, to join Fran Tarkenton as the only quarterbacks to throw for 300+ touchdowns. The Dolphins beat the Pats 39–35.

In the Hot Seats at Pro Player Stadium

Single-game seats usually go on sale in late spring or early summer, but don't worry too much about planning ahead. The Dolphins have a season ticket base of about 60,000, but as many as 5,000 seats are usually available right up to kickoff. Although the Dolphins sold out every home game for TV in 1995, this didn't happen until the Thursday prior to game day.

With so many tickets available for home games, folks who want to go on a whim generally are in luck; you'll likely wind up in the lower end zone or upper corners, as most other seats are held by season ticket holders or snapped up by those who live nearby. The hardest games to get into will be those against the Cowboys, Jets, and Giants. For a long time, the least attractive draw was the Indianapolis Colts, but this probably won't be so true as long as Marshall Faulk is around.

GOOD SEATS
Because of Pro Player Stadium's symmetrical design, no seats are obstructed. There are no poles, the bane of old-time parks.

BAD SEATS
If there's a place to avoid, it's the upper deck on the visitors' side; these seats have no protection from the sun, which can be fierce into late October.

SPECIAL PACKAGES
The Dolphins offer a family section that includes an area where alcoholic beverages are forbidden. These 5,000 seats are in the first 10 rows of sections 427–433, and are a bargain at $20, compared to the top price of $40 elsewhere in the park. All of Joe Robbie Stadium is designated smoke-free.

SCALPING
With tickets so freely available, scalping has not been a problem, which is just as well, since reselling tickets is illegal in Miami.

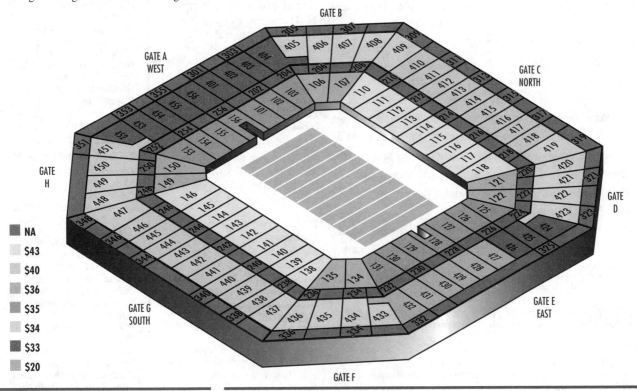

Legend:
- NA
- $43
- $40
- $36
- $35
- $34
- $33
- $20

HOME-FIELD ADVANTAGE

The weather always has been the Dolphins' friend and the visitors' enemy. With mean daytime temperatures of 82 degrees in September, conditioning is critical. For a team that practices in the cold to come down and play in December is an exercise in physical and mental fitness. The Dolphins have, for years, leaned toward somewhat undersized linemen because the bigger guys wilt too quickly in the heat.

GETTING TO PRO PLAYER STADIUM

Public transportation: Special, event-specific transportation is available from Dade, Broward, and Palm Beach counties. Call Dade Transit (305) 638-6700; Broward Transit (954) 357-8400; and Palm Beach County Transportation Authority (561) 233-1114 for details. Park and Ride service is available for games. From Miami call (800) 874-7245 for details.

By car: From Fort Lauderdale, take I-595 West to Florida Turnpike south, then 9 miles to exit 2 (N.W. 199th Street/Honey Hill Road). Exit to 199th and make a right. From Miami Airport, take I-95 north to Ives Dairy Road, then west for 9 miles (during which the road changes to 199th). The stadium is on the right.

TICKET INFORMATION
Address: 2269 N.W. 199th St., Miami, FL 33056
Phone: (305) 620-2578 or TicketMaster (305) 358-5885

Hours: Mon.–Fri. 8:30–6; Sat. 8:30–4.
Prices: $43: lower sidelines; $40: upper sidelines; $36: lower corners; $35: lower end zones; $34: upper corners; $33: upper end zones; $20: upper east side end zone,

family section, 1st 10 rows of sections 427–433.
Training camp: Nova University, Davie, FL

MINNESOTA VIKINGS

HHH Metrodome

Baseball purists complain about the Hubert H. Humphrey Metrodome, but football fans like it better. The team has done well at home since moving here, and fans have been treated to what, in general, is a comfortable environment. Vikings fans tend to be much older than Twins fans, and sitting indoors on a December day in Minnesota is just fine with most of them. The Vikings crowd is notoriously quiet except during the most exciting moments of the games. Younger fans who like to get rowdy get told to sit down and shut up by folks behind them. Tailgate parties are making a comeback, however, in a pedestrian plaza along three blocks of Washington Avenue that are closed to traffic two hours before game time; there's barbeque and music, and players sometimes swing through, giving out autographs.

Despite seats angled for the best football watching, the Metrodome recently has become a somewhat annoying place to watch a game—even for football fans. That's because the huge color replay scoreboards show commercials at least as often as they show replays, and with the roof holding the volume in, the ads are very loud. This can't have helped attendance, which has been down generally, although the stadium saw its two biggest crowds in Viking history in 1994.

Former Bears coach Mike Ditka often criticized the stadium. He once called it a big livestock hall, and the Vikings responded by putting fake cows on the field.

The Vikings miss Ditka.

PARKING
No attached or adjacent public parking. But many lots are in the blocks surrounding the facility. Anyone arriving an hour before kickoff should find fairly clear sailing. The nearest lots charge at least $10 a car, but fans willing to walk—fewer than 2 blocks in some cases—can find $5 lots. Chicago Avenue, north of the Metrodome, is closed to car traffic from Third to Sixth streets and becomes a pedestrian plaza two hours before game time, so fans have to go an extra couple of blocks either north or south to drive around.

WEATHER
Fortunately for the Vikings, the Twins have had to endure the brunt of the weather-caused calamities at the Metrodome. For whatever reason, most of the weather-induced collapses to the dome's Teflon roof have occurred during the baseball season. While coats aren't necessary once inside, earplugs are a must because of the volume of the commercials during time-outs.

MEDIA
Radio: All games can be heard on WCCO (830 AM). Dan Rowe and former Viking Darrin Nelson call the games.
TV: The local Fox affiliate is Channel 29, and the NBC station is KARE (Channel 11).

CUISINE
Mediocre at best, and sometimes not even that good. The hot dogs, popcorn, and the like are just OK; beer is offered in basic domestic brands. The best bet is the ice cream. Both hand-packed and soft-serve are good, and soft-serve sundaes are dished up in edible waffle-cone cups.

After the game, the best-kept secret is the Pickled Parrot (612-332-0673), near Target Center. It's more of an upscale bar and grill, but its ribs are tasty and tender with plenty of zing. If you don't like them quite so spicy, go to Market Barbecue (612-872-1111) or O'Brien's Decoy Pub & Smokehouse (612-623-3671). Sawatee (612-338-6451), just a few blocks east of the Metrodome on Washington Avenue, offers excellent Thai food.

LODGING NEAR THE STADIUM

Crown Sterling Suites
425 S. Seventh St.
Minneapolis, MN 55415
(612) 333-3111/(800) 433-4600
3 blocks from the stadium.

Holiday Inn Crown Plaza Northstar
618 Second Ave. S.
Minneapolis, MN 55402
(612) 338-2288/(800) 556-7827
7 blocks from the stadium.

THE VIKINGS AT THE METRODOME

Nov. 28, 1982: Tommy Kramer throws five touchdown passes in a 35–7 win over the Chicago Bears.

Sept. 16, 1984: Randy Holloway gets five sacks against the Atlanta Falcons in a 27–20 win.

Dec. 4, 1988: With one of their biggest victory margins ever, the Vikings demolish the New Orleans Saints 45–3.

Dec. 26, 1988: Wade Wilson throws for 253 yards and Anthony Carter logs 102 receiving yards, as the Vikes beat the Los Angeles Rams 28–17 in the first round of the NFC playoffs.

Oct. 4, 1992: Down 20–0 to the Bears after three quarters, the

Vikings roar back before a Monday night television audience to win 21–20.

In the Hot Seats at the HHH Metrodome

Most games eventually are filled by kickoff, but tickets for many games can be purchased the week of the game. Only a few are walk-up sales available on game days.

The toughest ticket is for the annual game against the NFC Central Division archrival Green Bay Packers. Scalpers have fetched upward of $300 apiece via agencies and $100 on the street for good seats to Packers games.

Many Minnesotans are old Packers fans, and many Wisconsinites cross the border to attend.

GOOD SEATS

Metrodome has no obstructed views, and many fans like to sit high, the better to see plays develop. For dollar value, the seats around the top rows of the stadium are hard to beat in the NFL.

SCALPING

Scalping is illegal in Minnesota but does happen. Most scalpers congregate near the intersection of Chicago Avenue and 6th Street, others near the will-call windows on the 11th Avenue side of the stadium. Purchasers who wait until after kickoff can buy for well below face value.

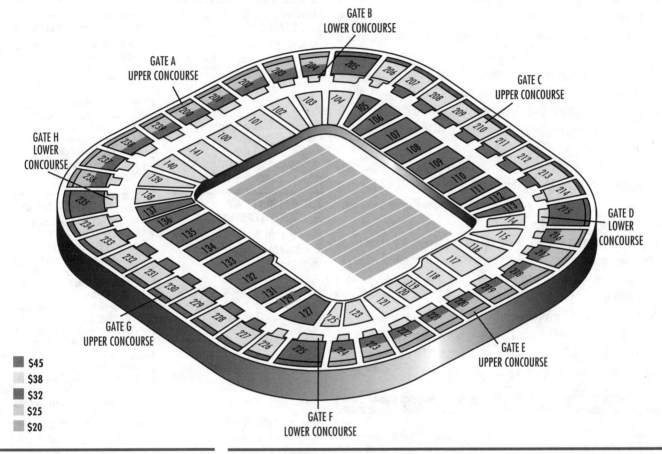

Legend:
- $45
- $38
- $32
- $25
- $20

HOME-FIELD ADVANTAGE

Like all other teams that play in domed stadiums, the Vikings have not gone to the Super Bowl since they moved into the Metrodome. Mike Lynn, the former general manager, said that the Metrodome worked against the team because it made them "soft" when playing playoff games outdoors. Moving out of Metropolitan Stadium in 1981, the Vikings lost one of best home-field advantages—an icy one. Still, in 1989 the Vikings won the NFC Central Division despite their 2–6 road record because they went 8–0 at the Metrodome. Since moving indoors, they've gone 70–43 at home.

GETTING TO THE HHH METRODOME

Public transportation: The 16A bus runs east along Fourth Street. The stop at Fourth Street and Chicago is the closest to the Metrodome. Call M.C.T.O. at (612) 373-3333 for additional bus information.

By car: From the north, go south on 35W to Washington Avenue and exit right. Go 2 blocks, left onto 11th Avenue, then right onto Fifth Street. The Metrodome is on the right. From the south, take 35W north to the Fifth Street exit. The Metrodome is on the right. From the east, head west on 94 to the Fifth Street exit. The Metrodome is on the right. From the west, follow 394 east to the Fourth Street exit. Turn on any street west of the Metrodome for parking, or east on 94 and follow Fourth Street north signs.

TICKET INFORMATION
Address: 500 11th Ave. S., Minneapolis, MN 55415
Phone: (612) 333-8828 or TicketMaster at

(612) 989-5151
Hours: Mon.–Fri. 8:30–5, plus Sat. 8–12 before home games (Mon.–Fri. 8:30–4 in the off-season).

Prices: $45, $38, $32, $25, $20.
Training camp: Mankato State University, Mankato, MN

NEW ENGLAND PATRIOTS

Foxboro Stadium

Foxboro Stadium is quintessential New England. The permanent home of the Patriots—thanks to stadium owner Bob Kraft, who purchased the team in 1993 using the lease as a purchasing wedge—is as raw as a New England winter and as chilly as a New England spring, with no frills and only intermittent thrills (6–10 record in '95). Being a Patriots fan is like serving on an Atlantic fishing boat: lots of ups and downs, plenty of wet weather, and not a lot of excitement.

Billy Sullivan owned the franchise when it played at Boston University. It "graduated" to Fenway Park, then to Boston College and Harvard, before Bay State Raceway owner E. M. Loew offered a piece of land less than an hour from Boston, Worcester, and Providence.

A vote was won from the townsfolk of Foxboro—the only town whose selectmen can decide NFL Monday Night Football schedules—and the first game was played less than a year after ground was broken.

It's a very basic stadium with one big bonus—great sight lines. There are good seats everywhere. And $10 million has been put into improvements since Kraft bought the stadium, with another $60 million promised. As of 1996, Foxboro is also the home of the New England Revolution professional soccer team.

Patriots' coach Bill Parcells says he became convinced of fan support when 42,810 showed up for a 1993 Jets game despite bone-chilling winds of 68 m.p.h. and relentless sheets of rain.

The stadium has upgraded food offerings to include Philly cheese-steak sandwiches, D'Angelo's, Papa Gino's pizza and fried dough as well as the usual fare.

LODGING NEAR THE STADIUM

Holiday Inn
700 Myles Standish Blvd.
Taunton, MA 02780
(508) 823-0430/(800) HOLIDAY
About 17 miles from the stadium.

Providence Marriott
Charles at Orms St.
Providence, RI 02904
(401) 272-2400/(800) 228-9290
About 20 miles from the stadium.

THE PATRIOTS AT FOXBORO STADIUM

April 4, 1970: The city of Foxboro is named the Patriots' new hometown.

Dec. 31, 1978: In the only playoff game in Foxboro, Patriots lose to the Houston Oilers 31–14.

Sept. 7, 1986: The 10-foot-wide by 15-foot-long 1985 AFC championship banner is raised at Sullivan Stadium in a pre-game ceremony.

Sept. 21, 1986: Tony Eason throws for 414 yards for a team record, exceeding Vito "Babe" Parilli's 400 yards. The Pats lose to the Seattle Seahawks, 38–31.

Dec. 4, 1988: Veteran wide receiver Stanley Morgan catches his 500th career pass with 26 seconds remaining in the first quarter against the Seahawks.

May 3, 1991: Natural grass is installed in what is now Foxboro Stadium.

Nov. 13, 1994: Down by 20, Drew Bledsoe throws for 426 yards in an NFL record 70 attempts as he leads the Pats back to a 26–20 win over the Vikings.

HOT TIPS FOR VISITING FANS

PARKING

If the coach wants to test how tough his players are, he should send them to the parking lots. If they can take the potholes, they can take NFL hits. The stadium has 18,500 licensed spaces, some 5,000 of those in private lots, and only controls the surrounding lots. Expect some traffic congestion after the game, although the recent widening of nearby Route 1 has helped a lot. The long-anticipated new off-ramp from I-95 is but a distant promise.

WEATHER

Yes, there's weather, a smorgasbord of it, and stories, too, like the infamous Snowplow Game, a 3–0 win over Miami in '82. A small plow cleared the space from which John Smith kicked the field goal on a day that started in sunshine and ended in a blizzard. Smith, now retired, calls the Foxboro winds the worst. "They swirl. In Buffalo it comes in one direction; at Foxboro they just swirl."

MEDIA

Radio: WBCN (104.1 FM). Gil Santos and Gino Cappelletti have been doing the play-by-play and color together since 1982.
TV: WCVB (Channel 5) is the ABC affiliate.

CUISINE

You can dine New England inn–style at the nearby Lafayette House, or visit The Red Wing on Route 1, which is famous for its fried clams and scallops, and for its old-style diner section.

In the Hot Seats at Foxboro Stadium

Owner Bob Kraft, who has had season tickets since the stadium opened, said he wants fans to "come here and know they are going to sit with the same people in the same area. The problems we've had are with the transient crowds. You never knew who would be next to you." Despite recent price hikes, season-ticket sales have been brisk; as proof, the whole 1995 season was sold out six months before it began.

BAD SEATS
The most expensive sections begin right behind the player benches and in spite of the field's being below the seats, the view here is still obstructed by players along the sidelines.

SPECIAL PROGRAMS
There is a family section for NFL games where security is more visible.

SCALPING
Patriots were known as pilgrims the last time anyone saw a scalper in Foxboro.

In 1993 a radio station, trying to promote a big home crowd for the final game against Miami, asked season ticketholders who weren't going to use their tickets to give them to the station to distribute. There were more givers than takers. If the Pats can ever put together two good seasons in a row, though, look for more action.

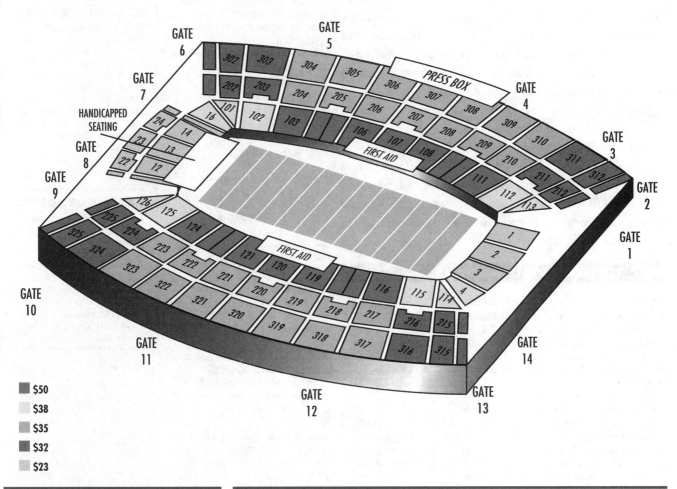

Legend:
- ■ $50
- ▨ $38
- ▨ $35
- ■ $32
- ▨ $23

HOME-FIELD ADVANTAGE

Or not. Since going back to grass in '91, the field has earned the reputation as one of the worst grass fields in the league. It simply doesn't root for the Pats. It comes up in clumps, though.

GETTING TO FOXBORO STADIUM

Public transportation: Train service from Boston stops within walking distance of the stadium. Call (617) 722-3200 for more information.

By car: From Boston, take Route 35 to Route 128N to Route 95S; exit 9 onto Route 1S, and proceed about 3 miles to Foxboro Stadium. From southern Connecticut or Rhode Island, take Route 95N to Route 495N; exit 14A onto Route 1N, then go approximately 4 miles to Foxboro Stadium.

From northern Connecticut or Rhode Island, take Route 295N to Route 495S; exit 14A onto Route 1N, then go approximately 4 miles to Foxboro Stadium.

TICKET INFORMATION
Address: Route 1, Foxboro, MA 02035
Phone: (800) WIN-PATS or TicketMaster (617) 731-2000

Hours: Mon.–Sat. 9–5.
Prices: $50; chairback sideline seats; $38: corner chairbacks; $35: sideline bench seats; $32: sideline corner; $23: end zones.

Training camp: Bryant College, Route 7, Smithfield, RI 02917

NEW ORLEANS SAINTS

Louisiana Superdome

New Orleans Saints linebacker Rickey Jackson has entered the Superdome many times in his NFL career, but never the way he did one Saturday night in mid-February 1994. Jackson rode into the arena on a float. He was the grand marshal of the parade of the Krewe of Endymion, the largest parading organization in the history of New Orleans' Mardi Gras. Located in downtown New Orleans, within walking distance of the French Quarter, a riverboat casino, and many shops and restaurants, the Superdome is the only pro sports stadium in the country that hosts a Carnival parade. And that's only one of the unique uses of this sports palace, which has become the favored destination of everything from Super Bowls to tractor pulls.

Truth is, it's always a party inside the Superdome, especially when the Saints are in town. As the only major-league sports franchise in the city, the Saints have enjoyed a love affair with New Orleans fans that has only intensified with the team's recent winning ways. Although the stadium is so big that the Astrodome could fit inside, Saints games have sold out for virtually seven years. The Superdome on game day is a prime example of a city letting the good times roll.

HOT TIPS FOR VISITING FANS

PARKING
The Superdome parking garage can hold 5,000 cars. Fans usually begin arriving at the Superdome about 2½ hours before kickoff; the traffic flow into the garages is steady. Parking costs $12. More than 10,000 additional parking spaces are within easy walking distance. But be careful. During special events, police are quick to tow illegally parked vehicles. Don't get waved into an area by someone who looks like an attendant and who'll then take your money while you get towed. If you're staying downtown, your best bet is to walk. Traffic after the game isn't bad because the stadium is next to an interstate highway.

WEATHER
The temperature inside the dome is 64 or 65 degrees before the game and about 72 once it starts. Outside, fall in New Orleans is warm and usually dry. Inclement weather during football season is more the exception than the rule.

MEDIA
Radio: WWL (870 AM).
TV: Preseason games that are not televised nationally are carried on WWL-TV (Channel 4) in New Orleans. WVUE (Channel 8) is the Fox affiliate.

CUISINE
Popeye's Fried Chicken, which originated in New Orleans, is sold here, but the rest of the choices usually run toward standard stadium fare. For something more substantial try the Dome Cafe, on the plaza level by Gate H. Open year-round, on game days it offers a buffet that starts two hours before kickoff and goes until game time. The plaza-level cafeteria is open game days. You can consume the libation of your choice, including mixed drinks, in your Superdome seat. This is New Orleans, the Big Easy, remember? The police are experts on crowd control; they're used to handling millions during Mardi Gras. Still, night games can get rowdy.

After the game you can find virtually any ethnic cuisine in New Orleans, from soul food at the Praline Connection (504-943-3934) to seafood at Ralph and Kacoo's (504-522-5226) and the Acme Oyster House (504-522-5973). Mulates (504-522-1492) has fine Cajun food, and Commander's Palace (504-899-8221) is known for serious gourmet fare—but make sure to call for a reservation.

LODGING NEAR THE STADIUM

Hyatt Regency
Poydras St. at Loyola Ave.
New Orleans, LA 70140
(504) 561-1234/(800) 233-1234
Next to the stadium.

Hotel Inter-Continental
444 St. Charles Ave.
New Orleans, LA 70130
(504) 525-5566/(800) 445-6563
About 7 blocks from the stadium.

THE SAINTS AT THE SUPERDOME

Oct. 30, 1977: A fake field-goal pass from Tom Blanchard to Elois Grooms helps upset the Los Angeles Rams 27–26.

Dec. 3, 1979: Though the Saints lose to the Raiders, Chuck Muncie rushes for 128 yards to become the first Saint to gain 1,000 yards in a season.

Sept. 4, 1983: George Rogers sets a team record by rushing for 206 yards against the St. Louis Cardinals. The Saints win 28–17.

Jan. 3, 1988: The Saints play their first playoff game, losing 44–10 to the Minnesota Vikings.

Nov. 20, 1988: The Saints secure their second consecutive winning season, 42–0 over the Denver Broncos.

Oct. 23, 1994: Tyrone Hughes returns two kickoffs for touchdowns, as he sets four NFL records. The Saints beat the Rams 37–34.

STADIUM STATS
Location: 1500 Poydras St., New Orleans, LA 70112
Opened: Aug. 3, 1975
Surface: AstroTurf
Capacity: 72,348
Services for fans with disabilities: Each section of the stadium has wheelchair-accessible seating.

STADIUM FIRSTS
Regular-season game: Sept. 28, 1975, 21–0 loss to the Cincinnati Bengals.
Points scored: 52-yard touchdown reception by Isaac Curtis of the Bengals.
Overtime game: Nov. 13, 1977, 10–7 loss to the San Francisco 49ers.
Playoff game: Jan. 3, 1988, 44–10 loss to the Minnesota Vikings.

TEAM NOTEBOOK
Franchise history: New Orleans Saints, 1967–present.
Division title: 1991.
Pro Football Hall of Fame: Jim Taylor, 1976; Doug Atkins, 1982; Earl Campbell, 1991.
Retired numbers: 31, Jim Taylor; 81, Doug Atkins.

In the Hot Seats at the Louisiana Superdome

The Saints' season-ticket base of about 41,000 is down a bit from previous years, but games can still fill up with loyal local fans by game time, depending on how well the home team has been playing. Tickets are sometimes available close to game day. Individual-game tickets—usually for the Plaza, padded Terrace, and Terrace levels—go on sale in mid-July, although applications are available in February. Since orders are filled on a first-come, first-served basis, apply early.

BAD SEATS

Even in the upper levels of the Terrace, seats for football offer excellent viewing with field glasses. If you're trying to get a last-minute ticket, you'll likely sit there, so bring those binoculars. New for 1996 are portals that lead directly into the upper level seats from beneath the stands, sparing fans with tickets in the stratosphere that long, long climb from the lower sections. And, if you do wind up in the upper reaches, at least you won't look like you're up there all by yourself (see Home-Field Advantage below).

SCALPING

Those who don't mind missing kickoff can usually get tickets for face value or less from one of the few scalpers outside. Reselling tickets for above face value is illegal, and scalping at all is forbidden within 100 yards of the dome.

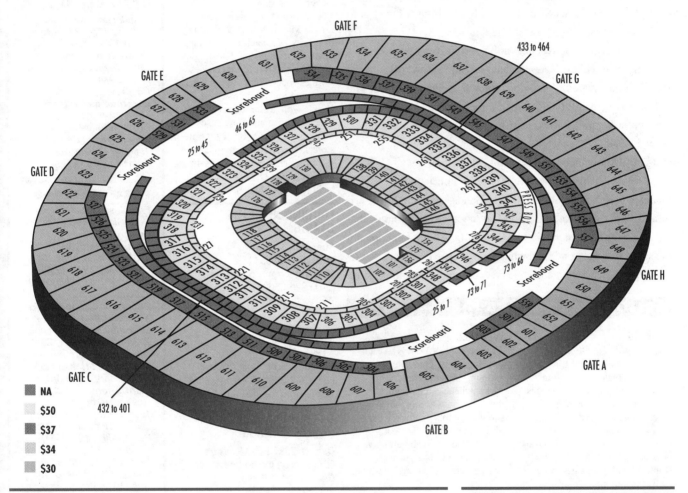

Legend:
- ▮ NA
- ▯ $50
- ▮ $37
- ▮ $34
- ▮ $30

HOME-FIELD ADVANTAGE

Since 1986 the Saints are 45–26 at the dome, so all those rowdy fans must really help. The Saints being the only pro sports team in town doesn't hurt, either. The new paint job on the terrace level is perhaps meant more to psych out or dispirit the opposing team's fans watching the game from home than to affect visiting players. The Superdome has painted these upper (and sometimes empty) seats in alternately light and dark colors, so that when TV cameras sweep over the section—even if it's mostly empty—viewers see what looks like the sorts of patterns created by seats filled with people. Maybe if this works they'll paint little binoculars on each seat as well.

GETTING TO THE LOUISIANA SUPERDOME

Public transportation: Many options exist for reaching the Superdome on public transportation. Call RTA at (504) 569-2700 for details.

By car: From New Orleans International Airport: I-10 east to New Orleans. I-10 forks. Stay on 10, following signs to Slidell. Take the Superdome exit (on left) ⅔ mile past the fork; exit left. The Superdome is on the right.

TICKET INFORMATION
Address: 1500 Poydras St., New Orleans, LA 70112
Phone: (504) 731-1700, TicketMaster at

(504) 522-5555 or (800) 488-5252
Hours: Mon.–Fri. 8–6, plus Sat. 8:30–3.
Prices: $50: club level suite; $37: loge (200 and 300 levels), padded terrace (500 level); $34:

plaza (100 level); $30: terrace (600 level).
Training camp: New Orleans Saints Training Facility, 5800 Airline Highway, Metairie, LA

NEW YORK GIANTS

Giants Stadium

Decked in red, white, and blue team colors, the 78,124-seat Giants Stadium offers terrific sight lines and the magical Manhattan skyline across the Hudson as a backdrop. Before what might be the league's best facility for football was built, this area, known as the Meadowlands, was a vast swampland filled with rats and abandoned car frames. Maybe the best way to explain why Giants Stadium is so football-fan friendly is to note that you can't fit a baseball field inside.

The Giants are strictly a blue-collar, grind-it-out team that has had only nine winning seasons (but two Super Bowl titles) since the stadium opened. The wind, known to the natives as the Hawk, has helped the Giants win a lot of games, as have their fans, unfairly reputed to be an affluent lot who sit on their hands. Attend an NFL East matchup with, say, the Philadelphia Eagles, and you'll know that the noise can be deafening.

Of course, it might not be only team spirit that drives the Giants when they play at the Meadowlands—it could be a spirit of a different sort. An outrageous but popular theory holds that long-missing Teamsters boss Jimmy Hoffa is buried underneath the stadium. Every once in a while someone makes the half-serious suggestion that the end zone be excavated just to make sure.

HOT TIPS FOR VISITING FANS

PARKING
The stadium lot, with 24,800 spots, is among the NFL's largest. Tailgaters arrive four hours before kickoff. The cost is $6. Some fans park at nearby hotels (Sheraton, Hilton, Days Inn) and run car pools to the game. It's not a good idea to walk because you have to cross busy Route 17 and walk a tightrope path along approach roads. Departing the stadium can tax your patience. The George Washington Bridge backs up routinely, and the addition of a few thousand cars makes the wait a good hour. The Lincoln Tunnel often is a better option for Manhattan. Travelers to Westchester County and Connecticut might prefer the Tappan Zee Bridge, although it also has heavy traffic on Sunday nights, especially in September when vacationers continue to return from the Catskill Mountains and other points north.

WEATHER
Autumn in New York is so exciting, as the song goes. But not late autumn, when the infamous Meadowlands winds begin howling, sometimes accompanied by snow. September games can be played in summer-like heat, accompanied by high humidity, but eight weeks later, heavy sweaters and parkas are in fashion.

MEDIA
Radio: WOR (710 AM) is the club's flagship station.
TV: Home and away games are carried on WYNY (Channel 5), the local Fox affiliate.

CUISINE
Along with traditional stadium fare (and which offers better-than-average hot dogs and pretzels), Giants Stadium introduced some more fun and upscale offerings in 1996, and expanded the number of concessions locations to 158. Giants fans can now chow down on fajitas, bratwurst, individual size pizzas, Philly cheese steak sandwiches, and Italian ices. Premium beers available include Heineken, Bud Ice, Miller Light, and Molson. Cappuccino and espresso also are sold, and if you're really adventurous, you can get a frozen margarita.

The favorite hangout for Giants fans is Manny's (201-939-1244) in nearby Moonachie. You can't beat the ambience and nostalgic mementos of old Giants heroes. Former coach Bill Parcells dined there on Sunday nights . . . if the Giants won. Manny's serves a terrific brunch and runs buses to home games. Two other favorite stops are in Manhattan—Gallagher's Steak House (212-245-5336) and the Dakota Bar and Grill (212-427-8889).

LODGING NEAR THE STADIUM

Sheraton Meadowlands
2 Meadowlands Plaza
East Rutherford, NJ 07073
(201) 896-0500/(800) 325-3535
Across the highway from the stadium.

Meadowlands Hilton
2 Harmon Plaza
Secaucus, NJ 07094
(201) 348-6900/(800) 445-8667
1 mile from the stadium.

THE GIANTS AT GIANTS STADIUM

Dec. 21, 1985: Joe Morris gains 202 yards on the ground as the Giants top the Pittsburgh Steelers 28–10.

Jan. 4, 1987: Joe Morris runs for 159 yards and defensive tackle Jim Burt knocks Joe Montana unconscious as the Giants romp past the San Francisco 49ers 49–3 in an NFC semifinal game.

Jan. 11, 1987: With wind gusting through Giants Stadium, the Giants defense stands firm. The 17–0 win over the Washington Redskins puts the Giants into their first Super Bowl.

Jan. 13, 1991: The Giants stop the

Location: East Rutherford, NJ 07073
Opened: Oct. 10, 1976
Surface: AstroTurf
Capacity: 78,148
Services for fans with disabilities: Seating available in sections 117–125.

STADIUM FIRSTS
Regular-season game: Oct. 10, 1976, 24–14 loss to the Dallas Cowboys.
Points scored: 8-yard touchdown by Robert Newhouse of the Cowboys.
Overtime game: Dec. 18, 1977, 12–9 loss to the Chicago Bears.
Playoff game: Dec. 29, 1985, 17–3 over the San Francisco 49ers.

TEAM NOTEBOOK
Franchise history: New York Giants, 1925–present.
Division titles: 1927, 1933–35, 1938, 1939, 1941, 1944, 1946, 1956, 1958, 1959, 1961–63, 1986, 1989, 1990.
Super Bowl appearances: XXI, Jan. 25, 1987, 39–20 over the Denver Broncos; XXV, Jan. 27, 1991, 20–19 over the Buffalo Bills.
Pro Football Hall of Fame: Hein, Henry, Hubbard, Mara, Thorpe, 1963; Guyon, Herber, Owen, 1966; Strong, Tunnell, 1967; McElhenny, 1970; Robustelli, Tittle, 1971; Brown, 1975; Flaherty, 1976; Gifford, 1977; Leemans, 1978; Badgro, 1981; Huff, 1982; Weinmeister, 1984; Tarkenton, 1986; Csonka, 1987.
Retired numbers: 1, Flaherty; 7, Hein, 11, Simms; 14, Tittle; 32, Blozis; 40, Morrison; 42, Conerly; 50, Strong; 56, Taylor.

Chicago Bears cold 31–3 in an NFC semifinal game. Again, the Giants defense makes the difference, snagging two interceptions and holding the Bears to 27 yards rushing and no first downs.

In the Hot Seats at Giants Stadium

The ticket office is bombarded each week with heart-wrenching stories, all designed to gain entrance to the stadium. They don't work. The more than 78,000 seats in Giants Stadium are held by season ticketholders. Another 10,000-plus names are on a waiting list that will take decades to fulfill. Tickets cost $35–$40 and are occasionally available from New York City ticket agencies (at a much higher price, of course).

GOOD SEATS

Giants Stadium boasts no obstructed seats on its three levels and good angles to the field.

There isn't a bad seat in the house, even in the lower rows that start 10 feet above the field. The very best seats are on the mezzanine level, particularly in sections 209–213. The lower tier, especially sections 128–134 and 108–114, also affords excellent sight lines; rows 30–35 have the added attraction of being under cover, just as in the mezzanine, but closer to the field. The front rows of upper-tier sections 309–313 and 329–333 have good sight lines, too. The sun hits the north-side stands, which can warm your toes in December but make you squint in September.

SCALPING

Stadium management prohibits the resale of tickets, even at face value, on its property. This is not to say no tickets change hands, only that discretion is required. The trade isn't brisk for Jets games, but on Giants game days, scalpers roam, offering tickets for double, sometimes triple, the face value. The state Sports Authority is perennially threatening a crackdown.

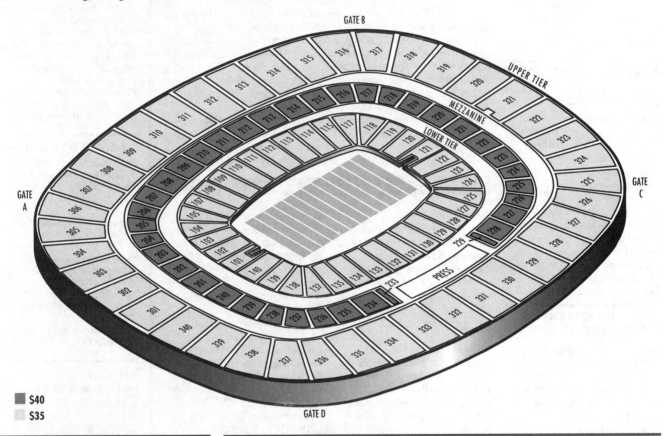

■ $40
■ $35

HOME-FIELD ADVANTAGE

The Giants have grown used to the gusting winds that blow across the Meadowlands later in the year, usually into the east-end tunnel. Spirals become wobblers and 60-yard punts travel 90 yards. The Giants' December home record since 1984 is 19–8.

GETTING TO GIANTS STADIUM

Public transportation: New Jersey Transit offers load-and-go bus service for all games from the Port Authority Bus Terminal in Manhattan. Call (201) 762-5100 for more information.
By car: From LaGuardia Airport, take Grand Central Parkway west to Triboro Bridge and follow directions to George Washington Bridge. Take I-95 to the New Jersey Turnpike. Take the western spur to the Sports Complex exit.

From JFK Airport, take Van Wyck Expressway to the Long Island Expressway (495 west) to the Midtown Tunnel. Cross 34th Street and follow signs to the Lincoln Tunnel. Go approximately 4 miles to Route 3 west to the Sports Complex.
From Newark Airport, take the New Jersey Turnpike north to exit 16W and follow signs to the Sports Complex.

TICKET INFORMATION
Address: East Rutherford, NJ 07073
Phone: (201) 935-8222

Hours: Mon.–Fri. 9–4:45.
Prices: $40: mezzanine; $35: lower and upper levels.

Training camp: The University at Albany, Albany, NY

NEW YORK JETS

Giants Stadium

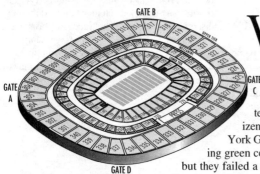

GATE B

GATE A

GATE C

GATE D

■ NA ▨ $25

HOME-FIELD ADVANTAGE

Wind is a big factor. It tends to swirl and often seems to blow in four directions at once, wreaking havoc on field-goal attempts and long passes. Often the ribbons hanging from the goal posts at each end of the field give different indications on the wind direction. Rumor has it that the home team can manipulate the wind by having a gate inside the tunnel behind the end zone raised or lowered, but this urban legend rates somewhere next to the one about Jimmy Hoffa being buried beneath the stadium's end zone.

IN THE HOT SEATS AT GIANTS STADIUM

The Jets sell more than 77,000 tickets for their games; the exact number varies slightly, depending on how many seats in the suites are sold. Of that total, some 74,000 are season tickets, and the Jets boast an annual renewal average of 96%-97%. The few that don't renew are generally in the end zone or the upper deck. A handful of single seats, usually no more than 300–400, go on sale in August at the stadium and at the Jets' training complex in Hempstead, New York. The remainder are allotted for club officials, Jets players, and visiting players. The week of a game against an unattractive opponent or a team based far from New York, tickets returned by the visiting club (which is allotted 500) go on sale on Wednesday at the stadium.

When the New York Jets departed the Big Apple for the Garden State in 1984, they left behind a dilapidated stadium and second-class citizenship foisted upon them by the New York Mets. What did they get when they crossed the rivers from Queens to Manhattan to alight in East Rutherford, New Jersey? More seats, better parking, a better financial deal, and second-class citizenship courtesy of the Stadium's prime tenants, the New York Giants. The Jets try to make the place homey by hanging green coverings and bunting over the (Giants') blue walls, but they failed a few years ago in an attempt to get the New Jersey Sports and Exposition Authority to rename the big cement dish.

Jets fans never will be mistaken for urban sophisticates attending the opera. They know the game, and make their displeasure known when all is not well. With the Jets, not having had a winning season since 1988, all has not been well in some time. And we're not just talking about boos and chants. At a Monday night game in 1988, with the home team badly trailing Buffalo, some fans set fire to their seats.

By contrast, Giants fans seem positively genteel. Tickets have been in their families longer, and they're more respectful of neighboring patrons. Jets fans tend to be younger and, well, more boisterous. Win or lose, you can expect a hot time at the ballpark when the Jets play.

HOT TIPS FOR VISITING FANS

PARKING
The cost is $6. And don't worry if you're a little late. The parking personnel are accustomed to sticking latecomers on roadways, grassy dividers, and other areas seemingly off-limits, bringing the actual capacity to about 32,000. (For traffic, see page 132.)

WEATHER
Bring sunblock in September and wear your woolies in December. This is generally a temperate place, but the wintry winds can make a late-afternoon game a thoroughly chilling experience.

MEDIA
Radio: All-sports WFAN (660 AM).
TV: Regular-season games generally are shown on WNBC (Channel 4); WYNY (Channel 5) is the local Fox station. WPIX (Channel 11) shows a limited number of games.

CUISINE
In 1996, Giants Stadium expanded the number and variety of the concessions stands. Along with the already better-than-average nachos, hot dogs, and pretzels, you can now nosh on fajitas, cheese steak sandwiches, bratwurst, individual-size pizzas, and Italian ices. The 158 food and beverage stands are spread throughout the stadium, and some 40 custom built food carts rove the arena. Beers range from premium imports to well-known domestics.

Many fans adjourn afterward to Manny's (201-939-1244), a sports bar and restaurant in nearby Moonachie, to rehash the game. Another popular restaurant not far from the stadium is The Park and Orchard (201-939-9292) in East Rutherford. The Tri-Boro Diner (201-343-7651) in Saddle Brook boasts a huge menu of everything from chef's salad to steaks and chops, and the portions are hefty. Adventurous sorts heading into New York City might like to try Runyon's (212-223-9592) for its sports-savvy patrons or Gallagher's Steak House (212-245-5336).

LODGING NEAR THE STADIUM

Sheraton Meadowlands
2 Meadowlands Plaza
East Rutherford, NJ 07073
(201) 896-0500/(800) 325-0500
Across the highway from the stadium.

STADIUM STATS
Location: East Rutherford, NJ 07073
Opened: Oct. 10, 1976
Surface: AstroTurf
Capacity: 78,148
Services for fans with disabilities: Seating available in sections 117–125.

STADIUM FIRSTS
Regular-season game: Sept. 6, 1984, 23–17 loss to the Pittsburgh Steelers.
Points scored: 6-yard touchdown reception by Louis Lipps of the Steelers.
Overtime game: Nov. 24, 1985, 16–13 over the New England Patriots.
Playoff game: Dec. 28, 1985, 26–14 loss to the New England Patriots.

TEAM NOTEBOOK
Franchise history: New York Titans, 1960–62; New York Jets, 1963–69 (AFL); New York Jets, 1970–present (NFL).
Division titles: 1968, 1969.
Super Bowl appearance: III, Jan. 12, 1969, 16–7 over the Baltimore Colts.
Pro Football Hall of Fame: Weeb Ewbank, 1978; Joe Namath, 1985; Don Maynard, 1987; John Riggins, 1992.
Retired numbers: 12, Joe Namath; 13, Don Maynard.

TICKET INFORMATION
Address: Weeb Ewbank Hall, Hofstra University, 1000 Fulton Ave., Hempstead, NY 11550
Phone: (516) 560-8200
Hours: Mon.–Fri. 9–5.
Training camp: Hofstra University, 1000 Fulton Ave., Hempstead, NY

Meadowlands Hilton
2 Harmon Plaza
Secaucus, N.J. 07094
(201) 348-6900/(800) 445-8667
1 mile from the stadium.

GETTING TO GIANTS STADIUM

(See page 133.)

OAKLAND RAIDERS

Oakland Coliseum

STADIUM STATS
Location: 7000 Coliseum Way, Oakland, CA 94621
Opened: 1966
Surface: Bluegrass
Capacity: 62,800
Services for fans with disabilities: Seating available.

STADIUM FIRSTS
Regular-season game: Sept. 18, 1966, 32–10 loss to the Kansas City Chiefs.
Playoff game: Dec. 31, 1967, 40–7 over Houston for the AFL Championship.

TEAM NOTEBOOK
Franchise history: Oakland Raiders, 1960–69 (AFL); Oakland Raiders, 1970–81 (NFL); Los Angeles Raiders, 1982–96; Oakland Raiders, 1996–present.
Division titles: 1967–70, 1972–76, 1978, 1982, 1983, 1985, 1990.
Super Bowl appearances: II, Jan. 14, 1968, 33–14 loss to the Green Bay Packers; XI, Jan. 9, 1977, 32–14 over the Minnesota Vikings; XV, Jan. 25, 1981, 27–10 over the Philadelphia Eagles; XVIII, Jan. 22, 1984, 38–9 over the Washington Redskins.
Pro Football Hall of Fame: Jim Otto, 1980; George Blanda, 1981; Willie Brown, 1984; Gene Upshaw, 1987; Fred Biletnikoff, 1988; Art Shell, 1989; Ted Hendricks, 1990; Al Davis, 1992.

It's déjà vu all over again. The Bay Area's prodigal sons of the gridiron are back. After a 14-year-long sojourn in sunny Southern California, the Raiders have come home to Oakland, where—most people agree—they truly belong. The Oakland–Alameda County Coliseum is welcoming the team home with a $100 million makeover of the stadium that was originally built for the Raiders, renovated a few years later to accommodate the Oakland A's, then turned into a baseball-only stadium when the Raiders decamped for Los Angeles, and now is back to being a two-sport venue.

To be ready for the Raiders' first home game of the 1996 season, construction of the new football seating sections went on during A's home games. But the local boys of summer also get some benefits from the new configuration for their trouble. Above the field-level football-only seating, two more sections will be permanent and at the ready for any baseball post-season play.

Modifications and new additions for the Raiders' return include an entirely new east wing, an array of luxury suites at different levels, new lights, two new video/matrix screen and scoreboard setups, a snazzy new plaza entrance on the stadium's west side, access ramps, an expanded ticket booth just north of the west entrance, new kitchen facilities, and direct BART station access. In addition, the Coliseum's old orange seating is being replaced with more comfortable—and green—seats. Seats on the club level along the first-base line (southwest end of the stadium) will have a padded bottom.

The Raiders' return has rekindled the long-simmering rivalry between Oakland and San Francisco; even though they won't play each other in the regular season, each team's record and style of play will stand in for its respective city's ego in a battle of civic pride and class consciousness. Raiders' fans are ready to rumble; they just hope that their team is, too.

late-season and playoff games, the highs are in the mid-50s and the lows in the low 40s. The heaviest periods of rainfall are in December and January.

MEDIA
Radio: KYCY (93.3 FM).
TV: KRON (Channel 4) is the local NBC affiliate and carries most home games; KTVU (Channel 2) is the Bay Area Fox station.

CUISINE
The Coliseum offers a wide variety of food, from traditional stadium fare such as hot dogs, all sorts of barbecued meats, and soft-serve ice cream to Chinese food. Roundtable pizza and Subway sandwiches are crowd favorites, as are the more health-conscious foods such as veggie burgers and salads (this is California, after all). The popular microbrewery stand offers boutique beers from Seattle and California. Brand names such as Miller and Budweiser also are sold.

Pre-kickoff tailgating is very popular, but most people go home after the games. Near the stadium, the Hyatt hotel is a popular haunt for visiting and hometown baseball players, as is the Hilton Sports Bar across the street. Francesco's (510-569-0653) is also nearby. Downtown, try the Pacific Coast Brewing Co. (510-836-2739) and the Old Spaghetti Factory (510-893-0222) in Jack London Square. Just across the bay, of course, the city of San Francisco is a gourmand's delight.

LODGING NEAR THE STADIUM

Oakland Airport Hilton
1 Hegenberger Rd.
Oakland, CA 94621
(510) 635-5000/(800) 445-8667
7 blocks from the stadium.

Waterfront Plaza
10 Washington St.
Oakland, CA 94607
(510) 836-3800/(800) 729-3638
About 5 miles from the stadium.

HOT TIPS FOR VISITING FANS

PARKING
The stadium has 11,500 spaces at $7 each. If the game is sold out, free overflow parking is across the freeway, a 10-minute walk away. Despite the convenience of a BART station with a footbridge that leads right to the east side of the Coliseum, most fans drive in, and the lots can fill up fast. Try to arrive at least half an hour to an hour before the game.

WEATHER
Big mood swings by Mother Nature are the norm in the Bay Area, so unexpected temperature drops should be expected. Oakland is always a few degrees warmer than San Francisco. During early-season games, the average highs generally hit the lower 70s and the lows dip to the lower 50s—with a sometimes stiff ocean and bay breeze. By the

In the Hot Seats at Oakland Coliseum

The much-touted private license seating sales weren't doing as well as expected as the Raiders' first season back in Oakland approached. When the team pulled an end run and began offering season tickets in the previously privileged sections without the obligation of a pricey long-term commitment, many fans who'd already shelled out major bucks for the PLSs felt like they'd been had, and some very unkind words were spoken about a certain football team's owner. This may result in more and better seats being available on a single-game basis, but with the actual number of single-game tickets yet to be decided, plan ahead.

GOOD SEATS

The first row of the plaza-level, removable, football-only section on the east side of the stadium is only 55 feet from the field.

BAD SEATS

There are no obstructed views or peculiarities that make any seats very bad, even with the new sections on the east side (the outfield to you A's fans), nor is the stadium so large that distance is a serious factor. The very top rows of the third, upper level on the east side, however, are up fairly high; they say it isn't that far, but bring binoculars anyway. You may well get distracted by spec-tacular sunsets over the bay during evening games.

SCALPING

Scalpers aren't allowed on stadium property. They should be fairly easy to find nearby, however. Expect to pay a hefty premium for any seat anywhere in the stadium—season tickets are $41 to $61 at face value, and single-game tickets may be only a wistful dream.

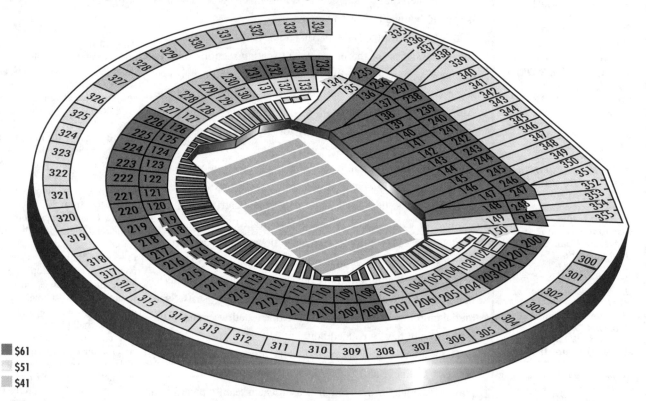

- ■ $61
- ▨ $51
- ▧ $41

HOME-FIELD ADVANTAGE

The home crowd. Period. This town is happy to see its team back, and not even the brouhaha over season ticket and private license seating could dampen the growing excitement of the Raiders' return to Oakland. When they take to the field at home it will be to a full house—a very noisy and excited full house. Buoyed by fan support, the Raiders could give the 49ers a run for their money as the Bay Area's football dynasty; Oakland football fans would like nothing better.

GETTING TO OAKLAND COLISEUM

Public transportation: Bay Area Rapid Transit (BART) trains go from San Francisco and other adjacent areas to the Coliseum BART station. For more information, call (510) 465-2278 or (510) 464-6000.

By car: The Coliseum is adjacent to I-880 on Coliseum Way, about 6 miles south of downtown Oakland. Take the 66th Avenue or Hegenberger Road exit off I-880.
From San Francisco, drive east over the Bay Bridge to I-580 toward Hayward. Take I-980 to Oakland and get on I-880 south. Get off at 66th Avenue and follow signs to the Coliseum. From Marin County, take I-580 over the San Rafael Bridge to I-80. Take I-80 to I-580 toward Hayward and follow the previous directions.
From Sacramento, take I-80 west toward Oakland. Get on I-580 toward Hayward and follow the previous directions.
From Contra Costa County, take Highway 24 through Caldecott Tunnel into downtown Oakland and get onto I-980. Follow the previous directions.

TICKET INFORMATION
Address: 7000 Coliseum Way, Oakland, CA 94621

Phone: (510) 864-5000/(800) 949-2626
Hours: Mon.–Sat. 9–6; on game days, the office is open until half an hour after the game.
Prices: (season tickets, per game) $61; $51; $41.

PHILADELPHIA EAGLES

Veterans Stadium

STADIUM STATS

Location: 3501 S. Broad St., Philadelphia, PA 19148
Opened: April 10, 1971
Surface: AstroTurf
Capacity: 65,352
Services for fans with disabilities: Call the ticket office (215-463-5500) for information.

STADIUM FIRSTS

Regular-season game: Sept. 26, 1971, 42–7 loss to the Dallas Cowboys.
Points scored: 1-yard touchdown run by Calvin Hill of the Cowboys.
Overtime game: Sept. 27, 1976, 20–17 over the Washington Redskins.
Playoff game: Dec. 23, 1979, 27–17 over the Chicago Bears.

TEAM NOTEBOOK

Franchise history: Philadelphia Eagles, 1933–present.
Division titles: 1947 (tie), 1948, 1949, 1960, 1980, 1988.
Super Bowl appearance: XV, Jan. 25, 1981, 27–10 loss to the Oakland Raiders.
Pro Football Hall of Fame: B. Bell, 1963; S. Van Buren, 1965; C. Bednarik, 1967; A. Wojciechowicz, 1968; E. Neale, 1969; P. Pihos, 1970; B. Hewitt, 1971; N. Van Brocklin, 1971; O. Matson, 1972; J. Ringo, 1981; S. Jurgensen, 1983; M. Ditka, 1988.
Retired numbers: 15, S. Van Buren; 40, T. Brookshier; 44, P. Retzlaff; 60, C. Bednarik; 70, A. Wistert; 99, J. Brown.

To Philadelphia's spirited football fans—who have an opinion on everything—Veterans Stadium always has been a huge open-air soapbox. Natives call it, simply, the Vet. Located in south Philadelphia, Veterans Stadium looks a lot like Cincinnati's Riverfront Stadium and Pittsburgh's Three Rivers. There's a hardness, though, about the stadium and an intimidating presence to the fans who pack the Vet on weekends to watch the Eagles—or "Iggles" in Phillytalk—that make a visit unique.

Despite the addition of plush penthouse suites, luxury boxes, fancy elevators, and the new blue seats that have replaced the uncomfortable earth-toned '70s-style molded plastic nightmares, the Vet is showing its age. Not even Big Bird, the unofficial mascot that roams the stands, the Eagle cheerleaders, or the new sound system can distract a visitor from that fact. The AstroTurf surface, often criticized for being dirty and brick-hard, has been replaced several times, most recently after the 1994 season. Talk of a new stadium is mostly wishful thinking, and besides, the co-tenant baseball Phillies have first dibs.

Even so, Eagles' fans remain a rowdy and loyal lot, even when they lose. Ask any Redskins' fan who has dared wear a headdress during his visit.

HOT TIPS FOR VISITING FANS

PARKING

Lots start filling with tailgaters about four hours before kickoff. The stadium complex has 14,000 spaces, and with another 6,500 in nearby lots. Cost is $5–$10. Wide boulevards and two major expressways help empty lots within an hour. Security at private lots can be a problem. Some fans park along Pattison Avenue and nearby side streets but must arrive several hours early.

WEATHER

Local weather runs the gamut from hot and muggy in September to gorgeously fresh in October and early November, to damp, wind-blown, and sometimes bitterly cold in December. When Leonard Tose owned the Eagles, his helicopter pilot refused to land inside the Vet because of the swirling winds. Fans wear shorts and T-shirts early in the season. But remember, the Vet is near a river on flat land, and temperatures, as well as rain, sleet, and snow, can fall unexpectedly in late fall. Wear hoods but don't bring an umbrella—fans behind will let you have it.

MEDIA

Radio: Many fans bring transistor radios to hear longtime WYSP (94.1 FM) announcer Merrill Reese's booming voice describe a touchdown. Sidekick Stan Walters, a former Eagle, is among the NFL's more underrated analysts.
TV: Eagles games are telecast on the Fox affiliate, WTXF (Channel 29).

CUISINE

The stadium's two food courts are behind the 50-yard line (south side) on the 200 and 500 levels. Both sell cheese steaks, the city's most popular nosh. Pizza Hut and a range of hoagies and grilled sandwiches are also offered. For the ultimate cheese steak, try Pat's King of Steaks (215-339-9872) on your way to the game. Stands offering a wider selection of domestic and imported beers were added in 1995.

South Street is nice for pre-game dining or post-game revelry. Café Nola (215-627-2590) serves excellent Cajun fare that visiting players love. The Legends sports bar at the Stadium Holiday Inn (215-755-9500), part owned by ex-Eagles quarterback Ron Jaworski, features a Bergey Brunch (named for former Eagles linebacker Bill Bergey), but the real action starts after the game, with patrons stacked five deep at the bar.

LODGING NEAR THE STADIUM

The Ritz Carlton
17th and Chestnut St. at Liberty Place
Philadelphia, PA 19106
(215) 563-1600/(800) 241-3333
7 miles from the stadium.

Sheraton Society Hill
1 Dock St.
Philadelphia, PA 19103
(215) 238-6000/(800) 325-3535.
7 miles from the stadium.

THE EAGLES AT VETERANS STADIUM

Sept. 23, 1974: Joe Lavender returns a Dallas Cowboy fumble 96 yards for a touchdown. The Eagles win 13–10.

Jan. 11, 1981: Wilbert Montgomery's 194 yards rushing help the Eagles to a 20–7 victory over the Cowboys and a trip to Super Bowl XV.

Nov. 10, 1985: Ron Jaworski throws a 99-yard touchdown to Mike Quick, tying the NFL record for longest touchdown pass. The Eagles beat the Atlanta Falcons 23–17 in overtime.

Dec. 24, 1989: The Eagles end the season with a 31–14 win over the Phoenix Cardinals. Reggie White leads the defense to a team-record 62 sacks for the season.

In the Hot Seats at Veterans Stadium

Win or lose, the Eagles sell more than 56,000 season tickets. Sunday home games are an autumn ritual. Starting in mid-May, 8,000 tickets per game go on sale. Those for Dallas, Washington, New York, and other traditional rivals are snapped up in a hurry. Each visiting team is allocated tickets (usually several thousand), that, if unsold, are returned late in the week. You might get lucky by calling on Friday before the game.

BAD SEATS

The worst seats are in the 100 level (sections 100–112, 125, and 152–166) behind the home and visiting benches. Other areas afford decent sight lines, although 700-level seats are far from the field. Some seats in the 300 level are obstructed. The Eagles will lose 1,200 seats (and gain back only 250) when a new disabled-accessible area is constructed in the 300 bleacher area (Gate F).

SCALPING

Scalpers roam the approach streets and near will-call windows on the concourse between Gates A and H. Typical cost: $75–$85 for the Cowboys, double face value for Giants games, and $55–$60 for non-rivals such as New Orleans and Baltimore. Bargaining is common; arrests are rare.

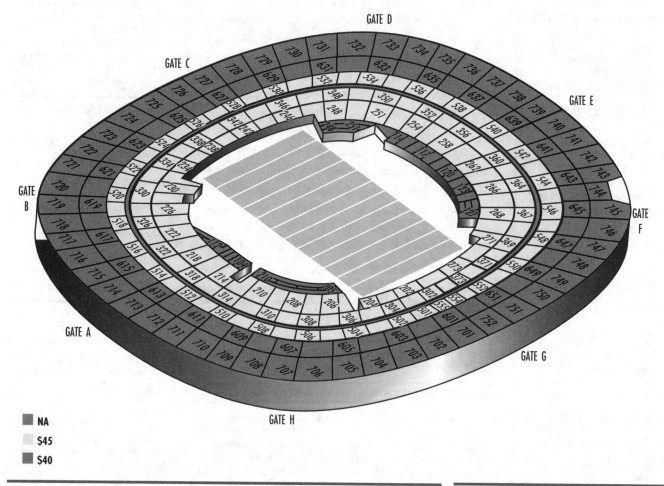

- NA
- $45
- $40

HOME-FIELD ADVANTAGE

Winds often whip off the nearby Delaware River, creating nightmares for visiting kickers; the turf doesn't help visitors much either. Former Eagles fullback Ronnie Bull once said he could run blindfolded and tell directions by the feel of the synthetic grass. Whatever direction, the Vet's turf is hard and sometimes causes visiting runners to take a pratfall. Full-throated home fans can also intimidate visiting teams, but fickle Eagles' rooters can flip-flop. For example, during a 42–3 Monday night loss to the Los Angeles Rams, Eagles fans tossed dog bones onto the field.

GETTING TO VETERANS STADIUM

Public transportation: The Broad Street/Orange Line of the subway stops at the Pattison Avenue exit, across the street from the stadium.
By car: From Philadelphia International Airport, take I-95 north to the Broad Street exit. Proceed 1 mile past JFK Stadium and the Spectrum. Turn right on Pattison Avenue; Veterans Stadium is on the left.

TICKET INFORMATION
Address: 3501 S. Broad St., Philadelphia, PA 19148.

Phone: (215) 463-5500 or TicketMaster at (215) 336-2000.
Hours: Mon.–Fri. 9–5.

Prices: $45, $40.
Training camp: Lehigh University, Bethlehem, PA

STADIUM STATS

Location: 300 Stadium Circle, Pittsburgh, PA 15212
Opened: July 16, 1970
Surface: AstroTurf
Capacity: 59,600
Services for fans with disabilities: Seating available on the third level by Gate A and in sections 312–313.

STADIUM FIRSTS

Regular-season game: Sept. 20, 1970, 19–7 loss to the Houston Oilers.
Points scored: 22-yard touchdown reception by Jerry LeVias of the Oilers.
Overtime game: Sept. 24, 1978, 15–9 over the Cleveland Browns.
Playoff game: Dec. 23, 1972, 13–7 over the Oakland Raiders.

TEAM NOTEBOOK

Franchise history: Pittsburgh Pirates, 1933–39; Pittsburgh Steelers, 1940–present.
Division titles: 1972, 1974, 1975, 1976, 1977, 1978, 1979, 1983, 1984, 1992, 1994, 1995.
Super Bowl appearances: IX, Jan. 12, 1975, 16–6 over the Minnesota Vikings; X, Jan. 18, 1976, 21–17 over the Dallas Cowboys; XIII, Jan. 21, 1979, 35–31 over the Dallas Cowboys; XIV, Jan. 20, 1980, 31–19 over the Los Angeles Rams; XXX, Jan. 28, 1996, 27–17 loss to the Dallas Cowboys.
Pro Football Hall of Fame: Bert Bell, Johnny (Blood) McNally, 1963; Arthur J. Rooney, 1964; Bill Dudley, 1966; Walt Kiesling, 1966; Bobby Layne, 1967; Marion Motley, 1968; Ernie Stautner, 1969; Len Dawson, 1987; Joe Greene, 1987; John Henry Johnson, 1987; Jack Ham, 1988; Mel Blount 1989; Terry Bradshaw, 1989; Franco Harris 1990; Jack Lambert, 1990; Chuck Noll, 1993.

Cozy is not a word most folks would use to describe Three Rivers Stadium, which has the uninspiring concrete-and-steel ambience of those circa-'70 stadiums. But this is Pittsburgh, a town concrete and steel helped build, and somehow the hard-nosed Steeler fans and their no-nonsense team match up well with this arena.

Set at the confluence of the Allegheny, Ohio, and Monongahela rivers, Three Rivers Stadium holds fond memories for Steeler fans. The Steelers had been perennially mediocre since their founding as the Pirates in 1933, but the move to Three Rivers in 1970 seemed to signal a turnaround. In 1972, anchored by the feared Steel Curtain, the team captured its first division title, and before the decade was over the names Terry Bradshaw, Joe Greene, Jack Ham, Franco Harris, and Jack Lambert became synonymous with greatness.

The atmosphere remains highly charged, much as it was during the Steelers' heyday. Banners saluting individual players and the team are draped over the walls, and some fans still wear the team's black-and-gold jerseys with numbers commemorating star players from the glory years, such as No. 32 for Franco Harris and No. 56 for Jack Lambert. When the team's fortunes fell, there were empty seats, especially in bad weather, but the AFC title in 1995 has brought back the fans. Generally speaking, though, the crowd is pure Pittsburgh, a shot-and-beer kind of town that's not for the faint of heart.

HOT TIPS FOR VISITING FANS

PARKING
There are only about 4,000 spaces, which go for $4. Several additional lots are on the North Side in neighborhoods near the stadium. Those who don't want the hassles of last-minute parking should arrive at least three hours prior to kickoff.
Pre- and post-game tailgating is not only permitted but also encouraged. The team suggests arriving by 9 a.m., when the gates open for 1 p.m. games.

WEATHER
Beautiful fall football weather abounds in September and October, when temperatures are in the 60s and 70s. It drops to the 40s and 50s in November and plunges to who-knows-what by December and January.

MEDIA
Radio: Tune in Bill Hargrove and analyst Myron Cope on the Steelers' flagship station, WTAE (1250 AM). Cope's high-pitched, nasal "Pittsburghese" is filled with "Cope-isms," local flavor that will give visitors a taste of what it's like rooting for the hometown team. Cope is the man who popularized the Terrible Towel of the '70s.
TV: If the games are sold out, which they usually are, WPXI (NBC) and WTAE (ABC) are the network television affiliates. WPGH (channel 53) is the local Fox affiliate.

CUISINE
Try the hamburgers and sausages, which are cooked on a charcoal grill. Primanti Brothers, a well-known local restaurant chain, offers made-to-order sandwiches, and Benkovitz Fish has fresh fish sandwiches. Iron City is the town's best-known beer, and it's ideal for washing down a kielbasa sandwich. At night games liquor sales are halted generally by the end of the third quarter.
Across the river, The Grand Concourse at Station Square (412-261-1717) tops the chow-down list. Also try Ruth's Chris for steaks (412-391-4800), The Carlton (412-391-4099) for American fare, or Tambellini's (412-481-1118) for Italian. Froggy's (412-471-3764) offers a pre-game brunch followed by bus service to the stadium. Among the top sports bars is the Clark Bar & Grill (412-231-5720), located near the stadium.

LODGING NEAR THE STADIUM

Westin William Penn
530 William Penn Pl.
Pittsburgh, PA 15219
(412) 281-7100/(800) 228-3000
9 blocks from the stadium.

Doubletree Hotel at Liberty Center
100 Penn Ave.
Pittsburgh, PA 15222
(412) 281-3700/(800) 222-8733
1 mile from the stadium.

THE STEELERS AT THREE RIVERS STADIUM

Dec. 23, 1972: In the first playoff game at Three Rivers Stadium, Franco Harris makes his "Immaculate Reception" in the final minute and the Steelers beat the Raiders 13–7.

Dec. 22, 1974: The Steelers defeat the Bills 32–14 in the AFC playoffs, on their way to their first Super Bowl win.

Dec. 15, 1985: Down 21–0 to Buffalo in the second quarter, the Steelers win 30–24; their biggest comeback ever.

Jan. 14, 1996: The Steelers beat the Colts 20–16, clinching their fifth Super Bowl appearance.

In the Hot Seats at Three Rivers Stadium

The Steelers have been sold out on a season-ticket basis since 1972. The team withholds a few thousand tickets for every game, which go on sale to the public for $30 in May of each year. Get 'em quick: Typically they sell out within a few weeks. Mail orders are accepted, starting in mid-May. On the rare occasion that an opposing team returns a block of its allotted tickets during the season, they are available at the box office on game day.

BAD SEATS

If you're not sitting between the 30-yard lines, you're a long post pattern from the field, particularly if you're in either end zone. If you have a choice, try to stay away from lower field box seats behind the teams' benches, as they tend to have obstructed views. Seats in the second level and above allow wider viewing.

SCALPING

Scalpers are kept off stadium property, but there are plenty of sellers standing on street corners, mostly in surrounding neighborhoods on the North Side. Prices drop on bad-weather weekends, when tickets are often available for face value.

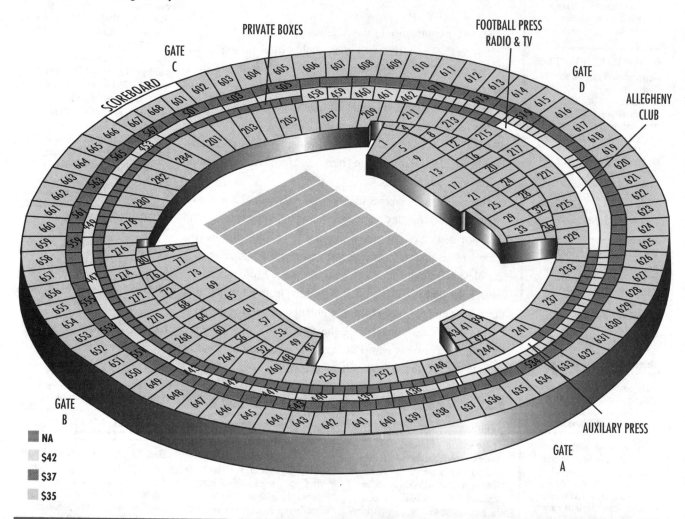

HOME-FIELD ADVANTAGE

Emerging victorious at Three Rivers Stadium is not an easy proposition for visiting teams, particularly as nasty weather rolls in during the winter months. The Steelers have never posted a losing season at Three Rivers. From 1970 to 1995 the team forged a 163–57 mark (74%) at home.

GETTING TO THREE RIVERS STADIUM

Public transportation: Starting 90 minutes before game time, the 96C shuttle buses run along Wood Street in downtown Pittsburgh to the stadium every 10 to 15 minutes. Call (412) 442-2000 for more information.
By car: From the east, take the Pennsylvania Turnpike to I-376 west to downtown and the stadium exit.

From the west, take the Ohio Turnpike to the Pennsylvania Turnpike, then south on I-79 to I-279 south to the stadium exit.
From the north, take I-79 south to I-279 south to the stadium exit.
From the south, take 79 north to I-279 north to the stadium exit.

TICKET INFORMATION
Address: 300 Stadium Circle, Pittsburgh, PA 15212
Phone: (412) 323-1200, ext. 205

Hours: Mon.–Fri. 9–5, plus Sat. 9–12 before home games, and 9–halftime on game days.
Order by mail: c/o Pittsburgh Steelers, P.O. Box 6763, Pittsburgh, PA 15212

Prices: $42, $37, $35.
Training camp: St. Vincent College, Latrebe, PA

ST. LOUIS RAMS

Trans World Dome

STADIUM STATS

Location: 701 Convention Plaza, St. Louis, MO 63101
Opened: 1995
Surface: AstroTurf
Capacity: 66,053
Services for fans with disabilities: Seating for those with mobility impairment is available on the concourse and terrace levels along the sidelines.

STADIUM FIRSTS

Regular-season game: November 12, 1995, 28–17 over Carolina.
Points scored: Jerome Bettis of the Rams.

TEAM NOTEBOOK

Franchise history: Cleveland Rams, 1937–45; Los Angeles Rams, 1946–94; St. Louis Rams, 1995–present.
Division titles: 1945, 1949, 1950, 1951, 1955, 1967, 1969, 1973, 1974, 1975, 1976, 1977, 1978, 1979, 1985.
Super Bowl appearance: XIV, Jan. 20, 1980, 31–19 loss to the Pittsburgh Steelers.
Pro Football Hall of Fame: B. Waterfield, 1965; D. Reeves, 1967; E. Hirsch, 1968; T. Fears, 1970; A. Robustelli, 1971; N. Van Brocklin, 1971; O. Matson, 1972; B. George, 1974; D. Lane, 1974; D. Jones, 1980; M. Olsen, 1982; S. Gillman, 1983; J. Namath, 1985; T. Schramm, 1991.
Retired numbers: 7, B. Waterfield; 74, M. Olsen.

Nobody seems particularly sorry that the Rams left Southern California, least of all the Rams themselves. After being eclipsed in popularity and play by the arriviste Raiders, the Rams languished in Anaheim Stadium, declining into season after season of dismal play and suffering the slings and arrows of the crowd's hostility. Most people in the stands came to root for the the visiting team—any visiting team.

In 1995 the Rams relocated to St. Louis, and it was a match made in football heaven—a true sports town hungry for football and a once-great team looking for new home. Until the Trans World Dome was ready, the Rams played at nearby Busch Stadium, going 3–1, egged on, no doubt, by the cheering crowds and the appearance for the first time in a long while of the team colors throughout the stands. They sold out every 1995 home game, and tickets were hard to get in 1996.

Part of a massive convention center complex in downtown St. Louis, the Trans World Dome was designed to host a variety of events, and its football capabilities were intended to attract an NFL team. The sports complex architects at HOK had a hand in the dome's design, and it shows. Views of the field are good from almost everywhere in the stands, and getting around the place is a snap. Concessions offer a local flavor, with various ethnic favorites reflecting the city's diverse population.

Although it is named for Trans World Airlines, which was founded in St. Louis in the 1920s and still uses the city as its main hub, it's not the TWA Dome. Most people just call it "the dome," explaining that "it's the only dome in town." This city knows how to treat a home team, and the Rams seem eager to return the favor.

HOT TIPS FOR VISITING FANS

PARKING
The dome offers parking only for season ticketholders. There are, however, lots with spaces for 25,000 cars within a 10-block radius; prices range from $5–$7.

WEATHER
The dome is comfortable in any weather. Since it was built to accommodate a wide variety of events, climate control is adjustable to virtually any condition or crowd size. Remember, though, that St. Louis winters can be brutal, so bundle up for your trip to and from the game.

MEDIA
Radio: KSD (550 AM and 93.7 FM).
TV: KTVI (channel 2). Gary Bender and former Ram Jack Snow call the games on radio.

CUISINE
Because the dome is a multipurpose exhibition hall and part of a massive convention center accustomed to feeding huge numbers of people hungry after dozing through trade shows, the food here is better than average, and in some cases flat-out terrific. Along with traditional stadium fare—hot dogs, popcorn, nachos—the dome offers such local specialties as toasted ravioli, meatball heros, gyros, and barbecued just about anything. At the southeast entry bay, a stand run by the nearby J. F. Sanfilippo's restaurant offers delicioso Italian specialties. Since St. Louis is the headquarters of beer giant Anheuser-Busch, a full range of their products is available. There is also a microbrewery with more esoteric choices.

The triangle of downtown St. Louis anchored by the dome, Busch Stadium, and Kiel Center has no shortage of pre- or postgame watering holes. Just look for a big-screen TV and listen for the hoots and hollers of those inside. Mike Shannon's (314-421-1540) on North Seventh Street, which has steaks and seafood and lots of sports memorabilia, is a popular spot near Busch Stadium. Players of all sports have been seen at the Alligator Alley Bar & Broiler (314-231-4287) on South Seventh after games. Head for Chestnuts restaurant in the Adams Mark Hotel (314-241-7400) for a pregame brunch. One of the best steakhouses in the Midwest is Dierdorf & Hart's Restaurant (ex-football-Cardinals Dan Dierdorf and Jim Hart are part owners) in Union Station (314-421-1772). Laclede's Landing, a Mississippi River waterfront complex of shops and restaurants, has a microbrewery, a blues bar, and a variety of restaurants.

LODGING NEAR THE STADIUM

Adams Mark Hotel
Fourth and Chestnut
St. Louis, MO 63102
(314) 241-7400/(800) 444-2326
5 blocks from the dome.

The St. Louis Marriott Pavilion
1 S. Broadway
St. Louis, MO 63102
(314) 421-1776/(800) 228-9290
6 blocks from the dome.

In the Hot Seats at the Trans World Dome

In their first season in St. Louis, the Rams sold out all eight home games, and not just to fans who wanted to root for the visiting team. They played the first half of the 1995 season at Busch Stadium, then moved into their new home in the dome. Only 4,000 seats are held for game day sales. The team's popularity has made getting the better seats something of a challenge.

GOOD SEATS

Even though it is a multi-purpose structure, football was always intended to be one of those purposes, and the seating configuration shows that foresight. Seats directly behind the players' benches are better than at some stadiums because they are four-and-a-half feet above the field level, allowing folks who've shelled out big bucks to be near the action to see more than the backs of players' heads.

BAD SEATS

There are about 600 semi-obstructed seats scattered thoughout the stands, and buyers are told that's what they're getting.The $25 seats are hardly ideal, but the sight lines are still pretty good, and these may well be the only seats you can get.

SCALPING

A hot team and a limited number of game-day tickets is a recipe for scalping, but reselling tickets—even at face value—is illegal in Missouri, and the police in St. Louis occasionally crack down on scalpers. Ticket brokers just over the border in Illinois, however, may have decent seats for a not too-obscene markup over face value.

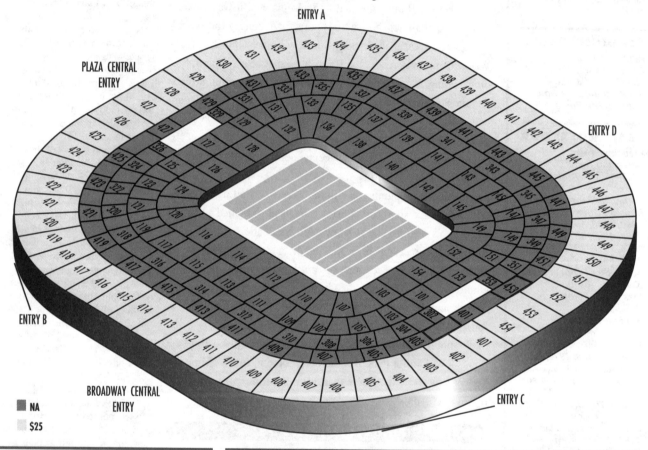

HOME-FIELD ADVANTAGE

Feeling welcome by the home crowd is a big boost to any team, especially one that's been so abused by its former host town. Besides being brand-spanking new and state-of-the-art, there isn't anything inherent in the dome's field or configuration that gives the Rams an edge. That they're considered worthy of this fine new arena, and deserving of the cheers of the home-team fans, however, is a vote of confidence that can be a powerful motivator.

GETTING TO THE TRANS WORLD DOME

Public transportation: The Convention Center stop on St. Louis' MetroLink light rail line is about 100 yards from from the dome's entrance. The fare is $1.
By car: From the east, take I–55/I–70 to the Poplar Street Bridge, exit onto Memorial Drive (one way, north), turn left on Wash-ington Ave. to the Washington entrance. From the west, take I–64 to Broadway (last Missouri exit), at the end of the ramp go right onto 7th Street/Stadium Plaza until you reach Washington Avenue, go left on Washington to the America Center entrance.

TICKET INFORMATION
Address: 701 Convention Plaza, St. Louis, MO 63101

Phone: (314) 425-8830
Hours: Mon-Fri, 9-5.
Prices: $25.

Training camp: Western Illinois University Macomb, IL.

San Diego Jack Murphy Stadium

STADIUM STATS

Location: *9449 Friars Rd., San Diego, CA 92108*
Opened: *Aug. 20, 1967*
Surface: *Grass*
Capacity: *60,794*
Services for fans with disabilities: *Seating available in plaza level sections 17, 25, 31, 43–46, and 57–59.*

STADIUM FIRSTS

Regular-season game: *Sept. 9, 1967, 28–14 over the Boston Patriots.*
Points scored: *7-yard touchdown by Paul Lowe of the Chargers.*
Overtime game: *Oct. 12, 1975, 13–10 loss to the Los Angeles Rams.*
Playoff game: *Dec. 29, 1979, 17–14 loss to the Houston Oilers.*

TEAM NOTEBOOK

Franchise history: *Los Angeles Chargers, 1960; San Diego Chargers, 1961–69 (AFL); San Diego Chargers, 1970–present (NFL).*
Division titles: *1960, 1961, 1963, 1964, 1965, 1979, 1980, 1981, 1992, 1994.*
Super Bowl appearances: *XXIX, January 29, 1995; lost 49–26 to the 49ers.*
Pro Football Hall of Fame: *Lance Alworth, 1978; Ron Mix, 1979; Johnny Unitas, 1979; David (Deacon) Jones, 1980; Sid Gillman, 1983; John Mackey, 1992; Dan Fouts, 1993; Larry Little, 1993; Kellen Winslow, 1995.*
Retired number: *14, Dan Fouts.*

After some proud years in the AFL and the NFL, the Chargers went through a lean decade in the 1980s and early '90s without making the playoffs, but the AFC West championships in 1992 and 1994, and their Super Bowl XXIX appearance, put the Chargers at the top of the San Diego—as well as national—sports scene. Despite their city's laid-back reputation, Chargers fans enjoy game day with the same fervor as fans in Cleveland or Washington, D.C. The stadium walls are covered with signs, fans wear their team's colors, and some—the Bolt Heads—wear huge foam lightning bolts on their heads. Even though large contingents from colder cities often follow their teams to enjoy the warm weather, they never outcheer the Chargers fans.

Like many arenas built in the late 1960s, "the Murph" is a multi-purpose stadium for baseball and football, slated for an expansion that will seat 10,000 more fans. It was renamed San Diego Jack Murphy Stadium in 1981 in honor of the late *San Diego Union* sports editor who was instrumental not only in bringing the Chargers to San Diego but also in construction of the stadium and acquiring the Padres expansion franchise. If not one of the more interesting football experiences the league has to offer, game day at Jack Murphy Stadium still is one of the most enjoyable.

HOT TIPS FOR VISITING FANS

PARKING

The lot that surrounds the stadium has room for 17,800 cars and 120 buses. Parking costs $5. For games that are sold out, the lot is usually filled and closed about an hour before kickoff. Satellite lots with shuttle service are available. Many fans arrive early and have tailgate parties. The lot has only four entrances, and traffic is slower as game time nears. After the game, getting out of the lot requires extreme patience.

WEATHER

San Diego has a mild climate, but fans bring sweaters and jackets to afternoon and night games to guard against chilly evenings.

MEDIA

Radio: All-sports station XTRA (690 AM) carries all games live. Lee Hamilton does play-by-play, while former Charger Jim Laslavic provides analysis.
TV: Most Chargers games are telecast on local NBC affiliate KNSD (Channel 39).

CUISINE

Concessions stands offer the standard fare of beer, hot dogs, popcorn, and nachos. In addition, the stadium offers franchise outlets for such local favorites as Rally's Hamburgers and Rubio's fish tacos—a San Diego culinary concoction of fish, cabbage, salsa, and lime that's tastier than it sounds. Other stands feature espresso, sausages, and hand-dipped Häagen-Dazs ice cream. The Sports Club is on the plaza level on the closed end zone side. It offers table seating, food, and a bar. A picnic area on the concourse near the scoreboard at the open end provides an area where groups can to hold tent parties before the game.
Trophy's Bar & Grill (619-296-9600) is on Friars Road near the ballpark, and Bully's East (619-291-2665) on Texas Street.

About 6 miles away downtown is the Gaslamp Quarter, a turn-of-the-century district known for its nightlife. Try Kansas City Barbecue (619-231-9680), downtown near the Marriott.

LODGING NEAR THE STADIUM

Sheraton Harbor Island East and West Towers
1380 Harbor Island Dr.
San Diego, CA 92101
(619) 291-2900/(800) 325-3535
7 miles from the stadium.

Marriott Mission Valley
8757 Rio San Diego Dr.
San Diego, CA 92108
(619) 692-3800/(800) 228-9290
1 mile from the stadium.

THE CHARGERS AT SAN DIEGO JACK MURPHY STADIUM

Sept. 30, 1973: *Johnny Unitas becomes the first quarterback to pass for more than 40,000 yards when he connects with Mike Garrett in a 20–13 loss to the Cincinnati Bengals.*

Dec. 17, 1979: *The Chargers take their first division title in 14 years when they beat the Denver Broncos 17–7.*

Sept. 14, 1980: *Dan Fouts throws a touchdown pass to John Jefferson in overtime to give the Chargers a 30–24 victory over the Raiders.*

Dec. 20, 1982: *The Chargers gain 661 total yards in a 50–34 win over the Cincinnati Bengals.*

Jan. 2, 1993: *Behind Marion Butts's 119 rushing yards, the Chargers beat the Kansas City Chiefs 17–0 in an AFC wild-card game.*

Jan. 8, 1995: *The undefeated Chargers recover from a third-quarter 21–6 deficit to defeat the Miami Dolphins 22–21, clinching an AFC championship spot as a record home crowd of 63,381 cheers them on.*

In the Hot Seats at San Diego Jack Murphy Stadium

The Chargers enjoy a season-ticket base of about 50,000 and frequently sell out home games, although some tickets may be available during the week leading up to several games. When the baseball season ends, bleacher seats are added to both end zones, in front of the stadium's permanent seats. These seats, just a few feet from the end zones, are sold on an individual-game basis.

Tickets on game day have always been hard to get, and now with the Chargers riding high, nearly impossible to find. The toughest tickets usually are for AFC West Division rivals Raiders, Kansas City Chiefs, and Denver Broncos, as well as for the 49ers. Single-

game tickets go on sale in mid-July. While most of the luxury boxes are leased year-round, a few may be available on a game-to-game basis.

BAD SEATS

The lowest seats on the field level on both sides are too low for fans to see over the players and coaches. That means the seats closest to the field between the 30-yard lines, including some right on the 50, have obstructed views. The team clearly marks all these tickets with obstructed-view warnings. East end-zone seats on the plaza level in the open end have a poor view of the main score-

board that towers above. Extended plaza seats in the open end zone provide no view of the main scoreboard at all. A second scoreboard in the west end zone is planned to be up for the 1998 season.

SCALPING

It's illegal to resell tickets on stadium grounds, but scalpers can be found on Friars Road and Mission Center Drive, which lead to the stadium. With the large season-ticket base and the Chargers' momentum, it's a seller's market.

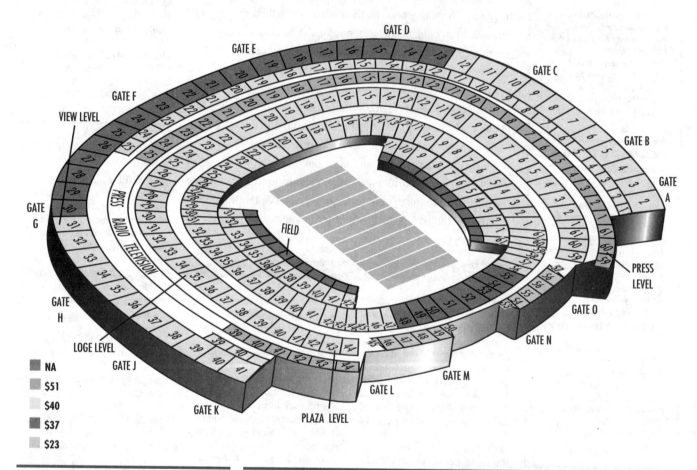

HOME-FIELD ADVANTAGE

Wind and weather are rarely factors, but before the baseball season ends, teams heading toward the closed end of the stadium encounter the dirt of the baseball infield. This can cause problems with footing for runners and kickers. When the baseball season ends, the dirt portion is sodded.

GETTING TO SAN DIEGO JACK MURPHY STADIUM

Public transportation: San Diego Transit offers a Chargers Express directly to the stadium, with departures from several locations. Call (619) 233-3004 for more information. North County Transit offers similar service from suburban Oceanside and Escondido.

Call (619) 967-2828 for more information. **By car:** From Lindbergh Field, Harbor Drive to Grape Street. Left on Grape through three traffic lights. Right onto I-5 south to I-163 north. Exit east on Friars Road 2 miles to the stadium.

TICKET INFORMATION
Address: P.O. Box 609100, San Diego, CA 92160

Phone: (619) 280-2121 or TicketMaster (619) 220-TIXS
Hours: Daily 8–5.

Prices: $51, $40, $37, $23.
Training camp: University of California at San Diego, La Jolla, CA

STADIUM STATS

Location: San Francisco, CA 94124
Opened: April 12, 1960
Surface: Grass
Capacity: 70,207
Services for fans with disabilities: Seating available throughout the stadium. Call (415) 468-2249 for information.

STADIUM FIRSTS

Regular-season game: Oct. 10, 1971, 20–13 loss to the Los Angeles Rams.
Points scored: 24-yard field goal by Bruce Gossett of the 49ers.
Overtime game: Sept. 14, 1980, 24–21 over the St. Louis Cardinals.
Playoff game: Dec. 26, 1971, 24–20 over the Washington Redskins.

TEAM NOTEBOOK

Franchise history: San Francisco 49ers, 1946–49 (AAFC); 1950–present (NFL).
Division titles: 1970, 1971, 1972, 1981, 1983, 1984, 1986, 1987, 1988, 1989, 1990, 1992, 1993, 1994, 1995.
Super Bowl appearances: XVI, Jan. 24, 1982, 26–21 over the Cincinnati Bengals; XIX, Jan. 20, 1985, 38–16 over the Miami Dolphins; XXIII, Jan. 22, 1989, 20–16 over the Cincinnati Bengals; XXIV, Jan. 28, 1990, 55–10 over the Denver Broncos; XXIX, Jan. 29, 1995, 49–26 over San Diego.
Pro Football Hall of Fame: Leo Nomellini, Joe Perry, 1969; Hugh McElhenny, 1970; Y. A. Tittle, 1971; O. J. Simpson, 1985; John Henry Johnson, 1987; Bob St. Clair, 1990; Bill Walsh, 1993; John Johnson, 1994.
Retired numbers: 12, John Brodie; 34, Joe Perry; 37, John Johnson; 39, Hugh McElhenny; 70, Charles Krueger; 73, Leo Nomellini; 87, Dwight Clark.

The name has officially been 3Com Park since 1995, when a local computer software company paid to get its name attached to the stadium formerly known as Candlestick. Many locals stubbornly continue to call the place by its old name or by its affectionate nickname, "the Stick," using the excuse that the stadium is on land called Candlestick Point. Whatever the name, the stadium's incomparable aura is as much a definitive part of the San Francisco 49ers' tradition as their great stars. The place has presence, and its menacing structure can give you the chills.

Start with the breathtaking view of San Francisco Bay. Add the aroma of the tailgate parties. Witness hot-dog wrappers swirling in the unpredictable wind. Bundle up for typically brisk and damp conditions, and brace for a sea of 49ers-red clothing in the stands. These are some of the things that make "the Stick" perhaps the NFL's most flavorful venue. Like the Golden Gate Bridge, 3Com/Candlestick Park is a true slice of San Francisco.

Unless you're tailgating, save your appetite for the stadium's fare, and bring a jacket, even if it's 70 degrees and sunny when you head for the game. All in all, it's a unique experience—and the football is pretty good, too. Getting a ticket can be difficult, but if you haven't been to a 49ers game at the Stick, the experience could be worth the price you have to pay.

HOT TIPS FOR VISITING FANS

PARKING
The stadium lot holds 8,000 cars. Spots cost $20, but without pre-paid parking tickets, forget about getting into them. Another 11,000 spaces on perimeter roads also cost $20, but some of these are in unpaved lots; mud can be a factor. The upside to parking lots on the outskirts is quick access in and out of the stadium to avoid the often murderous traffic congestion. Side streets aren't the best idea for night games, as spots are extremely limited, a long walk from the stadium, and leaving your car unattended in the neighborhood is a little risky.

WEATHER
Big mood swings by Mother Nature are the norm in the Bay Area, so unexpected temperature drops should be expected. During early-season games, the average highs generally hit the lower 70s and the lows dip to the lower 50s—with a stiff ocean breeze. By the late-season and playoff games, the highs are in the mid-50s and lows 40s. The heaviest periods of rainfall are in December and January.

MEDIA
Radio: KGO (810 AM).
TV: KTVU (Channel 2, Fox); KGO (Channel 7, ABC).

CUISINE
No one need go hungry at the Stick—even vegetarians, who can buy veggie burgers, baked potatoes, yogurt, fruit, trail mix, and bottled water. Seafood lovers can choose among crab cakes, prawns, gumbo, and seafood salad. The Stick also has a number of grill stands featuring hamburgers, specialty sausages and grilled chicken sandwiches. Candlestick offers imported and specialty beers such as Anchor Steam, Heineken, Killian's Red, and Gordon Biersch. Napa Valley wines are also available. Your best bet for after the game is downtown San Francisco or North Beach, about 20 minutes away. Two favorites: Izzy's Steaks and Chops (415-563-0487) in the Marina for a thick T-bone, or John's Grill (415-986-0069) on Ellis Street. If the lamb chops at John's were good enough for Sam Spade, they're good enough for you.

LODGING NEAR THE STADIUM

King George Hotel
334 Mason St.
San Francisco, CA 94102
(415) 781-5050/(800) 288-6005
About 5 miles from the stadium.

Westin San Francisco Airport
One Old Bayshore Highway
Millbrae, CA 94030
(415) 692-3500/(800) 228-3000
About 10 miles from the stadium.

THE 49ERS AT 3COM PARK

Dec. 19, 1971: The 49ers clinch their second consecutive divisional title, beating the Lions 31–27 in the last game of their debut season at Candlestick.

Dec. 7, 1980: Down 35–7 at halftime to the Saints, the 49ers make the biggest comeback in NFL history and win 38–35 in overtime.

Jan. 10, 1982: Despite six turnovers, the 49ers defeat the Dallas Cowboys 28–27 and advance to their first Super Bowl.

Dec. 6, 1992: Jerry Rice breaks Steve Largent's record for touchdown receptions by making his 101st against the Miami Dolphins. The 49ers win 27–3.

Sept. 5, 1994: A 38-yard reception against the Raiders gives Jerry Rice 127, the NFL record for career touchdowns.

Jan. 15, 1995: A 38–28 win over the Cowboys in the NFC championship game puts the Niners into their fifth Super Bowl.

In the Hot Seats at 3Com Park

Except for preseason games, it's virtually impossible to purchase a ticket from the 49ers, who have sold out every home game since 1982 and have a waiting list of 17,000 for season tickets.

GOOD SEATS

The very best seats are between the 40-yard lines and about 15 to 20 rows up on the east side, opposite the press box. This is the side of the stadium that gets the most extended sunlight, and naturally its seats are among the toughest to get. But if you're lucky, you'll sit in odd-numbered sections 43–47.

BAD SEATS

If your tickets are in the back rows of the lower end zone on the east side, you might get a taste of 3Com, but you won't see much of the game. Try to avoid tickets for seats in the back rows of odd-numbered sections 1–21 or even-numbered sections 2–8. The upper-reserved seats are pretty good. A few bad seats are in the upper deck—especially in sections 28 and 18, which are obstructed by a protruding press box.

SCALPING

Walking up to the box office at 3Com and

buying a ticket is, well, a baseball thing, so the best bet is to shop around. Experienced patrons say a quick mention at one of the top sports bars in the Bay Area—Ricky's in San Leandro, Pat O'Shea's in downtown San Francisco, the Flatiron in Marin, or Kip's in Berkeley—usually produces results. If this fails, scalpers usually can be spotted near the freeway exit ramps. The Golden Rule: If you're willing to pay, no game is impossible to attend.

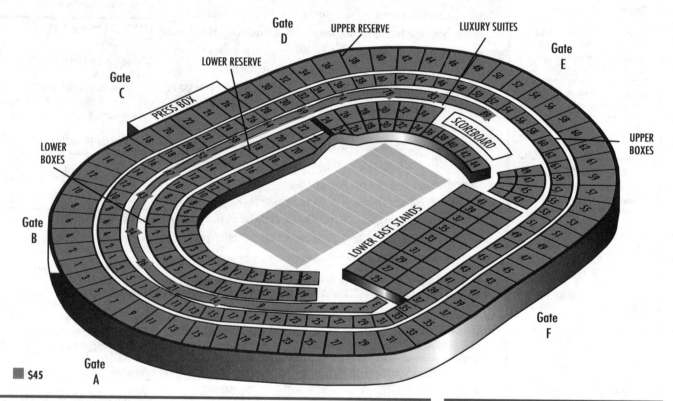

 $45

HOME-FIELD ADVANTAGE

The grass field holds water, and while the 49ers have learned to cope with slippery surfaces, visitors can have problems. Wearing the proper shoes is always a major concern.

Then there's the wind, which has a penchant for oddly changing directions during the course of the game. Joe Montana made getting a feel for the wind a routine part of his pregame warmups. The wind is tough on kickers and punters, too. It's no coincidence the 49ers punters and kickers almost never rank among the NFL leaders.

As long as the 49ers share 3Com with baseball's Giants (until 1999, when the Giants move out) they'll have an advantage down the stretch. Because of the baseball season, the 49ers play very few home games in September and early October, so they're often left with a home-heavy schedule in December, when playoff implications become clearer.

These quirks often—but not always—benefit the 49ers. In two of the last three NFC title games at Candlestick—with Super Bowl berths at stake—the 49ers lost.

GETTING TO 3COM PARK

Public transportation: "The Ballpark Express" is available on game day from a number of locations, or take the No. 29 directly to 3Com. Call (415) 673-6864 for more information.

By car: From downtown and the East Bay, take U.S. 101 south to either the Third Street or 3Com Park/Candlestick Point exit. From San Jose, take U.S. 101 north to same exits. The 3Com/Candlestick Point exit leads to the stadium lots. If you take the Third Street exit, go 3 blocks to Jamestown Avenue. Turn right and continue for 1 mile; the parking lots and stadium are on the left.

TICKET INFORMATION
Address: 3Com Park, San Francisco, CA 94124

Phone: (415) 468-2249
Hours: Mon.–Fri. 9–5.
Prices: $45.

Training camp: Sierra Community College, Rocklin, CA

Kingdome

STADIUM STATS

Location: 201 S. King St., Seattle, WA 98104
Opened: Aug. 1, 1976
Surface: AstroTurf
Capacity: 66,000
Services for fans with disabilities: Seating available in various sections on the 200 level, with a smaller number on the 100 level.

STADIUM FIRSTS

Regular-season game: Sept. 12, 1976, 30–24 loss to the St. Louis Cardinals.
Points scored: 28-yard field goal by Jim Bakken of the Cardinals.
Overtime game: Oct. 29, 1978, 20–17 loss to the Denver Broncos.
Playoff game: Dec. 23, 1983, 31–7 over the Denver Broncos.

TEAM NOTEBOOK

Franchise history: Seattle Seahawks, 1976–present.
Division title: 1988.
Pro Football Hall of Fame: Franco Harris, 1990; Steve Largent, 1995.
Retired number: 12, "Fans—the 12th man."

When the Kingdome opened in 1976, it was viewed as the Emerald City's ultimate jewel—a multipurpose complex that could house a football team, a baseball team, as well as a Rolling Stones concert and the occasional tractor pull. But after weathering 20-plus Seattle winters, the old gray dome just ain't what she used to be—as evidenced by the collapse of a roof section in 1994.

An ongoing $6 million face-lift is aimed at correcting a situation that got the Kingdome dubbed the "world's largest Chia Pet." The roof of the dome got stripped to its concrete base and the discolored white foam layer (who knew it was white?) was replaced with sheets of a sturdy high-tech vinyl. Inside, the ceiling tiles have been replaced with a sprayed-on acoustical substance that "evens out the noise," according to stadium officials, and reduces echoes.

Although the Mariners are packing up to move out of the Kingdome and into their new stadium in 1999, the Seahawks' lease runs for another decade or so. There's a lot of talk about what can, might, or should be done once the Mariners depart, but for the moment it's all just talk.

What the Kingdome does have in its favor is location, location, location. It sits just north of Interstate 90, the main freeway linking the city to the suburbs east of Lake Washington. And it's just west of Interstate 5, providing easy access from the south and north. It's also just south of downtown, so the Kingdome anchors Seattle's ever-growing skyline.

It also helps that Seattle has always been a football town. Fans embraced the Seahawks from the very first kickoff, and on game days they arrive early, leave late, and scream themselves silly in between.

HOT TIPS FOR VISITING FANS

PARKING
The Kingdome offers 4,000 spaces in three lots. Spots are $6 ($5 for cars carrying 3 or more people), but these fill up quickly so get there early. Another 30,000 spaces are available within a mile of the dome; don't count on finding a freebie on the street unless you plan to arrive several hours before kickoff. Prices at the adjacent lots top out at $10 for the closest ones.

MEDIA
Radio: All games are broadcast on KIRO radio (710 AM) and its network. Steve Thomas does the play-by-play and former Seahawk wide receiver Steve Raible provides the color commentary. **TV:** KING (Channel 5), Seattle's NBC affiliate.

CUISINE
Options include Pizza Hut pizza, frozen yogurt, as well as local favorites Ezell's fried chicken, Fletcher's hot dogs, and Cow Chip cookies. A variety of Starbucks coffee and espresso drinks is available. The concessions stands offer microbrews from the numerous local breweries. Don't let names like Ballard Bitter scare you off; Seattle was at the forefront of the microbrewery trend, and they've got something for just about any particular taste in beer—be bold, the beers are. If you want to quench your thirst or clear your palate with nothing more than some tasty bottled water, they've got Crystal Geyser.

Instead of tailgating, most fans opt for a pre-game brunch at one of the many restaurants in nearby Pioneer Square, the area where Seattle grew into a city in the 1890s. Among the most popular is F. X. McRory's (206-623-4800), which features an oyster bar and a great liquor list. A short walk to the northwest of the Kingdome is the waterfront area, which has several outstanding seafood restaurants. No visit to Seattle would be complete without a visit to the justly famous Ray's Boathouse (206-789-3770), about a half-hour drive north, on the beach of Elliot Bay.

LODGING NEAR THE STADIUM

Holiday Inn Crown Plaza
1113 Sixth Ave.
Seattle, WA 98101
(206) 464-1980/(800) HOLIDAY
About 1 mile from the stadium.

Westin Hotel Seattle
1900 Fifth Ave.
Seattle, WA 98101
(206) 728-1000/(800) 228-3000
About 2 miles from the stadium.

THE SEAHAWKS AT THE KINGDOME

Dec. 23, 1983: Dave Krieg completes 12 of 13 passes for 200 yards and three touchdowns, giving the team its first playoff win.

Dec. 22, 1984: Dan Doornink rushes for a career-high 126 yards in a 13–7 win over the Los Angeles Raiders in which the Seahawks score only one touchdown.

In the Hot Seats at the Kingdome

There's a Now Available sign on those once-impossible-to-come-by season tickets. Single-game tickets go on sale in early June. Games against the Raiders, the Denver Broncos, and the Kansas City Chiefs traditionally sell quickly.

GOOD SEATS

Seats on or near the 50-yard line are the best, of course, but any of the 200-level seats—which offer a more intimate atmosphere because of the limited number of rows and overhead television sets—are fine, too.

BAD SEATS

Because the Kingdome is not a football-only stadium, the 100-level seats nearest the field have a restricted view, and the top-of-domers in the 300 level, especially in the south end zone, make binoculars a must.

SCALPING

Busy every Sunday on corners around the Kingdome, but recently, there have been more sellers than buyers.

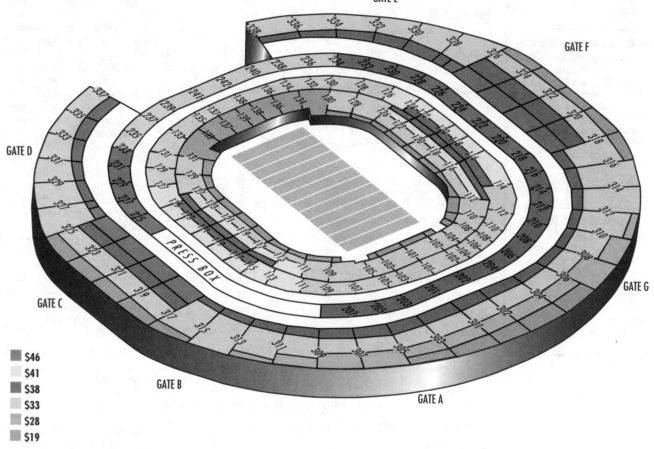

- $46
- $41
- $38
- $33
- $28
- $19

HOME-FIELD ADVANTAGE

Opposing teams have been known to practice with huge speakers blasting crowd noise or rock music at full volume to prepare for the painfully loud Seahawks fans' cheers, taunts, and chants that resonate within the Kingdome. How the Seahawks themselves cope with the decibel level is unknown, but they seem to manage; in 1995 they posted a 5–3 record at home.

GETTING TO THE KINGDOME

Public transportation: On game day a shuttle runs downtown every 10 minutes, starting 90 minutes before kickoff and running as long as it's needed. Nearly all regularly scheduled buses stop within easy walking distance of the dome. Call (206) 553-3000 for information.
By car: From the north, I-5 south to exit 164. Follow signs to Dearborn Street and the Kingdome. Go right onto Dearborn, then right onto Airport Way after about 5 blocks. At Fourth Avenue South, go right or left into Kingdome parking. From the south, I-5 north to exit 163/Spokane Street. Follow the Spokane Street off-ramp to Fourth and make a right. Take Fourth south to Royal Brougham Way. Turn left onto Royal Brougham, Kingdome parking is on the right.

TICKET INFORMATION
Address: 11220 N. E. 53rd St., Kirkland, WA 98033
Phone: (206) 827-9766

Hours: Mon.–Fri. 8–5 (8–4 in off-season).
Tickets: $46: 100, 200, 300 levels along sidelines; $41: 200, 300 level along sidelines near corners; $38: 200, 300 levels;
$33: end zones; $28: 300 level of end zone; $19: low 100, high 300 levels.
Training camp: 11220 N.E. 53rd St., Kirkland, WA

SEATTLE SEAHAWKS / KINGDOME

STADIUM STATS

Location: *4201 N. Dale Mabry Highway, Tampa, FL 33607*
Opened: *Nov. 7, 1967*
Surface: *Bermuda grass*
Capacity: *74,301*
Services for fans with disabilities: *Seating available in the north end zone, next to the field.*

STADIUM FIRSTS

Regular-season game: *Sept. 19, 1976, 23–0 loss to the San Diego Chargers.*
Points scored: *48-yard field goal by Toni Fritsch of the Chargers.*
Overtime game: *Oct. 12, 1980, 14–14 tie with the Green Bay Packers.*
Playoff game: *Dec. 29, 1979, 24–17 over the Philadelphia Eagles.*

TEAM NOTEBOOK

Franchise history: *Tampa Bay Buccaneers, 1976–present.*
Division titles: *1979, 1981.*
Pro Football Hall of Fame: *Lee Roy Selmon, 1995.*
Retired number: *63, Lee Roy Selmon.*

THE BUCCANEERS AT TAMPA STADIUM

Dec. 18, 1977: *The Bucs get their first home victory, 17–7 over the St. Louis Cardinals.*

Dec. 16, 1979: *In a driving rainstorm, the Bucs edge the Kansas City Chiefs 3–0 to clinch their first NFC Central Division title. Ricky Bell gains 137 yards.*

Sept. 11, 1980: *A 10–9 win over the Los Angeles Rams avenges a playoff loss the year before.*

Jan. 2, 1983: *Down by 17 at the half, the Bucs, led by quarterback Doug Williams, win in overtime 26–23 over the Chicago Bears to clinch a playoff spot.*

Sept. 13, 1987: *Steve DeBerg throws five touchdown passes as the Bucs trounce the Atlanta Falcons 48–10.*

Some places are known for moments when everything went right. Famous touchdown catches. Record-setting runs. Classic playoff games. Tampa Stadium is known for moments when everything went wrong.

The stadium's most notable tenants, the Buccaneers, entered the NFL in 1976 and lost their first 26 games. The Bucs didn't break the streak until the 13th game of their second season, and that happened at New Orleans. The tradition of losing continues to this day. The Bucs have put together an NFL record for futility—12 consecutive seasons with at least 10 losses, a string finally broken in 1995.

But the problems aren't limited to the Bucs. It was here that a last-second Buffalo field-goal attempt went wide to the right in the New York Giants' 20–19 victory in Super Bowl XXV to begin the Bills' streak of four consecutive Super Bowl defeats. It was here, when Tampa Stadium often hosted pre-season NFL games, that Joe Namath suffered one of the knee injuries that cut his career short.

Some locals will tell you the place is cursed. A few years ago, a radio station hired a witch doctor to remove the curse. The witch doctor stood in the parking lot, chanted some magic words, and said the Bucs would begin winning. They did win that Sunday, but at the next home game, things returned to normal. The Bucs not only lost, they were shut out.

New ownership in 1995 raised hopes for improvement on many fronts, but also prompted fears of the Bucs being relocated. Win-loss record aside, locals love their team and don't want them to leave. "They're like an ugly baby," says one Tampa fan, "They're ugly, but they're ours."

HOT TIPS FOR VISITING FANS

PARKING

The stadium's unusual grass parking lots make Tampa popular for tailgating. But most spots close to the stadium are sold for the season. Single-game parking is available for $5 in spots south of Tampa Bay Boulevard. The best bet for single-game visitors, however, may be the lot for Tampa Bay Center, a shopping mall across the street that so far is free. Traffic backs up on game days. One way to avoid some of the mess is to exit I-275 onto MacDill Avenue, go north approximately 1 mile to Columbus, turn left, and follow it to Dale Mabry.

WEATHER

On an average Sunday afternoon in October the place turns into the world's largest sauna. On special occasions, it throws in lightning. Before one game in the late '70s, the Bucs' then-public-relations director Bob Best warned officials that forecasters were saying a nasty storm was on its way. Legend has it that an official looked at Best and said, "This is the NFL; we play no matter what the weather." Legend also has it that when the lightning started ripping through the air above Tampa Stadium, a certain official was the first one off the field, calling for what turned into a 40-minute delay.

MEDIA

Radio: Gene Deckerhoff and former Buccaneer David Logan are the announcers on WQYK (1010 AM, 99.5 FM).
TV: Pre-season games are on WTOG (Channel 44). Jim Kelly and former Cincinnati Bengal Cris Collinsworth are the announcers.

CUISINE

You'll find a decent variety—pizza, subs, chicken wings, and frozen yogurt. Cuban sandwiches are a local favorite and as filling as they are tasty. And while fans are not allowed to bring in beverages, stadium officials say you can get a cup of ice at the concessions stand at no cost and fill it at a drinking fountain. The stadium offers a Safe Ride Home program for fans who've got too much of a beer buzz on to drive home; Tag-A-Kid bracelets with a child's name and seat number on them can be worn by youngsters, making it easier to reunite lost kids with their parents. South of the stadium on Dale Mabry are all kinds of fast-food options and chain restaurants. But if you want something more unique and are willing to drive 15 minutes, you can eat Spanish cuisine at the Columbia (813-248-4961), a fixture in historic Ybor City since 1905, or splurge and visit Bern's Steak House (813-251-2421), one of a handful of good restaurants on Howard Avenue.

LODGING NEAR THE STADIUM

Hyatt Regency Westshore
6200 Courtney Campbell Causeway
Tampa, FL 33607
(813) 874-1234/(800) 223-1234
10 miles from the stadium.

Radisson Bay Harbor Inn
7700 Courtney Campbell Causeway
Tampa, FL 33607
(813) 281-8900/(800) 333-3333
6 miles from the stadium.

In the Hot Seats at Tampa Stadium

Unless the Chicago Bears or the Green Bay Packers are in town, you can walk up and buy tickets the day of the game, which stuns visitors from places such as Denver and Washington, D.C. With the exception of the glory years—a brief stretch in the late 1970s and early '80s—it has been that way through Buccaneers' history. In more than a dozen years, the team sold out only 11 games. For those Chicago games, more than 20,000 Bears' fans—some visitors from up North, some transplanted residents—show up at Tampa Stadium. Before the "Battle of the Bays," thousands of Packers' fans gather in the parking lot for a giant tailgate party.

BAD SEATS

"The Big Sombrero," as ESPN's Chris Berman has dubbed it, is a giant bowl. That's good (no obstructed-view seats) and bad (no obstructed-sun or obstructed-rain seats). The west side of the stadium falls into the shade in the late afternoon, which is why the locals prefer those seats. The east side stays in the sun throughout the game, which to some visitors is a plus. Some fans like sitting in the south end zone because the players enter and leave the field near those seats. But the JumboTron scoreboard installed before the last Super Bowl sits behind those seats, so if you want to watch instant replays, go for the north end zone.

SCALPING

Scalping is illegal in Florida, and, in regard to the Bucs, completely unnecessary. Late in the season, scalpers practically give away tickets.

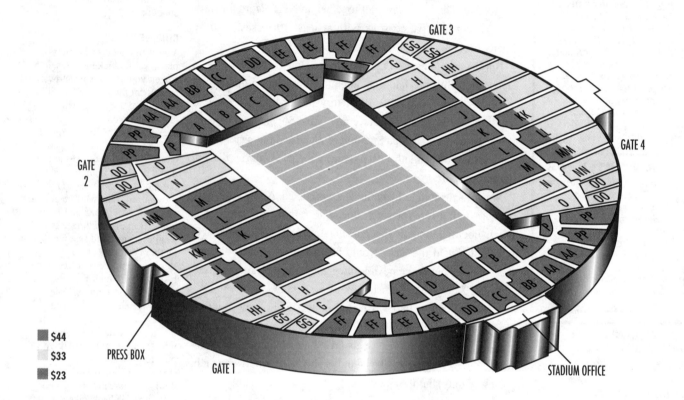

- ■ $44
- ▨ $33
- ▤ $23

PRESS BOX

GATE 1

GATE 2

GATE 3

GATE 4

STADIUM OFFICE

HOME-FIELD ADVANTAGE

In theory, the Buccaneers should have a home-field edge because of the heat and humidity. They go through training camp in it, they practice in it, they live in it. So when the Chicago Bears or the Green Bay Packers come to visit on a steamy Sunday in October, they should wilt in the fourth quarter, right? So the theory goes. In fact, over the years, the team's coaches have played down the importance of the heat. Ray Perkins went so far as to have the team's bench moved from its traditional west side location, with the sun on their backs, to across the field. Perkins insisted that real men wouldn't be bothered by having the sun in their faces. Of course, by the time he was fired in 1990, Perkins had moved the home bench back to the west. All in all, the Bucs have shown they can blow a fourth-quarter lead at Tampa Stadium just as well as at Soldier Field.

GETTING TO TAMPA STADIUM

Public transportation: The Nos. 7, 11, 14, 15, 32, 36, and 41 buses run to the Tampa Bay Center, which is across the street from the stadium. Call (813) 623-5835 for more information.

By car: From St. Petersburg, take I-275 North, across the Howard Franklin Bridge. Go left onto Dale Mabry Highway approximately 1 mile. The stadium is on the right. From the north, take I-275 south. Go right onto Dale Mabry Highway approximately 1 mile. The stadium is on the right.

TICKET INFORMATION

Address: Tampa Stadium, 4201 N. Dale Mabry Highway, Tampa, FL 33607
Phone: (813) 879-BUCS, (800) 282-0683, or

TicketMaster at (904) 353-3309, (813) 287-8844, or (407) 839-3900.
Hours: Mon.–Fri. 9–5, Sat. 9–1, Sat 9–6 before Sun. home games.

Prices: $44: prime sidelines, rows 1–79; $33: sidelines above row 80; $23: end zones.
Training camp: University of Tampa, Tampa, FL

STADIUM STATS

Location: 2400 E. Capitol St. S.E., Washington, DC 20003
Opened: Oct. 1, 1961
Surface: Grass
Capacity: 56,454
Services for fans with disabilities: Seating available on levels 2, 3, and 4.

STADIUM FIRSTS

Regular-season game: Oct. 1, 1961, 24–21 loss to the New York Giants.
Points scored: 17-yard touchdown reception by Kyle Rote of the Giants.
Overtime game: Nov. 2, 1975, 30–24 over the Dallas Cowboys.
Playoff game: Dec. 24, 1972, 16–3 over the Green Bay Packers.

TEAM NOTEBOOK

Franchise history: Boston Braves, 1932; Boston Redskins, 1933–36; Washington Redskins, 1937–present.
Division titles: 1936, 1937, 1940, 1942, 1943, 1945, 1972, 1982, 1983, 1984, 1987, 1991.
Super Bowl appearances: VII, Jan. 14, 1973, 14–7 loss to the Miami Dolphins; XVII, Jan. 30, 1983, 27–17 over the Miami Dolphins; XVIII, Jan. 22, 1984, 38–9 loss to the Los Angeles Raiders; XXII, Jan. 31, 1988, 42–10 over the Denver Broncos; XXVI, Jan. 26, 1992, 37–24 over the Buffalo Bills.
Pro Football Hall of Fame: Sammy Baugh, Earl Lambeau, George Preston Marshall, 1963; Bill Dudley, 1966; Cliff Battles, Wayne Millner, 1968; Turk Edwards, 1969; Vince Lombardi, 1971; Ray Flaherty, 1976; David Jones, 1980; Sam Huff, 1982; Christian Jurgensen, Bobby Mitchell, 1983; Charley Taylor, 1984; Hen Houston, 1986; Stan Jones, 1991; John Riggins, 1992.
Retired number: 33, Sammy Baugh.

Cramped, aging, on the verge of being replaced, Robert F. Kennedy Memorial Stadium nonetheless shakes and shimmies to the incessant drumbeat of Washington Redskins fans' cheers eight Sundays a year. Sure, the crowds have looked a little sparse recently, but don't think that means tickets have suddenly become available for Washington's other sporting passion (aside from politics and rumormongering).

The tight squeeze at RFK stems from its cozy confines. At 56,454 seats, it is the second-smallest venue in the NFL. Part of RFK's appeal is that closed-in feeling that allows cheering to reverberate and give the Redskins a true home-field advantage. The end-zone seats are closest to the field, allowing fans to ride visiting quarterbacks when their teams must operate in the shadow of the goal posts.

RFK Stadium lacks many of the modern conveniences. It has no luxury boxes, no premium seating, and has an open press box cursed by sportswriters. Stadium employees work for the city, not the Redskins, and are known to give civil servants an uncivil reputation.

The club hopes to have a new stadium, seating 78,000, open for the 1997 season. That, however, would move the Redskins from the nation's capital, their home since 1937, to suburban Laurel, Maryland, just 18 miles from Baltimore.

HOT TIPS FOR VISITING FANS

PARKING
The stadium offers 12,500 spaces, which doesn't seem like much but has proved adequate for a venue of this size. About 3,000 of the spaces closest to the entrances are reserved and sold in advance through the stadium/armory offices. General parking costs $6. Stadium gates open 90 minutes before kickoff, so to ensure parking at a close lot, arrive an extra 90 minutes early. The lots are dimly lighted at night.

WEATHER
Lovely in autumn, cold in winter.

MEDIA
Radio: The Redskins' flagship radio is WJFK (106.7 FM).
TV: Regular-season television will generally be Fox (Channel 5).

CUISINE
The stadium food is, well, stadium food, and includes hot dogs, knackwurst and sauerkraut, nachos, French fries, chips, soft pretzels, and popcorn. Wine and mixed drinks are available at some concessions locations, as is cappuccino. Available beers are Miller and Budweiser.
You're really better off saving your appetite for after the game, and the dining choices greatly improve outside the stadium, in terms of both cuisine and atmosphere. Sophisticated fans party before or after on Capitol Hill—The Hawk and Dove (202-543-3300) is popular—or in the area around refurbished Union Station, which is on the Metro's Red Line. Try The Dubliner (202-737-3773) for a taste of the brogue. And there's always Georgetown; Irish Times (202-543-5433) and Mad Hatter's (202-833-1495) are popular hangouts in that neighborhood.

LODGING NEAR THE STADIUM

Loews L'Enfant Plaza
480 L'Enfant Plaza S.W.
Washington, DC 20024
(202) 484-1000/(800) 235-6397
About 5 miles from the stadium.

Crystal City Marriott
1999 Jefferson Davis Hwy.
Arlington, VA 22202
(703) 920-3230/(800) 228-9290
About 5 miles from the stadium.

THE REDSKINS AT RFK STADIUM

Nov. 28, 1965: Sonny Jurgensen passes for more than 400 yards and three touchdowns, leading the Redskins back from a 21–0 deficit for their greatest comeback ever, 34–31 over the Dallas Cowboys.

Nov. 27, 1966: The Redskins wallop the New York Giants 72–41, as the two teams combine to score the most points ever in an NFL game.

Dec. 31, 1972: The Redskins beat the defending NFL champion Cowboys 26–3, earning the right to challenge Miami in Super Bowl VII.

Jan. 15, 1983: John Riggins' 185 rushing yards lead the way for the Redskins, who cruise past the Minnesota Vikings 21–7 to win a spot in the NFC championship game.

Jan. 12, 1992: The Redskins' 41–10 victory over the Detroit Lions in the NFC championship game puts them into their fourth Super Bowl under coach Joe Gibbs and the fifth in the team's history.

Oct. 12, 1992: Art Monk catches his 820th pass to become the NFL's all-time leading receiver. The Redskins beat the Denver Broncos 34–3.

In the Hot Seats at RFK Memorial Stadium

No way. Every home game since the season opener in 1966 has been sold out in advance—every single game, spanning more than 200 consecutive regular-season games. The waiting list for season tickets runs about 45,000 names, with only a few dozen—at most—moving up each year.

GOOD SEATS

End zone, if you like to yell at the players and know they can hear you. Mezzanine, for protection from the elements and for sight lines.

BAD SEATS

The first 10 rows, practically at field level, permit a great view of player necks.

SCALPING

Since tickets aren't available to the general public, desperate Redskin fans turn to scalpers or ticket brokers. Often tickets can be obtained through advertisements in the local newspapers, but the markup can be two or three times the face value. Games against Dallas, the New York Giants, and Philadelphia—all division rivals—are particularly hard to come by and can easily be marked up 300%.

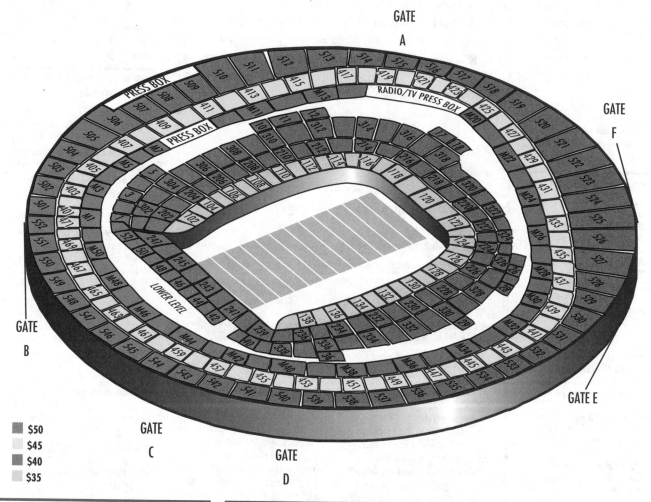

- $50
- $45
- $40
- $35

HOME-FIELD ADVANTAGE

Prescription athletic turf (a fancy type of real grass) always makes the game more colorful than the phony stuff. The history RFK has seen and the noise and intensity of Redskins' fans also help to give the home side a definite edge.

GETTING TO RFK MEMORIAL STADIUM

Public transportation: The Stadium/Armory station on the Orange and Blue lines of the Metro is 1 block away.
By car: From the north, take I-295 south to East Capitol Street. Go west on East Capital directly to the stadium.
From the south, take I-395 north to Sixth Street S.E. Go north on Sixth to East Capitol.

From the east, take Route 50 to I-295 south to East Capitol. Go west on East Capitol Street directly to the stadium.
From the west, take I-495 to Route 66. Take 66 into Washington. Go right onto Independence Avenue and follow Independence to the stadium.

TICKET INFORMATION
Address: 2400 E. Capitol St. S.E., Washington, DC 20003

Phone: (202) 546-2222
Hours: Mon.–Fri. 9–5.
Prices: $50: mezzanine; $45: 400 level; $40:

200, 300, 500 levels; $35: 100 levels.
Training camp: Redskin Park, Frostburg, MD

basketball

- - - - - - - - - - - - - - -

ATLANTA HAWKS

The Omni

One could argue that the Atlanta Hawks deserve more respect than they receive. In 1949, in a prior incarnation as the Tri-Cities Blackhawks, this franchise was one of the original members of the NBA. In their current hometown, however, the Hawks' founding role in the league is not a consideration for fans when they are deciding which team to support. When it comes to local interest, the Hawks take a backseat to the baseball Braves, as well as to college basketball at Georgia Tech. Don't expect any tomahawk chops or anything else near an electric, vibrant atmosphere at the Omni when the Hawks hit the floor.

There might also be a surprising number of empty seats. The Hawks have not had one season in which their per-game average neared the arena's basketball capacity of 16,378. One local reporter believes part of the explanation for Atlanta's relative indifference to pro basketball lies with the character of the city's population. As in Houston, many people grew up elsewhere, and still follow other teams.

Some cite the downtown address, and the problems people associate with the inner city, as yet another reason why the Hawks have trouble attracting fans, even though the area around the Omni is cosmopolitan and usually quite busy. There was talk of relocating to a new arena north of Atlanta, but that idea has since been abandoned. The Hawks will stay in the city and hope that maybe the Olympics, and the addition of Dikembe Mutombo, will get Atlantans back in the habit of coming downtown for a sport other than baseball.

HOT TIPS FOR VISITING FANS

PARKING
Given its downtown location, the Omni benefits from being surrounded by parking facilities. There are roughly 300 spaces at the Omni, each costing $7. The CNN Center and World Congress Center offer additional parking; the cost ranges from $7 to $10. The local mass-transit system, MARTA, which has a station next to the Omni, is a favorite way for fans to come for a game.

MEDIA
Radio: WSB (750 AM).
TV: WATL-TV (Channel 36) and SportSouth (regional cable). Mike Glenn, a 10-year NBA veteran and a commentator on TBS's coverage, is also an analyst for WATL and SportSouth.

CUISINE
Popular items include smoked sausage and chicken wings with sauce. There is also a specialty coffee stand that serves espresso and cappuccino as well as fudge made at the Omni. Two beer stands sell Heineken and Amstel Light, among other brews. Jocks 'n' Jills (404-688-4225), next to the Omni in the CNN Center, is popular with Hawks fans and NBA personalities after games. A sports bar and grill with nearly 60 television sets, Jocks 'n' Jills is owned in part by former players Doc Rivers, Scott Hastings, Randy Wittman, and John Battle. The food court in the lower portion of the CNN Center also features a good variety of fast, convenient places to eat before or after games.

LODGING NEAR THE ARENA

Marriott Marquis
265 Peachtree Center Ave.
Atlanta, GA 30303
(404) 521-0000/(800) 228-9290
½ mile from the arena.

Hyatt Regency
265 Peachtree Street N.E.
Atlanta, GA 30303
(404) 577-1234/(800) 233-1234
Fewer than 3 miles from the arena.

THE HAWKS AT THE OMNI

April 13, 1979: The Hawks win their first home playoff game in six years, topping Houston 100–91 to advance to the Eastern Conference semifinals.

Dec. 10, 1986: Dominique Wilkins scores 57 points against Chicago, an Omni record. The Hawks win 123–95. Four months later, Wilkins ties the record, against New Jersey.

May 7, 1989: After beating the Bucks in all six meetings during the regular season, the Central Division-champion Hawks fall to Milwaukee 96–92 and are eliminated, three games to two, in the first round of the playoffs.

Feb. 2, 1993: Wilkins breaks Bob Pettit's 29-year-old franchise record of 20,880 career points with 31 versus Seattle. The Hawks win 118–109.

Feb. 2, 1994: A 118–99 win over Orlando marks Lenny Wilkens' 900th win as a coach, second to Red Auerbach's 938.

May 8, 1994: Mookie Blaylock has 18 assists, leading the Hawks to a 102–91 win over Miami in the decisive fifth game of their first-round playoff series.

March 1, 1996: Lenny Wilkens becomes the first NBA coach ever to reach 1,000 wins when the Hawks beat Cleveland 74–68.

ARENA STATS
Location: 100 Techwood Dr. N.W., Atlanta, GA 30303
Opened: Oct. 15, 1972
Capacity: 16,378
Services for fans with disabilities: Seating varies, though it is always on the mezzanine level. Seats in the first 10 rows are available for the visually impaired. Call (404) 681-2100.

ARENA FIRSTS
Regular-season game: Oct. 15, 1972, 109–101 over the New York Knicks.
Overtime game: Nov. 7, 1972, 109–107 over the Baltimore Bullets.
Playoff game: April 4, 1972, 126–113 loss to the Boston Celtics.

TEAM NOTEBOOK
Franchise history: Buffalo Bisons, 1945–46 (NBL); Tri-Cities Blackhawks, 1946–49 (NBL); Tri-Cities Blackhawks, 1949–51 (NBA); Milwaukee Hawks, 1951–55; St. Louis Hawks, 1955–68; Atlanta Hawks, 1968–present.
Division titles: 1956–57, 1957–58, 1958–59, 1959–60, 1960–61, 1967–68, 1969–70, 1979–80, 1986–87, 1993–94.
Conference titles: 1956–57, 1957–58, 1959–60, 1960–61.
NBA championship: 1957–58.
Basketball Hall of Fame: Ed Macauley, 1960; Andy Phillip, 1961; Arnold "Red" Auerbach, 1968; Bob Pettit, 1970; Clifford Hagan, 1977; Slater Martin, 1981; Red Holzman, 1985; Bob Houbregs, 1986; Pete Maravich, 1986; Clyde Lovellette, 1987; Lenny Wilkens, 1988; Connie Hawkins, 1992; Walt Bellamy, 1993.
Retired numbers: 9, Bob Pettit; 23, Lou Hudson.

In the Hot Seats at The Omni

The Hawks' season-ticket base is approximately 6,000. Tickets for single games are sold starting in early October, but they are consistently available on game nights, mainly for seats in the upper deck. As in the rest of the NBA, games against the league's better teams are the big attractions, as are games against such southeastern rivals as the Charlotte Hornets and the Orlando Magic.

GOOD SEATS

The $20 seats in sections 206–212 and 224– 230 at center court in the upper deck offer excellent views for a decent price. If these are unavailable, check out upper-deck sections 213–216 and 231–234. In terms of comfort and sight lines, the Omni is a pretty good place to watch basketball.

BAD SEATS

Most of the bad corner seats have been taken out of the arena, but it's still a good idea to avoid the last several rows of the $10 seats behind the baskets—sections 201, 217–219, and 235–236—which are far from the floor. Other seats that require a hike are in the last several rows of sections 206–212 and 224– 230; they cost $15.

SCALPING

There are rarely scalpers outside the Omni, probably because good tickets are usually available at the box office.

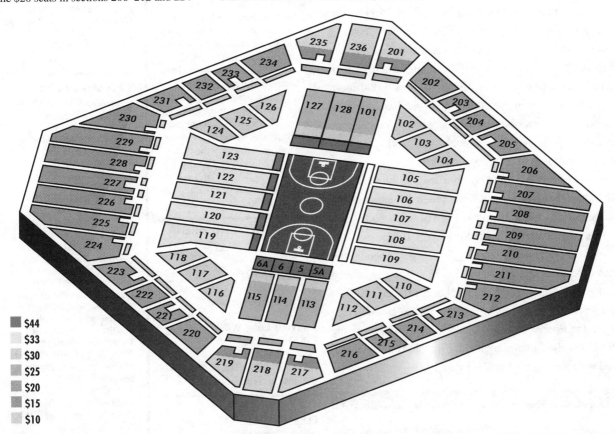

Legend:
- $44
- $33
- $30
- $25
- $20
- $15
- $10

HOME-COURT ADVANTAGE

With a relatively subdued crowd in a city where pro basketball is not the prime attraction, it might seem as though there is little benefit to the Hawks when they play at home. Nevertheless, this team still posts very respectable home records. Atlanta's 36–5 mark in 1993–94, for instance, was the second-best in the NBA. Maybe the players thrive on the home cooking and extra rest they get when they're not on the road.

GETTING TO THE OMNI

Public transportation: Take MARTA to the Five Points Station and get on a westbound train. The Omni is the first stop after Five Points.

By car: From the airport, take I-75/85 north to the International Boulevard exit and turn left onto International. Drive west past Marietta Street, then turn left at the signal. The Omni Hotel is on the corner; the arena is just past. Call (404) 681-2100 for directions to the Omni from anywhere else in the Greater Atlanta area.

TICKET INFORMATION

Address: One CNN Center, Suite 405, South Tower, Atlanta, GA 30303
Phone: (404) 827-3865 or TicketMaster at (404) 249-6400
Hours: Mon.–Fri. 10–5.
Prices: $44: 5, 5A, 6, 6A, first seven rows sections 101, 127, 128, first two rows sections 119–123; $33: sections 105–109, and 119-123; $30: middle of sections 101, 113–115, 127–128, sections 102–104, 110–112, 116–118, and 124–126; $25: back of sections 101, 113–115, 127, and 128; $20: sections 202–205, 213–216, 220–223, 231–234, and lower rows in sections 206–212 and 224–230; $15: lower rows in sections 201, 217–219, 235–236, and upper rows in sections 206–212 and 224–230; $10: upper rows of sections 201, 217–219, and 235–236.

BOSTON CELTICS

FleetCenter

The championship banners and retired jerseys, the parquet floor with the dead spots, and the booming ancient organ made Boston Garden one of the great buildings in NBA history. There were no gimmicks, mascots, dancers—there wasn't even any air conditioning, which made the place a sweatbox during the NBA Finals in June.

But those days are gone. The Celtics have moved to a privately financed new home adjacent to the Garden: FleetCenter, a 755,000-square-foot sports-and-entertainment complex that sits atop a five-story parking structure. The luxurious, high-tech arena—which seats 18,624 for basketball, almost 4,000 more than the Garden—has a multimillion-dollar video scoreboard, two full-service dining club areas, seven elevators, 13 escalators, 34 restrooms, 36 permanent concession stands, and 2,681 preferred seats, including 104 "executive suites."

But there's one thing it has that no other arena in the world can claim: the Celtics' beloved parquet floor. When the team moved, they took the floor with them. Built in 1946 of hardwood scraps left over from the construction of World War II barracks, the floor consists of 247 panels (5 feet by 5 feet) held together by wood planks and brass screws. It still takes an entire crew of men known as the "Bull Gang" two and a half hours to piece it together before a game—a ritual the Celtics wouldn't dream of giving up. After all, the floor was part of the team's history before the Garden was. It was originally created for the old Boston Arena, and moved with the team to the Garden in 1952.

HOT TIPS FOR VISITING FANS

PARKING
At the old Garden, parking was expensive and often impossible, but the new FleetCenter arena is perched atop a five-story parking garage run by the public transit authority (MBTA) and provides 1,150 reasonably priced spaces at the arena itself. The other 17,000 or so fans will have to park a few blocks away and brave the icy Boston winter, or take public transportation to avoid both the parking shortage and the traffic jams.

MEDIA
Radio: WEEI (590 AM).
TV: WSBK (Channel 38), SportsChannel (cable). A replica of the late, legendary announcer Johnny Most's microphone hangs from the rafters with the retired Celtics jerseys, a fitting tribute to one of the greatest but most biased announcers of all time. Glenn Ordway, Most's longtime partner, has taken over on the radio. Former Celtics greats Bob Cousy and Tommy Heinsohn team on television.

CUISINE
Fans can still enjoy the same Celts' cuisine they gobbled up at the Garden—huge pretzels, plump hot dogs (great mustard), fresh-popped popcorn, and fresh-baked pizza—along with new treats provided at the 36 concession stands at FleetCenter. There are also two upscale full-service restaurants, but you must reserve well in advance.

The Sports Café (617-723-6664) at the Garden will do just fine for after the game. It's at street level and is a good place in which to wait out the crowds; grab a beer, soft drink, or sandwich; and rehash the game. You're close enough to downtown to hit one of the great seafood restaurants, such as Legal Seafood (617-864-3400). The Bull and Bear (617-227-9600), a.k.a. the *Cheers* bar, is inside the Hampshire House hotel in the Copley Square district, about 2 miles from Fleet-Center, but the sign is about the only thing that resembles the bar in the show. Closer by the arena, in Quincy Market, is The Black Rose (617-742-2286), an Irish bar that will keep your Celtic mood going.

LODGING NEAR THE ARENA

Westin Copley Plaza
10 Huntington Ave.
Boston, MA 02116
(617) 262-9600/(800) 228-3000
2 miles from the arena.

Marriott Long Wharf
296 State St.
Boston, MA 02109
(617) 227-0800/(800) 228-9290
2 miles from the arena.

THE CELTICS AT FLEETCENTER

January 6, 1996: With 18 points from team captain Dee Brown, the Celtics break a five-game losing streak with a 93–77 win over the Cavaliers.

February 1, 1996: Boston beats the new expansion Vancouver Grizzlies team 131–98.

March 18, 1996: After two overtimes, the Celtics win 107–106 over the New Jersey Nets.

ARENA STATS
Location: Causeway St., Boston, MA 02114
Opened: Nov. 13, 1995
Capacity: 18,624
Services for fans with disabilities: Seating varies for each game.

ARENA FIRSTS
Regular-season game: Nov. 3, 1995, 101–100 loss to the Milwaukee Bucks.
First points: Rick Fox of the Celtics.

TEAM NOTEBOOK
Franchise history: Boston Celtics, 1946–48 (BAA); 1948–present (NBA).
NBA championships: 1956–57, 1958–59, 1959–60, 1960–61, 1961–62, 1962–63, 1963–64, 1964–65, 1965–66, 1967–68, 1968–69, 1973–74, 1975–76, 1980–81, 1983–84, 1985–86.
Basketball Hall of Fame: Ed Macauley, 1960; John Russell, 1964; Red Auerbach, 1968; Bob Cousy, 1970; Bill Russell, 1974; Frank Ramsey, Bill Sharman, 1981; John Havlicek, Sam Jones, 1983; Tom Heinsohn, 1985; Bob Houbregs, Pete Maravich, 1986; Clyde Lovellette, 1987; K. C. Jones, 1988; Dave Bing, 1989; Nate Archibald, Dave Cowens, 1991; Bill Walton, 1993.
Retired numbers: 1, Walter Brown; 2, Red Auerbach; 3, Dennis Johnson; 6, Bill Russell; 10, Jo Jo White; 14, Bob Cousy; 15, Tom Heinsohn; 16, Tom Sanders; 17, John Havlicek; 18, Dave Cowens and Jim Loscutoff; 19, Don Nelson; 21, Bill Sharman; 22, Ed Macauley; 23, Frank Ramsey; 24, Sam Jones; 25, K. C. Jones; 32, Kevin McHale; 33, Larry Bird; 35, Reggie Lewis.

In the Hot Seats at FleetCenter

Perhaps the best news about the Celtics' move to FleetCenter is that there are almost 4,000 more seats for basketball than at Boston Garden, and it is usually possible to see a game without being a five-generation season ticketholder. The Celtics hold aside 500 to 1,000 seats for purchase at the walk-up window at each game.

GOOD SEATS

Every seat at FleetCenter is not only cool and comfortable (quite a switch from the Garden) but also is angled toward the court, with a clear sight line. If you want to get close enough to smell the sweat, the best seats in the house are about 10 rows behind the bench ($60-$68). Order them far in advance; they are not sold out to season ticketholders yet, but they are very hot tickets.

BAD SEATS

There are no obstructed views at FleetCenter.

The only way to get a bad seat is to sit so far away that the players look like tiny clay figures. You might want to stay away from those high-elevation $10 seats.

SCALPING

Scalping is illegal, but enforcement isn't particularly tough. Scalpers are everywhere around the arena; prices vary according to supply and demand.

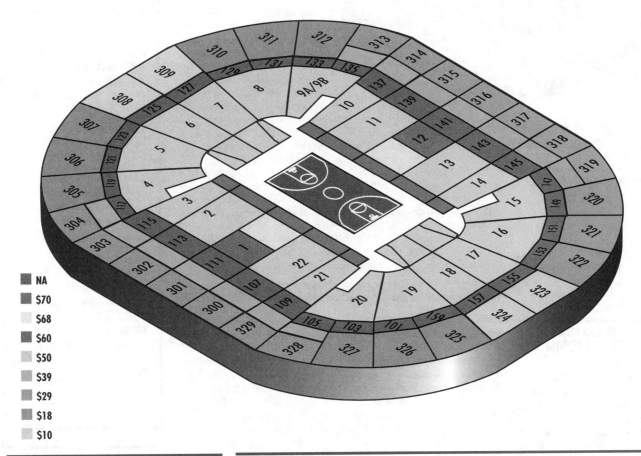

- ▓ NA
- ▓ $70
- ░ $68
- ▓ $60
- ▒ $50
- ▒ $39
- ▓ $29
- ▓ $18
- ░ $10

HOME-COURT ADVANTAGE

The ghosts and mystique of Boston Garden may be gone, but the Celtics' home-court advantage remains at Fleet-Center in the form of the parquet floor. Legendary former coach Red Auerbach summed it up in an interview on the Celtics' web site: "If teams felt it was a poor floor, I used it for advantage by playing with their minds. That usually worked." You can take the floor out of the Garden, but you can't take the Garden out of the floor.

GETTING TO FLEETCENTER

Public transportation: Take the Green or Orange MBTA lines to the North Station stop. North Station is also a commuter rail terminus.
By car: From the south, follow I-95 north to I-93 toward exit 25 (Causeway Street). Make a left at the bottom of the ramp; FleetCenter will be to your right.

From the west, take Massachusetts Turnpike (Route 90) to Route 93 north to exit 25. From the north, take I-93 south to Boston, or take I-95 south to Route 1 south across the Tobin Bridge. Merge with I-93 south. Take exit 26 (Storrow Drive). Bear right, following signs toward North Station.

TICKET INFORMATION
Address: Causeway St., Boston, MA 02114

Phone: (617) 523-3030 or TicketMaster at (617) 931-2000
Hours: Mon.–Fri. 9–5.

Prices: $70, $68, $60, $50, $39, $29, $18, $10.

CHARLOTTE HORNETS

Charlotte Coliseum

$70 $50 $45 $36 $31
$29 $22 $17 $12 $8

The circular Coliseum is a great place to watch basketball. The Hornets lead the league in attendance, selling out practically every game in this 24,042-seat arena. Owner George Shinn mingles with the crowd, and because so many season tickets are sold, it seems that everyone in the crowd knows everybody else. Fans treat the game like a big family night out and frequently come early for tailgate parties.

The fans and players have a great relationship. Most of the players make their homes in the area, and they are treated like genuine heroes. People here are basketball-hungry, and while ACC fans and NBA fans aren't the same animal, the atmosphere can be decidedly collegiate in its enthusiasm and unquestioning support.

But this high-tech arena has attractions other than the fans. The scoreboard has crystal-clear replays, and six other message boards are scattered throughout the arena. SuperHugo, the Hornets' mascot, wears a blue bodysuit with black sunglasses and is a three-time winner of the NBA mascot slam-dunk championship. Hugo is such a celebrity in Charlotte that his likeness—a 21,000-square-foot mural—covers nine stories on the side of an office building in downtown Charlotte (Two First Union Center). The mural, which was unveiled in January 1995, depicts the blue buzzer bursting through the bricks.

HOME-COURT ADVANTAGE

The fans and the noise can drive opponents crazy. The Hornets have had a winning home record four of their first six seasons. Sometimes when the Hornets are on defense, instead of chanting "dee-fense, dee-fense," the fans make a particularly unnerving buzzing sound.

IN THE HOT SEATS AT CHARLOTTE COLISEUM

Not a bad ticket in the house. Each seat is cushioned and comfortable, and the sky boxes are unobtrusive. Usually the only tickets available are the $8 seats high in the end zones, an area in which the sound can get deafening. They're not bad seats, though, especially for the price. Partitioned areas and elevators aid visitors with disabilities, and the main concourse is wider than normal at 30 feet, so you can easily get to your seat.

SCALPING

Scalpers get little business, because anyone who has tickets usually holds on to them. Buyers get lucky—people with extra tickets often will gladly sell them at only face value or close to it.

HOT TIPS FOR VISITING FANS

PARKING

Special roads and exit ramps were built to make getting here as easy as following a sign. Traffic is re-routed on game days to get people in and out as quickly as possible. Still, make sure you arrive early. The parking lot can accommodate 8,000 cars at $4 each, among the lowest prices in the league. There's an overflow lot for 1,500 more cars, but it's seldom needed.

MEDIA

Radio: WBT (1110 AM).
TV: WJZY (Channel 46), WFUT (Channel 55), SportSouth Cable.

CUISINE

The Crown Club is a 900-seat restaurant with 12 large television monitors. Fourteen permanent concessions stands and 10 specialty carts offer food ranging from Carolina barbecue and baked chicken to pizza and baked potatoes. Of course, you can get things like popcorn,

candy, and peanuts. The NBA recently singled out the coliseum for having the widest variety of concessions at the lowest prices. After the game, stop across the street at Jack and Jills (704-423-0001) to join the local fans for a beer and some post-game analysis. You'll have to drive to any other choice of post-game activities, but not far: The arena is only 10 minutes from Executive Park, which has clubs and restaurants, and is about 20 minutes from downtown.

LODGING NEAR THE ARENA

Embassy Suites
480 S. Tryon St.
Charlotte, NC 28217
(704) 527-8400/(800)EMBASSY
Less than a mile from the arena.

Hyatt
5501 Carnegie Blvd.
Charlotte, NC 28209
(704) 554-1234/(800) 233-1234
10 miles from the arena.

ARENA STATS

Location: 100 Paul Buck Blvd., Charlotte, NC 28266
Opened: Aug. 11, 1988
Capacity: 24,042
Services for fans with disabilities: Seating available around the perimeter of the upper concourse behind sections 103, 106, 108, 110, 112, 115, 118, 121, 124, 126, 128, 130, 133, and 136, and access to the floor level from rear entrance.

ARENA FIRSTS

Regular-season game: Nov. 4, 1988, 133–93 loss to the Cleveland Cavaliers.
Overtime game: April 1, 1989, 124–121 loss to the Portland Trail Blazers.
Playoff game: May 3, 1993, 119–89 over the Boston Celtics.

TEAM NOTEBOOK

Franchise history: Charlotte Hornets, 1988–present.
Rookie of the Year: Larry Johnson, 1991.

TICKET INFORMATION

Address: 100 Hive Dr., Charlotte, NC, 28217
Phone: (704) 357-0489 or TicketMaster at (704) 522-6500.
Hours: Mon.–Fri. 10-5.

GETTING TO CHARLOTTE COLISEUM

Public transportation: The coliseum can't be reached by public transportation.
By car: From I-77, take the Tyvola Road exit and follow signs to the coliseum. From I-85 get off on Billy Graham Parkway, take the Tyvola Road exit, and follow signs to the coliseum.

ARENA STATS

Location: 1901 W. Madison St., Chicago, IL 60612
Opened: August 18, 1994
Capacity: 21,711
Services for fans with disabilities: Seating available in four 100-level sections, five 200-level sections, and 12 300-level sections.

ARENA FIRSTS

Regular-season game: Nov. 4, 1994, 89–83 over the Charlotte Hornets.
Overtime game: Nov. 5, 1994, 99–100 loss to the Washington Bullets.
Playoff game: Apr. 28, 1995, 108–100 over the Charlotte Hornets.
NBA Finals game: June 5, 1995, 107–90 over the Seattle SuperSonics.

TEAM NOTEBOOK

Franchise history: Chicago Bulls, 1966–present.
Division titles: 1974–75, 1990–91, 1991–92, 1992–93, 1995-96.
Conference titles: 1990–91, 1991–92, 1992–93, 1995–96.
NBA championships: 1990–91, 1991–92, 1992–93, 1995–96.
Most Valuable Player: Michael Jordan, 1987–88, 1990–91, 1991–92, 1995–96.
Rookie of the Year: Michael Jordan, 1984–85.
Basketball Hall of Fame: Nate Thurmond, 1984.
Retired number: 4, Jerry Sloan; 10, Bob Love; 23, Michael Jordan.

The United Center, which opened for the 1994–95 NBA season, is across the street from the site of Chicago Stadium on the city's West Side, but until the 1995–96 season, it felt light-years away in history.

The old stadium had character, from the standing-room-only upper balcony to the hard seats, narrow aisles, and down-home charm. The scoreboard was old and outdated, and the players, emerging from the small locker rooms, had to duck to get upstairs to the floor. But the stadium had mystique, the kind of atmosphere that comes from moments such as June 14, 1992, when Michael Jordan—standing on the press table with tears in his eyes, a cigar in his mouth, and a bottle of champagne gripped in one hand—hoisted the Bulls' second championship trophy high to the cheering throng. Chicago Stadium's noise was incredible, and when the lights were turned down for the introduction of the Bulls, it was simply electrifying.

The world's greatest basketball player retired in 1993, before United Center opened, vowing that he loved the old stadium too much to play across the street. The Bulls retired his number (23), erected a bronze statue of him in the lobby of their new arena, and carried on without him. But on March 18, 1995, Michael Jordan decided he missed basketball and rejoined the Bulls in their opulent new arena. Apparently the high-tech replay scoreboard and 21,711 plush, theater-style seats haven't cramped His Airness's style too much—he got the Bulls to the 1994–95 conference semifinals and was the league's 1995–96 MVP en route to the Bulls' fourth NBA championship in six years.

The football-bowl shape of the arena provides good sight lines even in the farthest seats, and with the addition of "illustrated man" Dennis Rodman to their team, Chicago fans have plenty to look at—and cheer about. The triumvirate of Rodman, Jordan, and Scottie Pippen has been called the best combination in the game, and at the moment, nobody's arguing. In just two years the United Center has become the site of sports history and has guaranteed a place for itself in Chicago's heart.

HOT TIPS FOR VISITING FANS

PARKING
When the Bulls played at Chicago Stadium, parking attendants would start flagging you down 6 blocks from the building, trying to get you to park in their lot. The streets were narrow and bumpy, and that slowed traffic. The streets have now been widened, and the United Center has taken over most of the parking. These new lots have 25 entry lanes and are well lighted, clearly marked, fenced, and patrolled, so drive right past the lots on Madison. Get to the game early to make sure you get in (club-seat and luxury-box patrons have a guaranteed parking spot included in their ticket price). Street parking is available, but it's risky.

MEDIA
Radio: WMAQ (670 AM—English), WIND (560 AM—Spanish).
TV: WGN (Channel 9), SportsChannel (cable). Former Bulls coach Johnny "Red" Kerr, the television analyst, is a show unto himself. He works both WGN and SportsChannel.

CUISINE
The arena has 46 permanent concessions stands with computerized ordering in each line on the club levels. Themed concessions such as the West Side Deli, Mexican Fiesta, Windy City Grill, and Italian Piazza offer a broad range of items that reflect the city's diverse population. Local favorite Old Style leads the list of 25 beers available to chase down the food.

You can buy Bulls and other NBA merchandise at 22 places. The members-only, 285-seat Chicago Stadium Club (a full-service restaurant) and a 100-seat lounge, as well as private function rooms, are also available. Michael Jordan's Restaurant (312-644-3865) downtown is the obvious place to go. Michael is there most nights he's in town, and if you call the restaurant, you'll get his voice on the answering machine telling you his eatery is "just a free throw away from the Loop." Planet Hollywood (312-266-7827), the Hard Rock Cafe (312-943-2252), and Ed Debevic's (312-664-1707) are all 15 to 30 minutes away.

LODGING NEAR THE ARENA

Westin Hotel
909 N. Michigan Ave.
Chicago, IL 60611
(312) 943-7200/(800) 228-3000
5½ miles from the arena.

The Drake
140 E. Walton St.
Chicago, IL 60611
(312) 787-2200
3½ miles from the arena.

In the Hot Seats at the United Center

This place caters to big spenders, with three levels of private luxury suites (216 in all), and each level is serviced by a private concourse and elevators. The lower-level suites are only 19 rows (18 yards) from the floor. The Club Level suites are 27 rows up (32 yards). The Penthouse suites are at the top, above the 300-level seating. In addition to the luxury suites are 3,000 club seats on a private level. All 100- and 200-level seats are sold out to season ticketholders.

The 300-level seats will be the only seats available. If you sit in the high-up-behind-the-basket seats, you'll be looking through the backboard, but you'll get used to it. Just get in the building—the experience is worth it. Unlike at old Chicago Stadium, there are no standing-room tickets.

SCALPING

At Chicago Stadium, scalpers would stop cars a mile away, along Madison Street, to offer tickets; that probably won't change. Twice face value has been about the normal markup.

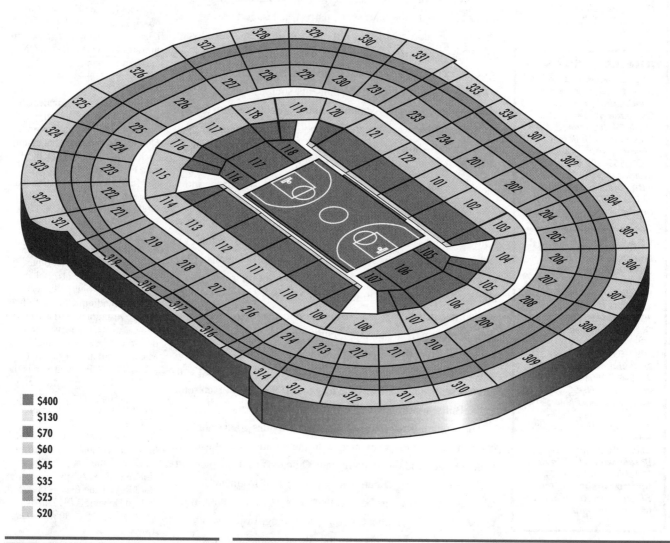

- ■ $400
- ▫ $130
- ■ $70
- ▨ $60
- ▨ $45
- ▨ $35
- ▨ $25
- ▨ $20

HOME-COURT ADVANTAGE

In recent seasons, the Bulls have had one of the best home records in the league. They may have lost something in atmosphere by leaving Chicago Stadium, but fans seem to love their new home, especially since Michael Jordan returned to play there.

GETTING TO THE UNITED CENTER

Public transportation: From downtown, take the No. 20 Madison bus westbound or the No. 19 Stadium Express, which runs to the stadium every 10 minutes from 90 minutes before the game until 30 minutes after. For more information, call the CTA at (312) 836-7000.

By car: From O'Hare International Airport, take I-90/94 East (Kennedy Expressway) to the Madison Street exit. Turn right on Madison (heading west). The United Center is on the left side.

TICKET INFORMATION

Address: 1901 W. Madison St., Chicago, IL 60612
Phone: (312) 455-4000 or TicketMaster at

(312) 559-1212.
Hours: Mon.–Fri. 12–6.
Prices: $400: courtside floor; $130: main floor; $70: 100 level, rows 1–11 sections

105–107 and 116–118 rows A–M; $60: 100 level, rows 12–19; $45: 200 level; $35: 300 level, rows 1–7; $25: 300 level, rows 8–12; $20: 300 level, rows 13–17.

CLEVELAND CAVALIERS

Gund Arena

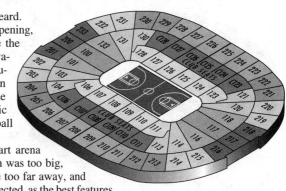

ARENA STATS

Location: One Center Court, Cleveland, OH 44115
Opened: Oct. 17, 1994
Capacity: 20,562
Services for fans with disabilities: 1% of seating in all price classes is set aside. Headsets for people with hearing impairments are also available.

ARENA FIRSTS

Regular-season game: Nov. 8, 1994, 100–98 loss to Houston Rockets.
First points scored: Bobby Phills, Houston Rockets.
Overtime game: Nov. 15, 1994, 89–86 over Charlotte Hornets.
Playoff game: May 4, 1995, 93–80 loss to the New York Knicks.

TEAM NOTEBOOK

Franchise history: Cleveland Cavaliers, 1970–present.
Division title: 1975–76.
Basketball Hall of Fame: Nate Thurmond, 1984; Lenny Wilkins, 1988.
Retired numbers: 7, Bingo Smith; 22, Larry Nance; 34, Austin Carr; 42, Nate Thurmond.

TICKET INFORMATION

Address: One Center Court, Cleveland, OH 44115
Phone: (216) 420-2200 or TicketMaster at (216) 241-5555.
Hours: Mon.–Sat. 10–6.

Forget all the Cleveland jokes you've heard. Downtown Cleveland is where it's happening, especially if you're a sports fan. While the city gets a bad rap for not being pretty, the Cavaliers' new home is a beautiful building in a beautiful part of town. Richfield Coliseum was out in the middle of nowhere, but Gund Arena is in the heart of downtown, three blocks from Public Square, in the same complex as the new baseball stadium, Jacobs Field.

Gund Arena is a brand-new, state-of-the-art arena built with the fan in mind. Richfield Coliseum was too big, with wasted space; the inexpensive seats were too far away, and the sight lines weren't good. That has been corrected, as the best features of all the new arenas were adopted when this facility was constructed.

The Cleveland Lumberjacks hockey team shares the building with the Cavaliers, but it was built for basketball. Besides containing the Cavaliers' practice facility, the arena has a sports bar with street-level access and a 40-by-100-foot bay window through which you can view downtown Cleveland and the Flats.

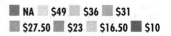

HOT TIPS FOR VISITING FANS

PARKING
Two on-site garages with 3,300 spaces are connected to the arena by covered walkways. Because Cleveland gets cold in the winter, it's worth paying $6 for these spaces. Another 7,000 parking spaces are within a 10-minute walk. Lots near the arena range from $3 to $8 for evening.

MEDIA
Radio: WWWE (1100 AM).
TV: WUAB (Channel 43) and SportsChannel Ohio (cable). At 6-11, former Cavs player Jim Chones might be the tallest color man in the league. He's fresh, funny, and knowledgeable. Play-by-play man Joe Tait is a legend. He has been the voice of the Cavaliers for a quarter of a century. He broadcast his 2,000th game on March 14, 1996.

CUISINE
Sammy's at the Arena (216-420-2900) might be one of the best restaurants in town, considering both ambience and location. The 350-seat full-service restaurant, operated by well-known local restaurateurs Denise Fugo and Ralph DiOrio, has a wide variety of meals priced from $5 to $25. Children can have pizza and cookies, while their parents can enjoy a juicy burger and a beer.

Low-cal meals are also available. After the game, Gordon's Sports Bar is at street level at the arena, or head out into Cleveland. John Q's Public Bar and Grill (216-861-0900), Sweetwater's Cafe Sausalito (216-696-CAFE), and Shooter's Waterfront Cafe (216-861-6900) are popular.

LODGING NEAR THE ARENA
Stouffer Renaissance Hotel
24 Public Sq.
Cleveland, OH 44113
(216) 696-5600/(800) 468-3571
2 miles from the arena.

Ritz-Carlton
1515 W. Third St.
Cleveland, OH 44113
(216) 623-1300/(800) 241-3333
Next to the arena.

GETTING TO GUND ARENA
Public transportation: RTA provides service to Tower City Rapid Station, which has an enclosed walkway to the arena. Park and Ride services are available. Call (216) 566-5100, ext. 4312, for more information.
By car: From the airport, take I-71 north to the Ontario Street exit (or East Ninth Street) and proceed north on Ontario. Follow signs to Gund Arena, on the corner of Ontario and Huron streets, just past Jacobs Field.

HOME-COURT ADVANTAGE
Historically in the NBA, teams play well in brand-new buildings. The Cavaliers also have the great advantage of practicing in the same building where they play. The Cavs have had one of the best home records in the league since 1991.

IN THE HOT SEATS AT GUND ARENA
If close is what you like, this is the building for you, because 60% of the seats are in the lower concourse. The seats are wider and plusher than in most places, and the luxury suites are closer to the floor than in any other arena (15 and 30 rows up).

GOOD SEATS
Try to sit opposite the benches and the scorer's table to get a view of the players and the interplay that goes on with the coaches. Corner seats are good in most basketball arenas, something that's especially true here because you're so close to the action.

BAD SEATS
The building has no bad seats. All the sight lines were done by computer to guarantee the best possible view.

■ NA ▨ $49 ▨ $36 ■ $31
■ $27.50 ▨ $23 ▨ $16.50 ■ $10

DALLAS MAVERICKS

Reunion Arena

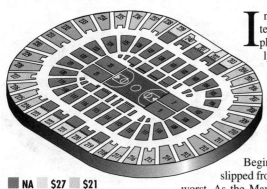

■ NA ■ $27 ■ $21
■ $15 ■ $9

I n the 1980s the Mavericks were the hottest sports team in Dallas. They were successful, making the playoffs each year from 1984 to 1988, and immensely popular. As the Cowboys slid into the NFL's cellar, Mavericks games at Reunion Arena became social events at which the big names in Dallas came to see and be seen. Players around the league liked the place, too, for its glamorous, exciting atmosphere and the fast pace of those Maverick teams.

But, as they say, all good things come to an end. Beginning with the 1990–91 season the franchise slipped from being among the NBA's best to being among its worst. As the Mavs declined, the Super Bowl–champion Cowboys supplanted them as the kings of Dallas. Many fans, frustrated with the team's poor play, began to stay home, and those who came had little patience. Boos cascaded down from the stands—boos more often directed at the Mavs than the visitors. There remains, perhaps surprisingly, a fairly large reservoir of goodwill about the Mavs, feelings bolstered by changes in management and coaching, plus the presence of such promising young players as Jamal Mashburn and Jim Jackson.

To top off the growing disappointment, the 1995–96 season started with the loss of leading scorer Jamal Mashburn to injury, and ended with the sale of the team. There is hope, however: After the Chicago Bulls won the 1995–96 NBA championship, their highly respected assistant coach, Jim Cleamons, became the Mavericks head coach.

HOME-COURT ADVANTAGE

Given the team's poor play, fans are often less than enthusiastic during games, but they can get loud if the game is close or the team is doing well. And while the Mavs have become synonymous with basketball futility, they also have a reputation for staging some of the most imaginative halftime shows in the NBA.

IN THE HOT SEATS AT REUNION ARENA

While the Mavericks' poor play is a source of frustration for fans, it's a boon for those seeking tickets. Excellent seats are available for virtually every game.

GOOD SEATS

Sight lines from the upper deck are good. Best buys are in upper-deck sections 235–238, 224–227, 215–218, and 204–207. Those corner seats cost only $21 and may be one of the league's best bargains.

BAD SEATS

If you really want to save money, $9 seats are available at the back of sections 228–234 and 208–214 behind the baskets.

SCALPING

A local ordinance prohibits ticket scalping on city-owned property, which includes Reunion Arena. The Mavericks and the Dallas police make an effort to enforce this law by occasionally using undercover officers to seek out scalpers.

HOT TIPS FOR VISITING FANS

PARKING
The arena is surrounded by approximately 6,000 spaces, which cost $6. Lot G costs $5. There is no on-street parking in the area, but additional parking garages are available downtown and at the nearby Hyatt Regency. Access into and out of the arena's lots is fairly easy and quick.

MEDIA
Radio: KLIF (570 AM).
TV: KDFI (Channel 27) and PrimeSports cable. The Mavs' television announcer is Jim Durham, who called the Chicago Bulls games for 23 years (1973-91). Veteran Dallas broadcaster Ted Davis is in his eighth season as radio announcer.

CUISINE
Fans can sample a variety of grilled selections, or burger and hot-dog baskets. Corn dogs, chicken fingers, and Pizza Hut pizza are also available. Imported bottled beers are also sold. The Hyatt Regency (214-651-1234) is across the street from the arena and has two popular restaurants. Fausto's Oven (712-651-7144), a bistro-style restaurant, serves such Italian dishes as pesto pizza and the Lonestar Legend, a pizza with jalapeño peppers, smoked chicken, and ham. Café Esplanade (214-953-3115) is in the hotel's atrium and features southwestern cuisine.

LODGING NEAR THE ARENA
Hyatt Regency Dallas
300 Reunion Blvd.
Dallas, TX 75207
(214) 651-1234/(800) 233-1234
Across the street from the arena.

Marriott Courtyard Market Center
2150 Market Center Blvd.
Dallas, TX 75207
(214) 653-1166/(800) 228-9290
Less than 1 mile from the arena.

ARENA STATS
Location: 777 Sports St., Dallas, TX 75207
Opened: April 28, 1980
Capacity: 17,502
Services for fans with disabilities: Reserved wheelchair seating available behind sections 101, 108, 116, and 122.

ARENA FIRSTS
Regular-season game: Oct. 11, 1980, 103–92 over San Antonio.
Points scored: Abdul Jeelani, Mavericks.
Overtime game: Nov. 28, 1980, 119–117 loss to Denver.
Playoff game: April 17, 1984, 88–86 over Seattle.

TEAM NOTEBOOK
Franchise history: Dallas Mavericks, 1980–present.
Division title: 1986–87.
Retired number: 15, Brad Davis.

TICKET INFORMATION
Address: 777 Sports St., Dallas, TX 75207
Phone: (214) 939-2800 or Dillard's at (800) 654-9545.
Hours: Mon.–Fri. 10–5.

GETTING TO REUNION ARENA
Public transportation: The No. 30 Marsalis bus goes to the arena. Call (214) 979-2712 for more information.
By car: From downtown, take I-35 east north to I-635 west. Exit I-635 at MacArthur Boulevard. Go north on MacArthur to Valley Ranch Parkway and turn right. Take the first left onto Cowboys Parkway; the arena will be ½ mile up on your left.

McNichols Arena

ARENA STATS

Location: 1635 Clay St., Denver, CO 80204
Opened: Aug. 22, 1975
Capacity: 17,171
Services for fans with disabilities: Seating available in 13 sections on the loge level.

ARENA FIRSTS

Regular-season game: Oct. 25, 1975, 118–101 over the Spirits of St. Louis.
Overtime game: Dec. 16, 1977, 117–112 loss to the Washington Bullets.
Playoff game: April 20, 1977, 101–100 loss to the Portland Trail Blazers.

TEAM NOTEBOOK

Franchise history: Denver Nuggets, 1967–76 (ABA); Denver Nuggets, 1976–present (NBA).
Division titles: 1976–77, 1977–78, 1984–85, 1987–88.
Retired numbers: 2, Alex English; 33, David Thompson; 40, Byron Beck; 44, Dan Issel.

Although Denver has long been associated with recreation and sporting activities, Rocky Mountain fans support their resident pro teams with as much fervor as they attack the ski slopes. The Broncos have sold out for many years, and since their debut in 1993, the Rockies have set records for drawing some of the largest crowds in baseball history. At that time the Nuggets became a hot item as well, selling out two-thirds of their home games.

McNichols Arena, an oval building on the west side of the South Platte River, opened for basketball in 1975, when the Nuggets were in the ABA. In 1987 McNichols underwent a $14 million renovation that included several improvements, such as installation of a new DiamondVision scoreboard, an improved audio system, and closed-circuit television monitors.

The next step for the Nuggets is a scheduled move to the $132 million Pepsi Center complex, an ultramodern 620,000-square-foot, five-acre arena that seats 19,100 for basketball. Expected to open in 1998, Pepsi Center will offer all of the amenities that have become typical of flashy NBA arenas—gigantic video scoreboard at center court; special-effects sound and lighting systems; and, of course, a 300-seat full-service restaurant.

HOT TIPS FOR VISITING FANS

PARKING
There are 4,700 parking spaces at McNichols and 5,300 at Mile High Stadium. Prices are about $5. There is some on-street parking in the area.

MEDIA
Radio: KFFN (950 AM). Jerry Schemmel is the Nuggets' play-by-play man for radio and television. When he's on television, Mike Evans takes over on KKFN.
TV: KWGN (Channel 2) features Schemmel on play-by-play and Prime Sports (cable) relies on Drew Goodman and Walter Davis for coverage and commentary.

CUISINE
McNichols has three full-service restaurants and a bar, all of which are open to all ticketholders. The Butcher Block serves a selection of hoagies, grilled chicken, and beef. Wong Gong's mixes a Chinese decor with alternating buffets ($7.95 per person) of Mexican and Italian foods. The Arena Club opens at 5:30 and offers a buffet for $14.95 per person. Underneath the Arena Club is the Fastbreak Lounge, open at halftime and for up to two hours after the game. Players occasionally stop by after the game.
In addition to providing several restaurant choices inside McNichols, the Nuggets also offer some Denver-area foods at their concession stands. Perhaps the most unusual are a number of buffalo-meat items. Other popular offerings include Greek gyros, quarter-pound hot dogs, and a Chicago dog that's topped with peppers, tomatoes, onions, and pickles. Imported beers can be found in section 31.
After the game there's Brooklyn's (303-572-3999), a comfortable bar in a Victorian-style building. Players and Nuggets executives are occasional customers. Wynkoop Brewing Co. is about 10 minutes from McNichols (303-297-2700). This was Colorado's first brew pub, and it is located in a mercantile building that dates from the 19th century. Sample some of the seven homemade beers on tap while enjoying buffalo steak, elk medallions, homemade sausage, or a pheasant quesadilla.

LODGING NEAR THE ARENA

The Westin Hotel Tabor Center
1672 Laurence St.
Denver, CO 80202
(303) 572-9100/(800) 228-3000
2 miles from the arena.

Hyatt Regency
1750 Walton St.
Denver, CO 80202
(303) 295-1234/(800) 233-1234
3½ miles from the arena.

THE NUGGETS AT McNICHOLS ARENA

Dec. 13, 1983: Denver and Detroit battle in a triple overtime game that ends 186–184 Pistons. It's the highest-scoring game in NBA history. Kiki Vandeweghe scores 51, Alex English 47.

May 8, 1986: Despite English's team playoff record of 50 points, the Nuggets fall to Houston, 126–122, losing the Western Conference semifinals four games to two.

May 19, 1994: Mutombo and Bryant Stith each make two free throws in the last 30 seconds to give the Nuggets a 94–91 victory over the Jazz, forcing a seventh game, in their playoff series.

April 14, 1996: Dale Ellis becomes the 13th active NBA player to score 16,000 career points.

In the Hot Seats at McNichols Arena

The Nuggets capped season-ticket sales at 13,000, so at least 4,000 seats are available for single-game purchases. Single-game tickets go on sale in early October. All are balcony seats; the rest of the arena is sold out. Any unsold tickets, mostly for seats in the upper deck, are available on game nights, though these are becoming more scarce as the Nuggets' following increases. Tickets for games against the better teams will be very difficult to find.

GOOD SEATS

Even though it is somewhat older than many NBA facilities, McNichols still offers plenty of good seats. For $25 you can sit in the center balcony area of the upper deck—sections 1, 3, 5, 29, 31, 33, 35, 59, 61, and 63—where the view is very good. Center-court seats in the lower deck are sold to season ticketholders. If you're looking for a bargain, spend $14.50 for seats in the lower two-thirds of upper-deck sections 10, 12, 14, 16, 17, 19, 44, 46, 47, 48, 51, and 53.

BAD SEATS

The top rows of seats behind the baskets—sections 10, 12, 14, 15, 16, 19, 21, 42, 44, 46-48, 51, and 53—are a long way from center court. However, with the growing popularity of the Nuggets and the increased difficulty of getting good tickets, seats here may be all that's available for selected games.

SCALPING

Ticket scalping is illegal in Denver. Nonetheless, scalpers can easily be found, especially for big games, along the way to McNichols from the Mile High Stadium and arena parking areas.

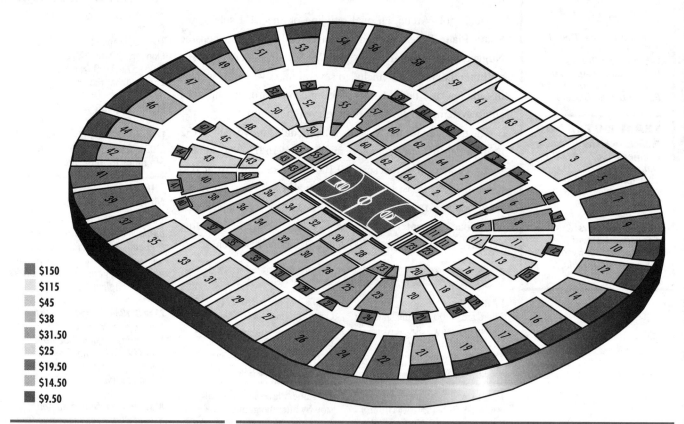

- ■ $150
- ▢ $115
- ▨ $45
- ▨ $38
- ▨ $31.50
- ▢ $25
- ■ $19.50
- ▨ $14.50
- ■ $9.50

HOME-COURT ADVANTAGE

Denver's altitude—5,280 feet above sea level—is an advantage the Nuggets seek to exploit. The Nuggets play an uptempo, full-court style at McNichols, particularly in the beginning of each game. The front office also gets into the act, rubbing in the atmospheric advantage by announcing before the opening tipoff, "Welcome to McNichols Arena, 5,280 feet above sea level," and playing upbeat music to accompany the Nuggets' fast-paced basketball.

GETTING TO MCNICHOLS ARENA

Public transportation: Catch the No. 31 Champa bus on 16th Street and go to 17th Street and Federal. Walk east 2 blocks to the arena. Call (303) 299-6000 for more information.

By car: From the east, take Colfax Avenue west to Bryant Street. The arena will be on the right.

From the west, take Colfax east to Bryant. The arena will be on the left.
From the north, take U.S. 87 south to the 17th Street exit. The arena will be on the left.
From the south, take U.S. 87 north to the 17th Street exit. The arena will be on the left.

TICKET INFORMATION

Address: 1635 Clay St., Denver, CO 80204
Phone: (303) 893-DUNK or TicketMaster at (303) 290-TIXS.

Hours: Mon.–Fri. 8:30–5:30.
Prices: $150: courtside; $115: end court-side; $45: prime loge; $38: center loge; $31.50: corner loge, end risers; $25: end loge, center balcony; $19.50: corner balcony; $14.50: lower end balcony; $9.50: upper end balcony.

The Palace of Auburn Hills

ARENA STATS

Location: 2 Championship Dr., Auburn Hills, MI 48326
Opened: Aug. 13, 1988
Capacity: 21,454
Services for fans with disabilities: Several dozen wheelchair-accessible seats are available. Call (810) 377-0154 for more information.

ARENA FIRSTS

Regular-season game: Nov. 5, 1988, 94–85 over the Charlotte Hornets.
Overtime game: Nov. 5, 1988, 94–85 over the Charlotte Hornets.
Playoff game: April 28, 1989, 101–91 over the Boston Celtics.
NBA Finals game: June 6, 1989, 109–97 over the Los Angeles Lakers.

TEAM NOTEBOOK

Franchise history: Fort Wayne Pistons, 1948–49 (BAA); Fort Wayne Pistons, 1949–57 (NBA); Detroit Pistons, 1957–present.
Division titles: 1954–55, 1955–56, 1987–88, 1988–89, 1989–90.
Conference titles: 1954–55, 1955–56, 1987–88, 1988–89, 1989–90.
NBA championships: 1988–89, 1989–90.
Basketball Hall of Fame: Dave DeBusschere, 1982; Dave Bing, 1989.
Rookies of the Year: Don Meineke, 1952–53; Dave Bing, 1966–67; Grant Hill, 1994–95 (tie).
Retired numbers: 11, Isiah Thomas; 15, Vinnie Johnson; 16, Bob Lanier; 21, Dave Bing; 40, Bill Laimbeer.

As one arrives at the Palace, three things immediately become apparent: First, in an effort to make sure all fans are thinking about the home team, the Pistons broadcast the pregame show over loudspeakers in the parking lot. Second, the arena has a distinctive exterior decoration—adorned with intricately arranged glazed-brick tiles that have a yellow/orange hue. Third, once you enter the building, television monitors bombard you with highlights of recent games, information on upcoming opponents, and updates on home-team players.

As striking as these things are, they don't make up for a bad team. The Detroit Pistons were recently at the top of the NBA world, with consecutive championships in 1989 and 1990. The Palace was sold out for 245 consecutive games until December 14, 1993. But as the team's play deteriorated, attendance dropped to an average of just over 17,500 per game—still a respectable crowd in the NBA.

Fans tend to be more subdued than they used to be, especially since the loss of their most visible self-appointed cheerleaders. Joe Diroff, a retired schoolteacher nicknamed "the Brow" because of his large, bushy eyebrows, used to run around the lower deck, hazing the opposing team and leading cheers. He has since suffered a stroke. His counterpart in the Palace's upper reaches was "Dancing Ernie," who distracted opponents with his modified striptease act. Ernie's gone, too. Without the Brow, Dancing Ernie, or Dennis Rodman, the Pistons have definitely lost their own eccentric version of the "triangle offense," but the presence of Grant Hill—basketball's answer to Ken Griffey, Jr.—has the Pistons hoping that the Palace will rock again soon.

HOT TIPS FOR VISITING FANS

PARKING
No on-street parking nearby, so you will need to park in the Palace's lot, which has space for 8,200 cars. The price is $6. The Palace sits astride two major roads, I-75 and Route 24. Perhaps because of its location, fans report that traffic moves fairly smoothly before and after the game.

MEDIA
Radio: Pistons Network WWJ (950 AM). Color analyst Vinnie Johnson, a former Pistons guard, joins George Blaha or Mark Champion.
TV: WKBD (Channel 50) and PRO-AM Sports (PASS) cable. George Blaha, who has been broadcasting Pistons' games for more than 20 years, is known for such phrases as "Isiah with the high glasser, and it goes!" He is joined by color commentator Kelly Tripucka, a former Pistons forward.

CUISINE
Each of the arena's four corners has its own unique concessions: Mexican Fiesta (nachos, fajitas, margaritas), and Mexican beer on tap); Little Italy (meatball subs, wines, Italian sausages); delicatessen (made-to-order subs, soups in sourdough-bread bowls, gourmet popcorn); and the Grill (sausages, chicken, Philly cheese steaks).

Draft beers, including Labatt's, Molson, Stroh's and Frankenmuth Pilsner, a local microbeer, are sold throughout the concourse. A large number of bottled brews, such as Bass, Amstel Light, Karlsberg, and Old Detroit, a microbeer, are also available.

If you want a pre-game meal, the arena has the Palace Club, which is a restaurant before the game and more of a bar afterward. Mountain Jacks (810-340-0585), a five-minute drive from the Palace, specializes in steak, prime ribs and seafood. Pistons and Detroit Lions players are occasionally customers after the game. Patrick's (810-852-3410) is about 10 minutes from the Palace and features a popular chicken-and-scallop combo, steak and pan-fried chicken.

LODGING NEAR THE ARENA

Troy Marriott Detroit
200 Big Beaver
Troy, MI 48084
(810) 680-9797/(800) 777-4096
8 miles from the arena.

Auburn Hills Hilton Suites
2300 Featherstone Rd.
Auburn Hills, MI 48326
(810) 334-2222/(800) HILTONS
3 miles from the arena.

THE PISTONS AT THE PALACE

June 8, 1989: Detroit beats the Los Angeles Lakers 108–105 in Game 2 of the NBA Finals. They end up sweeping the series, four games to none, to win the championship.

June 3, 1990: The Pistons beat the Chicago Bulls 93–74 in Game 7 of the Eastern Conference finals to advance to their second NBA Finals.

March 4, 1992: Dennis Rodman pulls down 34 rebounds against the Indiana Pacers.

In the Hot Seats at The Palace of Auburn Hills

With an average attendance of just over 17,500, there are usually 3,000 tickets available per game, and good seats are usually available. Season tickets go on sale in July; single-game tickets go on sale in the fall.

GOOD SEATS

The Palace has a reputation for being an excellent place in which to watch basketball. Not only are the seat locations and sight lines very good, but the plush, theater-style seats are also quite comfortable. It is difficult to find a bad seat, even in the top rows of sections 204-209 and 227-222. Seats there go for $14. Check out the $31 seats in sections 201–202, 214–217, and 229–230, which offer good center-court sight lines from the upper deck; the seats directly above are $26. Another worthwhile buy is an $20 seat in sections 203–205, 211–213, 218–220, or 226–228.

SCALPING

Illegal, but it still goes on. However, few scalpers are outside the Palace because of its relatively isolated location and the recent fortunes of the club.

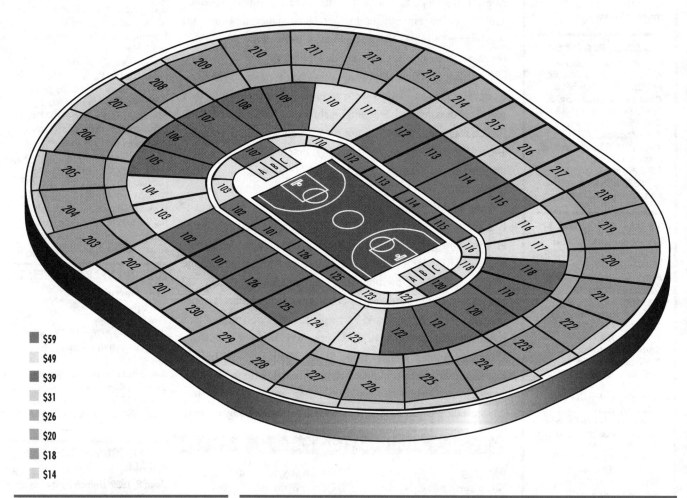

- $59
- $49
- $39
- $31
- $26
- $20
- $18
- $14

HOME-COURT ADVANTAGE

In an effort to pump up their fans, the Pistons succumbed to the NBA formula for frenzy: a mascot. Their knight in shining armor is Sir Slam-A-Lot, whose repertoire includes trampoline tricks and tossing balls into the crowd. Sir Slam will be assisted by another mascot whose identity will be determined in a fan contest; he (or she) is scheduled to debut in 1997.

GETTING TO THE PALACE OF AUBURN HILLS

Public transportation: You can't reach the Palace by public transportation.
By car: From the airport, head north on Merriman Road to I-94 east, then to south-field freeway north. Proceed north to I-696 east. Take I-696 to I-75 north; take exit 81 (Lapeer Road). Turn right (north). The Palace is on the immediate left.

TICKET INFORMATION
Address: 2 Championship Dr., Auburn Hills, MI 48326
Phone: (810) 377-0100 or TicketMaster at (810) 645-6666
Hours: Mon.–Fri. 10–6, Sat. 10–4, Sun. 10 a.m.–30 minutes after the game.
Prices: $59, 49, $39, $31, $26, $20, $18, $14.

San Jose Arena

ARENA STATS

Oakland Coliseum Arena
Location: *7000 Coliseum Way, Oakland, CA 94621*
Opened: *Nov. 9, 1966*
Capacity: *19,200*
Services for fans with disabilities: *The renovation will offer many services. Call for details.*

San Jose Arena Location: *525 W. Santa Clara St., San Jose, CA 95113*
Opened: *Sept. 8, 1993*
Capacity: *17,910*
Services for fans with disabilities: *Seating is available in several sections on the 200 level, and a few on the 100 level.*

ARENA FIRSTS

Regular-season game at Oakland Coliseum Arena: *Nov. 29, 1966, 108–101 over the Chicago Bulls.*
Overtime game: *Dec. 10, 1966, 123–120 over the Cincinnati Royals.*
Playoff game: *March 21, 1967, 124–108 over the Los Angeles Lakers.*
NBA Finals game: *May 20, 1975, 92–91 over the Washington Bullets.*

TEAM NOTEBOOK

Franchise history: *Philadelphia Warriors, 1946–49 (BAA); Philadelphia Warriors, 1949–62 (NBA); San Francisco Warriors, 1962–71; Golden State Warriors, 1971–present.*
Division titles: *1946–47, 1950–51, 1955–56, 1963–64, 1966–67, 1974–75, 1975–76.*
Conference titles: *1946–47, 1947–48, 1955–56, 1963–64, 1966–67, 1974–75.*
NBA championships: *1946–47, 1955–56, 1974–75.*
Basketball Hall of Fame: *Wilt Chamberlain, 1978; Rick Barry, 1986.*
Retired numbers: *14, Tom Meschery; 16, Al Attles; 24, Rick Barry; 42, Nate Thurmond.*

Perhaps unbeknownst to many NBA fans, the Golden State Warriors are a hot item in the Bay Area. All their games since 1989 have been sellouts. While such popularity is often reserved for a championship-caliber team, the Warriors have not won a title since 1975, making them a local phenomenon and their ticket sales all the more noteworthy.

With a $100 million renovation and an upgrade from 15,000 to more than 19,000 seats, the enthusiasm inside a Warriors game may finally match the frenzy at the ticket window. In the old arena—one of the oldest and smallest in the NBA—the crowd noise was amplified by the size and acoustics of the building, but far too often the cheering stopped and the squeak of sneakers echoed through the house. An extra 5,000 fans should add more vitality, but the fast-paced team will have to start winning more consistently to keep the crowd cheering.

The arena—located in the same complex that contains the Oakland/Alameda County Coliseum, home of the Raiders and the A's—opened in 1966 and was known for its no-frills, traditional atmosphere. The renovated arena will offer more of the amenities of the newer NBA arenas, including luxury suites, a retail store, and a sports bar. Bay Area sports fans, accustomed to a more low-key approach, may squawk about the bells and whistles, but they'll have had a year to get used to it: During the renovation (1996–97 season), the Warriors will play their home games at the modern San Jose Arena, home of the NHL's Sharks.

HOT TIPS FOR VISITING FANS

PARKING

San Jose Arena has 1,800 spaces in two lots. Private and city lots within half a mile have 7,000 more. Free parking is also available west of the railroad tracks on the west side of the arena. Beware of parking in residential neighborhoods; they're safe, but you need permits for many of them.

MEDIA

Radio: KNBR (680 AM—English), KIQI (1010 AM—Spanish). **TV:** KPIX, (Channel 5); KICU, (Channel 36); and SportsChannel (cable). Greg Papa, the play-by-play "voice of the Warriors," gets so involved in the game that he lost his voice twice during the frustrating 1995-96 season.

CUISINE

The food at San Jose Arena isn't cheap, as Sharks' fans will attest, but it's a notch above what you get in most stadiums. Along with the usual arena food, there are stands for Roundtable Pizza, Mexico Lindo, and Sausage Haus. Those lucky enough to be watching from a suite can try the Club, which has upscale California cuisine. Quality beers such as Pete's Wicked, local favorite Anchor Steam, and Tide House can be had here, along with imports at the Beers of the World kiosk.

After the game, much of the action is oriented to Sharks' fans, but the red carpet will surely be out for the visiting Warrior faithful. Henry's (408-453-5325), is hidden away under the Highway

87, but lots of Sharks' fans manage to find it after games. San Jose Live (408-294-5483), across First Street from the Hyatt, is perfect if you haven't gotten enough sports for the evening; there are pool tables, dartboards, foosball tables, and even a 20-foot-plus basketball cage along with 10 big-screen TVs, if you're happy to just sit and cheer.

LODGING NEAR THE ARENA

DeAnza Hotel
233 W. Santa Clara St.
San Jose, CA 95113
(408) 286-1000/(800) 843-3700
3 blocks from the arena.

Hilton
300 Almaden Blvd.
San Jose, CA 95110
(408) 287-2100/(800) HILTONS
1 mile from the arena.

THE WARRIORS AT OAKLAND COLISEUM ARENA

March 26, 1974: *Rick Barry scores a career-high 64 points against Portland, leading the Warriors to a 143–120 win.*

May 14, 1975: *The Warriors edge Chicago 83–79 to win the Western Conference final, four games to three. Golden State goes on to win the championship by sweeping Washington in the finals.*

March 30, 1979: *Robert Parish becomes the first Warrior since Nate Thurmond to get 30 points and 30 rebounds in a single game, a 114–98 win over New York.*

Jan. 7, 1984: *The Warriors score a team-record 154 points against San Antonio. Purvis Short sets an NBA high for the season, with 57, in the 154–133 win.*

May 10, 1987: *Eric "Sleepy" Floyd leads the Warriors to a 129–121 victory over the Lakers in Game 4 of the Western Conference semifinals with the year's NBA-playoff high—51 points. The Lakers take the series, four games to one.*

In the Hot Seats at San Jose Arena

In what had become the Warriors' annual rite of autumn, nearly 13,000 tickets were bought by season ticketholders at the start of the season. The remaining 2,000 or so tickets for individual games were snapped up within hours of going on sale. In the renovated, 19,200 seat arena, the rite will remain the same, but the numbers may change slightly to make a few more individual-game tickets available. Although the Warriors often announce on game nights that a limited number of tickets is available, there might not be two seats together; even so, they go fast.

GOOD SEATS

The old arena's small size meant many good seats for basketball, and the new arena promises even better sight lines. San Jose Arena has good views from all sections.

SCALPING

Many scalpers frequent the coliseum, starting about two hours before the game, but they must remain a certain distance from the building. In San Jose, though illegal, they casually work Santa Clara between downtown and the arena.

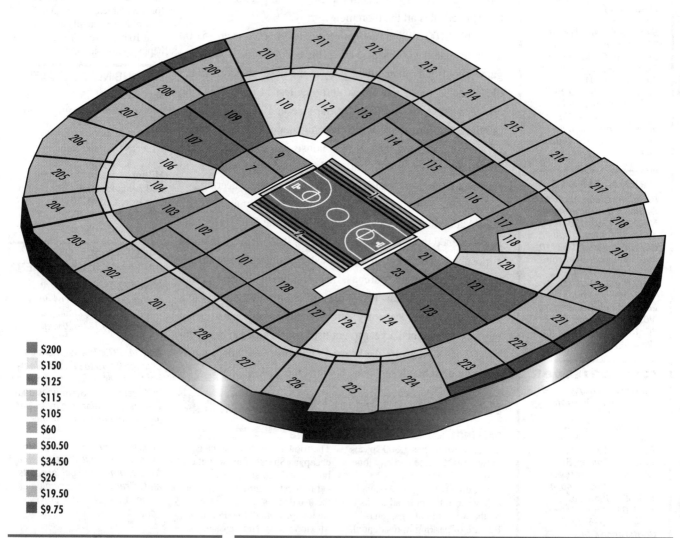

- ■ $200
- □ $150
- ■ $125
- ▨ $115
- ▨ $105
- ▨ $60
- ■ $50.50
- ▨ $34.50
- ■ $26
- ▨ $19.50
- ■ $9.75

HOME-COURT ADVANTAGE

Despite Warriors' fans tendency to become somewhat subdued when there is a lull in the action, they actually can make noise when they need to. Hopefully the addition of 5,000 fans—and fancy new acoustics—will pump up the volume a bit more consistently in the renovated arena.

GETTING TO SAN JOSE ARENA

Public transportation: From San Francisco, take Amtrak/CalTrain to Cahill Station, across the street from the arena. Call (800) 660-4287 for more information. In San Jose, take Light Rail to the Santa Clara Street station downtown, then a 15-minute walk along Santa Clara Street. Call (408) 321-2000 for more information about Light Rail.

By car: From the north, take 101 south to Guadalupe Parkway (Route 87). Exit right onto Park Avenue approximately 3 blocks to Autumn Street. Go right on Autumn Street for about 2 blocks. The arena is on the left. From the south, take Route 87 north. Exit at Santa Clara Street, turn left, and follow Santa Clara Street about 2 blocks.

TICKET INFORMATION
Address: 7000 Coliseum Way, Oakland, CA 94621

Phone: (510) 382-2305 or Bass at (510) 762-2277
Hours: Mon.–Fri. 8:30—5.

Prices: $200, $150, $125, $115, $105, $60, $50.50, $34.50, $26, $19.50, $9.75.

HOUSTON ROCKETS

The Summit

ARENA STATS

Location: 10 Greenway Plaza, The Summit, Houston, TX 77046
Opened: Nov. 2, 1975
Capacity: 16,285
Services for fans with disabilities: Seating available at the top of the 100 level.

ARENA FIRSTS

Regular-season game: Nov. 2, 1975, 104–89 over the Milwaukee Bucks.
Overtime game: Jan. 14, 1976, 107–103 loss to the New York Knicks.
Playoff game: April 19, 1977, 111–101 loss to the Washington Bullets.
NBA Finals game: May 9, 1981, 94–71 loss to the Boston Celtics.

TEAM NOTEBOOK

Franchise history: San Diego Rockets, 1967–71; Houston Rockets, 1971–present.
Division titles: 1976–77, 1985–86, 1992–93, 1993–94.
Conference titles: 1980–81, 1985–86, 1993–94, 1994–95.
NBA championship: 1993–94, 1994–95.
Most Valuable Player: Moses Malone, 1978–79, 1981–82.
Basketball Hall of Fame: Calvin Murphy, 1993.
Retired numbers: 23, Calvin Murphy; 45, Rudy Tomjanovich.

Until they beat the New York Knicks in the 1993–94 NBA Finals, the Rockets were just another of Houston's disappointing sports teams. The Rockets had never won a championship, despite reaching the NBA Finals twice. The Astros and the Oilers had also crushed the expectations of Houston fans, earning the town the nickname "Choke City."

As the 1993–94 NBA playoffs advanced, many Houston fans seemed afraid of the same letdown from the Rockets—a fear they've expressed countless times over the years with empty seats and a fickle affection born of too many trips to the altar with no championship rings to show for it. Disappointment hung in the air of the Summit, and the city was abuzz over complaints from some Rockets' players about a perceived lack of enthusiasm among the fans. The fans still waited to throw in their lot, but once they finally saw the championship trophy in Hakeem Olajuwon's hands, they poured out years of pent-up emotion in a huge victory parade later that week. Now that the Rockets have won back-to-back titles, it's official: Houston definitely loves the Rockets.

The Summit is readily accessible to the waves of Rockets' fans who now come to see their championship team. It's just outside of downtown Houston in an office/hotel complex known as Greenway Plaza. Inside the arena, banners hang from the rafters honoring the only two Rockets to have their jerseys retired—Hall of Famer Calvin Murphy, now a Rockets broadcaster, and Rudy Tomjanovich, the team's head coach. It's only a matter of time before 34, Olajuwon's number, hangs in the Summit, along with the banners that prove Houston no longer deserves to be called "Choke City."

HOT TIPS FOR VISITING FANS

PARKING

Greenway Plaza has ample parking. No fee is charged for parking in the Rockets' lots. Traffic after the game occasionally moves slowly out of these lots. Several other lots as well as some on-street parking are in the area, and traffic moves faster there.

MEDIA

Radio: KTRH (740 AM—English), KLAT (1010 AM—Spanish). **TV:** KTXH (Channel 20) and Prime Sports (cable). Hall of Famer Calvin Murphy, the Rockets' all-time leading scorer, does color commentary on both cable and broadcast TV.

CUISINE

A multimillion-dollar upgrade of the Summit's concessions operation includes an addition to the arena near section 108 on the north side of the building that houses a 13-stand food court with such varied cuisine as fajitas and Texas-style barbecued brisket and sausage, as well as sushi and margarita bars. Carts serving imported and domestic beers are stationed in sections 101 and 115 and in the food court.
After the game, stop by Los Andes (713-622-2686), which is occasionally visited by such Rockets' luminaries as Hakeem Olajuwon. This glass-roofed restaurant, about a block from The Summit, specializes in South American cuisine. House of Pies (713-528-3816) is also a short distance from The Summit. Open 24 hours for breakfast, lunch, and dinner, the House of Pies is decorated with pictures of celebrity customers and features 40 kinds of pies and cakes.

LODGING NEAR THE ARENA

Stouffer Presidente Hotel
6 Greenway Plaza E.
Houston, TX 77046
(713) 629-1200/(800) 468-3571
Across from the arena.

Westin Galleria
5060 W. Alabama St.
Houston, TX 77056
(713) 960-8100/(800) 967-2324
3 miles from the arena.

THE ROCKETS AT THE SUMMIT

March 18, 1978: Calvin Murphy sets a Summit record by scoring 57 points in a 106–104 win over the New Jersey Nets.

May 14, 1981: The Rockets reach the sixth game of the NBA Finals, but the Boston Celtics take the crown 102–91.

Feb. 11, 1982: Moses Malone grabs a record 21 offensive rebounds in a 117–100 win over the Seattle SuperSonics.

June 5, 1986: A 111–96 Rockets' win over the Celtics tightens the championship series to three games to two. Boston goes on to win the title.

June 22, 1994: Led by MVP Hakeem Olajuwon, the Rockets win the NBA title with a 90–84, Game 7 win over the New York Knicks, snaring the first professional sports championship for Houston.

June 1, 1995: Again led by Olajuwon, the Rockets beat the Orlando Magic 100–95 to win their second straight NBA title.

In the Hot Seats at The Summit

The Summit opened more than 20 years ago, but it shows few signs of age. The seats are still plush and comfortable and the sight lines are great—there are no obstructed views, and no seat is more than 128 feet from the floor. What has changed is the Rockets' fortune. The formerly lukewarm team became the league's best for two straight seasons. Houston fans have fallen madly in love with their home boys, and the house is always packed. Times are so good that front-office execu-tives believe the small arena will be entirely sold out to season ticketholders for some time to come.

GOOD SEATS

Any seats that might become available on an individual-game basis are certain to be on the upper level, probably in the end zones (sections 206-236 on one end and 216-226 on the other). Seats in the lower rows go for $20.50, while the top rows are $12.50. Don't be dis-couraged by the location; the view is still very good and you can't beat the price.

SCALPING

Scalpers start approaching fans within a few blocks of the arena. It's a seller's market now, so don't expect any bargains. These street vendors know that just about the only way you're going to get in to see the Rockets is to buy a ticket from them.

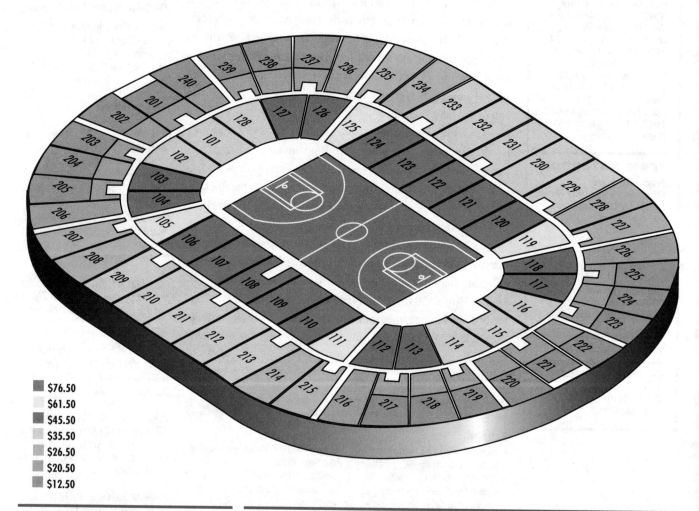

- ■ $76.50
- □ $61.50
- ■ $45.50
- ▨ $35.50
- ▨ $26.50
- ▨ $20.50
- ■ $12.50

HOME-COURT ADVANTAGE

The Rockets' back-to-back titles, along with their post-season bid in 1995–96, turned around Houston fans' cautious atti-tude. The newly boisterous crowds have made the Summit one of the tougher places to play in the league.

GETTING TO THE SUMMIT

Public transportation: METRO city buses stop just a few blocks from the Summit. Catch either the No. 25 Richmond on Main Street or the No. 53 Westheimer on Walker Street. Call (713) 635-4000 for more information.

By car: From Intercontinental Airport in the north, take Will Clayton Parkway east to High-way 59 South. Exit off Highway 59 at Edloe Street. The Summit will be on your right. From Hobby Airport in the south, take Mon-roe Road east to I-45 north; go to Highway 59 south, and proceed as above.

TICKET INFORMATION
Address: 10 Greenway Plaza, Houston, TX 77046

Phone: (713) 627-DUNK or TicketMaster at (713) 629-3700
Hours: Mon.–Sat. 10–6.

Prices: $76.50, $61.50, $45.50, $35.50, $26.50, $20.50, $12.50.

INDIANA PACERS
Market Square Arena

ARENA STATS

Location: *300 E. Market St., Indianapolis, IN 46204*
Opened: *Sept. 15, 1974*
Capacity: *16,530*
Services for fans with disabilities: *Seating and ticket prices vary. The restaurant on the seventh floor offers Braille and large-type menus. TDD and sound enhancement headphones are available.*

ARENA FIRSTS

Regular-season game: *Oct. 18, 1974, 129–121 loss to the San Antonio Spurs.*
Overtime game: *Oct. 18, 1974, 129–121 loss to San Antonio in double over-time.*
Playoff game: *(ABA) April 10, 1975, 113–103 over San Antonio. (NBA) April 2, 1981, 124–108 loss to the Philadelphia 76ers.*

TEAM NOTEBOOK

Franchise history: *Indiana Pacers, 1967–76 (ABA); Indiana Pacers, 1976–present. (NBA).*
Most Valuable Players: *Mel Daniels, 1968–69, 1970–71; George McGinnis, 1974–75 (ABA).*
Rookie of the Year: *Chuck Person, 1986–87.*
Retired numbers: *30, George McGinnis; 34, Mel Daniels; 35, Roger Brown.*

TICKET INFORMATION

Address: *300 E. Market St., Indianapolis, IN 46204*
Phone: *(317) 639-2112 or TicketMaster at (317) 239-5151.*
Hours: *Mon.–Fri. 10–5, Sat. 10–4.*

To say that Indiana—where almost everyone follows the Indiana University Hoosiers, and where people have been known to wait in line for hours to see high-school hoops—loves basketball is to put it mildly. Despite Indiana's basketball obsession, fans have been somewhat subdued in reacting to the NBA Pacers. The ABA Pacers won three titles between 1967 and 1976, but after the team joined the NBA, fans grew disappointed with a team unable to duplicate past ABA achievements.

And then came 1994. A rousing performance in the playoffs brought back memories of championship glory. Pacer Mania was born, complete with screaming fans and the loud sounds of Indy cars playing over the arena's speakers. The seats are still empty, but now it's because the faithful are standing and cheering from start to finish. The young Pacers have remained competitive, and Market Square has become one of the NBA's loudest, most frenzied places to watch basketball. As one fan puts it, "You put a winner on the floor, and you'll have Hoosier Hysteria."

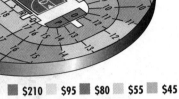

■ $210 ■ $95 ■ $80 ■ $55 ■ $45
■ $35 ■ $25 ■ $13 ■ $10

HOT TIPS FOR VISITING FANS

PARKING
Two garages connected to the Arena have spaces for approximately 1,300 cars. The price is $5. Additional lots, with prices ranging from $3 to $5, are in the surrounding neighborhood; on-street parking is limited.

MEDIA
Radio: WIBC (1070 AM).
TV: WTTV, (Channel 4), Pacers' Cable. Bob Leonard, who coached the Pacers to three ABA titles, is a radio broadcaster—as is Clark Kellogg, who played five seasons for Indiana.

CUISINE
Fans enjoy the jumbo hot dogs and barbecue sandwiches. Mixed-drink stands, which also serve domestic beer, can be found at aisles 3 and 22.
Market Square Gardens, the arena's sit-down restaurant, opens two hours before game time and closes about an hour after the final buzzer. It has large windows looking down onto center court, so fans can watch the game while they eat.
The Legal Beagle (317-266-0088), 1 block from Market Square and near the city's court-houses, is a popular hangout for fans and players.

LODGING NEAR THE ARENA
The Westin Hotel
50 S. Capital Ave.
Indianapolis, IN 46204
(317) 262-8100/(800) 228-3000
4 blocks from the arena.

Hyatt Regency
1 S. Capital Ave.
Indianapolis, IN 46204
(317) 632-1234/(800) 233-1234
5 blocks from the arena.

GETTING TO MARKET SQUARE ARENA
Public transportation: City bus routes begin and end in downtown Indianapolis, so they all come within 1 block of Market Square Arena. Call Metro Bus for more information at (317) 635-3344.
By car: From I-70 east take the Ohio Street exit to Alabama Street; the arena is on the left. From I-70 west take the Market Street exit. Enter on Alabama Street or New Jersey Street. From the north or south take I-65 downtown. Exit at Market Street and follow Market 3 blocks west. The arena will be on the left.

HOME-COURT ADVANTAGE
This building was transformed in 1994 from an occasionally placid,

even staid, venue into a raucous center of local basketball mania. Now even some fans admit that Market Square Arena is louder during Pacers games than those of the Indiana Hoosiers.

IN THE HOT SEATS AT MARKET SQUARE ARENA

With its small size, Market Square Arena offers good sight-lines and makes fans feel close to the action. Before 1994, finding tickets was not a challenge, but it may no longer be as easy.

GOOD SEATS
Excellent seats are available for $45 on the lower level in the four corners of the court. In the upper deck check out the $35 and $25 seats at center court, aisles 5–8 and 17–20. Aisles 2–4, 9–11, 14–16, and 20–23, in the corners of the upper deck, offer good views and cost only $25.

BAD SEATS
For $10 you can sit in the last several rows of the center-court sections. The view is decent compared to like seats in other arenas, but better seats have been available.

SCALPING
There are often a fair number of legal scalpers, mostly along the approaches to the arena. With the team's resurgence they do not necessarily offer a good bargain, and sometimes scalpers sell counterfeit tickets.

LOS ANGELES CLIPPERS

Memorial Sports Arena

$275 $140 $110
$40 $35 $24
$18 $14 $10

The Clippers are L.A.'s "other" team, taking a back seat to the Lakers in both name recognition and prestige. Unlike their neighbors to the south, the Clippers have never reached the final round of the playoffs, either in their present incarnation or when they were the San Diego Clippers or the Buffalo Braves. Still, this is Los Angeles, and you might spot Arsenio Hall, Raiders owner Al Davis, screenwriter Dan Mazur, or Clippers convert Billy Crystal.

Memorial Sports Arena is one of the oldest in the NBA, and though the Clippers have occasionally talked about relocating, they are still very much at home in the arena that housed the Lakers from 1960 to 1968. They continue to play several games each season at Arrowhead Pond of Anaheim, ostensibly to build their fan base.

The arena is well maintained and doesn't show its age. But because the Clippers don't have a fancy, high-tech scoreboard, among other extras, a game here is unique: At a time when most teams compete to see which has the best mascot or electronic presentation, the Clippers stress the action on the court.

IN THE HOT SEATS AT MEMORIAL SPORTS ARENA

The Clippers have a season-ticket base of approximately 6,000. Tickets for individual games go on sale the first Saturday of October. Unsold seats are sold on game nights. Beginning in the 1994–95 season tickets for games at Anaheim were made available through TicketMaster and at the Anaheim box office, but not through the Clippers at the Sports Arena.

GOOD SEATS

One distinct benefit of the Clippers over the Lakers is low ticket prices. For a good bargain and a good view, check out the $10 and $14 seats in the middle concourse, sections 1–4, 14–18, and 28A–30. Excellent seats are also available in the middle loge at center court.

BAD SEATS

Sight lines are generally good, although the seats at the top of the arena behind the baskets—sections 8, 8A, 9, 23, 23A, and 24—seem farther from the floor than comparable seats at newer NBA venues.

SCALPING

Police have been known to enforce the local ordinance against scalping.

HOT TIPS FOR VISITING FANS

PARKING

Ample spaces are available in lots adjoining the arena; the price is $7. Some on-street parking is available in the area. Generally, cars move quickly in and out of the lots. While this is not the best place to take a long walk late at night, the Clippers and the police do a good job with security. The nearby parking lots are well lighted.

MEDIA

Radio: KMPC (710 AM).
TV: Prime Sports Network.

CUISINE

The Clippers offer a good assortment, ranging from salads, veggie sandwiches and fruit-and-cheese plates to burritos and Jody Maroni sausages.

The Clipper Club, next to section 2, is a full-service restaurant and popular bar. It opens one hour before the game and stays open approximately 30 minutes after the final buzzer. Occasionally players stop by.

After the game head across from the arena to Julie's Trojan Bar and Grill (213-749-2575), a local institution among U.S.C. faithful for more than 50 years. This is a sports bar, decorated with U.S.C. memorabilia. Margarita Jones (213-747-4400), 1 block north of the arena, is a good Mexican restaurant.

LODGING NEAR THE ARENA

Westin Bonaventure Hotel and Suites
404 South Figueroa Blvd.
Los Angeles, CA 90071
(213) 624-1000/(800) 228-3000
2 miles from the arena.

Los Angeles Airport Doubletree
5400 W. Century Blvd.
Los Angeles, CA 90045
(310) 216-5858/(800) 222-8733
11 miles from the arena.

GETTING TO MEMORIAL SPORTS ARENA

Public transportation: Take the No. 81 bus west to Figueroa Avenue and 39th Street. Walk ½ block to the arena. Call (213) 626-4455 for more information.

By car: From the airport, follow signs to Century Freeway (105) east. Take 105 to the Harbour Freeway (110) north and exit at Martin Luther King, Jr., Boulevard. Turn left (west) onto King Boulevard and turn right at the second traffic light (Hoover)

ARENA STATS

Location: 3939 S. Figueroa St., Los Angeles, CA 90037
Capacity: 16,021
Services for fans with disabilities: Seating available at the top of the first loge level; exact placement changes each game.

ARENA FIRSTS

Regular-season game: Nov. 1, 1984, 107–105 over the New York Knicks.
Overtime game: March 3, 1985, 126–122 over the Kansas City Kings.
Playoff game: April 28, 1992, 98–88 over the Utah Jazz.

TEAM NOTEBOOK

Franchise history: Buffalo Braves, 1970–78; San Diego Clippers, 1978–84; Los Angeles Clippers, 1984–present.
Most Valuable Player: Bob McAdoo, 1974–75.
Rookies of the Year: Bob McAdoo, 1972–73; Ernie DiGregorio, 1973–74; Adrian Dantley, 1976–77; Terry Cummings, 1982–83.

TICKET INFORMATION

Address: 3939 S. Figueroa St., Los Angeles, CA 90037
Phone: (213) 745-0500 or TicketMaster (213) 480-3232.
Hours: Mon.–Fri. 10–6.

to enter the Sports Arena grounds.

HOME-COURT ADVANTAGE

The Clippers' record may be poor, but they are known for playing hard. Their long-suffering fans tend to love the game and be very knowledgeable—and can be very loud when the occasion calls for it. Players love this court, and the emphasis is definitely on basketball, not on mascots and special effects.

Great Western Forum

ARENA STATS

Location: *3900 W. Manchester Blvd., Inglewood, CA 90305*
Opened: *Dec. 30, 1967*
Capacity: *17,505*
Services for fans with disabilities: *Seating available at the top of the loge, in sections 1, 18, 19, and 36.*

ARENA FIRSTS

Regular-season game: *Dec. 31, 1967, 147–118 over the Houston Rockets.*
Overtime game: *Feb. 17, 1968, 135–134 loss to the Philadelphia 76ers in double overtime.*
Playoff game: *March 24, 1968, 109–101 over the Chicago Bulls.*
NBA Finals game: *April 26, 1968, 127–119 loss to the Boston Celtics.*

TEAM NOTEBOOK

Franchise history: *Minneapolis Lakers, 1947–48 (NBL); 1948–49 (BAA); 1949–60 (NBA); Los Angeles Lakers, 1960–present.*
Conference titles: *1948–49, 1949–50, 1951–52, 1952–53, 1953–54, 1954–55, 1958–59, 1961–62, 1962–63, 1964–65, 1965–66, 1967–68, 1968–69, 1969–70, 1971–72, 1972–73, 1979–80, 1981–82, 1982–83, 1983–84, 1984–85, 1986–87, 1987–88, 1988–89, 1990–91.*
NBA championships: *1948–49, 1949–50, 1951–52, 1952–53, 1953–54, 1971–72, 1979–80, 1981–82, 1984–85, 1986–87, 1987–88.*
Basketball Hall of Fame: *George Mikan, 1959; Bill Sharman, 1975; Elgin Baylor, Jim Pollard, 1977; Wilt Chamberlain, Pete Newell, 1979; Jerry West, 1980; Slater Martin, 1981; John Kundla, Vern Mikkelsen, Kareem Abdul-Jabbar, 1995.*
Retired numbers: *13, Wilt Chamberlain; 22, Elgin Baylor; 32, Earvin Johnson; 33, Kareem Abdul-Jabbar; 44, Jerry West.*

This is one of the classiest-looking arenas in the NBA. Aptly named the Forum, the circular building is ringed by white Roman columns. The only problem is that it's in a bad neighborhood. Players have been robbed across the street.

Nonetheless, stars still come out to see the Lakers—the Forum's in Inglewood, but it might as well be in Hollywood. Jack Nicholson still has his customary seat a few feet away from the visitors' bench. Dyan Cannon and Arsenio Hall are also diehard regulars, although Hall has been known to sneak across town and catch the Clippers, too. Even the cheerleading dancers, the Laker Girls (Paula Abdul is an alumna), had a movie made about them. The players enter through the rear tunnel, but if you want to star-gaze, arrive early and wait near the canopy at the main entrance to watch the limos drop off the big shots.

The retired jerseys of Wilt Chamberlain, Elgin Baylor, Jerry West, Magic Johnson, and Kareem Abdul-Jabbar are there to see. Johnson thrilled fans by returning to the Lakers in January 1996, and for a few months there truly was magic in the Forum once again. But after a first-round, 3–1 defeat in the playoffs, Johnson again announced his retirement from the game. Shaquille O'Neal's arrival in the 1996–97 season may lead Magic back onto the court, or start a whole new version of Showtime.

HOT TIPS FOR VISITING FANS

PARKING
Don't park on the street. You don't want to be walking around after dark. The closest lots are for preferred seating, but you can park across the street at Hollywood Park or behind the Forum for $7. This is Los Angeles, everybody drives, and traffic can be murder before and after games. Be patient going home, and leave for the game with time to spare. Traffic patterns change on game days, so make sure you get in the correct lane, because switching lanes is difficult once traffic gets congested.

MEDIA
Radio: KLAC (570 AM), with the legendary Chick Hearn, simulcast on television.
TV: KCAL (Channel 9), Prime Ticket cable.

CUISINE
Concessions stands are plentiful, and the lines are the most orderly in the league. The usual hot dogs, nachos, popcorn, and ice cream are available, as well as mixed drinks, wine, and bottled water. Budweiser and a number of imported beers are available. The place to go is the Forum Club, near the main entrance, but you have to be a season ticketholder or know somebody. It's like a nightclub after the game, with players and celebs stopping by. You can grab a bite there before the game, too. Tony Roma's (310-674-1679) in Inglewood is good. The Chart House (310-822-4144) in Marina del Rey is an easy drive away. Don't plan to walk anywhere; nothing is close enough, or safe enough, to try.

LODGING NEAR THE ARENA

Marriott Marina del Rey
13480 Maxella Ave.
Marina del Rey, CA 90292
(310) 822-8555/(800) 228-9290
5 miles from the arena.

Ritz-Carlton
4375 Admiralty Way
Marina del Rey, CA 90292
(310) 823-1700/(800) 241-3333
8-10 miles from the arena.

THE LAKERS AT GREAT WESTERN FORUM

Feb. 9, 1969: *Wilt Chamberlain sets a Forum record, scoring 66 points against the Phoenix Suns.*

March 19, 1972: *The Lakers trounce the Golden State Warriors 162–99, the largest margin of victory in an NBA game.*

May 7, 1972: *A 114–100 win over the New York Knicks in Game 5 of the NBA Finals gives the Lakers their first championship in Los Angeles.*

Oct. 28, 1973: *Elmore Smith sets an NBA record with 17 blocks against the Portland Trail Blazers.*

June 8, 1982: *The Lakers take Game 6 of the NBA Finals over the Philadelphia 76ers to clinch the championship.*

June 3, 1984: *The first Boston Celtics–Lakers NBA Finals of the Magic Johnson–Larry Bird era comes to Los Angeles. The Lakers beat Boston in Game 3, 137–104.*

June 14, 1987: *The Lakers win Game 6 of the NBA Finals 106–93 over the Celtics to win another title.*

April 15, 1991: *In a game against the Mavericks, Magic Johnson breaks Oscar Robertson's all-time NBA assist record of 9,887.*

January 30, 1996: *Magic Johnson returns to basketball as a Laker after having retired from the game in 1991.*

In the Hot Seats at Great Western Forum

The place, big and spread out, looks like it should hold more than 17,505. The seats might seem far from the action, but the farthest is only 170 feet from the playing surface. You can rent binoculars for $5, but be prepared to leave a deposit.

The Lakers have the most expensive tickets in the NBA. Prices are $110, $67, and $45 for the best seats.

GOOD SEATS

The arena has no obstructed-view seats. Each upholstered seat is angled to the center spot on the playing floor. The best seats are on the floor, of course, because you can see the game and the stars better, but they cost big bucks and you have to know someone.

BAD SEATS

Don't get suckered into buying seats on the end lines, because people will be walking in front of you all the time. Sit opposite the benches if possible.

SCALPING

This used to be the only way to get in, and now that Shaq's in town it may be again.

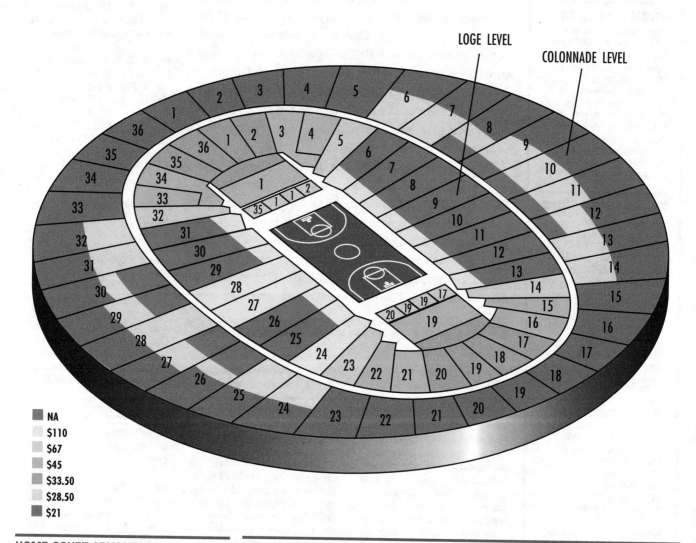

LOGE LEVEL

COLONNADE LEVEL

- ■ NA
- $110
- $67
- $45
- $33.50
- $28.50
- ■ $21

HOME-COURT ADVANTAGE

The stars and the history of the building can be intimidating, and the lifestyle of Hollywood gets opponents in trouble sometimes. The clubs, all-night spots, and hobnobbing with celebrities can take a player's legs away.

GETTING TO GREAT WESTERN FORUM

Public transportation: Take the No. 40 bus on South Broadway to Market Manchester. Transfer to an eastbound No. 211 bus. For more information, call (310) 320-9442.
By car: From Highway 110, exit at Manchester Boulevard and head west to the Forum. From the San Diego 405 Freeway, exit at Manchester and head east. Also accessible from Highway 105.

TICKET INFORMATION
Address: P.O. Box 10, Inglewood, CA 90306

Phone: (310) 419-3182 or TicketMaster at (213) 480-3232, (714) 740-2000, or (805) 583-8700

Hours: Mon.–Fri. 10–6.
Prices: $110, $67, $45, $33.50, $28.50, $21.

ARENA STATS

Location: *701 Arena Blvd., Miami, FL 33136*
Opened: *July 8, 1988*
Capacity: *15,008*
Services for fans with disabilities: *Seating available on the north side of the arena in the top rows of sections 101, 113, 114, 119, 121, and 126.*

ARENA FIRSTS

Regular-season game: *Nov. 5, 1988, 111–91 loss to the Los Angeles Clippers.*
Points scored: *Norm Nixon, Los Angeles Clippers.*
Overtime game: *Nov. 18, 1988, 123–117 loss to the Golden State Warriors.*
Playoff game: *April 29, 1992, 119–114 loss to the Chicago Bulls.*

TEAM NOTEBOOK

Franchise history: *Miami Heat, 1988–present.*

TICKET INFORMATION

Address: *SunTrust International Center, One SE Third Ave., #2300, Miami, FL 33131*
Phone: *(305) 577-HEAT*
Hours: *Mon.–Fri. 10–5.*

The Heat might be the most appropriate nickname among all of the NBA's 27 teams. Anyone who spends time in South Florida, especially during the summer, will be convinced. They'll have no trouble spotting Miami Arena either, which is painted a pastel shade of pink, in harmony with the Art Deco architecture for which Miami is known.

Inside, the basketball action is hot and the air blessedly cool. With the hiring of legendary Pat Riley as president and head coach, Miami fans have warmed to their team. Within the intimate confines of this arena, they can match the noise level of some of the more established NBA venues, often without the scoreboard telling them to yell.

Although Heat fans have had a lot to cheer about recently, including a new stadium that will open in the 1998–99 season, many have more on their minds than their team's success when they come to Miami Arena. The arena is on the edge of a section of Miami known as Overtown, portions of which were rocked by rioting several years back. Consequently the team and the city of Miami make a concerted and visible effort to provide security. While some might not feel comfortable taking a postgame stroll through the neighborhood, it should not stop anyone from checking out the Heat.

■ **$50** ■ **$41** ■ **$28** ■ **$21** ■ **$14**

HOT TIPS FOR VISITING FANS

PARKING
Prices at area lots range from $6 to $10. Lots in the $5 to $6 range tend to be several blocks away. Fans who are concerned about security generally park at the higher-priced lots. Panhandling in the area has been cited by Heat faithful as another reason to park as close to the arena as possible.

MEDIA
Radio: WINZ (940 AM-English), WACC (830 AM-Spanish). **TV:** UPN-WBFS (Channel 33), Sunshine Network. Eric Reid and coaching legend Jack Ramsay are the broadcast team.

CUISINE
Miami Arena offers standard fare, but the grilled cheeseburger is recommended. The arena also serves several distinctive Miami offerings: the Miami Heat tropical drink, made with rum and piña colada mix; potato knishes; kosher hot dogs; Miami Heros, with ham, cured pork, cheese, pickles, and mustard, served grilled on Cuban bread; and arepas, deep-fried patties of sweet corn and cheese.
After the game, Bayside Market Place (305-577-3344), a complex of restaurants and bars on 16 acres, is 5 blocks west of the arena. Along Biscayne Boulevard, there's the 1800 Club (305-373-1093), where some of the Heat coaching staff goes after the game. Jimmy Buffett and Heat players are occasional customers.

LODGING NEAR THE ARENA
Mayfair House
3000 Florida Ave.
Coconut Grove
Miami, FL 33133
(305) 441-0000/(800) 433-4555
6½ miles from the arena.

Don Shula's Hotel and Golf Club
15255 Bull Run Rd.
Miami, FL 33014
(305) 821-1150/(800) 247-4852
10 miles from the arena.

GETTING TO MIAMI ARENA
Public transportation: Take Metro Rail to Overtown Station, across the street from the arena. Call (305) 638-6700 for more information.
By car: From the airport, take 836 east to the Biscayne Boulevard exit. Make a right at the bottom of the ramp onto Biscayne, and proceed to Northwest 8th Street. Take a right. Miami Arena is 2 blocks, on the left.

HOME-COURT ADVANTAGE
Engaged, enthusiastic fans, plus the size of the arena, work to enhance and magnify the noise level, especially when there's a sellout. This is especially true against better teams, whom the Heat tend to play well against at home.

IN THE HOT SEATS AT MIAMI ARENA
Miami's season-ticket base is between 12,000 to 13,000. All available single-game tickets are put on sale in early October. Any tickets that remain are sold on game nights; although most are for upper-deck seats, there may be scattered singles.
This is one of the smallest arenas in the NBA, and its size translates into a large number of good seats. The $28 seats, located upstairs, offer a good view for the money. The Heat are building a larger facility, which will promise all the frills of other modern NBA venues.

BAD SEATS
Though this is a small arena, the seats in the upper deck are a long way up.

SCALPING
The police, with more pressing concerns involving crowds and security, generally seem to leave scalpers alone.

MILWAUKEE BUCKS

Bradley Center

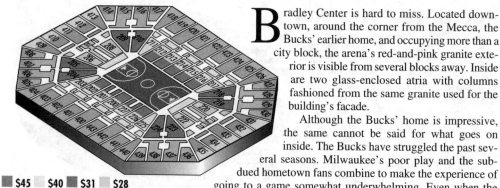

$45 **$40** **$31** **$28**
$22 **$19** **$14** **$10**

Bradley Center is hard to miss. Located downtown, around the corner from the Mecca, the Bucks' earlier home, and occupying more than a city block, the arena's red-and-pink granite exterior is visible from several blocks away. Inside are two glass-enclosed atria with columns fashioned from the same granite used for the building's facade.

Although the Bucks' home is impressive, the same cannot be said for what goes on inside. The Bucks have struggled the past several seasons. Milwaukee's poor play and the subdued hometown fans combine to make the experience of going to a game somewhat underwhelming. Even when the decibels rise, the sound seems to get lost.

Although the non-basketball entertainment at Bradley Center is not particularly noteworthy either, the local mascot, Bango—a buck with big antlers—is popular. A house band called StreetLife also does its best to get things going during the game. Rather than anticipating the basketball experience of a lifetime, you should expect a quieter kind of NBA evening. The highlight of your visit likely will be Bradley Center itself, a comfortable, well-built facility.

HOME-COURT ADVANTAGE

The Bucks have little or no edge at Bradley Center. The crowd can be so quiet at times that caustic comments by courtside fans can be heard in much of the lower level. In the past, several players have actually complained about fans' not being enthusiastic enough during games.

IN THE HOT SEATS AT BRADLEY CENTER

Single-game tickets go on sale in October, but tickets can be purchased on virtually any game night for seats at various locations around Bradley Center, although most are in the upper tier.

GOOD SEATS

Most of the sight lines are good, and the seats are comfortable. Preferred seats are in the lower half of the center. Check out the $19 seats in sections 400–404, 418–426, and 440–443 of the upper deck's center-court area. Center-court seating near the floor in sections 200–202, 212–216, and 226–227 costs $45, a bargain compared to similar seats at other NBA arenas.

BAD SEATS

Seats in the upper-deck end zones—sections 431–435 and 409–413—seem more suited to watching hockey than basketball. These seats cost $10 and $14.

SCALPING

Scalpers don't have a high profile outside, as the Bucks are not known for selling out games.

HOT TIPS FOR VISITING FANS

PARKING

Although Bradley Center has no on-site parking, plenty is available in the area, with prices ranging from $4 to $7. Some street parking is available. After games, traffic moves fairly smoothly.

MEDIA

Radio: WTMJ (620 AM).
TV: WVTV (Channel 18). Jon McGlocklin, one of the original Bucks, is a color analyst on radio and on TV during road games.

CUISINE

Milwaukee is best known for sausages and beer, both of which are well represented at the center. Fans also enjoy the pizza, grilled burgers, and chicken. Miller products are widely available, as well as local favorites Old Style and Leinenkugel's.
After the game, Major Goolsby's (414-271-3414) is a block away. This sports bar, popular with fans and players, once was known as the Liquid Locker Room of the NBA. Water Street Brewery (414-272-1195) is fewer than three blocks from the Bradley Center. It features eight made-on-the-premises brews, plus more than 20 other beers.

LODGING NEAR THE ARENA

Hyatt Regency Milwaukee
333 W. Kilbourn Ave.
Milwaukee, WI 53203
(414) 276-1234/(800) 233-1234
2 blocks from the arena.

Wyndham Milwaukee Center
139 E. Kilbourn Ave.
Milwaukee, WI 53202
(414) 276-8686/(800) 822-4200
4 blocks from the arena.

GETTING TO BRADLEY CENTER

Public transportation: The No. 30 bus stops one block from the arena. Call (414) 344-6711 for more information.
By car: From the south, take I-94 north to the Kilbourn/Civic Center exit. Go to the second stoplight and make a left onto North Fourth Street. Bradley Center is two blocks ahead on the left. From the north, take I-94 south to the Fourth Street/Civic Center exit, then take Fourth Street to the arena.
From the west, take I-94 east to the Civic Center exit (No. 1H). Take the right fork in the ramp to St. Paul Avenue. Make a left onto North Fourth Street and go six blocks. The arena will be on the left.

ARENA STATS

Location: 1001 N. Fourth St., Milwaukee, WI 53203
Opened: Oct. 1, 1988
Capacity: 18,633
Services for fans with disabilities: Seating available throughout; call (414) 227-0400/TTY (414) 227-0445.

ARENA FIRSTS

Regular-season game: Nov. 5, 1988, 107–94 loss to the Atlanta Hawks.
Points scored: R. Breuer, Milwaukee Bucks.
Overtime game: March 25, 1989, 113–109 over the Cleveland Cavaliers.
Playoff game: May 2, 1989, 117–113 over the Atlanta Hawks.

TEAM NOTEBOOK

Franchise history: Milwaukee Bucks, 1968–present.
Division titles: 1970–71, 1971–72, 1972–73, 1973–74, 1975–76, 1979–80, 1980–81, 1981–82, 1982–83, 1983–84, 1984–85, 1985–86.
Conference titles: 1970–71, 1973–74.
NBA championships: 1970–71.
Basketball Hall of Fame: Oscar Robertson, 1979; Bob Lanier, 1992; Kareem Abdul-Jabbar, 1995.
Retired numbers: 1, Oscar Robertson; 2, Junior Bridgeman; 4, Sidney Moncrief; 14, Jon McGlocklin; 16, Bob Lanier; 32, Brian Winters; 33, Kareem Abdul-Jabbar.

TICKET INFORMATION

Address: Bradley Center, 1001 N. Fourth St., Milwaukee, WI 53203
Phone: (414) 227-0500, or (608) 225-4646 in Madison, (414) 276-4545 in Milwaukee, (312) 559-1212 in Chicago.
Hours: Mon.–Fri. 9–5:30.

Target Center

After the Lakers moved to Los Angeles in 1960, NBA basketball didn't come back to Minneapolis for 27 years. But it might be a short visit. In 1994, the state legislature and NBA commissioner David Stern intervened on separate occasions to keep the Timberwolves in the Twin Cities area, which is already smarting from the loss of its NHL North Stars.

The loss of the Timberwolves would mean more to Minneapolis than just the loss of a basketball team. Target Center has brought people back downtown to an area known as the Warehouse District, full of artists' studios, restaurants, and bars.

Visitors to Target Center should not be surprised to hear the fans howling like wolves at various points during the game. Minneapolis's version of the noisemeter is a "Howl-O'Meter" shown on the large videoscreen over center court. Given the Timberwolves' record since entering the league, one might think these are howls of pain, but they're really a sign of fans learning to love their team. Only time will tell if Minneapolis fans will lose another pro sport.

| ■ $174 | □ $86 | ▨ $66 | ■ $48 |
| ▨ $35 | ▨ $29 | ▨ $17 | ■ $10 |

HOME-COURT ADVANTAGE

The Timberwolves have Crunch, a gray wolf mascot, and award-winning video displays to pump up the faithful, and after nearly losing the team, local fans could come to Target Center in record numbers to show their support for keeping the franchise in Minneapolis. Or they could go snowmobiling.

HOT TIPS FOR VISITING FANS

PARKING

Because Target Center is downtown, plenty of parking is in the area, either on the street or in flat lots. Two city-owned parking garages are connected to the center by ramps. Parking is $5. Cars move fairly quickly into and out of area lots.

MEDIA

Radio: KFAN (1130 AM).
TV: WB23 (Channel 23) and KARE (Channel 11) both broadcast games. Play-by-play announcer Kevin Harlan, known for his high-energy broadcasts, calls games on both radio and television.

CUISINE

Among the notable items are the Italian hoagies, steak sandwiches, Italian sausages—and, for a uniquely Minnesota dish, a fried walleye fish sandwich. Fans can also buy fruit and cheese platters and a veggie plate.
Frontrunners, a restaurant and lounge with a sports-bar theme and big-screen TVs, is on the main level, behind sections 101 and 140. Before the game, Frontrunners serves a variety of hot dishes and sandwiches; afterward, it swings into a lounge mode.
The Loon Cafe (612-332-8342) is a block from the arena. The

bar/restaurant has a comfortable, old-saloon atmosphere that's perfect for an after-game drink or meal. Rosen's (612-338-1926), another restaurant/bar, is housed in a former warehouse with high ceilings and hardwood floors. They have excellent pastas and a good selection of beers.

LODGING NEAR THE ARENA

Minneapolis Marriott
30 S. Seventh St.
Minneapolis, MN 55402
(612) 349-4000/(800) 228-9290
2 blocks from the arena.

Hyatt Regency
1300 Nicollet Mall
Minneapolis, MN 55403
(612) 370-1234/(800) 233-1234
About 5 blocks from the arena.

GETTING TO TARGET CENTER

Public transportation: All buses that go downtown go near the arena. Call Metro Transit at (612) 349-7000 for information.
By car: From the north, take 35W to the Washington Avenue exit. Turn right onto Washington and follow it until First Avenue North. Turn left, and the arena will be in front of you.
From the south, take 35W into downtown. Take the Fifth

Avenue downtown exit, then turn left onto Seventh Avenue. Take Seventh to First Avenue North. From the east or west, take 94 toward downtown, and exit at Fourth Street. Turn right onto First Avenue Center.

IN THE HOT SEATS AT TARGET CENTER

Good seats are available for most home games. Despite worries about whether the 'Wolves will stay, interest in basketball remains high in the Twin Cities. The team's home attendance has been among the best in the league. The season-ticket base is only about 10,000, though, meaning many tickets are sold on a walk-up basis. Single-game seats go on sale a week or two before the season starts.

GOOD SEATS

Virtually all the seats are comfortable and have good views. The top eight rows of sections 206–236 and 216–226 are a good deal at $17, considering that the view from here is decent.

SCALPING

Scalping is illegal in Minneapolis, but some scalpers can be found around the Center. However, you should have no difficulty buying what you want at the box office.

NEW JERSEY NETS

Continental Airlines Arena

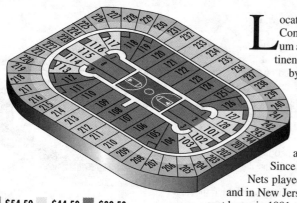

■ $54.50 ■ $44.50 ■ $39.50
■ $20 ■ $16 ■ $10

L ocated in the sprawling Meadowlands Sports Complex, which also includes Giants Stadium and a racetrack, the gleaming white Continental Airlines arena can be seen for miles by motorists speeding past on the nearby highway. While the arena, Madison Square Garden, and their respective basketball tenants share a geographic proximity, that's as far as the similarities go. The Knicks are a big-city team, and the Nets are a creature of the suburbs. Since their first game in the ABA in 1967, the Nets played at four suburban sites on Long Island and in New Jersey before finally moving into their present home in 1981.

Nets fans are divided in their opinions about Continental Airlines Arena, including its name change from Brendan Byrne Arena. Some like its atmosphere, which is less hectic than the Garden's, but others say the constant, family-oriented, non-basketball entertainment detracts from the games. The crowd is often fairly quiet; on most nights, the arena is a place to enjoy a relaxing evening rather than an intense basketball experience, especially in the post–Derrick Coleman/Kenny Anderson era. The exceptions are when the Knicks and many of their fans cross the Hudson River. On those nights the fans and the two teams, which have a mutual dislike, turn up the heat.

HOME-COURT ADVANTAGE

The crowd at the arena is not usually the raucous type that helps win games. When fans get going, it's often with the help of film clips on the videoscreen. Being the area underdog seems to help them against the Knicks.

IN THE HOT SEATS AT CONTINENTAL AIRLINES ARENA

The Nets have become a fairly popular attraction, but good seats should be available at the box office for most games, except against the Knicks.
After unloading their contracts with Derrick Coleman and Kenny Anderson, the Nets signed former UMass coach John Calipari to a huge contract to take Butch Beard's place on the bench, a move that gave them yet another reason to raise ticket prices.

GOOD SEATS

This is a fairly large building, more spread out than other arenas. Most seats are good.

BAD SEATS

Upper-deck seats cost $16, and though they're perfectly acceptable, given the general availability of tickets, you can probably do better if you're willing to pay.

SCALPING

Very few scalpers are around even when the Knicks are in town.

HOT TIPS FOR VISITING FANS

PARKING

Parking for approximately 4,000 cars is available at the Arena. An additional 25,000 spaces are available elsewhere in the Meadowlands. Parking costs $5. The Nets operate free shuttle service to and from the Arena.

MEDIA

Radio: WQEW (1560 AM) and WOR (710 AM).
TV: SportsChannel on cable. Play-by-play announcer Ian Eagle moved from the Nets' radio network to broadcast on cable TV. Color analyst Bill Raftery, a former coach of nearby Seton Hall University, is an analyst for college basketball games on CBS.

CUISINE

Local favorites include Carvel soft ice cream, potato knishes and a Hebrew National hot dog, either plain or with chili and onions. The arena also has two midcourt, mall-type food areas where you can find hot dogs, burgers, pizza, and grilled chicken. Three portable carts stock imported beer, including Molson and Heineken.

After the game, the Jersey Sports Cafe (201-933-3308) in East Rutherford heads the list.

LODGING NEAR THE ARENA

Embassy Meadowlands
455 Plaza Dr.
Secaucus, NJ 07094
(201) 864-7300/(800) 362-2779
2 miles from the arena.

Sheraton Meadowlands
2 Meadowlands Plaza
East Rutherford, NJ 07073
(201) 896-0500/(800) 325-3535
½ mile from the arena.

GETTING TO CONTINENTAL AIRLINES ARENA

Public transportation: New Jersey Transit runs load-and-go buses from the Port Authority Bus Terminal in Manhattan. Call (201) 762-5100 for more information.
By car: From Manhattan, take the Lincoln Tunnel, then follow Route 3 West directly to the sports complex.
From the New Jersey Turnpike, take the western spur to 16W and follow signs to the sports complex.

ARENA STATS

Location: East Rutherford, NJ 07073
Opened: July 2, 1981
Capacity: 20,029
Services for fans with disabilities: Seating available in sections 103–105, 111–114, 116–119, 125, and 127–128. Tickets are $44.50 or $54.50. Call (201) 935-8888 for more information.

ARENA FIRSTS

Regular-season game: Oct. 30, 1981, 103–99 loss to the New York Knicks.
Playoff game: April 20, 1982, 96–83 loss to the Washington Bullets.

TEAM NOTEBOOK

Franchise history: New Jersey Americans, 1967–68 (ABA); New York Nets, 1968–76 (ABA); New York Nets, 1976–77 (NBA); New Jersey Nets, 1977–present.
ABA championships: 1973–74, 1975–76.
Basketball Hall of Fame: Julius Erving, 1993.
Most Valuable Player: Julius Erving, 1973–74, 1974–75, 1975–76 (ABA).
Rookie of the Year: Brian Taylor, 1973 (ABA); Buck Williams, 1982; Derrick Coleman, 1991.
Retired numbers: 3, Drazen Petrovic; 4, Wendell Ladner; 23, John Williamson; 25, Bill Melchionni; 32, Julius Erving.

TICKET INFORMATION

Address: The Meadowlands, East Rutherford, NJ 07073
Phone: (201) 935-3900 or TicketMaster at (212) 307-7171, (201) 507-8900, (516) 888-9000, (609) 665-2500, (914) 454-3388, or (203) 624-0033
Hours: Mon.–Fri. 9–6, Sat. 10–6, Sun. 12–5.

Madison Square Garden

ARENA STATS

Location: 4 Pennsylvania Plaza, New York, NY 10001
Opened: Feb. 11, 1968
Capacity: 19,763
Services for fans with disabilities: Call Guest Services for information at (212) 465-6225.

ARENA FIRSTS

Regular-season game: April 14, 1968, 114–102 over the San Diego Clippers.
Overtime game: Feb. 20, 1968, 115–112 over the San Francisco Warriors.
Playoff game: March 23, 1968, 128–117 over the Philadelphia 76ers.
NBA Finals game: April 6, 1969, 108–100 loss to the Boston Celtics.

TEAM NOTEBOOK

Franchise history: New York Knickerbockers, 1946–48 (BAA); 1948–present (NBA).
Division titles: 1952–53, 1953–54, 1969–70, 1970–71, 1988–89, 1992–93, 1993–94.
Conference titles: 1950–51, 1951–52, 1952–53, 1969–70, 1971–72, 1972–73, 1993–94.
NBA championships: 1969–70, 1972–73.
Basketball Hall of Fame: Ned Irish, 1964; Joe Lapchick, 1966; Tom Gola, 1975; Jerry Lucas, 1979; Willis Reed, 1981; Slater Martin, 1981; Bill Bradley, 1982; Dave DeBusschere, 1982; Red Holzman, 1985; Walt Frazier, 1986; Earl Monroe, 1990; Harry Gallatin, 1991; Al McGuire, 1992; Dick McGuire, 1993; Walt Bellamy, 1993.
Retired numbers: 10, Walt Frazier; 12, Dick Barnett; 15, Earl Monroe; 15, Dick McGuire; 19, Willis Reed; 22, Dave DeBusschere; 24, Bill Bradley; 613, Red Holzman.

The reverence attached to Madison Square Garden goes beyond its three decades at 33rd Street and Seventh Avenue, an honor conferred as much by the Garden's proud lineage as by the many memorable moments this structure has seen. The current MSG is the fourth building so named. The first MSG once housed P. T. Barnum's Hippodrome. The second, built in 1890, was designed by Stanford White, who later was murdered in its roof gardens. In the late '40s and early '50s, college basketball was the real attraction at the third MSG, while pro ball was just an afterthought. But after the point-shaving scandals of the '50s, the Knicks and the NBA began to eclipse college ball in the minds of New Yorkers. The classic 1969–70 Knicks stole the limelight once and for all.

Though MSG has been gussied up in recent years, the memories of those championship teams are still responsible for much of the atmosphere. The high standards to which Knicks fans hold their team derive in large part from those glory years, a comparison that has burdened recent Knicks teams. Like their city, no other fans can be more unforgiving or more wholeheartedly enthusiastic; new addition Larry Johnson will soon find out if he can stand tall in a city of skyscrapers.

HOT TIPS FOR VISITING FANS

PARKING

Since the Garden is in midtown Manhattan, many scattered, private lots can be found in the area, averaging $15. Though some of the lots are on side streets and not particularly well lighted, the neighborhood is active on game nights, so safety is no more a concern than in any other part of midtown. Traffic can move slowly in the streets leading up to the Garden, especially if you're going crosstown. Plan an extra half hour or so.

MEDIA

Radio: WFAN (660 AM) and WEVD (1050 AM). Former Knick Walt "Clyde" Frazier is the analyst, offering outspoken opinions and colorful patter. **TV:** MSG Network (cable). Marv Albert has been a Knicks announcer for more than 25 years, as well as doing NBA games on NBC. He's responsible for play-by-play, and John Andriese handles color.

CUISINE

Given that midtown has no shortage of restaurants, many Knicks fans have a ritual meal at a favorite place and then head to the game. If you decide to rely on the concessions, though, you won't be too badly off. The renovations made to the Garden a few years ago included upgrading the food, which doesn't stray too far beyond the usual arena fare but is tasty nonetheless. Charley O's (212-630-0343), in the same complex as the Garden at 9 Penn Plaza, is very popular with Knicks fans. The Play-By-Play (212-465-5888) is another sports bar in the complex; after games, a show that features interviews with players and other famous guests is broadcast from here on the MSG Sports Network.
A few blocks up, there's P. J. Clarke's (212-759-1650), an old-time New York bar with lots of cigar smoke and atmosphere.

LODGING NEAR THE ARENA

Best Western Hotel Pennsylvania
401 W. 33rd St.
New York, NY 10001
(212) 736-5000/(800) 233-8585
Across the street from the arena.

Park Lane
36 Central Park South
New York, NY 10019
(212) 371-4000
Just over a mile from the arena.

THE KNICKS AT MADISON SQUARE GARDEN

May 8, 1970: An injured Willis Reed limps onto the court and starts Game 7 of the NBA Finals. Reed hits his first two shots and leads the Knicks to an emotional 113–99 win over the Los Angeles Lakers.

Nov. 18, 1972: The Knicks come back from an 86–68 deficit by scoring 19 straight points in the last 5 minutes and 11 seconds to beat the Milwaukee Bucks 87–86.

April 22, 1984: After scoring 46 points against the Detroit Pistons three nights earlier in Game 2 of the first round of the playoffs, Bernard King matches that total in Game 3. The Knicks win 120–113.

May 14, 1992: Despite spraining his ankle in the third quarter, Patrick Ewing leads the Knicks to a dramatic 100–86 win over the Chicago Bulls, forcing a seventh game in their Eastern Conference final.

June 2, 1993: The Knicks fall 97–94 to the Bulls in the pivotal Game 5 of the Eastern Conference final when Charles Smith is unable to convert on a series of last-second layups.

June 5, 1994: Patrick Ewing's slam dunk with 27 seconds left gives the Knicks a 94–90 win in Game 7 of their Eastern Conference final over the Indiana Pacers.

In the Hot Seats at Madison Square Garden

The Knicks have sold out every game since 1992. Season tickets account for a large number of the seats, but the Knicks put single-game tickets on sale twice a year—once before the season for the first half, and again during the first half for the second half. Tickets go quickly; those calling on the second day might find slim pickings in terms of available games and seat selection.

BAD SEATS

The sight lines are generally good, although the nosebleed seats at the top of the Garden, in sections 401–428, are far from the court. The seating area also rises quickly from the floor, making for a steep climb to the upper sections. But even up there, the view can be decent. Throughout most of the Garden there is not a lot of legroom, so it can get cramped, especially if you are above average size.

SCALPING

All along Seventh and Eighth avenues, between 34th and 31st streets, though signs warn that it's illegal. With Knicks tickets hard to get, it's definitely a seller's market.

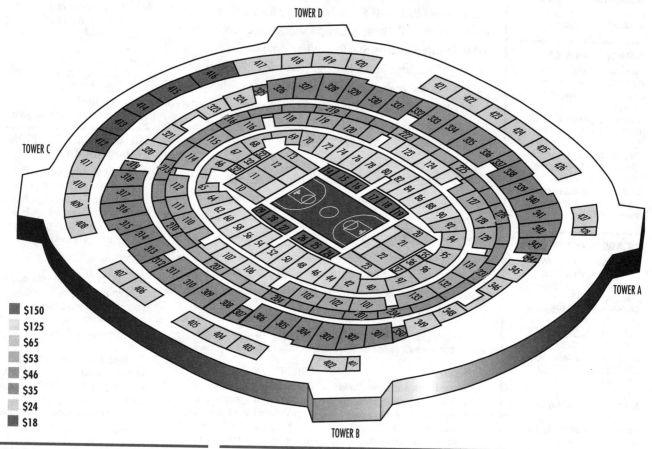

- ■ $150
- □ $125
- ▨ $65
- ▨ $53
- ▨ $46
- ■ $35
- ▨ $24
- ■ $18

HOME-COURT ADVANTAGE

Even though this is a more upscale, suit-and-tie crowd than you'll see at Rangers games, don't expect quiet stands. Unlike at many other arenas in the league, the scoreboard has to keep up with the crowd. Knicks fans can generate enough electricity and noise to seriously affect the performances of players, many of whom are already a bit starstruck by the famous faces at courtside and the history of this place. A Knicks game at the Garden is not a diverting way to spend an evening; it's an intense and exhilarating experience shared between the fans and their team. Clearly the team responds—they're 69–13 at home since 1992.

GETTING TO MADISON SQUARE GARDEN

Public transportation: Take the B, D, F, Q, N, or R train to the 34th Street station; MSG is 2 blocks west. The A, C, E, 1, 2, 3 and 9 trains all stop at Pennsylvania Station–34th Street, which is directly below MSG.
By car: From New Jersey and south, enter Manhattan via the Lincoln Tunnel. Follow signs for downtown and turn left on 34th Street.
From Connecticut and the north, take Route I-95 to Route 9A-south. Exit at 34th Street.

TICKET INFORMATION
Address: 4 Pennsylvania Plaza, NY, NY 10001
Phone: (212) 465-6741 or TicketMaster at

(212) 307-7171, (201) 507-8900, (516) 888-9000, (609) 665-2500, (914) 454-3388, or (203) 624-0033
Hours: Mon.–Sat. 12–6.

Prices: $150, $125, $65, $53, $46, $35, $24, $18.

Orlando Arena

ARENA STATS

Location: 1 Magic Place, Orlando, FL 32801
Opened: Jan. 29, 1989
Capacity: 17,248
Services for fans with disabilities: Seating is available in sections 109–115 and 104–120, with a special entrance on the east side of the building, north of the arena box office. More than 200 temporary and permanent seats are available throughout the stadium.

ARENA FIRSTS

Regular-season game: Nov. 4, 1989, 111–106 loss to the New Jersey Nets.
Points scored: Jerry Reynolds of Orlando.
Overtime game: Feb. 14, 1990, 135–129 over the Chicago Bulls.
Playoff game: April 28, 1994, 89–88 loss to the Indiana Pacers.
NBA Finals game: June 7, 1995, 120–118 overtime loss to the Houston Rockets.

TEAM NOTEBOOK

Franchise history: Orlando Magic, 1989–present.
Rookie of the Year: Shaquille O'Neal, 1992–93.
Conference titles: 1994-95.

In the land of Disney, the Orlando Magic go to great lengths to supply fans at the "Orena"—how the locals refer to the Orlando Arena—with as much entertainment and glitz as possible. Between what one reporter described as "nuclear rock music" and the contests, giveaways, prizes, and roving magicians, the Orena on game nights can often seem as much a circus tent as a basketball arena. The man behind this extravaganza is former general manager Pat Williams (now senior executive vice president), whom one local reporter describes as a "Bill Veeck disciple." A big part of the off-court "Magic Act" is the mascot Stuff the Magic Dragon. An energetic entertainer, he is successful at raising the noise level of the crowd. Stuff is joined by a freelance act, a 40-something gentleman known as the "Fat Guy" for reasons that are apparent.

Stuff and the Fat Guy will have to work a lot harder now. The other men responsible for the excitement were Shaquille O'Neal and Penny Hardaway, but now that Shaq has gone Hollywood and donned the Lakers' purple and gold, it's all up to Penny to provide on-court interest. During the Shaq years, some fans suggested the Magic went too far with all of the non-basketball amusements, creating a carnival-like atmosphere that seemed to match the attention paid to Shaq wherever he went. That ambience, coupled with the youthful character of the team, made this an exciting place for an NBA game. Whether or not Orlando really loves this team—still a threat with Hardaway, Horace Grant, and Dennis Scott—and not just the hype, will now be seen.

HOT TIPS FOR VISITING FANS

PARKING
There are 3,500 on-site parking spaces at Orlando Arena. To avoid delays after the game, you can park several blocks away in the downtown area, where there are more than 7,500 spaces within a ¾-mile radius of the arena, priced from $2 to $4. The team operates a free shuttle from downtown lots to the arena. There is also a free shuttle to Church Street Station, a local entertainment complex, from the arena.

MEDIA
Radio: WDBO (580 AM).
TV: WKCF (Channel 18) and Sunshine Network (cable). Chip Caray, the Magic's television play-by-play man, comes from the well-known broadcasting family.

CUISINE
Popular items include tacos, burritos, churros, and assorted Italian fare. A grill serves burgers, fries, and chicken. Pizza Hut pizza and Subway sandwiches also are available. Imported and specialty beers, including Molson, Sam Adams, Fosters, and Heineken, are on tap in each of the arena's four corners.
An easy stop after the game, Church Street Station (407-422-2434), is about five minutes from the arena. This entertainment complex contains several restaurants and nightclubs. There is a $16.95 general charge covering admission to the clubs. A shuttle leaves approximately one hour before the game and departs from the arena one hour after the final buzzer. Given its huge tourism business, though, Orlando has a lot more to offer in the way of dining. Try Charley's Steak House (407-851-8400) for huge, beautiful slabs of meat, or Straub's Seafood (407-273-9330) for local fish served any way you want. Crab House (407-352-6140) has a terrific all-you-can-eat raw bar and blue crab out of the shell.

LODGING NEAR THE ARENA

Omni Marriott Downtown
400 W. Livingston St.
Orlando, FL 32801
(407) 843-6664/(800) 574-3160
Across the street from the arena.

Harley Hotel of Orlando
151 E. Washington St.
Orlando, FL 32801
(407) 841-3220/(800) 321-2323
8 blocks from the arena.

THE MAGIC AT ORLANDO ARENA

Dec. 30, 1990: Scott Skiles dishes an NBA record 30 assists. The Magic beat the Denver Nuggets 155–116.

April 20, 1994: Shaquille O'Neil sets the team single-game scoring mark with 53 points in a 121–101 win over the Minnesota Timberwolves.

April 17, 1995: Shaq's 34 points and 12 rebounds lead the Magic to a 111–110 win over the Bullets, clinching their division.

May 16, 1995: The Magic take Game 5 of their conference semifinal series against the Chicago Bulls 103–95.

June 4, 1995: The Magic beat the Pacers 105–81 to advance to the NBA Finals.

In the Hot Seats at Orlando Arena

Since the Magic's debut in 1989, the team has become a hot ticket; virtually every game is sold out. Only 1,000 non-season tickets are sold to each game, usually at the end of September. With a basketball capacity of 17,248, the arena is one of the smaller facilities in the NBA, but its size creates a certain intimacy. This state-of-the-art building also has good sight lines and a large number of comfortable seats.

GOOD SEATS

All lower-level seats are sold out to season ticketholders, but corner sections, such as 226 and 227, have seats in the F range for $20 that offer good views at a decent price. The $14 seats, the G price, are in the end zones; they're good bargains, but the F seats are better.

SCALPING

Scalpers can be found around the arena, although not in great numbers. Fans shouldn't expect to bargain down the price of a ticket very much—there are more than enough potential buyers for scalpers to get close to what they're asking.

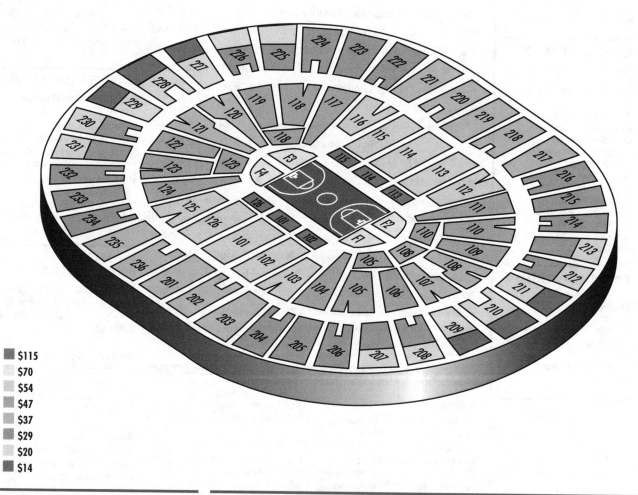

- ■ $115
- □ $70
- ▨ $54
- ▨ $47
- ▨ $37
- ■ $29
- ▨ $20
- ■ $14

HOME-COURT ADVANTAGE

The decibel increase is magnified by the building's small size, which amplifies the roars from the crowd. The Orlando faithful's cheering has a very definite impact on the players, a young team driven as much by emotion as by talent.

GETTING TO ORLANDO ARENA

Public transportation: A free shuttle runs from various stops on Orange Avenue to the arena entrance. Call (407) 841-8240 for more information.
By car: From the airport, get on Semoran (I-436) and continue 4 to 5 miles to the East/West Expressway. Go west on the expressway and connect to I-4; exit I-4 at Amelia Street. Turn left; the arena is on the left.

TICKET INFORMATION
Address: 600 W. Amelia St. Orlando, FL 32801
Phone: (407) 649-BALL (2255) or

TicketMaster at (407) 839-3900; (407) 89-MAGIC for tickets for fans with disabilities only.
Hours: Mon.–Fri. 10–5.

Prices: $115, $70, $54, $47, $37, $29, $20, $14.

CoreStates Center

ARENA STATS

Location: Broad St. and Pattison Ave., Philadelphia, PA 19147
Opened: Aug. 31, 1996
Capacity: 18,168
Services for fans with disabilities: Seats are available throughout the arena, depending on ticket availability at each game. Call (215) 339-7600 for more information.

TEAM NOTEBOOK

Franchise history: Syracuse Nationals, 1946–48 (NBL); Syracuse Nationals, 1948–63 (NBA); Philadelphia 76ers, 1963–present.
Division titles: 1949–50, 1951–52, 1954–55, 1965–66, 1966–67, 1967–68, 1976–77, 1977–78, 1982–83, 1989–90.
Conference titles: 1949–50, 1953–54, 1954–55, 1966–67, 1976–77, 1979–80, 1981–82, 1982–83.
NBA championships: 1954–55, 1966–67, 1982–83.
Basketball Hall of Fame: Dolph Schayes, 1972; Harry Litwack, 1975; Frank McGuire, 1976; Wilt Chamberlain, 1978; Hal Greer, 1981; Billy Cunningham, 1985; Jack Ramsay, 1992; Julius Erving, 1993.
Retired numbers: 6, Julius Erving; 13, Wilt Chamberlain; 15, Hal Greer; 24, Bobby Jones; 32, Billy Cunningham.

Philadelphians are well known for their sports knowledge and their impatience. If the home team is losing, fans make their feelings clear by booing players during the game and venting their disappointment on the city's sports talk-radio programs afterward. Now the 76ers are the team on the hot seat. Fans are frustrated by losing seasons, unpopular trades, and an ownership perceived as unresponsive.

This sense of disaffection permeated the Spectrum for almost 30 years. Even when the team won its last championship, in 1983, the Sixers drew only 646,788 (a franchise high) to the Spectrum. Some ascribe this less-than-overwhelming support not only to lack of interest but also to the popularity of such local collegiate basketball rivals as Penn, La Salle, Temple, St. Joseph's, and Villanova. It may also have to do with things such as signing Shawn Bradley—a favorite Spectrum whipping boy—then trading him for Derrick Coleman, a malcontent extraordinaire sure to please the Philly crowds.

But there is new hope on the horizon in the form of a snazzy new arena about 100 yards away, where JFK Stadium used to be. The Sixers' new 21,000-seat home—CoreStates Center—leaves the fans with little to grumble about in terms of amenities. Its oval design provides a good sight line from every seat in the house, there are twice as many restrooms as there were in the Spectrum (a consistent focus of the recalcitrant Philly crowd's ongoing gripe), and the fancy videoscreens and scoreboard are on a par with the best in the NBA. There's even a microbrewery (Red Bell) on the premises, as well as a sports bar and restaurant and a view of the Philadelphia skyline.

It's tough to say whether Sixers fans will embrace their new stadium with loving arms, especially after the negotiations for its construction dragged beyond the bounds of their limited patience—and followed threats to move the team to New Jersey. But even if the fans may be a bit disagreeable at first, CoreStates Center is going to be a good place to watch a game.

HOT TIPS FOR VISITING FANS

PARKING

Access to CoreStates Center is very good, with on-site parking for more than 12,000 cars at a cost of $4.50 per vehicle. Cars move fairly quickly after the game because the entrance to I-95 is just blocks away. There is also on-street parking next to the naval hospital on the west side of Broad Street, which runs past the arena. However, there have been reports of broken windows in cars parked on this block.

MEDIA

Radio: WIP (610 AM).
TV: Prism/SportsChannel (cable). Mark Zurnoff, the Sixers' play-by-play announcer on television, is joined by commentator Steve Mix.

CUISINE

CoreStates Center features such local favorites as pretzels with mustard and cheese steaks. But there's a lot more than hoagies in the 30 concession stands, including a wide variety of ethnic foods and an on-site Red Bell microbrewery that will brew beer right there at the arena and sell eight varieties on tap. For fancier eats, try the arena's own full-service club restaurant, Victor's.

After the game, try Pat's Steaks (215-468-1546) for a slice of true Philly gastronomy. Open 24 hours and offering only counter service with several tables out front, Pat's has been serving up a variety of steak sandwiches since 1930. While the most popular selection is the mushroom cheese steak with onions, you can get pizza steak, steak and peppers, as well as roast pork and sausage. Ask for a "cheese wit," as the locals do, meaning a cheese steak with onions.

Melrose Diner (215-467-6644) is about 10 blocks north of the arena. A favorite late-night haunt of Philadelphians since 1935, many local sports figures, including Dr. J., have been customers over the years. For Italian and another dose of Philly atmosphere, try Dante and Luigi's (215-922-9501). Though well known for its fine food, it's even better known in the area for a recent Mob hit that took place there.

LODGING NEAR THE ARENA

Sheraton Society Hill
1 Dock St.
Philadelphia, PA 19106
(215) 238-6000/(800) 325-3535
7 miles from the arena.

Franklin Plaza Hotel
2 Franklin Plaza
Philadelphia, PA 19103
(215) 448-2000/(800)822-4200
6 miles from the arena.

In the Hot Seats at CoreStates Center

The Spectrum was one of the oldest arenas in the NBA, and fans had several complaints, including insufficient lighting and not enough restrooms and concession stands. All of these concerns have been addressed at CoreStates Center.

GOOD SEATS

Although the Sixers' premium seats are sold out to season ticketholders, there are still plenty of very good seats available—virtually every seat at CoreStates Center has a good sight line. For the best value, check out the seats in the lower level behind the basket (sections 106–108 and 108–120); at $28, they're a steal. Also well worth the $28 are sections 223–224, 211–215, and 201–203.

SCALPING

Scalpers are usually in front of the arena; near the subway station across the street; and a block away, near a naval hospital. Scalpers are sometimes willing to bargain the price down to get rid of the tickets they have.

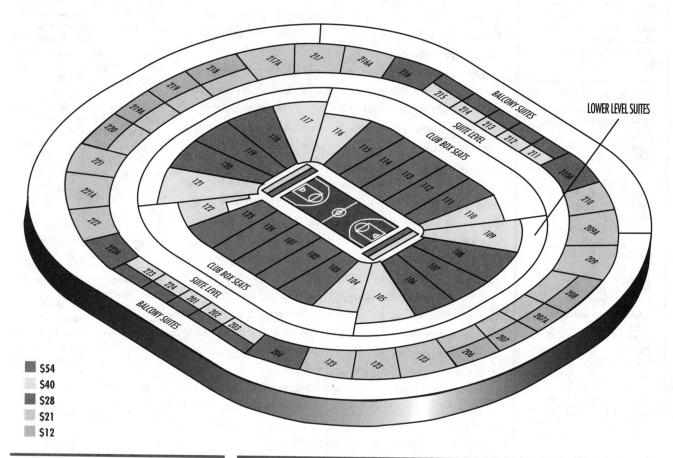

- ■ $54
- ▨ $40
- ▨ $28
- ▨ $21
- ▨ $12

HOME-COURT ADVANTAGE

Since Philly fans often boo the home team more than they do the visitors, there's almost an advantage for the visiting team when the Sixers play poorly. Some fans also have little patience for any entertainment-oriented attempts to liven things up when the team is losing. Philadelphia is just a tough town when the locals are not faring well. Fans lament the death of Dave Zinkoff, the team's famous public-address announcer, whose distinctive voice and style—"Now entering the game, Julius Errrrrrrrving"—is sorely missed.

GETTING TO CORESTATES CENTER

Public transportation: Catch the Broad Street subway at 15th and Market southbound to the last stop, Broad and Pattison. The arena is 1 block away. Call (215) 580-7800 for more information.

By car: From the north, take I-95 south to the Broad Street exit. Follow Broad Street to the first light (Zinkoff Boulevard) and turn right. The arena is on the left.
From the south, take I-95 north to the Broad Street exit. Follow Broad Street to the first light (Zinkoff Boulevard) and turn right.
From the west, take I-76 east. At Center City, stay to the right and follow signs for New Jersey and the Sports Complex heading toward the Walt Whitman Bridge. Take the Broad Street exit, No. 45 (Sports Complex), and make a right at the bottom of the ramp onto Broad Street. Follow Broad Street (stay to the far left) to Pattison Avenue. Follow Pattison Avenue to the arena.
From the east, take the Walt Whitman Bridge to I-76 west through the tolls. Continue on I-76 west to exit 46B (South Seventh Street). Follow ramp and go straight through one traffic light and continue on to Pattison Avenue. Take a right onto Pattison Avenue and follow to 11th Street, the first traffic light. Turn left.

TICKET INFORMATION
Address: P.O. Box 25050, Philadelphia, PA 19147

Phone: (215) 339-7676 or TicketMaster at (215) 336-2000, (609) 665-2500, (302) 984-2000, or (717) 693-4100

Hours: Mon.–Fri. 9–5.
Prices: $54, $40, $28, $21, $12.

ARENA STATS

Location: 201 E. Jefferson St., Phoenix, AZ 85004
Opened: June 1, 1992
Capacity: 19,023
Services for fans with disabilities: Seating available in sections 105, 106, 110, 111, 117, 118, 122, 123, 211, and 227. Each suite has two wheelchair-accessible spaces.

ARENA FIRSTS

Regular-season game: Nov. 7, 1992, 111–105 over the Los Angeles Clippers.
Overtime game: March 22, 1994, 124–118 win over the Miami Heat.
Playoff game: May 11, 1993, 94–89 over the San Antonio Spurs.
NBA Finals game: June 9, 1993, 100–92 loss to the Chicago Bulls.

TEAM NOTEBOOK

Franchise history: Phoenix Suns, 1968–present.
Division titles: 1980–81, 1992–93, 1994–95.
Conference titles: 1975–76, 1992–93.
Basketball Hall of Fame: Connie Hawkins, 1992; Gail Goodrich, 1996.
Most Valuable Player: Charles Barkley, 1992–93.
Rookies of the Year: Alvan Adams, 1975–76; Walter Davis, 1977–78.
Retired numbers: 5, Dick Van Arsdale; 6, Walter Davis; 33, Alvan Adams; 42, Connie Hawkins; 44, Paul Westphal.

Timing is everything. For the 1992–93 NBA season, the Suns got a new coach in Paul Westphal, a new star in Charles Barkley, and a new building in America West Arena. Even the players voted it the best arena in the league in a 1994 *USA TODAY* survey.

The Suns hired former player Alvan Adams to tour the finest arenas in the world; the best of their features were incorporated into the arena's design. Everything is state-of-the-art, built with not only the fans but also the players in mind. Unlike most NBA teams, the Suns practice where they play, in a gym built next to the locker rooms at the arena.

All the seats, even the less expensive ones, have great sight lines. America West Arena is pretty, too, with the Suns' team colors—purple, orange, and copper—everywhere. No expense has been spared. The downtown location is perfect. Crime is low, and plenty of police and security officers help with traffic and directions into and out of the arena's 11 acres.

Get here early and stroll around. Before game time, bands play outside on the plaza, and Suns fans love to mingle and chat with tourists and visitors before tipoff. Owner Jerry Colangelo's office overlooks the arena plaza so he can watch the people coming in. Wave to him. He'll wave back. Or, if you are too excited about the game to leave your seat, come back later for a guided tour—it's worth it.

HOT TIPS FOR VISITING FANS

PARKING

A 900-space parking garage is attached, a 1,500-space garage is across the street, and more than 11,000 parking spaces in less expensive lots are within an eight-minute walk of the entrances. The garage across the street is $6. The farther you park from the building, the less expensive the parking is, and the quicker you can get out of the traffic congestion.

MEDIA

Radio: KTAR (620 AM).
TV: KUTP (Channel 45) and Cox Cable (ASPN). All away games are televised on Channel 45 (with the exception of nationally televised games); cable has the home games. The Channel 45 games are simulcast on KTAR, and some are available on pay-per-view.

CUISINE

Popcorn, nachos, beer, soda, peanuts, ice cream—all the regular fare—are prepared on site. The service is excellent, too: If you end up buying more food than you can carry, attendants might help you tote it to your seat. The Copper Club is a 10,000-square-foot bar and restaurant with a view of the court on the second concourse level. It serves a buffet on event nights and is open to the public for lunch on weekdays. The first concourse has its own food court, featuring Whataburger, Subway, Pizza Hut, and Miss Karen's Frozen Yogurt. It is also open for lunch on weekdays.

The place to go after the game is Majerle's Sports Grill (602-253-9004). Former Suns star Dan Majerle drops in and mingles when he's in town, as do most of the players from both teams. It's just up the street at 24 North Second Street, and it stays open from 11 to 11 every day. The Arizona Center, at 455 North Third Street, has Sam's Café (602-252-3545), Lombardi's (602-257-8323), and Players (602-252-6222) eateries.

LODGING NEAR THE ARENA

The Ritz-Carlton
2401 E. Camelback Rd.
Phoenix, AZ 85016
(602) 468-0700/(800) 241-3333
12 miles from the arena.

Hyatt Regency
122 N. Second St.
Phoenix, AZ 85004
(602) 252-1234/(800) 233-1234
1 block from the arena.

THE SUNS AT AMERICA WEST ARENA

Dec. 30, 1992: The Suns stretch their home winning streak to 14 games when they top the Houston Rockets 133–110.

March 23, 1993: A brawl erupts during a game against the New York Knicks. Six players are ejected, and $159,500 in fines are levied. The Suns win 121–92.

April 11, 1993: The Suns beat the Utah Jazz 112–99, giving them the Pacific Division title.

May 9, 1993: After dropping the first two games of the series at home, the Suns come back to beat the Los Angeles Lakers in Game 5 of their playoff series.

June 5, 1993: Dan Majerle sets an NBA playoff record with eight three-pointers in a 120–114 win over the Seattle SuperSonics in the fifth game of the Western Conference final.

May 20, 1995: Kevin Johnson scores 46 points and Charles Barkley pulls in 23 rebounds in a 115–114 loss to the Houston Rockets in Game 7 of the Western Conference semifinals.

In the Hot Seats at America West Arena

The arena seats 19,023 for basketball and has few bad seats. The Suns capped their season ticket sales at 16,000 to keep 3,000 seats available for individual games, but it is still tough to get a ticket. Try Dillard's ticket system by phone and plan ahead. You can use the on-site ticket office on the main plaza at the northwest entrance, too.

GOOD SEATS

No floor seats are available for individual games, but try to sit opposite the benches so you can watch the interplay on the sidelines between the coach and the players and see what's going on at the scorer's table. The row of seats on the floor is for the high rollers. The rest of the seats are on risers; you're going to feel close to the action no matter where you sit.

BAD SEATS

If you can help it, don't sit right behind the basket at any level, because you're often looking through the backboard at a skewed perspective. You don't need to sit at center court, either. You'll see all you need to see from any corner, as long as you aren't too low.

SCALPING

Scalping is legal in Phoenix but can't be done on arena grounds, so sellers cross the street to do business. The markup is about $20 for a regular-season game. For playoffs and special games, fans pay $50 or more above face value for prime seats.

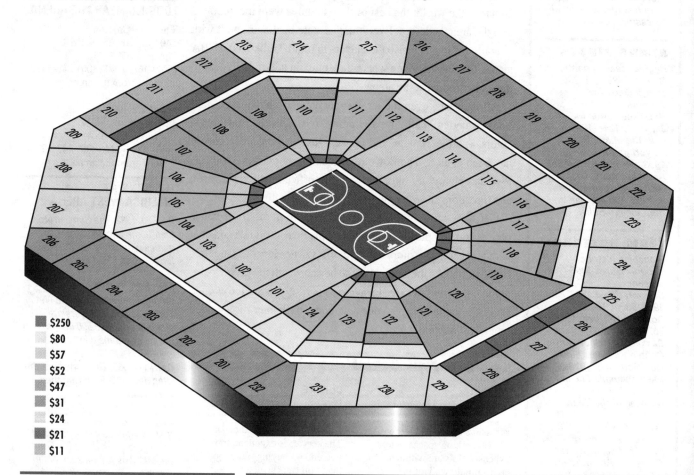

Legend:
- $250
- $80
- $57
- $52
- $47
- $31
- $24
- $21
- $11

HOME-COURT ADVANTAGE

The luxury in which the Suns bask can be intimidating to visiting players. The fans are loud and loyal. Even the Suns' front-office personnel are notorious for sitting courtside and riding the refs. The fact that the Suns practice where they play makes a difference as well. They're completely at home here—and what a home!

GETTING TO AMERICA WEST ARENA

Public transportation: Phoenix transit buses stop ½ block from the arena. The main bus station is across the street. Any bus coming into downtown passes near America West Arena. Call (602) 253-5000 for more information.

By car: From the north, take the I-17 Black Canyon Freeway to Washington Street. Go left onto Washington, then left on First Street. The arena will be on the left.

From the south, take the I-10 Maricopa north to Jefferson Street. Go left onto Jefferson. The arena will be on the right.

From the east, take the SR-360 Superstition Freeway to the I-10 Mariciopa, heading north.

From the west, take the I-10 Papago to First Street. Go right onto First Street. The arena will be on the right.

TICKET INFORMATION

Address: P.O. Box 515, Phoenix, AZ 85001
Phone: (602) 379-SUNS (7867) or Dillard's at (602) 678-2222

Hours: Mon.–Fri. 8–5, Sat. 10–4.
Prices: $250, $80, $57, $52, $47, $31, $24, $21, $11.

The Rose Garden

ARENA STATS

Location: One Center Court, Portland, OR 97208
Opened: October 13,1995
Capacity: 21,300
Services for fans with disabilities: In addition to reserved parking for fans with mobility impairments, the Rose Garden provides a wide range of services. Call (503) 797-9617 for further information.

ARENA FIRSTS

Regular-season game: Nov. 3, 1995, 92–80 loss to the Vancouver Grizzlies.
Overtime game: Dec. 10, 1995, 103–101 win over the Houston Rockets.
Playoff game: April 29, 1996, 94–91 win over the Utah Jazz in overtime.

TEAM NOTEBOOK

Franchise history: Portland Trail Blazers, 1970–present.
Division titles: 1977–78, 1990–91, 1991–92.
Conference titles: 1976–77, 1989–90, 1991–92.
NBA championship: 1976–77.
Basketball Hall of Fame: Jack Ramsay, 1992; Bill Walton, 1993.
Retired numbers: 1, Larry Weinberg; 13, Dave Twardzik; 15, Larry Steele; 20, Maurice Lucas; 32, Bill Walton; 36, Lloyd Neal; 45, Geoff Petrie; 77, Jack Ramsay.

Only seven years after playing their first game, the Portland Trail Blazers won the NBA championship in 1977, and "Blazermania" swept this portion of the Pacific Northwest. After 25 years at the NBA's smallest arena (12,888 seats), where the team drew more than 13 million fans and 809 consecutive sold-out games, Portland's beloved Blazers moved from their cozy home at Memorial Coliseum to the $262 million high-tech Rose Garden next door.

Though Portland's failure to win another title had diminished the deafening roar in the Coliseum to what one fan described as "intermittent showers," the crowd noise was still enough to distract visiting teams. Some fans worried that the huge, new Rose Garden—which seats 21,300 for basketball—might dampen the noise, but the Blazers are taking no chances on losing their home-court advantage: The $2 million acoustics system includes rotating panels that reverberate crowd noise and reflect it back down to the court.

While some mourn the loss of one of the few remaining traditional basketball courts to another flashy NBA-spectacle arena, there are some major advantages to the move. For one thing, according to the arena's fact sheet on the Internet, the Rose Garden prides itself in being one of the most "bladder-friendly" arenas in the NBA, with 32 public restrooms. If you do get stuck in line at the loo, however, you won't have to worry about missing any of the action—there are 700 televisions within the concourse, and one of them is bound to be nearby.

HOT TIPS FOR VISITING FANS

PARKING

Parking is not a problem at the Rose Garden. The Rose Quarter complex has four on-site parking facilities (almost 2,500 spaces at $10 apiece), and runs free shuttle buses before and after every game to additional lots in the nearby Lloyd District ($7). Parking (with free shuttle passes) may be purchased in advance with your ticket.

MEDIA

Radio: KEX (1190 AM).
TV: KGW-TV (Channel 8). In the past 20 years, Bill Schonley has broadcast more than 2,000 Blazers games on radio and TV.

CUISINE

There are 19 concession stands inside the Rose Garden, with different themes: The Blaze has flame-broiled burgers; the Flying Wok has "anti-gravity Asian cuisine"; Houndogs has "Viva Las hot dogs"; Meschugenah Mama's is a New York-style deli; I Scream is ice cream; Arena Roma has Italian food; Bridgetown Cantina and Truck Stop has Mexican food; and Rosie's Frying Circus does sandwiches and French fries. One stand you might not find in other arenas is Havanas, which serves not only espresso drinks but also wines and cigars. There are also several restaurants within the Rose Quarter complex, including Cucina! Cucina! Italian Cafe (503-238-9800) and Friday's Front Row Sports Grill (503-235-0907). Jake's Famous Crawfish (503-226-1419), a popular spot with Blazer fans, players, and opponents, is about 10 minutes from the arena in a historic building with stained glass and paintings. When Jake's first opened, more than 100 years ago, the crawfish were raised in the basement. Champions American Sports Bar (503-274-2470) is in the Marriott Hotel across from the arena. Visiting teams often stay there, so players are frequent customers.

LODGING NEAR THE ARENA

Hotel Vintage Plaza
422 S.W. Broadway
Portland, OR 97205
(503) 228-1212/(800) 243-0555
4 miles from the arena.

Red Lion Lloyd Center
1000 N.E. Multnomah St.
Portland, OR 97232
(503) 281-6111/(800)547-8010
6 blocks from the arena.

THE TRAIL BLAZERS AT THE ROSE GARDEN

Nov. 3, 1995: The Blazers open their season in their new home with a 92–80 loss to the expansion Vancouver Grizzlies.

March 8, 1996: A 117–105 victory over the Sacramento Kings propels the Blazers to a record 18–4 run over the next six weeks. They would not lose at home until the final day of the season.

April 29, 1996: In Game 3 of the first round of the playoffs—a sellout at the Rose Garden—the Blazers hold the Utah Jazz, best-shooting team in the NBA, to a .378 shot chart (34–90) and win 94–91 in overtime. It is the Blazers' 14th consecutive playoff appearance (18th in 19 years), the longest active streak in the league and the fourth-longest in professional sports.

May 1, 1996: The second straight NBA playoff sellout game at the Rose Garden extends the Blazers' record of consecutive playoff sellouts to 73, dating back to 1977. The Blazers beat Utah 98–90.

In the Hot Seats at The Rose Garden

More than 85% of the Rose Garden's 21,300 seats are sold to season ticketholders. The remaining 3,000 tickets are offered first in multi-game packages, then for individual games. The Blazers try to keep a variety of seats available for individual games so that those who are lucky enough to get tickets can get good seats. The best bet is to call the ticket office in August to find out when tickets will go on sale, and purchase them immediately.

GOOD SEATS

Though individual-game ticket buyers will not have access to premier seats, there are excellent seats available in some of the best sections. Corner sight lines are best: Seats in lower-level sections 103, 110, 114, and 121 cost $80.30 and are the best that can be bought for a single game; upper-level sections 205, 212, 220, and 227 are next-best, at $72.85. Other great view options are the side-court upper-level seats in sections 302–333 at $47.65.

BAD SEATS

There are no overhangs, posts, or pillars inside the Rose Garden, so technically speaking there are no obstructed views. However, seats in end-zone sections 223, 224, 208, and 209 will put a backboard between you and the action, and are a bum deal at $50.40.

SCALPING

Where there are sellouts, there are scalpers, and the Rose Garden is no exception. But the demand for tickets is far greater than the supply, so don't expect the sellers to negotiate.

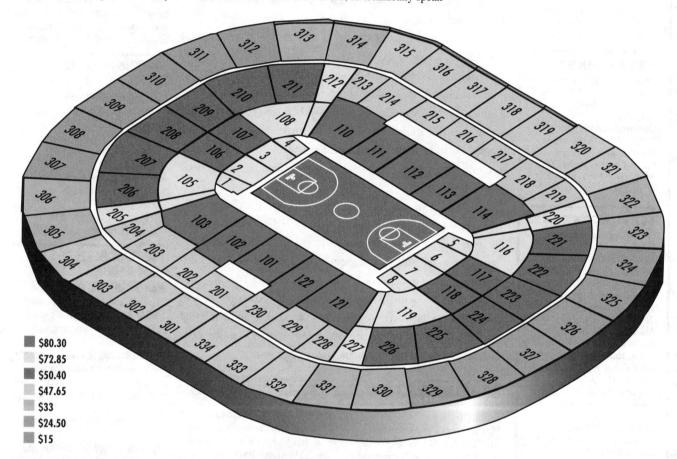

- $80.30
- $72.85
- $50.40
- $47.65
- $33
- $24.50
- $15

HOME-COURT ADVANTAGE

The Blazers' home record has consistently been among the best in the NBA, and with the league's longest consecutive sellout streak (more than 800 games), fan support has been a major factor. That trend seems to be continuing at the Rose Garden, where a special acoustical system aids the cause by reverberating the crowd noise back toward the court.

GETTING TO THE ROSE GARDEN

Public transportation: The Rose Quarter Transit Center is across the street from the front door to the Rose Garden. It is served by MAX light rail and 10 Tri-Met buslines.
By car: From Portland International Airport, take Airport Way to I-205 south. Exit I-84 west, proceed to I-5 north and take the Broadway–Weidler/Rose Quarter exit. Turn left at the second light onto Broadway. Follow signs to the Rose Garden.

TICKET INFORMATION
Address: P.O. Box 4448, Portland, OR 97208.
Phone: (503) 231-8000

Hours: Mon.–Fri. 8–6:30, Sat. 10–5.
Prices: $80.30, $72.85, $50.40, $47.65, $33, $24.50, $15.

ARCO Arena

ARENA STATS

Location: *1 Sports Parkway, Sacramento, CA 95834*
Opened: *Nov. 8, 1988*
Capacity: *17,317*
Services for fans with disabilities: *Seating varies for each game. Call (916) 928-6900 for more information.*

ARENA FIRSTS

Regular-season game: *Nov. 8, 1988, 97–75 loss to the Seattle Super-Sonics.*
Points scored: *Reggie Theus of the Kings.*
Overtime game: *Dec. 1, 1988, 133–126 loss to the Denver Nuggets.*
Playoff game: *April 26, 1996, 97–85 loss to the Seattle SuperSonics.*

TEAM NOTEBOOK

Franchise history: *Rochester Royals, 1945–48 (NBL); Rochester Royals, 1948–49 (BAA); Rochester Royals, 1949–57 (NBA); Cincinnati Royals, 1957–72; Kansas City-Omaha Kings, 1972–75; Kansas City Kings, 1975–85; Sacramento Kings, 1985–present.*
Division titles: *1948–49, 1951–52, 1978–79.*
Conference title: *1950–51.*
NBA championship: *1950–51.*
Basketball Hall of Fame: *Bob Davies, 1969; Jerry Lucas, 1979; Oscar Robertson, 1979; Jack Twyman, 1982; Nate Archibald, 1991.*
Most Valuable Player: *Oscar Robertson, 1963–64.*
Rookies of the Year: *Maurice Stokes, 1955–56; Oscar Robertson, 1960–61; Jerry Lucas, 1963–64; Phil Ford, 1978–79.*
Retired numbers: *1, Nate Archibald; 11, Bob Davies; 12, Maurice Stokes; 14, Oscar Robertson; 27, Jack Twyman; 44, Sam Lacey.*

S acramento is considered the gateway to California's gold country, and while the city's resident NBA franchise has not struck gold on the court, it certainly has at the box office. Despite no winning seasons since moving from Kansas City in 1985, the Kings have sold out ARCO Arena for every game since it opened in 1988, the third-longest sellout streak in the league, behind Portland's and Boston's. This success is not surprising, considering the Kings are the only game in town in one of the NBA's smallest markets.

Even when the Kings are not tearing down the hoops, ARCO Arena does its best to please. The arena is a large, tan rectangle sitting alone amid 105 acres of largely undeveloped land. Inside, it's another story. As fans enter, they are greeted by countless television monitors showing the Kings' in-house pre-game show—unique in the NBA. Once the game starts, the crowd takes over. ARCO has a reputation among players for being one of the loudest arenas in the league, a prime reason being wood floors in the stands so fans can stomp their feet.

Tickets have always been hard to come by, and now that the Kings have made the playoffs, they're worth much more than their weight in gold.

HOT TIPS FOR VISITING FANS

PARKING
ARCO Arena is surrounded by a spacious, well-lighted lot with spaces for 12,000 cars. Cost is $6. The Kings also make an effort to keep traffic moving after the game, keeping waiting time to a minimum.

MEDIA
Radio: KHTK (1140 AM—English), KRCX (1110 AM—Spanish).
TV: KPWB, Channel 31.

CUISINE
Besides the standard fare, ARCO offers such options as Mexican and Italian cuisine, barbecued beef, and the cheddar dog—a fan favorite consisting of a hot dog baked with cheese inside, surrounded by bagel-like dough. ARCO also features a Java City concessionaire that sells specialty coffees.
The Skyline Club, a buffet restaurant in the south corner above sections 202 and 203,
serves hot entrées such as prime rib. The club opens at 5:30, one hour before the arena gates open, for fans with a ticket to that night's game. After the game, fans flock to the Locker Room, a nightclub at the north end above sections 214 and 215. Besides a full bar, it offers make-your-own sandwiches. The Locker Room is also open before the game. Players have been known to stop by. About 15 minutes south is America Live!, a multi-entertainment complex containing six night-clubs and two restaurants. The Sports City Café (916-447-4600) has a varied menu featuring Louisiana crab cakes, Cornish game hen, and an extensive selection of California wines. Next door, the Original Sports Bar not only has the obligatory sports memorabilia and big-screen televisions but pool tables, a caged basketball court, and a video arcade as well. America Live! also includes the Gatlin Brothers Music City Grille (916-447-5483), which showcases local country bands.

LODGING NEAR THE ARENA

Hyatt Regency Sacramento
1209 L St.
Sacramento, CA 95814
(916) 443-1234/(800) 233-1234
10 miles from the arena.

Courtyard by Marriott-Natomas
2101 River Plaza Dr.
Sacramento, CA 95833
(916) 922-1120/(800) 443-6000
6 miles from the arena.

THE KINGS AT ARCO ARENA

Feb. 9, 1989: *Sacramento makes 16 of 31 shots from three-point range while beating the Golden State Warriors 142–117.*

Dec. 27, 1989: *Danny Ainge tries for revenge against his former team, but his nine points in over-time are not enough and the Kings fall to the Boston Celtics 115–112.*

Dec. 29, 1992: *The Kings beat the Dallas Mavericks 139–81. Four nights later, they beat the Philadelphia 76ers 154–98, setting a record for the largest back-to-back margins of victory in NBA history.*

April 28, 1996: *The Kings play their second postseason game ever at ARCO Arena, beating the Seattle SuperSonics 90–81, as Mitch Richmond scores 11 points in the fourth quarter, eight in the final six minutes, for a total of 37 in the game.*

In the Hot Seats at the ARCO Arena

ARCO was built primarily for basketball, so the sight lines are excellent no matter where you sit. Although the best seats have already been purchased by season ticketholders, the remaining ones, ranging in price from $28 to $12, are sold on a game-by-game basis. The season-ticket base is more than 15,000.

Tickets for individual games are sold during the first week of October. Choice games sell out quickly. Remaining tickets can often be had on game night. These are mainly for seats in the upper deck, although you can buy tickets for scattered single seats elsewhere in the arena.

SCALPING

The paucity of scalpers is due as much to ARCO Arena's isolated location as to the ordinance prohibiting scalping on the grounds. Local fans in search of the best seats usually consult the newspaper for ads offering tickets.

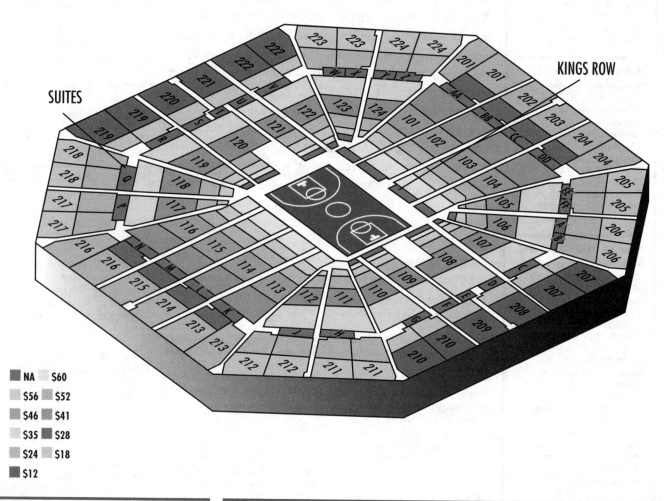

SUITES

KINGS ROW

Legend:
- NA
- $60
- $56
- $52
- $46
- $41
- $35
- $28
- $24
- $18
- $12

HOME-COURT ADVANTAGE

Being a loud and loyal fan base, the Sacramento crowds make their presence felt when the Kings are holding court. The team encourages fans not only with the wooden floor but also with things such as the "Fan-O-Meter" next to the main scoreboard hanging over center court. Its lights are tuned to the amount of noise the fans make, and if the decibels light the Fan-O-Meter all the way to the top, it "explodes" into a multicolored spelling of the team's name.

GETTING TO ARCO ARENA

Public transportation: There is no way to reach the ARCO Arena by public transportation.
By car: From the north or south, take I-5 to the Del Paso Road exit. The arena will be visible, so follow signs.
From the east or west, take I-80 or U.S. 50 to I-5, then proceed as above.

TICKET INFORMATION
Address: 1 Sports Pkwy., Sacramento, CA 95834

Phone: (916) 928-6900 or BassCharge at (916) 923-BASS
Hours: Mon.–Fri.10–6, Sat. 12–5.

Prices: $60, $56, $52, $46, $41, $35, $28, $24, $18, $12.

Alamodome

ARENA STATS

Location: *100 Montana St., San Antonio, TX 78203*
Opened: *May 15, 1993*
Capacity: *20,662*
Services for fans with disabilities: *About 300 wheelchair positions are located next to fixed seats for companions.*

ARENA FIRSTS

Regular-season game: *Nov. 5, 1993, 91–85 over the Golden State Warriors.*
Points scored: *David Robinson of the Spurs.*
Overtime game: *Dec. 8, 1993, 109–107 loss to the Seattle SuperSonics.*
Playoff game: *April 28, 1994, 106–89 over the Utah Jazz.*

TEAM NOTEBOOK

Franchise history: *Dallas Chaparrals, 1967–70 (ABA); Texas Chaparrals, 1970–71 (ABA); Dallas Chaparrals, 1971–73 (ABA); San Antonio Spurs, 1973–76 (ABA); San Antonio Spurs, 1976–present (NBA).*
Division titles: *1977–78, 1978–79, 1980–81, 1982–83, 1989–90, 1990–91, 1994–95, 1995–96.*
Rookie of the Year: *David Robinson, 1990.*
Retired numbers: *13, James Silas; 44, George Gervin.*

San Antonio's rich history is a source of civic pride, and even with an NBA team that won two straight division titles in 1995 and 1996, the city misses no opportunity to evoke its storied past: The Spurs, therefore, play in the Alamodome. The original Alamo, only a short distance from the A-Dome, still stands in tribute to the dashing heroes of the frontier. While Davy Crockett and Jim Bowie would have been too short to play pro ball, the Spurs have found an equally colorful team to wage war on the court, led by "the Admiral," David Robinson. Should the energy level lag a bit, the team has another piece of southwestern heritage on call: Coyote, a Native American trickster figure, stirs up the crowd as the Spurs' mascot.

Viewing the Alamodome from outside, however, the name appears to be a misnomer. Not only (as you might suspect) does the stadium look nothing like the Alamo, it also has no conventional dome. Instead, the Spurs' new home features a slightly angled roof that is suspended from cables and attached to four enormous concrete pillars. Inside, the building is equally unusual: Although the Alamodome was built to house the Spurs, it can also host football games. When the Spurs play, the unused sections of the stadium are blocked off by two large blue curtains that hang perpendicular to each other.

HOT TIPS FOR VISITING FANS

PARKING
All Alamodome parking is sold to season ticketholders. However, numerous indoor and outdoor lots, priced from $5 to $8, are nearby; the neighborhood is safe. The most convenient place to park is the Rivercenter Mall garage, across the street. If you have your ticket validated at the mall, you'll get two hours off.

MEDIA
Radio: WOAI (1200 AM—English), Jay Howard does the play-by-play; KCOR (1350 AM—Spanish), with announcer Paul Castis.
TV: KSAT (Channel 12) and KABB (Channel 29). Some games are also broadcast on pay-per-view. Dave Barrett handles the play-by-play and Coby Dietrich does color.

CUISINE
The Alamodome features several items from local restaurants, including Whataburger and Rosario's fajitas, tacos, and hot-and-spicy nachos. The corn dogs and spicy sausages also are popular. For a healthy non-meat alternative try the Caesar salad or the veggie plate.

After the game head north to the heart of downtown and San Antonio's Riverwalk. Here you will find a large number of good restaurants. Champions Sports Bar (210-226-7171) has 16 TV monitors and two satellite dishes and serves Tex-Mex food. The Zuni Grill (210-227-0864), along the river, serves southwestern fare.

LODGING NEAR THE ARENA

Airport Hilton
611 N.W. Loop 410
San Antonio, TX 78216
(210) 340-6060/(800) HILTONS
10 miles from the arena.

Marriott Riverwalk
711 E. Riverwalk
San Antonio, TX 78205
(210) 224-4555/(800) 228-9290
Across the bridge from the arena.

THE SPURS AT THE ALAMODOME

April 28, 1995: *Led by 21 points from Sean Elliott and 12 rebounds by Dennis Rodman, the Spurs beat the Denver Nuggets 104–88 in Game 1 of their first playoff series.*

May 8, 1995: *The Spurs beat the Lakers 97–90 in overtime to take Game 2 of their conference semifinal series.*

February 10–12, 1996: *The Spurs host the 46th annual All-Star Game, featuring David Robinson in his seventh All-Star Game appearance and Sean Elliott in his second.*

March 31, 1996: *A 97–83 win over the Phoenix Suns gives the Spurs an NBA record 16–0 slate for March.*

April 18, 1996: *Down 80–59 in the third quarter, the Spurs come back to edge the Lakers 103-100.*

In the Hot Seats at the Alamodome

The Spurs season-ticket base is well over 13,000. Single-game tickets go on sale in early October. Tickets are sometimes available on game nights.

GOOD SEATS
Because this arena was built with basketball in mind, the vast majority of seats are good ones. When popular opponents come to town and on certain weekends, the Spurs sometimes expand the Alamodome's capacity to 35,000 by opening the upper level. Extra upper-deck seats go on sale for 14 games during the season, selling for only $9 and $5, the latter being arguably the best buy in the NBA.

SCALPING
Ticket scalping is legal off the Alamodome's grounds. When the top teams play the Spurs, scalpers can readily be found the farther a buyer is from the dome.

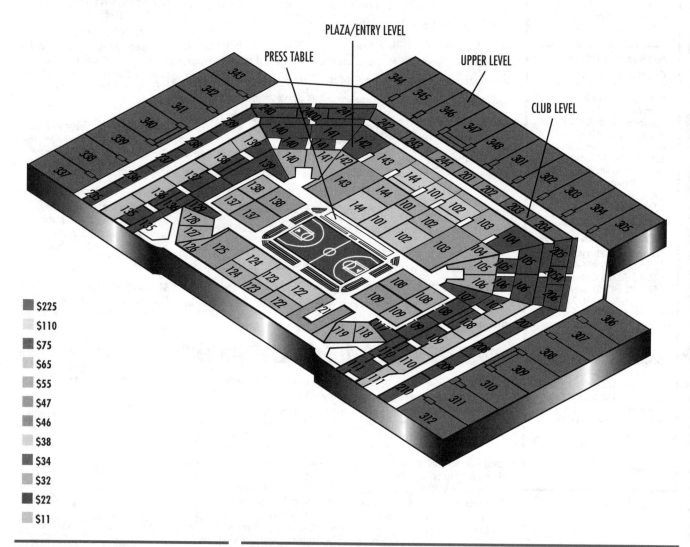

PLAZA/ENTRY LEVEL
PRESS TABLE
UPPER LEVEL
CLUB LEVEL

■ $225
□ $110
■ $75
▨ $65
▨ $55
▨ $47
▨ $46
▨ $38
■ $34
▨ $32
■ $22
▨ $11

HOME-COURT ADVANTAGE

San Antonio fans have responded well to the Alamadome, not only because the Spurs are the only major-league pro sport in town, but also because they've topped their division the past two years, drawing among the best attendance in the NBA. Unfortunately, the dome is so big it tends to diffuse the crowd noise.

GETTING TO THE ALAMODOME

Public transportation: VIA Metropolitan Transit offers transportation options to the Alamodome, including Park & Ride, shuttle service, and VIAtrans service for the mobility impaired. For more information, call VIAinfo at (210) 227-2020.
By car: From San Antonio International Airport, take Highway 281 south for approximately 7 miles, exit at Durango, take the turnaround, and go south on the access road that runs along the west side of the dome.

TICKET INFORMATION
Address: 100 Montana St., San Antonio, TX 78203

Phone: (210) 554-7787.
Hours: Mon.–Fri. 8–5.

Prices: $225, $ 110, $75, $65, $55, $47, $46, $38, $34, $22, $11.

ARENA STATS

Location: *190 Queen Anne Ave. N., Seattle, WA 98109*
Opened: *April 21, 1983*
Capacity: *17,072*
Services for fans with disabilities: *Ramp access on east and west sides of building; 155 wheelchair locations; 171 seats with retractable armrests for the motion-impaired.*

ARENA FIRSTS

Regular season game: *November 4, 1995, 103–89 over the Los Angeles Lakers.*
Overtime game: *January 19, 1996, 100–97 loss to the New York Knicks.*
Playoff game: *April 27, 1996, 97–85 over the Sacramento Kings.*
NBA Finals game: *June 9, 1996, 108–86 loss to the Chicago Bulls.*

TEAM NOTEBOOK

Franchise history: *Seattle SuperSonics, 1967–present.*
Division title: *1978–79, 1993–94.*
Conference titles: *1977–78, 1978–79.*
NBA championship: *1978–79.*
Basketball Hall of Fame: *Lenny Wilkens, 1988.*
Retired numbers: *19, Lenny Wilkens; 32, Fred Brown; 43, Jack Sikma.*

Though some Seattle fans insist that the new Key Arena is still the old Coliseum and should never have changed its name, the majority are thrilled with the renovated 17,072-seat arena where the Sonics' capped their 1996 return to Seattle Center by beating the Chicago Bulls in two out of three NBA Finals games. Both teams credited the fans with having a major impact on the outcome of those games. The Bulls' Scottie Pippen said the crowd lifted the momentum for the Sonics, noting it is so loud in Key Arena that "when the pressure is on, we aren't executing." The *Seattle Post-Intelligencer* runs a NoiseMeter chart that measures the crowd's decibel levels in comparison to the relative loudness of a rock concert or a jet taking off at close range.

And the noise isn't limited to the arena. Directly across the street is a boisterous tavern/pizzeria that is packed with Sonics fans during and after every game—and that is known to produce its own wall-shaking volume at particularly exciting moments. Ironically it is called Chicago's, which so irked the fans during the NBA Finals that the owners covered the logo with a huge banner renaming the bar "Seattle's."

The Sonics' home—a stone's throw from the Space Needle—offers all of the typical special effects of the flashy new NBA arenas: a new eight-sided, 57,000-pound video scoreboard; an ear-shattering public address system, light shows that would put a Madonna concert to shame; billows of colored smoke that emit from the ceiling while the announcer is shouting out the names of the players; and, of course, a mascot who performs amazing acrobatics and whips the crowd into an even greater frenzy.

What separates Key Arena from most other NBA sites is that it was created with the Pacific Northwest's special devotion to the environment—which also saved the city a handy $1.5 million in renovation costs. The original building was recycled rather than torn down and rebuilt; pieces of the old ceiling were cleaned and reused; demolition and scrap materials were recycled. Even the cobblestones in and around the building were recycled from old city streets.

HOT TIPS FOR VISITING FANS

PARKING

Simply stated, there is nowhere to park at Key Arena. The arena structure holds just over 650 cars, most of which are used by season ticketholders. There are a few tiny lots in the immediate area, but they gouge prices on game nights and fill up quickly. You can park for free (at night) on neighboring streets—the area is safe—but you often have to get there several hours ahead of time to get a spot (and be sure to keep feeding the meter until 7 p.m.) and be prepared for the free-for-all. Best bet: Take public transportation.

MEDIA

Radio: KJR (950 AM).
TV: KSTW-TV (Channel 11), Cable Prime Sports Network. Kevin Calabro does play-by-play on all 82 radio games and all televised games. The color analyst is Marcus Johnson.

CUISINE

You can get anything from Thai food to pizza at Key Arena's 22 concession stands, but it's the fresh seafood that gives the place its unique Pacific Northwest flavor. Prawns, crab, shrimp, and even salmon are popular—and delicious—in season.
Or cross the street for some local flavor at the most popular Sonics fans' haunt in town: Chicago's (206-282-7791). It is jammed to the rafters with noisy, happy fans—before, during, and after games. The big-screen TV is augmented by four smaller ones, and if a Sonics game is not broadcast on local, national, or cable TV, they'll get it on pay-per-view.

LODGING NEAR THE ARENA

Best Western Executive Inn
200 Taylor Ave. N.
Seattle, WA 98109
(206) 448-9444/(800) 351-9444
Across the street from the arena.

Travelodge
200 Sixth Ave. N.
Seattle, WA 98109
(206) 441-7878/(800) 578-7878
About 1 block from the arena.

In the Hot Seats at Key Arena

The Sonics have more than 14,000 season ticketholders, leaving just 3,000 seats for special multigame package sales and individual games. Tickets for individual games usually go on sale a couple of days before the season starts, and they sell fast. The best bet is to call the ticket office in September for details.

GOOD SEATS

There are simply no bad seats at Key Arena. The slope is so steep that all of the sight lines are good. The best deal—especially for families—is a $7 seat, which includes a free hot dog and soda on the family plan. Early in the 1995–96 season, reporters from the *Seattle Post-Intelligencer* bought tickets anonymously to try the $7 seats and pronounced both the view and the price to be excellent.

SCALPERS

There are scalpers near the arena, but don't expect any bargains. The Sonics are a hot ticket in town, especially after their run at the Bulls in the 1996 NBA Finals, when single tickets in the lower sections were selling for as much as $1,500 apiece. Classified ads in local newspapers do offer tickets, but there are often as many ads from buyers as there are from sellers.

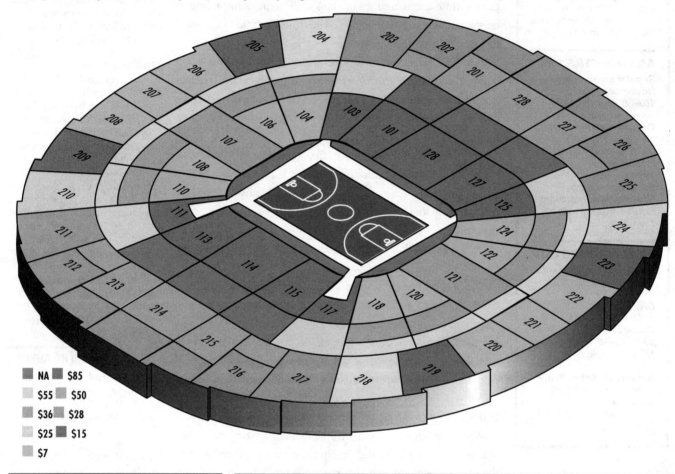

Legend:
- NA
- $85
- $55
- $50
- $36
- $28
- $25
- $15
- $7

HOME-COURT ADVANTAGE

There are three key factors to the Sonics' home-court advantage: noise, noise, and noise. The fans are so loud and distracting to visiting players, in fact, that Chicago Bulls coach Phil Jackson was said to have accused the Sonics of using canned noise on the public address system to pump up the volume during the 1996 NBA Finals. At one point during Game 5, the decibel level was measured at 114, just shy of a full-scale heavy-metal rock concert.

GETTING TO KEY ARENA

Public transportation: The Monorail stops right at Seattle Center. Board at Westlake Center, Pine Street, between Fourth and Fifth avenues.
By car: From I-5 take the Mercer Street exit and follow signs to Seattle Center. Key Arena is on the corner of the grounds, with street access on First Avenue north and Fifth Avenue north, and lower Queen Anne Avenue.

TICKET INFORMATION
Address: 190 Queen Anne Ave. N., P.O. Box 900911, Seattle, WA 98109

Phone: (206) 283-DUNK or TicketMaster at (206) 628-0888
Hours: Mon.–Fri. 10–5, Sat. 10–2.

Prices: $85, $55, $50, $36, $28, $25, $15, $7.

ARENA STATS

Location: 300 Bremner Blvd., Toronto, ON M5V 3B3, Canada
Opened: June 5, 1989
Capacity: 22,911 (basketball)
Services for fans with disabilities: Wheelchair seating is available behind sections 111, 112, and 113.

ARENA FIRSTS

Regular-season game: Nov. 3, 1995, 94–79 victory over New Jersey Nets.
Overtime game: Nov. 11, 1995, 123–117 loss to the Charlotte Hornets.

TEAM NOTEBOOK

Franchise history: 1995–present.
Rookie of the Year: Damon Stoudamire, 1995-96.

TICKET INFORMATION:

Address: 20 Bay St., Suite 1702, Toronto, ON M5J 2N8, Canada
Phone: (416) 366-DUNK or (416) 872-5000, TicketMaster.
Hours: TicketMaster is open 24 hours.

Contrary to popular opinion, the Raptors are not Toronto's first professional basketball team. Forty-nine years before the Raptors ever heard of Sky-Dome, the Toronto Huskies were charter members of one of the NBA's forerunners, the Basketball Association of America, losing their first home game at Maple Leaf Gardens to the New York Knicks, 68–66, in front of a crowd of 7,090 fans. The Huskies were so bad that they folded after the first year, but they didn't have JumboTron and dizzying light shows and a 5-foot-10 point guard named Damon Stoudamire, who had more playing time than anyone in the NBA and took Rookie of the Year honors in the inaugural season of pro basketball's long-awaited return to Toronto.

The two million-square-foot SkyDome is not the ideal spot to watch a basketball game, as any local fan will tell you, but it's only temporary. The Raptors are scheduled to start the 1997–98 season in the state-of-the-art Air Canada Centre, a three-level bowl-shaped arena with 22,500 seats for basketball, including 330 in restaurants overlooking the court.

Meanwhile, if you want to see what legendary former Detroit Pistons star Isiah Thomas (director of basketball operations) has put together, you'll have to put up with a strange brew of temporary-style bleacher stands on one side of the court, facing a semicircular seating configuration that stretches way out on the Blue Jays' first-base line and all the way to the upper reaches of the dome. Some of the seats are so far away that the best—if not only—view of the game is on the video monitors.

HOT TIPS FOR VISITING FANS

PARKING

There are 5,000 parking spaces within a 20-minute walk, but lot owners tend to jack up the prices for games, sometimes more than double the normal cost. Prices tend to increase the closer it gets to game time. They usually start around C$8 and can go up to about C$20 by the time the game starts. And beware of parking on the streets—there are very strict regulations, and cars parked illegally are regularly towed away.

MEDIA

Radio: CFRB (1010 AM)
TV: City TV (Channel 7) and New VR (Channel 20). John Saunders does the television play-by-play, with Leo Rautins, a former player with the 76ers and the Hawks, providing color commentary.

CUISINE

If you like McDonald's, you're in luck: The company runs Sky-Dome concessions. There are other Canadian favorites as well—Italian sausages, corned beef, Country Style Donuts, and, of course, plenty of beer. Both Molson and Labatt's are on tap.

The closest restaurant is the 360 Revolving Restaurant in the CN Tower next door (416-868-6937). Al Frisco's (416-595-8201), about 5 blocks away, has home-brewed beers on tap.

LODGING NEAR THE ARENA

Westin Harbour Castle
1 Harbour Sq.
Toronto, ON M5J 1A6
Canada
(416) 869-1600/(800) 228-3000
About 1¼ miles from the arena.

Toronto Hilton
145 Richmond St. W.
Toronto, ON M5H 2L2
Canada
(416) 869-3456/(800) 445-8667
5 blocks south of the arena.

HOME-COURT ADVANTAGE

Most fans will be happy to tell you that SkyDome is a rotten place to watch basketball. Despite all of that Labatt's on tap, Canadians aren't known for high volume at sporting events, but their enthusiasm for the home team is endearing if not intimidating.

■ NA	■ C$84	■ C$82	■ C$58
■ C$37	■ C$26.25	■ C$16	■ C$13
■ C$10.50	■ C$5		

IN THE HOT SEATS AT SKYDOME

The Raptors have actually lowered the price of most of their tickets. Their season ticket base is just over 15,000, leaving about 7,000 seats available for individual games. The "Hoops Club," C$5 seats up high in the section that put the "sky" in SkyDome, don't go on sale until two weeks before each game. You can't see the court from up there, but the JumboTron provides an excellent video view. The best part is that the Raptors open up the entire section during games versus popular teams such as the Bulls and the Lakers, which has allowed more than 36,000 fans to get in at once.

GOOD SEATS

The best seats in the house are the temporary grandstand seats that surround the court (sections 5–12). They're not cheap—C$84 and up—and they're not particularly easy to get, but they do give the feel of a college stadium.

BAD SEATS

The worst seats are in the "purple" section on the 500 level. You're up as high as the C$5 seats, but you have to pay C$26.25 because in theory you are aligned with the court. In fact, it would take a telescope to see the players.

SCALPING

There are plenty of scalpers, they have plenty of tickets, and they're usually willing to bargain.

GETTING TO SKYDOME

Public transportation: Take the Yonge–University Spadina subway line to Union Station at Front and Bay Streets. For more information, call the Toronto Transit Commission at (416) 393-4636.
By car: From the south, take the Queen Elizabeth Expressway east toward Toronto. Exit at the Gardener Expressway and proceed to the Spadina Avenue exit. Go north on Spadina to Blue Jay Way; SkyDome is on the left. From the east, take the Gardener Expressway and follow above directions. From the west, take the Don Valley Parkway to the Gardener Expressway and continue as directed above.

UTAH JAZZ

Delta Center

S alt Lake City is nestled between the Great Salt Lake and its adjacent desert, to the west, and the Wasatch National Forest and Uinta Mountains, to the east. The Utah Jazz are the beneficiaries of the scenic beauty surrounding this community, because they play in the heart of it all. Located in downtown Salt Lake City, the Delta Center is also near renowned attractions such as Temple Square and the Mormon Tabernacle, and about 2 blocks from the Salt Palace, the team's first home after it moved from New Orleans in 1979. The Jazz played their home games there until the 1991–92 season.

The Delta Center is a large concrete-and-silver, cubelike structure with plenty of windows; from the front, it looks more like an imposing office building than the home of an NBA team. One way to make sure you're at the home of the Jazz is to look in the parking lot for a distinctive 18-wheel truck painted with various depictions of western scenery and owned by Jazz All-Star forward Karl "the Mailman" Malone.

Because of the size of Salt Lake City—the population is about 160,000—and the strong influence of the Mormon religion here, you are less likely to find alcohol-induced rowdiness or obnoxious fan behavior than in other NBA arenas. Still, while the Jazz faithful tend to be less vocal than fans in larger cities, the team has one fan who likes to get very involved: Owner Larry Miller usually sits in the first row, across from his team's bench. Before the game he is on the court, greeting his players while they warm up and dishing out high fives during the introductions.

HOT TIPS FOR VISITING FANS

PARKING
Abundant in the area surrounding the Delta Center, which has no on-site facility. Numerous private lots and garages are available that charge between $3 and $6. Plenty of on-street parking can be found. A consortium of 17 area businesses offers another parking alternative: They run free shuttle buses from their establishments to the Delta Center. The shuttles begin 90 minutes before the game and continue for approximately one hour afterward. Call Chris Patterson at Market Street Grill (801-322-4668) for more information.

MEDIA
Radio: KISN (570 AM).

TV: KJZZ (Channel 14) and Prime Sports Network on cable.

CUISINE
The concessions are run by the Marriott Corporation. Offerings include such brand-name items as Pizza Hut pizza, Russell hand-dipped ice cream, and Golden Swirl frozen yogurt, which is sold from four portable carts. On the plaza level in quad one in the western corner of the building, a food court offers such items as chef and garden salads, baked potatoes with several toppings, and kosher hot dogs. Squatter's Pub Brewery (801-363-BREW) is only a short distance from the Delta Center. Located in the old Boston Hotel,

Squatter's brews its own beer, including six homemade ales. You can watch the brewmasters at work from the restaurant, which serves a diverse menu. D. B. Cooper's (801-532-2948) is a restaurant and nightclub; listen to live jazz, blues, or rock while dining on such popular items from the scaled-down menu as Utah smoked trout and fresh fish.

LODGING NEAR THE ARENA

Salt Lake City Marriott
75 W. South Temple
Salt Lake City, UT 84101
(801) 531-0800/(800) 345-4754.
4 blocks from the arena.

Doubletree
215 W. South Temple
Salt Lake City, UT 84101
(801) 531-7500/(800) 553-0075.
Across the street from the arena.

THE JAZZ AT THE DELTA CENTER

Feb. 3, 1992: The Jazz play their longest game ever, a 126–123 triple-overtime win against the Chicago Bulls. The game lasts three hours and 11 minutes.

May 14, 1992: Utah beats the Seattle SuperSonics 111–100 to advance to its first Western Conference final.

May 24, 1992: Karl Malone's 33 points help the Jazz beat the Portland Trail Blazers 121–112 in Game 4, tying the Western Conference final at two games apiece. Portland goes on to win the series, four games to two.

Feb. 21, 1993: John Stockton and Karl Malone lead the West to a 135–133 overtime win over the East in the All-Star Game, played at the Delta Center. Stockton and Malone are co-MVPs.

ARENA STATS
Location: 301 W. South Temple, Salt Lake City, UT 84101
Opened: Oct. 4, 1991
Capacity: 19,911
Services for fans with disabilities: Seating available behind sections 4 and 21 and in front of sections 115, 129, and 139.

ARENA FIRSTS
Regular-season game: Nov. 7, 1991, 103–95 loss to the Seattle Super-Sonics.
Points scored: Karl Malone of the Jazz.
Overtime game: Jan. 31, 1992, 117–116 over the Phoenix Suns.
Playoff game: April 24, 1992, 115–97 over the Los Angeles Clippers.

TEAM NOTEBOOK
Franchise history: New Orleans Jazz, 1974–79; Utah Jazz, 1979–present.
Division titles: 1983–84, 1988–89, 1991–92.
Basketball Hall of Fame: Pete Maravich, 1986.
Rookie of the Year: Darrell Griffith, 1980–81.
Retired numbers: 1, Frank Layden; 7, Pete Maravich; 35, Darrell Griffith.

In the Hot Seats at the Delta Center

Salt Lake City has been quite supportive of its NBA franchise. Since the Delta Center opened, only four games have not sold out. Utah has approximately 15,500 season-ticketholders. Single-game tickets are sold during mid-October. During the season, with the exception of a handful of games against Phoenix and Seattle that sell out quickly, remaining tickets are sold one week before the game. All are for upper-deck seating only. Any unsold tickets are available at the box office on game night.

BAD SEATS

Because the arena was built primarily for basketball, it has good sight lines. Still, the $9.50 seats that reach around the top five rows of the corner and end sections are a fair distance from the court.

SCALPING

Although it's legal in Salt Lake City, the team does not allow scalping on the grounds of the Delta Center. It takes place on the neighborhood streets along the approach to the arena. Some might have lower-deck seats available that they bought from season-ticketholders.

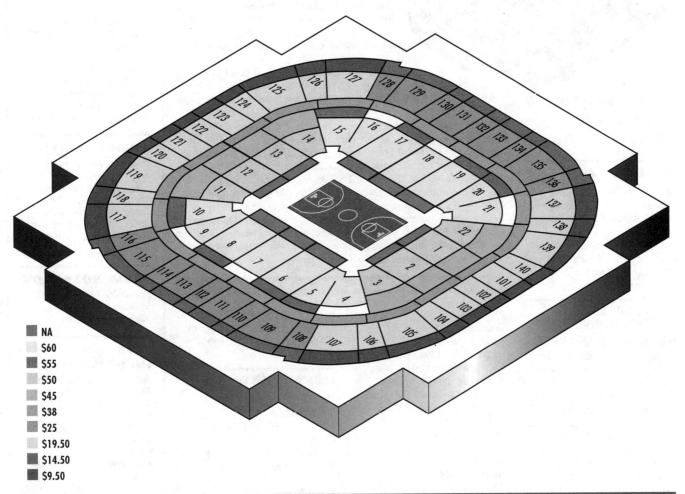

- ■ NA
- ▫ $60
- ■ $55
- ▫ $50
- ▪ $45
- ▪ $38
- ▪ $25
- ▫ $19.50
- ▪ $14.50
- ■ $9.50

HOME-COURT ADVANTAGE

Don't get the idea that just because Jazz fans have a reputation for being better behaved than some of their NBA brethren, they sit on their hands all night. The Jazz keep things lively with exciting play on the court and entertainment provided on a JumboTron scoreboard/video system. The energetic atmosphere has rubbed off on the players, who have won nearly 80% of their home games since the early '90s.

GETTING TO THE DELTA CENTER

Public transportation: UTA buses stop within a block of the Delta Center. Call (801) 287-4636 for more information.
By car: From the north or south, take I-15 to the 6th South Street exit. Stay in the right-hand lane. After approximately five blocks, take the Third West Street exit, which will circle and head north on Third West. Follow Third West for about a mile to the arena, on your right.

TICKET INFORMATION
Address: 301 W. South Temple, Salt Lake City, UT 84101

Phone: (801) 325-7328 or (801) 355-DUNK
Hours: Mon.–Fri. 9–6.
Prices: $60, $55, $50, $45, $38, $25, $19.50, $14.50, $9.50.

VANCOUVER GRIZZLIES

General Motors Place

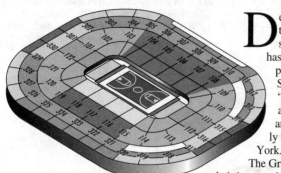

■ NA	■ C$64.50	■ C$56
■ C$49	■ C$43	■ C$37
■ C$30	■ C$22.50	■ C$16.50

Despite its state-of-the-art architecture, sound system, video scoreboard, and all of the other requisite amenities of a new NBA arena, GM Place has a friendly, homey feel generated by fans whom point guard Greg Anthony likes better than their Stateside counterparts. He says the Canadians are "much friendlier" and much more eager to learn about the game. "They accept the fact that they are not experts," he says, describing what is surely a welcome switch from his former home: New York.

The Grizzlies thrilled their wide-eyed fans by opening their inaugural season with two consecutive victories, only the second team in NBA history to do so. Then they tested their loyalty with 19 consecutive losses.

If the team isn't exactly great, they've got a great home. The 475,000-square-foot arena not only provides a good sight line from every seat in the house but also pumps in 270,000 cubic feet of fresh, outdoor air per minute through its ventilation system to keep the air not just comfortable but also clean. Fans with disabilities have their own ease-of-use entrance and seven elevators to take them to their seats. Guide dogs get their own aisle seats. They'll even bring a cellular phone to your seat if you're expecting an emergency phone call. Things are so nice at GM Place that when players were given the chance to air their complaints, the only problem they expressed was getting used to the "funny money," Canada's multicolored currency.

HOME-COURT ADVANTAGE

It may be difficult for those who are accustomed to the deafening tumult of, say, Chicago Bulls fans, to recognize the abiding enthusiasm good-natured Grizzlies fans have for their new team. Don't count them out just because they are mannerly.

IN THE HOT SEATS AT GENERAL MOTORS PLACE

In order to get an NBA franchise, every team must first guarantee sales of at least 12,500 season tickets; the Grizzlies initially sold just 10,000, so a Canadian supermarket chain bought the other 2,500. But when the games began, Vancouver sports fans came through. The Grizzlies averaged 17,183 per game during their first season (1995–96). That leaves about 2,000 empty seats for every game, and with a good sight line from virtually every seat, fans are practically guaranteed a good spot.

GOOD SEATS

Any seat in center court sections 104–111 or 113–121 is going to be fantastic; tickets range from C$16.50 to C$64.50, depending on the location.

SCALPING

All sporting events have scalpers somewhere, but there's no need to patronize them at GM Place, because you can almost always walk up to the ticket window and get a good seat.

HOT TIPS FOR VISITING FANS

PARKING

Good news. There are 14,000 parking spaces within a 15-minute walk of the arena (about C$5) in addition to the limited parking on site (595 spaces, C$12). If you have a computer, you can pick your spot in advance on the detailed parking map on the arena's World Wide Web site.

MEDIA

Radio: CKNW (980 AM).
TV: BCTV (Channel 11).

CUISINE

There are more than 25 concession stands at GM Place, and the food reflects Vancouver's broad ethnic diversity. A variety of Asian and Mexican foods complements classic stadium hot dogs and British fish and chips. Fresh-roasted espresso and cappuccino are also available. There are also three full-service restaurants in the arena, seating a total of 823 and catering primarily to executive suite customers.

To mingle with other sports fans after the game (or any other time), head for Double Overtime Sports Grill (604-683-7060), Malone's (604-684-9977), or the Shark Club Bar & Grill (604-687-4275).

LODGING NEAR THE ARENA

Pan Pacific Hotel
999 Canada Ave.
Vancouver, BC V6C 3B5
Canada
(604) 662-8111/(800) 937-1515
Walking distance to arena.

Hyatt Regency
655 Burrard St.
Vancouver, BC V6C 2R7
Canada
(604) 683-1234/(800) 233-1234
Walking distance to arena.

GETTING TO GENERAL MOTORS PLACE

Public transportation: SkyTrain's Stadium stop is right at GM Place. The SeaBus connects to SkyTrain, and extra sailings on BC Ferries are scheduled between Vancouver Island and the city on game days. For more information, call BC Transit at (604) 521-0400.
By car: From the airport, cross the Arthur Laing Bridge and exit at Marine Drive East. After about a mile, turn left onto Cambie Street and drive north about 5 miles toward downtown Vancouver. Cross Cambie Bridge and exit at Pacific Boulevard East, which will take you directly to the arena.

ARENA STATS

Location: 800 Griffiths Way, Vancouver, BC V6B 6G1, Canada.
Opened: Sept. 21, 1995
Capacity: 19,193 (basketball)
Services for fans with disabilities: A wheelchair-only section (serviced by a special elevator) with 102 seats is available in addition to individual floor seats; service animals are welcome and will be given an aisle seat if necessary; easy-use access is available at gate 5. Hotline: (604) 899-7445.

ARENA FIRSTS

Regular-season game: Nov. 5, 1995, 100–98 victory over the Minnesota Timberwolves.
Overtime game: Nov. 5, 1995, 100–98 victory over the Minnesota Timberwolves.

TEAM NOTEBOOK

Franchise history: Vancouver Grizzlies, 1995–present.

TICKET INFORMATION

Address: General Motors Place, 800 Griffiths Way, Vancouver, BC V6B 6G1, Canada
Phone: (604) 899-HOOP or TicketMaster (604) 280-4400
Hours: Mon.–Fri. 8–8; Sat. 9:30–8; Sun. 11–5.

WASHINGTON BULLETS

USAir Arena

ARENA STATS

Location: 1 Harry S. Truman Dr., Landover, MD 20785
Opened: Dec. 2, 1973
Capacity: 18,756
Services for fans with disabilities: Seating available on the concourse level between the red and blue sections.

ARENA FIRSTS

Regular-season game: Dec. 2, 1973, 98–96 over the Seattle SuperSonics.
Overtime game: Nov. 8, 1975, 99–95 loss to the Milwaukee Bucks.
Playoff game: March 31, 1974, 98–87 over the New York Knicks.
NBA Finals game: May 18, 1975, 101–95 loss to the Golden State Warriors.

TEAM NOTEBOOK

Franchise history: Chicago Packers, 1961–62; Chicago Zephyrs, 1962–63; Baltimore Bullets, 1963–73; Capital Bullets, 1973–74; Washington Bullets, 1974–present.
Division titles: 1968–69, 1970–71, 1971–72, 1972–73, 1973–74, 1974–75, 1978–79.
Conference titles: 1970–71, 1974–75, 1977–78, 1978–79.
NBA championship: 1977–78.
Basketball Hall of Fame: Wes Unseld, 1987; Earl Monroe, 1989; Elvin Hayes, 1989.
Retired numbers: 11, Elvin Hayes; 25, Gus Johnson; 41, Wes Unseld.

A look at the souvenir apparel worn by residents of Washington, D.C., tells a lot about what a visit to USAir Arena is like. Redskins paraphernalia is followed in popularity by those of the Baltimore Orioles and Georgetown, George Washington, and Howard universities. Also seen are a fair number of Washington Capitals T-shirts. But a Bullets hat or T-shirt is the hardest to find. The local NBA team just does not have a loyal following among D.C. sports fans, and USAir Arena is far from a mecca for local sports.

The arena is on the eastern edge of the Capital Beltway, and many fans express as much frustration with the location of the Bullets' home as they do with the team's lackluster play. Hopefully all that will change when the team moves to its new home at the modern MCI Center in downtown Washington, D.C. Not only will the Bullets have a new address, but a new name as well—they'll become the Wizards when they begin play at the MCI Center in 1997–98. The new moniker, designed to remove any suggestion of violence from the inner-city team's name, was chosen by fans who voted by phone. Their other options were the Dragons, Express, Sea Dogs, and Stallions.

Bullets fans are not known for being boisterous, and don't expect a new name to change that. Only some new star power on the court will help transform them into diehard Wizard fans.

HOT TIPS FOR VISITING FANS

PARKING
USAir Arena is surrounded by a large parking area with spaces for approximately 7,000 cars. The cost is $6. No on-street parking is available. The wait to get out of the lot after the game can be lengthy—all cars must funnel out of one location to reach the access road for the Beltway.

MEDIA
Radio: WTEM (570 AM).
TV: WBDC (Channel 50), and Home Team Sports on cable. Phil Chenier, who averaged nearly 18 points a game in nine years with the Bullets, including their championship season in 1977–78, is the color commentator.

CUISINE
Among the most popular items here are the colossal pretzels, twice as large as the standard size, and the kosher hot dogs, which you can get topped with onions, chili, and hot peppers. Freshly made 8-inch pepperoni and cheese pizzas are available, too, along with burgers and cheese steaks. A variety of imported bottled beers and cocktails are also sold.

The Showcase Pub and Eatery, open two hours before the game, is a cafeteria-style restaurant. The grilled burgers and onion rings are better than those at the concession stands, and it has a salad bar. Fans can watch the game on one of several television screens. Fewer than five minutes from the arena is The American Cafe (301-808-0200), which has the atmosphere of a neighborhood saloon. The continental menu includes crab cakes or Kentucky-style London broil. Several draft beers are available, including many local microbrews. T.G.I. Friday's (301-345-2503) is about 10 minutes away, in Greenbelt. Wash down a plate of blackened-chicken alfredo, ribs, or steak with one of the more than 40 types of beer, including Killian's and Foster's on tap. Players are occasional customers at both places.

LODGING NEAR THE ARENA

The Greenbelt Marriott
6400 Ivy Lane
Greenbelt, MD 20770
(301) 441-3700/(800) 228-9290
15 miles from the arena.

Best Western Capital Beltway
5910 Princess Garden Pkwy.
Lanham, MD 20706
(301) 459-1000/(800) 528-1234
5 miles from the arena.

THE BULLETS AT USAIR ARENA

April 6, 1975: Wes Unseld gets 30 rebounds in a 119–103 win over the New Orleans Jazz.

May 11, 1975: The Bullets beat the Boston Celtics 98–92, advancing to the championship series against the Golden State Warriors.

June 4, 1978: The Bullets win Game 6 of the championship series 117–82 over the Seattle SuperSonics. Three days later Washington clinches the title by topping the Sonics in Seattle.

Dec. 29, 1990: Bernard King scores 52 points—a USAir Arena record—as the Bullets crush the Denver Nuggets 161–133. The 161 points also set an Arena record.

In the Hot Seats at USAir Arena

GOOD SEATS

Despite its drawbacks, USAir Arena has many fine seats. Check out sections 105–109 and 119–123 on the lower level. The center-court view from these seats is excellent, and the price ($50) compares favorably to the going rate around the NBA. Sections 203–209, 217, and 219–223 offer good views as well. These seats, at $30, are perhaps the best bargain. Recently the Bullets have sold out about half of their home games, mostly against the better teams in the league.

BAD SEATS

The "cheap seats," costing $12, are at the top of the upper-deck center-court sections. Along with the seats behind the baskets—sections 211–216 and 225–228, which cost $22, or $30—these seats can seem very far away. Also avoid sections 104, 110, 116, and 124, where you must sit at an awkward angle to follow the game.

SCALPING

Scalpers begin their approach to fans in the parking lot. But unless those fans are trying to get in to see the Knicks, the Bulls, the Suns, or the like, they would probably do just as well at the box office.

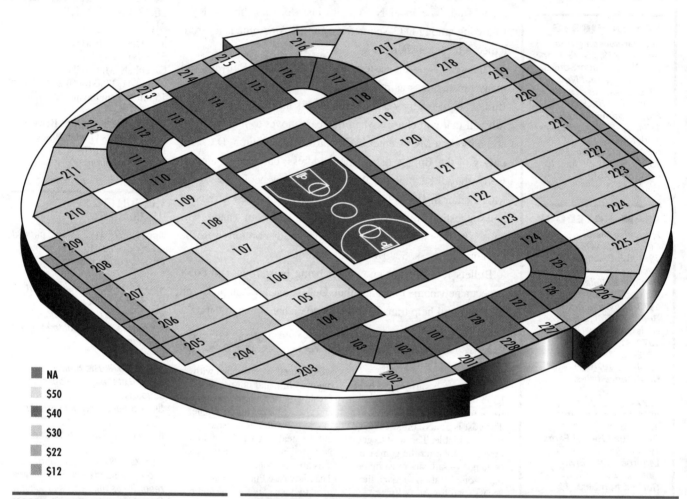

■ NA
□ $50
■ $40
□ $30
□ $22
▨ $12

HOME-COURT ADVANTAGE

Although Washington crowds know their basketball, this does not translate into fervent support. More often than not, fans come to USAir Arena to see the visiting team from their former hometown or to root for such former local heroes as Patrick Ewing, Dikembe Mutombo, and Alonzo Mourning, all of whom played college hoops for Georgetown in this very building.

GETTING TO USAIR ARENA

Public transportation: USAir Arena cannot be reached by public transportation.
By car: From downtown Washington, go east on New York Avenue (Route 50). About 5 miles outside of Washington, it intersects with the Capital Beltway. Go south to exit 15A or 17A. The arena is visible from the highway.
From Baltimore, take the Baltimore–Washington Parkway or I-95 to the Beltway south, to exit 15A or 17A.

TICKET INFORMATION
Address: 1 Harry S. Truman Dr., Landover, MD 20785

Phone: (301) NBA-DUNK or TicketMaster at (202) 432-SEAT
Hours: Mon.–Fri. 10–5:30.

Prices: $50, $40, $30, $22, $12.

hockey

EASTERN CONFERENCE

WESTERN CONFERENCE

BOSTON BRUINS

FleetCenter

The Bruins' retired jerseys that hang from high above the ice at FleetCenter are bigger than they were over at Boston Garden; they have to be. From their new, higher perch in this vast new arena, the old jerseys looked like postage stamps from below and were just barely visible.

The Celtics, with whom the Bruins share this luxurious 755,000-square-foot, high-tech sports complex, got to bring over their beloved parquet floor, but the Bruins didn't bring their smaller-than-regulation rink. FleetCenter's ice is the full 200 by 85 feet, but the extra nine feet of length and two feet of width didn't seem to faze the Bruins, who posted a winning home season their first year here.

FleetCenter holds some 3,000 more hockey fans than Boston Garden did, and has a multimillion-dollar, state-of-the-art video scoreboard, two full-service dining areas, seven elevators, 13 escalators, 36 permanent concessions stands, 34 restrooms, a couple of thousand preferred seats, and more bells and whistles than you'd have time to notice during a hockey game. Happily, none of this interferes with watching the game. Sight lines are terrific from everywhere, and—unlike the beloved Garden—there are no obstructed-view seats.

The storied history of Boston Garden was only part of what made seeing a game there such a wonderful experience. The fans, who range from rowdy to wild, have adapted nicely, and are as enthusiastically behind their team as ever. If you get to feeling nostalgiac for the Garden, have a look at the old scoreboard clock that now resides in the FleetCenter's lobby. As you gaze at it wistfully, remember the Garden's rock-hard seats, the fog that could form over the ice on warm days (no air conditioning—remember?), and views blocked by luxury boxes and the balcony's overhang. Chances are that you'll stroll to your seat in the newfangled FleetCenter with a spring in your step and a kind thought for progress.

HOT TIPS FOR VISITING FANS

PARKING
FleetCenter sits atop a five-level parking garage run by the public transit authority (MBTA) that has room for 1,150 cars. Everybody else will have to fend for themselves. The next nearest parking, although only a few blocks away, can seem like a cross-country trek against the freezing winds of a Boston winter. Boston's charmingly crooked and narrow streets can make traffic a nightmare. The best bet is to stick with public transportation.

MEDIA
Radio: WEEI (590 AM); former Bruin Barry Pederson does analysis.
TV: WSBK (Channel 38) and NESN (cable); Fred Cusick has done Bruins play-by-play for four decades, and ex-Bruin Derek Sanderson provides analysis.

CUISINE
Bruins fans can still get the same sorts of arena food they enjoyed at the Garden. The huge pretzels, plump hot dogs (and the great mustard), fresh-popped popcorn, and pizza made on the premises that people clamored for at the old place are all here, along with new treats at the Fleet's 36 concession stands. The center's two upscale full-service restaurants have gotten rave reviews, but you need to reserve far in advance.

After the game, many Bruins fans head to North Station's Sports Café (617-723-6664), which has two crowded, noisy bars and five TVs. Bruins players often pop in. Also recommended is The Harp (617-742-1010), an upscale Irish spot nearby. Expect a 20-minute wait after a game. Bruins or visiting players often come by. If you're in the mood for Italian food, head for the North End and take your pick among the numerous fine choices. Downtown is Legal Seafood (617-864-3400); it's a Boston landmark and one of the best seafood restaurants anywhere. The Bull & Bear (617-227-9600), inside the Hampshire House hotel in the Copley Square district, will be instantly recognizable to anyone with a television as the inspiration for the TV show *Cheers*. Just across the Charles River is Cambridge, a hotbed of trendy nighspots that cater to the college crowd.

LODGING NEAR THE ARENA
Westin Copley Plaza
10 Huntington Ave.
Boston, MA 02116
(617) 262-9600/(800) 228-3000
2 miles from the arena.

Marriott Long Wharf
296 State St.
Boston, MA 02109
(617) 227-0800/(800) 228-9290
2 miles from the arena.

ARENA STATS
Location: Causeway St., Boston, MA 02114
Opened: Nov. 13, 1995
Capacity: 17,565
Services for fans with disabilities: Seating varies for each game.

ARENA FIRSTS
Regular-season game: Oct. 7, 1995, 4–4 tie with the New York Islanders.
Goal: Sandy Moger of the Bruins.
Playoff game: Apr. 24, 1996, 4–2 loss to the Florida Panthers.

TEAM NOTEBOOK
Franchise history: Boston Bruins, 1924–present.
Stanley Cups: 1928–29, 1938–39,1940–41, 1969–70, 1971–72.
Hockey Hall of Fame: A. H. Ross, E. Shore, 1945; A. Clapper, 1947; M. MacKay, 1952; S. Cleghorn, F. Frederickson, 1958; C. Denneny, C. Thompson, 1959; C. F. Adams, S. Mantha, 1960; M. Schmidt, 1961; W. Brown, N. Stewart, G. Wilson, 1962; A. Siebert, 1964; M. Barry, 1965; F. Brimsek, W. Pratt, 1966; H. Oliver, 1967; Bill Cowley, 1968; T. Johnson, 1970; H. Jackson, T. Sawchuk, R. Weiland, 1971; W. Adams, R. Smith, 1972; B. Burch, 1974; B. Quackenbush, 1976; J. Plante, 1978; Bobby Orr, 1979; H. Lumley, 1980; J. Bucyk, A. Stanley, 1981; Harry Sinden, 1983; B. Parent, P. Esposito, 1984; G. Cheevers, J. Ratelle, 1985; L. Boivin, 1986; B. Park, 1988; F. Flaman, 1990; W. Dumart, 1992; G. Lapointe, 1993.
Retired numbers: 2, E. Shore; 3, L. Hitchman; 4, B. Orr; 5, A. Clapper; 7, P. Esposito; 9, J. Bucyk; 15, M. Schmidt.

In the Hot Seats at FleetCenter

With 3,000 more seats for hockey than at Boston Garden, many fans at FleetCenter may be able to sit through their first Bruins game ever, or at least their first without craning their necks for a view of the ice and/or scoreboard from their obstructed-view seat. There is a season ticket base of about 13,000 and a very long waiting list. Single-game tickets go on sale in September.

GOOD SEATS

Every seat in FleetCenter is angled toward the ice and has a clear sight line. Those sitting along the sidelines will be virtually at ice level and may have to peer around the backs of benched players' heads; the first rows of seats at the corners and in the end zones are about a foot above the ice level.

BAD SEATS

With no obstructed seats, the only real drawback might be sitting too high up; but if you like to watch plays develop and strategy unfold, the upper seats can provide a diagrammatic view.

MOVING DOWN

Tickets are checked, and there is less tolerance for those trying to move down than there was at Boston Garden.

SCALPING

Scalping is illegal in Boston, but enforcement of this ordinance doesn't seem to be a high priority. Scalpers are everywhere and can easily be found; prices vary according to supply, demand, and the Bruins' fortunes.

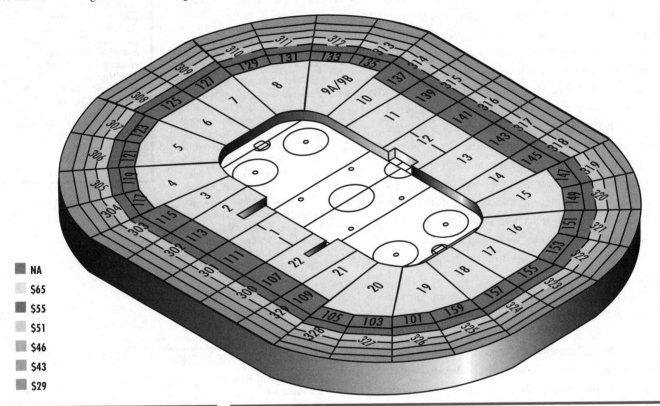

- ■ NA
- ■ $65
- ■ $55
- ■ $51
- ■ $46
- ■ $43
- ■ $29

HOME-ICE ADVANTAGE

Boston Garden had the smallest ice surface in the NHL, 191 feet by 83 feet. FleetCenter's rink is the regulation 200 by 85. The smaller surface gave the Bruins an edge, making it easier for rushing defensemen or defensemen good at outlet passes, such as Bobby Orr and Ray Bourque. The standard-size ice now means that the Bruins won't have to adjust their playing style while on road trips, but it also means that visiting teams won't have to adapt to the Bruins' home ice. In their first season in FleetCenter, the Bruins went 22–14–5, so apparently they're coping well with all their new extra space.

GETTING TO FLEETCENTER

Public transportation:
The North Station stop on both the Green and Orange lines of the MBTA is right outside FleetCenter. North Station is also a commuter tail terminus. Call (617) 722-3200 for more information.

By car:
From the south, follow I-95 north to I-93 toward exit 25 (Causeway Street). Make a left at the bottom of the ramp. Boston Garden will be visible to your right, and Fleet-Center is right next door.

From the west, take Massachusetts Turnpike (Route 90) to I-93 north to exit 25.
From the north, take I-93 south to Boston, or take I-95 south to Route 1 south, cross the Tobin Bridge, and merge onto I-93 south. Take exit 26 (Storrow Drive). Bear right and follow signs toward North Station. At the stop sign, make a left onto Lamancy Way. At the first traffic light, make a left onto Causeway Street. FleetCenter is ¼ mile farther.

TICKET INFORMATION
Address: Causeway St., Boston, MA 02114

Phone: (617) 624-1950 or TicketMaster at (617) 931-3100

Hours: Mon.–Sat. 11–7, Sun. 12–6.
Prices: $65, $55, $51, $46, $43, $29.

BUFFALO SABRES

Marine Midland Arena

Out of "the Aud" and into the new—that's the Sabres' story in 1996. Marine Midland Arena, the $127 million new home of the Buffalo Sabres, is set to open for the 1996–97 season and will host more than 125 events in its first year of operation, including everything from professional indoor soccer, lacrosse, and collegiate sports to circuses, concerts, and ice shows.

The Sabres will now have a regulation-size rink, and how well their rock-'em, sock-'em style of play will travel to the new arena remains to be seen. Fans will like the new, improved amenities: better sight lines, more food courts, more parking, and over 3,000 more seats for hockey.

Many of the Sabres' blue-collar faithful, however, may feel a bit left out of this corporate suite- and luxury box–filled new arena. What effect the snazzier surroundings will have on their usually rowdy behavior is unknown. Those lucky enough to have club-level suites will be able to get to and from the indoor parking through covered walkways and corridors, sparing them from what's been called the coldest walk in all of hockey—from the parking lot to the arena. Everyone else will still have to contend with the biting winter winds that sweep in from Lake Erie and blast through downtown Buffalo, and the mounds of snow they can bring with them.

Built in 1940, Memorial Auditorium was no beauty—at least on the outside. Its gray-granite, WPA-look facade and brown roof were not alluring. But inside, hockey was king, and that gave the Aud all the charm it needed. Set just diagonally across the street from the Aud, Marine Midland Arena will have to win over the hearts of the locals; if the Sabres play well in their new venue, it may not be too hard to do.

HOT TIPS FOR VISITING FANS

PARKING

Marine Midland Arena will offer 5,200 parking spaces; 2,200 of these will be weather-protected, and club-level ticketholders will be able to get from their cars to the stands through covered walkways. The expanded parking may ease the need to get to the arena an hour or more early just to get a decent spot. There are also plenty of smaller lots, usually at $5, within a 10-block radius. The one-way streets (and having Main Street closed to traffic) can make it tough to circle around looking for the ideal spot—the best bet is just to get in one and walk.

MEDIA

Radio: WGR (550 AM). Former Sabres player Danny Gare calls the games for radio. Also, WWKB 1520 AM and CJRN 710 AM on the Empire Sports Network.

TV: WUTV (Channel 29), the Fox affiliate, broadcasts away games.

CUISINE

Traditional arena fare such as hot dogs, burgers, popcorn, and nachos that was served at the Aud will be readily available at Marine Midland, including a tasty local peculiarity, "beef on weck," roast beef on kümmelweck (a crusty roll) served up with horseradish (no wonder the crowd was so rowdy); it isn't yet known whether another local delicacy, grilled bologna sandwiches with onions, will make the move as well. A great emphasis is being put on the upscaling of the overall ambience at Marine Midland, and the food courts, and especially concessions serving the luxury boxes and suites, are going for more sophisticated grub.

A wider variety of beers than the Aud had is on tap for Marine Midland, although Busch, long the only beer from Aud concessions, will continue to be available. Given Buffalo's proximity to Canada and the city's taste for their northern neighbor's beer, you can count on still getting Molson Canadian, Molson Ice, and O'Keefe at individual stands.

Plenty of choices after the game are within walking distance. A hot spot is Jim Kelly's Sport City Grill (716-849-1200), just 4 blocks down Main Street. It's like walking into a sports museum. Also try Garcia's Irish Pub; it's sometimes a post-game hangout for players.

LODGING NEAR THE ARENA

Buffalo Hyatt Regency
2 Fountain Plaza
Buffalo, NY 14202
(716) 856-1234/(800) 233-1234
4 blocks from the arena.

Buffalo Hilton
120 Church St.
Buffalo, NY 14202
(716) 845-5100/(800) HILTONS
2 blocks from the arena.

ARENA STATS

Location: *Main St. and South Park Ave., Buffalo, NY 14202*
Opened: *September 1996*
Capacity: *19,500*
Services for fans with disabilities: *Seating is available in all sections.*

TEAM NOTEBOOK

Franchise history: *Buffalo Sabres, 1970–present.*
Rookies of the Year: *Gil Perreault 1971–72; Tom Barrasso 1983–84.*
Hockey Hall of Fame: *Tim Horton, 1977; Marcel Pronovost, 1978; Punch Imlach, 1984; Gil Perreault, 1990; Scotty Bowman, 1991; Seymour H. Knox III, 1993.*
Retired number: *11, Gil Perreault.*

In the Hot Seats at Marine Midland Arena

Though it's a bigger building, getting seats for a Sabres game at Marine Midland Arena hasn't necessarily gotten easier. Granted, it wasn't that tough to get into the Aud, even on a Friday, when the Sabres often happened to be playing at home. The new arena has more seats, but a greater proportion of them are private suites and luxury boxes owned by season ticketholders and corporations. From the old auditorium to the new it should be about a wash in terms getting a single-game ticket close to the day of the game. Call ahead or check with the box office.

GOOD SEATS

Marine Midland has been designed to offer good sight lines, plusher and wider seats with more leg room, and seamless glass around the ice. What's not to like? Well, large sections of the arena, including food courts and parking, are for the exclusive use of those with the bucks for the private suites and luxury boxes. Those with seats at rinkside will be pleased to find that they are raised about 6 inches above the ice level, allowing for better visibility.

MOVING DOWN

The more rigid and visible hierarchy of seating in Marine Midland will make moving down from the upper seats both more difficult and less rewarding, even if you get away with it. You can bank on arena management cracking down on usurpers and protecting the sanctity of the pricier seats' owners.

SCALPING

Reselling of tickets is not allowed within 500 feet of the arena. Whether there will be much of a market with Marine's larger capacity, and whether the team's play in this new spot will increase the demand remain to be seen. Scalpers of tickets to the old Memorial Auditorium gathered at the corner of Main and Terrace.

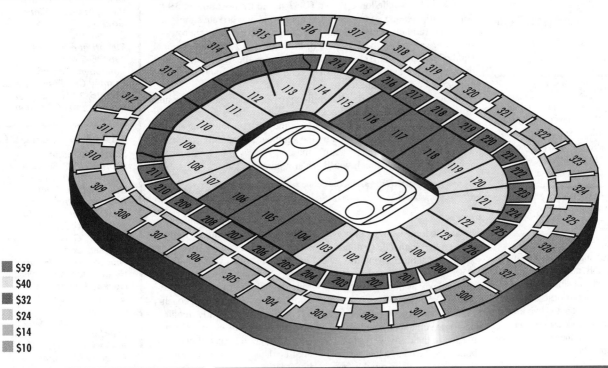

- $59
- $40
- $32
- $24
- $14
- $10

HOME-ICE ADVANTAGE

The Sabres will have to get used to playing on a regulation-size rink at home. The Aud's ice surface measured 193 feet by 84 feet, 7 feet shorter and 1 foot narrower than NHL standards, so the Sabres had built their teams to take full advantage of the smaller rink, with a tighter skating style. The plusher surroundings may or may not have any effect on the players, but if the luxury-suite crowd at Marine Midland isn't as vocal as the Aud's thank-God-it's-Friday blue-collar fans, that could bring down the adrenaline levels on the ice.

GETTING TO MARINE MIDLAND ARENA

Public transportation: The No. 8 Main light rail transit goes directly to the arena. Metro buses also stop at the arena. Call (716) 855-7211 for more information.
By car: Take the New York State Thruway to the Buffalo exit, then Route 33 west into the city. Exit at Oak Street. Go right onto Swan Street, then left onto Washington Street. Marine Midland Arena is at the corner of Main Street and South Park Avenue, diagonally across the street from the Aud.

TICKET INFORMATION
Address: Main St. and South Park Ave., Buffalo, NY 14202
Phone: (716) 856-8100 or TicketMaster at (716) 852-5000, (716) 232-1900 or (800) 755-5589
Hours: Mon.–Fri. 9–5
Prices: $59: club level (100–200); $40: 100 level; $32: 100 level behind the goals; $24: upper deck (1st two rows of 300 level); $14: upper deck (3rd and higher rows of 300 level); $10: 300 level behind the goals.

CALGARY FLAMES

Canadian Airlines Saddledome

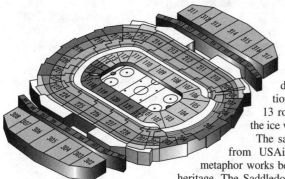

■ C$83	C$78	■ C$60	C$50
C$46	■ C$41	C$33	
C$28	■ C$21	C$9	

The thing that sets the Saddledome apart from other arenas constructed in the early 1980s is its original purpose, which was to host the 1988 Winter Olympics. It was the first building in North America designed to accommodate the larger, international-size playing surface. Accordingly, the first 13 rows of the 100-level seats are perched where the ice was for the Olympic hockey matches.

The saddle-style design of the roof was borrowed from USAir Arena in Landover, Maryland, but its metaphor works better in Calgary because of the city's cowboy heritage. The Saddledome got a C$37 million renovation in 1995. Along with creating some 1,500 revenue-producing private suites, and club seats (and the private dining room to go with them), eight rows of seats were added on the 200 level of the north end zone, an octagonal JumboTron and matrix were installed above the ice, traffic flow throughout the arena was improved, and several new and improved concessions were introduced.

The acoustic tiles covering the ceiling provide excellent concert sound but make for an eerily quiet hockey arena. These fans aren't exactly rowdy to begin with (they like to claim they're concentrating on the game), and have to be prompted by the signboard to audibly root, root, root for the home team. The team's mascot, Harvey the Hound, is the about the only wacky touch you'll see around here.

HOME-ICE ADVANTAGE

Since they moved from Atlanta, the Flames have never had a losing home record. Schedule permitting, visiting teams come in a day early to get used to the altitude, which is about 3,000 feet above sea level.

IN THE HOT SEATS AT CANADIAN AIRLINES SADDLEDOME

Despite their quiet crowds, the Flames are usually in the top five teams for NHL attendance. Apart from a handful of single tickets available at the box office for most games, every seat in the two lower bowls is sold on a season-ticket basis. Tickets for the upper loges go on sale at the start of each month.

GOOD SEATS

There are virtually no bad seats in the two lower bowls, but these seats are rarely available. The first row of the second tier is among the priciest, but the cost drops dramatically as you move up only a few rows, and the view isn't all that different. Some fans like the new 200-level seats in the north end zone.

BAD SEATS

Seeing the game from the third tier is like watching table hockey.

SCALPING

Toronto and Montreal are the two top draws. Scalping is illegal on the Stampede Grounds, but scalpers usually get warned by security before the police step in.

HOT TIPS FOR VISITING FANS

PARKING

The Saddledome isn't the only venue on the Stampede Grounds, so if there's another event, its 1,050 C$10 spots fill up fast, but not as quickly as the Stampede's 2,400 C$3.50 spaces.
Some residents of Victoria Park will allow you to park on their lawns or in their driveways for about C$3. Two large lots off Olympic Way fill up quickly once the Stampede Grounds is full.

MEDIA

Radio: CFR (660 AM).
TV: CITC (Channel 7).

CUISINE

Better food came with the renovations. Along with upgraded versions of traditional stadium fare, Wendy's, Little Caesar's Pizza, and Subway Sandwiches now all have outlets here, as does Canadian favorite, Tim Horton's donuts. The beer is mostly Molson. The Olympic Lounge, on the terrace level, serves a wider variety of beers, finger foods and snacks. On the concourse level, the Penalty Box offers more extensive menu items. Dutton's Hall of

Fame Sports Lounge is adjacent to the club seats; its dining room is open during Flames' games, and the bar is open year-round. Dusty's Saloon, a cowboy bar roughly 3 blocks from the Saddledome, attracts out-of-town coaches and players. A slightly trendier hangout is Hy's (403-263-2222), which has good steaks. If players aren't at Dusty's, they are probably at Hy's.

GETTING TO THE CANADIAN AIRLINES SADDLEDOME

Public transportation: LRT stops at Stampede Park, just across the street from the Saddledome. The C train offers service from the University of Calgary to the arena door. Call (403) 262-1000 for more information.
By car: From Highway 1, take Center Street south. Go left onto Ninth Avenue, then right onto First Street. S.E. and left onto 12th Avenue. Go right onto Olympic Way, directly to the Saddledome.

LODGING NEAR THE ARENA

Westin
320 Fourth Ave. S.W.

ARENA STATS
Location: Olympic Way, Calgary, AL T2P 3B9 Canada
Opened: Oct. 15, 1983
Capacity: 20,140
Services for fans with disabilities: 85 seats are available in the Main Concourse, another 12 in the upper level.

ARENA FIRSTS
Regular-season game: Oct. 15, 1983, 4–3 loss to the Edmonton Oilers.
Goal: Jari Kurri of Edmonton.
Playoff game: April 4, 1984, 5–3 over the Vancouver Canucks.
Stanley Cup Finals game: May 16, 1986, 5–3 over the Montreal Canadiens.

TEAM NOTEBOOK
Franchise history: Atlanta Flames, 1972–80; Calgary Flames, 1980–present.
Stanley Cup: 1988–89
Rookies of the Year/Calder: Eric Vail, 1974–75; Willi Plett, 1976–77; Gary Suter, 1985–86; Joe Nieuwendyk, 1987–88; Sergei Makarov, 1989–90.
Hockey Hall of Fame: Glenn Hall, 1975; Bob Johnson, Lanny McDonald, 1992; Guy Lapointe, 1993.
Retired number: 9, Lanny McDonald.

TICKET INFORMATION
Address: P.O. Box 1540, Station "M," Calgary, AB T2P 3B9,Canada
Phone: (403) 261-0475 or (403) 270-6700.
Hours: Mon.–Fri. 9–5.

Calgary, AB T2P 2S6
Canada
(403) 266-1611/(800) 228-3000
½ mile from the arena.

Palliser
133 Ninth Ave. S.W.
Calgary, AB T2P 2M3
Canada
(403) 262-1234/(800) 441-1414
Less than a mile from the arena.

CHICAGO BLACKHAWKS

United Center

ARENA STATS

Location: 1901 W. Madison St., Chicago, IL 60612
Opened: August 18, 1994
Capacity: 20,500
Services for fans with disabilities: Seating available in all levels of the end zone corners.

ARENA FIRSTS

Regular-season game: Jan. 25, 1995, 5–1 over the Edmonton Oilers.
Goal: Joe Murphy of the Blackhawks.
Overtime game: Feb. 16, 1995, 2–2 tie with the Calgary Flames.
Playoff game: May 7, 1995, 5–3 loss to the Toronto Maple Leafs.

TEAM NOTEBOOK

Franchise history: Chicago Blackhawks, 1926–present.
Stanley Cups: 1933–34, '37–38, '60–61.
Most Valuable Players/Hart: M. Bentley, 1945–46; Rollins, '53–54; Hull, '64–65, '65–66; Mikita, '66–67, '67–68.
Rookies of the Year/Calder: Karakas, 1935–36; Dahlstrom, '37–38; Litzenberger, '54–55; Hay, '59–60; T. Esposito, '69–70; Larmer, '82–83; Belfour, '90–91.
Hockey Hall of Fame: Gardiner, Morenz, 1945; MacKay, '52; Hay, Irvin, Keats, Lehman, '58; Denneny, '59; Boucher, '60; Norris, '62; McLaughlin, '63; D. Bentley, Seibert, Stewart, '64; Mosienko, '65; M. Bentley, Brimsek, Lindsay, '66; Abel, '69; Dye, Gadsby, '70; A. Wirtz, '71; Burch, Coulter, Ivan, '74; Hall, Pilote, '75; B. Wirtz, '76; Orr, '79; Lumley, '80; Stanley, '81; Hull, Mikita, '83; P. Esposito, '84; Mariucci, Olmstead, Pilous, '85; T. Esposito, '88; Poile, '90; Smith, '91.
Retired numbers: 1, Hall; 9, Hull; 21, Mikita; 35, T. Esposito.

Across the street from the old Madhouse on Madison Street stands the $175 million United Center, home away from home for Blackhawks (and Bulls) fans.

More than twice as large as the old Chicago Stadium, United Center provides the best of the new while doing its best to carry on some of the stadium's traditions—and without the cockroaches. The building's exterior design borrows heavily from 1920s architecture, making it appear older and more homey than most modern arenas. Inside, the seats are wide and comfortable. Sight lines, sometimes nonexistent from the old stadium's mezzanine and second balcony, are outstanding, with no obstructions. The sound quality of the stadium's stately Barton organ has been painstakingly re-created, a process that took more than a year. Notes from the original organ were recorded and then used as the basis for creating the sound of the new Allen organ. The result bears a great resemblence to the original, but it just doesn't shake you in your seat the way the Barton could on the low notes. In addition, sound absorbers and deflectors have been installed to help re-create and amplify the roar of noise that made the stadium famous, a roar made by lifetime fans, not luxury box visitors snacking on appetizers. Again, the sound is close, but not quite the real thing.

In the Center's first few years the Bulls have dominated the limelight, but the Blackhawks and their fans seem to like it here just fine. The team capped its inaugural season here by reaching the Western Conference finals and also setting a record as the first NHL team to average attendance of more than 20,000 patrons per game. Though the spirit of Mikita, Hull, and Esposito hasn't quite made it across the street yet, nor the popular standing-room-only tickets that packed the stadium with rabid fans, the Hawks have played well enough here to begin creating new memories.

HOT TIPS FOR VISITING FANS

PARKING

Up to 5,500 official parking spots are within a 4-block area. Prices are $10. A number of lower-priced lots nearby hold approximately 2,000 cars, but few are patrolled or completely secure, so the likelihood of vandalism and break-ins is high. Street parking is forbidden in a 4-block radius.

MEDIA

Radio: WMVP (1000 AM).
TV: SportsChannel for road games only. Broadcasters are Pat Foley for play-by-play and former Blackhawk Dale Tallon.

CUISINE

Chicagoans love to eat. With that in mind, United Center has a considerably larger menu than at Chicago Stadium. In addition to the usual hot dogs and nachos, themed concessionaires abound, which offer deli sandwiches, Mexican and Italian specialties, and grilled meats. To wash down all that food, the United Center offers 25 different beers. After the game, head across Jackson Street to Moretti's (312-850-0208), or try Cheli's Chili Bar (312-455-1237), which is owned by Hawks defenseman Chris Chelios and offers 20 kinds of chili. Another hangout is Hawkeyes (312-226-3951), a sports bar with many Blackhawks players among its clientele. If you're still in a rowdy mood, try Dick's Last Resort on the North Pier (312-836-7870). It's loud, messy, and as close to a frat as you'll find south of Northwestern.

LODGING NEAR THE ARENA

The Drake
140 E. Walton St.
Chicago, IL 60611
(312) 787-2200
5 miles from the arena.

Westin
909 N. Michigan Ave.
Chicago, IL 60611
(312) 943-7200/(800) 228-3000
5 miles from the arena.

THE BLACKHAWKS AT UNITED CENTER

May 19, 1995: A 5–2 win over the Toronto Maple Leafs in Game 7 puts the Hawks into the conference semifinals.

June 8, 1995: Down 3–0 in their conference final series, the Blackhawks stay alive, beating the Detroit Red Wings 5–2.

February 22, 1996: Blackhawks right wing Tony Amonte recorded the first hat trick at the United Center against the St. Louis Blues.

In the Hot Seats at the United Center

Some 20,500 seats are available for hockey, nearly 2,000 more than at Chicago Stadium. The team offers some single-game tickets on either the day before a game or on game days, but selection is limited, and most available seats will likely be in the upper levels.

GOOD SEATS
If you can get one, the 3,000 club seats offer private parking, waitress service, and an attached computer keypad through which you can place food orders from your seat.

MOVING DOWN
Crowd-control personnel positioned at the entrance to each seating section inspect every ticket. If you manage to sneak past and are caught, you'll be politely asked once to go back to your original seat. If you are caught again, you'll be evicted.

SCALPING
Scalping is illegal here, and United Center management has been strict about enforcement, coming down hard on both sellers and buyers. Nonetheless, there are scalpers out front, and their prices are high. Police aren't as plentiful in the 2 to 4 blocks surrounding the arena, but that area also brings with it the potential for crime.

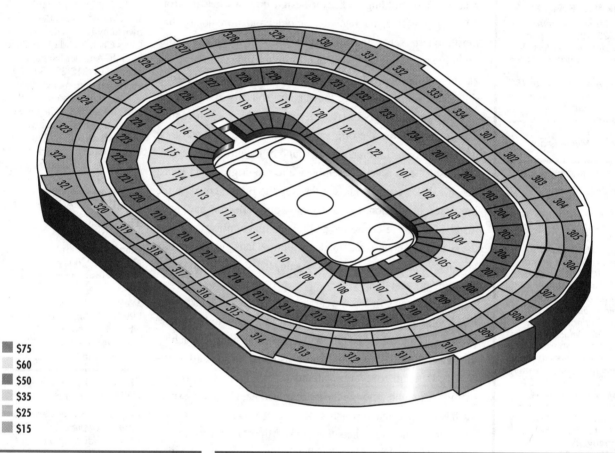

- $75
- $60
- $50
- $35
- $25
- $15

HOME-ICE ADVANTAGE

The United Center's ice surface is about 9 feet longer than Chicago Stadium's was, and whatever slight edge that tighter space gave the Blackhawks is long gone. Still, they went 22–13–6 at home in the 1995–96 season. United Center's acoustics amplify the crowd noise, making the visitors play amid a roar of antipathy. However nostalgic people get about the old Chicago Stadium, nobody misses the hordes of cockroaches that lived in both locker rooms.

GETTING TO THE UNITED CENTER

Public transportation: The No. 19 Stadium Express bus operates every 10 minutes from 1½ hours before each game until half an hour after. For more information, call (312) 595-3900.

By car: From O'Hare International Airport, take I-90 east to the Madison Street exit. Turn right on Madison, and follow it for about a mile. The United Center will be on the right.

TICKET INFORMATION
Address: 1901 W. Madison St., Chicago, IL 60612

Phone: (312) 943-7000 or (312) 455-7000
Hours: Mon.–Sat. 10–6.

Prices: $75, $60, $50, $35, $25, $15.

McNichols Arena

ARENA STATS

Location: *1635 Clay St., Denver, CO 80204*
Opened: *Aug. 22, 1975*
Capacity: *17,022*
Services for fans with disabilities: *Seating available in 13 sections on the loge level.*

ARENA FIRSTS

Regular-season game: *Oct. 6, 1995, 3–2 win over the Detroit Red Wings.*
Goal: *Valeri Kamensky*
Playoff game: *April 16, 1996, 5–2 win over the Vancouver Canucks.*
Stanley Cup game: *June 4, 1996, 3–1 win over the Pittsburgh Panthers.*

TEAM NOTEBOOK

Franchise history: *Quebec Nordiques, 1972–79 (WHA), 1979–94 (NHL); Colorado Avalanche, 1995–present.*
Division title: *1996*
Stanley Cup: *1996*
Rookie of the Year/Calder: *Peter Forsberg, 1994–95.*
Most Valuable Player/Hart: *Joe Sakic, 1995–96.*

TICKET INFORMATION

Address: *1635 Clay St., Denver, CO 80204*
Phone: *TicketMaster (303) 839-8497*
Hours: *Mon.–Fri. 8:30–5:30.*

GETTING TO McNICHOLS ARENA

Public transportation: Catch the No. 31 Champa bus on 16th Street and go to 17th Street and Federal. Walk east 2 blocks to the arena. Call (303) 299-6000 for more information.
By car: From the east, take Colfax Avenue west to Bryant Street. The arena is on the right. From the west, take Colfax east to Bryant. The arena is on the left. From the north, take U.S. 87 south to the 17th Street exit. The arena will be on the left. From the south, take U.S. 87 north to the 17th Street exit. The arena is on the left.

There hasn't been this much excitement in McNichols Arena since the pope was here a few years ago. The Colorado Avalanche, a slightly modified version of the Quebec Nordiques transplanted in Denver, win first the Pacific Division, then the Western Conference championship, and then go and win the Stanley Cup in their very first year of existence! Talk about Rocky Mountain Fever.

The Avalanche is actually the fifth professional hockey team to call McNichols Arena home, and this international bunch looks like they're settling in for a good long while.

Opened in 1975, McNichols got a $14 million facelift in 1987 that brought it up to par with most newer arenas. Rocky Mountain residents have as much fervor for their local pro sports teams as they do for their personal recreational activities—the Broncos frequently sell out, and the Rockies have been setting baseball attendance records since they started playing in 1993.

McNichols Arena has come a long way since a Lawrence Welk concert opened the place in 1975. The Nuggets helped make it an "in spot" in Denver, and the Avalanche look to keep it that way.

$100 **$75** **$65** **$55**
$45 **$32** **$19** **$10**

HOT TIPS FOR VISITING FANS

PARKING
There are 4,700 parking spaces at McNichols and another 3,000 at nearby Mile High Stadium; $5 gets you a spot in either one. There is some on-street parking in the area, but several blocks near the arena are no-parking zones patrolled by tow trucks.

MEDIA
Radio: KKFN (950 AM).
TV: KTVD (Channel 20), PrimeSports; KDVR (Channel 31) is the local Fox affiliate.

CUISINE
McNichols Arena operates three full-service restaurants and a bar, all of which are open to all ticketholders. The Butcher Block serves a selection of hoagies, grilled chicken, and beef. Wong Gong's mixes a Chinese decor with alternating buffets of Mexican and Italian foods. The Arena Club opens a couple of hours before face-off and offers a reasonably priced buffet. Underneath the Arena Club is the Fastbreak Lounge, open at halftime and for up to two hours after the game. Players occasionally stop by after the game. In addition to providing its own restaurants, McNichols also features Denver-area foods at their concession stands. Buffalo-meat items are popular, as are Greek gyros, quarter-pound hot dogs, and a Chicago dog that's topped with peppers, tomatoes, onions, and pickles. Imported beers can be found in Section 31.
After the game, there's Brooklyn's (303-572-3999), a comfortable bar in a Victorian-style building right across the street from McNichols. Denver Nuggets players and execs are occasional customers. About 10 minutes' drive from the arena is the Wynkoop Brewing Co. (303-297-2700), Colorado's first microbrewery.

LODGING NEAR THE ARENA

The Westin Hotel
1672 Laurence St.
Denver, CO 80202
(303) 572-9100/(800) 228-3000
2 miles from the arena.

Hyatt Regency
1750 Walton St.
Denver, CO 80202
(303) 295-1234/(800) 233-1234
3½ miles from the arena.

HOME-ICE ADVANTAGE

Winning the Stanley Cup on the first try is about the best advantage a team could wish for. Denver's altitude—5,280 feet above sea level—is always a boost to the home teams, who are still going strong when the visitors are beginning to gasp for air.

IN THE HOT SEATS AT McNICHOLS ARENA

GOOD SEATS
Even though it is an older facility, and not originally built for hockey, McNichols still offers plenty of good seats. From the center balcony area of the upper deck, the view is very good. Center-rink seats in the lower deck are held almost exclusively by season ticketholders. A bargain with a surprisingly good view can be had in the lower two-thirds of the upper-deck sections.

BAD SEATS
The top rows of seats behind the end zones are a long way from the ice, although they do afford the big picture. Given the Avalanche's strong start and their popularity, these may be the only seats available.

SCALPING
Ticket scalping is illegal in Denver. Nonetheless, scalpers can easily be found along the way to McNichols from the Mile High Stadium and McNichols Arena parking areas.

DALLAS STARS

Reunion Arena

D on't think Dallas isn't a hockey town. Though the Stars have been here only since 1993, minor-league teams here and in neighboring Fort Worth had already introduced local fans to the game, and they quickly came to understand NHL hockey. Even since the team cooled off after a hot start in Dallas, hockey has carved out a niche in the Dallas sports market.

Don't get too attached to Reunion, though. The arena opened in 1980 and is already considered out of date because it lacks luxury suites. Another major problem is the decibel level. All arenas play loud music, and home teams welcome the roar of their crowd, but the sound in Reunion is so loud that players can't hear their own coach's instructions when they are standing right next to him. It may be a while before it happens—probably not until the Stars and Mavericks both improve tremendously—but it will be a sad day for fans if and when the arena is replaced. It has some of the best sight lines in the NHL and is an intimate place in which to watch a game.

■ $110	■ $82.50	■ $72.50
■ $57.50	■ $44	■ $36
■ $27.50	■ $19.50	■ $14

ARENA STATS

Location: 777 Sports St., Dallas, TX 75207
Opened: April 28, 1980
Capacity: 16,924
Services for fans with sis-abilities: Seating available behind upper-level sections 101, 108, 115, and 122. Tickets are $14.

ARENA FIRSTS

Regular-season game: Oct. 5, 1993, 6–4 over the Detroit Red Wings.
Goal: Neal Broten of the Stars.
Overtime game: Oct. 9, 1993, 3–3 tie with the Winnipeg Jets.
Playoff game: April 17, 1994, 5–3 over the St. Louis Blues.

TEAM NOTEBOOK

Franchise history: Minnesota North Stars, 1967–93; Dallas Stars, 1993–present.
Rookies of the Year/Calder: Danny Grant, 1969; Bobby Smith, 1979.
Hockey Hall of Fame: Harry Howell, 1979; Gump Worsley, 1980; John Mariucci, 1985; Leo Boivin, 1986; Bob Gainey, 1992; Al Shaver, 1993.
Retired numbers: 8, Bill Goldsworthy; 19, Bill Masterton.

TICKET INFORMATION

Address: 211 Cowboy Pkwy., Irving, TX 75063
Phone: (214) GO-STARS or Dillard's at (800) 654-9545
Hours: Mon.–Fri. 10–5.

HOT TIPS FOR VISITING FANS

IN THE HOT SEATS AT REUNION ARENA

The Stars sold out 21 of 40 games in 1993–94, including 15 of their last 16, but only 16 of 45 in 1995–96. Advance single-game tickets are sold only 3 months in advance, and tickets to most games lately have been available right up to face-off.

GOOD SEATS/BAD SEATS

This is one of the best arenas in which to watch a game; only the seats near the glass should be avoided.

MOVING DOWN

Reunion Arena attendants seem less than vigilant. Some will stop you, but others seem to recognize squatters' rights if a seat is empty. Should the Stars suddenly become a hot ticket, you can bet that moving down won't be much of an option.

SCALPING

There isn't much of a market for scalping Stars tickets lately. If, however, the team gets hot, and there's no other way to find tickets, look for scalpers on the corner closest to Reunion Tower. Reselling tickets on arena property is not allowed.

PARKING

Plenty of parking (costing $6) is adjacent to the arena, including a five-level, 2,100-space parking structure. Downtown traffic can be very hectic close to game time, so give yourself some extra time, or walk if you're at a downtown hotel.

MEDIA

Radio: WBAP (820 AM).
TV: KDFI (Channel 27), KDFW (Fox, Channel 4) and Prime Sports (cable).

CUISINE

Though you can get chili, you won't find any other Texas treats in the concessions stands. The more popular items are Pizza Hut individual-size pies, frozen yogurt, and nachos. Miller, Bud-weiser, and Coors Light are available on tap, and you can also get bottled Heineken and Molson or chardonnay, white zinfandel, and wine coolers. If you get a Stars Club seat (a few are available on a single-game basis), you have access to the private Stars Club outside the arena, which has a fully stocked bar, sandwiches, snacks, and a pre-game buffet. Given the downtown location, fans have plenty of nightspots from which to choose after the game. Many opposing teams stay at the Hyatt, across the street.

Some fans head there, but many head to West End Marketplace, Dallas's version of Boston's Faneuil Hall. The city's most popular sports bars are Humperdinks on Greenville (214-368-6597), Randy White's restaurant (214-351-3261), Slap Shot's (214-392-4092), and Christie's (214-954-1511). Because Stars players live 20 to 30 miles from the arena, if they congregate, it's usually at the Stars Club.

LODGING NEAR THE ARENA

Hyatt Regency
300 Reunion Blvd.
Dallas, TX 75207
(214) 651-1234/(800) 233-1234
Across the street from the arena.

Holiday Inn
1933 Main St.
Dallas, TX 75201
(214) 741-7700/(800) 465-4329
7 blocks from the arena.

GETTING TO REUNION ARENA

Public transportation: The No. 30 Marsalis bus goes to the arena. Call (214) 979-2712 for more information.
By car: From DFW Airport, take the South Airport exit and go east on Highway 183 to I-35E south. Get off at the Reunion Boulevard exit and follow signs to the arena.

HOME-ICE ADVANTAGE

After a strong start in Dallas, the Stars dipped to a disappointing 14–18–9 in 1995–96. Dallas fans were hungry for a new contender, and the Stars came through at first, going 10–1–7 in their first 18 home games. The ice at Reunion is said to play "slow."

DETROIT RED WINGS

Joe Louis Arena

ARENA STATS

Location: 600 Civic Center Dr., Detroit, MI 48226
Opened: Dec. 12, 1979
Capacity: 19,383
Services for fans with disabilities: 200 seats available in the concourse level.

ARENA FIRSTS

Regular-season game: Dec. 27, 1979, 3–2 loss to the St. Louis Blues.
Goal: Brian Sutter of the Blues.
Playoff game: April 7, 1984, 4–3 loss to the Blues.
Stanley Cup Finals game: June 17, 1995, 2–1 loss to the New Jersey Devils.

TEAM NOTEBOOK

Franchise history: Detroit Cougars, 1926–30; Detroit Falcons, 1930–32; Detroit Red Wings, 1932–present.
Stanley Cups: 1935–36, 1936–37, 1942–43, 1949–50, 1951–52, 1953–54, 1954–55.
Hockey Hall of Fame: Connell, Foyston, Frederickson, Hay, Keats, Norris Sr., 1958; Adams, Thompson, 1959; Walker, 1960; Conacher, 1961; J. D. Norris, 1962; Goodfellow, Seibert, 1963; Stewart, 1964; S. Howe, Barry, 1965; Lindsay, 1966; Abel, Kelly, B. Norris, 1969; Gadsby, 1970; Sawchuk, Weiland, 1971; Holmes, G. Howe, 1972; Harvey, 1973; Ivan, Voss, 1974; Hall, 1975; Quackenbush, 1976; Delvecchio, 1977; Bathgate, Provonost, 1978; Lumley, 1980; Bucyk, Mahovlich, 1981; Ullman, 1982; Lynch, 1985; Boivin, 1986; Giacomin, Ziegler Jr., 1987; Park, 1988; Lewis, Sittler, 1989; Martyn, 1991; Dionne, 1992.
Retired numbers: 1, Sawchuck; 6, Aurie; 7, Lindsay; 9, G. Howe; 10, Delvecchio; 12, Abel.

The Red Wings haven't won the Stanley Cup since 1955, but their fans may be among the most loyal in the world. The Red Wings have been among the NHL leaders in attendance for nearly ten seasons now. When the team is playing well, the building rocks with excitement, but with the Cup slipping yet again through the Wings' hands in 1995–96, one has to wonder if that loyalty will soon be tested.

The arena was dubbed the "Joe Louis Warehouse" when it first opened in 1979 because of its vast, stark look, but when Mike and Marian Ilitch bought the team in 1982, they immediately spruced up the building. Though Joe Louis Arena hasn't known an NHL championship, the Red Wings' seven Stanley Cup banners hang from the rafters, as do recent divisional title banners and the retired numbers of Gordie Howe, Larry Aurie, Alex Delvecchio, Ted Lindsay, Terry Sawchuk, and Sid Abel.

The Red Wings' most eagerly anticipated tradition is the throwing of an octopus on the ice during the playoffs. This ritual began back when only four NHL teams made the playoffs, and the eight legs symbolized the eight victories needed to win the Stanley Cup. As 16-legged creatures are rare, an octopus is still used. Attendants who use a shovel to remove the octopus from the ice are booed, but those who use their bare hands are cheered wildly.

HOT TIPS FOR VISITING FANS

PARKING
If you don't know your way around Detroit, park in the lots adjacent to the arena; costs will range from $7 to $10. The Joe Louis parking structure, on Jefferson Avenue, is fewer than 50 yards from a main entrance. It's easily accessible from the Lodge Freeway (U.S. 10); the exit off the Lodge is marked as Joe Louis parking. A ramp leads you right into the parking structure on the second level, which is well lighted and safe. Some street parking is available on Fort Street, running parallel to Jefferson, but most knowledgeable fans consider that risky.

MEDIA
Radio: WJR (760 AM); Ken Kal and Paul Woods call the games.
TV: WKBD (UPN, Channel 50), PASS (Pro-Am Sports Service), and pay-per-view's Special Order Sports. Dave Strader calls the play-by-play and Mickey Redmond does the color commentary.

CUISINE
Since Red Wings' owner Mike Ilitch made his fortune with the Little Caesars pizza chain, pizza (guess whose?) is clearly the top item on the Detroit menu. The Coney Island stand offers kielbasa, bratwurst, and other sausages. A sub shop offers all sorts of sandwiches, a turkey stand offers turkey salads, and Mr. Pita puts all sorts of stuffings into this tradtional Middle Eastern pocket bread. Fresh fruit, ice cream, and frozen yogurt are also sold. The beer selection is wide, including Miller, Stroh's, Molson, Labatt's, and Löwenbräu on tap or in bottles. Lines move quickly.
After a Red Wings game fans (and sometimes players) head to Galligan's (313-963-1955) on Jefferson. Fans coming to the game by car can stop at Andrews on the Corner (313-259-8325) or Dunleavy's (313-259-0909), both on Joseph Campau Avenue, and take advantage of the bus service to and from Joe Louis Arena. The Loco Bar (313-965-3737) in the nearby Greektown neighborhood is also a popular hangout. Some fans cross the bridge into Windsor, Ontario, to have a drink at former NHL coach Don Cherry's bar.

LODGING NEAR THE ARENA

Omni Detroit
333 E. Jefferson Ave.
Detroit, MI 48226
(313) 222-7700/(800) 843-6664
3 blocks from the arena.

Westin Hotel
Renaissance Center
Detroit, MI 48243
(313) 568-8000/(800) 228-3000
½ mile from the arena.

THE RED WINGS AT JOE LOUIS ARENA

Feb. 11, 1982: The Red Wings score two goals on penalty shots; Tom Gradin and Ivan Hlinka are the shooters, and Gilles Gilbert of the Vancouver Canucks is the goalie.

Dec. 23, 1987: Bob Probert racks up an NHL-record eight penalties as the Buffalo Sabres beat the Red Wings 5–2.

April 12, 1991: Detroit is called for 33 penalties in a game against the St. Louis Blues, tying an NHL record, and the team sets a record with 152 penalty minutes.

March 24, 1992: Pittsburgh Penguins great Mario Lemieux scores his 1,000th point, but the Red Wings win 4–3.

June 11, 1995: Vyacheslav Kozlov scores in the second overtime to give the Red Wings a 2–1 win over the Blackhawks and a place in the Stanley Cup Finals.

In the Hot Seats at Joe Louis Arena

Order your tickets early, or be prepared to sit well above the ice. The Red Wings sold out all but one of their home games in 1995–96 and average crowds of more than 19,000.

GOOD SEATS

The best seats are in the lower bowl, and they are all owned by season ticketholders. The only way to find a lower-bowl seat is to pay a hefty premium to a private ticket service. Several are listed in Detroit newspapers. Though most offer some very good seats, fans should exercise caution, because not all are equally reputable. One of the best seats for Red Wings games isn't a seat at all. Standing-room tickets allow patrons to stand

in the aisle above the lower bowl. One word of warning: If you purchase a standing-room ticket, you had better be in good shape and first in line when the door opens at 6 p.m.— the sprint to secure prime standing spots often resembles the Oklahoma land rush.

BAD SEATS

Built in 1979 with fans in mind, the arena has no obstructed views. However, the higher-lettered rows in the upper bowl are a long way from the ice. If you have to choose among a group of higher seats, most Joe Louis fans will tell you to avoid behind the net, because it's difficult to see what's happening at the other end. If you're a Red

Wings fan and have to be at one end of the arena, choose the east side because Detroit shoots for two periods at that end.

MOVING DOWN

All lower-bowl seats are sold for each game, and no-shows are rare. Finding a lower seat unoccupied doesn't happen very often.

SCALPING

The resale of tickets, even at face value, is illegal in Detroit, and the police have been known to enforce this law with vigor. However, several people buy and sell tickets near the Joe Louis parking structure.

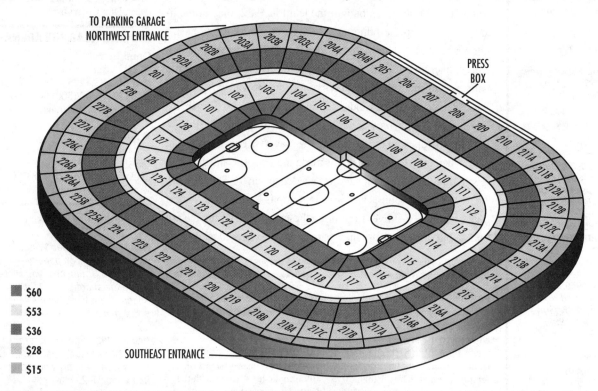

TO PARKING GARAGE
NORTHWEST ENTRANCE

PRESS BOX

SOUTHEAST ENTRANCE

- $60
- $53
- $36
- $28
- $15

HOME-ICE ADVANTAGE

Though Joe Louis doesn't have the reputation of a Madison Square Garden in its ability to intimidate opposing teams, home ice has been good to the Red Wings. They have 10 consecutive winning seasons there, including 1989–90, when they didn't make the playoffs but still went 20–14–6 at home. In 1995–96 the Red Wings went 36–3–2 in Joe Louis. But even the most loyal of fans can turn, as evidenced in 1993–94, when fan booing of goaltender Tim Cheveldae helped convince the team to trade him.

GETTING TO JOE LOUIS ARENA

Public transportation: A Detroit People Mover station is at the arena, and a bus stop is at Cobo Hall, which is adjacent to the arena. Call (313) 933-1300 for more information.

By car: From the south, go north on I-75 to the exit for U.S. 10. Exit southbound onto

U.S. 10 and head south for 1 mile. Take the Joe Louis exit, which will lead to the arena. From the north, go south on 1-75 until it meets I-375 south. Exit onto I-375 south and continue to the Jefferson Avenue exit. Go west on Jefferson Avenue for 1½ miles; the arena will be on the left.

TICKET INFORMATION

Address: 600 Civic Center Dr., Detroit, MI 48226

Phone: TicketMaster at (810) 645-6666
Hours: Mon.–Fri. 10–6.
Prices: $60: rows 1–7, lower level; $53:

rows 8–20, lower level; $36: rows 2–12, upper level; $28: rows 13–21, upper level; $15: rows 22–27, upper level.

Edmonton Coliseum

ARENA STATS

Location: 7424 118th Ave., Edmonton, AB T5B 4M9 Canada
Opened: Nov. 10, 1974
Capacity: 16,900
Services for fans with disabilities: 100 seats available throughout the arena.

ARENA FIRSTS

Regular-season game: Oct. 13, 1979, 3–3 tie with the Detroit Red Wings (NHL).
Overtime game: Oct. 9, 1983, 4–3 over the Minnesota North Stars (NHL).
Playoff game: April 11, 1980, 3–2 loss to the Philadelphia Flyers (NHL).
Stanley Cup Finals game: May 10, 1983, 2–0 loss to the New York Islanders.

TEAM NOTEBOOK

Franchise history: Alberta Oilers, 1972–73 (WHA); Edmonton Oilers, 1973–79 (WHA); Edmonton Oilers, 1979–present (NHL).
Stanley Cups: 1983–84, 1984–85, 1986–87, 1987–88, 1989–90.
Most Valuable Players/Hart: Wayne Gretzky, 1979–1980, 1980–81, 1981–82, 1982–83, 1983–84, 1984–85, 1985–86, 1986–87; Mark Messier, 1989–90.
Retired number: 3, Al Hamilton.

It may still be known as the house that Gretzky built, but he'd hardly recognize it anymore. Edmonton Coliseum—formerly Northlands Coliseum—got a major face-lift in 1994. The good news is that the arena still has not a single obstructed-view or bad-angle seat, and the better news is that—at least inside—the Coliseum is no longer a cousin to those functional but impersonal baseball parks, Three Rivers and Veterans stadiums. Outside, it still looks like a hubcap if viewed from an airplane. And the history is still here. Outside the main doors stands a bronze statue with No. 99 hoisting the Stanley Cup overhead. From the rafters hang no fewer than 22 banners, including five denoting Stanley Cup victories won in a building where Gretzky, Mark Messier, Paul Coffey, Grant Fuhr, Glenn Anderson, and Jari Kurri played the best hockey of their careers.

The multimillion-dollar renovation upgraded everything in the building. Oiler fans now sit in plusher seats everywhere, have more club and luxury seats to choose from, more and better concessions, and an eight-sided scoreboard with snazzy graphics and instant replay capability.

Oiler fans still remember the Great Gretzky too well to get very excited over recent seasons. This comfy new arena, however, and a maturing young team may win them back yet.

HOT TIPS FOR VISITING FANS

PARKING

Stadium parking is C$5 in one of the 1,100 first-come, first-served lots for the general public, or you can pay a little extra for closer parking off Capilano Freeway on the east side of the building. No cheaper neighborhood parking is nearby; even if you find an on-street spot, the savings are not worth the walk in January. On cold winter nights, wise fans find heated underground parking downtown (about C$6) and take the Light Rail Transit subway. If you are driving, avoid the Capilano Freeway exit south of 118th Avenue. It can be backed up a long way.

MEDIA

Radio: CHED (630 AM). Radio play-by-play announcer Rod Phillips has called games since 1972 in the WHA. Many locals hit the mute button on their TVs and listen to Phillips while they watch the game.

TV: CFRN (Channel 2).

CUISINE

The food at Edmonton Coliseum aims to please. For at least the first season, a variety of concessions will be offered on a trial basis; if the fans don't like it, it doesn't come back next year. Fan comment on the food, both pro and con, is also being heeded. The arena hot dogs are now from Oscar Mayer, smaller and tastier than their predecessors, but the real attention-getters are the exotic meat burgers, made from caribou, buffalo, and venison. If your taste in meat runs more toward the traditional, head for Coliseum Steak and Pizza (403-474-1640) before the game; it's 2 minutes west on 118th Avenue and was frequented by Gretzky and Messier in their Oiler days. If you're determined to eat in the arena, the best variety is on the lower-level concourse. Molson beer and wine coolers are also available.

After the game, the LRT rider gets a good deal, with several good options by stops downtown, but not much near the rink. Sherlock Holmes Pub (403-426-7784), about a block from the Central Station LRT drop, is favored by fans for a post-game pint. The players frequent Barry T's (403-438-2582). It's not a relaxing setting, but it's great for singles.

LODGING NEAR THE ARENA

Forum Motor Inn
11845 73rd St.
Edmonton, AB T5B 4R4
Canada
(403) 471-1231
Across the street from the arena.

Hilton
10235 101st St.
Edmonton, AB T59 3E9
Canada
(403) 428-7111/(800) HILTONS
6 miles from the arena.

THE OILERS AT EDMONTON COLISEUM

Feb. 15, 1980: Wayne Gretzky ties an NHL record with seven assists in an 8–2 win against the Washington Capitals.

Feb. 18, 1981: Gretzky scores four goals in one period, tying an NHL record, in a 9–2 win against the St. Louis Blues.

May 19, 1984: The Oilers beat the New York Islanders 5–2 to clinch their first Stanley Cup.

Dec. 19, 1984: Gretzky scores his 1,000th point in a 7–3 win against the Los Angeles Kings.

May 30, 1985: An 8–3 victory over the Philadelphia Flyers gives Edmonton its second consecutive NHL championship.

Oct. 15, 1989: Gretzky returns to Northlands Coliseum with his new team, the Kings, and becomes the NHL's all-time scoring leader with a goal at 19:07 of the third period. His 1,851 points move him past Gordie Howe.

In the Hot Seats at Edmonton Coliseum

The sight lines were always good, and now they're also comfortable. The Coliseum's renovation included seats with two inches of padding, although the extra ¾-inch came out of the leg room. The only tough tickets are for Montreal's annual Christmas season visit, the two Maple Leafs games, and visits from Calgary, Pittsburgh, and anyone from the Original Six. Excitement over the renovated arena may pull in more fans, but unless the team heats up, it won't really make a difference, and good seats will be easy to get.

GOOD SEATS

All seats are decent values. The budget-conscious should try the first four or five rows of the colonnade rather than the executive seats.

The low blues are excellent seats—particularly the first row, where you have no "leaners" obstructing your view.

BAD SEATS

As with most arenas, if you sit up close to the ice, the glass can distort your view. The C$15 seats are very high up.

MOVING DOWN

This town has little traffic, which means people who buy the more expensive season tickets are either in their seats by the 10-minute mark or they're not coming. The "expansion seat boogie" works especially well on cold midweek nights from December to February, when many older folks with good seats opt to

stay home and watch the game on TV. Buy a C$15 seat and pick out a pair down below after the 15-minute mark of the first period. Grab those seats right at the start of the first intermission when ushers aren't guarding the aisles, and be sitting there when people arrive for the second period. You'll get some stares, but only until the puck drops.

SCALPING

With so few sellouts, scalpers don't make a great living. They are outside the Coliseum for every game, however, on the south side of the building by the subway exit, and on the pedestrian bridge over 118th Avenue.

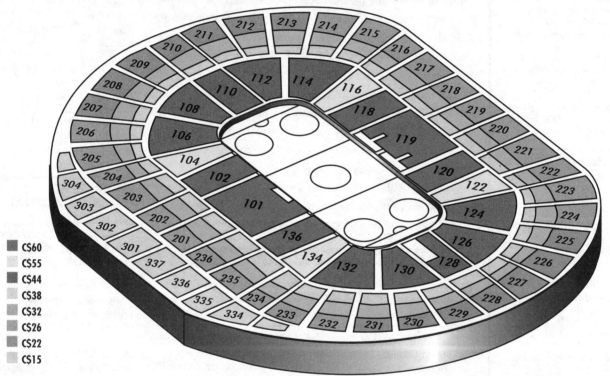

C$60
C$55
C$44
C$38
C$32
C$26
C$22
C$15

HOME-ICE ADVANTAGE

Little home-ice advantage remains at the Coliseum, where visiting teams used to be happy to escape with their jockstraps. With the Oilers still rebuilding after the selloff of all the team's stars, they hardly strike fear in their opponents.

Fans are purists, so they're more intent on watching a game they deeply understand than disturbing their concentration with clapping. No sirens, spotlights, or foghorns going on here, and almost no

signs either, except for the families of visiting players from Alberta, British Columbia, or Saskatchewan.

One note: Crowds dwindled as hatred for owner Pocklington grew, but the newly revamped and fan-friendly arena, along with a maturing team, may just pull them back in. The most fun you'll have here is a Saturday night game against the Canadiens, the Maple Leafs, or the Rangers now that Gretzky has signed on.

GETTING TO EDMONTON COLISEUM

Public transportation: Light Rail Transit stops at the Coliseum, as do the Nos. 5, 11, 18, 20, 23, 28, and 70 buses. Call (403) 421-4636 for more information.
By car: From Municipal Airport, take 118th Avenue 3 miles straight into the city; 118th Avenue runs right past the Coliseum. From Route 16, the Yellowhead Trail, take 82nd Street south. Turn left onto 118th Avenue.

TICKET INFORMATION
Address: 7424 118th Ave., Edmonton, AB T5B 4M9, Canada
Phone: (403) 471-2191 or TicketMaster at

(403) 451-8000.
Hours: Mon.–Fri. 9–5.
Prices: C$60: gold; C$55: silver; C$44: executive end zone; C$38: executive terrace;

C$32: terrace; C$26: side colonnade; C$22: end colonnade; C$15: gallery.

FLORIDA PANTHERS

Miami Arena

ARENA STATS

Location: 701 Arena Blvd., Miami, FL 33136
Opened: July 8, 1988
Capacity: 14,700
Services for fans with disabilities: Seating available in all price ranges in sections 101, 113, 114, 119, and 121.

ARENA FIRSTS

Regular-season game: Oct. 12, 1993, 2–1 loss to the Pittsburgh Penguins.
Goal: Martin Straka of the Penguins.
Regular-season win: Oct. 14, 1993, 5–4 over the Ottawa Senators.
Overtime game: Oct. 17, 1993, 3–3 tie with the Tampa Bay Lightning.
Playoff game: April 17, 1996, 6–3 over the Boston Bruins.
Stanley Cup final: June 8, 1996, 3–2 loss to the Colorado Avalanche.

TEAM NOTEBOOK

Franchise history: Florida Panthers, 1993–present.

Fog at Boston Garden. Puddles at New York Rangers games. So how, you ask, does a South Florida hockey team have some of the best ice in the NHL? Director of Operations Preston Williams credits the combination of two Zambonis, a water-treatment system, training of the staff at an ice school in Canada, and the fact the ice surface stays down almost season-round. Or perhaps it's because the building is kept very cold. Game-time temperatures dip into the 50s, even high up in the arena. No matter the cold air, the atmosphere inside the arena is hot.

Miami Arena opened in 1988 but was not used for hockey until the Panthers began play in 1993. But the Panthers quickly made up for lost time by compiling the best record ever of any first-year NHL team, and followed up in 1995–96 with a playoff victory and a trip to the Stanley Cup finals, where they faced off against the newly formed Colorado Avalanche (formerly the Quebec Nordiques) for a series that ended in a thrilling triple overtime victory by Colorado.

The Panthers pack 'em into the 14,700 available seats. Even before the team proved its mettle, hockey-starved Floridians—many of them transplanted Northerners—were lined up to see some action on the ice. Plenty of young families are in attendance, as are groups of high school girls hoping for a glimpse of their favorite player. The great fan activity is rat-throwing. Emulating the Detroit tradition of throwing live octopi onto the ice, Miami fans took to lobbing rubber rats rinkward during the '96 run for the Cup. The best that can be said about this ritual is that the rats aren't real.

Although the fans here now know their hockey, the Panthers also accommodate newcomers to the game, providing a pamphlet on hockey rules. This pamphlet is available at the Guest Relations booths, near sections 237 and 217.

HOT TIPS FOR VISITING FANS

PARKING
The closest lots, across the street, cost $10. Lots one block away cost $5. For the extravagant, valet parking is available for $12. Most fans park in the $5 lots. Security guards are positioned around the arena and the parking lots. The price for lots goes down dramatically after just a couple of blocks, and if you don't mind a slightly longer walk, you can probably find a lot for $2–$3. A limited number of metered street spaces are available around the outside of the $5 lots; the meters are off at night, but the neighborhood, on the edge of Overtown, can be risky at that time.

MEDIA
Radio: WQAM (560 AM—English). WCMQ (1210 AM—Spanish).
TV: Sunshine Network and occasionally WBFS (Channel 33). Denis Potvin and Jeff Rimer are on the mikes.

CUISINE
The food is only average, but the selection is remarkably wide and diverse—especially the liquor. Frozen-drink stands are spread throughout the concourse, offering everything from piña coladas to mixed drinks and draft beer. Pizza Hut pizza is available at a couple of locations in the arena, and other food stands offer the typical arena fare, but the stands near section 232 also offer pizza, hero sandwiches, shrimp or wings, and fries and Polish sausages. You can also get a Boca Burger (a tasty—really—veggie burger), and arepa, a Latin-American pancake-like concoction that's very popular hereabouts. Popular bars in nearby Bayside include Hooter's and the Hard Rock Cafe. Or if you're going north of Miami, try the Penalty Box (305-565-6658) in Fort Lauderdale. Owned by Rosie Paiement, former NHL right wing and brother of ex-NHL player Wilf Paiement, it's a hockey fan's heaven. Rosie organizes bus trips for some games. The cost is about $50, and reservations should be made at least a week in advance.

LODGING NEAR THE ARENA

Doral Ocean Resort
4833 Collins Ave.
Miami, FL 33140
(305) 532-3600/(800) 22DORAL
8 miles from the arena.

Sonesta
350 Ocean Dr.
Key Biscayne, FL 33149
(305) 361-2021/(800) 766-3782
10 miles from the arena.

THE PANTHERS AT MIAMI ARENA

March 31, 1994: A 3–3 tie with the New Jersey Devils gives the Panthers 74 points, the most ever for a team in its first season.

June 10, 1996: In a marathon contest that goes to three overtimes and lasts 4 hours and 58 minutes, the Panthers fall to the Colorado Avalanche by a score of 1–0 in the last game of the Stanley Cup Finals.

In the Hot Seats at Miami Arena

The lower-bowl seats are filled with season ticketholders and are not available on an individual-game basis. The Panther Pack seats, which go on sale for $9 at 10 a.m. on the day of the game, usually sell out very quickly. Individual seats may also be available for the mezzanine and the reserved section. You can bet that games against the Colorado Avalanche will be nearly impossible to get into. Teams from the Northeast (the Bruins and any from the New York area) will find many fans among the Pan-thers crowd, since so many Florida residents have moved south from that region.

GOOD SEATS
The Panther Pack seats offer a good view. Whichever of the other upper sections you prefer, the best view is between the blue lines, in sections 230–232 and 210–212. Sections 210–212 also afford a view of the player benches.

BAD SEATS
In the lower bowl, the first 10 rows are partially blocked by the glass and have reduced vision of the boards and corners.

SCALPING
Scalping is illegal in Miami, and although the market for Panthers tickets is way up after their quick rise to the Stanley Cup Finals, the city does an effective job of preventing scalping and isn't particularly tolerant of sellers or buyers.

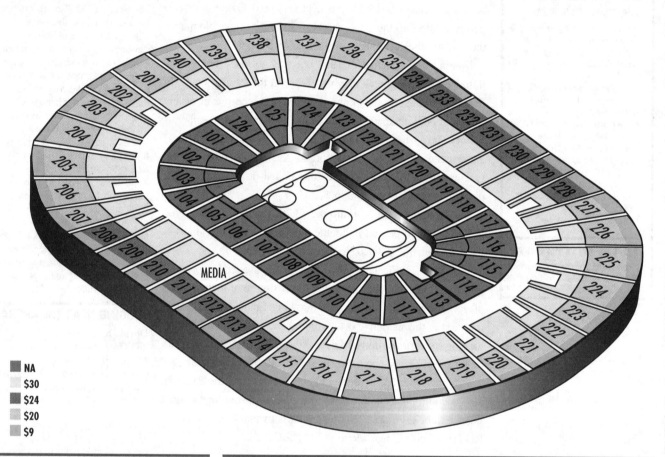

- ■ NA
- ▨ $30
- ■ $24
- ▧ $20
- ▨ $9

HOME-ICE ADVANTAGE

Good ice can be a disadvantage for a clutch-and-grab team such as the Panthers. The team's biggest advantage is having proven themselves contenders so early in their history. This also means that they have to live up to their own record, which can be a burden. Perhaps the fan noise, which seems louder because of a low roof, will help spur them on. Ironically, visitors look forward to having rubber rats tossed onto the ice after Panther goals; they say it gives them time to regroup.

GETTING TO MIAMI ARENA

Public transportation: The Overtown Metrorail stop is just across the street from the arena. Call (305) 638-6700 for more information.
By car: From the airport, take 836 east to Biscayne Boulevard. Exit right at the bottom of the ramp onto Biscayne Boulevard. Proceed to Northwest Eighth Street and make a right. The arena is 2 blocks on the left.

From Miami Beach, take I-395 west to the Biscayne Boulevard exit. Go left onto Biscayne Boulevard and south 3 blocks to Northeast Eighth. Take a right onto Northeast Eighth for 3 blocks. The arena is on the left.

TICKET INFORMATION
Address: 701 Arena Blvd., Miami, FL 33136

Phone: (305) 530-4435 or TicketMaster at (800) GO-PANTH. In Dade County, (305) 358-5885; in Broward County, (954) 523-

3309; in Palm Beach, (407) 966-3309
Hours: Mon–Fri. 10–4.
Prices: $30, $24, $20, $9

HARTFORD WHALERS

Hartford Civic Center

ARENA STATS

Location: *242 Trumbull St., Hartford, CT 06103*
Opened: *Jan. 11, 1975*
Capacity: *15,635*
Services for fans with disabilities: *Seating available in the last two rows of sections 101, 106, 107, 112, 113, 118, 119, and 124. For more information, call (860) 249-7528.*

ARENA FIRSTS

Regular-season games: *Jan. 11, 1975, 4–3 over the San Diego Mariners in overtime (WHA); Oct. 11, 1979, 4–1 loss to the Minnesota North Stars (NHL).*
Overtime games: *Jan. 11, 1975, 4–3 over the San Diego Mariners (WHA); Nov. 26, 1983, 4–3 over the New York Rangers (NHL).*
Playoff game: *April 11, 1980, 4–3 overtime loss to the Montreal Canadiens (NHL).*

TEAM NOTEBOOK

Franchise history: *New England Whalers, 1972–79 (WHA); Hartford Whalers, 1979–present (NHL).*
Retired numbers: *2, Rick Ley; 9, Gordie Howe; 19, John McKenzie.*

TICKET INFORMATION

Address: *242 Trumbull St., Hartford, CT 06103*
Phone: *(860) 728-6637, 800-WHALERS or TicketMaster at (860) 525-4500*
Hours: *Mon.–Sat. 10–6 (Mon.-Fri. 10-6 in the off-season).*

HOME-ICE ADVANTAGE

Not much. The Whalers are barely better than .500 at home, and in recent years they've gone below that.

The Hartford Civic Center is located inside a mall—appropriate, since the Whalers are still shopping for an identity. The team has moved around, starting in Boston in 1972 as the World Hockey Association's New England Whalers, then to Springfield, Mass., in 1974, then to the new Civic Center in Hartford in 1975, back to Springfield for two years (the arena's roof collapsed during a 1978 snowstorm), and finally to the National Hockey League in 1979. The team had a good WHA history, but its NHL tenure has been undistinguished. It doesn't help matters that the Whalers play in a state where half the residents tend to root for Boston teams, and the other half for New York teams; local sports enthusiasm seems to be saved for the University of Connecticut basketball teams.

All this and a poor economy leave a lot of empty seats at the Civic Center. Attendance averages fewer than 10,000 at the 15,635-seat arena. Businessmen and children are noticeably scarce.

Inside, the arena provides good sightlines and its center-ice scoreboard/video screen has excellent resolution and can be seen from all angles. Nothing else stands out about the arena. If the Whalers are playing well, the arena can be exciting. If not, this can be a dreary place.

■ $50 $40   ■ $30 $25

HOT TIPS FOR VISITING FANS

PARKING
Lots beneath the Civic Center and at the Sheraton-Hartford have spaces for $7. City lots farther from the arena can go as low as $4 or $5, but the walk can get cold.

MEDIA
Radio: WTIC (1080 AM).
TV: SportsChannel New England.

CUISINE
Prices are low, but so are the quality and variety, and lines are long. Season ticketholders have access to the Coliseum Club, which offers a lavish buffet before games, or you can buy a dinner and ticket package. Several bars in the neighborhoods are open after the game, but going to the mall is more convenient. The mall has more than 70 restaurants and shops, plus the Sheraton-Hartford Hotel. Recommended restaurants: Chuck's Steak House (860-241-9100) and Gaetano's (860-249-1629).

LODGING NEAR THE ARENA

Sheraton Centre
315 Trumbull St.
Hartford, CT 06103
(860) 728-5151/(800) 325-3535
Adjacent to the arena.

Goodwin Hotel
1 Haynes St.
Hartford, CT 06103
(860) 246-7500/(800) 922-5006
Across the street from the arena.

GETTING TO THE HARTFORD CIVIC CENTER

Public transportation: Shuttle buses from commuter lots downtown are available. Call (860) 728-6637 for more information.
By car: From the north or south, I-91 to Trumbull Street, exit 32B. The Civic Center is five lights ahead.
From the east, take I-84 west to Main Street, exit 50. Go right past the Holiday Inn, then go left at the traffic light onto Main Street. At the second traffic light, go right onto Church Street. The Civic Center is at the next intersection.
From the west, take I-84 east to Ann/High Streets. Go right onto High Street and, at the first light, left onto Church Street. The Civic Center is at the next intersection.

IN THE HOT SEATS AT THE HARTFORD CIVIC CENTER

Tickets go on sale in August, but with a small season-ticket base and an average attendance of fewer than 10,000, you can easily get tickets in the middle of the price range on game day, and often in all sections.

GOOD SEATS
Even with the empty seats, same-day discounted tickets aren't offered. Most of the 100-level seats go to season ticketholders. The 200-level seats offer the best combination of view and price. The steepness of the 300 level makes it ideal for watching plays develop.

BAD SEATS
The lowest seats in the 100-level often have views distorted by the glass and/or blind spots, particularly if you're sitting in the bottom five rows behind the nets. In the bottom 10 rows of the 200 and 300 levels, railings or fans–who are allowed to move about during play–can obstruct your view. Rows AA through GG in the 300 level require a hike of up to 60 steps.

MOVING DOWN
Don't bother. Ushers are instructed to check all tickets.

SCALPING
Because of the empty seats, there is little need, except when the Bruins or the Rangers are in town and huge convoys of their fans come. The Whalers post guards to discourage scalping.

LOS ANGELES KINGS

Great Western Forum

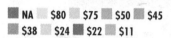

NA $80 $75 $50 $45
$38 $24 $22 $11

The Great Western Forum, which opened in 1967, was already on its last legs when the Kings began to thrive. Now that the Kings are no longer thriving, the Forum is still on its last legs, and the talk of building a modern arena with sky boxes and all sorts of high-tech bells and whistles has pretty much been silenced. The reason for both? Wayne Gretzky. He came, he conquered, he left.

Many Southern Californians were barely aware that L.A. even had a hockey team until Gretzky arrived in 1988. But when he did, and the Kings started winning, a Kings ticket became almost as hot as a courtside seat for the Lakers. Celebrities and well-off wannabes crowded the place, and as long as the team was doing well, it was easy to cheer. The Kings made it to the Stanley Cup Finals in 1993, and it looked like just maybe Los Angeles had become a hockey kind of town.

But when Gretzky left, so did a huge percentage of the crowd. His legacy was to elevate hockey's standing in the hierarchy of L.A. sports; now it's up to the Kings to keep it there. The good news for true L.A. hockey fans is that good seats are plentiful, and the place isn't so crowded with glitterati anymore.

IN THE HOT SEATS AT THE GREAT WESTERN FORUM

Only a handful of Kings games sold out in 1995, and even on those rare occasions there were tickets for good seats available until the very last minute. Now that the fickle Hollywood types have ditched hockey, anyone else who wants to get into a Kings game can pretty much show up fifteen minutes before the face-off and get an excellent seat, partly because the $24 and $11 tickets tend to sell before the $80 and $45 tickets. Those $11 tickets, by the way, are very decent seats.

BAD SEATS

Some spots high in the corner are located as far as 170 feet from the ice. If you sit next to the glass, it's rather difficult to see what's happening along the boards on your side.

MOVING DOWN

Things haven't reverted to the BG (before Gretzky) days when you could buy the cheapest ticket, then sit anywhere. But someone in the pricier sections who isn't wearing Armani doesn't look so conspicuous anymore. Ushers are still pretty vigilant, though.

SCALPING

Nobody's seen a scalper hereabouts since Gretzky left.

HOT TIPS FOR VISITING FANS

PARKING

The lots surrounding the Forum are the safest. Overflow parking goes across the street to Hollywood Park, which some fans say is easier to exit. Both charge $6. After the game, traffic controllers keep the cars moving, so you can get out of the lots quicker than you get in. Don't park on the side streets; they're permit-only.

MEDIA

Radio: XTRA (690 AM–English), KWIZ (1480 AM–Spanish). **TV:** Prime Sports. Bob Miller has been "the Voice of the Kings" since 1973. He's also provided voice-overs for both of the Mighty Ducks movies.

CUISINE

Yes, this is Los Angeles, but there's no sushi here, like at Dodger Stadium. What you'll find is more along the lines of traditional hot dogs and cheeseburgers than anything "Californian," although burritos and various Mexican dishes are available. You can get carved roast-beef sandwiches and salads at the Whistle Stop Restaurant, a stand-up deli. Of the concessions-stand food, fans seem to like the chicken sandwiches best. Domestic beers are Miller, Budweiser, and Coors. Heineken and Molson are also on tap, and there's an imported bottled-beer stand. Postgame, much of the hockey crowd, including players, heads to Harry O's (310-545-4444) in Manhattan Beach. Owned by former Kings player Billy Harris, this sports bar is always hopping and usually jampacked. To dine, players and fans seem to like Jerry's Deli (310-821-6626) in Marina Del Rey.

LODGING NEAR THE ARENA

Marriott Airport
5855 W. Century Blvd.
Los Angeles, CA 90045
(310) 641-5700/(800) 228-9290.
8 miles from the arena.

Radisson Hotel
1400 Parkview Ave.
Manhattan Beach, CA 90267
(310) 546-7511/(800) 333-3333.
8 miles from the arena.

GETTING TO THE GREAT WESTERN FORUM

Public transportation: Take a No. 40 bus to Market Manchester. Transfer to an eastbound No. 211. For information, call (310) 320-9442.
By car: From Highway 105, exit at Prairie Avenue and head north for a few blocks to the Forum.

ARENA STATS

Location: 3900 W. Manchester Blvd., Inglewood, CA 90305
Opened: Dec. 30, 1967
Capacity: 16,005
Services for fans with disabilities: About a dozen seats for the mobility-impaired are available in each end zone.

ARENA FIRSTS

Regular-season game: Dec. 30, 1967, 2–0 loss to the Philadelphia Flyers.
Goal: Brian Kilrea of the Kings.
Overtime game: Oct. 5, 1983, 3–3 tie with the Minnesota North Stars.
Playoff game: April 4, 1968, 2–1 over the Minnesota North Stars.
Stanley Cup Finals game: June 5, 1993, 4–3 overtime loss to the Montreal Canadiens.

TEAM NOTEBOOK

Franchise history: Los Angeles Kings, 1967–present.
Most Valuable Player/Hart: Wayne Gretzky, 1988–89.
Rookie of the Year/Calder: Luc Robitaille, 1986-87.
Retired numbers: 16, Marcel Dionne; 30, Rogatien Vachon; 18, Dave Taylor.

TICKET INFORMATION

Address: 3900 W. Manchester Blvd., Inglewood, CA 90305
Phone: (310) 419-3182 or TicketMaster at (213) 480-3232, (714) 740-2000, (619) 278-8497, or (805) 583-8700
Hours: Mon.–Fri. 10–6.

HOME-ICE ADVANTAGE

Though it's not as pronounced as it used to be, even pre-Gretzky, opposing teams didn't seem to play well at the Forum. The Great One's presence used to help explain it, but some theorize that it's because eastern teams are in the midst of long road trips when they hit L.A.

MIGHTY DUCKS OF ANAHEIM

Arrowhead Pond of Anaheim

ARENA STATS

Location: 2695 E. Katella Ave., Anaheim, CA 92803
Opened: June 17, 1993
Capacity: 17,174
Services for fans with disabilities: Seating available throughout the 200 level.

ARENA FIRSTS

Regular-season game: Oct. 8, 1993, 7–2 loss to the Detroit Red Wings.
Goal: Aaron Ward of Detroit.
Overtime game: Dec. 12, 1993, 2–1 loss to the St. Louis Blues.

TEAM NOTEBOOK

Franchise history:
The Mighty Ducks of Anaheim, 1993–present.

TICKET INFORMATION

Address: 2695 E. Katella Ave., Anaheim, CA 92803
Phone: (714) 704-2786 or TicketMaster at (714) 740-2000
Hours: Mon.–Fri. 10–6, Sat. 10–4, Sun. for three hours before the game.

HOME-ICE ADVANTAGE

The team played better on the road than at home during their first season, but they improved quickly, and posted a 22–15–4 record at home in 1995–96. General Manager Jack Ferreira has fashioned a very physical team that knows how to assert itself. Most visiting teams have learned better than to dismiss this arena as a hockey theme park.

The Pond might be the Taj Mahal of NHL arenas or, more properly, the Magic Kingdom. With marble concourses, a granite exterior, glass archways, and brass fittings, it is the most luxurious and aesthetically pleasing building in the league.

Disney's focus on family-style entertainment is evident at Ducks games. The arena hosted the movie version of the Mighty Ducks before the NHL team hit the ice. Game scenes from *The Mighty Ducks: D2* were shot in the arena in the summer of 1993. Even now, games are as much fun-for-all-ages events as they are hockey showdowns. Pre-game, the team's "Wild Wing" mascot drops from the rafters, and fans blow merrily on their duck callers (an average of 2,000 are sold each game) when the Ducks score.

The fans' appreciation can be measured in dollars: The Mighty Ducks surpassed the Sharks in merchandise popularity right from the start. The arena's team store does a brisk business, game day or not. The initial novelty aspect of the Ducks has been quickly replaced by a genuinely credible team that is taken seriously by its fans and by its opponents.

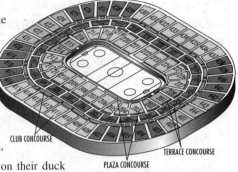

CLUB CONCOURSE · TERRACE CONCOURSE · PLAZA CONCOURSE

■ NA ■ $125 ■ $75 ■ $55 ■ $45
■ $35 ■ $30 ■ $24.50 ■ $21 ■ $20

From the east, take the 57 or 91 freeways to I-5 and follow the directions above.

HOT TIPS FOR VISITING FANS

PARKING

Come early and park in the adjacent lots. There are about 4,500 arena spaces available at $6. Some nearby restaurants—Mr. Stox, The Catch, and Charlie Brown's—offer shuttles to the Pond from their lots.

MEDIA

Radio: KEZY (95.9 FM); Charlie Simmer, a member of the Los Angeles Kings' famed "Triple Crown" line, does analysis on radio.
TV: KCAL (Channel 9) and PrimeSports on cable.

CUISINE

Mexican food from the Chili Peppers stand is the best-selling of the Pond's tasty and diversified menu. Many varieties of hot dogs are offered, and Yoshinoya's Japanese-style cooking is also very popular. Pizza Hut makes the pies, and another stand's spicy grilled chicken is many fans' favorite. Barbecued beef and pork sandwiches are also gaining a following. Bottled beers include Tecate, Modelo Especial, and Corona Extra, plus beers from Germany, Canada, Australia, and northern California. Concessions are clustered in each corner of the arena. The club level, which you can't access without purchasing a club seat, has the best selection

and four bars. Players tend to go to The Catch (714-634-1829) or El Torito (714-956-4880), a Mexican restaurant chain that has good margaritas. If you don't mind a drive, head to Harry O's (310-545-4444) in Manhattan Beach, a hangout for hockey fans and players. It's owned by former Kings player Billy Harris and is always hopping.

LODGING NEAR THE ARENA

Anaheim Hilton & Towers
777 Convention Way
Anaheim, CA 92802
(714) 750-4321/
(800) HILTONS1
1 block from the arena.

Embassy Suites Brea
900 E. Birch St.
Brea, CA 92621
(714) 990-6000/(800) EMBASSY
1 mile from the arena.

GETTING TO THE POND

Public transportation: A bus stop is in front of the Pond. The city also runs a shuttle from Anaheim Stadium. For more information, call (714) 635-6010.
By car: From the north or south, take I-5 (a.k.a. the Santa Ana Freeway) to the Katella Avenue exit. Exit west and follow Katella approximately half a mile. The arena and parking will be to the right.

IN THE HOT SEATS AT ARROWHEAD POND OF ANAHEIM

The Ducks' season-ticket base is at about 14,000 and climbing. From early on, any seat you could get was a good seat because of the frequent sellouts. This is still true. The Ducks planned to hold back a few hundred seats to sell on a game-by-game basis, but even those were expected to sell out before the first game.

GOOD SEATS

If you have a choice, get into the first row in the terrace. It's high enough to give you perspective on strategy and see the whole game, but close enough to see players sweat.

BAD SEATS

As in any arena, high in the corner is high in the corner. The row under the press box should be avoided.

SCALPERS

Because the Mighty Ducks are a hot item, scalping is a cottage industry. When fans exit Highway 57 at Katella Avenue, scalpers are waiting. Other scalpers wander through the parking lot. Prices can start at a 40% markup or higher, depending on the game. Scalping is strictly illegal hereabouts, and the law is actively enforced.

MONTREAL CANADIENS

Molson Centre

Once you're inside the Molson Centre, the Canadiens' new home in the heart of downtown Montreal, you could almost believe that you're in a larger, spiffed-up version of the old Montreal Forum. The red, white, and blue color scheme and the overall look are nearly identical, but the Molson Centre has a few new twists that may help ease fan anguish over leaving the hallowed hockey shrine that was the Forum: Curved glass around the ice, 3,388 more seats, a steeper rise to the stands, club seats, better food, three restaurants, and no more standing room.

The Canadiens brought their history with them. The 24 Stanley Cup banners that hang from the rafters are larger than the old ones (the Forum's were auctioned for charity and brought millions of dollars) so they can be seen in their higher perch. Throughout the arena are pictures and memorabilia. Still, it's been difficult to bid *adieu* to the old Forum, where eleven Cup-clinching games were played and more than 70 years of history were played out. The Forum is slated to become a multiplex movie theater, with the exterior left largely unaltered. Whether they'll devote one of the many screens to continual showings of *Slap Shot* is not known.

Canadiens' crowds are a mixture of corporate types and die-hard hockey fans. Until the playoffs, you won't see the folks in the lower-level red seats getting too wild. But if you look beyond the corporate seats, you'll find a knowledgeable and demanding hockey crowd. Fans tend to arrive late and become more intense as the game goes on. They expect excellence and let the team know when it falls short.

HOT TIPS FOR VISITING FANS

PARKING
For a lucky 580 Canadiens fans there is finally arena parking. These spots are mostly taken by season ticketholders. The rest of us will have to make do with one of the 15,000 spaces in lots around the Molson Centre. Prices start at about C$12, and drop the farther away you get. Canadiens fans tend to arrive at the very last minute, so you shouldn't have trouble finding a place unless you hit the rush.

MEDIA
Radio: In English, Hall of Famer Dick Irvin handles play-by-play on CJAD (800 AM) and CBMT (Channel 6). Games in French are broadcast on CBF (690 AM). **TV:** CBFT (Channel 2), CBC (Channel 6), and RDS (cable).

CUISINE
The 38 concession stands' fare has improved considerably over the Forum's, but it still ain't exactly gourmet. The grilled hot dogs are standouts, as are the smoked meat sandwiches. This being Canada, Tim Horton's donuts are served, and the beer is mostly Molson—hardly a surprise given the arena's name and team ownership. Of the Centre's three restaurants, only Ovation, a casual sports bar, is open to non-club seat holders.

Nearby, Crescent Street has several fine restaurants, ranging from the distinguished Les Halles (514-844-2328) to the Hard Rock Cafe (514-987-1420). For deli fare, try Dunn's (514-866-4377). Many of the nicer spots require gentlemen to wear jackets. If you want informal, a few fast-food and sit-down restaurants are on Ste. Catherine, near the old Forum; also the mall across Atwater Street offers several options.

LODGING NEAR THE ARENA

Bonaventure Hilton
1 Pl. Bonaventure
Montreal, PQ
Canada H5A 1E4
(514) 878-2332/(800) 445-8667
Across the street from the arena.

Marriott Chateau Champlain
1050 W. Legeuche-Tiere
Montreal, PQ
Canada H3B 4C9
(514) 878-9000/(800) 200-5909
Across the street from the arena.

ARENA STATS
Location: 1260 rue de La Gauchetiere Ouest, Montreal, PQ, H3B 5E8, Canada
Opened: March, 1996
Capacity: 21,347
Services for fans with disabilities: Seating in lower level.

ARENA FIRSTS
Regular-season game: March 16, 1996, 4–2 over the New York Rangers.

TEAM NOTEBOOK
Franchise history: Club de Hockey Canadien 1909–10, 1916–17; Club Athlétique Canadien, 1910–16 (NHA); Montreal Canadiens, (NHL) 1917–present.
Stanley Cups: 1915–16, 1923–24, 1929–30, 1930–31, 1943–44, 1945–46, 1952–53, 1955–56 to 1959–60, 1964–65, 1965–66, 1967–68, 1968–69, 1970–71, 1972–73, 1975–76 to 1978–79, 1985–86, 1992–93.
Hockey Hall of Fame: Morenz, Vezina, 1945; Joliat, Northey, 1947; Lalonde, Malone, 1950; Cleghorn, Gardiner, Raymond, 1958; Mantha, Selke, 1960; Hall, Hainsworth, M. Richard, 1961; Laviolette, O'Brien, Pitre, 1962; Dandurand, Gorman, 1963; Durnan, B. Siebert, 1964; Blake, Bouchard, Lach, Reardon, 1966; T. Johnson, 1970; Beliveau, Geoffrion, 1972; Harvey, Molson, 1973; Moore, 1974; Cattarinich, 1977; Plante, Pollock, 1978; H. Richard, 1979; Worsley, 1980; Mahovlich, 1981; Cournoyer, 1982; Dryden, 1983; Lemaire, 1984; Olmstead, 1985; Savard, 1986; Laperriere, 1987; Lafleur, O'Connor, 1988; Bowman, 1991; Gainey, 1992; Lapointe, Shutt, 1993; Robinson, 1995.

In the Hot Seats at the Molson Centre

With 3,388 more seats than the Forum, tickets are somewhat easier to get at the Molson Centre; however much of the arena is still sold out on a season-ticket basis. Between 3,000 and 4,000 tickets are available on an individual-game basis, but most are gone as soon as they go on sale. The club designates a day in September (for games in the first half of the season) and another in early December (second-half games) for sale of individual-game tickets. As each approaches, call the club and get the exact date. Orders are limited to a maximum of four tickets a game for four games.

Standing-room tickets are no longer sold, in part because of the additional seating, but also due to new building fire codes.

GOOD SEATS

The Molson Centre's interior greatly resembles the Forum: same colors, same overall look, but bigger, taller, and with more seats. One big improvement is the absence of obstructed views. The club seats are about midway up and are considered the best seats in the house; try to get seated just above or below them for a close second-best view. The curved glass allows for unblocked views from rinkside, and the first row of seats starts about a foot up from ice level. It was said that there was not a bad seat in the Forum, and that's certainly true at the new Molson Centre—plus you'll never have to stand through a game.

SCALPING

The municipal ordinance against reselling tickets doesn't seem to stop anyone, and when the Canadiens moved over from the Forum, so did the scalpers. Look for them on the block or two leading to the Centre's main entrance. It's a sellers' market, so expect significant markups.

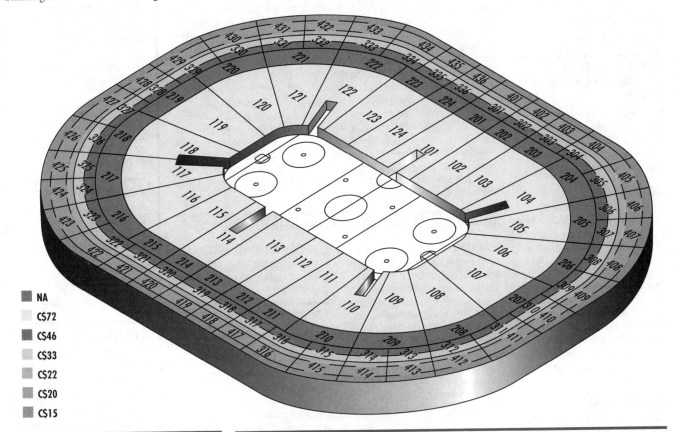

Legend:
- NA
- C$72
- C$46
- C$33
- C$22
- C$20
- C$15

HOME-ICE ADVANTAGE

The excellent ice from the Forum has been re-created at the Molson Centre, allowing the Canadiens to carry on their tradition of speed and finesse. The "Flying Frenchmen" lost some altitude, however, when they moved to their new digs, going a disappointing 5–4–1 in their first 10 games there, probably jarred by switching arenas in midseason. Once they're fully comfortable in their new home, the Canadiens will no doubt get back to their winning ways.

GETTING TO THE MOLSON CENTRE

Public transportation: The Lucien-l'Allier and Bonaventure metro stations stop near the Centre. Buses also stop nearby. Call (514) 288-6287 for more information.

By car: From the south, take Route 15 north to route 10 west. Follow Route 10 across the Champlain Bridge, then turn right at the Wellington exit; go right onto Peel Street, then left onto Ste. Antoine. The Molson Centre garage is another 500 feet.

From the west, take Route 401 in Ontario, which becomes Route 20 in Quebec. Follow this road into Montreal, where it becomes Route 720. From Route 720, follow signs to the Molson Centre.

TICKET INFORMATION

Address: 1260 rue de La Gauchetiere Ouest, Montreal, PQ, H3B 5E8, Canada.

Phone: (514) 932-2582 or Admission at (514) 790-1245.
Hours: Mon.-Fri. 10–6.

Prices: C$70, C$40, C$30, C$33, C$22, C$20, C$17, C$15.

NEW JERSEY DEVILS

Continental Airlines Arena

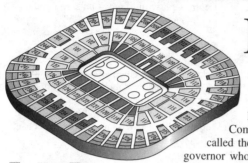

■ NA ■ $50 ■ $45
■ $35 ■ $26 ■ $18

Looking east from the Meadowlands' Continental Airlines Arena parking lot, you can see the tops of the Empire State Building and the World Trade Center. New York City is only 6 miles away, and it overshadows much of what happens here in East Rutherford, New Jersey.

One of the better-kept secrets in the NHL, the hockey/basketball venue at the Meadowlands Sports Complex is a sight to behold. The arena was originally called the Brendan Byrne Arena, in honor of the New Jersey governor who put his political weight behind the building of the Meadowlands complex; it was renamed in 1996 when Continental Airlines bought the right to put their name on it. Finished in 1981, this arena features amenities that NHL teams push for nowadays: concourse-level luxury boxes, wide concourses, plentiful concession stands, and state-of-the-art scoreboards. The arena's most impressive aspect, though, is its size. To get its true impact, arrive early and walk into the seating area when it's mostly empty—you'll feel like you're inside a canyon.

The franchise, plucked from Denver and plopped down in Rangers territory, slowly built a loyal fan base of its own. Local fans were grateful to have a truly New Jersey team at the Meadowlands, not just a New York team using it as an outpost. A cross-river rivalry has built up between the Rangers and the Devils during their respective championship seasons, and the crowd for these games can be evenly split for the home team and the visitors. It can get loud.

IN THE HOT SEATS AT CONTINENTAL AIRLINES ARENA

Seats are generally available in all sections, but one warning: Rangers–Devils games and late-season Saturday matinees sell out, so order early for those.

BAD SEATS

Just a few minor annoyances. Down low, the folding chairs on the metal risers are not as comfortable as the chairs bolted into the cement risers. In sections 203 (5–10), 204 (rows 6 and 7), 226 (6 and 7), and 227 (5 and 6), a railing cuts across your view of the goal. Noisy rooms of machinery sit at the top of sections 207, 217, 228, and 238, but you'll quickly get used to the sound. The building is very cold, so bring a jacket if you're sitting down low.

MOVING DOWN

Arena managment is strict about this, but it's a big arena. Possible in the upper section, but wait until the second period.

SCALPING

Reselling tickets recently became legal in New Jersey on an open-ended experimental basis; the exceptions are certain special events (playoffs, concerts, etc.). The unofficial official scalpers' area is around Gate D. Since the Devils won the Cup, fewer tickets are available for face value, but it still happens. Expect a higher markup if the Rangers or Red Wings are the opponent. Scalpers may also buy your extra tickets, but not at full face value.

HOT TIPS FOR VISITING FANS

PARKING

You're stuck with the stadium lot, which costs $6. If you park on the access roads, you might get ticketed or towed. The arena lots have only 4,500 spaces; the overflow parking at Giants Stadium adds another 20,000, but it's a hike. If you need to get on the turnpike when you leave, park in the front or back and work your way to the northeast corner. That puts you right at the on ramp.

MEDIA

Radio: WABC (770 AM).
TV: SportsChannel.

CUISINE

Pretty much standard stadium fare. The Hebrew National hot dogs are better than the regular ones. The jumbo pretzels may seem pricey at $3, but they're the size of a loaf of bread and will last you an entire game. Budweiser and Miller are offered on tap, and Heineken, Beck's, and Molson as well as wines are available at portable stands. After the game, most of your choices are in Secaucus. A popular fan hangout is the Jersey Sports Cafe (201-933-3308), and Devils fan-club members often congregate afterward at Rutt's Hut, a hot dog and beer joint in Clifton.

LODGING NEAR THE ARENA

Sheraton Meadowlands
2 Meadowlands Plaza
East Rutherford, NJ 07073
(201) 896-0500/(800) 325-3535
½ mile from the arena.

Meadowlands Hilton
2 Harmon Plaza
Secaucus, NJ 07094
(201) 348-6900/(800) HILTONS
1 mile from the arena.

GETTING TO CONTINENTAL AIRLINES ARENA

Public transportation: New Jersey Transit offers bus service from the Port Authority Terminal in Manhattan. Call (201) 762-5100 for more information.
By car: From the Lincoln Tunnel, take Route 3 west directly to the sports complex. Northbound on the New Jersey Turnpike, take the western spur to 16W and follow signs to the sports complex. Southbound on the Garden State Parkway, leave the parkway at exit 163 and follow Route 17 south to Paterson Plank Road east to the sports complex.

HOME-ICE ADVANTAGE

For the teams' first years, the New York media focused more on the Rangers and Islanders, allowing the Devils to grow into a Stanley Cup–winning team at their own pace. The credibility of a Stanley Cup win and the cheers of the home crowd are the advantages these days.

ARENA STATS

Location: East Rutherford, NJ 07073
Opened: July 2, 1981
Capacity: 19,040
Services for fans with disabilities: Seating available on the concourse and in lower lobby. Call (201) 935-3900 for information.

ARENA FIRSTS

Regular-season game: Oct. 5, 1982, 3–3 tie with the Pittsburgh Penguins.
Goal: Don Lever of the Devils.
Overtime game: Nov. 12, 1983, 4–3 loss to the Calgary Flames.
Playoff game: April 9, 1988, 3–0 over the New York Islanders.
Stanley Cup game: June 22, 1995, 5–2 over the Detroit Red Wings.

TEAM NOTEBOOK

Franchise history: Kansas City Scouts, 1974–76; Colorado Rockies, 1976–82; New Jersey Devils, 1982–present.
Rookie of the Year/Calder: Martin Brodeur, 1993–94.
Stanley Cup: 1994–95.

TICKET INFORMATION

Address: East Rutherford, NJ 07073
Phone: (201) 935-3900 or TicketMaster at (201) 507-8900, (212) 307-7171, (914) 454-3388, or (516) 888-9000
Hours: Mon.–Fri. 9–6, Sat. 10–6, Sun. 12–5.

NEW YORK ISLANDERS

Nassau Veterans Memorial Coliseum

ARENA STATS

Location: Uniondale, NY 11553
Opened: May 29, 1972
Capacity: 16,297
Services for fans with disabilities: Seating in sections 202 and 222. Call (516) 794-9303 for tickets or more information.

ARENA FIRSTS

Regular-season game: Oct. 7, 1972, 3–2 loss to the Atlanta Flames.
Overtime game: March 10, 1984, 5–4 loss to the Calgary Flames.
Playoff game: April 10, 1975, 8–3 loss to the New York Rangers.
Stanley Cup Finals game: May 17, 1980, 6–2 over the Philadelphia Flyers.

TEAM NOTEBOOK

Franchise history: New York Islanders, 1972–present.
Stanley Cups: 1979–80, 1980–81, 1981–82, 1982–83.
Most Valuable Player/Hart: Bryan Trottier, 1978–79.
Rookies of the Year/Calder: Denis Potvin, 1973–74; Bryan Trottier, 1975–76; Mike Bossy, 1977–78.
Hockey Hall of Fame: Mike Bossy, Denis Potvin, 1991; Billy Smith, 1993.
Retired numbers: 5, Denis Potvin; 9, Clark Gillies; 22, Mike Bossy; 23, Bob Nystrom; 31, Billy Smith.

The view of the ice from Nassau Coliseum's section 329 takes you under the New York Islanders' four Stanley Cup banners and over a lot of empty seats. Just as the Islanders' play turned ordinary when the team grew old, the Coliseum, which opened in 1972, is showing signs of age. The color scheme—or what passes as one—makes the arena look darker. Seats added over the years have obstructions. The sound system—or clock radio, as one fan calls it—is so-so in most seats and unintelligible from the upper section. Crowds can be sparse, and fans are tough on the team. Also, the arena is pretty much accessible only by car. In a metropolitan area that boasts hockey at Madison Square Garden and the Meadowlands, the Coliseum comes in third.

But that's not to say going to a game isn't fun. The Islanders shut out the lights for pre-game announcements, plays James Bond–like theme music, and then turn on the lights as the team bursts onto the ice, and the fans can shout as loud as any in the league. And if you can get a ticket to a Rangers–Islanders game, by all means go. With about a 50-50 ratio of home and visiting team fans, the back and forth in the stands can be as exciting as the action on the ice.

Talk of renovations to Memorial Coliseum has been a perennial topic of conversation for the past several seasons, but so far no formal requests have been made and no plans have been announced. In the meantime, don't go to an Islanders game expecting to relive the magic of the 1980s, especially on the uniforms. The new logo—a fisherman in a slicker—bears a startling resemblance to something you'd see on a box of fish sticks. Just ask a Ranger fan.

HOT TIPS FOR VISITING FANS

PARKING
The lot has 6,800 spaces, and on a night with a sparse crowd, that's more than enough. But arrive early, just in case. The price is a reasonable $4.75. Roads from the parking lot to Hempstead Turnpike back up after the game. If you work your way to the west exit and leave by Earle Ovington Boulevard, you'll encounter less traffic on your way to the Hempstead Turnpike and Meadowbrook Parkway.

MEDIA
Radio: WRCN (94.3 & 103.9 FM). Barry Landers and former Isle Bob Nystrom handle the games.

TV: SportsChannel. Howie Rose and Ed Westfall are the TV duo.

CUISINE
The food is so-so. Your best bets are the Hebrew National hot dogs (they taste better after the first intermission) and the French-bread pizza. A Pizza Hut Express is scheduled to open in 1994. The chicken sandwiches are OK. The on-tap beers are Budweiser and Miller, and you also can get Heineken and Beck's. Bottled water sells for $2. Mixed drinks, beer, and wine are also available at the downstairs bars. Mulcahy's (516-785-9398) in Wantagh traditionally drops its

cover charge on Friday and Saturday nights if you have an Islanders ticket stub. The bar has eight giant screens, 50 monitors, and occasionally features prominent entertainment acts. Many of the section 329 fans go to the T.G.I. Friday's (516-832-8320) in Westbury.

LODGING NEAR THE ARENA

Marriott Long Island
101 James Doolittle Blvd.
Uniondale, NY 11553
(516) 794-3800/(800) 228-9290
Next door to the arena.

Huntington Hilton Hotel
598 Broad Hollow Rd. (Rte. 110)
Mellville, NY 11747
(516) 845-1000/(800) 445-8667
10 miles from the arena.

THE ISLANDERS AT NASSAU VETERANS MEMORIAL COLISEUM

Dec. 23, 1978: Bryan Trottier sets an NHL record with six points in one period—three goals and three assists—as the Islanders beat the New York Rangers 9–4.

May 24, 1980: At 7:11 of overtime, Bobby Nystrom scores to give the Islanders a 5–4 win over the Philadelphia Flyers in Game 6 of the finals for the team's first Stanley Cup.

May 17, 1983: A 4–2 win over the Edmonton Oilers clinches the Islanders' fourth consecutive Stanley Cup.

April 10, 1984: Ken Morrow scores in overtime against the Rangers, boosting the Isles to a 3–2 win in the final game of the Patrick Division final.

Jan. 12, 1985: In his eighth season, Mike Bossy scores his 400th career goal during a 5–3 win over the Flyers. It was the quickest anyone had scored 400 goals in NHL history.

Jan. 28, 1986: Denis Potvin scores his 271st goal, passing Bobby Orr's NHL record for goals by a defenseman.

In the Hot Seats at Nassau Veterans Memorial Coliseum

With an average attendance of just 11,350 in a 16,297-seat arena, seats are available in all price ranges.

GOOD SEATS

The lower bowl is your best bet if you're willing to pay. The glass doesn't interfere too much with your vision, but it's better to sit a little higher. The best deal is the 200 level. The 300 level is good, too, except up high. If you want the higher, less expensive seats and want to be able to see the scoreboard, sit in sections 328–339. If you're looking for some off-ice entertainment, sit in or next to section 329, but the rowdy fans there warn that you shouldn't bring the kids.

BAD SEATS

The upper two rows are horrendous: There is little shoulder room; luxury boxes cut off your view of the scoreboard above row N in sections other than 328–339, and in section 319, above row P, part of your view of the ice is cut off. TV monitors are provided in obstructed sections.

MOVING DOWN

The ushers check tickets and are very serious about not letting anyone sneak down. Ushers sit on the stairways during play, and to get to the 100 level, you'll have to walk over them. Moving down is possible in the 300 level, but wait until the second period.

SCALPING

A few operate in the main parking lot, south of the arena. Because of the infrequent sell-outs, it's not worth their while. It's illegal in Uniondale to sell tickets for more than face value, so if you're selling extras, be advised that that's all you'll get.

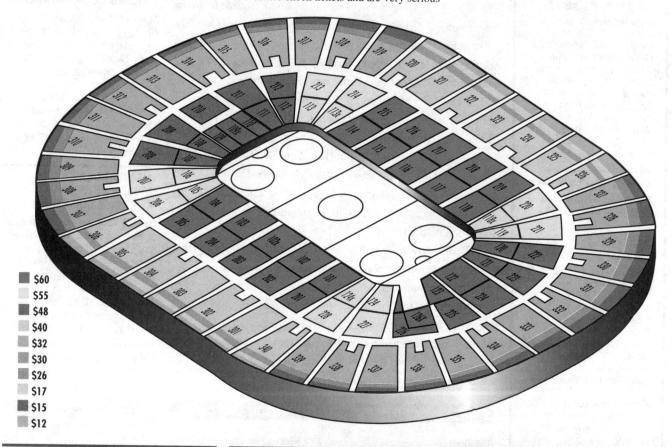

- $60
- $55
- $48
- $40
- $32
- $30
- $26
- $17
- $15
- $12

HOME-ICE ADVANTAGE

Three reasons for the Islanders' home-ice advantage. The fans: When things are going well, the fans are among the loudest in the league. New York bragging rights: With two rivals in the metropolitan region, the Islanders carry the banner for the city's eastern suburbs. The playoff mystique: The Islanders save their best for the playoffs, particularly when their backs are against the wall. When they make the playoffs, that is.

GETTING TO NASSAU VETERANS MEMORIAL STADIUM

Public transportation: Take the Long Island Railroad to Hempstead Station. Walk 1 block to the Hempstead Bus Terminal. The N70, N71, and N72 buses will drop you off on Hempstead Turnpike opposite Nassau Coliseum. Call (516) 222-1000 for bus information.

By car: From Connecticut and northern New York state, take I-95 to Throgs Neck Expressway. Cross Throgs Neck Bridge and continue about 3 miles to the Long Island Expressway east (I-495). Take the LIE about 7 miles to exit 38 (Northern State Parkway east). Go south to exit 31A (Meadowbrook Parkway south), then to exit M4 (Nassau Coliseum).

From Manhattan: take the Midtown Tunnel to the LIE east and follow the same directions as above.

TICKET INFORMATION
Address: Uniondale, NY 11553
Phone: (800) 882-ISLE (4753) or

TicketMaster at (516) 888-9000 or (212) 307-7171
Hours: Mon.–Sat. 10:45–5:30.

Prices: $60; $55; $48; $40; $32; $30; $26; $17; $15; $12.

Madison Square Garden

ARENA STATS

Location: 4 Pennsylvania Plaza, New York, NY 10001
Opened: Feb. 11, 1968
Capacity: 18,200
Services for fans with disabilities: Seating available in the 200 sections.

ARENA FIRSTS

Regular-season game: Feb. 18, 1968, 3–1 over the Philadelphia Flyers.
Playoff game: April 4, 1968, 3–1 over the Chicago Blackhawks.
Stanley Cup Finals game: May 4, 1972, 5–2 over the Boston Bruins.

TEAM NOTEBOOK

Franchise history: New York Rangers, 1926–present.
Stanley Cups: 1927–28, 1932–33, 1939–40, 1993–94
MVP/Hart: O'Connor, 1947–48, Rayner, 1949–50, Bathgate, 1958–59, Messier, 1991–92.
Rookies of the Year/Calder: MacDonald, 1939–40; Warwick, 1941–42; Laprade, 1945–46; Lund, 1948–49; Worsley, 1952–53; Henry, 1953–54; Vickers, 1972–73; Leetch, 1988–89.
Hockey Hall of Fame: Morenz, L. Patrick, 1945; Cook, 1952; Boucher, Johnson, 1958; O. Siebert, 1961; E. Siebert, 1963; D. Bentley, 1964; M. Bentley, Pratt, 1966; Colville, 1967; Hextall, 1969; Gadsby, 1970; Sawchuck, 1971; Geoffrion, 1972; Harvey, Rayner, 1973; Coulter, 1974; Bathgate, Plante 1978; Howell, 1979; Patrick, Worsley, 1980; Gilbert, Francis, 1982; P. Esposito, 1984; Ratelle, 1985; Giacomin, 1987; Lafleur, O'Connor, Park, 1988; Smith, 1991; Dionne, 1992; Laprade, 1993.
Retired numbers: 1, Giacomin; 7, Gilbert.

Madison Square Garden is New York—big, loud, jam-packed, and proud of it. In keeping with the city's vertical landscape, even the ice surface is five stories above the street. Owned by entertainment and gambling conglomerate ITT, this Garden is the fourth in a line that stretches all the way back to Stanford White's turn-of-the-century original.

A visit to the circular Garden will stir your senses. It is one of the loudest arenas in the league, and its 18,000-plus fans match the volume of the fabulous sound system. Self-proclaimed "true" Ranger fans sit in the upper tier, still known as the blue seats even after a renovation changed them to teal. Rhythmic "Let's go, Rangers" chants cascade down from that level as well as rude comments about opposing players. Still, it's nothing compared to the rowdiness back in the days of the real blue seats.

This crowd is loyal (witness the 1975 standing ovation for returning goaltender Eddie Giacomin); totally unforgiving (as when former Islanders star Denis Potvin was booed unmercifully at a Heroes of Hockey game); and proud, since the Rangers finally brought home the Stanley Cup in 1994. Disappointments the past few seasons have done little to dampen enthusiasm, and expect it to reach Cup fever level as Wayne Gretzky and Mark Messier join forces once again for what will probably be the last run for the title for each of them.

HOT TIPS FOR VISITING FANS

PARKING

Lots of lots can be found around the area, and prices start at about $15. The neighborhood surrounding the Garden is bustling, and the Garden itself is above Penn Station, one of New York's commuter hubs, so it's well traveled and generally safe. Traffic down Seventh Avenue and on crosstown streets can be knotty before games, so give yourself extra time.

MEDIA

Radio: WFAN (660 AM) and WEVD (1050 AM).
TV: MSG Network. Former Ranger goaltender John Davidson does analysis.

CUISINE

Pretty much standard arena fare, though the quality is relatively high. You can get New York deli food near gate 76. Numerous vendors walk through the lower-level seats, which keeps down the lines at the food courts. Beer-only stands have the same effect. The End Court bar, which offers mixed drinks, is near gate 64. No food courts in the upper level. Streets surrounding the Garden are packed with bars and restaurants. Some nearby postgame hangouts are Penn Bar, Blarney Rock, and Blarney Stone. Charley O's and Play-By-Play are in the Penn Plaza complex. For Italian, try Carmine's (212-221-3800) or Dock's (212-986-8080) on the East Side for seafood. Up Third Avenue from Dock's, there's P. J. Clarke's, the perfect wood-paneled and stained-glass bar for an after-game drink and cigar. If you still want to keep that hockey thing going, try the All-Star Cafe in Times Square (212-221-3800); Wayne Gretzky owns a piece of it.

LODGING NEAR THE ARENA

Hotel Pennsylvania
401 W. 33rd St.
New York, NY 10001
(212) 736-5000/(800) 223-8585
Across the street from the arena.

Essex House
Hotel Nikko New York
160 Central Park S.
New York, NY 10019
(212) 247-0300/(800) 645-5687
1 mile from the arena.

THE RANGERS AT MADISON SQUARE GARDEN

Nov. 21, 1971: The Rangers score the most goals in team history when they beat the California Golden Seals 12–1.

May 4, 1972: The Rangers win their first Stanley Cup Finals game at this Madison Square Garden, beating the Boston Bruins 5–2.

April 8, 1982: Mikko Leinonen gets an NHL-playoff-record six assists as the Rangers beat the Philadelphia Flyers 7–3 in the first round of the playoffs.

Feb. 23, 1983: Mark Pavelich ties a team record when he scores five goals against the Hartford Whalers in an 11–3 win.

April 13, 1985: Tim Kerr of the Philadelphia Flyers sets an NHL-playoff record with four goals in the second period of a 6–5 win over the Rangers.

April 16, 1992: The Rangers beat the Pittsburgh Penguins 7–1, clinching the President's Trophy for the league's best record.

May 27, 1994: Stéphane Matteau scores in the second overtime to give the Rangers a 2–1 win over the New Jersey Devils in Game 7 of the Eastern Conference finals.

June 14, 1994: Mark Messier scores the winning goal as the Rangers beat the Vancouver Canucks 3–2 in Game 7 of the Stanley Cup Finals, giving New York its first Cup since 1940.

In the Hot Seats at Madison Square Garden

Sight lines are generally good. An eight-sided center-suspended scoreboard has four television screens that follow all the action and show any view that might be obstructed. Home games usually sell out, particularly since the Rangers' Stanley Cup win in 1994. If you want to see a game here, you'll have to plan ahead.

GOOD SEATS

The best seats are down low, but these tend to be held by corporate owners and season ticketholders and are rarely available. The newest hot ticket is in one of the 20 or so seats next to the penalty boxes; these are sold as season tickets only.

BAD SEATS

The arena has three interior concourses in the lower tier. If you're sitting in the first two rows behind each of these, your view may be blocked by the occasional passing fans and vendors. If you're sitting behind the goal in the 300 level, the net closer to you is hard to see. If you sit in section 406, next to the broadcast booth, a good chunk of your view is cut off.

MOVING DOWN

Don't bother. With average attendance of 18,000 in an 18,200-seat arena, empty seats are rare.

SCALPING

Scalping is illegal in New York, but so is jay-walking. Plenty of scalpers are around the arena, and with the law of supply and demand, it's a seller's market. But as with most scalpers, buyers who wait until the game starts find that prices go down dramatically.

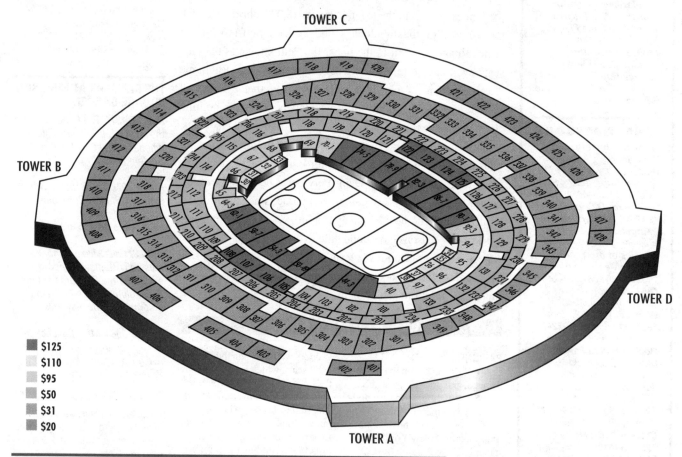

$125
$110
$95
$50
$31
$20

HOME-ICE ADVANTAGE

The Rangers say their fans are worth a goal a game. Besides being a little intimidating and occasionally just plain rude, Rangers fans are very knowledgeable. A good pass will start them cheering. The large season-ticket base brings camaraderie in the stands and a strong identification with the team. At games against the Islanders and Devils, the arena may have a sizable visiting team cheering section.

The ice at MSG isn't remade as often as it used to be; various methods of covering and maintaining the ice under the flooring for other events (the Garden hosts about 320 events a year) have meant improved quality, but its reputation lingers. Visiting teams still arrive expecting less than good skating conditions and bouncing pucks.

GETTING TO MADISON SQUARE GARDEN

Public transportation: Take the B, D, F, or Q train to the 34th Street Station; MSG is 2 blocks west. Or take an A, C, E, 1, 2, 3, or 9 train to Pennsylvania Station–34th Street, which is directly below MSG.

By car: From New Jersey and the south, enter Manhattan via the Lincoln Tunnel. Follow signs for downtown and turn left on 34th Street.

From Connecticut and the north, follow I-95 to Route 9A-south. Exit at 34th Street.

TICKET INFORMATION
Ticket Office: 4 Pennsylvania Plaza, New York, NY 10001

Phone: (212) 465-MSG1 or TicketMaster (212) 307-7171
Hours: Mon.–Sat., 10–8; Sun., 11–7

Prices: $125: rink side; $110: club level; $95: club level; $50: 100 and 200 levels; $31: 300 level; $20: 400 level.

OTTAWA SENATORS

Corel Centre

ARENA STATS

Location: 1000 Palladium Dr., Kanata, ON K2V 1A4 Canada
Opened: January 1996
Capacity: 18,500
Services for fans with disabilities: Most seating is on the 300 level, but there is some seating on the 100 and 200 levels.

ARENA FIRSTS

Regular-season game: January 17, 1996, 3–0 loss to the Canadiens. **Goal:** Yves Duchesne of the Senators. **Overtime game:** January 27, 1996, 2–2 tie with the Toronto Maple Leafs.

TEAM NOTEBOOK

Franchise history: Ottawa Senators, 1992–present. **Rookie of the Year/Calder:** Daniel Alfredsson, 1995–96. **Retired number:** 8, Frank Finnigan.

TICKET INFORMATION

Address: 1000 Palladium Dr., Kanata, ON K2V 1A4 Canada
Phone: (613) 721-4300 or TicketMaster (613) 755-1111
Hours: Mon.–Sat. 10–6.

GETTING TO COREL CENTRE

Public transportation: Buses stop at the corner of Terry Fox and Palladium drives, a short walk from the arena. The transit authority runs shuttles to the arena from several park-and-ride locations along the line. Call (613) 741-4390 for more information.
By car: From the United States, cross at Ogdensburg, New York, and go north on Highway 16 toward Ottawa. Take Highway 417 (the Queensway) west, to the Palladium Drive exit or the Terry Fox exit; each runs next to the arena. From downtown Ottawa, take 417 west and follow the directions above.
From the airport, take Airport Parkway north (it becomes Bronson Avenue) to 417 west, then follow the directions above.

A fter three seasons in their temporary home in the Ottawa Civic Centre, the Senators moved into permanent digs at the new Corel Centre in the nearby Ottawa suburb of Kanata in January 1996.

Designed by Rossetti, the same firm that built the NBA Detroit Pistons' award-winning Palace of Auburn Hills, Corel Centre was originally dubbed the Palladium, but it wasn't called that long enough for the name change to cause much confusion.

Corel Centre's 18,500 seats are all cushioned—even the non-luxury sections. The sight lines are unsurpassed for maximum viewing, and the farthest seat from the ice is only 138 feet away, the closest in the NHL. Now that they've got a place to call home, maybe the Senators will find their own identity and create some hockey history of their own. This expansion franchise adopted the name Senators from a team that had ceased play in 1934 (Frank Finnigan, who played on that team, was instrumental in bringing the NHL back to Ottawa), and inherited its eight Stanley Cup banners; but it is a distant heritage, and the struggling new team is still trying to live up to it. The Senators say their job now is for the team to get the fans going, but the best way to do that is to get the team going (they went 6–16–4 in their first season at Corel). As with most fans in Canada, Senators fans are knowledgeable—but quiet.

HOT TIPS FOR VISITING FANS

PARKING

The arena lot has room for 6,500 cars; the cost is C$10. There isn't much other parking nearby, and the closest street parking is less than a mile away.

MEDIA

Radio: CFRA (580 AM—English) and CJRC (1150 AM—French).
TV: CHRO (Channel 20) and CGOH (Channel 7).

CUISINE

This being Canada and all, you can get Tim Horton donuts at the Corel Centre, and the beer is mostly Molson, although the Beers of the World stand serves up suds from all over the globe. Other concessions offer pizza, and grilled and barbecued foods. Of greatest interest to many is that the arena has its very own Hard Rock Cafe. It's open year-round and has all the rock-and-roll trappings of the franchises's other locations worldwide. The Palladium Club, and Brad Marsh's Marshy's Bar-B-Q & Grill, are also open to fans before or after games and in the off-season.
Kanata is a nice place to live, but you don't come here for the

nightlife; the three restaurants within the Corel Centre are pretty much all of it. For some hopping post-game action head to Elgin Street in downtown Ottawa, where there is a string of bars and nightclubs. Some players and fans head across the river to Le Mirage Bistro, in Hull, Quebec (819-778-1852).

LODGING NEAR THE ARENA

Westin
11 Colonel By-Driveway
Ottawa, ON K1N 9H4
Canada
(613) 560-7000/(800) 228-3000
15 miles from the arena.

Radisson Ottawa
100 Kent St. at Queen
Ottawa, ON K1P 5R7
Canada
(613) 238-1122/(800) 333-3333
15 miles from the arena.

HOME-ICE ADVANTAGE

The old Civic Center was no lion's den, but the Corel Centre may prove to be. State-of-the-art ice-making has rectified the perpetually below-average surface that the Senators had to play on at the Civic Center; and now that the team has a permanent home,

■ C$55 ■ C$44 ■ C$40
■ C$32 ■ C$28.50 ■ C$25
■ C$22 ■ C$18.50 ■ C$14.24

they might just get to defend it with a vengeance.

IN THE HOT SEATS AT COREL CENTRE

There aren't any bad seats in Corel Centre. Really. The most you'll miss are the expressions on the players' faces.
Tickets for the second half of the season go on sale in mid-December. Sections 1–12 offer at-your-seat service, but these are taken up by season ticketholders. Standing room is available in that section for less than half the price. If these are unavailable, try to get a seat in the lower bowl or mid-bowl. No alcohol is allowed in parts of sections 16, 23, and 27.

BAD SEATS

Above row MM, the luxury boxes cut off your view of the scoreboard. If you like to keep track of shots, the shot counter isn't visible up high in sections 16–23. This upper section also can feel claustrophobic because insulated pipes and girders are over you.

MOVING DOWN

Don't even think about it. Management is strict, and frankly, there aren't a lot of empty seats. Besides, even the seats high up aren't that high up, and visibility from the cheap seats is very good.

SCALPING

With some 8,000 more seats than the Civic Center, there isn't much need for scalping.

PHILADELPHIA FLYERS

CoreStates Center

Rocky Balboa's statue is still at the Spectrum, but the Flyers aren't. The Broad Street Bullies have moved down the block to the brand-new CoreStates Center. The Spectrum may be a shrine to the team's Stanley Cup years, but it was never the best place to watch a hockey game.

CoreStates Center, however, might just be. It has more than 2,000 more seats than the Spectrum, nearly twice the overall square footage, and vastly improved fan amenities even for those fans not in a superbox, club box, balcony suite, luxury suite, or the fancy on-site restaurant. Having more than one concourse makes getting to and from the two-level seating at CoreStates much easier than at the one-concourse-for-all-three-levels Spectrum. There are twice as many restrooms (whew!), and foot traffic moves briskly between the seats and the 30 concession stands. Inside and out, the place seems to have been designed to eliminate waiting long for anything; the arena is only two blocks from the entrance to I-95.

Flyers' fans are among the most loyal, knowledgeable, and demanding in the league. The relationship has been strained by a couple of poor seasons, although in their last year in the Spectrum the Flyers went 27–9–5. Maybe this new, cushier arena will put fans in a better mood and make them more inclined to root for the Flyers, regardless.

treats. At various "Action Station" stands, fans can sample an ever-changing roster of foods on "themed food nights" that might offer various ethnic cuisines (or at least their stadium cousins) such as Chinese and Italian; the Broad Street Bistro handles the hoagies. At the Red Bell microbrewery you can get all sorts of beers you've never heard of, but those who want to stay with the tried and true will not have to go thirsty.

Sometimes players go to the bar at the Coliseum in Voorhees, New Jersey, their practice facility. Closer to the arena, the Legends sports bar is a few blocks away, in the Holiday Inn. Partially owned by former Eagles quarterback Ron Jaworski, it draws more of a Phillies and Eagles crowd, but there is Flyers memorabilia on the walls. The atmosphere is loud and the crowd is young. South Street offers the most possibilities for pre-game dining or post-game revelry. Café Nola (215-627-2590) serves excellent Cajun fare that visiting ballplayers love. Susanna Foo (215-545-2666) has first-rate Chinese food. Better yet, go to the Italian Market in South Philadelphia and find your way to Pat's King of Steaks (215-339-9872) for that Philadelphia specialty, the cheese steak. Philadelphia's major nightclub district is also along South Street.

HOT TIPS FOR VISITING FANS

PARKING

There is on-site parking for more than 12,000 cars for $4.50 at CoreStates Center. Traffic to and from moves fairly quickly because the nearest entrance to I-95 is only two blocks away. There is also on-street parking next to the naval hospital on the west side of Broad Street, which runs past the arena; locals warn that car windows frequently get broken along here, however. The old Spectrum lot is also likely to be used for Flyers games, and sometimes the Veterans Stadium lot nearby is available. Street parking in the small neighborhood just north of Veterans Stadium should be avoided as residents are quick to call in the tow trucks. If the Phillies or the Eagles are also playing at home, traffic will be a nightmare.

MEDIA

Radio: WIP (610 AM).
TV: WPHL (Channel 17). Play-by-play announcer Gene Hart has been with the team—on TV and/or radio—since its inception in 1967. Prism and SportsChannel Philadelphia (cable) have been covering most home games.

CUISINE

There are 30 food concessions spread around the arena. Along with the indispensable cheese steak sandwiches (for the full cheese steak experience, get it smothered in onions), plenty of renowned Philadelphia delicacies are available. Handmade soft pretzels served in the traditional style—with mustard—are a must, especially if you haven't sampled this local specialty. Pizza Hut slices and dices the pies, and Dannon Yogurt provides a range of smooth taste

LODGING NEAR THE ARENA

Holiday Inn
10th Packer Ave.
Philadelphia, PA 19148
(215) 755-9500
2 blocks from the arena.

Sheraton Society Hill
1 Dock St.
Philadelphia, PA 19106
(800) 325-3535
4 miles from the arena.

In the Hot Seats at CoreStates Center

Although there are only two levels of seating in CoreStates Center, the views of the ice are remarkably similar to those in the Spectrum. There are more than 2,000 more seats available than at the Spectrum. Season ticket sales at the Spectrum often reached the 99% of capacity mark, and they'll probably come close to that here as well. You can bet that season tickets will sell from the ice up. Games with the Capitals or Rangers will be almost impossible to get into. Even with the larger capacity, if you want two seats together, order them early. Single seats may be eas-ier to get. Either way, unless you're a season ticketholder, you'll end up in the upper rows. Single-game tickets go on sale in October.

BAD SEATS

There are no obstructed-view seats in CoreStates Center, unlike the old Spectrum. The sight lines are good from everywhere, but, as anywhere, the seats farther up and back are, well, up and back. Still, there's nothing to compare to the corner seats at the Spectrum, where you could barely see from the blue line in.

MOVING DOWN

Not even worth trying. Ushers will know you're a stranger.

SCALPING

The Flyers used to broadcast that scalpers' tickets might be forged or stolen, and—it is illegal, after all—police officers are posted quite visibly in the parking lot and around the arena. Still, where's there's a buyer, there's a seller, and scalpers work as close to the front entrance as they dare, and near the subway station across the street.

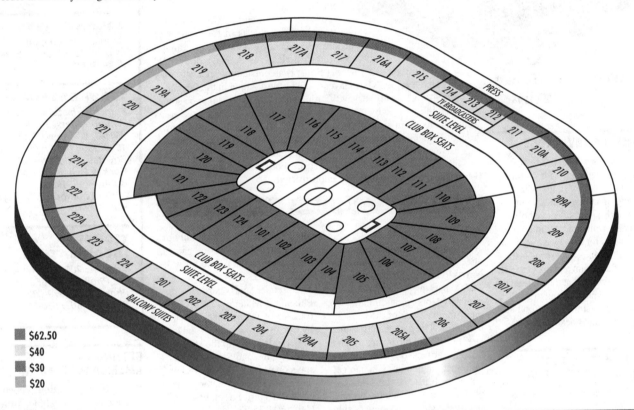

$62.50
$40
$30
$20

HOME-ICE ADVANTAGE

They left the Rocky statue at the Spectrum, and nobody's saying what will become of Kate Smith. The singer's rousing rendition of "God Bless America" first spurred the Flyers onto victory on December 11, 1969, and every game at which the song was played for a good long time afterwards. She performed it live three times, including once before a Stanley Cup game against the Bruins in 1974 (the Flyers won the game and the Cup). If the Flyers are smart (and they are) they won't leave a good luck charm like that just lying around.

GETTING TO CORESTATES CENTER

Public transportation: Take the Broad Street subway from 15th and Market southbound to Broad and Pattison. The arena is a block away. Call (215) 580-7800 for more information.
By car: From I-95, north or south, take the Broad Street exit. You'll see CoreStates Center on your right. Follow signs to the arena parking lots.
From New Jersey via the New Jersey Turnpike, look for signs announcing 295 south and the Walt Whitman Bridge. Follow these signs to the bridge, then follow signs to the Broad Street exit. Turn left onto Broad Street. The arena will be on the left.
From the west, take I-76 (Pennslyvania Turnpike) east. Follow signs for the Walt Whitman Bridge/Sports Complex to exit 45, Broad Street. At the end of the ramp, turn right at the light. The arena will be on your left.

TICKET INFORMATION
Ticket office: One CoreStates Complex, 3601 S. Broad St., Philadelphia, PA 19148
Phone: (215) 336-3600 or TicketMaster at (215) 336-2000, (609) 339-9000.
Hours: Mon.–Fri. 9–6, Sat. 10–4:30, Sun. game days 10–4:30.
Prices: $62.50; $40; $30; $20.

PHOENIX COYOTES

America West Arena

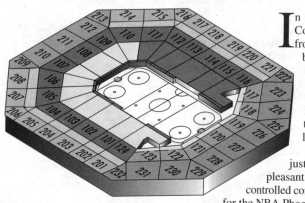

■ NA ■ $70 ■ $49.75 ■ $45.75
■ $37.75 ■ $26.75 ■ $15.75 ■ $8.75

In moving from Winnipeg to Phoenix, the Coyotes—formerly the Jets—have gone from one extreme to another, from freezer burn to sunburn. Winnipeg Jets fans often left the arena to face temperatures of 30 below, and wondering if their cars would start up. Now, Phoenix Coyotes fans step inside America West Arena for air-conditioned relief from the searing desert sunlight.

Anyone who attends a Coyotes game just to escape the heat is in for a series of pleasant surprises far beyond the fact of climate-controlled comfort. America West Arena, built in 1992 for the NBA Phoenix Suns, is an outstanding place to play or watch a game. NBA players voted it Best Arena in the League in a 1994 *USA Today* survey. Visiting teams are even said to be somewhat intimidated by the luxurious surroundings. Ideas for the arena were gathered from visits to the world's finest sports venues, and it shows. Adapting the arena for hockey was no strain. All seats here, even the less-expensive ones, have great sight lines. In at least one way, it's even better for hockey than for basketball: No backboards block the view, so seats behind the goals are completely unobstructed.

ARENA STATS

Location: 201 E. Jefferson St., Phoenix, AZ 85004
Opened: June 1, 1992
Capacity: 18,013
Services for fans with disabilities: Seating available in sections 105, 106, 110, 111, 117, 118, 122, 123, 203, 211, and 227. Each suite has two wheelchair-accessible spaces.

ARENA FIRSTS

Regular-season game: Oct. 10, 1996, vs. the San Jose Sharks.

TEAM NOTEBOOK

Franchise history: Winnipeg Jets, 1972–79 (WHA); Winnipeg Jets, 1979–1996 (NHL); Phoenix Coyotes, 1996–present.
Hockey Hall of Fame: Bobby Hull, 1983.
Retired number: 9, Bobby Hull.

TICKET INFORMATION

Address: 201 E. Jefferson St., Phoenix, AZ 85004
Phone: (602) 379-7825 or Dillard's (602) 678-2222

HOME-ICE ADVANTAGE

The Coyotes won't be fazed by home crowds filled with visiting-team fans, as they surely will be playing in a town with so many snowbirds and residents who've relocated from colder climes. The good news for the newest addition to the Phoenix sports scene is the surge of attention and excitement; the bad news is that there might not be enough sports mania to go around, at least while the football, basketball, and hockey seasons overlap.

IN THE HOT SEATS AT AMERICA WEST ARENA

The Coyotes are anticipating a season-ticket base of about 12,500, which should leave plenty of seats available for single-game buyers; even the snowbirds and vacationers probably won't fill up the place too often.

GOOD SEATS

The row of seats on the floor is for the high-rolling season ticket-holders. The rest of the seats are on risers, so you'll feel close to the action no matter where you sit. There aren't any truly bad seats, especially without basketball backboards blocking the view from behind each end zone.

SCALPING

Scalping is legal in Phoenix but not on arena grounds; sellers cross the street to conduct their business.

HOT TIPS FOR VISITING FANS

PARKING

A 900-space parking garage is attached, a 1,500-space garage is across the street, and more than 11,000 parking spaces in less expensive lots are within an eight-minute walk of the entrances. The garage across the street is $5; the others are $4 and $3. The farther you park from the building, the quicker you can get out of the traffic congestion; plus, as you approach the arena before the game, the view of the building is spectacular.

MEDIA

Radio: At press time, no flagship radio station had been chosen.
TV: KSAZ (Channel 10) is the local Fox affiliate.

CUISINE

Popcorn, nachos, beer, soda, peanuts, ice cream—all the regular fare—are prepared on site. The food court on the first concourse features Whataburger, Whatataco, Subway, Pizza Hut, and Miss Karen's Frozen Yogurt, and is open for lunch on weekdays year-round. The Copper Club is a 10,000-square-foot bar and restaurant on the second councourse level with a terrific

view of the ice; it's open only to suite ticketholders during games, but is open to the public for lunch on weekdays.

The premier sports bar in Phoenix is Majerle's Sports Grill (602-253-0118), which is owned by Suns star and local hero Dan Majerle. It's just up the street at 24 North Second Street, and it stays open from 11 to 11 every day. The Arizona Center, a mall on North Third Street, has Sam's Café (602-252-3545), Lombardi's (602-257-8323), and Players (602-252-6222) eateries. And, like any self-respecting North American city these days, Phoenix now has its own brew-pub, Coyote Springs (no relation to the team), downtown at First and Washington streets.

LODGING NEAR THE ARENA

Hilton Suites at Pheonix Plaza
10 E. Thomas Rd.
Phoenix, AZ 85012
(602) 222-1111/(800) HILTONS
2 miles from the arena.

Hyatt Regency
122 N. Second St.
Phoenix, AZ 85004
(602) 252-1234/(800) 233-1234
1 block from the arena.

GETTING TO AMERICA WEST ARENA

Public transportation: Phoenix transit buses stop ½ block from the arena. The main bus station is across the street, and any bus through downtown passes near the arena. Call (602) 253-5000 for more information.
By car: From the north, take the I-17 Black Canyon Freeway to the Jefferson/Washington exit. Go left onto Washington Street, then left on First Street. The arena will be on the left. From the south, take the I-10 Maricopa north to Jefferson Street. Go left onto Jefferson. The arena will be on the right. From the east, take the SR 360 Superstition Freeway to the I-10 Maricopa, heading north. From the west, take the I-10 Papago to First Street. Go right onto First Street. The arena will be on the right.

PITTSBURGH PENGUINS

Pittsburgh Civic Arena

ARENA STATS

Location: *300 Auditorium Pl., Pittsburgh, PA 15219*
Opened: *Sept. 17, 1961*
Capacity: *17,181*
Services for fans with disabilities: *Seating available in sections B5 and B11. Special arrangements can also be made before the game by calling (412) 642-1326.*

ARENA FIRSTS

Regular-season game: *Oct. 11, 1967, 2–1 loss to the Montreal Canadiens.*
Goal: *Andy Bathgate, Penguins.*
Overtime game: *Oct. 12, 1983, 4–3 loss to the Winnipeg Jets.*
Playoff game: *April 23, 1970, 3–2 over the St. Louis Blues.*
Stanley Cup Finals game: *May 15, 1991, 5–4 over the Minnesota North Stars.*

TEAM NOTEBOOK

Franchise history: *Pittsburgh Penguins, 1967–present.*
Stanley Cups: *1990–91, 1991–92.*
Most Valuable Player/Hart: *Mario Lemieux, 1987–88, 1992–93.*
Rookie of the Year/Calder: *Mario Lemieux, 1984–85.*
Hockey Hall of Fame: *Andy Bathgate, 1978; Leo Boivin, 1986; Scotty Bowman, 1991; Bob Johnson, 1992.*
Retired number: *21, Michel Briere.*

The round home of the Pittsburgh Penguins is cold and forbidding, hunched halfway up The Hill like an artifact from the Arctic. That's why fans call the Civic Arena the Igloo and the locals take a lot of pride in it. The roof was built in 1961 of 2,950 tons of Pittsburgh stainless steel, something not so plentiful today. It's one of the few retractable roofs that actually works well even if it isn't opened very often, and never for hockey.

The Arena was designed for use by the Civic Light Opera, and the conditions of a $1 million grant from Edgar J. Kaufman required the retractable roof so the CLO could play *en plein air*. Unfortunately, when the roof was opened, the sound blew out, so the CLO and the symphony moved on to better concert halls, leaving the Igloo to the Penguins, who came in 1967.

In the early days, fans often were heard to grumble that the AHL Hornets, the league-champion team whom the Pens supplanted, were better than the Penguins, but you don't hear such grumbling now. In fact, some would say you don't hear much of anything in the arena now that going to hockey games has become the thing to do in Pittsburgh. A lot of suits and ties are seen in the arena these days, and the crowd isn't as rollicking as it once was, unless Jean-Claude Van Damme is around (The movie *Sudden Death* was filmed here). Some might even call it dull, but that tends to be the price of success, even in the home of Pittsburgh steel.

HOT TIPS FOR VISITING FANS

PARKING
The cost is $6 to park in one of the five arena lots, but the two closest to the arena are permit-only parking for season ticketholders. Arrive 45 minutes early to get a spot in one of the other three; of those, the East Lot, above the arena, offers the speediest exit. Parking at nearby Chatham Center and St. Francis Central Hospital is also $6. Limited street parking is available a few blocks away, on Forbes Avenue.

MEDIA
Radio: WTAE (1250 AM).
TV: KBL (cable), KDKA (Channel 2), and Penvision (pay-per-view).

CUISINE
Nothing to die for, but nothing will kill you. Actually, the nachos are quite tasty, and the vendors are generous with the hot peppers. The rest is your basic arena food. No Pittsburgh specialties are available, except for beer: locally brewed Iron City and I. C. Light are sold, as well as standard domestics. Afterward, many people head to an area of bars and restaurants along Forbes and Fifth avenues: Souper Bowl (412-471-0416), Loafers Restaurant & Bar (412-391-4087), and Corleone's Pizza (412-281-8181). Clientele ranges from blue-collar to BMW. Equally close to the arena but a little more upper-crust are the Ruddy Duck in the Ramada Inn (412-281-3825), and Anthony's (412-261-2215). The nearby Strip District is also filled with several nightspots.

LODGING NEAR THE ARENA
Ramada Inn
1 Bigelow Sq.
Pittsburgh, PA 15219
(412) 281-5800/(800) 228-2828
1 block from the arena.

Marriott
1 Chatham Center
112 Washington Place
Pittsburgh, PA 15219
(412) 471-4000/(800) 228-9290
Across the street from arena.

THE PENGUINS AT PITTSBURGH CIVIC ARENA

Nov. 22, 1972: *The Penguins score five goals during two minutes and seven seconds of a 10–4 rout of the St. Louis Blues, the fastest five goals by one team in NHL history.*

Dec. 31, 1988: *Mario Lemieux becomes the first NHL player to score a goal in each of the five possible ways during a single game: even handed; shorthanded; power play; penalty shot; and, as time ran out, into an empty net.*

April 25, 1989: *Mario Lemieux scores five goals, four of them in one period, as the Penguins win Game 5 of the division final against the Philadelphia Flyers 10–7. The five goals ties an NHL playoff record.*

May 11, 1991: *The Penguins down the Boston Bruins 5–3 to advance to their first Stanley Cup Finals. Pittsburgh goes on to beat the Minnesota North Stars, four games to two, for the title.*

May 26, 1992: *The Penguins defeat the Blackhawks 5–4 in the first game of the Stanley Cup finals. Pittsburgh sweeps the series for its second consecutive title.*

April 10, 1993: *Kevin Stevens' third-period goal clinches the Penguins 4–2 victory over the Rangers and an NHL record-setting 17 consecutive wins.*

Feb. 7, 1995: *An assist by Joe Muller makes him the first American-born player to score 1,000 career points.*

In the Hot Seats at the Pittsburgh Civic Arena

Tickets go on sale in September and sell well, but not quickly. Sellouts aren't as common these days, although Rangers and Flyers games might be harder to get into. Tickets on game day are usually for seats in sections F and D.

GOOD SEATS

The best seats for your money are probably the 3,000 spots in the two E-level balconies. These are at the ends of the ice, so you don't have to twist around to follow the action. Section A, close behind the glass and the penalty box, is considered choice, since you can hear the players. But you're paying $60 to sit behind Plexiglas.

BAD SEATS

Unless you really can't afford anything else, skip the limited-view seats in D-7 and D-25. Section F is very high both in altitude and price, considering its location. Fans can't see the scoreboard from the last rows of section C because the balconies block the view. The only poles are those supporting the super boxes and the press box; the seats behind those poles, in sections D-25 and D-7, go for $20.

MOVING DOWN

Some fans say that ushers will move you down for a couple of bucks.

SCALPING

There isn't much of a need, and it's illegal, but scalpers can easily be found within two blocks of the arena, and their prices are not too high. Even for sellouts or playoffs, tickets are often only $10 or $15 above face value.

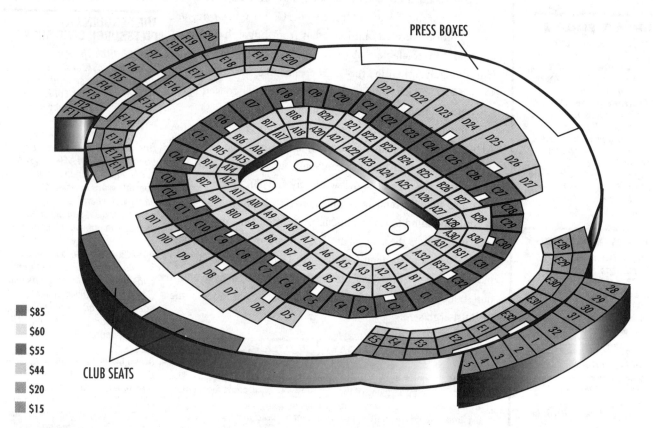

PRESS BOXES

CLUB SEATS

- ■ $85
- □ $60
- ■ $55
- ▨ $44
- ▨ $20
- ▨ $15

HOME-ICE ADVANTAGE

The Penguins were bad for a lot longer than they've been good, and despite a couple of good seasons (they went 32–9 at home in 1995–96) the home crowd isn't all that revved up.

The fan factor is next to negligible unless the Rangers or Flyers are in town, and even larger crowds aren't very boisterous. Arena organist Vince Lascheid's witty musical accompaniment has been overshadowed by the new JumboTron scoreboard.

GETTING TO THE PITTSBURGH CIVIC ARENA

Public transportation: The Port Authority Transit Subway stops less than a block away, at Steel Plaza. Also, the USX Tower, Fifth Avenue and Washington, and St. Francis Central Hospital bus stops are within 1 block of the arena. Call (412) 442-2000 for more information.

By car: From the south, take 279 North through the Fort Pitt Tunnel to Liberty Avenue. Go right off Liberty Avenue onto Seventh Avenue, cross Grant Street, then right onto Centre Avenue.

From the north, take 79 south to the Route 279 south exit, about a mile past the Wexford exit. Follow 279 south over Veterans Bridge to the Sixth Street exit. Go left at the light onto Bigelow Boulevard.

TICKET INFORMATION

Address: 300 Auditorium Pl., Pittsburgh, PA 15219
Phone: (412) 642-1326 or TicketMaster

(412) 323-1919
Hours: Mon.–Fri. 8:30–5:30.
Prices: $85: club seats; $60: A, B levels; $55: C levels; $44: D level, E level, A–E;

$20: F–K and scattered limited-view seats; $15: L–P.

ST. LOUIS BLUES

Kiel Center

ARENA STATS

Location: 1401 Clark Ave. (at 14th St.), St. Louis, MO 63102
Opened: Oct. 14, 1994
Capacity: 19,260
Services for fans with disabilities: Seating available throughout the arena.

ARENA FIRSTS

Regular-season game: Jan. 26, 1995: 3–1 win over the Los Angeles Kings.
Goal: Craig Johnson, St. Louis Blues
Overtime game: April 23, 1995: 2–2 tie with the Chicago Blackhawks.
Playoff game: May 7, 1995, 2–1 win over the Vancouver Canucks.

TEAM NOTEBOOK

Franchise history: St. Louis Blues, 1967–present.
Most Valuable Player/Hart: Brett Hull, 1990–91.
Hockey Hall of Fame: D. Harvey, 1973; D. Moore, 1974; G. Hall, 1975; J. Plante, 1978; J. L. Patrick, 1980; E. Francis, 1982; D. Kelly, 1989.
Retired numbers: 3, B. Gassoff; 8, B. Plager; 11, B. Sutter; 24, B. Federko.

TICKET INFORMATION

Address: 1401 Clark Ave., St. Louis, MO 63102
Phone: (314) 968-1800
Hours: Mon.–Sun. 10-6.

LODGING NEAR THE ARENA

The St. Louis Marriott Pavilion
1 S. Broadway
St. Louis, MO 63102
(314) 421-1776/(800) 228-9290
½ mile from the arena.

Hampton Inn
2211 Market St.
St. Louis, MO 63103
(314) 241-3200/(800) 426-7866
5 blocks from the arena.

Needing to replace aging St. Louis Arena, developers and city officials put into practice Missouri's motto as the Show Me State.

The result: the $135 million, 12-story, glass and concrete Kiel Center. Built on the site of the old and renowned Kiel Auditorium and adjacent to the historic Kiel Opera House, the 664,000-square-foot, 19,000-seat arena is picking up for hockey's Blues where St. Louis Arena, opened in 1929, left off. Rather than being a multipurpose building first and a hockey arena second, Kiel Center is a hockey facility that can also accommodates other purposes. A $3.5 million video scoreboard with animation and replay capability hangs over center ice. The arena's neutral colors, plants, and artsy neon signs might seem more fitting for California than Missouri, but St. Louis Arena's noise level, trademark Budweiser song, and foghorn after goals are all part of the Blues games at Kiel Center.

Even though it preserves some familiar aspects, Kiel Center borrows from The Pond of Anaheim, Boston Garden, Market Square Arena, and Calgary's Olympic Saddledome. The next step is to build its own tradition for the Blues, which, before Gretzky's departure, was off to a flying start. Hopefully new fixtures such as "Towel Man," in section 315–316, who vigorously swings a towel around after every goal, will stick around post-Wayne.

■ $55 ▨ $45 ■ $37 ▨ $30

HOT TIPS FOR VISITING FANS

PARKING

More than 6,000 parking spaces are available within a 3-block radius, including a 1,240-space parking garage that adjoins the arena. Prices range from $7 to $10. You can park on nearby streets, but some consider the neighborhood more than 3 or 4 blocks away to be risky.

MEDIA

Radio: KMOX (1120 AM).
TV: KPLR (Channel 11) and Prime Sports (cable).

CUISINE

The richest food—in calories and cost—is in the Club Restaurant, which is open only to those in the luxury suites and club seats. It offers a huge buffet, with different selections daily.

On the concourse is the usual selection of hot dogs, nachos, and pretzels. The Kiel Grill booth offers chicken wings, French fries, hamburgers, barbecue, and steak sandwiches. Other specialty booths include Taste of the Hill, at which you can get the local Italian specialty, toasted ravioli, the Italian Deli, and Sweets And Such. Kiel Center sits in the shadow of an Anheuser-Busch brewery, so Budweiser and Bud Light are inescapable, but there's also a wide selection of imported beers and microbrews at The Brew Room.

Your best bets after the game are Union Station, a former railroad terminal that has been converted into a mall, and Laclede's Landing, a riverfront complex of shops and restaurants. A popular new fan hangout is Maggie O'Brien's (314-397-5010) on Market Street.

GETTING TO KIEL CENTER

Public transportation: A MetroLink station is directly south of Kiel Center at 14th Street and Clark Avenue. The city's Bi-State bus system also has service to the center; call (314) 231-2345 for more information.

By car: From the west, take I-44 east, exit at Jefferson Avenue, and proceed north. Turn right at Chouteau Avenue, then left at 18th Street, and follow signs. From the south, take I-55 north, then take the Downtown exit to Memorial Drive. From Memorial Drive, turn left at Market Street, then left at Tucker. At Clark Avenue, turn left or right.

From the north, take I-70 east. Then take the Memorial Drive exit to Market Street. Proceed west on Market Street to 16th Street and make a left.

From the east, take I-64 west to the Ninth Street exit. Turn left on Clark Avenue and proceed to the arena.

IN THE HOT SEATS AT KIEL CENTER

With the Blues having a season-ticket base of 14,000 and playing at 98.4% capacity, tickets can be hard to come by, but Gretzky's quick leave-taking may change that. Designers increased the angle between seats so fans will have a higher plane of seating, giving an overhang type of view.

GOOD SEATS

The best seats, if you can get them, are the 1,640 premium club-level (center mezzanine) seats, which offer seat-side food and beverage service.

BAD SEATS

Kiel Center has no obstructed views, but as with any arena, if you sit too close to the glass, your view of parts of the ice can be distorted.

SCALPING

Scalping is illegal. The city has continued to be hard on scalpers at Kiel Center.

SAN JOSE SHARKS

San Jose Arena

Nary a discouraging word escapes the lips of Sharks fans when they talk about their Men of Teal and San Jose Arena, which stands a few blocks west of downtown San Jose on Santa Clara Street. Indeed, in their first season in the arena, the Sharks played to 96.5% capacity, selling out most games. This happened despite pricey tickets (up to $73), concessions, and parking ($10), and hasn't dropped too far in the less than stellar couple of seasons that followed.

Fans who brave the prices are treated to an enjoyable experience. It starts with a breathtaking entrance, which leads into a 60-foot, glass-enclosed, terrazzo-tiled cathedral lobby. The sound system cranks out 70,000 watts through 32 speaker clusters. Seats are comfortable, with good legroom and cupholders, and sight lines are excellent. Even at the highest seats, the circular, state-of-the-art replay scoreboard guarantees a great view.

And make sure you get to the game on time—the Sharks provide one of the greatest openings in the NHL. The players skate through the fog-belching mouth of a 17-foot shark's head, complete with glowing red eyes. It's enough to raise the noise to feeding-frenzy level.

If the Sharks' play can once again match the popularity of their logo merchandise and the fervent support of their fans, the arena will become one of the most treacherous places for visiting teams to swim and one of the best places in which to watch a hockey game.

HOT TIPS FOR VISITING FANS

PARKING
Of the 1,800 spaces in two arena lots, many are immediately west and are reserved by suite and club seatholders. Late-arriving or early-leaving fans should pay the $10 and park close. Almost 7,000 more spaces are available in private and city lots within half a mile. Downtown you can park for as little as $3 and catch a free shuttle bus. Free parking is available west of the railroad tracks on the west side of the arena. The neighborhoods are safe, but beware of "permit only" residential areas. The fine if you are caught is $51.

MEDIA
Radio: KFRC (610 AM).
TV: KICU (Channel 36), KGO (Channel 7) and SportsChannel.

CUISINE
The fare is pricey but worth it. The 22 point-of-sale stands offer quality and variety. Along with traditional sports arena fare, San Jose's Roundtable Pizza and Mexico Lindo stands are quite popular, as is the Sausage Haus. The Club offers more upscale and rather tasty California cuisine treats but is open only to suite ticketholders. The locally made beers Anchor Steam, Pete's Wicked, and Tide House are available here, and the Beers of the World kiosks offer imported suds. Mixed and specialty drinks include margaritas and wine.
Scott's Seafood Bar & Grill (408-971-1700) downtown offers a seafood menu; visiting players, many of whom stay at the nearby Hyatt Regency or Hilton, stop by for one entrée—the shark.
After games, Henry's (408-453-5325), two blocks down a side street from the arena and tucked under the superstructure of Highway 87, is packed with Sharks fans. If you're looking for more action, head for San Jose Live (408-294-5483), upstairs in the pavilion across First Street from the Hyatt. The centerpiece is a 20-foot-plus basketball cage, plus a dozen pool tables, plenty of dartboards, foosball, and table-hockey games, and 10 big-screen TVs tuned to sporting events. The heart of San Jose's burgeoning nightclub scene is only a few blocks away from the arena, in a few blocks of South First and Second streets.

LODGING NEAR THE ARENA

DeAnza Hotel
233 W. Santa Clara St.
San Jose, CA 95113
(408) 286-1000/(800) 843-3700
3 blocks from the arena.

Hilton
300 Almaden Blvd.
San Jose, CA 95110
(408) 287-2100/(800) HILTONS
1 mile from the arena.

THE SHARKS AT SAN JOSE ARENA

March 20, 1994: Wayne Gretzky reaches Gordie Howe's mark of 801 goals when he ties the game between the Los Angeles Kings and the Sharks at 6–6.

March 29, 1994: Sergei Makarov scores the Sharks' first penalty-shot goal as they beat the Winnipeg Jets 9–4.

April 23, 1994: Goalie Arturs Irbe has a pass stolen from him behind the net, resulting in a Detroit Red Wings goal, but the Sharks rally and win 4–3 to tie their playoff series at two games each.

April 26, 1994: The Sharks take Game 5 against the Red Wings to gain a 3–2 lead in their series.

ARENA STATS
Location: 525 W. Santa Clara St., San Jose, CA 95113
Opened: Sept. 8, 1993
Capacity: 17,190
Services for fans with disabilities: Seating is available in several sections on the 200 level, and a few on the 100 level.

ARENA FIRSTS
Regular-season game: Oct. 14, 1993, 2–1 loss to the Calgary Flames.
Goal: Kip Miller, San Jose.
Overtime game: Oct. 16, 1993, 1–1 tie with the Boston Bruins.
Playoff game: April 22, 1994, 3–2 loss to the Detroit Red Wings.

TEAM NOTEBOOK
Franchise history: San Jose Sharks, 1991–present.

May 10, 1994: Sergei Makarov notches four points as the Sharks beat the Toronto Maple Leafs 5–2, taking a 3–2 edge in their Western Conference semifinal series.

May 17, 1995: Down 3–2 in their series, the Sharks put out the Flames 5–3 and go on to win the series.

In the Hot Seats at San Jose Arena

The Sharks' season-ticket base jumped to between 13,000 and 14,000 after the 1993–94 season. It used to be that tickets could be had up to 48 hours of game time, but with the team playing well, tickets are much harder to come by even the week before a game. Local fans are still fairly new at rooting for a hot team, so the Sharks' performance on the ice will greatly affect ticket availability. Single-game tickets for the remaining 3,000 to 4,000 seats go on sale in the fall. Team officials are considering holding back a block of tickets for each game, but for the time being what's available close to game time are tickets returned by the visiting team. Don't expect any seat you get on short notice to be in a great spot.

GOOD SEATS

Every seat gives an unimpaired view of the playing area. Try the $45 seats in sections 101 and 115; they are the top six or seven rows of the lower level, between the blue lines, and are high enough to see all the action, strategies, and angles. For value, try the $32 seats.

Be aware that by being only a couple of rows higher, you might be able to save $11 or more a seat. For example: The first row of the second level is $43, but the second row is $32, or $28 at the ends.

SCALPING

Reselling tickets isn't allowed on arena property, but with tickets harder to come by, it's a seller's market; scalpers ply their trade discreetly (it's illegal in San Jose) along Santa Clara Street in the 2 blocks between downtown and the arena.

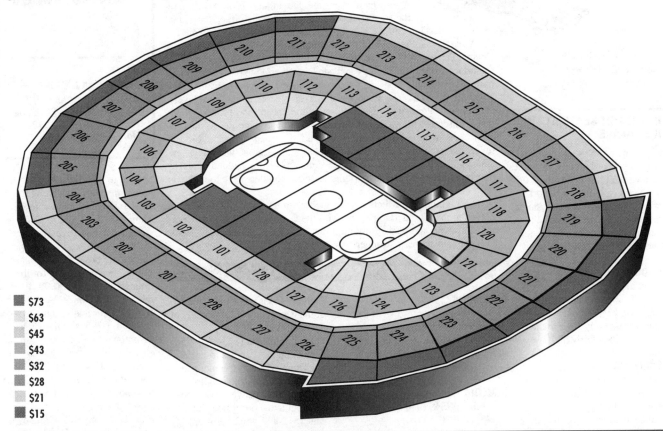

Legend:
- ■ $73
- □ $63
- ▨ $45
- ▨ $43
- ▨ $32
- ■ $28
- ▨ $21
- ■ $15

HOME-ICE ADVANTAGE

In the Sharks' first season in San Jose Arena, teal-clad fans erupted into a frenzy at every goal or great play, doing their group chomp, arms acting like jaws and fingers like teeth. The loud mutual love fest boosted the team's regular-season play and carried over into their suprising run through the playoffs. Sharks fans have been called the best in the league, and even the team's disappointing home record in 1995–96 (12–26–3) did little to dampen the noise level or fan enthusiasm.

GETTING TO SAN JOSE ARENA

Public transportation: From San Francisco, take Amtrak/CalTrain to Cahill Station, across the street from the arena. Call (800) 660-4287 for more information. In San Jose, Light Rail goes to the Santa Clara Street station downtown; a 15-minute walk along Santa Clara Street gets you to the arena. Also, shuttles run to and from the arena during Sharks games. For more information about Light Rail and buses, call (408) 321-2300.

By car: From San Francisco and the north, take 101 south to Guadalupe Parkway (Route 87). Exit right onto Park Avenue approximately 3 blocks to Autumn Street. Go right on Autumn Street for about 2 blocks. The arena is on the left.
From the south, take Route 87 north to San Jose. Exit at Santa Clara Street, turn left, and follow Santa Clara approximately 2 blocks. The arena is on the right.

TICKET INFORMATION
Address: 525 W. Santa Clara St., San Jose, CA 95113
Phone: (408) 999-5765 or Bass Tickets at

(408) 998-BASS, (510) 762-BASS, (707) 546-BASS, (916) 923-BASS, (209) 226-BASS, (209) 952-BASS, or (800) 225-BASS
Hours: Mon.–Fri. 9:30–5:30, Sat. 9:30–1.

Prices: $73, $63, $45, $43, $32, $28, $21, $15.

TAMPA BAY LIGHTNING

Ice Palace

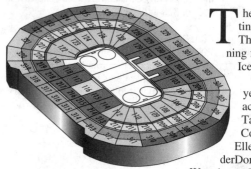

NA	$66	$56
$42	$33	$27
$25	$20	$15

ARENA STATS
Location: 401 Channelside Drive, Tampa, FL 33602
Opened: October 1996
Capacity: 19,500
Services for fans with disabilities: Seating will be available throughout the arena.

TEAM NOTEBOOK
Franchise history: Tampa Bay Lightning, 1992–present.

TICKET INFORMATION
Address: 401 Channelside Dr., Tampa, FL 33602
Phone: (813) 223-4919
Hours: Mon.–Fri. 9–6.

There's no place like home. After a season in Tampa's tiny Expo Hall, then three at the converted-from-baseball ThunderDome in St. Petersburg, the Tampa Bay Lightning finally have a place in which to hang their skates: the Ice Palace, in downtown Tampa.

Although it will also host 15 or so other events each year, the Ice Palace is a hockey-first arena. Set on a 17-acre spot in the Garrison Channel area of downtown Tampa, between the Florida Aquarium and the Tampa Convention Center, the Ice Palace is a creation of Ellerbe Becket, the same firm that transformed the ThunderDome into a hockey rink and also designed the America West Arena, FleetCenter, Gund Arena, Kiel Center, and CoreStates Center. The 660,000-square-foot, $153 million arena features state-of-the-art ice-making technology and can be converted to or from a rink in hours. The arena's first-level suites are only 19 rows from the ice—closest in the NHL. The arena's seating rises steeply up its seven levels, creating excellent sight lines from even the cheap (and they are inexpensive) seats. Three sides of the arena will have windows to the outdoors. As with so many new arenas, the focus here is on the revenue-generating luxury suite and club seat sections, which are lavished with all manner of creature comforts, from padded seats to gourmet foods, and private parking; lesser seatholders have to make do with merely good views.

The Lightning and their fans formed a strong bond when the team played at the ThunderDome, and with the team now installed in a permanent home, the hockey tradition that began here in the early 1990s will continue to grow stronger.

IN THE HOT SEATS AT THE ICE PALACE

Single-game sales usually start in September; order early for games against the Florida Panthers, or any team from the New York area. Precisely how many single-game tickets will be available depends upon suite, club-seat, and season-ticket sales.

GOOD SEATS

Sight lines are good from everywhere, and the steep rise of the seats will keep even those in the cheap seats fairly close to the action—albeit fairly high above it.

SCALPING

With fewer seats overall (and fewer non-suite and club box seats) for hockey in the Ice Palace than there were at the ThunderDome, scalping may be a growth industry. They won't be allowed on arena property, and it's too soon to know where they'll set up shop. At the ThunderDome the markup for premium games was generally $8 to $10 above face value, more for a ticket if the Panthers were the opponent.

HOT TIPS FOR VISITING FANS

PARKING
A 1,500-space, city-owned lot is adjacent to the arena; prices have not yet been set. Another 16,000 spaces are in lots within a half mile of the arena.

MEDIA
Radio: WFNS (910 AM) and WSUN (620 AM).
TV: WTOG (Channel 44) and the Sunshine Network (cable); WTVT (Channel 13) is the local Fox affiliate.

CUISINE
The specific vendors were still being chosen at press time (summer '96). SportService, who provides concessions and catering for several major-league baseball stadiums and NHL arenas, is in charge of the Ice Palace concessions. A restaurant club with two stories of glass will look out onto Tampa Bay as well as affording views of the rink.
The Ybor City neighborhood in northeastern Tampa, five minutes' drive from the Ice Palace, is a center of nightlife and entertainment.

Lightning fans were pretty fond of the generously sized pitchers of beer and decent menu at Ferg's Sports Bar (813-360-9558) back in St. Pete, across from the old ThunderDome. If looking at all that ice leaves you wanting to sift some sand between your toes, head out to the beachside Hurricane (813-822-4562); it offers good food, good music, and a great view of the Sunshine Skyway Bridge from the rooftop.

LODGING NEAR THE ARENA

Hilton
2225 Lois Ave.
Tampa, FL 33607
(813) 877-6688/(800) HILTON1
15 minutes north of downtown.

Wyndham Harbour Island
725 South Harbour Island Blvd.
Tampa, FL 33602
(813) 229-5000/(800) 996-3426
3 blocks from the arena.

GETTING TO THE ICE PALACE

Public transportation: The Ybor Trolley (actually a bus painted to look like an old-fashioned streetcar) runs along Channelside Drive from downtown Tampa northeast out to Ybor; it stops at Marion Street, just a block from the Ice Palace. Special shuttle buses for Ice Palace events are a possibility for the future. Call (813) 530-9911 for more information.

By car: Four major highways—I-75, I-4, I-275, and the Crosstown Expressway—run close by the Ice Palace.
From St Petersburg: I-75 to Ashley exit onto Jackson Street. Turn onto Morgan Street, then Channelside Drive.
From Brandon: Take Crosstown Expressway to the first downtown exit. Turn east onto Kennedy, then left onto Morgan Street and then onto Channelside Drive.

HOME-ICE ADVANTAGE

The intense rivalry with the Florida Panthers continues, hotter than ever. Many in Tampa Bay still hold a grudge against Marlins owner H. Wayne Huizenga, whom they believe got the baseball franchise that the ThunderDome was built for. The ThunderDome's out-of-town scoreboard referred to the Panthers as "Miami" instead of Florida. Matches between these two teams will always be hot contests.

TORONTO MAPLE LEAFS

Maple Leaf Gardens

ARENA STATS

Location: 60 Carlton St., Toronto, ON M5B 1L1, Canada
Opened: Nov. 12, 1931
Capacity: 15,642
Services for fans with disabilities: Seating in the gold sections.

ARENA FIRSTS

Regular-season game: Nov. 12, 1931, 2–1 loss to the Chicago Blackhawks.
Goal: Mush March, Chicago Blackhawks.
Overtime game: Nov. 14, 1931, 1–1 tie with Montreal Canadiens.
Playoff game: March 29, 1931, 6–0 over the Blackhawks.
Stanley Cup finals game: April 9, 1932, 6–4 over the New York Rangers.

TEAM NOTEBOOK

Franchise history: Toronto Maple Leafs, 1926–present.
Stanley Cups: 1931–32, 1941–42, 1944–45, 1946–47, 1947–48, 1948–49, 1950–51, 1961–62, 1962–63, 1963–64, 1966–67.
Hockey Hall of Fame: Hewitt, 1947; Clancy, Irvin, Smythe, 1958; Selke, 1960; Apps, Conacher, Day, Hainsworth, 1961; Schriner, 1962; Hewitt, Horner, S. Howe, 1965; M. Bentley, Kennedy, Pratt, Primeau, 1966; Broda, 1967; Dye, 1970; Jackson, Kelly, Sawchuck, 1971; Carl Voss, 1973; Moore, Nighbor, 1974; Armstrong Bailey, Drillon, Pilote, 1975; Bower, 1976; Ballard, Horton, 1977; Bathgate, Bickell, Plante, Pronovost, 1978; Lumley, 1980; Mahovlich, Stanley, 1981; Ullman, 1982; Imlach, Parent, 1984; Olmstead, Pilous, 1985; Keon, 1986; Sittler, 1989; Flaman 1990; Poile, 1990; Pulford, 1991; Mathers, McDonald 1992.
Retired numbers: 5, Barilko; 6, Bailey.

Walking down Carlton Street in downtown Toronto, there's little to tell you that you're approaching a hockey shrine. You pass the Pizza Hut, the Days Inn—then, suddenly, there's a small building made of yellow brick with a marquee above the doors. That's Maple Leaf Gardens.

But it's that very, well, nondescriptness that makes Maple Leaf Gardens arguably the most hallowed building in all of hockey. Indeed, now that the Canadiens, Bruins, and Blackhawks have moved into their new high-tech digs, it is the last remaining building still in use from the days of the "Original Six."

For hockey fans—especially Canadians—the Gardens represents the last remnant of a bygone era, a time when going to an NHL game meant dressing up in your Sunday best. Toronto tourism executives say they receive more requests for directions to the Gardens than any other site in the city.

The Gardens has changed little since it was built in 1931. It is a place of reverence for many people—they're the ones wandering around each of the concourses, staring at the old pictures of past Maple Leafs teams and great moments in Leafs history. For them, this isn't just an arena, it's also a monument to hockey.

HOT TIPS FOR VISITING FANS

PARKING

Since the Gardens is downtown, a number of small lots are around. Generally, any within about a five-block radius of the building charge C$20 for game parking. The farther away you get, the cheaper parking is, down to about C$5 near the lake, but that's a good half-hour walk up Yonge Street from the Gardens.

MEDIA

Radio: Q107 (107.1 FM).
TV: Global CBC.

CUISINE

Mostly standard arena fare, but the prices aren't bad. Nearly both sides of each concourse are concessions stands. The hot dogs are a great value. The all-beef frank is about nine inches long, grilled in front of you, and served on a poppy-seed bun. It almost qualifies as a sausage—though there are those, too. A Canadian hockey tradition is a meat sandwich on rye; there are three stands where the beef is hand-carved.

Pizza-Pizza, a regional chain, provides its namesake. Believe it or not, beer only became available recently at Maple Leaf Gardens. Now you can get Molson and a regional brew, Sleeman's, along with non-alcoholic offerings. A favorite postgame snack is beer and doughnuts. Don't ask, it's a Canadian thing. For the doughnuts, go to a Tim Horton's—it's The Gap of doughnut shops, there's one on every street corner. For the beer, head just a few steps away to Yonge Street. Two Maple Leafs fan hangouts are on Carlton: P. M. Toronto (416-962-8607) and M. L. Gardoonies (416-598-1033). Another choice is the Boosters bar at the Days Inn next to the Gardens—surprisingly, it rocks with hockey fans. Also, Wayne Gretzky has a restaurant (416-979-7825), near the corner of King and Peter streets, by SkyDome, though, of course, he's usually off playing somewhere else.

LODGING NEAR THE ARENA

Days Inn
30 Carlton St.
Toronto, ON M5B 1L1
Canada
(416) 977-6655/(800) AAA-DAYS
Adjacent to the arena.

Howard Johnson Plaza Hotel
Downtown
475 Yonge St.
Toronto, ON M4B 1L1
Canada
(416) 924-0611
Behind the arena.

THE MAPLE LEAFS AT MAPLE LEAF GARDENS

April 9, 1932: Led by Ace Bailey, King Clancy, and Harvey "Busher" Jackson, the Maple Leafs take their first Stanley Cup by beating the Rangers 6–4.

Nov. 1, 1946: A new sport edges into the spotlight—the first NBA game is played in Maple Leafs Gardens. The New York Knickerbockers defeat the Toronto Huskies 68–66.

April 16, 1949: A 3–1 victory over the Detroit Red Wings gives Toronto the Stanley Cup, its fourth in five years.

April 18, 1963: Dave Keon ties an NHL record with two shorthanded goals in Game 5 of the Stanley Cup Finals. The goals prove to be the margin of victory as the Maple Leafs win the game 3–1 over the Red Wings and take their second consecutive Cup.

Feb. 7, 1976: Darryl Sittler sets an NHL record with a total of 10 points—six goals and four assists—leading the Maple Leafs to an 11–4 win over the Bruins.

Oct. 15, 1983: Toronto and the Chicago Blackhawks explode for five goals during one minute and 24 seconds of the second period. Three belong to the Hawks and two are Toronto's, but the Leafs go on to win 10–8.

In the Hot Seats at Maple Leaf Gardens

The size of Maple Leaf Gardens limits the seating choices available, and nearly 95% of the games are sellouts. The Maple Leafs, who have a season-ticket base of 13,800, put all remaining tickets on sale during the first week of October. It's best to order then, because they tend to go quickly. Games against Montreal or one-time visitors with marquee players, such as Pittsburgh, sell out. For other games, you can sometimes get gray seats, the highest level, on game nights.

GOOD SEATS

Any of the middle five sections in the red and green seats probably are better deals than at many other rinks, given the exchange rate. The ends are fun; the steepness of the seats gives you the feeling you're almost hanging from the wall. But during play you have to sit forward—a bar in front of each seat (so you don't pitch forward on the person in front) blocks part of the near zone if you sit back.

BAD SEATS

The end sections in all color groups could cause a stiff neck. Because the seats were built facing forward, when you sit straight up, you're actually looking at the seats beyond the end of the rink. The grays are a long way from the action, and in the top two rows you can only see the very bottom of the scoreboard.

In some places, standing room can be the best deal in the house. But not here. Only 108 tickets are available, and you have a reserved standing place that's completely cut off from the action.

SCALPING

If the Leafs are doing well, it's the toughest ticket in town. Scalpers are tough; they get top dollar and allow little room for negotiation. Scalping is illegal, but sellers are brazen; fans are sometimes approached as they walk up Carlton from Yonge Street.

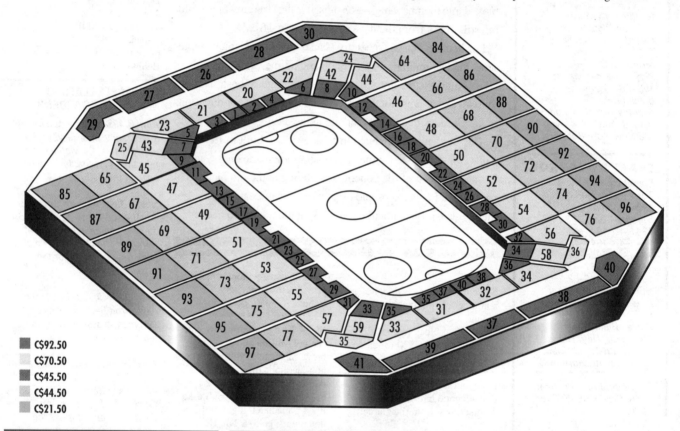

C$92.50
C$70.50
C$45.50
C$44.50
C$21.50

HOME-ICE ADVANTAGE

Torontonians tend to be a little conservative, and Leafs fans are certainly the same. Surprisingly, when the Canadiens come to town, there are almost more red sweaters in the building than blue. The big rivals these days are Montreal, Colorado, Pittsburgh, and Detroit. The Red Wings are also an Original Six team, but the rivalry is more by virtue of the conference setup. Still, the Leafs–Wings battles of the '40s for the Stanley Cup are legendary.

GETTING TO MAPLE LEAF GARDENS

Public transportation: The College Station subway stops at the corner of Yonge and Carlton. The Carlton streetcar stops directly in front of the arena. Call (416) 393-4636 for more information.

By car: From the airport and Niagara Falls, take 427 south to QEW east. Take the Jarvis Street exit north to Carlton Street. Turn left. The Gardens will be on the left.

TICKET INFORMATION
Address: 60 Carlton St., Toronto, ON M5B 1L1, Canada

Phone: (416) 977-1641
Hours: Mon.–Fri. 10–8, Sat. 10–5.
Prices: C$92.50: gold; C$70.50: red;

C$45.50: blue. C$44.50: green; C$21.50: gray.

VANCOUVER CANUCKS

General Motors Place

ARENA STATS

Location: 800 Griffiths Way, Vancouver, BC V6B 6G1, Canada
Opened: Sept. 21, 1995
Capacity: 18,422
Services for fans with disabilities: Seating available in each of the endzone corners.

ARENA FIRSTS

Regular-season game: Oct. 9, 1995, 5–3 loss to the Detroit Red Wings.
First goal: Oct. 9, 1995; Red Wing Mike Ridley at 19:44 in the first period.

TEAM NOTEBOOK

Franchise history: Vancouver Canucks, 1970–present.
Rookie of the Year/Calder: Pavel Bure, 1991–92.
Hockey Hall of Fame: Jim Robson, 1992; Frank Griffiths, 1993.
Retired number: 12, Stan Smyl.

TICKET INFORMATION

Address: 800 Griffiths Way, Vancouver, BC V6B 6G1, Canada
Phone: TicketMaster at (604) 280-4400
Hours: Mon.–Fri. 9–5.

GETTING TO GENERAL MOTORS PLACE

Public transportation: The Orca Bay complex is only 50 feet from its own stop (Stadium Station) along the SkyTrain monorail line that runs from the Seabus dock out to the suburbs. B.C. Transit bus 17 stops one block from the arena. Call (604) 521-0400 for information.
By car: From the airport, take the Arthur Laing Bridge to Cambrie Street north to Thornton, north over the Cambrie Bridge to Pacific Boulevard east; General Motors Place is a mile farther, on the left.

They've done it again. Although Vancouver is one of North America's younger cities, it has a long history of progressive hockey arenas. General Motors Place, part of the larger Orca Bay Sports & Entertainment complex, is only the latest of the state-of-the-art arenas that Vancouver teams have called home. In about 1915, the Vancouver Millionaires played in the Denman Street Arena, the first building in western Canada to have artificial ice. In 1968, Vancouver again became the envy of other hockey towns when the Pacific Coliseum opened and the Vancouver Canucks of the Western Hockey League moved in.

The salmon-colored concrete-and-steel GM Place holds 18,422 for hockey and is designed to have good sight lines from every seat. The number and lavishness of luxury suites aside, average fans will benefit from the well-thought-out design; getting in and out of the building is smooth; numerous and well-placed concessions minimize time away from the action; and restaurants offer seating from which you can take in the whole game as you eat. As if the whole place didn't already feel that it had leaped back from the 21st century, the arena has its own monorail stop, just 50 feet from the entrance.

Vancouver's knowledgeable fans are louder than typical Canadian rooters but less boisterous than U.S. fans. The crowd is polite and well behaved but hardly sedate. Though nobody disliked Pacific Coliseum, its passing didn't generate much nostalgia either, and fans have brought their love (and their towels) for their team to the Canucks' new home.

| ■ NA | ▨ C$58 | ■ C$51 | ▨ C$44 |
| ■ C$37 | ▨ C$30 | ■ C$23 | |

have to practice elsewhere, and the ice is made fresh for nearly every game. The place can get very loud, and the team's play seems to correspond to the crowd's enthusiasm or lack of it.

HOT TIPS FOR VISITING FANS

PARKING

Only about 550 spaces are available in the Orca Bay complex's underground parking lots; if you're lucky enough to get one it'll cost you C$14. Within a few blocks, however, are 14,000 spaces in a variety of private lots costing about C$10. There is also limited street parking nearby.

MEDIA

Radio: CKNW (980 AM).
TV: BCTV (Channel 8).

CUISINE

The British influence is evident by the fish and chips stands at General Motors Place, but they're only the beginning. Other offerings range from popcorn to caviar. A wide variety of deli favorites are at the Georgia Street Deli, and elsewhere such regional favorites as Whitespot burgers (with a highly touted "secret sauce"), Grimm's hot dogs (try the spicy Cajun dog) are sold, along with Boston Pizza, and Chinese, Mexican, and Japanese food (including sushi). Starbucks coffees are inescapable. At the upscale Orca Bay Grill you

can sample nouvelle West Coast cuisine. Beer lovers may miss several plays trying to decide among the host of domestic, imported, regional, and microbrewery options. Nearby watering holes geared toward sports fans include Courtnall's Sports Grill (604-683-7060), Malone's (604-684-9977), and the Shark Club Bar & Grill (604-687-4275). For a look at Vancouver at its most chic, try Bar None (604-689-7000).

LODGING NEAR THE ARENA

Westin Bayshore
1601 West Georgia St.
Vancouver, BC V6G 2V4
Canada
(604) 682-3377/(800) 228-3000
2½ miles from the arena.

Pan Pacific
300-999 Canada Place
Vancouver, BC V6C 2B5
Canada
(604) 662-8111/(800) 937-1515
8 blocks from the arena.

HOME-ICE ADVANTAGE

Because GM Place hosts so many other events, the Canucks usually

IN THE HOT SEATS AT GENERAL MOTORS PLACE

With some 2,000 more seats than Pacific Coliseum, the Canucks are playing to larger crowds but also leaving more single-game tickets available. You can usually get a ticket close to game day.

GOOD SEATS

The arena has been designed as a state-of-the-art sports venue, and the sight lines are good from everywhere. The glass around the rink is seamless, creating no distortions for close-up viewers. The big surprise is that even up high in the less expensive seats (the 200 level in particular), the steep angle affords excellent views and allows you to watch plays develop.

MOVING DOWN

Ushers are more vigilant here than at Pacific Coliseum, but with the upper-level seats being better than okay, there's less incentive to try moving down.

SCALPING

Scalping is not allowed on the grounds of the Orca Bay complex. It's not illegal in Vancouver, however, so expect to see scalpers on the sidewalk across the street or near the Stadium Station monorail stop. With some 2,000 seats available for each game, there isn't much of a market.

WASHINGTON CAPITALS

USAir Arena

■ NA ■ $45 ■ $38
■ $35 ■ $25 ■ $12

As happens to so many in nearby Washington, D.C., the USAir Arena, located just off the Capital Beltway in Prince Georges County, Maryland, is a lame duck. The 1996–97 season will be the last that the Washington Capitals play in this potato-chip-shaped arena (known for 19 of its years as the Capital Centre). The arena is also a lot like the hockey team that plays there: not very flashy, no star attractions, just good enough to get the job done. Inadequate lighting adds to the problem, making the arena dreary. Because of the Capitals' traditional slow starts and playoff disappointments, fans tend to sit on their hands early in the season. When a game isn't going well, they can be almost eerily quiet and have to be egged on by a noisemeter. Sometimes they are even outshouted by large contingents of out-of-town fans.

The multimillion-dollar plans for upgrading USAir Arena have been supplanted by the impending construction of the MCI Center in downtown D.C., where the Caps will relocate in 1997. The new arena will hold an additional 2,000 fans—many of them in revenue-producing suites and luxury boxes—and feature all of the latest high-tech bells and whistles that team owners insist their fans can't do without.

IN THE HOT SEATS AT USAIR ARENA

Easy to come by, especially early in the season. Arena sellouts matched a franchise record during the 1995–96 season, but tickets were still usually available right up to game day.

GOOD SEATS

The best seats are in sections 222 and 209, which allow views of the whole ice and all scoreboards. If you're a fan of the opponent, sit in the $38 seats.

BAD SEATS

With a few exceptions, sight lines are good. However, unless you sit in the corners, you'll find the Telscreen blocks your view of either the out-of-town scoreboards or the shot counter. If you're sitting in sections 106 and 108, you'll be watching on TV if the action is in the far end. Make sure you're either in the very front or at least eight rows up. In the second level, particularly in the corners, railings can obstruct your view in rows AA through CC. Avoid row D: no legroom.

MOVING DOWN

Possible within the upper level. Wait until the second period to move down.

SCALPING

Though there is little need to buy a scalped ticket, scalpers abound. Reselling tickets is legal in Maryland but not permitted on arena property, so scalpers gather around the footbridge leading from the auxiliary parking lot and near the Stars and Stripes entrance.

HOT TIPS FOR VISITING FANS

PARKING

The arena lot holds 7,400 cars, and parking costs $6. About a dozen spots are available on Largo Drive, off the Central Avenue exit, but you'll have to come early. If you're coming in the Central Avenue entrance, make sure to arrive early and stay to the left, or you'll get directed into a large auxiliary lot that takes forever to exit.

MEDIA

Radio: WTEM (570 AM). Play-by-play announcer Ron Weber has never missed a Capitals game.
TV: WBDC, (Channel 50) and Home Team Sports (cable).

CUISINE

Pretty much standard fare, most of it on the expensive side. The pretzels are huge, the pizzas are made fresh on the premises, and you can get your kosher hot dogs topped with onions, hot peppers, and/or chili. One stand features kid-oriented fare. The Showcase Pub and Eatery offers burgers and grilled foods a notch or two above the concessions fare in quality (and price), a wider variety of food, and mixed drinks. Monitors in the restaurant show the game in progress.
The favorite postgame hangout is the American Café (301-808-0200), a quarter mile from the arena at the Hampton Inn. It offers casual dining in a cozy atmosphere; players sometimes show up here. The Penalty Box (703-683-0313), a sports bar in Alexandria, Virginia, on the other side of D.C., is a hockey-oriented sports bar.

LODGING NEAR THE ARENA

Hampton Inn
9421 Largo Dr. W.
Landover, MD 20785
(301) 499-4600
Less than ¼ mile from the arena.

Holiday Inn—USAir Arena
9100 Basil Ct.
Landover, MD 20785
(301) 773-0700/(800) 874-0322
2 miles from the arena.

GETTING TO USAIR ARENA

Public transportation: The arena can't be reached using public transportation.
By car: From downtown, take New York Avenue to Route 50. Take the Beltway (I-95) south to exit 17A or 15A.
From Baltimore, take Baltimore–Washington Parkway or I-95 to the Beltway, then south to exit 17A or 15A.

ARENA STATS

Location: 1 Harry S. Truman Dr., Landover, MD 20785
Opened: Dec. 2, 1973
Capacity: 18,130
Services for fans with disabilities: Seating available on the concourse level between the red and blue sections.

ARENA FIRSTS

Regular-season game: Dec. 15, 1974, 1–1 tie with the Los Angeles Kings.
Goal: Yvon Labre of the Capitals.
Overtime game: Oct. 8, 1983, 8–7 loss to the New York Islanders.
Playoff game: April 9, 1983, 6–2 loss to the New York Islanders.

TEAM NOTEBOOK

Franchise history: Washington Capitals, 1974–present.
Retired number: 7, Yvon Labre.

TICKET INFORMATION

Address: 1 Harry S. Truman Dr., Landover, MD 20785
Phone: (301) 386-7000 or TicketMaster at (202) 432-SEAT
Hours: Daily 10–5.

HOME-ICE ADVANTAGE

After Rod Langway arrived in 1982–83 and the team began making the playoffs, the Capitals became tough at home. Only in one season, 1989–90, did they struggle even a bit (19–18–3). In 1985–86 they were an astounding 30–8–2; even in their current doldrums, the Caps managed a 21–15–5 record at home in 1995–96.

The fans can be disturbingly quiet, especially early in the season when Redskins and Orioles fever afflicts them, but when the Capitals begin their traditional January run to the playoffs, fans get into the game.